THE CAMBRIDGE WORLD HISTORY
OF SLAVERY
Volume 4: AD 1804–AD 2016

Slavery and coerced labor have been among the most ubiquitous of human institutions both in time – from ancient times to the present – and in place – having existed in virtually all geographic areas and societies. This volume covers the period from the independence of Haiti to modern perceptions of slavery by assembling twenty-eight original essays each written by scholars acknowledged as leaders in their respective fields. Issues discussed include the sources of slaves, the slave trade, the social and economic functioning of slave societies, the responses of slaves to enslavement, efforts to abolish slavery continuing to the present day, the flow of contract labor and other forms of labor control in the aftermath of abolition, and the various forms of coerced labor that emerged in the twentieth century under totalitarian regimes and colonialism.

David Eltis is an Emeritus Professor of History at Emory University and a Research Associate at the Hutchins Center, Harvard University and at the University of British Columbia. His publications include *Atlas of the Transatlantic Slave Trade* (co-authored with David Richardson), *The Rise of African Slavery in the Americas*, and *Economic Growth and the Ending of the Transatlantic Slave Trade*.

Stanley L. Engerman is Professor Emeritus at the University of Rochester and a Research Associate at the National Bureau of Economic Research. Among his books are *Time on the Cross: The Economics of American Negro Slavery* (co-authored with Robert William Fogel), *Slavery, Emancipation, and Freedom: Comparative Perspectives*, and *Economic Development in the Americas since 1500: Endowments and Institutions* (co-authored with Kenneth L. Sokoloff).

Seymour Drescher is Distinguished University Professor Emeritus of History and Sociology at the University of Pittsburgh. His numerous publications include: *From Slavery to Freedom: Comparative Studies in the Rise and Fall of Atlantic Slavery*, *The Mighty Experiment: Free Labor vs. Slavery in British Emancipation*, and *Abolition: A History of Slavery and Antislavery*.

David Richardson is Professor of Economic History at the University of Hull, and the former Director of the Wilberforce Institute for the study of Slavery and Emancipation. He is co-author (with David Eltis) of the *Atlas of the Transatlantic Slave Trade*, and co-editor of *Routes to Slavery: Direction, Ethnicity and Mortality in the Transatlantic Slave Trade*, *Extending the Frontiers: Essays on the New Transatlantic Slave Trade Database*, and *Networks of Transcultural Exchange: Essays on the Slave Trade in the South Atlantic*.

THE CAMBRIDGE WORLD HISTORY OF SLAVERY

General editors

David Eltis, *Emory University*
Stanley L. Engerman, *University of Rochester*

Volume I: The Ancient Mediterranean World
Edited by Keith Bradley and Paul Cartledge

Volume II: AD 500–AD 1420
Edited by Craig Perry, David Eltis, Stanley L. Engerman
and David Richardson

Volume III: AD 1420–AD 1804
Edited by David Eltis and Stanley L. Engerman

Volume IV: AD 1804–AD 2016
Edited by David Eltis, Stanley L. Engerman,
Seymour Drescher, and David Richardson

THE CAMBRIDGE WORLD HISTORY OF SLAVERY

VOLUME 4
AD 1804–AD 2016

DAVID ELTIS
Emory University

STANLEY L. ENGERMAN
University of Rochester

SEYMOUR DRESCHER
University of Pittsburgh

DAVID RICHARDSON
University of Hull

CAMBRIDGE
UNIVERSITY PRESS

CAMBRIDGE
UNIVERSITY PRESS

University Printing House, Cambridge CB2 8BS, United Kingdom

One Liberty Plaza, 20th Floor, New York, NY 10006, USA

477 Williamstown Road, Port Melbourne, VIC 3207, Australia

4843/24, 2nd Floor, Ansari Road, Daryaganj, Delhi – 110002, India

79 Anson Road, #06–04/06, Singapore 079906

Cambridge University Press is part of the University of Cambridge.

It furthers the University's mission by disseminating knowledge in the pursuit of education, learning, and research at the highest international levels of excellence.

www.cambridge.org
Information on this title: www.cambridge.org/9780521840699
10.1017/9781139046176

© Cambridge University Press 2017

First published 2017

Printed in the United States of America by Sheridan Books, Inc. in 2017

A catalogue record for this publication is available from the British Library.

ISBN 978-0-521-84069-9 Hardback

CONTENTS

MAPS

FIGURES

TABLES

CONTRIBUTORS

Gareth Austin, Professor of Economic History, University of Cambridge

Kevin Bales, Wilberforce Institute for the Study of Slavery and Emancipation

Alan Barenberg, Department of History, Texas Tech University

Laird W. Bergad, Department of Latin American and Puerto Rican Studies, Lehman College, City University of New York

Alex Borucki, Department of History, University of California, Irvine

Gwyn Campbell, Department of History, McGill University

Celso Thomas Castilho, Department of History, Vanderbilt University

Indrani Chatterjee, Department of History, University of Texas, Austin

Peter A. Coclanis, Department of History, University of North Carolina, Chapel Hill

Pamela Crossley, Department of History, Dartmouth College

Seymour Drescher, Department of History, University of Pittsburgh

David Eltis, Department of History, Emory University and the University of British Columbia

Pieter C. Emmer, Department of History, University of Leiden

Stanley L. Engerman, Department of Economics, University of Rochester

Michael Ferguson, Department of Sociology, The New School for Social Research

David Geggus, Department of History, University of Florida

B. W. Higman, School of History, Research School of Social Sciences, Australian National University

Rosemarijn Hoefte, Royal Netherlands Institute of Southeast Asian and Caribbean Studies

Jessica Millward, Department of History, University of California, Irvine

David Northrup, Department of History, Boston College

Shane O'Rourke, Department of History, York University

Robert L. Paquette, Executive Director, Alexander Hamilton Institute

João José Reis, Departamento de História, Universidade de Federal da Bahia

David Richardson, Wilberforce Institute for the Study of Slavery and Emancipation

Richard Roberts, Department of History, Stanford University

Christopher Schmidt-Nowara, Department of History, Tufts University (deceased)

Pamela Scully, Department of Women's, Gender, and Sexuality Studies, Emory University

Alessandro Stanziani, Department of Sociology, École des hautes études en sciences sociales

James Brewer Stewart, Department of History, Macalester College

Ehud R. Toledano, Department of Middle Eastern and African History, Tel Aviv University

Kerry Ward, Department of History, Rice University

Rudolph T. Ware III, Department of History, University of Michigan

SERIES EDITORS' INTRODUCTION

This is the fourth volume of *The Cambridge World History of Slavery*, exploring the various manifestations of coerced labor in Africa, Asia, and the Americas between the formal creation of the new nation of Haiti and the end of the twentieth century. Slavery has been among the most ubiquitous of all human institutions, across time and place, from earliest history until, some would argue, the present day. Yet its durability and ubiquity are not widely recognized and, where they are, they seem poorly understood by the general public and scholars alike. A central aim of these volumes, which cover many different times and places, is to help to place the existence and nature of slavery against the backdrop of the broader human social condition.

Slavery has appeared in many different forms and is not always easy to separate from other forms of coerced labor. Nevertheless, there are basic similarities that emerge from the contributions that follow. Most critical of these is the ownership of one human by another, and the ability to buy and sell the human chattel such ownership creates. A second common characteristic is the fact that chattel status is a heritable condition passed down through the mother. Such characteristics are not to be found in the more general category of "coerced labor" as normally practiced. The latter typically involves a general loss of citizenship rights, but does not necessarily mean ownership of one person by another and inherited status. Some scholars regard slavery as part of a spectrum of coerced labor and dependency, but the institution has maintained a distinctive legal existence in almost all societies.

PART I

OVERVIEW

CHAPTER 1

INTRODUCTION

DAVID ELTIS, STANLEY L. ENGERMAN, SEYMOUR DRESCHER,
AND DAVID RICHARDSON[*]

From the long-run perspective concerning the global history of coerced labor, the more than two centuries covered by this final volume of *The Cambridge World History of Slavery* witnessed both the rapid growth of the more extreme forms of chattel slavery – particularly in the Americas – and their even more rapid decline everywhere. The period from the 1783 establishment of the Quaker Meeting for Sufferings to establish a sub-committee on the slave trade, through to the League of Nations' Convention to Suppress the Slave Trade and Slavery in 1926 saw the formal proscription of all labor practices designed to extract involuntary labor. Efforts to make these proscriptions effective began in 1808 but, given that forms of involuntary labor continue to the present day, it is clear that such efforts have not been completely effective. The best we can say is that the incidence of coercive labor practices is lower today than ever before in relative terms and possibly even in absolute terms.

The present volume spans the timing of the independence of Haiti in 1804 to the present day, but any discussion of involuntary labor in this era must be set within a framework of an even broader set of global socio-economic trends. Not only was slavery made illegal, but the major form of coerced labor in Continental Europe, serfdom, was finally eliminated via government decrees by 1864, most dramatically in France in 1789 and in Russia in 1861. These past two centuries have brought dramatic change in both the magnitude of the world's populations and the terms under which that population has labored. Life expectancy, nutritional trends (as measured by stature and household consumption), female control over reproductive rights, access to education, and economic opportunities have all risen dramatically, as have levels of education achieved by most people. By contrast, the incidence of famines, the proportion of people living in poverty (however defined), and the ratio of violent deaths to total deaths have declined precipitously. The causes and implications of these revolutionary patterns in the human experience have yet to be fully understood. Collectively, they mean a vast increase in the supply of labor, especially

[*] We extend special thanks to both Sophie Rosinke, the copy-editor, and William Jack, the indexer, of this volume.

3

skilled, and an equally vast improvement in the quality of the longer life which humans now experience compared to earlier centuries. Global populations have increased sevenfold since 1800 and with the expanding opportunities for females, longer productive lives for both men and women, and better nutrition, the share of this larger number of global inhabitants (currently 7 billion) prepared to work, as well as the labor effort that they can generate, is also larger than ever before. Therefore, human beings today are far more productive than were their forebears in 1800.

An associated pattern is the decline in the share of locally produced goods that global populations consume and the weakening of the family, not only as the center of production, but also as center of decision-making both for the consumption of goods and the allocation of resources, including labor. Perhaps the key global-wide shift in social relations that has occurred in the last two centuries is the gradual breakdown of traditional social ties and obligations between individuals, and the appearance of conditions where free labor in the modern sense could emerge. Nevertheless, probably a great majority of the world's peoples lived through at least the nineteenth century without any change in the terms of labor governing their work. Rural South and East Asia, indigenous Latin America, and nomadic peoples generally, produced little for world markets and consumed a small share of global exports prior to the onset of our period. Any understanding of the causes of these changes in the categories of dependency in most societies, particularly changes in personal status over time, remain largely beyond the understanding of the scholar. Slavery and other forms of exploitation certainly continued to exist, but after 1888, there remained no slave societies at least as defined by Moses Finley. Our volume is necessarily preoccupied with the changes in the way people worked in response to the dramatic trends described above. In addition to the massive population increases, the global movement of peoples and merchandise has never been greater. Coercive labor practices, acceptable and widely practiced two centuries ago, are now universally and officially condemned, though, as catalogued in this volume, they have not completely disappeared. Notwithstanding the horrors of the twentieth century such as those in Soviet Russia and other Communist nations and in Nazi Germany, it is not easy to anticipate anything that might interfere with, or reverse, the global march of possessive individualism, or the shift from familial dependence to the legal autonomy of the individual. The pace of change has varied widely, and, of course, there remain areas where the protection of individual rights and liberties is partial and fragile.

The trends that began to emerge after 1800 were unimaginable to even the most insightful and socially aware of contemporaries. The dystopian vision of writers as diverse as Arthur Young, Adam Smith, and Karl Marx was widely held. One of the major tropes of late enlightenment discourse was that about 90 percent of the world's peoples, almost all living outside Western Europe and its American offshoots, lived in a state of dependency. As late as the 1850s many writers in the US South and elsewhere frequently pointed out that free labor was confined to only a small part of the populated globe. Marx and many others saw slavery as typically characterizing one of the stages (there were usually four of them) through which societies evolved on their way from hunter-gathering to modernity. Jefferson and Lincoln, among others, saw slavery lasting for many years beyond 1800, and increasing numbers of contemporary writers agreed with them. Following the lead of Kevin Bales' 1999 book, estimates from UN agencies and a range of NGOs suggest that there are 20 to 30 million slaves at work today, perhaps as many as 2.5 million annually supplied by human trafficking with its obvious parallels to the slave trade. The estimates vary over time and by the agency providing the estimates. The International Labour Organization estimates 20.9 million within a probable range of 19.5 to 22.3 million. However, at www.walkfree.org, the current estimate (2016) is 45.9 million. According to Barry Higman, such numbers are no more than the global peak of 45 million chattel slaves attained in 1800, and, of course, constitute a much smaller share of the world's population – 4.7 percent in 1800 compared to 0.7 percent today.

As Higman points out, however, such comparisons can be misleading. "Modern slavery" as it is increasingly coming to be called is not heritable, about two-thirds of the group to which the term is applied are in debt bondage – mostly in China and India – and while such arrangements can continue for long periods, a duration of five years approximates the norm. Thus, the status of a chattel slave in 1800 is not the same as that of a modern slave as construed by twenty-first-century NGOs. The "Introduction" of Volume 3 in this series pointed to the lack of a broadly accepted definition of slavery. To complicate matters, the mandate of *The Cambridge World History of Slavery* is to go beyond slavery, however defined, and examine other forms of coerced labor. How much less likely is a consensus definition on what today constitutes coerced labor?

In the several thousand years since the onset of the agricultural revolution, very few societies around the globe evolved what could be considered to be egalitarian social structures characterized by equality, whether status, income, or between gender. In most, the majority has owed obligations to, or been dependent on, the few. The major population centers of the world, in China, India, East Asia, and the Indonesian archipelago, developed a wide range of categories of coercion and obligations to elites. Throughout recorded history, coerced dependents have been of Asian rather than African descent and, among the enslaved sub-group of this category, they have been female rather than male according to Orlando Patterson.[1]

[1] Orlando Patterson, *Slavery and Social Death: A Comparative Study* (Cambridge, MA, 1982), pp. 120–1.

An attempt at a taxonomy of coerced labor dependency for the eighteenth century should begin with recognition that in the indigenous Americas, much of Africa, and the Islamic world, an incorporative form of bondage prevailed. If plantation slavery aimed primarily at extracting labor, the incorporative variety evolved in part as a device to extend the size and prestige of a lineage, a fictive kin-group, or a religion in a social environment where an existence without such associations was inconceivable. Full social integration for a slave or her descendants was a possibility. Slaves in China and Korea (termed nu for male, bi for female, in China, and nobi in Korea), by contrast, had few prospects of changing status. They were created by foreign conquest, the court system (convicts), or were simply drawn from the lowest social stratum of base people, and all were "invisible as legal persons," and thus without protection. Yet the concept of property in persons that characterized slavery in the European Americas and the Islamic worlds never evolved in China.[2] India, as we might expect given the Islamic influence, occupied a large middle ground. Collective ownership of slaves by Hindu and Buddhist monastic lineages survived alongside ownership by individuals. Islamic incursions introduced military, and extended royal court, slavery. But across Islamic, Hindu, and Buddhist communities slave holding and transfers of property-in-persons entailed responsibilities. Ownership was circumscribed by law, such that slaves had some rights, including rights to inherit, own, and dispose of their own property.

European imperial expansion led to an increase in the land/labor ratio for Europeans. Also, as exemplified by British India, it expanded the political control of Europeans which eroded indigenous forms of bondage and tended to replace them with the chattel slavery of the Atlantic World. But Europeans also adopted other forms of servile labor for their own purposes. Dutch historian Peter Boomgaard recognizes three broad categories of coerced labor in Java in a typography that has relevance for other parts of Eurasia: "slaves, who can be bought and sold, serfs, who can neither be traded nor leave their masters, and debt bondmen and bondwomen who in principle can regain freedom by paying off their debts."[3] The intermittent threat of famine, the continued need for credit, and conflict within and between communities and polities, ensured a steady supply of candidates for these categories well into the twentieth and early twenty-first centuries.

---

[2] Pamela Crossley, "Slavery in Early Modern China," in David Eltis and Stanley L. Engerman (eds.), *Cambridge World History of Slavery*, Vol. 3: *1420–1804* (Cambridge, 2011), p. 187 (hereafter, *CWHS*).

[3] Peter Boomgaard, "Human Capital, Slavery and Low Rates of Economic and Population Growth in Indonesia, 1600–1910," in Gwyn Campbell (ed.), *The Structure of Slavery in Indian Ocean Africa and Asia* (London, 2004), p. 87.

To allow us to parse the different interpretations of how the terms of labor have evolved in the last two centuries it may be useful to begin with the familiar and review the essentials of a free market in labor, rather than approach coercion from its most extreme manifestation – that of chattel slavery. The years since 1804 are replete with declarations against slavery and laws abolishing it. Why this occurred is of great interest and is taken up below, but abolition immediately raises the question of what replaced slavery. The answer ranges from waged labor at one end of the free/coerced spectrum to indentures and long-term contracts at the other.

Slavery and contract (indentured) labor have normally been associated with the movement of labor over long distances. The period covered by this volume straddles what was (and is) a stage of unprecedented global migration interrupted only by two world wars. The largest and best known of these movements was from Europe to the Americas. Between 1800 and 1920, 50 million people left Europe compared to a European population in the mid nineteenth century of 276 million. Prior to 1850, some thousands of these migrants travelled under indenture (Spanish to Cuba, English to Jamaica, Portuguese to British Guiana, and, until 1827, British to the United States), but most Europeans going to the Americas – at least after the American Revolution – left free of formal restrictions on their labor. The second largest flow was between Asian countries. Asian transoceanic emigration was smaller than that from Europe. Between 1834 and 1937, 30 million overseas migrants left India, of whom 24 million returned, 7.5 million left China, and another 1 million left Indonesia, Japan, and the Pacific Islands. Many of the Chinese, Japanese, and Indonesians returned. Net transoceanic migration from all Asian countries could not have exceeded 12 million compared to a population in 1850 of around 850 million. The great majority of these 12 million were free migrants.[4] Finally, after 1800, about 6 million people were forcibly removed from sub-Saharan Africa for the Americas, Indian Ocean destinations, and the Middle East, almost all of them slaves (but including about 60,000 who were indentured). The sub-Saharan population in 1850 has been estimated at around 80 million.[5]

While the long-run big picture suggests that after 1800 – unlike before – coerced migration (however defined) was of lesser importance, it nevertheless faded very gradually. The minor flow of European indentured servants was ended with the arrival of Canary Islanders in Cuba in the late

---

[4] This paragraph is based on Walton Look Lai, "Asian Contract and Free Migrations to the Americas," in David Eltis (ed.), *Coerced and Free Migrations: Global Perspectives* (Stanford, CA, 2002), pp. 229–58, especially, p. 230.

[5] Ewout Frankema and Morten Jerven, "Writing History Backwards or Sideways: Towards a Consensus on African Population, 1850–2010," *Economic History Review*, 67 (2014): 907–31.

nineteenth century, and the African slave trade, by now confined to the Middle East, ended shortly thereafter. The Asian flow of contract laborers continued until the Indian Government banned the traffic in 1917 – but long before this point, probably around 1870 – free migration from China, India, Indonesia, and Japan had come to greatly exceed the numbers travelling under obligations to a future employer. Globally, there was a clear progression from 1800 when the slave trade was the dominant form of moving labor across oceans, to 1917, by which time most movement was nominally free – except for convicts sent from France to French Guiana (Cayenne).

The late emergence of free labor transoceanic migration in global history points to a much more fundamental innovation in social relations. Agreements to exchange wages for labor unencumbered by non-financial penalties or additional obligations on the part of either the buyer or the seller are of very recent origin. Such transactions assume either a degree of possessive individualism or the existence of an atomized society rarely found in the historical record. Contracts are as ancient as market activity and probably pre-date written language. Contracts treating labor as a commodity are at least as old as slavery. But contracts that gave one party access to the temporary use of the labor of another on the assumption that both parties are equal before the law emerged gradually, only after 1800. And only since the mid twentieth century have these become the global norm as household autarky disappeared and compulsory labor of any form has become illegal. Taking these profound transitions into account gives us a better understanding of the ebb and flow (though ultimately the ebb) of coercive labor practices since 1804.

The degree of coercion in any arrangement that commits an individual to future work hinges on two key issues. First, is the degree of volition at the point of entry into the arrangement – were there alternative options available to the laborer? The second is whether there are sanctions other than dismissal or damages that might be used to enforce the terms of the contract. As recently as 1987, the US Supreme Court was still struggling to draw a clear distinction between involuntary servitude and free labor.[6] For some, extreme poverty in itself constitutes coercion in the sense that there is no real alternative to committing to future labor. Such a decision is analogous to a free person selling him- or herself into slavery during a famine or at times of low income. But there is nevertheless a distinction between forcible enslavement or the inherited slave (or serf) status on the one hand, and recruitment into a

---

[6] Robert Steinfeld, "Changing Legal Conceptions of Free Labor," in Stanley L. Engerman (ed.), *Terms of Labor: Slavery, Serfdom and Free Labor* (Stanford, CA, 1999), pp. 140–44.

fixed term of labor on the other. In the course of the nineteenth and early twentieth centuries, a shift of emphasis from the former to the latter is clearly discernible in all sectors that produced goods for global markets. In tropical areas, contract labor was often seen as an intermediate step toward waged labor (though in densely populated Caribbean islands such as Antigua, the change from slave to waged labor was immediate). In those temperate regions where serfdom was prevalent, the obligations of former serfs were gradually reduced before disappearing altogether and waged labor emerged as the dominant pattern in labor relations.

But how much volition was there for prospective migrants to commit their future labor? The story is complicated, but some generalizations are possible. Neither the British nor US 1807 slave trade abolition Acts permitted slaves captured in the course of enforcement of those Acts to become free laborers in the modern sense of that phrase. The US Act until 1820 provided for a recaptured slave to be disposed of by the state in which they were landed. For most, this meant being sold into the slave population of Georgia because the state's coastline was where US coastguards and cruisers detained most illegal slave ships. Thus, several thousand African slaves did in fact land in the United States between 1808 and 1820 and remained enslaved until the Civil War. The very few taken into US "abolitionist" ports, such as Philadelphia, were apprenticed out for a period of years, depending on their age, under master-servant laws. The British Act required recaptives to be apprenticed out for seven years (albeit in some occupation other than sugar production) ostensibly in order to acquire skills and the means to sustain themselves, but in reality to provide labor in return for food and shelter. Between 1808 and 1863, 185,000 Africans were removed from captured slave ships or coastal barracoons. For most of the nearly 100,000 arriving in Sierra Leone, there was initially some land for them to grow subsistence crops, and they very quickly formed communities with some government support, probably because the colony had no export crops and far too few masters to take on so many apprentices. Before 1848, the only large group of emancipated slaves that truly had unrestricted volition immediately after leaving slave status was the 60,000 Africans disembarked in Sierra Leone from captured slave ships that were not subsequently sent to the West Indies, or forcibly recruited by British armed forces. The 33,000 that *were* sent from Sierra Leone and Saint Helena to the British Caribbean came nowhere near meeting the demand for labor there. Initially, unrestricted volition was uncommon even in Haiti, where slaves had freed themselves. The Haitian Government forced ex-slaves to work on their former plantations and suppressed subsequent rebellions. Both Toussaint and Dessalines expressed interest in obtaining slaves from British slave traders to revive sugar production. Wage labor was presumably not what they had in mind.[7]

By far the largest nineteenth-century group who travelled under terms that committed the laborer to work for an employer was Asian. A far greater number of Indian, Chinese, and Indonesian migrants travelled to relatively nearby work sites in the Indian Ocean world than went to the Americas, and the terms of labor varied. For Indians going to Indian Ocean sites, a Kangani (an Indian recruiter), often relying on family or community ties, would negotiate the obligations of the laborer, and while no formal contract was involved, the plantations would pay the travel costs. More distant destinations did involve contracts, and often Kanganis were also involved in these. For the Chinese, a credit ticket system developed for the streams heading for South and Southeast Asia, Australia, and North America, controlled by a Chinese money broker. Under the credit ticket system, the fare would be advanced and the worker would pay it off after arrival under terms of varying length. Under indentures, supplying labor to more remote destinations in British, French, Dutch, and Spanish sugar colonies, free passage went along with, often unreliable, promises of remuneration and a fixed term of work enforced by draconian laws.

There was clearly coercion involved in or resulting from recruitment into both contract and non-contract systems. With the Kanganis, this might result in pressure from the extended family or community to which the Kangani belonged, in contrast to the indenture where the obligation was entirely between the individual worker and employer. The free credit ticket system for Chinese migrants, operating without much state intervention in China, could lead to what today would be considered debt slavery. Like modern slavery, it was usually temporary. In Macao, the source of most Asian migrants to Latin America, abuses were rife and shipboard rebellions frequent. But the major problem for Asian contract workers was misleading information on destinations, wages, and working conditions. Among Chinese passing through Macao, outright kidnapping was also claimed to be common. The volition issue defies simple generalizations, even though most historians see contract labor as a new system of slavery from the point of "recruitment" onward. There were, however, laborers who chose to re-engage when their term was complete and others – especially in Mauritius – who were able to return to Asia. In addition, most

---

[7] Daniel Domingues da Silva, David Eltis, Philip Misevich, and Olatunji Ojo, "The Diaspora of Africans Liberated from Slave Ships in the Nineteenth Century," *Journal of African History*, 55 (2014): 369; Philippe R. Girard, "Black Talleyrand: L'Ouverture's Diplomacy," *William and Mary Quarterly*, 66 (2009): 112–20; and Philippe R. Girard, "Jean-Jacques Dessalines and the Atlantic System: A Reappraisal," *William and Mary Quarterly*, 69 (2012): 549–82.

historians would accept that living standards in the Americas, even in the tropical Americas, were higher than those in rural India and China. Did people leaving Asia have an alternative that slaves leaving Africa did not have? For the most part, the answer is yes. Staying put or going elsewhere were options for most. With or without volition contract workers entered a status that was not free labor as it is construed today, but neither was it chattel slavery.

Scholars focus on the rights of laborers under contract as much as on methods of recruitment. But here, too, a broader perspective on "freedom" described above is useful. Youval Rotman notes that in the ancient world "in fact no one was free *de facto* since freedom in its political sense according to modern definitions did not exist."[8] At the beginning of the period covered by this volume, Arthur Young argued that this was still the case except for small parts of Western Europe and the Americas, but perhaps even this view was too optimistic. Breaches of contract made workers liable to penal sanctions in Germany throughout the nineteenth century and in England until the repeal of the Master and Servant Acts in 1875. Derivatives of master–servant legislation became law in Australia, Canada, South Africa, the Caribbean colonies, and New Zealand in the mid nineteenth century. A worker could be imprisoned for quitting before the end of the contract or even leaving work without permission, and the English law still provided for physical chastisement until 1867, even though such penalties had fallen into disuse in the previous century. All such legislation equated absence, disobedience, or insufficient work effort with stealing from the employer. At root was the tension "between commitments to liberty of person and commitments to liberty of contract." Over the course of the nineteenth century, the former gradually took precedence over the latter. The beginning of the process was perhaps marked in the late 1820s when a US canal company gave up its attempt to enforce indentured contracts agreed to in England despite obtaining a favorable court decision. It was the withering of indentured servitude in the United States prior to the ending of slavery and then the failure of US legislation to successfully bring it back in 1864 that signified the emergence of modern conceptions of free labor.[9]

The enforcement of indentured contracts on migrant Asians in the Americas, South Africa, and the Indian Ocean areas was not much different in principle from what was already in the statute books in Europe and the United States. When governments in British tropical possessions

[8] Youval Rotman, "Forms of Slavery," in Peregrine Horden and Sharon Kinoshita (eds.), *A Companion to Mediterranean History* (Chichester, 2014), p. 265.
[9] Robert J. Steinfeld, *The Invention of Free Labor: The Employment Relation in English & American Law and Culture, 1350–1870* (Chapel Hill, NC, 1991), pp. 166–72.

sought Colonial Office approval for immigration ordinances governing Asian plantation labor, they were able to cite the English Master and Servant Act – still in force – as a precedent. While physical punishment on the work site or in penal custody came to an end, penalties for non-performance of work remained extremely severe. Every sugar-producing region that took in contract laborers bound the laborer to a specific plantation, a requirement enforced with pass-laws. Fines and imprisonment underpinned very detailed regulations on work performance. In Cuba and Suriname, prisoners could be put in irons for contract violations. With rare exceptions, a judiciary that reflected the needs of planters, not workers, adjudicated disputes over the control of laborers and wages.

But despite the use of penal sanctions to ensure a desired supply of labor for plantations, and for building railroads and canals – in most cases the second best option compared to slaves – the numbers were not large compared to the population they left behind. The central story about coerced migration in the last two centuries should be the experiences in the countries that such migrants left. We know much less about coercive labor policies, practices, and trends over time among the 850 million (to cite a rough estimate of the population in 1800) who remained behind in India, China, Indonesia, Japan, and other Asian countries than we do about the fates and experiences of their 4 million confreres who left under various contracts for overseas work. Those left behind were, for the most part, not part of the global economy, and their absorption into that economy largely occurred after transoceanic contract labor had ended in the early twentieth century. Most non-Western societies had slaves, but they had also evolved forms of oppression and servitude that had little to do with Western conceptions of slavery and contract labor. Numerically, these other servitudes were of far greater importance and were not immediately affected by the global economy or by Western ideas of slavery and freedom. In rural China, especially the south, dominant lineages used Hsi-min or "minor people" as hereditary household slaves until well into the twentieth century, though in no sense did such usage underpin a slave economy. In 1956, the Chinese Government declared freedom for an estimated 10,000 slaves in a remote mountainous area of Yunnan Province and provided some compensation for owners and, surprisingly, land for former slaves. In all cases, there was a movement of former slaves into the peasant option wherever it was feasible, and the shift of the rural population into the modern labor market had to await the vast urbanization process of the twentieth century.

Because of the continued prominence of the rural sector in most parts of the globe, the vast differences in the way in which females experienced the terms of labor across the world in 1800 remained substantially unchanged until the second half of the twentieth century. The huge imbalances in sex ratios between Western Europe, Japan, and sub-Saharan Africa on the one

hand, and Asia and the Middle East, on the other, noted by Amartya
Sen in 1991, were certainly present in 1800. Women had fewer work
opportunities everywhere, but in the latter areas the particularly low
values placed on their labor triggered the title of Sen's essay, "More than
100 Million Women Are Missing."[10] Paradoxically, plantation owners in
the Americas were equal opportunity employers given their penchant for
placing their female slaves in the first gang on sugar plantations (though the
skills that slave women were permitted to acquire outside of field labor were
almost always domestic in nature). In the early modern period (and probably
long before), transoceanic migrants had always been overwhelmingly male.
Yet the slave trade contained many more females than was usual in transoceanic migration and the flow of Asian contract labor that succeeded it
initially reverted to the more typical very high male ratio. However, regulations put into effect in British India in the mid nineteenth century ensured
a female ratio closer to the one-in-three pattern of the transatlantic slave
trade – at least for the large Indian component of the indentured labor
stream. As under slavery, women worked in the sugar cane fields. Some
scholars see sex workers as forming a major component of female coerced
migration both in the nineteenth century and today, but a systematic
study of a time trend of this phenomenon has yet to be undertaken.

Three phenomena temporarily reversed the gradual emergence of the
legal autonomy of the individual in the terms of labor after 1800. The first
was European colonialism in post-slave trade Africa, and in parts of Asia, as
well as Japanese use of forced labor in Korea. The second was a worldwide
experimentation with Stalinism in the twentieth century – lasting less than
half a century in most countries. The third was the widespread resort to
forced labor by combatants during the Second World War – Germany in
Europe, Japan across occupied parts of Asia, and on a somewhat smaller
scale, Britain and especially France in Africa. These may also be seen as a
pushback against institutions built on possessive individualism and thus
modern conceptions of free labor, but none of these experiments with the
exception of Cambodia constituted an economy-wide re-imposition of
coerced labor. The re-emergence of slave labor in prison camps in these
countries as well as the regions controlled by Nazi Germany was a more
significant phenomenon.

It is clear from the above that both community conceptions and
toleration of coerced labor around the globe are still present. They have
shifted markedly since 1800, and, as the cases of early colonial Africa, the
Soviet Union, and Nazi Germany have shown, not always in the direction
of less coercion. Community norms have indeed moved measurably in

[10] Amartya Sen, "More than 100 Million Women Are Missing," *New York Review of Books*, 36(20)
(1991): 61–6.

recent years, and will no doubt continue to do so in the future. Thirty years ago, when likely an even larger proportion of the world's labor force worked in temporary debt servitude than at present, few scholars equated such status with chattel slavery on nineteenth-century plantations in the Americas. Activists and reformers used the term "modern slavery" somewhat rhetorically to draw attention to working conditions that required reform. But what is true of slavery is also true of a range of other moral issues, such as physical chastisement of children, child pornography, and sexual harassment, all now treated differently by legal codes and by police and prosecutors compared to a few decades ago. When community standards change in this fashion, citizens almost always believe that new laws, or new prosecutions of existing laws, which have lain unused on the statute books, are the "right thing to do." More remarkably, they also came to believe in the universality and absolute nature of the new values, and that it was both just and appropriate to apply the new standards to past behavior as though no shift in values had ever occurred. Perpetrators not prosecuted at the time of the offence, are, if they live long enough, likely to be charged, and their victims given redress. Ironically, organized religions, educational institutions, and even the police themselves – the supposed arbiters and gatekeepers of collective moral values – have been most affected by this tendency. Churches and government schools for native peoples in Canada and Australia have paid out millions in damages for offences that were not perceived at the time to warrant prosecution. The largest police force in the United Kingdom has come under investigation for not following up on complaints first made in 1970.

Tracking changing attitudes to the use of coercion in the workplace is rather easier than explaining them. The dates and events are well known, including:

1787 – the formation of the English society for effecting the abolition of the slave trade;

1789 – the last relics of the manorial system and serfdom abolished in France;

August 1791 – the beginning of the Saint Domingue revolution;

1804 – the independence of Haiti;

1807 – the abolition of the British and US slave trades;

1833 – the British abolition of slavery;

1861 – the abolition of serfdom in Russia;

1863 – the Emancipation Proclamation in the United States;

1888 – the ending of Brazilian slavery;

1910 – formal abolition of slavery in China; and

1926, 1930, and 1956 – several actions by the League of Nations and the United Nations.

Over the course of these events, the transatlantic slave trade was shut down and 8 million people in the Americas left slave status behind. In Russia, by 1907, 25 million serfs had exited from the last restrictions on their movement imposed by the emancipation law. More widely, in Eastern Europe, the remnants of the "second serfdom" of the seventeenth century resulting in rural subjection and the manorial system had already vanished by the first half of the nineteenth century. From a global perspective, these events were a mere prelude. By 1962, every country in the world had abolished chattel slavery, thereby releasing perhaps another 50 million slaves and many millions more living in servile conditions in Southeast Asia. Serfdom in Thailand ended in 1874, and there were changes in the status of the nobi caste in Korea between 1894 and 1896. More importantly, as we have seen, the various coercive terms of labor and restraints that replaced slavery and serfdom were also gradually phased out, leaving prison labor in some countries as the last legal vestige. Illegal activities continue to thrive as they have throughout history – usually comprising child exploitation, debt slavery, and various sectors of the sex trade industry. But in relative and possibly also even in absolute terms, the decline in the incidence of coercive labor practices around the world over the past two centuries has been truly dramatic.

The Western Hemispheric bias in the above catalogue of events – the idea that reduced emphasis on coercion was a concept that spread from the Atlantic to the rest of the world – remains a question. Slavery as an institution had existed in most societies formed in the aftermath of the transition from hunter-gathering to agriculture. Its incidence had fluctuated over time with its periods of dominance usually associated with the rise of empire and military hegemony. Moreover, the major slave societies – those with economies that drew primarily on slave labor – usually obtained their slaves from regions outside their immediate imperial domains. Prior to 1800, societies had experienced the decline and even the disappearance of slavery, often accompanied by its replacement with terms of labor that most would regard as less severe. In Japan, it had ended by the early seventeenth century; in Russia slaves became serfs in the early eighteenth century, a phenomenon that had occurred in Western Europe several centuries earlier. But the countries in all these cases subsequently moved on to establish systems drawing on slave labor when presented with the opportunity to do so. Japan colonized the Koreans, European countries turned to Africa and Asia. European expansion both to the east and to the west was initially built on coerced labor. The source of that labor was non-European. The completely new feature about the post-1800 pattern of force in the workplace was the growing acceptance of its immorality in the imperial heartlands. This happened first in the Western Hemisphere, whether one locates the initial impulse in Britain, France, or Haiti, and then elsewhere, if the laws and constitutions of the 195 modern nations are any guide. Today, nowhere is slavery or any other form of servitude recognized as legal. Moreover, unlike the pattern at the time of abolition, when it was the ex-slave-owners rather than the ex-slaves who received compensation, the descendants of the freed people today are calling on the nations that enslaved their ancestors to pay reparations.

There are two counter-examples to this interpretation represented in the present volume: one focusing on Islam and the other drawing on post-colonial scholarship. The first contends that abolitionism – the conviction that no one should be a slave – emerged in more than one location around the globe. This argument focuses on Islam as one alternative environment congenial to abolition. Islam had a long tradition, honored in the breach as much as in the observance, of banning adherents from selling Muslim slaves to non-believers. Islam expanded in early-nineteenth-century West Africa via two separate modes. The more militant version – associated with the creation of the Sokoto Caliphate and the destruction of the Oyo Empire, and stretching from northern Burkina Faso to the Cameroons – dispatched slaves to the Americas; the second, located in Upper Guinea and spreading through proselytization rather than jihad, has been described as quietist. Groups in the Gambia, it is argued, freed all slaves. How extensive this movement was is unclear, but it is notable that world religions, including Christianity and Islam, had existed for centuries in perfect harmony not only with slavery, but also with all forms of coercive labor practices as far back as written records exist, though often with a proviso for some leniency for the laborers.

A second counter-example to the Atlantic-centric view of how slavery and coercion became unacceptable to the modern world emerges from post-colonial scholarship. From this perspective, the abolition of slavery by Western powers in the nineteenth century (and by implication Haitian independence) had no significant impact. First, even in the Americas it was many years before abolition took effect and then it was replaced by other ways of coercing labor against the wishes of the laborer. Second, outside the Americas, especially in Asia and Africa, there were many forms of dependency and oppression that did not conform to the European slave/free dichotomy. These all lay beyond the reach of abolition decrees, so that the ending of chattel slavery by itself had little impact on social structures even in regions under European control. Third, it is argued that Western powers have promoted the abolition of slavery from the nineteenth century down to the present as a way of establishing ideological hegemony over the globe and thus reinforcing power structures that have changed little in essence since the age of high imperialism over a century ago. Post-colonial scholars thus do not see any diminution in coercion in the last two centuries, just changes in the means by which it is applied. Indeed, as

Chatterjee has argued, colonial powers eliminated existing regulations and traditions that in some limited sense favored slaves. Post-colonialists tend to ignore abolition except to argue that it was a device that Western powers used to validate their ideological pre-eminence and to ultimately deflect attention away from underlying global inequalities.[11]

Nevertheless, the change in attitudes toward coerced labor over our period remains striking. The recent historiography has tended to push the beginnings of abolitionism further back in time, with the first slaves in the Americas freed by the new 1777 Vermont Constitution, and the Royal African Company seen as moving toward an abolitionist stance in the last years of its operations in the 1730s.[12] But the Atlantic community's acceptance of the slave trade in the pre-1800 era is indicated by the over 100 ports located in thirty-eight nation states (or their colonies) around the Atlantic Ocean, which fitted out at least one successful transatlantic slave voyage. It was not only Rio de Janeiro, Liverpool, and Nantes. As soon as merchants in Saint Peter Port in the Channel Islands, Vannes in France, Portsmouth, New Hampshire, and many other tiny ports around the Atlantic became large enough to pool the necessary capital, they launched a transatlantic slave venture. Their vessels were named after the holy family, saints, owners, their wives and daughters, national heroes, or well-known public figures. This was regarded as a business like any other. The initial effect of the Saint Domingue rebellion was to trigger a boom in other slave-using regions, especially those of the British, Cubans, and Brazilians. Expectations of future growth of these slave systems as reflected in slave prices remained buoyant, and slave prices continued to rise through the nineteenth century for almost as long as slavery lasted.[13] But, by the middle of the nineteenth century, the traffic had become reviled outside slave-owning communities and, by the mid twentieth century, ideological defenses of coercion in a work environment had evaporated completely.

Why are the attitudes to coerced labor that have evolved in the nineteenth and twentieth centuries so different from those that held in the preceding millennia of recorded history? For many scholars of post-colonialism or subaltern studies, the question is not of particular interest,

---

[11] For example, James Epstein's *Scandal of Colonial Rule: Power and Subversion in the British Atlantic during the Age of Revolution* (Cambridge, 2012) covers the first dozen years of explosive plantation growth in British Trinidad with scarcely a mention of abolition. For the Indian case and Western misunderstanding of the cultural context of Asian labor relations, see Indrani Chatterjee's chapter in this volume.

[12] William Pettigrew, *Freedom's Debt: The Royal African Company and the Politics of the Atlantic Slave Trade, 1672–1752* (Chapel Hill, NC, 2013), ch. 7.

[13] Recent works on the British decline thesis completely ignore the potential growth of the slave trade on Trinidad and British Guiana and their enormous potential for sugar production – a potential achieved over the ensuing century via Asian contract labor.

since the differences between chattel slavery, "new slavery," and wage slavery are less important than the line between elite and non-elite. The literature on the issue is nevertheless extensive. Perhaps because of the quite sudden shift from total acceptance to condemnation, most historians link abolition of the slave trade and slavery as revolutions of one kind or another rather than temporal trends. In the aftermath of Eric Williams' work, industrialization held center stage for several decades – either as a response to the growth of slavery or as a cause of its decline. Revolution on the part of the slaves themselves is currently given more attention. The Haitian – and the immediately preceding French – Revolutions are now seen to have triggered the shift, though why slave resistance should suddenly have become more effective after millennia of successful suppression by masters remains unclear.[14] Slaves had always resisted, and the new element was the fracturing of the ruling class of what in 1800 was still the most powerful country in Western Europe. But even if we accept this interpretation, there is still the fact that over the next nine decades, the remaining New World slave powers – in the Southern United States, Cuba, and Brazil – buckled in response to armed invasion or abolitionist pressure from without, rather than to pressure below from slaves.

The same argument can be made for the disappearance of slavery in the rest of the world, and other forms of coercion after the ending of chattel slavery in the Americas. Contract labor, state servitude (in Russia, Nazi Germany, and colonial Africa), and many other forms of unfreedom around the globe were not eliminated as a direct result of resistance on the part of the exploited. Nor were there many cases where the employers of such labor voluntarily switched to reliance on what today would be recognized as free labor. Typically, the pressure for change came from outside the labor relationship and often outside the society that hosted the relationship. Where coerced labor after slavery was entered into voluntarily, it was likely the case that both parties to the contract might have preferred slavery to continue. Certainly, contract labor did not end because there were no more people willing to sign up for indentured work. Nor was there any shortage of prospective employers after 1917 willing to hire them. As with indentured servitude in the United States, and contract labor in China, the decision was made and enforced by authorities who believed the terms of employment had become demeaning and slave-like. This is no doubt why the estimated 20 to 45 million "modern slaves," including some adult sex workers who have not been trafficked into their profession, are so difficult to turn into "free workers" in the face of strong

---

[14] See most recently Claudius K. Fergus, *Revolutionary Emancipation: Slavery and Abolitionism in the British West Indies* (Baton Rouge, LA, 2013).

pressures to eliminate their status. Contracts by their nature offer something to both sides that is not otherwise available to them.

The shift, or perhaps more accurately given the slow process, drift in community values that in effect drives authorities to redefine what constitutes coercion in the workplace is poorly recognized and understood. Abolition of slavery was certainly underway long before 1800, and the change in values should be seen as affecting far more than just the issue of slavery. In Europe, rights for those enserfed, protection of children, and equal rights for women were live issues before the late eighteenth century.[15] All these groups were, of course, far more numerous than the enslaved population of the Americas. In the British case, the so-called "second serfdom," which saw thousands of Scottish colliers bound to and sold along with their place of work, was formally ended thirty-two years before the abolition of the slave trade, an initiative that has received a tiny fraction of the scholarly attention paid to the 1807 Act. In the US case, acceptance of slavery came to an end in several northern states over a period of eighty years before the outbreak of the Civil War. Full discussion of the shifts in the way coercive labor practices and constructions of race evolved after 1800 needs to begin with the seventeenth century or earlier, and lies outside the scope of this volume.

[15] Edgar Melton, "Rural Subjection in East Central Europe ca. 1500–1800," in Eltis and Engerman, *CWHS*, Vol. 3, pp. 296–322.

CHAPTER 2

DEMOGRAPHIC TRENDS

B. W. HIGMAN

In 1804, the world's population was about to achieve its first billion, after millennia of slow growth. By 2012, it had exploded to 7 billion. This dramatic global growth was not matched by growth in enslaved populations. In strong contrast to the experience of the seventeenth and eighteenth centuries, when more modest global growth was paralleled by the expansion of slave systems, the period after 1804 saw the eventual universal abolition of slavery as a legal category. Serfdom and most other forms of state-sanctioned coerced labor also came to an end, though replaced to some extent by temporary growth in indentured contract labor and by customary and illegal forms of labor coercion. Overall, the proportion of the world's population experiencing slavery and related forms of coercive social relations declined significantly.

This transformation suggests either that the end of slavery as a legal institution liberated population growth or that the increased density of populations made coercion less profitable to the exploiters of labor. The massive growth in world population resulted in part from the closer settlement of regions formerly occupied at low densities, generally as part of the process of European imperial expansion, but in the decades since 1950, when growth was most rapid, the world's people became highly urbanized and geographically concentrated in coastal regions. By 2007, more people lived in urban centers than in rural regions, and many cities were very large. These two conditions – the concentration of population and the growth of mega-cities – can be viewed as factors counter to the development of slavery systems, independent of moral or political attitudes. However, they also gave birth to new forms of inequality.

The growth of inequality within newly prosperous states, after about 1980, was matched by large-scale migration to urban centers where poor people often had little choice but to accept low-paid employment. Increasingly, potential employers were able to exploit these opportunities to engage workers without needing to consider active enslavement or coercion. Cities provided great reservoirs of workers, and also offered opportunities for people to acquire knowledge of alternative employment relations and to travel more easily to new work sites than was possible for the rural poor. An important consequence of this shift was that enslaved and coerced workers often became part of a hidden world. The more they were isolated and hidden, the harder they were to identify, define, and count.

COERCED POPULATIONS

Charting the global growth, decline, and resurgence of "coerced populations" depends very much on how "coercion" is defined. At the beginning of the period, there was a broad understanding in the West that "slavery" was equivalent to "chattel slavery," a status marked by the notion of property, in which one person could be bought and sold by another. The owner put a price on the enslaved and was entitled in law to exploit the labor and person of such individuals almost with impunity. The status was lifelong and hereditary. It was chattel slavery that was overturned by the revolution in Saint Domingue and abolished by European colonial empires and their descendant nation states in the Americas, where the final abolition occurred in Brazil in 1888.

Europeans sought to apply this definition of slavery and their model of abolition around the world. They were not immediately successful, even in their extensive colonial empires, but fully articulated "slave systems" founded on the chattel model disappeared. In the Muslim world, however, local customary law created a variety of degrees of servitude. Only where Sharia law held sway were slaves defined as chattels, and even there the enslaved had specific rights that recognized their humanity rather than being seen as outsiders. Instead of a simple slave/free dichotomy, it is necessary to think of a typology of dependency in which the chattel slave experience is just one way to be unfree. This should not, however, be taken as a reason to understand all forms of African and Asian dependency as benign and undeserving of the label "slavery"; and in the long run, the notion of a typology of dependency seems to fit most societies and faiths, though in different degrees. The linguistic nuances are considerable, with different societies applying their own terms to social relations that did not easily translate into simple, discrete comparable models.

This terminological complexity was paralleled by the emergence and resurgence of alternative forms of coercion, in a world where chattel slavery persisted in close proximity. In the nineteenth century, critics sometimes called this a "new system of slavery" and indeed some indentured contract laborers – notably the Chinese in Cuba – worked and lived alongside chattel slaves. The transportation of convicts and the forced migration of indentured laborers within the colonial empires of the British, French, and Dutch was also termed "slavery."

The first attempt to apply a universal standard – and to broaden the definition of slavery – came immediately after the First World War and the establishment of the International Labour Organization (ILO). The League of Nations responded to the capture of a slave trader taking people from Ethiopia to Arabia in 1922, by setting up a Temporary Slavery Commission. Four years later, a Slavery Convention was proclaimed, defining slavery as "the status or condition of a person over whom any or all of the powers attaching to the right of ownership were exercised." Although the Slavery Convention had no power to monitor and was vague in its definition, it was the first international legal document to condemn slavery and the slave trade in all its forms, and it remained in force until 2000.[1] A Supplementary Convention, agreed by the United Nations in 1956, added to chattel slavery four types of "servile status": debt bondage, serfdom, servile marriage, and the exploitative transfer of children. In 1975, the United Nations' Working Group on Slavery sought to expand the definition further to "any form of dealing in human beings leading to the forced exploitation of their labor" or, alternatively, "all institutions and practices, which by restricting the freedom of the individual, are susceptible of causing severe hardship and severe deprivations of liberty."[2]

In the late twentieth century, from about 1980, contemporary commentators and advocates began to talk about "new slavery." The term "slave labor" became increasingly common in the discourse of political policymaking and the language of religious activists. Definitions derived from the chattel slavery model were expanded to include an ever-increasing variety of forms of exploitation and oppression. The UN Working Group talked about street children (when forced to work as pimps), genital mutilation (because women had lost control of their bodies), honor killing, kidnapping, and organ harvesting.[3]

Expanding the definition of slavery in these ways served as a means of bringing attention to extreme forms of contemporary labor exploitation. It constitutes an explicit appropriation of the past, simplifying situations by applying an old word to a new concept, thus concealing the widely varied experience of exploitation. In Brazil, for example, the ILO initially employed the terms "coerced" or "forced" labor, but its local inspectors promoted the advantages of the alternative and by the early 1990s the ILO

---

[1] Kevin Bales and Peter T. Robbins, "'No One Shall Be Held in Slavery or Servitude': A Critical Analysis of International Slavery Agreements and Concepts of Slavery," *Human Rights Review*, 2 (2001): 21.

[2] Joel Quirk, *Unfinished Business: A Comparative Survey of Historical and Contemporary Slavery* (Paris, 2008), p. 27; Suzanne Miers, *Slavery in the Twentieth Century: The Evolution of a Global Problem* (Walnut Creek, CA, 2003), p. 415.

[3] Bales and Robbins, "'No One Shall be Held in Slavery or Servitude," 32; Miers, *Slavery in the Twentieth Century*, p. 416.

came to prefer the term "labor analogous to slavery." As early as 1940, the Brazilian penal code had put in place penalties for persons "reducing anyone to a condition analogous to that of a slave." Revised in 2003, the code repeated this formula and associated it with subjecting a person to "forced labor or to debilitating work days, or by subjecting him or her to degrading work conditions," or restricting their mobility because of debt to an employer.[4]

The demographic significance of these developments is that they make even more difficult the estimation of the numbers of people found in such circumstances and complicate comparison with earlier periods. If the wide range of social relations now proposed as "slavery" were to be reclassified and included in counts for the past, the numbers would be vastly greater for those earlier eras. Critics argue that the process of redefinition trivializes the extreme forms of chattel slavery experienced by people in the past.

GEOGRAPHICAL DISTRIBUTION

It is sometimes claimed that there are now more enslaved people than ever before. This claim is generally based on a broadly defined estimate of about 30 to 35 million people in "new slavery."[5] However, applying a narrow definition of "slavery" at the beginning of the nineteenth century, when chattel slavery remained dominant, indicates a larger total of about 45 million. If the definition is expanded, to include serfs and indentured laborers, the 1804 total is nearer to 75 million. The contrast is even greater in proportional terms. Whereas perhaps 0.5 percent of the world's people were in "new slavery" in 2014, the narrow definition shows 4.7 percent in slavery around 1804 and the broader definition 8.0 percent.

These global estimates rest on a combination of well-founded census data, surveys, and samples, together with the observations of contemporaries whose capacity was often limited and analogies of varied validity. For much of the period, our knowledge of global population totals is not vastly superior to our ability to count the enslaved. And although there have been substantial advances in our knowledge over recent decades, major regions remain inadequately studied. The numbers offered here are best estimates, with uncertain margins of error, to be refined by further research. With these caveats firmly in mind, it does appear that aggregating what is known from the diverse data sources shows significant variation over time and space.[6]

[4] Angela de Castro Gomes, "Labor Analogous to Slavery: The Constitution of a Problem," *Translating the Americas*, 1 (2013): 119–40.
[5] Miers, *Slavery in the Twentieth Century*, p. 455.
[6] The estimated 45 million enslaved in 1804 is derived from the following regional estimates: Asia – 37 million; Africa – 5 million; the Americas – 3 million. For 1850: Asia – 31 million; Africa – 11 million; the Americas – 4 million. For 1900: Asia – 11 million; Africa – 10 million. For 1950: Asia – 1 million;

The world's chattel slave population kept up its numbers – around 45 million – until the middle of the nineteenth century and declined only marginally in proportional terms, falling from 4.7 percent of total world population in 1804 to about 3.7 percent in 1850. It then declined rapidly, to 1.3 percent in 1900 and 0.1 percent in 1950. Adding serfs and contract laborers does not alter this pattern, but makes the great decline in the second half of the nineteenth century even more dramatic. The 0.5 percent found for "new slavery" in 2014 derives from a different – broader – definition, but does suggest that the long decline halted in the later twentieth century.

Beneath these global tendencies were important differences in the experience of world regions, and significant variations in the timing, growth, and varieties of coercion. Only in Europe and Oceania was slavery almost completely absent throughout the period from 1804 to the present. Asia always had the largest absolute number of enslaved people – and always had more than 50 percent of the world's population – but never ranked highest in proportional terms. In 1804, the Americas, with just 2.5 percent of the world's population, had the largest proportion in slavery (12.5 percent). This was the greatest proportion for any region and period. From 1850, the focus shifted to Africa, and it remains there today.

Although the importance of the Americas and plantation slavery is often exaggerated, it is certain that at the beginning of the nineteenth century enslavement was a more common experience there than anywhere else. The Americas accounted for the three major "slave societies" of the modern world, where slaves made up more than 30 percent of the total population. These were located in the Caribbean, the US South, and Brazil, which together had about 3.2 million enslaved people in 1804. The largest of these slave populations was the Caribbean, even though the Haitian abolition had freed more than 450,000 people. The late development of Cuba kept the total slave population of the Caribbean as high as 1.3 million in the 1820s – almost 60 percent of the total regional population – but the abolitions by the British, Danish, French, and Dutch reduced it to 200,000 in 1880. This brought to an end some of the most intense forms of plantation slavery associated with very high slave to free population ratios, high rates of forced migration, and extraordinary mortality.

Whereas the Caribbean slave population declined after 1804, that in the US South and Brazil continued to grow. In the South, growth persisted until the eve of the Civil War, when the slave population reached 4.0 million (35 percent of the regional population, 13 percent of the

Africa – 1 million. Estimated serf population: 1804 – 30 million; 1850 – 22 million. Contract laborers: 1850 – 1 million; 1900 – 1 million.

national total population). Brazil's peak occurred around the same time, reaching 2.3 million in 1860 (30 percent of the total). These populations were both larger than the maximum reached earlier in the Caribbean. Thus, in spite of the decline of the Caribbean, the total slave population of the Americas increased to a peak of about 5.9 million in 1860. However, the growth of the slave population did not keep pace with the free: about 10 percent of the peoples of the Americas were enslaved in 1804, but by 1860 this proportion had fallen to 7 percent. Both Brazil and the Caribbean had depended heavily on continued forced migration through the transatlantic slave trade, whereas the South's growth came to be almost entirely the product of natural increase. After 1820, the increasing flood of free (European) immigrants to North America shifted away from the South, so that the rapid growth of the slave population occurred parallel to this peopling of the North and West. Remnants of pre-colonial slave systems persisted in North America beyond 1804, and indigenous peoples within the frontiers of European expansion – notably the Cherokee – sometimes possessed Africans and adopted variants of plantation slavery.

Elsewhere in the Americas, chattel slavery had effectively disappeared by the beginning of the nineteenth century or had a limited lifetime under gradual emancipation schemes, though in some cases postponing formal abolition until the middle of the nineteenth century. Slavery was fully abolished in Chile in 1823, when the total slave population was less than 4,000. Abolition in the United Provinces of Central America in 1824, and Mexico in 1829, affected similarly small numbers. The largest slave populations in mainland Spanish America around 1804 were in New Granada, now north-eastern Colombia (about 50,000), where gradual emancipation was initiated in 1814, and Peru (90,000) and Venezuela (60,000), both of which abolished slavery in 1854. These numbers were significantly smaller than in earlier periods and throughout Spanish America there were roughly three times as many free people of color as slaves.

Although the Americas provided iconic examples of modern slave societies – and generated some of the most reliable data on demographic trends – the continent did not dominate the global pattern. In 1804, the Americas accounted for just 2.5 percent of the world's population and, though the proportion doubled to 4.8 percent in 1850, it remained a small part of the total. Europe had about 20 percent of the world's population in 1800, but chattel slavery had effectively disappeared on this continent. Oceania's population was tiny and European colonial enterprise did not install legal chattel slavery in this region. Africa had about 10 percent of the world's population, and chattel slavery persisted. However, roughly two-thirds of the world's people lived in Asia, and it is the pattern set in that continent that sets the pattern for the world. Thus, in order to calculate the size of the slave population before and after 1804, it is essential to know what was happening in Asia and Africa. Here, the regulation of slave systems rarely produced the census and registration data that were common in the Americas after 1804. These problems are compounded by the complex varieties of coercion that existed along with chattel slavery, and problems of definition as well as computation.

In some cases, abolitions directed at the Americas were imagined as applying to entire European empires, but in fact proved more limited. For example, the British imperial abolition of 1834 was effective in all of its colonies in the Americas, as well as the Cape of Good Hope and Mauritius, but not South Asia. In India, proportions of enslaved people varied greatly from province to province, making up 5 to 30 percent of the population. When detailed statistics first became available, in 1840, the Bengal Presidency counted some 4 million and together with Bombay and Madras, the total under the East India Company was perhaps 8 million. Slavery was equally common on the northern frontiers, beyond the Company's domain, and there were an estimated 9 to 16 million slaves in the subcontinent around 1840, some 4 to 10 percent of the Indian population – ten to twenty times more enslaved people than in the British colonies where abolition had been effected.

British abolitionists did not pay as much attention to Indian slavery because it was seen as an ancient scandal of the Indian polity rather than a product of British colonialism. They declared it mild and used it as a foil against the West Indian colonies. In fact, much labor in India was "unfree" and loosely related to caste, kinship, class, and debt bondage, as well as slavery. Domestic slaves were attached to noble households by heredity or supplied by an internal trade in women and children; and there was also an active slave trade from East Africa. In Indian agriculture, slaves and bonded laborers shared conditions of hereditary servitude. In the face of these complications and conflicted commercial interests, the British developed a model which sought not to upset "local" Indian traditions, declaring in 1843 that slavery no longer had legal status. They hoped it would die a natural death. The institution was not criminalized until 1860. This model was applied also to Ceylon, Malaya, and Hong Kong and, later, to Britain's colonies in Africa; but not to the Princely States of India, under British Protection, which occupied almost half the subcontinent.[7]

---

[7] Andrea Major, "'The Slavery of East and West': Abolitionists and 'Unfree' Labour in India, 1820–1833," *Slavery and Abolition*, 31 (2010): 501–25; Andrea Major, "Enslaving Spaces: Domestic Slavery and the Spatial, Ideological and Practical Limits of Colonial Control in the Nineteenth-Century Rajput and Maratha States," *Indian Economic and Social History Review*, 46 (2009): 318; Indrani Chatterjee, *Gender, Slavery and Law in Colonial India* (Oxford, 1999); Howard Temperley, "The Delegalization of Slavery in British India," *Slavery and Abolition*, 21 (2000): 177–83; Miers, *Slavery in the Twentieth Century*, pp. 30–31.

As well as the persistence of slavery in India, large populations of enslaved people existed in other regions of Asia. In China, the most populous place of all, the institution was in decline from the eighteenth century and had never accounted for a large proportion of the population, but even this small fraction meant large numbers absolutely. Chattel slaves (*ximin*) accounted for an estimated 2 percent of the total population, or about 8 million in the middle of the nineteenth century, in addition to the many girls sold into adoptive servitude (*mui tsai*). Household slaves performed domestic service, but the most demanding varieties of agricultural labor were gradually replaced by looser forms of servitude, including indenture. In other regions of Asia, however, a growing demand for slaves developed in the nineteenth century. This was particularly evident in lands along the Silk Road caravan route, in Central Asia, which had previously been a supplier of slaves rather than a receiver. By 1840, there were an estimated 900,000 slaves in the Muslim (Uzbek) states of Bukhara and Khiva. This nineteenth-century demand was mostly for female domestic slaves, which was filled from Persia and (Christian) Russia.

In the Russian Empire, serfdom effectively replaced slavery in the 1720s. The number of serfs remained steady in the nineteenth century, though their proportion of the population declined from 50 percent in 1811 to 36 percent in 1857. At the abolition of serfdom in 1861, some 23 million serfs were "emancipated," one-third of the total population of the Empire. By then, more than half of the peasants living on private estates had already become state peasants or city dwellers, and only about half of the remainder still owed labor services; but the end of serfdom did not mean the end of labor obligations.[8]

Elsewhere, the proportions were sometimes greater, but the numbers less. In Siam (Thailand), perhaps 50 percent of the population of Bangkok were slaves in the middle of the nineteenth century, most of them non-Chinese and often ethnic minorities (such as the Karen), employed as a show of political power by local elites. An active slave trade continued in the Philippines, Indonesia, and Malaya down to the middle of the nineteenth century, and in some regions slaves constituted up to a half of the population. Muslim princes and sultans clung to their slave retinues, as essential to their status and justified by law and religion, until the early twentieth century. Europeans played a role as slave-owners in parts of colonial Southeast Asia, but only in Java did a substantial system of

[8] Alessandro Stanziani, "Serfs, Slaves, or Wage Earners? The Legal Status of Labour in Russia from a Comparative Perspective, from the Sixteenth to the Nineteenth Century," *Journal of Global History*, 3 (2008): 185; David Moon, *The Abolition of Serfdom in Russia, 1762–1907* (London, 2001), pp. 16–20.

plantation agriculture emerge, and there slavery was largely replaced by other varieties of servitude and coercion.[9]

In spite of the British abolition of chattel slavery at the Cape in 1838 and in spite of the suppression of transatlantic slave trading, the slave population of Africa grew rather than shrank during the nineteenth century. For the first time, a variety of plantation slavery emerged in some regions of the continent, notably Northern Nigeria where the Sokoto Caliphate – established in 1804 – came to form a true slave society, created through enslavement in war, raiding, and demands for tribute. When Northern Nigeria became a protectorate in 1901, the Caliphate had an estimated 1 to 2.5 million slaves, some 25 to 50 percent of the total population, rivalling the earlier American slave societies. Across the broader West African region, it is estimated that 10 to 15 percent of the population was enslaved, and Muslim Africa generally had proportions larger than this down to the end of the nineteenth century. Slavery was fully functional, based on enslavement through capture and an active slave trade.

When European states scrambled to establish African colonies in the later nineteenth century, they generally adopted the model developed by the British in India. Where they found systems of slavery in place – particularly in territories treated as protectorates rather than formal colonies – the imperial powers hoped for a natural death, but did little to actively promote abolition, preferring to cultivate the support of local slave-owning classes without disturbing the structure of local economies. At the Gold Coast, children born from January 1, 1875 were declared free, but the courts were powerless to enforce claims, and the onus was on the enslaved to complain, a choice with unpredictable consequences. The Portuguese declared slavery illegal in their African colonies, but it persisted in new guises with new names; the French outlawed slavery throughout their West African territories in 1905, but this region proved one of the most resilient in the long run. In Northern Nigeria, the colonial courts denied slavery legal status, but the Islamic courts continued to recognize it; and in Southern Nigeria, at the beginning of the twentieth century, people were left to live in virtual slavery under the unhindered power of the masters of their households. The definitive abolition of slave status in colonial Nigeria (united in 1914) came only in 1936.[10]

At the beginning of the twentieth century, abolitionist efforts were directed at Africa and Asia, where slavery persisted in the face of efforts

---

[9] Andrew Turton, "Thai Institutions of Slavery," in James L. Watson (ed.), *Asian and African Systems of Slavery* (Berkeley, CA, 1980), p. 275; William Gervase Clarence-Smith, *Islam and the Abolition of Slavery* (Oxford, 2006), pp. 15–16, 122; Quirk, *Unfinished Business*, p. 43.

[10] Paul E. Lovejoy and Jan S. Hogendorn, *Slow Death for Slavery: The Course of Abolition in Northern Nigeria, 1897–1936* (Cambridge, 1993), p. 261; Miers, *Slavery in the Twentieth Century*, p. 37.

to extend freedom globally. In the Americas and Europe, no states owned to the presence of enslaved people. In Africa, slavery proved most resilient in a broad band stretching across the middle of the continent from west to east, though the institution was legal only in the Arabian Peninsula and Ethiopia, where slavery was widespread and an active slave trade persisted. It is estimated that around 1900 there were as many as 3 to 3.5 million slaves in French West Africa, more than 30 percent of the total population of the federation.[11] The French excluded Tunisia and Morocco from the expectations of the Slavery Convention of 1926; the British excluded the Princely States in India; and Saudi Arabia refused to sign, with about 10 percent of its population still enslaved in the 1920s. One excuse for the Italian attack on Ethiopia in 1935 was the need to suppress slavery, but it was not outlawed until 1943.

In Asia, slavery and the slave trade continued into the 1920s in Bukhara and Khiva, where 12,000 to 15,000 people worked as "heavy slave laborers" in irrigated cotton fields, even though Russia had bravely declared abolition when it conquered the emirates in 1868. Chattel slavery remained legal in China until 1909, and it took until the middle of the century for the edict to take full effect beyond Peking. It survived longer in some independent states. In Nepal, there were 60,000 slaves – 1 percent of the total population – in 1924, considered hereditary chattels. Remnants persisted in Korea, the Philippines, and Baluchistan (the southwestern corner of modern Pakistan). Slavery became illegal in Qatar (1952), Yemen and Saudi Arabia (1962), and Oman (1970). Mauritania formally abolished slavery in 1960, then in 1966 and again in 1980; and declared it a crime in 2007. At last, slavery was outlawed everywhere. However, as late as 1960, at the point of decolonization, there were still perhaps 500,000 slaves in the Arabian Peninsula. Most of the 15,000 to 30,000 in Saudi Arabia had been born in the region, of African heritage, and 70 percent belonged to the royal family and its immediate allies. There were also 200,000 slaves in French West Africa; and a similar slow reduction occurred in Northern Nigeria.[12]

The decline of chattel slavery, in law and practice, was paralleled by growth in new and revived systems of coerced labor. Some of the new settler colonies established by the British in Australia before 1838 were founded on convict labor, but none of them was allowed to create a law of slavery. The same applied to New Zealand and throughout the Pacific, though contract laborers were brought from India to work on the

---

[11] Martin Klein, *Slavery and Colonial Rule in French West Africa* (Cambridge, 1988), p. 256.

[12] B. D. Hopkins, "Race, Sex and Slavery: 'Forced Labour' in Central Asia and Afghanistan in the Early 19th Century," *Modern Asian Studies*, 42 (2008): 669; Miers, *Slavery in the Twentieth Century*, p. 350; Quirk, *Unfinished Business*, p. 45.

plantations of Fiji, and Melanesians to work in sugar in Queensland, through a mix of violent raids, deception, and voluntary movement.

Imperial states also supported localized forms of coercion, as in the continued use of unpaid communal labor on farms and public projects in British Kenya in the 1920s and in the grotesque use of intimidation, murder, amputation, fines, and hostage-taking to compel the labor of Africans in collecting rubber for the personal benefit of Belgium's King Leopold II, in the "Congo Free State" he established in 1885. In 1899, Portugal passed a law that led to "a system of sub-contracted labor" in its African colonies: Angola, Guinea-Bissau, Mozambique, and the islands of São Tomé and Principe. This law was applied to all adult male "natives," excluding only chiefs, police, men over the age of 60, boys under the age of 14, and the sick and invalid. Although officially referred to as "contract labor," people were rounded up by press gangs sweeping through villages. They were forced to work on plantations and in mines, as many as 20,000 in the mines of Mozambique in 1915. This system continued until 1962, when forced labor was abolished by the Portuguese, following the examples of France and Britain which had made it illegal in their African colonies in the 1940s.[13] In some places, particularly Northern Australia, indigenous peoples were forced to work for rations, well into the twentieth century.

The decline of chattel slavery between the wars was also balanced against the rise of forced labor camps in Russia, followed by the slave-labor concentration camps of the Nazis. In the Second World War, the Japanese forced the labor of colonized peoples, as in the mobilization of Indonesians to work in mining, railroad-building, and plantation agriculture, resulting in a massive relocation of labor. Post-war reconstruction and decolonization encouraged the United Nations to pass a series of conventions opposing slave-like institutions and forced labor, but significant examples appeared in Mao's China, North Korea, and elsewhere; trafficking persisted and, many argue, flourished in the late twentieth and early twenty-first centuries.

For the contemporary period, the most complete attempt to estimate the size of the world's enslaved/coerced populations is found in the Global Slavery Index, published by the Walk Free Foundation, for the years 2013 and 2014. The numbers offered in these tabulations are derived largely from the work of Kevin Bales, based on published reports for particular states, expert local opinion, and – for some countries – random sample surveys. The working definition is based on the Slavery Convention of 1926 (and supplement of 1956), which saw "slavery" as a matter of

---

[13] Eric Allina, *Slavery by Any Other Name: African Life under Company Rule in Colonial Mozambique* (Charlottesville, VA, 2012), pp. 4–6, 59–60, 178–82.

ownership, but included also debt bondage, forced or servile marriage, the sale or exploitation of children (including in armed conflict), and descent-based slavery. On this basis, the Global Slavery Index calculated an average estimate of 29.8 million persons in slavery in the year 2013, within a range from 28.3 to 31.3 million. This is somewhat higher than the 27 million calculated by Bales in 2007. The second edition of the Global Slavery Index, for the year 2014, found an even larger number of people in slavery – 35.8 million – the increase attributed mainly to improved reporting, and with a somewhat different regional distribution.

All of these estimates are larger than the ILO's 2012 count of 20.9 million in forced labor, people "trapped in jobs into which they were coerced or deceived and which they cannot leave." This number is understood as a conservative estimate, but not a minimum; its calculated standard error means that the estimate can range between 19.5 and 22.3 million. However, the ILO estimate is derived from reported cases, so the real total is certain to be much larger, and the regional weighting is not exactly the same as that of the Global Slavery Index. The ILO found forced labor most common per capita in Central and Southeastern Europe and the Commonwealth of Independent States (0.42 percent of the total population), followed by Africa (0.40), the Middle East (0.34), Asia and the Pacific (0.33), Latin America and the Caribbean (0.31), and lowest in the Developed Economies and the European Union (which permits free movement of labor between its member states).[14]

Of the 35.8 million slaves counted in the 2014 Global Slavery Index, the largest number are found in India (14 million) and India ranks fifth in the world, with 1.14 percent of its population placed in this status. Higher proportions are, however, found in Mauritania (4.00 percent, 155,000 slaves), Uzbekistan (3.97 percent, 1.2 million slaves), Haiti (2.30 percent, 237,000 slaves), and Qatar (1.36 percent, 29,000 slaves). China also has a large slave population (3 million), according to the Index, but a rate of only 0.24 percent; and Pakistan has 2 million (1.13 percent). At the other extreme, the smallest proportions are found in Iceland and Ireland, followed by a number of Western European states, New Zealand, Australia, and Canada. On a continental level, contemporary slavery is most common in Africa – especially in a belt stretching from Mauritania in the west to Ethiopia in the east – and Asia – notably Pakistan, India, Nepal, Thailand, Laos, and Myanmar. It is least common in North America, Europe, and Australasia. With the exception of the persistent belt across Africa, this map of contemporary slavery contrasts quite strongly with the geographical pattern at the beginning of the nineteenth century.

[14] International Labour Office, *ILO Global Estimate of Forced Labour: Results and Methodology* (Geneva, 2012), pp. 13, 15.

Explanations of the distribution of slavery in the contemporary world point to poverty, high fertility, and population pressure as causative factors, creating a youthful demographic profile of impoverished and socially vulnerable potential workers, growing up in corrupt polities. There is a complex correlation with the past existence of slavery, but its intensity is not a good predictor of the contemporary pattern. The slave societies of the Americas do not stand out, though in Brazil bonded labor systems seem to be direct descendants of slavery, expanded to Amazonia. New slavery also prospered in some newly rich regions, notably the "contract slavery" and debt bondage of domestic servants in the Middle East – including but not confined to the oil economies of the Persian Gulf – most of them women brought from Southeast Asia or Africa. Although bondage was officially illegal, the immigration schemes, which brought servants to the region based on systems of sponsorship, were often actively supported by governments. For their term of service, workers were effectively bonded to their sponsor, and unable to change employer; whereas the sponsor could return the worker to their home country at any time. In Lebanon in 2002, for example, there were an estimated 160,000 Sri Lankans, 30,000 Filipinos, and 20,000 Ethiopians, almost all of them domestic servants and most of them in conditions of "contract slavery."[15]

In the particular case of Mauritania, the persistence of slavery was striking, derived from the ethnically differentiated social hierarchy that existed across the drought-prone fringes of the Sahara. The continuity of the institution could be traced through the official outlawing of chattel slavery in 1980, to the survival of "vestiges" of slavery in 2013 that activists defined as manifestations of slavery, thus giving the country its place at the top of the table.

FORCED MIGRATION

Whereas oceanic population movements were dominated by forced migration in the seventeenth and eighteenth centuries – notably the slave trade – the period after 1804 witnessed both a great growth in total migration and a great increase in the proportion of people moving freely. For various reasons, including the settlement of colonial territories in the temperate regions of the world and the relative healthiness, speed, and cheapness of ocean voyages, migration became a more attractive option for European

---

[15] Ray Jureidini and Nayla Moukarbel, "Female Sri Lankan Domestic Workers in Lebanon: A Case of 'Contract Slavery'?" *Journal of Ethnic and Migration Studies*, 30 (2004): 591; Elizabeth Frantz, "Jordan's Unfree Workforce: State-Sponsored Bonded Labour in the Arab Region," *Journal of Development Studies*, 49 (2013): 1072–87.

peoples. On the other side of the balance, the abolition and suppression of slave trades greatly reduced the intercontinental flow of coerced people, and the numbers were only partially replaced by other forms of contract and forced migration. However, this shift did not occur until after the middle of the nineteenth century, just as the decline in slave populations did not commence until after this time.

At the beginning of the nineteenth century, the transatlantic slave trade was still near to the peak it recorded in the 1780s. It continued apace for several decades. A total of 3.9 million Africans was taken to the Americas after 1800, most of them in the first half of the century, making up almost one-third of the total for the whole period of the transatlantic slave trade, which had begun in the sixteenth century. The vast majority of these people were brought to Brazil (2 million) and Cuba (700,000); 90 percent of the total long-term slave trade to Cuba and 40 percent of that to Brazil occurred between 1800 and 1867. Britain and the United States abolished their transatlantic trades in 1807. The British then encouraged other European nations to follow suit, and used their Navy to suppress the illegal activities of their own and other traders. However, not all of the people aboard these captured vessels were returned to Africa. Between 1841 and 1867, some 36,000 "liberated" Africans were trans-shipped to the West Indies as indentured laborers.

With the exception of Cuba, the policing of the Atlantic meant the effective end of slave trading to the island plantation economies that had consumed so many in the eighteenth century. The slave population of the US South no longer needed the transatlantic slave trade in order to grow. It remained essential to Brazil, however, to where the trade from Africa remained legal south of the equator up until 1830, before going underground until it was finally outlawed in 1850.

These factors forced the nineteenth-century transatlantic slave trade to follow new patterns. Whereas previous centuries had seen massive numbers taken from ports west of the Bight of Biafra, proportionally the focus shifted – south of the equator – after 1800. The nineteenth century saw 440,000 enslaved people shipped from Southeast Africa to the Americas, the trade peaking in the 1840s, but this remained much less than the 3.4 million shipped from the west coast of Africa. Overall, at least 5.2 million sub-Saharan people entered the maritime slave trades of the Atlantic and Indian Oceans in the nineteenth century, compared to the eighteenth-century total of 7.2 million. In addition, the trans-Saharan trade took 1.2 million north in the nineteenth century, more than in earlier periods. Ottoman Egypt received close to 400,000 African slaves, and Ottoman North Africa (Algeria, Tunisia, Libya) almost as many. Further, a large number of enslaved people were traded within the Indian Ocean in the nineteenth century: at least 492,000 from Red Sea ports, 618,000 from

East Africa, and 202,000 from Madagascar. Thus, a minimum of 1.8 million enslaved people were caught up in the Indian Ocean trades of the nineteenth century. Adding this number makes the contrast between the eighteenth and nineteenth centuries less dramatic.[16]

As well as transoceanic forced migrations, enslaved people were often moved to new locations – more profitable for their owners – via internal slave trades, notably in Brazil and the United States. In the British Caribbean, a smaller movement of slaves from one colonial territory to another developed after 1807. Much larger internal slave trades persisted in Africa and the (Indian) subcontinent, which brought a visibility to the slavery that European colonizers pretended not to see.

In addition to the slave trade, between 1831 and 1920, more than 2 million people were moved around the world as contract labor, most of them "indentured," meaning that they agreed to serve for a fixed number of years, receiving in return wages, housing, medical care, and either return passages or rights to land. The extent to which such laborers were coerced or simply deceived varied from situation to situation. A significant proportion of the people were repeat migrants and many accepted land in lieu of return passages. Whereas the transatlantic movement of indentured servants in the seventeenth and eighteenth centuries had comprised mainly the migration of white men and women from Europe to the Americas, the new system of overseas indenture was dominated by Indians (1.3 million) and Chinese (0.4), with significant numbers from Africa, the Pacific Islands, Japan, Europe, and Java. There was a parallel migration of contract workers within continents, not included in these numbers; and parallel free migration of Chinese to the goldfields of Australia and California, and from India to the tea plantations of Ceylon.

The oceanic migration of contract labor was spread quite evenly across the period 1831 to 1920, but peaked in the 1850s and 1860s, with 800,000 moved in these two decades. Sugar plantation economies dominated the destinations of the indentured, often the same places that had featured during the slave trade. The Caribbean received the most (800,000), followed by Mauritius and Réunion (600,000), Africa (300,000), Peru, Hawaii, Fiji, and Queensland.[17]

Convict workers added to these numbers: the British sent 160,000 to Australia between 1788 and 1868 (peaking in the 1830s), and the French sent 103,000 to French Guiana and New Caledonia between 1852 and 1938. These convicts often called themselves "slaves" and, indeed, up until the 1830s a small number of them were enslaved people transported from

---

[16] Note that Northrup's estimates in his chapter in this volume are slightly lower.
[17] David Northrup, *Indentured Labor in the Age of Imperialism, 1834–1922* (Cambridge, 1995), pp. x, 156–59.

colonies in the Americas where they had committed crimes or been involved in rebellions. French Guiana was certainly a place of terror, with annual mortality of 25 percent in the first years of the transportation system. There, French convicts and deported ex-convicts joined Africans taken in the illegal slave trade but not returned to Africa. Death rates were also high in some of the earliest of the long voyages to Australia, but most of these convicts were "emancipated" within a few years and even fewer of the convicts than the contract laborers became return migrants. Critics claimed that persons committed crimes intentionally to be transported free of cost to Australia and, as with the flow of contract labor, the forced migration of convicts was quickly paralleled by a flow of free migrants. French Guiana never became a magnet.[18]

At the beginning of the twentieth century, a small active slave trade continued across the Red Sea and Indian Ocean, people being "smuggled" (trafficked) from East Africa, India, China, and Southeast Asia. Raiding for slaves became uncommon, though it persisted in some remote locations such as Mauritania and the southern fringe of the Sahara. The Portuguese operated a "virtual slave trade," taking contract workers to the "chocolate islands" of São Tomé and Principe to labor on European enterprises six months of each year. Slaves and ex-slaves were forced to move temporarily from West Africa to Europe during the First World War, where they performed heavy manual labor and suffered high rates of sickness and death in consequence; but on return in 1918 they refused to continue in bondage. Slave trading experienced a revival in the Red Sea in the 1950s, taking slaves from Eritrea, the people generally embarking voluntarily and discovering their fate only after their arrival in Arabia.

Intercontinental forced migration became relatively insignificant after 1920, but re-emerged in the later twentieth century, in response to regional differences in global wealth and income that drove an increasing flow from poorer to richer states. Free migrants were joined by a rapidly growing pool of desperate refugees – "coerced" in a variety of ways. Many of these willingly took great risks in being smuggled across borders and sometimes died in the process. Forced migrants fled local wars, ethnic and religious conflict, human rights abuses, and persecution, especially in Central and East Africa and the Middle East. The global refugee population grew erratically from a low 2.4 million in 1975 to exceed 50 million in 2013 for the first time since the Second World War.

People "smuggling," in which people freely choose to conceal themselves from the authorities, is distinguished from "trafficking," which is

---

[18] Miranda Frances Spieler, *Empire and Underworld: Captivity in French Guiana* (Cambridge, MA, 2012); Colin Forster, "Convicts: Unwilling Migrants from Britain and France," in David Eltis (ed.), *Coerced and Free Migration: Global Perspectives* (Stanford, CA, 2002), pp. 259–91.

characterized by the coercion of persons with a view to their exploitation, through recruitment, transportation, transfer, harboring, or receipt of such people. However, in contrast to practice in historic models, contemporary "slavery" does not necessarily involve coercion at every stage. In the recruitment phase, persons may readily agree to proposals put to them by strangers and even unwitting relatives. They may also agree to being transported to distant, unknown places, and pay for their own passages. Many share transport technologies with regular travellers, rather than the hazardous spaces used by the smuggled or the specialized vessel of bondage that was the slave ship. Coercion and attendant violence may only come into play in the "exploitation" phase, when the trafficked person finally becomes aware of what is required of them and their condition of "enslavement," and they are also often placed in debt. In the oil-rich Arabian Peninsula, the *kafala* or sponsorship system allows employers to hold the passports of migrant laborers and denies them any right to change employer – generally for a two-year term – creating what Human Rights Watch has labelled "slave states." The vital element is not the initial enslavement, but the difficulty or impossibility of exit.[19]

Much-publicized examples of abduction follow the ancient slave-raid model, as for example the violent kidnapping of hundreds of girls from their school in Northern Nigeria in 2014. On the other hand, in the global sex industry only a minority of migrant women – trafficked from Eastern Europe and Southeast Asia to Western Europe and North America – see themselves as coerced. Much the same applies to the large trade in domestic workers, in which women sometimes find themselves in "slave-like" conditions and exploited sexually, though having willingly migrated in order to escape forced marriage or bonded labor as well as generational poverty and inherited debt. Even when caught up in these situations, they may be able to send substantial remittances to their families, and it is this that encourages both individuals and governments to maintain their participation.

ILO data suggest that 2.4 million people were trafficked around the world in the decade 1995 to 2005, but larger numbers have been advanced for more recent periods: more than 1 million annually, including perhaps 20,000 into the United States. The source regions are concentrated in Southeast Asia, Africa, and South America, while the major receiving states are found in North America, Europe, and the Persian Gulf. Overall, according to the ILO, about 44 percent of contemporary forced labor involves internal or international migration, the latter most commonly

---

[19] Julia R. Pennington, A. Dwayne Ball, Ronald D. Hampton, *et al.*, "The Cross-National Market in Human Beings," *Journal of Macromarketing*, 29 (2009): 122–5. Cf. Robert J. Steinfeld, *Coercion, Contract, and Free Labor in the Nineteenth Century* (Cambridge, 2001), p. 238.

associated with sexual exploitation; with the majority exploited close to home.[20] In contemporary trafficking, the major flows are from Eastern to Western Europe, from Latin America to the United States, and from Southeast Asia to Europe and the United States.

The recent identification of internal trafficking in Haiti – and the state's high rank in the Global Slavery Index – stems largely from changed perceptions of the traditional practice of *restavèk* (meaning in Creole "one who stays with"), in which hard-pressed parents send their children, through intermediaries, to work as domestic servants for more wealthy households, generally in urban areas. The understanding is that these children will be fed, clothed, and given an education in return for household labor, but often they are exploited and subjected to domestic violence and emotional abuse. Contact between child and parents is severed. The ILO in 1993 found that *restavèk* children were forced "to work as domestics in conditions which are not unlike servitude." A 2009 survey estimated a *restavèk* population of 225,000, more than the total "slave" population estimated in the Global Slavery Index. A similar system existed in nearby Jamaica until the middle of the twentieth century, the young women euphemistically called "schoolgirls." The 1930s saw an attack on the Chinese practice of *mui tsai* (meaning "little sister" in Cantonese), in which girls were adopted into households, but were often reduced to ill-treated unpaid drudges. Some were trafficked to Hong Kong and Southeast Asia, until the practice was ended around 1950. Other children up to 10 years of age were purchased as domestic servants and never adopted; but a girl might also become the wife of her owner or a concubine, since the fixed patrilineal system meant she could not pose a threat to family fortunes.[21]

The recent growth of trafficking has in some cases been fueled by supply. China's "one child policy" instituted in 1979 resulted in the abandonment of many baby girls, due to gender preference (for the first child) and to avoid the fine (for a second). These children were trafficked for adoption, the traffickers at first paying parents for their babies, but more recently simply kidnapping them. At the same time, the sex imbalance created by the policy led to a shortage of women for marriage, and

[20] Kevin Bales, *Understanding Global Slavery: A Reader* (Berkeley, CA, 2005), p. 151; ILO, *ILO Global Estimate*, p. 17.

[21] Leslie Anderson, Edmund J. Kelly, and Zara Kivi Kinnunen, *Restavek: Child Domestic Labor in Haiti* (Minneapolis, MN, 1990); Ira L. Leeds, Patricia M. Engel, Kiersten S. Derby, *et al.*, "Case Report: Two Cases of Restavek-Related Illness: Clinical Implications of Foster Neglect in Haiti," *American Journal of Tropical Medicine and Hygiene*, 83 (2010): 1098; James L. Watson, "Transactions in People: The Chinese Market in Slaves, Servants, and Heirs," in James L. Watson (ed.), *Asian and African Systems of Slavery* (Berkeley, CA, 1980), p. 223; Jonathan Blagbrough, "Child Domestic Labour: A Modern Form of Slavery," *Children and Society*, 22 (2008): 182–3.

their trafficking for forced marriage and sexual exploitation. Throughout the Third World, examples of children being "given away" to adoptive parents, outside the legal process and in return for payment, continue to occur and are now considered to be "human trafficking." The motives for such transfers of children stem both from the poverty of the parents and the difficulties faced by hopeful adopters in finding children through official channels.

Chinese Triads smuggled people into Europe, the United States, and other richer states, then demanded that payments of money should continue, under threat of harm to the migrant as well as their families at home. The inability to pay saw such trafficked people forced into prostitution, or treated brutally as domestic servants, locked up by their employers, or forced to work in factories and mines. Locally, children were particularly vulnerable, sent by parents themselves mired in debt bondage, to work in Asian sweatshops and carpet factories. It is even harder to identify a voluntary element in the movement of children trafficked to gold mines in Africa and South America, or kept as prisoners on West African cocoa plantations, working long and dangerous hours for little remuneration, often in forms of debt bondage contracted by their parents.

SEX, AGE, ETHNICITY

Contemporary slavery and forced labor contrast strongly with earlier patterns, when males generally outnumbered females. The ILO's 2012 estimate of global forced labor finds a female majority (55 percent), with females almost completely dominant in sexual exploitation (98 percent) and males more common only in the exploitation of labor in the private economy (60 percent). Within Haiti, two-thirds of the *restavèk* population are girls. The feminization of coerced labor is even more stark in the contemporary transnational trafficking of people, in which perhaps 80 percent are female – 70 percent of them in the commercial sex trade and 30 percent consigned to forced labor. New slavery has also prospered in some newly rich regions, notably the "contract slavery" and debt bondage of domestic servants in the Middle East – including but not confined to the oil economies of the Gulf – most of them women brought from Southeast Asia or Africa. This pattern reflects the shift in total world migration, which, since the 1970s, has been about 50 percent female, compared to the earlier dominance of males in free migration, as well as in the slave and contract labor trades.

The feminization of slavery and coercion began relatively early in the Muslim world. By the end of the eighteenth century, the Ottoman slave trade, focused on Istanbul, was increasingly driven by the enslavement of women for domestic labor or sexual exploitation, whereas the recruitment of enslaved men to the military declined in response to the diminished resources of the contracting empire. Slaves were replaced by free soldiers in the nineteenth century. Male slaves sometimes rose to become respected retainers and high officials of state, but their numbers were few. Agricultural slavery, with its larger demand for males, was never prominent in the Ottoman Empire. Around the Mediterranean, black African males continued to be used in domestic roles, but they became a shrinking proportion of the black and white slave population that was dominated by females overall. Women might become beloved concubines and occasionally the mothers of rulers. Muslim slavery did not disapprove of sexual relations between master and slave, and the institution's power relations retained a strong sexual aspect throughout the nineteenth century.

Growing demand for female domestics came particularly from the wealthier urban classes in Istanbul and Cairo. In the middle of the nineteenth century, when about 12 percent of Istanbul's population were slave-holders and the city had a registered slave population of 52,000, some 90 percent of the slaves were female. Cairo had about 11,000 slaves, 5 percent of the city's population, and 75 percent of the slaves were female. The same applied in Central Asia and Afghanistan in the early nineteenth century, where the majority of those enslaved were female domestic slaves.[22]

In the Christian states and colonies of the Americas, the occupations of chattel slaves were typically limited to manual tasks, but men were much more likely than women to be taught marketable skills and females dominated the ranks of domestic servants. Males were a majority in the transatlantic slave trade, whereas females were more common within Africa. This balance shifted after 1804, but even in the US South, where natural increase drove population growth, male and female slaves did not become equal in numbers until 1850.

Children became more common in the transatlantic slave trade after 1804, accounting for as many as 40 percent of those taken from Benin and Biafra by 1820. Where poverty and famine ruled the land – especially in India and on the margins of the African desert – recruitment was often driven by the poor and starving themselves, offering to enter bondage in hope of food for themselves and their children, or offering one child in order to sustain the others.

The ending of slavery did not always mean the release of children from forced labor. In the British colonies in the West Indies, the Apprenticeship

---

[22] Madeline C. Zilfi, *Women and Slavery in the Late Ottoman Empire: The Design of Difference* (Cambridge, 2010), pp. 195–7; Terence Walz and Kenneth M. Cuno (eds.), *Race and Slavery in the Middle East: Histories of Trans-Saharan Africans in Nineteenth-Century Egypt, Sudan, and the Ottoman Mediterranean* (Cairo, 2010), p. 11.

instituted in 1834 went together with the absolute freeing of children under 6 years of age. Apparently uniquely, rural masters at the Cape quickly placed the freed children under indentures, before 1838, drawing on the established practice of bonding (officially free) Khoi children to work on their farms. This strategy served to give the former slave-owners power over the former enslaved, many of whom wished to leave the farms and establish independent lives.[23]

In 2002, the ILO estimated a global total of 6 million children in slavery, most of them in forced and bonded labor; this was part of the much larger total of 211 million children aged 5 to 14 years engaged in "economic activity," with about 8 million of these suffering the worst conditions, most of them in Asia. But children did not dominate the forced labor population. The ILO's 2012 global estimate found that 74 percent of those in forced labor were 18 years of age and above. In contemporary trafficking, the dominant age group is said to be 18 to 24 years of age. However, though children (under 18 years of age) are thought to be a substantial component (perhaps 50 percent) of the trans-national traffic, particularly in the global commercial sex trade, the ILO finds that only 21 percent of those caught up in sexual exploitation are children. These complexities are partly explained by regional variations in forced labor: within Africa, the Middle East, and South Asia, children are more likely to be used in forced labor – typically girls in domestic service – as well as being sexually exploited. In the gold mines of South America, boys as young as 8 are forced to lay dynamite.[24]

In state-sponsored "contract slavery" – taking mostly women from Southeast Asia and Africa to richer states in the Middle East – ethnicity is recognized as a distinguishing characteristic. However, the earlier gradual abolition and suppression of long-distance slave trading reduced the chances that masters and slaves would be people of different ethnicities and races. The slave society of Sokoto, for example, did not depend on "racial" difference. In more ancient systems, as in India, race was rarely an element. Caste did remain a significant factor, but coercion was not always applied to the lowest rank. For instance, because untouchables (*dallits*) were thought fit for the most unsavoury tasks, their pollution made them unemployable as the hand servants of the higher castes and in consequence those further up the scale were forced to fill such roles.

[23] Pamela Scully, *Liberating the Family? Gender and British Slave Emancipation in the Rural Western Cape, South Africa, 1823–1853* (Portsmouth, NH, 1997), pp. 58–9.

[24] Hans van de Glind and Joost Kooijmans, "Modern-Day Child Slavery," *Children and Society*, 22 (2008): 150; Blagbrough, "Child Domestic Labour," 179–90; Quirk, *Unfinished Business*, p. 49; ILO, *ILO Global Estimate*, pp. 14–15.

Where there was a significant period between the abolition of an external slave trade and the abolition of slavery itself – as was common throughout the Americas – the enslaved populations became increasingly "Creole" as a result of births, no longer balanced by new infusions. At the Cape of Good Hope, for example, at the time of abolition in 1834, some 50 percent of the enslaved population had been born in the colony since 1807. In the US South, the American-born proportion was possibly 99 percent by the time of the Civil War. In the British Caribbean, at the time of emancipation, the Creole proportion was as high as 97 percent in Barbados, where a natural increase was achieved relatively early. These differences had much to do with variations in natural increase.

FERTILITY, MORTALITY, NATURAL INCREASE

Normally, population growth is the product of births minus deaths plus net migration. Enslaved populations are more open, however, so the numbers depend on a more complex equation: births plus recruitment minus deaths, manumission, and escape, plus net (forced) migration. Throughout history, enslaved populations have been notable for the number of examples in which natural increase failed to support the reproduction of particular populations without dependence on constant recruitment through slave trading. In the eighteenth century, 25 to 50 percent of enslaved people brought to the plantation economies of the Americas died within the first three years. The period after 1804 continued this pattern, but the abolition of long-distance slave trades both removed the heavy mortality suffered by the newly arrived and made the survival of slave populations increasingly reliant on a surplus of births over deaths.

The strongest contrast in the capacity of slave populations to reproduce and grow occurred in the Americas. Whereas the slave population of the US South had grown vigorously since the colonial period, the other slave societies – the plantation economies of the Caribbean and Brazil – typically faced extinction and their growth was dependent on the transatlantic slave trade. The deficit derived from low birth rates as well as high mortality. The most convincing explanation for this contrast is the difference in labor requirements of large-scale plantation sugar production as against the demands of small-scale tobacco or cotton farming. However, some sugar plantation economies began to show positive natural increase by the end of the eighteenth century – Barbados, for example – suggesting a secular pattern of demographic change in response to developments in technology and the management of forced labor systems. Similarly, in South Africa, the enslaved population became self-reproducing in the early nineteenth century.

Fertility and slave marriage were generally encouraged by Indian slave-owners, and the same was true of Muslim societies. Where caste operated, as in India, intercourse between master and slave often indicated pollution, hence the desire of the ruling classes to encourage reproduction within the system. On the other hand, particularly in East Asia, one of the reasons eunuchs were valued as soldiers and officials was because they could not father rival dynasties. Among Muslims, the child of a free man and slave concubine was always born free, and the mother might also be freed. In the Americas, however, white men fathered numerous children with enslaved women, the children being born slaves and often not acknowledged by the men. Slave-owners, particularly in the antebellum South, are often said to have forced enslaved people to have children by means of so-called "slave breeding" and, though there seems to be little empirical support for the idea, it remains a feature of the literature on memory.[25]

The demographic dynamics associated with contemporary slavery are harder to define and measure. This stems directly from the illegal, isolated, and invisible character of the practice, with many enslaved people not part of a larger community or population, finding themselves in the status on only a temporary basis and their children not generally destined to inherit the rank. The ILO estimates that almost half of reported forced laborers endure spells of six months or less and only 9 percent beyond three years; though the rates are likely to be higher for unreported cases. Thus, it is not surprising that there seem to be no attempts to measure the fertility of contemporary coerced populations.

Coerced people suffered heavy mortality even when the period of their forced labor was projected to be short. Death rates were often as high in the coerced labor projects of the early twentieth century as they had been in plantation slavery, where extreme demands were made. In the 1920s, for example, perhaps 20,000 forced laborers died in the building of the French Congo Railway, and mortality was also high among men forced to work as miners in Mozambique. These numbers were, however, exceeded by the immense toll of twentieth-century genocides and localized "ethnic cleansing" which were sometimes associated with coerced labor, but often were simple murder.

ESCAPE

The great rebellion in Saint Domingue that freed near to half a million people had no successor. In most places, achieving freedom through escape

---

[25] Jack Goody, "Slavery in Time and Space," in Watson (ed.), *Asian and African Systems*, p. 41; Gregory D. Smithers, *Slave Breeding: Sex, Violence, and Memory in African American History* (Gainesville, FL, 2012).

was generally best attempted by individuals or small groups. It was always a hazardous business – especially so within the major slave societies – and accounted for only small numbers. Even where it occurred on a large scale, as in Northern Nigeria immediately before the First World War – encouraged by the British formal abolition of the legal status of slavery – only about 10 percent of the enslaved were able to escape successfully. Those most likely to escape tended to be the recently captured. Indentured laborers also deserted the plantations, and sometimes committed suicide, particularly the Chinese in Cuba living within slave society.

In nineteenth-century Brazil, a significant fluidity developed in the hierarchy of statuses from slave to free. Some individuals were said to be "living as if free," en route to gradual manumission, whereas on the other hand so-called "free Africans" might be forced to work by the state. Such fluidity was always greatest in cities and towns. Some slaves – both males and females – engaged in self-hire, living independent of their owners, as if free, paying a monthly or weekly amount to the owner, and finding their own jobs. Others – generally adult males – formed themselves into small gangs of autonomous workers, on a similar basis, to undertake larger manual labor tasks. Such slaves gained a level of independence and agency that enabled alternative family and household arrangements and eroded the core of the enslaved population.

Escape from contemporary new slavery is hard to analyze. The illegality of enslavement means that owners have an interest in isolating their victims, treating them brutally and locking them away, making escape very difficult. When the enslaved escape into the outside world, their chances of freedom are good, though once identified they may face deportation as illegal aliens. The worst treated take refuge in embassies. Setting up hidden "maroon" enclaves of compatriots is not a viable option. In contrast, earlier – legal – slave societies rarely applied such strict control because it was harder for escaping individuals to blend into the wider community without being quickly recognized or hunted down by the state. Maroon communities prospered up until the end of slavery wherever slavery accounted for a majority of the population, being relatively common in the Caribbean and Brazil. In Eastern Africa and Madagascar, numerous maroon communities flourished in response to the late-nineteenth-century spread of plantation systems; but they were rare in the Muslim zones of Arabia, the Persian Gulf, and South Asia, where domestic slavery was more common than agricultural.

MANUMISSION

Rates of manumission varied substantially between slave societies and other forms of coerced labor. In the Spanish and Portuguese territories of the Americas, manumission was relatively common, whereas rates were much lower in the colonies of the British and French. In the antebellum United States, the capacity to manumit was often limited by state legislatures, because freed people were thought dangerous to social peace. Throughout the Americas, manumitted people typically carried a burden of identification as "freed" people, commonly distinguished as "free colored" and "free black" to further locate their rank within slave society. This served to blur the line between slavery and freedom, and indeed individuals in the United States sometimes petitioned for re-enslavement because the personal social disruption and economic disadvantage flowing from "freedom" within slave society were too great. In Jamaica, the practice of manumitting old and disabled enslaved people, left without resources, was prohibited by law to limit vagrancy, theft, and dependence on parish welfare.

Muslim societies allowed manumission, and the children of slave concubines were particularly likely to be granted free status. However, social equality was rarely achieved and many persons remained dependent on the authority of their former masters, for permission to marry, for example. Outside the Muslim domain, many African societies lacked a formal mechanism of self-purchase. At the Cape of Good Hope, rural slaveowners rarely manumitted children they had by enslaved women or the women themselves.

Manumission was also a practice of Russian serfdom, but its frequency is disputed. In 1803, a law permitted the owners of serfs to free entire villages and ten years later the gradual emancipation commenced of serfs in the Baltic provinces of the empire, but these measures had little impact on the mass of the serf population. More often, serfs who obtained manumission were freed as family household groups, and were required to register in new occupational and social statuses that concealed their identity as "freed" people. This meant that they had a more normal demographic profile in terms of sex and age, and they disappeared into the larger population fairly easily, rather than forming a visible intermediate segment, though it has been argued that the non-serf population of Russia was systematically subjected to repressive regimes. As elsewhere, manumission in Russia often occurred only at the death of the owner, as a final expression of the owner's authority, written in a will or spoken on their deathbed. Again, this selfish generosity sometimes left newly freed people without subsistence, and was used as a means of avoiding responsibility for the aged and ailing. On the other hand, individuals and family groups seeking to buy their way out of serfdom were often required to pay substantial sums.[26]

---

[26] Alison K. Smith, "Freed Serfs without Free People: Manumission in Imperial Russia," *American Historical Review*, 118 (2013): 1030–3.

FAMILY AND COMMUNITY

Enserfed and enslaved peoples tied to the land always had better chances of maintaining family households and building local communities than those slaves whose lives were made fragile by separation and sale. In nineteenth-century rural India, for example, settled slave communities could not be sold separately from the land, thus preventing the sale and removal of individual family members.

Interpretations of slave family life in the Americas are a matter of continuing debate. Until the 1970s, there was focus on the model of a single woman raising her children single-handed, and her children being dispersed through sale and removal. Family reconstitution studies, however, led to a new picture in which the nuclear household played a greater role, and the strength of the family unit could be understood as a tool of resistance to the oppressive regime of slavery and the plantation. Everywhere, the ability of chattel slaves to form family households, identifiable in the documentary record, depended partly on the scale of slave holding. The larger the plantation community, the better the chances for family formation.

Really large plantations – of more than 200 slaves – were, however, relatively rare. This was particularly true of the United States, but even in Brazil slave holding was generally not on a large scale. Toward the end of slavery, in the province of Minas Gerais around 1870, the mining sector was dominated by slave-owners with fewer than five slaves. In Bahia, the region of the sugar latifundia, the average was less than sixty slaves per holding. However, many of the smaller slave-holders were by then black or "colored," often female, and often kin to the enslaved. Thus, two contrasting patterns of family structure existed in the last decades of slavery in the Americas. In the zones of intense plantation development, particularly in the Caribbean, free black and free colored people were few, and enslaved people living on large holdings were able to create nuclear family households to a significant degree. On the other hand, where slave owning was relatively small-scale, the free black and free colored populations were substantial, and the family unit was more complex, bringing together slave and free, black and white.

Family structure was not always a simple product of scale, however, and many variations occurred. At the Cape, for example, most rural slave-holders owned fewer than eight people, so that the household rather than the plantation or estate was the common unit. The intimacy of the social situation was complex. Enslaved women often bore children fathered by their white masters, but without having any right to acknowledge relations with the free household.

LEGACIES

With important exceptions, slavery is associated with low fertility and high mortality, for the free as well as the enslaved component of a population. Globally, slave populations appear to have peaked sometime between the end of the eighteenth century and the middle of the nineteenth, at the beginning of the Industrial Revolution which marked the initiation of the long period of sustained growth resulting from reduced mortality and heightened fertility known as the "demographic transition," first in Europe then spreading slowly elsewhere around the world. Broadly, then, the growth of freedom was associated with the growth of population. On the other hand, it might be argued that to the extent Atlantic slave systems underpinned the capitalization of the Industrial Revolution, long-term global population growth was stimulated by slavery rather than inhibited by it.

Within Africa, slavery is generally thought to have slowed population growth, notably in the "Middle Belt" of West Africa, the source of many of the peoples taken in the transatlantic slave trade and across the Sahara. A partial repopulation resulted when many of the perhaps 200,000 people who escaped slavery in Northern Nigeria in the early twentieth century moved south to the Middle Belt where they were less likely to be recognized and recaptured. However, a new emptying occurred in East Africa between 1820 and 1890 in the Indian Ocean slave trade. Overall, as much as one-half of the potential population of sub-Saharan Africa was lost.[27] Only since 1950 has Africa become the world's fastest growing region. Over the longer term, Africa's population increased eight-fold between 1800 and 2000, whereas the population of the Americas increased thirty-five times.

The African heritage of populations in the contemporary Americas varies directly with the role of the transatlantic slave trade in their creation. Maroon communities were unique in their ability to maintain their African genetic diversity. Those who were unable to escape slavery developed differently, with continued infusions through the transatlantic slave trade and hybridization, both with Europeans and Asians. Where natural increase occurred early in the establishment of slave populations, a "founder effect" may be identified, with significant genetic contributions from the first ethnic groups in the slave trade. Where natural increase was slow to emerge, and the masters persisted in replacing people through the slave trade, as in the sugar plantation economies of the Caribbean and Brazil, this founder effect was absent and the genetic heritage of the modern populations reflected more closely the profile of groups arriving

---

[27] Robert Harms, Bernard K. Freamon, and David W. Blight (eds.), *Indian Ocean Slavery in the Age of Abolition* (New Haven, CT, 2013), pp. 27–8.

later in the slave trade. In the case of Brazil, the population was sufficiently large to create persistent regional variation.[28]

The continuing visibility of the descendants of formerly enslaved and coerced populations depended on ethnic/racial difference. In Russia, emancipated serfs shared the ethnicity of their larger communities, and bodily markers such as beards and dress could be quickly transformed. Although the economic consequences of serfdom might persist for generations, the demographic markers did not. In much of Asia, enslaved people were taken from neighboring populations. At the other end of the scale, freed black and "colored" people in the Americas carried with them the public proof of their origins in Africa and, most often, slavery.

On a global scale, the demographic legacies of slavery and coerced labor appear vividly in the changed geographical distribution of the peoples of the world resulting directly and indirectly from forced migration. Typically, forced migration was one arm of imperial expansion, the other being the devastation of indigenous populations. From the middle of the nineteenth century, free migration became more important than forced, and this ushered in the great era of European migration to many parts of the temperate world, most of these people occupying regions not formerly sites of slave societies or coerced migration. The most dramatic changes in the world population map resulting from forced migration occurred in the tropics and subtropics, particularly in the Americas and Southeast Asia. Few of these people had the opportunity or chose to return to the homelands of their ancestors. Many live in persistent poverty, but most have come to share the demographic dynamics of the larger populations in which they find themselves and have come to participate in new (free) migration streams to richer regions, some of which are the homes of former imperial and colonial powers and some the same places to which people are trafficked in contemporary slavery.

A GUIDE TO FURTHER READING

The broad context of global demographic change since 1804 is surveyed in Massimo Livi Bacci, *A Concise History of World Population* (Oxford, 2012) and *A Short History of Migration* (Cambridge, 2012). The Global Slavery Index 2013 is available at www.globalslaveryindex.org.

---

[28] Nicolas Brucato, Olivier Cassar, Laure Tonasso, *et al.*, "The Imprint of the Slave Trade in an African American Population: Mitochondrial DNA, Y Chromosome and HTLV-1 Analysis in the Noir Marron of French Guiana," *BMC Evolutionary Biology*, 10 (2010): 1–19; Michael L. Deason, Antonio Salas, Simon P. Newman, *et al.*, "Interdisciplinary Approach to the Demography of Jamaica," *BMC Evolutionary Biology*, 12 (2012): 5; Wilson Araújo Silva, Maria Cátira Bortolini, Maria Paula Cruz Schneider, *et al.*, "mtDNA Haplogroup Analysis of Black Brazilian and Sub-Saharan Populations: Implications for the Atlantic Slave Trade," *Human Biology*, 78 (2006): 29–41.

Major works on Africa include Suzanne Miers and Igor Kopytoff (eds.), *Slavery in Africa: Historical and Anthropological Perspectives* (Madison, WI, 1977); Suzanne Miers and Richard Roberts (eds.), *The End of Slavery in Africa* (Madison, WI, 1988); Martin Klein, *Slavery and Colonial Rule in French West Africa* (Cambridge, 1998); Paul E. Lovejoy and Jan S. Hogendorn, *Slow Death for Slavery: The Course of Abolition in Northern Nigeria, 1897–1936* (Cambridge, 1993); Humphrey J. Fisher, *Slavery in the History of Muslim Black Africa* (New York, 2001); Eric Allina, *Slavery by Any Other Name: African Life under Company Rule in Colonial Mozambique* (Charlottesville, VA, 2012).

The Indian Ocean and its margins are covered by Gwyn Campbell (ed.), *The Structure of Slavery in Indian Ocean Africa and Asia* (London, 2004).

For Middle Eastern and Ottoman slavery, see Ehud R. Toledano, *Slavery and Abolition in the Ottoman Middle East* (Seattle, WA, 1998).

For Asia, see Indrani Chatterjee and Richard M. Eaton (eds.), *Slavery and South Asian History* (Bloomington, IN, 2006); Indrani Chatterjee, *Gender, Slavery and Law in Colonial India* (Oxford, 1999); Anthony Reid (ed.), *Slavery, Bondage and Dependency in Southeast Asia* (Saint Lucia, 1983); Cindy Yik-Yi Chu, "Human Trafficking and Smuggling in China," *Journal of Contemporary China*, 20 (2011): 39–52.

For the Americas, see Herbert S. Klein and Francisco Vidal Luna, *Slavery in Brazil* (Cambridge, 2010); B. W. Higman, *Slave Populations of the British Caribbean, 1807–1834* (Baltimore, MD, 1984); Robert William Fogel and Stanley L. Engerman, *Time on the Cross: The Economics of American Negro Slavery* (Boston, MA, 1974).

For sex and gender, see the two-volume collection edited by Gwyn Campbell, Suzanne Miers, and Joseph C. Miller, *Women and Slavery* (Athens, OH, 2007–08); Claire C. Robertson and Martin A. Klein (eds.), *Women and Slavery in Africa* (Madison, WI, 1983); and Madeline C. Zilfi, *Women and Slavery in the Late Ottoman Empire: The Design of Difference* (Cambridge, 2010).

Children are studied in Gwyn Campbell, Suzanne Miers, and Joseph C. Miller (eds.), *Child Slaves in the Modern World* (Athens, OH, 2011).

CHAPTER 3

OVERSEAS MOVEMENTS OF SLAVES AND INDENTURED WORKERS

DAVID NORTHRUP

INTRODUCTION

The labor migrations from the early 1800s to 1920 far exceeded those of any previous era in their magnitude and global scope. Despite concerted abolitionist efforts led by Great Britain, the slave trades from Africa remained substantial until the mid nineteenth century in the Atlantic and for much longer across the Sahara and in the Indian Ocean. As slavery declined, Britain and other countries initiated a new trade in indentured laborers, mostly from Asia, to meet the needs of sugar plantations, mines, and other labor-intensive industries. At much the same time, millions of other Asian and European overseas migrants, not necessarily bound by contracts, were transforming the demography of the Americas, Australia, and other lands. In addition to differences in their origins and status, the slave, indentured, and free labor migrations differed greatly in their magnitudes. Some 6.4 million slaves left Africa for the Americas, the Mediterranean, and Asia, and about 2 million indentured laborers moved overseas. Furthermore, some 160,000 convicts were forcibly transported from Britain to Australia between 1787 and 1868 and another 100,000 from France to French Guiana and New Caledonia between 1852 and 1938. Largest of all the overseas migrations were the 10 million other Asians who ventured abroad to work and the 50 million Europeans who emigrated by 1920. It is relevant to keep this larger context in mind, as this chapter examines the intercontinental movement of slaves and indentured laborers.

Moving people of whatever status was a big operation in this period, challenging technological capacities, ideas of freedom, and many government policies. The growing use of iron fastenings made it possible to build longer, taller, and faster wooden ships. Steam power first supplemented sails and, as engines became more efficient, replaced them. By the time the nineteenth century was turning into the twentieth, giant ships with steel hulls and powerful engines had become the new norm. Greater size and speed helped lower the risks and costs of sea travel, as did improvements in medical care and tighter government regulation. This was also a period that saw changing definitions of bondage and freedom. Abolitionists generally welcomed indentured labor as a free alternative to slavery, but over time critics high and low denounced indentured contracts as an unacceptable form of bondage. This reversal paralleled new perspectives in Western lands charging that supposedly "free" industrial workers were actually wage slaves and that supposedly "free" European women were in fact being held in domestic servitude. Evolving government policies reflected these changes. Slave trading and slavery became illegal. While often subsidizing the entry of European migrants into high-wage lands in temperate climes, policies first authorized indentured migration to more tropical plantation economies, then made it illegal.

The slave and indentured labor trades had close commonalities and striking differences. The most obvious commonality was the fact that transatlantic slaves and most indentured laborers went to plantation systems. Although in theory indenture was meant to be a free labor alternative to slavery, in practice the distinction might be blurred. The blurring was most obvious in places like Cuba, where the two labor systems coexisted for a time. However, indentured labor was more distinct from slavery in destinations where that institution no longer existed (such as British and French Caribbean colonies) or where it had not previously existed (such as Hawaii, Fiji, and Australia). Slaves and indentured laborers differed strikingly in other ways. The slaves transported overseas were nearly all Africans; nine out of ten indentured laborers were Asians, most coming from British India. The close government regulation of the indentured labor trade also sets it apart from the largely unregulated slave trades. Finally, while appreciating the similarities and differences of the economic, political, and ideological constructions of these labor systems, it is important not to lose sight of how they looked to those passing through them. Enslaved people might struggle to escape or resign themselves to a fate they had not chosen, but most indentured laborers, however constrained by their homeland circumstances and powerful external factors, had chosen to migrate and, like other voluntary immigrants, embarked on their journeys with hope.

SLAVE TRADES

While slaves of many origins existed in 1800, nearly all intercontinentally traded slaves came from sub-Saharan Africa, as had been the case for several centuries. This was true of not only the Western-dominated trades across the Atlantic and in the Indian Ocean, but also the Arab-dominated trades across the Red Sea, the Indian Ocean, and the Sahara. Despite the continuities of these trading patterns, other dynamics of the African slave trades changed significantly during the 1800s. Within sub-Saharan Africa, there was a great increase in enslavement associated with the growth of Islamic empires and other states in West Africa, the expansion of Ottoman

Egypt south into the Sudan, and the expansion of Omani Arab dominion into inland Eastern Africa from a new headquarters on the island of Zanzibar. Externally, the Western slave trades continued at a high level during the first half of the nineteenth century until British-led abolitionist efforts brought it to an end in 1867. The Arab slave trades from Africa remained strong during the nineteenth century and, though also diminished by international pressures in the latter decades, continued into the twentieth century.

Overall, 6.4 million slaves left sub-Saharan Africa during the nineteenth century. The carefully compiled records that in 2008 created *Voyages: The Transatlantic Slave Trade Database* (hereafter TAST2) enable the size of the transatlantic slave trade to the Americas in those years to be estimated at 3.9 million with a high degree of confidence. This was over 30 percent of the 12.5 million enslaved Africans entering the Atlantic slave trade after 1500. As the first column of Figure 3.1 shows, half of these came from ports in West Central Africa, a quarter from the Gulf of Guinea ports, and the rest from other parts of West Africa and an expanded trade from Southeast Africa. Western ships carried another 182,000 slaves from East and Southeast Africa to the Mascarene Islands of Réunion and Mauritius in that period. In contrast, the records of Arab slave trades from sub-Saharan Africa to the Islamic lands of North Africa, the Middle East, and elsewhere are too fragmentary to permit their volume to be estimated with equal confidence. The trans-Saharan slave trade may be considered "overseas" only metaphorically, as in calling camels "the ships of the desert" and in the Arabic designation of both southern and northern edges of the desert as a shore (*sahel*). Even so, to complete the picture it seems appropriate to include this important slave trade along with those crossing the conventionally recognized oceans. Scholarly estimates of the magnitude of trans-Saharan slave trade in the nineteenth century have ranged as high as 2 million, but the work of historian Ralph Austen suggests 1.5 million as a more reasonable estimate of how many enslaved Africans left sub-Saharan Africa, a volume higher than in earlier centuries. Of those slaves who reached North Africa, 80 percent or more remained there, the rest being shipped to other Mediterranean destinations. The Arab trades from Northeastern Africa across the Red Sea to Arabia and from ports on the Swahili Coast to destinations elsewhere on the Indian Ocean also increased in the nineteenth century to a total of about 800,000. The combined Arab slave trades from sub-Saharan Africa in the nineteenth century represented 44 percent of the estimated number of enslaved Africans entering on these routes since 1500. Overall, as Figure 3.1 shows, about 63 percent of the slave trades from Africa were in Western hands and the remainder under Arab egis. One should note that this tally does not include the very considerable slave trades within sub-Saharan Africa (see Chapter 8) nor

Figure 3.1 Origins, Destinations, and Volumes of African Slave Trade, 1801–1900

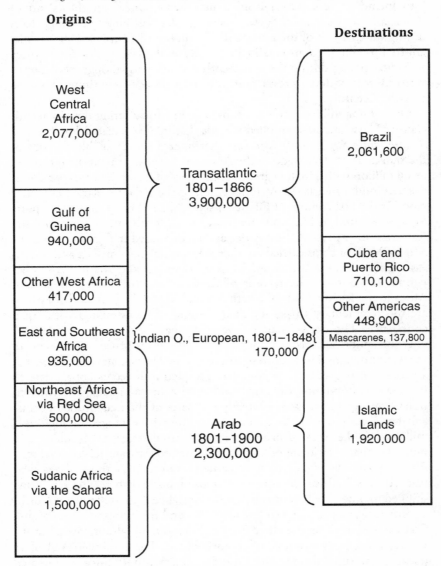

Origins

Destinations

West Central Africa 2,077,000

Gulf of Guinea 940,000

Other West Africa 417,000

East and Southeast Africa 935,000

Northeast Africa via Red Sea 500,000

Sudanic Africa via the Sahara 1,500,000

Transatlantic 1801–1866 3,900,000

}Indian O., European, 1801–1848{ 170,000

Arab 1801–1900 2,300,000

Brazil 2,061,600

Cuba and Puerto Rico 710,100

Other Americas 448,900

Mascarenes, 137,800

Islamic Lands 1,920,000

Sources: TAST2; Ralph A. Austen, "The 19th-Century Islamic Slave Trade from East Africa (Swahili and Red Sea Coasts): A Tentative Census," in William Gervase Clarence-Smith (ed.), *The Economics of the Indian Ocean Slave Trade in the Nineteenth Century* (London, 1989), pp. 22–44; Ralph A. Austen, "The Mediterranean Islamic Slave Trade out of Africa: A Tentative Census," *Slavery and Abolition*, 13 (1992): 214–48; Richard B. Allen, "Satisfying the 'Want for Labouring People': European Slave Trading in the Indian Ocean, 1500–1850," *Journal of World History*, 21 (2010): 45–73, tables 1 and 2.

the much smaller Indian Ocean slave trades from South and Southeast Asia (fewer than 10,000).

In the slave trade of the nineteenth century, there were major alterations in the nationality of the carriers and the destinations of the trades. During the half-century before Britain's withdrawal from the slave trade at the beginning of 1808, British merchants had been the greatest participants in the Atlantic slave trade. The TAST2 database estimates that over 40 percent of the slave ships in that period had been British. After British withdrawal, Portuguese and Brazilian vessels accounted for two-thirds of the Atlantic slave trade, with another quarter under Spanish (or Uruguayan) flags. (In this calculation ships flying American flags of convenience to evade interception have been allocated to their actual owners' nationalities.) This change also reflects the withdrawal of other former carriers: Denmark in 1803, the United States in 1808, the Netherlands in 1814, and France in 1831.

Many former markets for African-born slaves in the Americas closed under circumstances linked to different revolutionary movements. France's major market in the Americas collapsed as the result of the successful slave revolt in its Caribbean colony Saint Domingue (Haiti). During and after the American Revolution, the northern states had ended slavery, but the closing of the remaining US markets to new transatlantic slaves had less to do with liberal ideas than with slave-owners' fears that slaves who had once been free in Africa were more likely to lead a rebellion like Haiti's. In the wake of the revolutions in mainland Spanish America, liberal reformers ended the slave trade and slavery, a task made easier by the fact that slavery was generally an unimportant institution in those lands. Cuba and Brazil, where slavery persisted, became the largest destinations for slaves in the Americas and the last to end the importation of newly enslaved Africans.

A third factor in changing the dynamics of the Atlantic slave trade was British pressure on other European nations to participate in an abolitionist movement. Although French, US, and Portuguese patrols also functioned, their combined effect was dwarfed by the size and success of Britain's effort. Over a half-century, the British used armed patrols to intercept slave-trading vessels in the Atlantic trade, employing bullying, bribes, and diplomacy to get European and African states to sign treaties that provided a legal basis for abolitionist actions. British patrols gradually extended their range along the coast of West Africa, then south of the equator and around the southern tip of Africa. At its peak in the mid-1840s, the patrols employed 15 percent of Royal Navy ships and over 10 percent of naval personnel. Historian David Eltis has estimated that the patrols and other anti-slave trade efforts in the Atlantic cost £12.4 million, a sum comparable to all the profits British merchants had made from slave trading in the half-century before 1808. Under the authority of treaties, British naval patrols were able to intercept nearly 600 ships carrying slaves in the Atlantic and to emancipate and resettle some 160,000 liberated Africans. Another 1,000 ships without slaves were detained under treaties allowing the seizure of vessels carrying equipment usable in the slave trade. Most of the condemned vessels were destroyed. The total vessels intercepted represented more than a fifth of the ships engaged during the last six decades of the transatlantic slave trade. Once the transatlantic slave trade ended in 1867, British naval vessels and resources were devoted to suppressing the Indian Ocean slave trade, sanctioned by a new round of treaties, of which the 1873 treaty with the Omani Sultan of Zanzibar was of critical importance. Over three decades from 1860 to 1890, British patrols in the Indian Ocean intercepted over 1,000 vessels and liberated another 12,000 Africans from slavery.[1]

During the nineteenth century, the average duration of a slave voyage across the Atlantic decreased, as did the average mortality suffered by the enslaved passengers. The summary statistics in the TAST2 show that passages took an average of forty-five days in the years 1801 to 1866, compared to sixty-seven days in the years 1751 to 1800, and mortality averaged 10 percent, compared to 10.8 percent in the previous half-century. Mortality varied considerably by African coast of origin. For example, on voyages from the Bight of Benin or Slave Coast, mortality was 6.5 percent, lower than the average, and those from West Central Africa (Angola and adjoining regions) saw losses of about 8 percent. Higher than average mortality occurred on voyages from the Bight of Biafra (16.5 percent) and from Southeast Africa (18.7 percent). Some of the variation reflects differences in the length of the Middle Passage: an average of thirty-nine days for West Central Africa versus sixty-eight days from Southeast Africa. However, the four-day difference in average travel time from Bight of Benin compared to the neighboring Bight of Biafra cannot, by itself, account for the 10 percentage points difference in mortality, leading scholars to suspect that the relative health of slaves taken on from these coasts is a factor which must be taken into consideration.

The conditions endured by slaves on these journeys were grim and varied, but poorly documented. Vessels used in the transatlantic (and Indian Ocean) slave trades varied considerably in size, degree of crowding, and the treatment by ships' officers and crew. A small ship in the transatlantic trade at mid-century might provide the slaves stowed below deck little more than 14 inches of headroom, while the largest vessels had as much as 8 feet of head space. Most slaves in the transatlantic slave trade of

---

[1] David Eltis, *Economic Growth and the Ending of the Transatlantic Slave Trade* (Oxford, 1987), pp. 81–122; www.slavevoyages.org launched 2008 (hereafter TAST2); Raymond Howell, *The Royal Navy and the Slave Trade* (New York, 1987), p. 220. This chapter draws heavily on Eltis' book and the TAST2.

the 1800s were transported on mid-sized ships (100–250 tons) configured with half-decks that provided more space for slaves to lie down at the cost of headroom. Such ships generally carried quantities of water and food adequate for a normal crossing or for one somewhat longer than normal. On the whole, transatlantic slave ships in the first half of the 1800s were not much larger than those used in the previous half-century. Some determined slavers even bought Yankee Clippers to outrun the British patrols, though the members of the squadron also acquired such ships from those captured to use in pursuit. At mid-century, a few vessels had steam power, but the rapidly declining Atlantic slave trade kept the changes in ship technology from having much overall significance.

The Arab slave trades exhibit both similarities to the Atlantic trade and differences from it. The closest comparisons can be made with the Indian Ocean and Red Sea trades. The classic ship in these waters was the dhow, whose wooden planks were generally sewn together with stout cords. Dhows varied considerably in size, but those carrying slaves on the longer routes were fairly large. Working from the records of dhows the British captured for trading in slaves from East Africa between 1858 and 1873, historian Abdul Sheriff has shown that the average dhow displaced 132 tons (just over half the size of slave vessels in the Atlantic in that period). The largest vessels, generally from the Swahili port of Kilwa, carried over 100 slaves each, whereas the largest vessels in the transatlantic trade embarked an average of 360 slaves. In contrast to the Atlantic, where slaves either constituted the main cargo or were entirely absent, Indian Ocean dhows carried varying mixtures of slaves and goods, so that the number of slaves carried correlates poorly with vessel size. The movement of slaves across the Sahara shows the greatest differences from these maritime trades. First, slaves had to walk the distances. Infants had to be carried by their mothers, as did small children, unless they were allowed to ride atop the loaded camels. The only solace for the slaves in these arduous crossings was that the caravans moved at night when desert temperatures were cooler. Although storms could be dangerous for both land and sea trades, the trans-Saharan trade had additional perils. The risk of running short of food and water was greater in the desert, since the camels could not manage enough for the entire crossing. Thus, anything that delayed reaching the next oasis might have serious consequences. Additionally, slaves who became too ill to transport themselves might be left behind unlike those who became ill at sea, who remained on the vessel unless, as in the famous case of the *Zong*, they were thrown overboard.

No precise quantification of slave mortality in the Arab trades is possible, since only scattered records exist. However, the fact that these trades used the same techniques as in previous centuries suggests that mortality in transit would not have fallen as it did in the Atlantic.

Historian John Hunwick observes mildly, "The passage across the Sahara or up the Nile valley was, in many ways, as perilous and cruel as the crossing of the Atlantic," a comment one might interpret as suggesting a mortality of 10 to 11 percent. However, other historians believe that mortality in the trans-Saharan trade, as well as in the Arab slave trade of the Indian Ocean, may have been on the order of 20 or 25 percent, much higher than in the Atlantic in the nineteenth century. Historian Richard Allen uses similar estimates of mortality for the better-documented European slave trade in the Indian Ocean to the Mascarene Islands.[2]

Another difference among the slave trades was in the proportions of men, women, and children they transported. In the Atlantic, the proportion of male slaves rose to 67.6 percent, compared to 64.2 percent in the 1700s, and the increase in proportion of children was even more, jumping from 18.4 percent during the 1700s to 29.4 percent during the 1800s. However, there was notable variation in the proportions of males and children from different coasts of Africa, probably related to internal circumstances. The highest proportion of males came from Atlantic and Indian Ocean ports below the equator; the highest proportion of children came from the Bights of Benin and Biafra and Southeast Africa. In contrast to the greater demand for males in the Americas and Mascarenes, most slaves in the Islamic world were women, who were concentrated in domestic service (household servants, artisans, concubines). In Oman, African slaves played a significant role in clove production in the 1800s. Even there, agriculture was the principal occupation of only about a third of the slave population. The proportions of men, women, and children also varied in the Arab slave trades. Whereas females characteristically outnumbered males on trans-Saharan routes, the slave trade from Eastern African ports had a more balanced sex ratio, along with a higher proportion of children. For example, children numbered 110 out of the 192 slaves (57 percent) on a dhow bound for the Comoros that was captured by the British naval vessel *Dryad* in early September 1868.[3]

The sex and age of slaves, whether traveling overland or over water, also affected their experiences. Because of their greater propensity to

---

[2] TAST2, Summary Statistics, 1801–1866; John Hunwick and Eve Troutt Powell, *The African Diaspora in the Mediterranean Lands of Islam* (Princeton, NJ, 2002), pp. 67–81; Richard B. Allen, "The Mascarene Slave-Trade and Labour Migration in the Indian Ocean during the Eighteenth and Nineteenth Centuries," *Slavery and Abolition*, 24 (2003): Table 3; Richard B. Allen, "Satisfying the 'Want for Labouring People': European Slave Trading in the Indian Ocean, 1500–1850," *Journal of World History*, 21 (2010): Tables 1 and 2.

[3] Abdul Sheriff, *Slaves, Spices and Ivory in Zanzibar, 1770–1873* (London, 1987), pp. 35–41; ibid, "Localization and Social Composition of the East African Slave Trade, 1856–1873," *Slavery and Abolition*, 9 (1988): 136–38; Eltis, *Economic Growth*, p. 69 and App. B. For the *Dryad's* capture, see *Parliamentary Papers* 1868–69 [4131] Class A, Correspondence with the British Commissioners, no. 11, Commander Maxwell to Secretary to the Admiralty, Seychelles, September 12, 1868.

flight and otherwise resist enslavement, men were usually shackled with chains or ropes in the transatlantic and trans-Saharan trades. Once at sea, women were generally not bound, but were kept under watch. Young children were given the greatest freedom. On Arab vessels in the Indian Ocean, there seems to have been less use of bonds than in the Atlantic, but all slave transporters made ready use of whips and other punishments.

Although it is impossible to quantify these variations, a few individual cases may suggest the range of experiences. For example, the 466 enslaved Africans loaded onto the Spanish brig *El Almirante* at the port of Lagos in 1829 and headed for Cuba had the good fortune to have been intercepted by a British patrol, though eleven of the slaves perished during the strong resistance that accompanied the capture. Another thirty-nine died before they could be liberated by a Court of Mixed Commission (in this case, a court having both Spanish and British judges) in Sierra Leone. A young slave shipped to Brazil the next year later described the sufferings of his fellow captives to a parliamentary committee. As a youth, Augustino had not been put in chains, but he remembered the misery of the naked adults below deck, the poor diet, the inadequate water, and the many deaths. He believed many died of dehydration, while others, fearing they were going to be eaten, jumped overboard when they got the chance. In the Sahara, fear of wild animals kept most from venturing outside the camps where caravans halted during the day. An account from the 1830s tells of two men, braver or more desperate than most, who did take flight. To escape a lion that was stalking them, they managed to climb a tree, despite being chained together, but the lion grabbed and partly consumed the nearer of the two. The other was recaptured but died soon after, apparently due to the frightfulness of his experience. A rare account of the personal experience of a young woman comes from a 17 year old on a dhow captured by the British off the coast of Arabia in 1870: Sarhea had been captured by Arabs while she was on her way to the inland market town of Unyamyembe, capital of the East African Nyamwezi kingdom. After a three-month trek to the coast, she was shipped to the island of Zanzibar, where she remained for five months before being sold and sailing at night on a dhow to Muscat, the port of Oman. The details of these few individual accounts can hint at the variety of physical and psychological sufferings of the enslaved.[4]

---

[4] Great Britain, Parliamentary Papers 1830, X, 126, no. 29, HM Commissioners to the Earl of Aberdeen, Sierra Leone, March 23, 1829, enclosing Case of the Spanish Brig "El Almirante"; ibid. 1850, IX (53), *Report of the Select Committee of the House of Lords, on the African Slave Trade*, pp. 162–3; for the voyage see http://slavevoyages.org/voyages/b2cIW6tS; Hunwick and Powell, *African Diaspora*, pp. 65–81; Sarhea's story is recounted in P. H. Colomb, *Slave Catching in the Indian Ocean* (London, 1968 [reprint of 1873 edition]), p. 29.

Most studies of the slave trade concentrate on the passage from coast to coast, known in the Atlantic as the "Middle Passage," but, as this name suggests, the enslaved and their captors were part of much larger and more complex networks. Enslavement in Africa usually began well inland, as in the just-recounted story of Sarhea. Accounts by other individuals captured in interior regions describe being sold and bought several times before reaching the shore, whether in markets or through more private transactions. As a result of the alienation and disruption they experienced, slaves' physical and mental health was affected well before they embarked on an ocean or desert passage. From a business perspective, Western and Arab slave traders were also engaged in larger and more complex trading patterns. The "Middle Passage" in the Atlantic ended with the shipment to Europe of the products of slave plantations, notably sugar and cotton. The voyages had begun by assembling trade goods from around the world that would satisfy African customers. Cargoes varied by nationality of the ship and the African coast they visited, but Asian textiles, European metals and hardware, and New World rum and tobacco featured prominently. A French ship trading along the Bight of Benin in the late eighteenth century brought a cargo that may serve as an example: one-third European and Asian textiles, 27 percent Brazilian tobacco, 21 percent cowrie shells from the Indian Ocean (used by Africans as a currency), 11 percent French brandy, and 7 percent firearms, gunpowder, and other goods. In addition to slaves, foreign traders purchased African provisions, timber, hides, gold, and ivory, which could amount to a fifth or more of expenditures. During the last decades of their participation in the slave trade, for example, British merchants purchased significant quantities of ivory, palm oil, pepper, and redwood along the Bight of Biafra, and after 1808 this "legitimate" trade, especially in palm oil, grew to be of even greater economic value than the trade in slaves had ever been. American trade with East Africa also increased greatly after that nation withdrew from the slave trade. Similarly, Indian textiles underpinned the Arab trade with East Africa, and elephant ivory, copal resin, and Zanzibar-grown cloves accompanied slaves in the export trade.[5]

Slave trading in the 1800s was generally a big business, complex in its operations and full of risks to the uninitiated. Only those with specialized knowledge, trading connections, and reserve capital or credit could expect to weather the risks, which greatly increased when the Atlantic trade became illegal. In compensation, strong demand in the Americas increased the difference between the purchase price in Africa and the selling price in the

[5] David Northrup, "New Evidence of the French Slave Trade in the Bight of Benin," *Slavery and Abolition*, 24 (2003): 64–5; Stephen D. Behrendt, A. J. H. Latham, and David Northrup, *The Diary of Antera Duke: An Eighteenth-Century African Slave Trader* (New York, 2010), pp. 90–9; Sheriff, *Slaves, Spices*, pp. 249–56 and passim.

Americas. Eltis has shown that in the period 1815 to 1850, prime male slaves from Africa sold in Brazil for four or five times what they had cost in Africa. In Cuba, the difference was nearly seven times. However, the slave traders' profits were curtailed by much higher transport costs due to new risks of interception and having to pay bribes to land slaves illegally in the Americas.

The dominance of sophisticated British commercial and financial organization before 1807 demonstrated, in Eltis' words, that "the slave trade was one of the best examples of successful capitalism." Britain's withdrawal from the slave trade changed the nationality of the owners and direct investors, but did not fundamentally alter the dominance of big firms. Indeed, the growing risks posed by abolitionist patrols seem to have accelerated the growth of large new firms that spread risks across many investors. Some of these were individuals, including ship owners and captains, but, as Eltis has shown, the slave trades to Brazil and Cuba became increasingly concentrated in the hands of a few firms, generally dominated by Iberian owners, which were able to cultivate good connections with suppliers in Africa and buyers in the Americas, as well as with investors and suppliers of essential trade goods in Europe and elsewhere. Eltis further points out that British firms continued to supply many of the trade goods after 1807 and much of the financing. Those services were legal. Accepting slaves as collateral was not, though it was common. US firms were also important shipbuilders for the Atlantic slave trade. More than a hundred American-built vessels were used in the slave trade after the US withdrawal, a third constructed in Baltimore. The Baltimore clippers' speed enabled them to outrun slower British patrol ships and to cross the Atlantic faster.[6]

The slave trades of the Indian Ocean had a similar business model. While some small ships operated on a shoestring across the Red Sea and some Indian Ocean dhows carried only a handful of slaves, the major voyages from Ethiopia, Zanzibar, Kilwa, and other East African locations required substantial investments. As historian W. G. Clarence-Smith points out, the large dhows operating in the Indian Ocean were "the specialized business of a handful of wealthy Muslim merchants" and received financing from Indian merchants, especially those from the state of Gujarat. Gujaratis in Mozambique also served as brokers for the Spanish and Portuguese shippers in the transatlantic slave trade, just as they had been doing from the 1730s in transporting slaves from Mozambique to Portuguese enclaves in India.[7]

---

[6] Eltis, *Economic Growth*, pp. 51–5, 145–63, 260–4, 269–82, quotation 51; TAST2, consulted 3-14-13.
[7] William Gervase Clarence-Smith, "The Economics of the Indian Ocean Slave Trade in the Nineteenth Century: An Overview," in W. G. Clarence-Smith (ed.), *The Economics of the Indian Ocean Slave Trade in the Nineteenth Century* (London, 1989), pp. 11–12; Pedro Machado, "A Forgotten Corner of the Indian Ocean: Gujarati Merchants, Portuguese India and the Mozambique Slave-Trade, c.1730–1830," *Slavery and Abolition*, 24 (2003): 17–32.

In short, though the overseas slave trades were on their last legs in the nineteenth century, the vitality and complexity that had so long sustained them remained evident. As the slaves' origins, destinations, and transportation underwent changes, the underlying structures of the trades continued. Those seeking to profit from slavery and slave trading were participating in networks that extended far and wide from inner Africa across the Atlantic and Indian oceans and across the Sahara. In addition to the direct participants in slave trading and their customers, many others supplied financing, trade goods, and ships, few of whom would have seen themselves as part of the business of slaving. Despite their central importance to this history, the ordeals of the enslaved have left the scantiest documentation.

INDENTURED LABORERS

The new indentured labor trade of the period 1834 to 1920 played a major role in the transition from chattel slavery. The trade linked impoverished people seeking work with distant employers in low-population areas in need of a labor force. Initially indentured laborers were sought as an alternative or supplement to the declining slave trades to existing plantation economies in the Americas (notably Cuba) and Indian Ocean (Mauritius and Réunion), but the origins of the laborers and their far-flung destinations became quite different from those in the slave trade. Although the new indentured laborers came from many lands, most were Asians and most were employed in enterprises that were new or that had made only modest previous use of slave labor. Their destinations ranged from new sugar plantations around the Pacific to mining and railroad building in Africa.

Contracts of indenture provided free passage overseas to individuals otherwise unable to afford the costs of migrating and who, in return, agreed to work for a specified period of years for those who bought their contracts. The system had been widely used to recruit Europeans for British colonies in the West Indies and North American mainland in the seventeenth and eighteenth centuries. Indeed, the majority of Europeans crossing the North Atlantic before 1800 had been indentured. The new indentured laborers were bound to work for a set number of years, but, unlike slaves, their term of bondage was limited and not heritable. By the standards of the mid nineteenth century, indentured labor was free labor. The new system incorporated a number of new features, which varied with the supervising power and were refined over time. The contracts usually provided for wages to be paid and for government oversight and inspection, features that had not been part of older indentured labor systems. The period of indenture ranged from one to ten years, but the most common contract was for five years, with free return passage provided if a second contract was signed.

Figure 3.2 Sources, Destinations, and Volumes of Indentured Migrants, 1834–1922

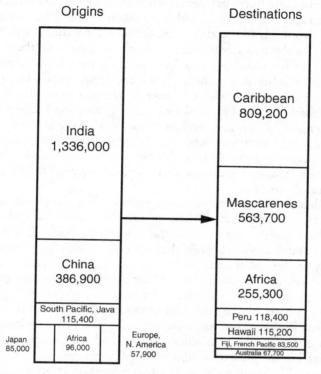

Source: David Northrup, *Indentured Labor in the Age of Imperialism, 1834–1922* (Cambridge, 1995), tables A1 and A.2.

Despite these improvements in contract terms, the system was brought to an end in the early twentieth century under accusations that it was a form of unfree labor and of a new system of slavery.[8]

During the nine decades from 1831 to 1920, over 2 million individuals were transported from one continent to another on contracts of indenture. That number includes some individuals who sailed from their native lands more than once; it does not take into account the large number of individuals who signed one or more additional contracts while overseas, often to secure a free passage back home. The new indentured laborers were more global in their origins than those in the slave trade. They included some 56,000 Europeans (mostly Portuguese from Madeira), 96,000

[8] This section draws heavily on David Northrup, *Indentured Labor in the Age of Imperialism, 1834–1922* (Cambridge, 1995), esp. ch. 4 and app. A.

Africans, and a similar number of South Pacific islanders, but, as Figure 3.2 shows, most came from Asia. Seven out of every eight indentured migrants came from South or East Asia, with most coming from British India, which supplied two-thirds of the entire indentured labor trade. Concerned with ensuring that this new labor trade was clearly different from the slave trade, British regulators added two new features to the contracts: Indian laborers were entitled to free passage home at the end of one or two contracts, and they were paid a modest monthly wage in addition to free housing, food, clothing allowances, and medical attention. British officials also policed the recruitment, transport, and working conditions of the laborers to ensure that the contract terms were observed. Since the conditions at their destinations are examined elsewhere in this volume, the most significant regulations for this chapter's purposes are those that governed their recruitment and transport overseas.

The destinations of the migrants were even more global than their origins, as Figure 3.2 shows. Most indentured laborers went to two large geographical areas: 810,000 to the Caribbean basin (including the Guianas) and 820,000 to lands that are now considered parts of Africa, primarily to the Mascarene Islands in the Indian Ocean, plus British mainland colonies in southern and eastern parts of the continent. The remaining 385,000 went to Pacific basin lands (in descending order of importance, Peru, Hawaii, Fiji, and Queensland, Australia). Most of these indentured laborers were employed on sugar plantations, initially to supplement or replace slaves in older colonies, and increasingly in lands that had never known plantation slavery, notably Hawaii, Queensland, Peru, Natal, and Fiji. Some indentured laborers worked at other occupations: Chinese mined gold in the Transvaal Republic and guano on Peruvian islands; Indians helped build the East African railroad from Mombasa to Uganda. Politically, the destinations were less diverse: two-thirds of indentured laborers went to parts of the British Empire, with the rest going (in descending order) to French colonies, Spanish Cuba, Peru, Hawaii, and Dutch Guiana.

Some observers have seen little difference between the slave and indentured labor trades. As other chapters explore, the transition from slavery to a free labor system was complex. In British colonies, for example, emancipated plantation slaves had been required to provide their former masters with 40.5 hours a week of unpaid labor for several years. Rather than serving as a transition to free labor, this "apprenticeship" extracted as much unpaid labor as possible while providing few hints of the incentives that lay at the basis of free labor. In the judgment of historian William Green, apprenticeship was "little more than a mitigated form of slavery." The transition from slave-like apprenticeship to free indentured labor was similarly flawed in the judgment of many historians. In the

1970s, Hugh Tinker entitled his influential study of indentured Indians overseas *A New System of Slavery* and historian François Renault called the labor systems that replaced slavery in French colonies a "new servitude." These sentiments are consistent with the views of some contemporaries, whose unflattering names for the indentured labor trades capture the involuntary nature of recruitment and transport: the Chinese trade was "pig trade"; that from India the "coolie trade"; labor recruitment in the South Pacific was known as "blackbirding." Among British officials, similar views are not hard to uncover. The British Secretary of State for the Colonies in 1840 expressed concern that the nascent trade in indentured Indian laborers might easily become "a new system of slavery," while the Viceroy of India, in urging its termination in 1915, charged that it has indeed become "a system of forced labor ... differing but little from ... slavery."[9]

The amount of freedom exercised by indentured laborers varied over time as the system worked out initial kinks and also varied by place of origin and destination. For Africans, the slave trade and indentured labor trade were closely linked. About a quarter (39,000) of the 160,000 enslaved Africans whom British patrols liberated from the transatlantic trade were persuaded to go to the British Caribbean as indentured laborers. Studies by Johnson Asiegbu and Monica Schuler both conclude that these African emigration schemes came close to slave trading or were indistinguishable from it. Renault concludes that the French efforts that supplied "labor to their Indian Ocean colony of Réunion after the end of slavery in 1848 by purchasing slaves in East Africa and then declaring them 'free' was an administrative fiction."[10]

On the other hand, close comparisons of the slave and the indentured labor trades reveal highly significant differences between the two, which raise doubts about such blanket conflations of the two trades. Despite serious lapses in the system, especially with regard to African and Chinese recruitment, these exceptions do not negate the fact that this was the best-run large-scale labor recruitment that had ever existed up until that time. The differences between the slave and indentured labor trades were due to three factors: the volunteers were more rigorously screened for physical and

[9] William A. Green, *British Slave Emancipation: The Sugar Colonies and the Great Experiment* (Oxford, 1976), p. 151; François Renault, *Libération d'esclaves et nouvelle servitude: les rachats de captifs africains pour le compte des colonies françaises après l'abolition de l'esclavage* (Abidjan, 1976), p. 71. Hugh Tinker, *A New System of Slavery: The Export of Indian Labour Overseas, 1830–1920* (London, 1974), pp. vi, 339–40, is the source of the quotations from British officials.

[10] Johnson U. J. Asiegbu, *Slavery and the Politics of Liberation, 1787–1861 A Study of Liberated African Emigration and British Anti-Slavery Policy* (London, 1969), p. 119; Monica Schuler, "The Recruitment of African Indentured Labourers for the European Colonies in the Nineteenth Century," in P. C. Emmer (ed.), *Colonialism and Migration: Indentured Labour before and after Slavery* (The Hague, 1986), pp. 125–7.

mental "defects" and many were rejected; shipboard conditions were strictly regulated; and there were significant advances in maritime transportation and medical science in the second half of the nineteenth century. In addition to these top-down factors, one should give ample weight to the substantial differences between the outlooks of indentured and enslaved individuals.

Like the slave traders before them, indentured labor recruiters and regulators made efforts to ensure that their passengers were fit to travel and to maintain their health en route. Effectiveness varied in both systems. In the East Asian indentured labor trade, for example, the achievements of the Japanese and Chinese governments could not have been more different. The reformist Meiji government in Japan directly and effectively supervised the recruitment and safe transport of 85,000 Japanese indentured laborers to Hawaii and Peru. In contrast, the imperial government of China refused to legalize labor migration to foreign destinations, but was unable to stop it. As a result, the fates of many of the 387,000 indentured Chinese migrants were left to the not-so-tender mercies of port officials, local recruiters, and foreign transporters, producing conditions that closely resembled those on slave ships.

Most recruiting was done by agents of British Government, whose concern to demonstrate this was free labor led to efforts to ensure that those who signed up did so voluntarily and were able to do the physical work for which they were recruited. Those seeking to emigrate were screened for physical impediments. To the extent possible, authorities made sure that recruits knew what was expected of them at their destinations and freely assented to the terms of their contracts. That shortfalls and lapses occurred does not negate the fact that overall standards were as good as could be expected under the circumstances. For example, British efforts to ensure a gender balance among recruited Indians was actually much more successful than most contemporaries would have believed possible. In contrast to the almost total absence of females among Chinese indentured laborers to destinations like Cuba and Peru, women came to constitute well over a quarter of Indian migrant laborers. The proportion of Indian females going to Mauritius, for example, rose from 12.4 percent in the early years of that trade to 26.4 percent in the 1860s. Similarly, the proportion of Indian women transported to British Guiana rose from 16.1 percent in the early 1850s to 30.6 percent in the period between 1868 and 1917. The standards of French authorities overseeing the indentured trade from India were similarly high since they had to abide by British regulations, because most of their recruits came from British India. One French physician became so distraught at the failure of his efforts to curb deaths among Indians under his supervision during a voyage to French Antilles that he committed suicide.

Additional close regulation at sea followed the screening and gender balancing in the ports. Historically, ships at sea had been under the authority of their captains, who had the power of life and death. Though the Portuguese introduced measures in 1684 to try to regulate slave-carrying ships, the first effective extension of national regulations to the high seas was the Dolben Act passed by the British Parliament in 1788, which limited the number of slaves in proportion to ship size on British vessels. Subsequent legislation in 1799 put a limit on the number of slaves to be carried per ship. In time, regulation was extended to other passenger vessels. After 1828, British Passenger Acts became increasingly detailed, specifying the amount of food, water, and medical supplies a passenger ship had to carry per person. These rules applied equally to all passenger ships, whether transporting indentured Asians or free Europeans. The Colonial Land and Emigration Commission created in 1840 by the British Government kept track of passenger mortality and issued detailed regulations to save lives. In 1840, ships from British possessions whose routes crossed the equator were required to provide accommodations of at least 15 square feet (1.4 square meters) per passenger with headroom of at least 5.5 feet (1.7 meters) that could be divided into no more than two tiers of berths. New regulations in 1855 increased space requirements and reduced densities. The enforcement of these regulations seems to have been as tight on ships carrying the indentured migrants as on those carrying free European passengers. These British shipboard regulations also governed French vessels carrying migrants from South Asia.[11]

Larger, faster ships were more important in the indentured labor trade than they were in the nineteenth-century transatlantic slave trade. Only a few clippers and steamers were used in the last years of the slave trade, but steam-powered ships became the norm from the 1870s on routes from India to Mauritius, Africa, and Southeast Asia. All indentured Japanese crossed the Pacific in steel-hulled steamships, and all of these ships were Japanese owned and built. While slaves in the transatlantic trade were crammed into vessels averaging under 200 tons, ships conveying indentured Chinese to the British West Indies between 1852 and 1873 averaged 870 tons and those transporting Indians to that destination averaged 968 tons.

Because of better regulation and better ships, there were dramatic differences in mortality between slave voyages and indentured labor voyages. As Table 3.1 shows, on voyages of similar duration to the Americas in the 1840s to 1860s, enslaved Africans perished at almost four times the rate

---

[11] Northrup, *Indentured Labor*, pp. 81–85.

Table 3.1 *Mortality on Mid-Nineteenth-Century Voyages*

Routes	Period	Average Days En Route	Deaths Per 1,000 Per Voyage	Deaths Per 1,000 Per Month
Enslaved Africans to the Americas	1841–66	36	130.0	108.3
Indentured Africans to British West Indies	1848–67	32	35.2	32.0
Indentured Indians to Mauritius	1858–68	38	21.6	17.0
Indentured Indians to Martinique	1853–58	85	27.1	9.7
Indentured Indians to British West Indies	1851–73	96	46.0	19.9
Indentured Chinese to British West Indies	1852–73	104	50.0	14.1
Indentured Pacific Islanders to Queensland	1873–94	111	11.1	3.0
British Convicts to Australia	1815–68	122	9.8	2.4
Free British to Australia	1838–53	109	26.9	7.4

Sources: TAST2, Summary Statistics, 1841–1866, consulted December 23, 2014; David Northrup, *Indentured Labor in the Age of Imperialism, 1834–1922* (New York, 1995), Table A.5.

of indentured Africans (130 vs. 35 per 1,000 passengers). The fact that most indentured Africans were recently liberated from slave ships may have increased their risk of dying on the indentured leg, since on voyages of only slightly greater duration in this period indentured Indians en route to Mauritius suffered a mortality of 22 per 1,000. On the much longer voyages from India to the British West Indies, the death rate was higher (46 per 1,000), though quite similar when the length of the voyage is factored in. On similarly long voyages to Australia in the same century, mortality among British convicts was only 10 per 1,000 on average, less than among free immigrants to the continent.

The statistics suggest that factors besides tight regulation and larger ships affected the mortality on these voyages. For example, in the case of indentured Indians leaving British India, there was a notable variation in mortality from different Indian ports, even though the recruits would have received similar screening for perceptible health problems and similar shipboard accommodations. In 1858, Indians leaving Calcutta perished at five times the rate on a voyage to Mauritius as did those leaving from the port of Madras. The one-third longer sailing time from Calcutta to Mauritius can account for only a small part of the difference, since a similar difference shows up on voyages of more equal length from these ports to the West Indies. The prime cause of the difference, as contemporary officials suspected, was that Indians from Calcutta were much more likely to be carrying cholera or to contract it from fellow passengers after departure. Despite serious efforts, detecting those suffering from cholera proved difficult, partly because Indians eager to emigrate concealed their symptoms. Nevertheless, it appears that better screening made a difference in the great variations in mortality on voyages from China. The lower mortality rate noted in Table 3.1 among Chinese going to the British West Indies, compared to those en route to Cuba, may be explained by the fact that the former were subject to the standard British inspection system and traveled on tightly regulated British ships. In contrast, sailings from the Portuguese colony of Macau or from mainland Chinese ports such as Canton were much more loosely screened and involved ships of various nationalities. Cholera outbreaks also occurred on some Chinese ships. But the general health of the recruits may be another factor that explains why Chinese mortality was higher than Indian on all routes. The evidence is not rigorous, but social and economic disruption seems to have weakened the constitutions of many. For the Chinese, warfare (both internal and external), famine, and displacement were constant features of life in the mid-1800s. Political weakness showed up as well in the inability of the imperial government to enforce its long-standing ban on any emigration. As in the slave trade, disease and social disruption among the embarking passengers in the indentured labor trade could be a significant factor in increasing mortality and one that was hard to eliminate. The famine years in Ireland also produced a very high mortality among those fleeing across the Atlantic, and there was a similar spike in mortality among Indians at the time of the Indian mutiny.

A final factor distinguishing the slave and indentured experiences was the mindset of the passengers. Although the evidence is anecdotal and circumstantial, the mental states of most slaves and of most indentured laborers were clearly worlds apart. It is evident that enslaved Africans were victims, not volunteers, and that the physical sufferings they endured on their long journeys were accompanied by deep psychological anguish, as some of the case studies presented earlier suggest. These captives were traveling into the unknown, with frightening ideas of what their fates might be. Many were deeply depressed by their alienation from their homelands, traumatized by rough treatment and the unfamiliar vessels, and sometimes terrified by a belief that they were to be eaten by the strange-looking men who now controlled them. This is why, while still in sight of the shore, some staged rebellions against their captors or threw themselves overboard in hopes of returning home. To prevent such uprisings, the men were fettered and kept in locked compartments and netting was strung around the main deck to impede those inclined to jump overboard. Once out of sight of land, captives' depression deepened or resignation set in: mutinies were less common, but some still tried to kill themselves by refusing to eat or finding a way to jump into the sea.

Although early indentured migrants might hold very imprecise ideas about where they were going and what they might find there, on the whole they boarded ships expecting that their future would be far better than what they were leaving behind. Instead of poverty and misery, they dreamed of riches; instead of marginalized existence, steady work, ample food, and adequate clothing; instead of danger and uncertainty, new and more stable beginnings. To be sure, homesickness was as inevitable as seasickness on the long voyages, but both were temporary problems on journeys of hope. Thus, except for some voyages from China, there were no chains, gratings, or attempted mutinies. The contract laborers arrived at their destinations eager to begin a new and better life. The reality they found was usually rougher than what they had imagined, but over time many became more realistic and contented with their new situations. Some Indians who completed their contracts and returned home subsequently signed new contracts to return to the same places. In addition, high percentages of indentured laborers chose to remain in their new countries after the expiration of their contracts: 65 to 80 percent of Indians in Mauritius, Natal, and the Caribbean, and similar shares of Japanese in Hawaii and Javanese in Dutch Guiana. As with other voluntary migrants overseas, decisions to return or to stay on do not suggest total satisfaction. Some may have been ashamed at their limited successes; others may have decided remaining overseas was preferable to attempting to reintegrate into their old communities. In any case, however constrained their choices, indentured laborers were choosing among the options open to them.

Despite these differences from the slave trade, indentured labor recruitment was eventually halted because of three changing perceptions that made indenture seem an unacceptable form of coercion or servitude. The first was the changes taking place in Western ideas of free labor following the abolition of slavery and reforms of labor contracts. American law had pioneered the banning of voluntary servitude in 1867, so that when the United States annexed Hawaii in 1900, indentured contracts became illegal there as well. Second, Indian nationalists charged that expecting India to provide other colonies with indentured laborers was unjust, racist, and akin to enslavement. During the First World War, the Government of India terminated indentured labor recruitment in 1916 to allay these criticisms. Finally, in destinations such as Australia and South Africa, there was mounting opposition from European settlers to the rising presence of "non-whites" who were not returning to their homelands after the expiration of their contracts. This led to the forced repatriation of many at the end of indentured contracts and the discontinuation of new imports. In some Caribbean colonies, there was also resentment among older black settlers of the competition from the new Asian immigrants. Changing economic circumstances, including rising labor costs and the greater availability of resident labor, also played a role. Recruitment fell sharply during the 1910s and stopped completely in 1922.

CONCLUSION

Although commonly studied separately, comparing the Western and Arab overseas slave trades with the overseas trade in indentured laborers reveals important commonalities, connections, and differences. All were geared to providing the labor demands of regional and global economic and social systems. In the nineteenth century, plantation agriculture expanded in the Atlantic, the Indian Ocean, and the Pacific, while transitioning to new labor supplies and systems. The indentured laborers replaced slaves in some older plantation economies and made possible new plantations (and other labor-intensive projects) in Australia, the East Indies, Hawaii, Fiji, Southern Africa, and South America. Capital investment was essential to all of these labor trades, and important innovations in shipping facilitated the movement of laborers over unprecedented distances at competitive costs. These trades also highlight the expanding imperial reach of Western governments, especially the British. After making a massive commitment of ships and men to ending the slave trades, Great Britain and its colonial dependencies organized the recruitment, transport, settlement, supervision, and eventual suppression of the indentured labor movement. For all their importance, these top-down inputs need to be balanced by attention to forces from below. Substantial African demand for imported goods was essential in sustaining its participation in overseas trade, whether in slaves or other "legitimate" goods. The indentured labor trade would have been impossible unless large numbers of young people were so eager to escape poverty and other miseries that they were willing to venture abroad as indentured laborers, a motivation shared by millions of European emigrants.

A GUIDE TO FURTHER READING

Allen, Richard B., "Satisfying the 'Want for Labouring People': European Slave Trading in the Indian Ocean, 1500–1850," *Journal of World History*, 21 (2010): 45–73.

Campbell, Gwyn (ed.), *The Structure of Slavery in the Indian Ocean, Africa, and Asia* (London, 2003).

Clarence-Smith, William Gervase (ed.), *The Economics of the Indian Ocean Slave Trade in the Nineteenth Century* (London, 1989). A special issue of *Slavery and Abolition*, 9 (1988).

Eltis, David, *Economic Growth and the Ending of the Transatlantic Slave Trade* (New York, 1987).

Hunwick, John and Eve Trout Powell (eds.), *The African Diaspora in the Mediterranean Lands of Islam* (Princeton, NJ, 2002).

Meagher, Arnold J., *The Coolie Trade, the Traffic in Chinese Laborers to Latin America, 1847–1874* (Bloomington, IN, 2010).

Northrup, David, *Indentured Labor in the Age of Imperialism, 1834–1922* (Cambridge, 1995).

Pétré-Grenouilleau, Olivier, *Les traits négrières: Essai d'histoire globale* (Paris, 2004).

Shlomowitz, Ralph, L. Brennan, and John McDonald, *Mortality and Migration in the Modern World* (Aldershot, 1996).

Voyages: The Transatlantic Slave Trade Database, launched 2008, www.slave voyages.org.

Wright, John, *The Trans-Saharan Slave Trade* (London, 2007).

PART II
SLAVERY

CHAPTER 4

THE NON-HISPANIC WEST INDIES

PIETER C. EMMER AND STANLEY L. ENGERMAN

BACKGROUND

The rapid growth of the plantation economy had made the Caribbean very susceptible to changes in the legal status of its labor force and in the tariffs for its products. During the eighteenth century, the region had become the fastest growing economy in the world and that growth continued into the nineteenth century in spite of severe hiccups caused by the American and French Revolutionary Wars. No wonder the Caribbean colonies were called "the darlings of empire" in Britain, and the same can be said for France, Spain, the Netherlands, and Denmark. During the nineteenth century, however, the abolition of the slave trade, of slavery itself, and of the protective tariffs in the home markets threw much of the Caribbean into abrupt economic decline notwithstanding the dramatic improvements in the processing of sugar cane, the working and living conditions of the labor force, and official attempts to concentrate as many resources as possible in the production of sugar cane. However, there were limits to the drive to increase productivity: the slaves on the sugar plantations spent less than half of their annual laboring hours actually working on sugar and no area of the Caribbean succeeded in putting more than half of the slaves into the sugar sector. In addition, the ending of the transatlantic slave trade in combination with an aging population resulted in a dramatic decrease in the number of productive slaves and a sharp increase in those slaves who were too old or too sick to work. After the ending of slavery and the period of apprenticeship, the number of active field laborers declined even more rapidly as workers left the plantations.

A good yardstick for the remarkable growth of the Caribbean economy before the abolition of the slave trade was the constantly rising volume of the slave imports from Africa. The number of slaves in the Caribbean colonies of the major European slave-owning colonies increased by over 2 percent annually from 1700 to 1790, achieving its all-time peak of almost 1.5 million in 1790. Between them, the British and French accounted for about 83 percent of this total, with the share of the French exceeding that of the British in the years around 1790. In addition to the relatively small

73

numbers of slaves on the Dutch, Danish, and Swedish islands, the Spanish colonies accounted for only about 9 percent of the Caribbean slave population. The major changes after 1790 were the very sharp decline in the number of slaves in the French colonies, the result of the Haitian Revolution, and the continued expansion of slavery in the Spanish colonies, such that Cuba and Puerto Rico accounted for more than one-quarter of all Caribbean slaves in the early nineteenth century – a period when the British share of the Caribbean slave population ranged between 50 and 60 percent. Nevertheless, as Table 4.1 shows, by 1830 the total population (free and slave) of the French islands and Haiti exceeded that of the British.[1]

In 1790, on the eve of the Saint Domingue uprising, the French colonies had the largest number of slaves of any European power in the West Indies. This was due to the very rapid expansion of slave imports in the 1780s. Saint Domingue alone had approximately one-third of all slaves in the West Indies. The Haitian Revolution had a huge impact on the economy of the former major French colony Saint Domingue. Exports and investments from abroad almost disappeared. Indeed, as is well known, the Haitian constitution of 1805 stipulated that no white man was allowed to possess any property in this first black republic. From 1789 to 1795, sugar exports in those areas of Saint Domingue controlled by the insurgents were reduced to 1.2 percent and coffee exports to 2.8 percent of their pre-revolution levels. The large plantations were gradually divided among ex-soldiers and squatters, and after some time Haiti must have been the only Caribbean country without landless laborers, albeit with landholdings of a constantly decreasing average size. Attempts were made to get some plantations started again, especially those in the hands of the former military commanders. In spite of the fact that Haiti had fallen apart into various warring sections, the new black elites of each of these sections tried to restrain the former plantation slaves from moving to the towns, punish vagabondage, restrict emigration to other parts of the Caribbean – the latter punishable by death – and ban the sale of small plots of land.[2]

These restrictive policies were soon reversed in an attempt to make Haiti less dependent upon imports and foreign currency. In 1826, the Haitian Government agreed to an indemnity of 150 million francs to be paid to France in the course of five installments, presumably to compensate the

[1] Stanley L. Engerman and B. W. Higman, "The Demographic Structure of the Caribbean Slave Societies in the Eighteenth and Nineteenth Centuries," in Franklin W. Knight (ed.), *General History of the Caribbean*, Vol. III: *The Slave Societies of the Caribbean* (London, 1997), pp. 45–104.

[2] Mats Lundahl, *Poverty in Haiti. Essays on Underdevelopment and Post-Disaster Prospects* (London, 2011), p. 6; Michel Hector, "Problèmes du passage à la société postesclavagiste et postcoloniale (1791–1793/1820–1826)," in Michel Hector and Laënnec Hurbon (eds.), *Genèse de l'état haïtien, 1804–1859* (n. p., 2009), pp. 93–117.

Table 4.1 *Caribbean Populations in 1830*

	White	Slave	Free Persons of Color	Total
British:				
Barbados	14,812	82,026	5,312	102,150
St. Kitts	1,498	19,094	2,808	23,400
Nevis	453	9,194	1,403	11,050
Antigua	1,187	29,600	5,513	36,300
Montserrat	352	6,300	848	7,500
Virgin Islands	603	5,148	1,699	7,450
	18,905	**151,362**	**17,583**	**187,850**
Jamaica	18,903	319,074	40,073	378,050
Dominica	703	14,706	3,591	19,000
St. Lucia	1,012	13,395	3,993	18,400
St. Vincent	1,400	23,100	3,500	28,000
Grenada	710	23,884	3,806	28,400
Tobago	453	12,551	1,146	14,150
Trinidad	3,323	22,757	15,985	42,065
Demerara and Essequibo	3,100	67,968	6,433	77,500
Berbice	601	20,698	1,802	23,100
	11,302	**199,059**	**40,256**	**250,615**
British Honduras	302	1,898	1,999	4,200
Cayman Island	350	1,000	150	1,500
Bahamas	5,007	9,503	2,520	17,030
Anguilla	300	2,600	399	3,300
Barbuda	3	500	—	503
	5,962	**15,501**	**5,068**	**26,533**
Sub-total	**55,072**	**684,996**	**102,980**	**843,048**
French:				
Martinique	9,362	86,499	14,055	109,916
Guadeloupe	10,900	97,339	11,424	119,663
French Guiana	1,381	19,102	2,379	22,862
	21,643	**202,940**	**27,858**	**252,441**
Haiti			880,202	880,202
Dutch:				
Suriname	2,029	48,784	5,041	55,854
Curaçao	2,602	5,894	6,531	15,027
St. Eustatius	132	1,614	527	2,273
Saba	?	?	?	?
St. Martin	500	4,000	1,500	6,000
Aruba	465	393	1,888	2,746
Bonaire	90	547	839	1,476
Sub-total	**5,818**	**61,232**	**16,326**	**83,376**

Table 4.1 *(cont.)*

	White	Slave	Free Persons of Color	Total
Danish:				
St. Croix	1,892	19,876	4,913	26,681
St. John	208	1,971	202	2,381
St. Thomas	1,977	5,032	5,204	12,213
Sub-total	**4,077**	**26,879**	**10,319**	**41,275**
Spanish:				
Puerto Rica	162,311	34,240	127,287	323,838
Cuba	332,352	310,218	113,125	755,695
Santo Domingo	38,272	15,000	38,272	91,544
Sub-total	**532,935**	**359,458**	**278,684**	**1,171,077**
Swedish:				
St. Bartholomew	1,723	1,387	906	4,016
TOTAL	**621,268**	**1,336,892**	**1,317,275**	**3,275,435**

Source: Stanley L. Engerman and B. W. Higman, "The Demographic Structure of the Caribbean Slave Societies in the Eighteenth and Nineteenth Centuries," in Franklin W. Knight (ed.), *General History of the Caribbean*, Vol. III: *The Slave Societies of the Caribbean* (London, 1997), pp. 50–2.

former owners of real estate and slaves on Saint Domingue. In 1838, the remaining debt was reduced to 60 million francs to be paid over a period of thirty years, and ultimately was paid in full.[3]

Unfortunately, it is impossible to measure the effects of the end of plantation agriculture on the average income of the former slaves in this unique Caribbean state. Did the average Haitian obtain a higher income, in both kind and money, than during the last decades of French rule? Some abolitionists pointed to the growing population of Haiti, suggesting that personal incomes had increased over those earned during slavery with its excess of deaths over births. Yet the opposite effect on the level of income seems more likely. The relatively high death rates and low birth rates during slavery were not the result of low incomes causing undernourishment, but of other factors such as the constant arrival of African and European pathogens. The decline in income was, in part, caused by the decline in labor productivity and the amount of labor performed by the freedmen in comparison with the high labor productivity and long working hours on the plantations. The rising poverty, in addition to the political instability,

---

[3] Mats Lundahl, *Peasants and Poverty: A Study of Haiti* (London, 1979), p. 272; David Nicholls, *Haiti in Caribbean Context: Ethnicity, Economy and Revolt* (London, 1985), pp. 92–100; Robert I. Rotberg, *Haiti: The Politics of Squalor* (Boston, MA, 1971), pp. 66–102, 398–9.

explains why the new republic never became a haven for those wanting to escape from slavery elsewhere in the Caribbean region. In spite of the growing population, land prices continued to decline, suggesting a long-time reduction in agricultural productivity and thus in peasant income.[4]

Haitians could certainly not benefit from amelioration policies such as were introduced in the other Caribbean colonies where the slave-owners were forced to increase the wages and benefits in kind to the workers and their families, or, after emancipation, from the influx of metropolitan money that the slave-owners received as compensation when their slaves were freed. The small amount of hard currency earned by exporting cotton and coffee – far less than before 1794 – was needed to pay the French indemnity, as well as for the importation of manufactured and luxury goods from the United States, the United Kingdom, and France. Over time, Haiti remained a nation of mainly peasant subsistence farmers with decreasing incomes, and it is presently the only area in the Americas with average personal incomes at sub-Saharan African levels. In addition, *restavèka*, or child slavery, has reappeared.[5]

THE SLAVE TRADE AND THE SUPPLY OF SLAVES

In contrast to Haiti in the early nineteenth century, the remaining French colonies, as well as the Dutch and Danish colonies, saw similar changes to those in the British Caribbean. The Danes ended their slave trade in 1802, the slave trade to the foreign colonies conquered by Britain during the Napoleonic Wars was ended in 1805, and in 1807 the British Parliament also abolished the slave trade to the British colonies. In 1813, under British pressure, the Dutch outlawed their slave trade and around 1830 the French finally suppressed the slave trade originating in their ports. The Spanish and Portuguese sent slave ships to their colonies and to Brazil for another three decades. Because of the suppression of the slave trade from Africa, the availability of slaves to planters became dependent upon the number of slaves on sale in the colony itself and on the slave trade between the slave-holding areas in the Caribbean. In actual practice, the number of slaves offered in the inter-island slave trade for sale constituted only a very small fraction of the numbers sold before the importation of slaves from Africa had been made illegal. The importation of Africans remained financially very attractive. After 1800, the British colonies received over 190,000 slaves, the French colonies imported around 86,000, the Danish colonies 22,244, and the Dutch colonies 25,244. These differences can be explained by the

---

[4] B. W. Higman, *A Concise History of the Caribbean* (Cambridge, 2011), pp. 161–2; Lundahl, *Peasants and Poverty*, p. 265.

[5] Nicholls, *Haiti in Caribbean Context*, p. 97.

fact that legislation regarding the suppression of the slave trade as well as the relevant government policies differed widely during the first decades of the nineteenth century. In addition, illegally imported slaves from Africa could be re-exported legally to other areas from the French and Danish colonies, as the inter-Caribbean slave trade was allowed to continue.[6]

With the ending of the illegal slave trade, imports from Africa could no longer compensate for the excess of deaths over births in the British, French, Dutch, and Danish Caribbean. Yet the causes for this decline varied. In the British islands mortality exceeded fertility while the numbers imported declined and, for older areas, the numbers sold in the inter-island trade were relatively small. The British also acquired new colonies by conquests, Trinidad from Spain in 1797, and the three colonies, Essequibo, Demerara, and Berbice, which eventually became British Guiana, from the Dutch in 1803. These new areas had enormous amounts of unsettled land.

After acquisition, the British severely limited the number of slaves these colonies could import. Not surprisingly, these areas had the highest slave prices in the British Caribbean when slavery ended, and after emancipation they brought in many indentured laborers from India and elsewhere. The British colonies had by far the largest number of slaves, and, when slavery ended in the 1830s and afterwards, had by far the largest number of slaves emancipated.

In Dutch Suriname, the demographic decline was also caused by mortality factors, the number of deaths exceeding that of births. In the small islands of the Dutch Antilles, numbers declined mainly because of voluntary emancipation and the sale of slaves to the neighboring Spanish colony of Puerto Rico. In the French Antilles, voluntary emancipation also increased, in addition to slaves being sold to Puerto Rico and Cuba. The slave population of the Danish West Indies declined from about 30,000 in 1815 to roughly 22,000 in 1846; while the number of freedmen and white people rose in those years from about 8,000 to 17,000.[7] (see Table 4.1).

A small part of the decline of the slave populations was also due to the fact that some slaves escaped to neighboring colonies, particularly after 1834 when British slavery had been abolished, though other downward pressure came from voluntary emancipation and sales of slaves to other parts of the

---

[6] David Eltis, *Economic Growth and the Ending of the Transatlantic Slave Trade* (New York, 1987), pp. 185–204; David Eltis, "Free and Coerced Migrations From the Old World to the New," in David Eltis (ed.), *Coerced and Free Migrations, Global Perspectives* (Stanford, CA, 2002), pp. 62, 63, and related data.

[7] Alex van Stipriaan, *Surinaams contrast. Roofbouw en overleven in een Caraibische plantagekolonie, 1750–1863* (Leiden, 1993), pp. 310–14; W. E. Renkema, *Het Curaçaose plantagebedrijf in de negentiende eeuw* (Zutphen, 1981), pp. 117–27; Josette Fallope, *Esclaves et citoyens: Les noirs à la Guadeloupe au XIX ième siecle* (Basse-Terre, 1992), pp. 120–25; Neville A. T. Hall, *Slave Society in the Danish West Indies: St. Thomas, St. John and St. Croix* (Kingston, 1992), p. 5.

Caribbean. Mention is made of about 2,000 slaves from Martinique and Guadeloupe escaping to the nearby British islands after 1833. In Suriname, the number of escaped slaves was smaller, in spite of the fact that the borders with British Guiana (after 1834) and French Cayenne (after 1848) were hardly patrolled. Some runaways did return, such as a group of slaves from Dominica, where they had been freed, in order to re-enslave themselves in Guadeloupe. They explained their return by stressing that they would rather work for an owner who, by losing his slaves, would lose his fortune.[8]

SLAVE WORK AND REBELLION

As already mentioned, in most plantation areas, the principal use of slave labor was increasingly in the production of sugar, with relatively few working in small-scale agriculture or located in urban areas. Slaves were used in decreasing numbers on smaller units than sugar plantations, to produce crops such as coffee, cotton, and cocoa, as well as on livestock-producing farms. The labor force participation of slaves was generally high: the only groups not working tended to be those under the age of 5 and over the age of 70. In Guadeloupe, for example, the majority generally worked as unskilled field laborers, with about 20 percent of males in skilled trades, and a small number in domestic service. The percentage of females working in the field was higher than the percentage of males, as were the numbers in domestic service. Females were more likely to be in urban areas than were males. The largest enslaved urban populations were in Cuba, primarily in Havana.

The Haitian Revolution of 1791 to 1804 was, historically, the only slave uprising that succeeded in ending white rule and replacing it with ex-slave rulers. It led to a permanent shift in the color of the Haitian ruling class. There were other slave rebellions that did not, however, achieve the same degree of success, though they did play a role in aiding antislavery sentiment in Britain, often because of white missionaries being jailed and killed. There were a number of documented slave revolts in the eighteenth century in Jamaica, Antigua, Berbice, and the Danish Virgin Islands, as well as continued internal warfare by the Jamaican Maroons. The major revolts in the first third of the nineteenth century were in Barbados (1816), Demerara (1823), and Jamaica (1831–32). The last one involved 60,000 slaves and the first two had a total of about 40,000 slaves. Killed in the three rebellions were less than twenty whites and over 1,000 slaves, two-thirds by judicial decree. The Jamaica uprising led to a parliamentary inquiry, followed one year later, by coincidence or not, by legislation leading to slave emancipation. A limited number of relatively minor slave

[8] J. P. Siwpersad, *De Nederlandse regering en de afschaffing van de Surinaamse slavernij, 1833–1863* (Groningen, 1979), pp. 1–5; Fallope, *Esclaves et citoyens*, p. 599.

revolts occurred on most slave islands, generally involving small numbers, and most provoked harsh reactions by the whites.

In the historiography, the slave uprising in Haiti has been allotted a special place as it was the only rebellion to succeed and turn into a veritable revolution. Some historians compare the slave uprising in Haiti to the French Revolution in that slave rebellions before the one in Haiti usually aimed at changing the plight of those slaves, who rebelled, while after Haiti the subsequent slave rebellions elsewhere not only aimed at liberating the insurgents themselves, but at removing the slave system wholesale. Yet there are several facts that do not support this hypothesis.

First of all, even after the Haitian Revolution, most slave-owners in the Caribbean continued to see slave uprisings and rebellions as an occupational hazard of a slave society just like most people in Europe and in the non-slave Americas viewed mutinies, rebellions, and even protracted wars as inevitable ingredients of human society. This stoic attitude toward slave rebellions can be deduced from the fact that the price of slaves for sale in the Caribbean continued to rise until a few years before the moment of slave emancipation, when slave prices tended to hover around the amount of compensation that was expected to be granted after abolition. Economically speaking, the more slave prices increased, the less sensitive the slave-owners had to be to slave resistance as the rise in slave prices was triggered by the fact that any alternative to slave labor – in spite of its rebelliousness – would increase labor costs.

Second, it is debatable whether after the Haitian Revolution the majority of the slaves in the wider Caribbean suddenly started to support the idea that colonial slavery was doomed. That idea was much more prominent among the abolitionists in Europe and North America. For them, protests, strikes, insurrections, and rebellions among the slaves and especially the harsh reaction by the colonial authorities became important arguments for abolition.

Third, slave insurrections did have an effect on emancipation, but only when there were strong prospects of metropolitan legislators approving abolition. The massive insurrection in Jamaica in 1831 to 1832 provided the last stages of the abolition debate in the House of Commons in London with a sense of urgency that this ongoing debate did not have before, while slave risings in Martinique and the Danish West Indies did not impact on the discussion on abolition at home – as the metropolitan legislatures had already set a date for slave emancipation. Rather, slave risings forced the local governors to free the slaves immediately.

AMELIORATION

Although some nations had laws regulating aspects of the slave trade and even slavery before 1800, in the course of the nineteenth century many of the colonies had introduced further amelioration measures in response to the attack by the abolitionists on slavery and to their attempt to increase the population of slaves. These policies aimed at improving the working and living conditions of the slaves. The slave-owners accepted these policies and the expense involved because of the rapid rise in slave prices. The ending of slave imports from Africa meant that any replacement or increase in the number of slaves could now come only from natural population growth, as the still legal internal slave trade in the Caribbean was very small. Amelioration policies were specifically aimed at increasing the birth rate and reducing the death rate.

Beginning in the early nineteenth century, the British introduced various measures to ameliorate the slaves' conditions. The registration of colonial slaves was introduced in 1813, primarily as a means of ensuring the halting of the slave trade by reducing illegal imports, but also to highlight the decline in the slave population and thus lead to a more favorable treatment of slaves. Measures regarding the care and treatment of slaves were introduced in 1823, establishing norms regarding food, work, and punishments. There were further improvements in regulations regarding slavery in 1826, with the introduction of rules for compulsory manumission of slaves, so they could legally purchase themselves for an agreed-upon price.

The French, Dutch, and Danish slave-owners were keenly aware of the sharp decline in the production of cash crops after emancipation in the British colonies in 1834 and also resorted to amelioration in the hope of reducing the decline of the slave population and postponing emancipation. That is why standards of slave housing and food rations were improved, better medical care and a maximum number of working hours were instituted, and the right of the slave-owners to punish their slaves was limited. In Suriname, slaves also obtained the legal right to complain when their owner did not comply with the new standards.[9]

TECHNICAL INNOVATION, MARKET CONDITIONS, AND METROPOLITAN TARIFFS

In spite of all the technical improvements in sugar production and the amelioration of the living and working conditions of the slaves, it was generally believed that the export economies of the West Indies were doomed and could not survive much longer, though in the British parliamentary debates some considered a rather long period of survival in the absence of political intervention. In spite of the fact that the profits of

[9] Fallope, *Esclaves et citoyens*, pp. 301–08; P. C. Emmer, *The Dutch in the Atlantic Economy, 1580–1880* (Aldershot, 1998), pp. 167–202. Justin Roberts, however, has argued that amelioration began earlier. See *Slavery and the Enlightenment in the British Atlantic, 1750–1807* (Cambridge, 2013).

British slavery had improved once Haitian sugar production fell to virtually zero and that British slave prices increased until the 1820s, the economic argument against slavery in favor of nominally free labor remained critical. Slave-owners were forced to provide more food and housing to the rapidly growing number of non-productive slaves, as the slave population was aging without new imports from Africa. The only way to combat competition from the expanding slave economies of Brazil and Cuba was technical innovation combined with protective tariffs in the metropolis. At first, the British aided their colonial sugar producers with tariff protection, until differential sugar duties for British colonial areas and other sugar-producing areas were equalized after a prolonged campaign by free traders.

After the French colonies of Martinique, Guadeloupe, and Cayenne (which had ended slavery in 1794) had been restored to France and slavery had been reintroduced in 1802 by Napoleon, the slave-owners concentrated on the production of sugar and foodstuffs, while the output of coffee and cotton declined. The protective tariffs for French colonial sugar created a small boom in sugar production between 1820 and 1830 as protective tariffs shielded the French colonial sugar producers from the competition of the expanding sugar producers in Cuba and Brazil. After 1830, however, the beet sugar industry in France started to produce sugar in quantities that equaled those from the French colonial sugar producers. Colonial property values began to decline. In order to raise productivity in the sugar-producing colonies, central plants for processing sugar cane were established, to which a number of plantations would send their cane to be processed.[10] Over the years, the central processing plants were able to increase the quantity and quality of their sugar and to acquire neighboring cane fields, thereby ensuring a steadier supply of cane. Small-scale growers, freed of the necessity to build and operate mills, were able to add to this supply. The end of slavery meant that Caribbean property values declined even further, a development that provided additional momentum to the separation of milling from cultivation.[11]

Except for the Spanish colonies and Brazil, the production of slave-grown sugar in Suriname continued longer than elsewhere as slavery was not abolished until 1863, and the period of apprenticeship ended only in 1873. During the last decades of slavery, Suriname experienced the same changes that had occurred elsewhere, such as the concentration of the slave labor force in the production of sugar, with a constant stream of amelioration measures. Between 1833 and 1860, the share of slaves employed in the sugar sector increased from 32 to almost 50 percent, while in that same period the percentage of slaves employed in the coffee sector declined from

---

[10] Paul Butel, *Histoire des Antilles françaises* (Paris, 2002), pp. 319, 378.
[11] Butel, *Histoire des Antilles françaises*, pp. 394–400.

28 to 11 percent. As in the French Caribbean, the number of slaves employed in food production and cattle-raising increased, while those employed in non-agricultural activities such as work in the household declined. But, unlike the French and British colonies, Suriname did not enjoy any protection for its products in the Dutch market, and thus had to compete with Brazil, Cuba, and Java. That is why the plantation owners in Suriname increased the size of their plantations, amalgamated plantations, and used new technology. In 1830, the average productivity of Suriname slaves on a sugar plantation was about the same as in British Guiana, higher than in Trinidad, and double that in Jamaica.[12] This impressive feat was largely achieved via the use of steam power – by 1853, the majority of the sugar plantations had steam engines to drive their mills.

On the smaller islands of the Dutch Antilles, slavery differed radically from that elsewhere in the Caribbean. There were few export plantations and the majority of the slaves were employed in the production of foodstuffs, household work, and as artisans and sailors. As could be expected, the rising slave prices in the new Caribbean sugar-producing colonies stimulated many owners of slaves in the less productive areas to sell their slaves to other parts of the Caribbean. Between 1819 and 1847, more than 4,000 slaves were sold to foreign owners. In some years, when the corn harvest was bad, the sale of slaves amounted to 6 percent of the resident slave population on Curaçao, the main island in the Dutch Caribbean. The majority of the slaves preferred to be sold to Puerto Rico, as the slave regime on that island seemed to offer better treatment, sufficient food, and monetary rewards, enabling the slaves to buy their freedom. A government premium that was paid to every foreign slave-owner who sold his or her slaves to Suriname had little effect.[13]

The Danish West Indies had, in 1830, a population of over about 45,000 persons, of whom 65 percent were slaves, 10 percent whites, and 25 percent freedmen (Table 4.1). As in most other Caribbean colonies, there was an excess of deaths over births and the black population in the Danish Caribbean declined until the 1880s, i.e. long after the abolition of slavery. The main cause for the high mortality was the inadequate treatment of newborn babies rather than living and working conditions on the plantations. Most plantations in the Danish West Indies produced sugar and about half of the slaves worked in the fields. There are strong indications that many of the

---

[12] Emmer, *The Dutch in the Atlantic Economy*, pp. 167–202; Fréderique Beauvois, *Indemniser les planteurs pour abolir l'esclavage? Entre économie, éthique et politique, une étude des débats parlementaires britanniques et français (1788–1848) dans une perspective comparée* (Paris, 2013), pp. 167–202; Van Stipriaan, *Surinaams contrast*, pp. 139, 179.

[13] W. E. Renkema, "De export van Curaçaose Slaven, 1819–1847," in P. Boomgaard (ed.), *Exercities in ons verleden: Twaalf opstellen over de economische en sociale geschiedenis van Nederland en koloniën, 1800–1950* (Assen, 1981), pp. 188–208.

Table 4.2 *Number of Slaves in Colonies of the Metropolitan Nations, 1810, 1830, 1850, 1880*

	Date of Abolition	1810	1830	1850	1880
British	1834	766,200	684,996		
French	1848	180,289	202,940		
Dutch	1863	67,289	61,232	48,762	
Danish	1848	31,632	26,879		
Swedish	1847	2,406	1,387		
Spanish	1886	252,936	359,458	369,437	171,087
Total		**1,300,752**	**1,336,892**	**418,199**	**171,087**

Source: Stanley L. Engerman and B. W. Higman, "The Demographic Structure of the Caribbean Slave Societies in the Eighteenth and Nineteenth Centuries," in Franklin W. Knight (ed.), *General History of the Caribbean*, Vol. III: *The Slave Societies of the Caribbean* (London, 1997), pp. 50–2, and worksheets.

plantations went through periods of severe losses and many planters went bankrupt. After 1815, an increasing number of plantations came into the hands of Irish and Scottish plantation owners and most plantation produce from the Danish West Indies was shipped to non-Danish ports.[14]

EMANCIPATION

Gradual emancipations were generally in areas with rather small plantations. What made the British emancipation different was that it affected a large number of slaves and, while gradual, would free the enslaved in four to six years. Emancipation, to take place on August 1, 1834, was to be followed by a period of apprenticeship of either four or six years, depending on the occupation of the emancipated. Later, due to abolitionist protests, all periods of apprenticeship were reduced to four years for all slaves. A compensation of £20 million was also paid to individual slave-owners based on the prices of slaves in each colony during a period in the 1820s. This amount was equal to about one-half of the market value of slaves. During the period of apprenticeship, the surplus earnings of slave-owners from the labor required from the apprentices was also equal to about one-half the value of slaves. With emancipation, the imperial government introduced stipendiary magistrates to control labor

---

[14] Niklas Thode Jensen, *For the Health of the Enslaved: Slaves, Medicine and Power in the Danish West Indies, 1803–1848* (Copenhagen, 2012), p. 250; D. H. Anderson, "Denmark-Norway, Africa, and the Caribbean, 1660–1917: Modernisation Financed by Slaves and Sugar?" in P. C. Emmer, O. Petre-Grenouilleau, and J. V. Roitman (eds.), *A "Deus ex Machina" Revisited: Atlantic Colonial Trade and European Economic Development* (Leiden, 2006), pp. 291–315.

bargaining, though these were soon considered to favor landowners in labor disputes, compelling apprentices to do plantation work.[15]

As Table 4.2 indicates, emancipation of the non-British Caribbean slaves was undertaken in the years from the British abolition of slavery in 1834 to the emancipation of all slaves in Cuba in 1886. Discussions regarding slave emancipation in all of the colonial mother countries other than Britain suffered from the fact that the aftermath of slave emancipation in the British colonies belied the theory that the transition to free labor would increase production. This is why the French and Danish Governments introduced gradual emancipation, which for political reasons they shifted to immediate emancipation, with compensation, in 1848. The Danish move to immediate emancipation coincided with a slave uprising in their West Indian colonies. Slave emancipation was debated by the Dutch beginning in the 1840s, but it was not passed until 1863, three years after the non-compensated emancipation of slaves in the Dutch East Indies. In 1863, the Dutch Government introduced a ten-year apprenticeship called "state supervision" for Suriname (but not for the small islands of the Netherlands Antilles). In all three of these cases, the pressure from abolitionist lobby groups was limited, in comparison to the British case.

The British passed an Emancipation Act in 1833, the first of the major New World slave powers to end slavery by a metropolitan political decision. Several of the northeastern states of the United States had passed legislation or imposed legal decisions to end slavery in the late eighteenth and early nineteenth centuries, and many of the states of Latin America, now independent from Spain, passed legislation to end slavery in the years after 1810. These were usually gradual emancipations, freeing those born to slave mothers subject to a period of apprenticeship of somewhere between fifteen to thirty years, but freeing none of those enslaved.

In 1845, the French Government enacted the Law Mackau envisioning gradual abolition by making it easier for slaves to buy their freedom. The law also outlawed the whipping of female slaves, and stipulated that slave families should have their own dwellings, in addition to which slaves had the right to a small garden plot and a free day per week to cultivate it. In 1848, after a regime change in Paris, a law providing for immediate emancipation was enacted. The amount of compensation to the slaveowners was to be decided later, while money was made available to build hospitals and courthouses. Because of a slave uprising, the governor of Martinique liberated the slaves before the text of the metropolitan emancipation law reached the island.[16]

---

[15] Robert W. Fogel and Stanley L. Engerman, "Philanthropy at Bargain Prices: Notes on the Economics of Gradual Emancipation," *Journal of Legal Studies*, 3 (1974): 377–401.

[16] Butel, *Histoire des Antilles françaises*, pp. 379–84.

A completely different procedure was followed in the Dutch and Swedish slave-holding colonies in the Caribbean. Unlike the French and the Danes, the Swedes and the Dutch enacted the emancipation of the slaves in their colonies without any interference from the colonial governors or legislators. In the case of Sweden, there were only about 600 slaves to be emancipated in its single colony in the Caribbean: Saint Bartholomew (Saint Barts). In 1847, the Swedish Government paid about 80 US dollars per slave. All slaves immediately obtained the same rights in the law as enjoyed by the free population. Saint Barts had no plantations and the freedmen had little choice but to continue working for their former masters or leave the island.[17]

The Dutch took longer to emancipate the slaves in their Caribbean colonies than any of the non-Iberian colonies. That was not because the Dutch Government or Parliament was more (or less) opposed to slave emancipation than the French and the Danish. In 1844, the Dutch minister for the colonies had already stated the view that there was no alternative to emancipation. In 1852, the pro-slavery lobby of Suriname planters also ended their opposition to emancipation. Nevertheless, it took five abortive government proposals to arrive at the final law of 1862 stipulating that the slaves in the Dutch Caribbean would be freed as of July 1, 1863. The law provided the slave-owners with a compensation of 300 guilders per slave, amounting to 12 million guilders, to be paid out of the public purse. The plantations were not expropriated, but there would be immediate emancipation, and the government would actively facilitate the recruitment of indentured laborers from Java and elsewhere for work on the plantations. And last but not least, for ten years after emancipation, all the field slaves in Suriname were required to conclude labor contracts with any Suriname employer according to a scale of wages set by the colonial government.[18]

In the Danish West Indies, the initiative to ameliorate slavery and to emancipate the slaves came from the governor of the Danish West Indies rather than from Copenhagen. During the 1830s, Governor Scholten had decreed several amelioration measures, such as the limitation of the control of the slave-owners over their slaves and a ban on the sale of slaves in public. During the 1840s, the slaves were freed from work on Saturdays, allowing them to go to the market. In addition, slaves were given a free Sunday, enabling them to attend religious services and other types of instruction. In 1847, a royal decree stipulated that the slaves in the Danish

[17] Ernst Ekman, "Sweden, the Slave Trade and Slavery, 1784–1847," *Revue française d'histoire, d'outremer*, 62 (1975): 221–31.

[18] M. Kuitenbrouwer, "De Nederlandse afschaffing van de slavernij," *Bijdragen en Mededelingen van het Historisch Genootschap*, 93 (1978): 69–98; Siwpersad, *De Nederlandse regering*, pp. 217–61.

West Indies would be free soon, but a slave uprising in 1848 forced the governor of the islands to grant immediate freedom to the slaves, with compensation paid to the owners.[19]

THE COMPENSATION PAYMENTS

Before 1804, five northern US states had gradually ended slavery by the "law of the free womb"; under which the labor of those born after legislation were to serve as apprentices for a period of years, thus providing compensation to the slave-owners, at no cost to the government. Paying compensation to end the slave trade was a tradition that began with the British campaign to suppress the slave trade of other nations. In order to obtain the cooperation of Spain, Portugal, and some West African states, Great Britain paid varying sums of money to their governments and rulers in order to allow them to compensate shipping firms and traders for their loss of income. The French Government was offered no money by the British, as they had been defeated in the Napoleonic Wars, while London more or less forced the Dutch to abolish their slave trade in exchange for at least some parts of their colonial empire that had fallen into the hands of the British during the Napoleonic Wars.[20]

The British debates about slave emancipation saw slave-owners arguing that they should be compensated for the confiscation of what had been legally held property. The first proposal was for a £15 million loan, but the final legislation provided for an indemnity of £20 million, to be allocated among slave-owners based on the value of their slaves in the 1820s. To provide a supplementary benefit to slave-owners, as well as to allow time to "educate" the slaves for freedom, a period of apprenticeship, with compulsory plantation labor was mandated. The British had already introduced a system of apprenticeship in 1807 for slaves captured on board illegal slave ships who were required to work in the Caribbean for a period up to fourteen years.[21]

The French debate on compensation payments started when the internal wars in Saint Domingue drove out a great number of slave-owners. In the beginning, the French metropolitan authorities only supported those most in need, but over time these relief payments became part of the financial claims made by France to the government of independent Haiti. Originally, the French demanded the payment of 160 million francs,

[19] Hall, *Slave Society in the Danish West Indies*, p. 209.
[20] Beauvois, *Indemniser les planteurs*, pp. 221–4. This book has the most comprehensive coverage of compensation for ending slavery.
[21] Alvin O. Thompson, "'African Recaptives' under Apprenticeship in the British West Indies, 1807–1828," *Immigrants & Minorities*, 9 (1990): 123–44.

based on a complicated calculation of the value of the estates in 1791, but eventually settled for 150 million francs in 1825. The payments from the Haitian Government no longer favored those most in need, but instead those who had possessed the largest estates. Many of the small proprietors only received a few francs in compensation, since the claim on the Haitian state was reduced from 150 to 60 million francs in 1838.[22]

The compensation for the slave-owners in the other French colonies was discussed after their slaves had been freed. In the end, it was based on principles that were different from those used in calculating the compensation for property owners on Saint Domingue. Some participants in the compensation debate pointed out that by 1848 the slave-owners in the French Caribbean hardly possessed any slaves that had been purchased from Africa since the slave trade had ended decades earlier. Thus, it was argued, the actual slave population had not been purchased and its value should not therefore be the basis of any compensation. Instead, the French Finance Minister offered to pay half the daily wage of the liberated slaves during a period of five years with the exception of children and the aged. Half of that sum would be paid immediately in cash, the other half in eight installments. This arrangement was intended to prevent a repetition of what happened in the British colonies, where most of the compensation money never reached planters in the islands, but ended up with their creditors in the United Kingdom itself. Yet estimates suggest that the same happened in the French case in spite of the complicated payment regulations.

Over time, compensation payments became an important issue in the Netherlands. The French and Danish cases had clearly demonstrated that once the slaves had been freed, their owners could no longer influence the amount of compensation or the ability to obtain coerced labor, and were dependent on the goodwill of the metropolitan legislators. In the end, the Dutch Parliament decided to pay about half the average sale prices of the slaves in Suriname and in the Dutch Antilles, 300 and 200 guilders, respectively. An exception was made for the slaves on the Dutch part of Saint Maarten, who had all fled to the French side of the island in 1848 and no longer served their owners. The Dutch Government offered only 30 guilders in compensation, which was later increased to 100 guilders. Again, an unknown amount of the compensation paid to slave-owners was used to pay off the metropolitan creditors of the plantations. With the end of slavery, the price of plantations, now without slave laborers, declined dramatically. Many were bought by proprietors from inside Suriname, as the capital costs for a purchase had decreased considerably. The new

[22] Nicholls, *Haiti in Caribbean Context*, pp. 96, 97.

owners only needed to pay for the real estate, while the workers were paid by the day. In both the Swedish and Danish emancipations, the governments agreed to compensate the slave-owners by paying a flat fee of 50 and 80 dollars per slave respectively; in the Swedish cases, this amount was to be paid out over a period of five years.[23]

In sum, the former British, French, Danish, Dutch, and Swedish ex-slave-holding areas saw only a moderate increase in their net worth, as a substantial part of the money remained in the metropole. The British slave-owners were permitted to keep their land, but with limits on the coercion of labor in the apprenticeship period. Property values fell thereafter. The years 1823 to 1830 had seen slave prices decrease as a result of parliamentary debates, and the ending of tariff protection in 1846 caused a reduction in British West Indian sugar sales in England and elsewhere. Similar types of issues were present in the compensation schemes of the other European nations, suggesting that the losses in net worth suffered by the slave-owners were not fully offset by the compensation payments.[24]

The compensation payments weighed most heavily on the Haitians. They had to pay for their own freedom or that of their parents, thus 608,400 inhabitants of the first black republic had to pay the equivalent of 5.9 British pounds per person. The total amount constituted 116 percent of the yearly state budget of Haiti. Second was Great Britain, where there were twenty-one metropolitan inhabitants for every colonial slave. Each individual Briton had to pay on average 1.4 pounds to compensate the slave-owners, an amount that could be earned in nine days' work by a farmer or in twenty-eight days by a domestic servant or weaver. The total compensation payment amounted to 40.8 percent of the yearly budget. Elsewhere, the costs were much lower: in France, 0.1 pound sterling per metropolitan taxpayer, in the Netherlands 0.3 pound sterling, in Denmark 0.1 pound sterling, and even less in Sweden.

Usually, the payment of compensation money took several years and the percentage of the value of the slaves that was in fact compensated varied widely. Adding the artificially low labor costs during the period of apprenticeship to the compensation paid in cash, the slave-owners in the British West Indies and in Dutch Suriname received about 70 to 80 percent of the value of their slaves. Those in the Danish West Indies received about 60 percent, and in the French West Indies (other than Saint Domingue), about 45 percent. In the Dutch Antilles, the ratio was not less than 23

[23] Beauvois, *Indemniser les planteurs*, pp. 260–67; Kuitenbrouwer, "De Nederlandse afschaffing," 69–98.

[24] This and the next two paragraphs are based on Beauvois, *Indemniser les planteurs*, esp. pp. 284–96.

percent. Former slave-owners from Saint Domingue only recovered about 15 percent of the value of their human property.

APPRENTICESHIPS: BRITISH WEST INDIES, 1834–1838
AND SURINAME, 1863–1873

The British West Indies period of apprenticeship lasted for four years, and was accepted by all colonies except Antigua and Bermuda, where it was felt that the high population density made the legal coercion of the freedmen to work unnecessary. The legislation for this period included a set number of hours to be worked per week, though how they were divided by days was an issue for negotiation. This system led to controversy between apprentices and planters, and the apprenticeship period for plantation slaves was reduced from the six years as legislated in the original law to four years.

Denmark, in 1847, legislated a twelve-year period of apprenticeship, but due to uprisings it was terminated after one year. The Dutch legislators enacted a period of apprenticeship of ten years' duration, but only for the former field slaves in the plantation colony of Suriname. The belated slave emancipations as well as the long apprenticeship period in the Dutch West Indies were made possible by the absence of an influential abolitionist lobby in the Netherlands and the concerns inspired by large slave rebellions in the other colonies. Another factor that contributed to the long period of apprenticeship, or "state supervision" as it was called, were the negative effects of slave emancipation on the labor supply already demonstrated in the British and French Caribbean.

On paper, the advantages of apprenticeship for the plantation owners in Suriname seemed impressive. In exchange for paying a daily wage, they no longer needed to support those who were too young, too old, or too ill to work. In addition to wages, the former slave-owners were obliged to provide housing, medical care, and provision grounds as part of the wage, but only to those who had concluded a labor contract with the owner. In reality, however, a reduction in the labor costs was sometimes difficult to achieve. In order to retain a good laborer, the employers had to extend the housing, medical care, and garden plots to the unproductive family members. Wages were set by the government, but employers sometimes had to pay a premium for those laborers who were more productive and had to be lured away from competitors.[25]

For the freedmen, apprenticeships seemed a bothersome extension of slavery. It forced them into more labor on the plantations, but probably

[25] Emmer, *The Dutch in the Atlantic Economy*, pp. 227–54.

also to earn more money than they would have done voluntarily. During the apprenticeship period, the number of freedmen available to conclude labor contracts shrank by 15 percent. Healthy, adult freedmen earned more than they had received in kind as slaves, but the incomes of the young, the old, and the sick probably declined. Right from the start of the period of apprenticeship, there was a tendency among female slaves and their children to withdraw from plantation work and instead squat on the available plots of land. Family incomes declined as a result. Some of that decline, however, was probably offset by the income in kind derived from peasant farming. Employers complained about the strange, to them, reaction to an increase in wages: it reduced rather than increased the amount of labor offered, a phenomenon to be later called by economists "the backward bending supply curve of labor," which also was said to characterize the European proletariat in the first phase of the Industrial Revolution.

The new freedom not only increased the differences in income among the ex-slaves, it also raised the possibility of changing employers, and the subsequent internal migrations also had some widening effects on the income distribution within the black community. Some missionary reports indicate that the freedom to move sometimes destroyed family ties as men would leave their families and seek employment elsewhere. School attendance dropped as families moved away from the plantations when possible. Yet the freedom to move did not induce many ex-slaves to migrate to the neighboring English and French colonies.

THE POST-SLAVERY CARIBBEAN

The most frequent outcomes after the ending of slavery were that the plantation system in the non-Spanish Caribbean, as it had operated for two centuries, became far less able to compete on the international market for tropical cash crops, as the laborers probably worked for fewer hours and with less intensity than when enslaved. The initial result in most of the slave emancipations was a reduction in the output of cash crops and thus in exports. This occurred most dramatically in the case of Haiti, but as seen in Table 4.3, most Caribbean colonies experienced declining output levels, particularly for sugar. This led to attempts to explain what some called the failure of "free labor," and stimulated planters to seek alternative methods for economic recovery.

The changes in the economy of the post-slavery Caribbean depended on four factors: (1) the ratio between land and the number of inhabitants, i.e. the population density; (2) the willingness of the colonial governments to limit access to land and to coerce the freedmen to offer their labor in the plantation sector; (3) the ability to recruit laborers from elsewhere; and (4) the modernization of the export plantations.

Table 4.3 *Average Annual Sugar Production before and after Emancipation* (*'000 tons*)

	Five Years before Abolition	Five Years after Abolition or End of Restrictions	% Change	Period in Which Pre-Emancipation Level Regained
Haiti	71.7	1.2	−98.3	1960s
Martinique	29.1	(1847) 20.1	−29.6	1857–61
Guadeloupe	31.9	(1847) 17.7	−44.5	1868–72
St. Croix	9.7	(1848) 7.3	−24.7	c. 1890
Louisiana	177.1	(1865) 44.0	−75.2	1887–91
Suriname	15.7	(1873) 9.7	−38.2	1927–31
Puerto Rico	94.0	(1876) 74.4	−20.9	1900–04
Cuba	595.4	(1886) 745.7	+25.2	−
Brazil	254.0	(1888) 170.6	−32.8	1905–09

Source: Stanley L. Engerman, "Economic Change and Contract Labor in the British Caribbean: The End of Slavery and the Adjustment to Emancipation," *Explorations in Economic History*, 21 (1984): 133–50.

The first major legislated slave emancipation, in the British West Indies, illustrated the importance of these four factors. Most areas experienced an initial decline in sugar output, but some, after several decades, recovered and exceeded their output levels under slavery. While most of the plantation areas did continue to produce sugar as the major crop, it took several decades before the total sugar output of the British West Indies recovered to its pre-emancipation level. The outcome for individual colonies did differ, reflecting the influence of the four factors noted above.[26]

There were three basic patterns in the British West Indies. As seen in Table 4.4, Barbados and Antigua, islands with high population density, sustained a plantation economy, given that the freedmen had no access to land, and thus the only opportunities to make a living were to keep working on the plantation or to migrate. Sugar output rose and these islands became sources of outmigration when permitted. British Guiana and Trinidad had considerable land to which the ex-slaves could move to establish small farms. Sugar plantations needed to obtain more labor to maintain sugar production. After about twenty years, contract labor was obtained, mainly from India (legal until 1917), but also from China, Madeira, Africa, and elsewhere. The total number of contract laborers coming to the British Caribbean between 1834 and 1917, mainly from India, was 525,404. The labor contracts were generally for eight- to ten-

---

[26] For discussions of British slave emancipation, see William A. Green, *British Slave Emancipation: The Sugar Colonies and the Great Experiment, 1830–1865* (Oxford, 1976); Seymour Drescher, *The Mighty Experiment: Free Labor versus Slavery in British Emancipation* (New York, 2002).

Table 4.4 *Changes in Sugar Production in the British Slave Colonies prior to and after Emancipation*

	% Change in Average Annual Sugar Production, 1824–1833 to 1839–1846	Period in Which Pre-Emancipation Level of Sugar Production Regained	Ratio of Sugar Production in 1887–1896 to Sugar Production in 1839–1846
1. Antigua	+8.7	–	1.5
Barbados	+5.5	–	3.5
St. Kitts	+3.8	–	2.7
2. Trinidad	+21.7	–	3.0
British Guiana	+43.0	1857–66	3.4
Mauritius	+54.3	–	3.1
3. Dominica	−6.4	1847–56	0.7
St. Lucia	−21.8	1857–66	1.7
Nevis	−43.1	1867–76	–
Montserrat	−43.7	1867–76	2.5
St. Vincent	−47.3	Never	0.7
Tobago	−47.5	–	–
Jamaica	−51.2	1930s	0.6
Grenada	−55.9	Never	–

Source: same as Table 4.3.

year terms, with some providing return passage when these years passed. These areas underwent a very rapid growth of sugar output in the second half of the nineteenth century. On the other hand, Jamaica, and most other smaller British islands, had enough land to allow ex-slaves to move into highland areas or to move elsewhere and leave the plantations. Jamaica, for example, suffered a sharp reduction in sugar output (and did not regain its pre-emancipation levels until 1930). Overall economic expansion in Jamaica did not recur until after 1850, with the development of the banana industry.[27]

In all of the French Caribbean as well as in Dutch Suriname, the population density was such that the freedmen also could establish themselves as subsistence farmers by squatting on non-occupied plots. At the same time, those colonies maintained large export plantations with a high demand for labor, often met with the import of indentured labor from Asia. In principle, the colonial governments were unable to coerce the freedmen to remain on the plantations. Yet colonial policies did make a difference. It took the Dutch colony of Suriname more than half a century to increase its sugar production to the level it had reached before the

[27] J. R. Ward, *Poverty and Progress in the Caribbean, 1800–1960* (London, 1985), pp. 31–45; David Northrup, *Indentured Labor in the Age of Imperialism* (Cambridge, 1995), p. 159.

abolition of slavery, while French Guadeloupe and Martinique managed to do this within twenty-two and eleven years, respectively. Laws to curb vagrancy and squatting were adopted in all ex-slave colonies, but it seemed that they were best enforced in the French Caribbean. In addition, a *livret* system required the former slaves to prove at any moment in time that they had concluded a labor contract.[28]

Another feature that explains the relatively rapid return to pre-emancipation sugar production levels in the French Caribbean was the division of many sugar-cane fields between the original owner and the former slaves, allowing the latter to produce sugar cane on their own account. Central mills took care of processing the cane and marketing the sugar. This allowed ex-slaves to become new entrepreneurs and to grow sugar cane employing a small number of additional laborers. This might have made the freedmen more reluctant to leave the plantations in the French Caribbean than in the British Caribbean and Suriname.[29]

A further factor that could explain the relatively quick recuperation of the sugar exports in the French Caribbean was the early onset of immigration. Unlike the Dutch, between 1854 and 1862, the French imported more than 19,000 African indentured laborers into their Caribbean colonies. Also, the French were able to start recruiting indentured laborers from India earlier than the Dutch. Between 1853 and 1888, around 79,000 Indian laborers arrived in the French West Indies. Whether these immigrants forced the freedpeople out of their jobs or simply offset previous decline in the labor supply has not been established. Evidence from Suriname suggests that "the flight from the plantations" was an autonomous process sharply reducing the amount of labor offered by women and children, while the males previously enslaved seemed to have had a preference for forming "jobbing gangs" and offering their labor only during harvest time. The number of immigrant laborers under indenture arriving in Dutch Suriname after slave emancipation ranged from 953 in 1864 to 2,230 in 1872, mainly from China. The immigration of 34,500 indentured immigrants from India took place from 1873 to 1917, and that of 32,965 Javanese lasted from 1853 to 1920.[30]

---

[28] Herbert S. Klein and Stanley L. Engerman, "The Transition from Slave to Free Labor: Notes on a Comparative Economic Model," in Manuel Moreno Fraginals, Frank Moya Pons, and Stanley L. Engerman (eds.), *Between Slavery and Free Labor: The Spanish Speaking Caribbean in the Nineteenth Century* (Baltimore, MD, 1985), pp. 225–69; Fallope, *Esclaves et citoyens*, pp. 401, 402.

[29] Butel, *Histoire des Antilles françaises*, pp. 400–05.

[30] Emmer, *The Dutch in the Atlantic Economy*, p. 157; Northrup, *Indentured Labor in the Age of Imperialism*, pp. 27–8, 156, 159; Northrup, "Freedom and Indentured Labor in the French Caribbean, 1848–1900," in Eltis (ed.), *Coerced and Free Migrations*, pp. 204–28; R. Hoefte, *In Place of Slavery: A Social History of British Indian and Javanese Laborers in Suriname* (Gainesville, FL, 1998).

In the Danish West Indies, immigration was also seen as a means to combat the declining number of freedmen who offered to work on plantations. In spite of regulations enacted in 1849 and lasting until 1878, stipulating that each freedman should accept yearly labor contracts with daily wages set by the government, the number of freedmen working on the plantations had declined by 25 percent by 1854. That is why Saint Croix, the main sugar-exporting island, received about 10,000 immigrants between 1850 and 1917, mostly from Barbados, but to a lesser extent from other parts of the Caribbean. Only one ship with 321 indentured laborers from India arrived, in 1863.[31]

Unlike parts of the British and Spanish Caribbean – basically Trinidad, British Guiana, and Cuba – the French, Dutch, and Danish Caribbean colonies did not have areas where plantation agriculture was still expanding. The sugar producers in the French Caribbean could only stay in business because of the protective tariff. Their only competitors were the beet sugar producers in France itself. The Dutch did not protect the sugar coming from Suriname and the only way for the Suriname planters to sell their sugar was in competition with Cuba, Brazil, and Java, which produced cheap sugar by a system of forced cropping, was also a source (as was India) of contract labor for Suriname.

THE LEGACY OF SLAVERY AND REPARATIONS

Without slavery, most of the plantations in the non-Spanish Caribbean could not compete with sugar producers elsewhere in the world and over time the Caribbean economies reoriented to other activities such as the exportation and refining of oil, the exportation of bauxite, financial services and – most importantly – tourism. As in many parts of the world, the average personal income of the inhabitants of the former plantation colonies never reached that of the former colonizers. That is why the interstate organization of cooperation in the Caribbean region, the Caribbean Community and Common Market or CARICOM, issued a press statement in December 2013 in which each Caribbean nation was asked to set up a national reparations committee, while CARICOM would institute a reparations commission of which all chairs of those national committees would become members. At present, eight Caribbean countries have set up such reparation committees: Antigua and Barbuda, Barbados, Belize,

---

[31] Lomarsh Roopnarine, "Re-Indenture, Repatriation and Remittances of Ex-Indentured Indians from Danish St. Croix to British India, 1863–1873," *Scandinavian Journal of History*, 35 (2010): 247–267.

Guiana, Jamaica, Saint Lucia, Saint Vincent and the Grenadines, and Suriname.[32]

The press statement mentions the following reasons for reparations: native genocide, the transatlantic slave trade, and a racialized system of chattel slavery. The press statement further points out that slavery has impaired the health of the present-day descendants of Caribbean slaves as they now have: (1) "the highest incidence in the world of chronic diseases," especially hypertension and diabetes; (2) a low level of literacy; (3) few museums and research institutes dealing with colonial history; (4) a low self-esteem as African culture was "criminalized" during slavery, resulting in "broken structures" and "diminished family values"; (5) experience of psychological damage based on the fact that the ancestors of the present-day Afro-Caribbeans "as slaves were denied recognition as members of the human family." Finally, they were unable to build up an industrial society as technological progress was confined to the colonial mother countries.

Some of these claims are difficult to verify, but those regarding health and literacy are not supported by the available statistical evidence. In contrast to what the press statement says, the literacy rates in the Caribbean are among the highest in the world, more than 90 percent with the exception of Haiti (around 50 percent) in spite of the fact that the period of slavery was shorter there than elsewhere in the New World. Similarly, life expectancy in the Caribbean is somewhat lower than in Europe, but higher than other tropical countries in Africa and South Asia. Two countries with a particularly strong history of plantation agriculture and chattel slavery, Cuba and Barbados, have the highest life expectancy in the region. Furthermore, it should be noted that the number of universities per capita, the rate of industrialization, and the prevalence of two-headed families differ widely among the nations of the world, making it virtually impossible to establish a direct link with the legacy of slavery in the Caribbean.

A GUIDE TO FURTHER READING

Beauvois, Frédérique, *Between Blood and Gold: The Debates over Compensation for Slavery in the Americas (European Expansion & Global Interaction)* (New York, 2017).
Beckles, Hilary McD., *Britain's Black Debt: Reparations for Caribbean Slavery and Native Genocide* (Kingston, 2013).
Butel, Paul, *Histoire des Antilles françaises* (Paris, 2002).

---

[32] Hilary McD. Beckles, *Britain's Black Debt: Reparations for Caribbean Slavery and Native Genocide* (Kingston, 2013); Sandew Hira, *20 Questions and Answers about Reparations for Colonialism* (The Hague, 2014).

Drescher, Seymour, *The Mighty Experiment: Free Labor versus Slavery in British Emancipation* (New York, 2002).

Eltis, David, *Economic Growth and the Ending of the Transatlantic Slave Trade* (New York, 1987).

Emmer, P. C., *The Dutch in the Atlantic Economy, 1580–1880* (Aldershot, 1998).

Engerman, Stanley and B. W. Higman, "The Demographic Structure of the Caribbean Slave Societies in the Eighteenth and Nineteenth Centuries," in Franklin W. Knight (ed.), *General History of the Caribbean*, Vol. III: *The Slave Societies of the Caribbean* (London, 1997), pp. 45–104.

Green, William A., *British Slave Emancipation: The Sugar Colonies and the Great Experiment, 1830–1865* (Oxford, 1976).

Hall, Neville A. T., *Slave Society in the Danish West Indies: St. Thomas, St John and St. Croix* (Kingston, 1992).

Higman, B. W., *A Concise History of the Caribbean* (Cambridge, 2011).

Jensen, Nicholas Thode, *For the Health of the Enslaved: Slaves, Medicine and Power in the Danish West Indies, 1803–1848* (Copenhagen, 2012).

Lundahl, Mats, *Peasants and Poverty. A Study of Haiti* (London, 1979).

Lundahl, Mats, *Poverty in Haiti. Essays on Underdevelopment and Post-Disaster Prospects* (London, 2011).

Nicholls, David, *Haiti in Caribbean Context: Ethnicity, Economy and Revolt* (London, 1985).

Northrup, David, *Indentured Labor in the Age of Imperialism* (Cambridge, 1995).

Northrup, David, "Freedom and Indentured Labor in the French Caribbean, 1848–1900," in David Eltis (ed.), *Coerced and Free Migration: Global Perspectives* (Stanford, CA, 2002), pp. 204–28.

Rotberg, Robert I., *Haiti: The Politics of Squalor* (Boston, MA, 1971).

CHAPTER 5

SLAVERY IN CUBA AND PUERTO RICO, 1804 TO ABOLITION

LAIRD W. BERGAD

INTRODUCTION

In the aftermath of the British and US actions in 1808 banning slave imports to the British colonies and to the United States, Cuba became the principal destination of the trans-Atlantic slave trade to the Caribbean. More than 700,000 slaves disembarked during the nineteenth century until the trade was finally curtailed in 1866. Puerto Rico experienced a surge in slaving as well, but the volume of the trade was small in comparative perspective, perhaps some 30,000 to 40,000 Africans arriving on the island. This rapidly growing slave-labor force was a critical factor in transforming Cuba into the largest sugar exporter in the world by the 1820s. The sugar economy of Puerto Rico also expanded during the early nineteenth century, though output and exports were dwarfed by those of Cuba.

In some ways, the trajectory of slave-based sugar production in nineteenth-century Cuba and Puerto Rico mirrored the development of the seventeenth-century Brazilian sugar/slave complex in Bahia and Pernambuco and the British and French Caribbean plantation models of the eighteenth century. The first African slave society in the Americas emerged in the Brazilian northeast in the late sixteenth and early seventeenth centuries, where slave labor and sugar production were closely linked. This Brazilian model was adopted and transformed by the British in their Caribbean colonies beginning with Barbados during the 1640s, then in the smaller British Leeward Island possessions, and finally on an unprecedented scale in Jamaica, after initial experiments with indentured labor. The French followed suit in their eastern Caribbean colonies and then in Saint Domingue, the future Haiti, after the western side of Hispaniola was occupied in the late seventeenth and early eighteenth centuries. In each of these colonial societies the expansion of sugar production would have been much slower without African slaves. Indeed, it has been estimated that approximately two-thirds of all slaves crossing the Atlantic were destined for regions where sugar drove economic systems, though slave labor was employed in many other sectors, urban and rural.

From their inceptions, the Brazilian northeast and the British and French Caribbean were slave societies.[1] Slavery not only created wealth for slave-holders, but it was central to social, economic, cultural, and political life for all people, irrespective of legal or racial status. As the slave trade escalated in each region, slaves came to comprise the vast majority of total populations in plantation zones, often over three-quarters or more of all inhabitants.

Although these dynamics were characteristic of nineteenth-century Cuba, the historical evolution of slavery on the island was altogether different. Cuban slavery dated from the sixteenth century and the onset of Spanish colonization. Although African slaves were found on relatively small-scale sugar plantations through the colonial period, slavery as a labor system was not exclusively associated with the development of sugar production as was the case in Brazil, British Jamaica, and French Saint Domingue. Colonial Cuba was a society with slaves, rather than a slave society, and Africans and their descendants labored in nearly every occupational category and economic sector in cities, small towns, and in the rural regions surrounding them. Slavery was important to the pre-nineteenth-century Cuban colonial economy to be sure, but it was not the exclusive labor system utilized by elites who often relied upon nominally free workers of diverse racial backgrounds.

These same observations may be made for Puerto Rico, though the development of slavery and labor systems in general was altogether different from Cuba owing to the critical role that Havana came to play in the Spanish colonial trading system. After the establishment of a fleet system to transport Mexican and Peruvian silver back to Spain in the 1570s, the port of Havana became the rendezvous point for silver-laden ships heading to Europe from Veracruz and Panama. This transformed the city into a dynamic urban center and an important market for a diverse array of products from food, to provision the swollen population when the fleet was docked, to hides that filled empty spaces in cargo holds. Ships needed to be serviced and repaired, and had to take on all kinds of supplies to prepare for the trans-Atlantic crossing to Seville. Havana eventually became the third largest city in the Americas behind Mexico and Lima. In the city and its environs, slaves and free laborers were found in every occupational category.[2]

---

[1] In his *Ancient Slavery and Modern Ideology* (London, 1980), Moses I. Finley distinguished between societies with slaves and slave societies. For Finley, slave societies were dependent on slave labor for production and the wealth of elite groups who were heavily comprised by slave-owners. Slavery governed nearly all social relationships because of the legal distinctions between slaves and free people, irrespective of race.

Clearly, these characteristics applied to Brazil and the British and French Caribbean. Cuba, however, was a society with slaves that was converted into a slave society by the 1820s. Puerto Rico was never a slave society, though in particular micro geographical regions shaped by sugar production in the early nineteenth century there were characteristics of slave societies.

[2] See Alejandro de la Fuente, *Havana and the Atlantic in the Sixteenth Century* (Chapel Hill, NC, 2008).

There was no such parallel dynamic in Puerto Rico. San Juan was an important, if substantially smaller, port, largely because it was the easternmost extension of Spanish colonial power in the Caribbean. Its strategic location guaranteed that fortifications were built and maintained and that a colonial bureaucracy was supported. But San Juan never became the economic or strategic center that made Havana one of the most important Spanish colonial cities in the Americas during the sixteenth and seventeenth centuries. This meant that labor needs in Puerto Rico were comparatively smaller, and that slavery did not develop in the same way that it would in Havana and throughout Western Cuba in regions contiguous to the port city. Even at slavery's apex in the first half of the nineteenth century, slaves in Puerto Rico never comprised more than 15 percent of the total population of the island, while in Cuba, by the 1820s, slaves were a majority of all inhabitants.

GEOGRAPHY AND HISTORY

Cuba

From its early history, slavery in Cuba was concentrated in the western regions of the island and this was a pattern which would continue through the nineteenth century, even until final abolition in 1886. The driving force for the slave trade from the sixteenth to mid eighteenth centuries was the labor demands of a fairly diversified economy which revolved around the port of Havana. The association of slavery with sugar production in Cuba would emerge in the late eighteenth and early nineteenth centuries, but sugar only became the island's principal export product in the 1820s. Prior to sugar's expansion after 1750, slaves labored in every conceivable urban occupation, from domestics, nannies, liverymen, and drivers to carpenters, stevedores, shipbuilders, and iron-workers. Surrounding Havana, truck farms, cattle ranches, tobacco farms, and small-scale sugar mills were worked by slave labor, usually in fairly small numbers per farm. The large-scale concentration of slaves on specialized plantations found in the British and French Caribbean and Brazil would not emerge in Cuba until well into the nineteenth century.

Reliable late-eighteenth-century slave population estimates date from the 1774 Spanish census, which found a slave population of about 44,000, about one-quarter of all residents in Cuba. The slave trade had increased substantially after the 1762 English occupation of Havana, which opened the island to unrestricted slave trading. This was essentially legalized after Spain regained Havana from the British in the following year. Perhaps as many as 10,000 slaves entered the island during the 1760s. By 1792, the slave population had nearly doubled from 1774 to about 85,000 slaves, comprising over 30 percent of Cuba's total population.

Puerto Rico

Scholars have recently revised the pre-nineteenth-century history of slavery in Puerto Rico. Once considered a marginal institution until the expansion of sugar production after 1800, slaves played an important role from the sixteenth century onward in the port of San Juan and in comparatively small-scale commercial agricultural activities such as ginger, tobacco, and sugar cultivation, as well as in cattle ranching. The first systematic census of Puerto Rico, published in 1765, enumerated about 5,000 slaves out of a total population of some 45,000. This relatively small number leaves open the possibility that at times during the sixteenth and seventeenth centuries slave populations may have been substantially larger. Since there was no center of ongoing dynamic economic activity analogous to the role played by Havana in Cuba, Puerto Rico's colonial economy experienced cycles of growth and contraction and this affected the volume of the slave trade to the island, as well as the overall size of the slave population.[3]

It is certain, however, that the slave population increased considerably after 1765. The reformist policies enacted by Spain led to an extraordinary surge in the Puerto Rican slave trade. Estimates indicate that as many as 10,000 slaves may have been imported in the five-year period between 1766 and 1770, double the size of the slave population in 1765, though how many of these slaves may have been re-exported to other regions in the Caribbean is unknown. Strikingly, this was about the same volume as the slave trade to Cuba during the 1760s. Commercial agriculture in Puerto Rico began to expand on an unprecedented scale and surviving archival population censuses reveal that by 1800 there were over 20,000 slaves on the island or quadruple the number found in 1765.[4] Although this was about a quarter of the size of Cuba's slave population at the turn of the nineteenth century, both islands were poised for economic expansion and the increased importance of the slave trade and slavery to each island's history.

ECONOMIC DEVELOPMENT

Cuba

To understand the quantitative dimensions of slavery and the slave trade, it is necessary to understand patterns of economic development and their

---

[3] See Elsa Gelpi Baiz, *Siglo en blanco: estudio de la economía azucarera en Puerto Rico, siglo XVI (1540–1612)* (San Juan, 2000); and David M. Stark, "A New Look at the African Slave Trade in Puerto Rico through the Use of Parish Registers: 1660–1815," *Slavery and Abolition*, 30 (2009): 491–520.

[4] Francisco A. Scarano and Katherine J. Curtis, "Agrarian Change and Population Growth in Late Colonial Spanish America: The Case of Puerto Rico, 1765–1815," Center for Demography and Ecology, University of Wisconsin-Madison, Working Paper No. 2011-04.

accompanying labor requirements that fueled the demand for slave labor. The meteoric expansion of Cuban slavery and sugar production after the onset of the Haitian slave revolt in the early 1790s, which disrupted European import markets and led to sharp short-term price rises for both sugar and coffee, was in many ways the intensification of processes which began in the mid eighteenth century rather than any sharp break with the past. Sugar production and slavery were fixtures in colonial Cuba and to a lesser extent in Puerto Rico from the sixteenth century, but never on any significant scale for periods of time and there was no continuous growth of the industry. There were cyclical periods of expansion followed by con- traction as mills were established and later closed for a variety of reasons so that from a secular perspective the industry was incapable of sustaining any long-term expansion from the sixteenth through the mid eighteenth century.

Conditions improved in Cuba during the 1740s, some two decades prior to the 1762 British seizure of Havana. This is usually cited as the watershed in the development of the sugar/slave complex on the island due to increased slave imports facilitated by slave traders who descended on Havana while it was under British control for eleven months. Spain eliminated import duties for Cuban sugar during the 1740s and a rise of prices for raw sugar in Europe led to an expansion of sugar and slavery in the Havana region. In 1750, about sixty mills were found near the port city and the number increased to ninety-six in 1761 on the eve of the British invasion. There is no question that the opening of Havana to unrestricted slave imports in 1762 accelerated this extant process of expansion. By 1792, there were 225 mills grinding cane close to Havana and the area planted in cane had risen from 320 *caballerías* in 1762 to 5,000 *caballerías* of land.[5] Throughout Western Cuba, sugar cane planting moved toward the south- ern coastal town of Batabanó and slowly eastward toward the plains of Matanzas and further east. In 1792, some 529 mills, large and small, were found throughout Cuba, mainly in the west. By 1827, there were 1,000 sugar mills; 1,439 in 1846; and 1,531 mills in 1862.

The key to explaining rising demand for slave labor in the sugar sector of the nineteenth-century Cuban economy requires an understanding of both the agricultural and the industrial sides of the industry. It is not simply a matter of increasing numbers of plantations. The mills built as the nineteenth century progressed bore little resemblance to the animal- or human-driven *ingenios* of previous centuries. Technological innovations from Europe in the processing of sugar and in transportation led to substantial increases in the productive capacity of the industry, particularly

---

[5] A *caballería* was roughly equivalent to 33 acres.

in the refining of cane into sugar. The application of steam engines in mills, Jamaican trains, vacuum-pan evaporators, and centrifuges during the 1850s and after resulted in sharp rises in industrial sugar yields at the mill and in the profitability at these plantations which were able to install the most advanced technological innovations. The utilization of railroads during and after the 1840s, to move cane from field to mill and from mill to port cities, also resulted in increased efficiency. The substantial investments in processing technology and in an efficient transportation infrastructure meant that the capacity to grind cane increased enormously. There was a need for greater quantities of cane to justify capital investments in expensive processing equipment and internal railroad systems. This is central to understanding the extraordinary increase in the demand for slave labor to serve in the production of sugar cane, sugar, and a wide variety of ancillary economic sectors.

While there was an ongoing technological revolution in processing sugar cane and in transportation, the methods of cultivating and harvesting cane were virtually timeless. Cane was cut by gang laborers working by hand with machetes; it was stacked in piles by cane cutters; loaded by hand onto oxen-pulled carts, and increasingly after 1840, onto small railway carts which were pulled by oxen on moveable railroad tracks for transportation from fields to mills for processing. Cane cutting would not be mechanized until the middle of the twentieth century. There was a very simple equation for mill owners. The only way to expand the acreage planted in cane, which was mandatory to meet the ever-increasing processing capacity of mechanized mills, was to increase the number of workers in the agricultural sector. With a limited internal labor market composed of free people who worked for wages or other forms of compensation, the only alternative for the expansion of the sugar industry was the importation of outside laborers. This meant slaves from Africa who were readily available despite repeated and ongoing efforts by the British to curb the slave trade.

As British and Dutch Caribbean import markets for slaves evaporated after the abolition of the slave trade to the British colonies and the United States by the US and British restrictions of 1808, and as French slave markets receded after the onset of revolution in Saint Domingue in 1791, there was an over-supply of slaves for purchase in African coastal slave-trading regions which were the embarkation points for the trans-Atlantic crossing to the Americas. The end of British slaving and the gradual decline of the French trade did not result in a contraction of West-African slave markets, but rather increased the availability of slaves for high-labor-demand regions such as Cuba, Puerto Rico, and Brazil, as well as Africa.

The slave population in Cuba continued to be found not only in sugar, but in all occupational categories and economic sectors, and would not become concentrated in the sugar plantation complex until the 1850s, the decade when technological innovation in processing intensified and railroad construction began on a significant scale.

By 1827, the slave population of the island had risen to about 287,000 slaves from about 85,000 in 1792. About one-quarter of all slaves in 1827 worked on sugar plantations; another 25 percent were found on coffee farms, an important sector of the Cuban export economy until the 1840s. As "late" as 1830 it has been estimated that about as much capital was invested in the coffee sector as in the production of sugar. Another quarter of Cuban slaves lived and worked in urban areas, mainly Havana; and the remaining 25 percent of the slave population labored on small-scale food-producing farms and cattle ranches. An undetermined number of these slaves worked in activities that supported the sugar sector: producing food for *ingenios*; transporting sugar to ports; working as stevedores on the docks loading sugar onto ships; and in a wide variety of urban and rural occupations which in some way helped sustain the expanding sugar economy.

By 1846, about one-third of the nearly 324,000 slaves in Cuba were found on sugar plantations, a significant increase from the late 1820s, though not on the scale that would have been encountered in eighteenth-century Jamaica or Saint Domingue. By 1862, the slave population had expanded to 370,000 and nearly half of all slaves labored directly on sugar plantations. The Cuban coffee economy experienced a sharp collapse in the 1840s, in part because of the devastating impact of hurricanes in the early 1840s. This resulted in a transfer of slaves from coffee farms to sugar plantations, as well as to other economic sectors. Urban slavery remained extraordinarily important and slave labor was also found on non-sugar rural farms and ranches – to be the case until abolition in the 1880s. Once again, the diversity of Cuban slavery must be stressed, even within the context of an economic system shaped in many ways, but not exclusively, by the sugar plantation complex.

The geographical distribution of slaves in Cuba also was closely related to the development of the sugar-export economy. From the late sixteenth century onward, there had always been an overwhelming concentration of slaves in Western Cuba, specifically within and around the port city of Havana because of its dynamic role in the fleet system and as the island's center of economic activity. Cuban agriculture – sugar, tobacco, coffee, and a wide variety of food crops – spread from the environs of the port toward the southern coast in the late eighteenth century and gradually eastward toward Matanzas as sugar cultivation expanded in the first half of the nineteenth century. However, the nineteenth-century sugar plantation economy never moved further eastward than the geographical center of the island. The most technologically advanced mills and the largest slave populations were located in Western Cuba. In 1827, about 70 percent of the total Cuban slave population lived and worked in Western Cuba and

Table 5.1 *Distribution of Slaves in Cuba in Broad Geographical Zones,
1792–1862*

	1792		1827		1846		1862	
	Slaves	% of Total Population	Slaves	% of Total Population	Slaves	% of Total Population	Slaves	% of Total Population
West	52,025	62%	197,415	69%	227,813	70%	248,781	67%
Center	18,381	22%	42,028	15%	46,985	15%	69,994	19%
East	14,184	17%	47,499	17%	48,961	15%	51,778	14%
Total	84,590	100%	286,942	100%	323,759	100%	370,553	100%

Source: Cuban census for corresponding years.

of these more than half were found in Havana and its contiguous regions. In 1846, the same percentage (70 percent) of the overall slave population was concentrated in Western Cuba, but there had been clear movement of the slave population away from the regions in and near the port city eastward toward the center of the island. Little had changed by 1862 in terms of the geographical distribution of slaves, with about 67 percent residing in the west, and with a greater concentration in sugar plantation districts than ever before (see Table 5.1 and Map 5.1).

Puerto Rico

Similar occupational data for slaves are not found for Puerto Rico, though the late-eighteenth- and nineteenth-century census materials provide fairly precise quantitative information on the geographical distribution of slaves on the island. These suggest that Puerto Rican slavery may have been more closely tied with sugar expansion than was the case in Cuba, partially because of the comparative lack of occupational diversity among slaves. Urban slavery in San Juan dated from the early colonial period, but it was not on the same scale as found in Havana. San Juan was a fortified port in the eastern Caribbean serving the broader colonial empire, rather than a dynamic center of international trade, a port city from which significant quantities of agricultural and pastoral products were shipped to European markets.

This was the case until the late eighteenth century, when coffee and sugar production began their ascent. It is conspicuous that these product-ive activities did not emanate outward from San Juan in the way that export agriculture expanded away from Havana, but rather took hold primarily in the western and southern coastal regions of the island. Most agricultural endeavors in Puerto Rico in the late eighteenth and early

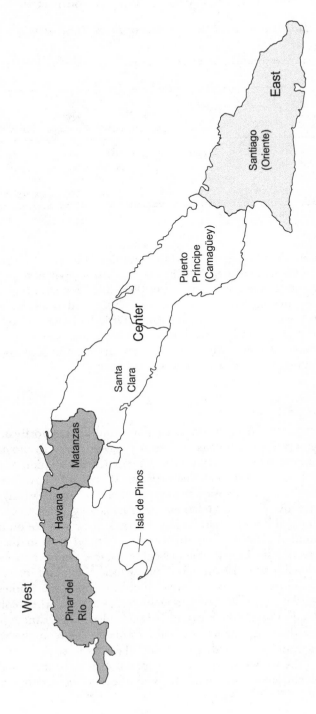

Map 5.1 Approximate Administrative Subdivisions in Cuba during the Nineteenth Century

nineteenth centuries were fairly small scale, utilizing family labor and relatively few slaves.

In 1802, when the island's slave population numbered about 25,000, some 11 percent of the total slave population was concentrated in the San Juan region, with slaves along the western, southern, and eastern coastal areas of Puerto Rico and no great concentrations found in any one district (see Table 5.2). Both sugar and coffee took hold in the coastal regions during the second half of the eighteenth century, which accelerated because of the arrival of French planters fleeing the upheaval in nearby Saint Domingue, where war raged between 1791 and 1804.

Yet despite the influx of French entrepreneurs, many of whom brought their slaves with them, significant growth in the Puerto Rican sugar economy only occurred after 1815, and during the 1820s and 1830s sugar production expanded impressively. Thus, the timing of sugar's ascent varied from the Cuban case where significant growth, along with the demand for slaves, occurred from the mid eighteenth century. The geographical distribution of slaves on the island suggests another major difference with Cuba. The sugar sector in Puerto Rico was almost the sole driving force in the growth of nineteenth-century slavery, a somewhat different pattern of development compared with more diversified Cuba.

Slave populations increased in Puerto Rican coastal enclaves where sugar plantations were established, expanded, and prospered during the 1820s through the 1840s. In 1828, about 38 percent of all slaves in Puerto Rico were found in five regions along the western and southern coasts: Mayagüez, Ponce, Guayama, San Germán, and Aguadilla. By 1854, these districts accounted for 37 percent of the island's slaves and this rose to 40 percent in 1865, each increasingly driven by the production of sugar, though earlier in the nineteenth century coffee was of primary importance (see Table 5.2 and Map 5.2).

Other fundamental differences between the two colonies were the scale of production and the changing technological parameters of the sugar industry. These were connected and they affected both the size of individual plantations and the accompanying demand for slave labor. There is no question that Puerto Rican sugar plantations were considerably smaller than those found in Cuba. In part, this was related to milling capacity. There was a direct correlation between the installation of ever-changing technologies in sugar processing and the size of individual plantations. Specialization that divided sugar-cane farming from sugar production did not emerge until very late in the nineteenth century. Planters in Puerto Rico modernized their mills as much as was feasible during sugar's rise in the 1820s and 1830s, but they were never able to install internal rail systems or the most modern processing technologies on a significant scale during and after the 1840s. This limited both the need for the physical extension

Table 5.2 *Slave Populations in the Fifteen Largest Slave-Holding Districts of Puerto Rico, 1802–1865*

	1802			1828			1854			1865		
District	Slaves	% of Total	District	Slaves	% of Total	District	Slaves	% of Total	District	Slaves	% of Total
San Juan	2,405	9.8%	Mayagüez	3,860	12.9%	Ponce	4,431	9.4%	Ponce	4,720	12.1%
Humacao	1,556	6.3%	Ponce	3,204	10.7%	Guayama	4,269	9.1%	Mayagüez	3,823	9.8%
Cabo Rojo	1,448	5.8%	Guayama	2,303	7.7%	Mayagüez	4,065	8.7%	Guayama	3,087	7.9%
Aguada	1,376	5.6%	San Germán	1,673	5.6%	San Germán	2,761	5.9%	San Germán	2,885	7.4%
Coamo	1,244	5.1%	Aguadilla	1,306	4.4%	Isabela	2,034	4.3%	Arecibo	1,398	3.6%
Ponce	1,023	4.2%	Río Piedras	969	3.2%	Aguadilla	1,950	4.2%	Añasco	1,298	3.3%
Yauco	1,014	4.1%	Arecibo	915	3.1%	San Juan	1,938	4.1%	Juana Díaz	1,240	3.2%
Caguas	943	3.8%	Bayamón	899	3.0%	Cabo Rojo	1,660	3.5%	Cabo Rojo	1,238	3.2%
Loíza	933	3.8%	Cabo Rojo	851	2.9%	Arecibo	1,603	3.4%	Aguadilla	1,209	3.1%
Arecibo	853	3.5%	Yauco	834	2.8%	Añasco	1,332	2.8%	Humacao	958	2.5%
Guayama	842	3.4%	Caguas	808	2.7%	Vega Alta	1,077	2.3%	Yabucoa	859	2.2%
San Germán	842	3.4%	Loíza	742	2.5%	Juana Díaz	1,079	2.3%	Manatí	769	2.0%
Añasco	788	3.2%	Añasco	627	2.1%	Guayanilla	895	1.9%	Isabela	728	1.9%
Mayagüez	690	2.8%	Moca	625	2.1%	Yabucoa	777	1.7%	Cayey	706	1.8%
Río Piedras	668	2.8%	Cayey	555	1.9%	Patillas	727	1.5%	Guayanilla	697	1.8%
Total slaves	**24,591**			**29,929**			**46,923**			**39,057**	

Sources: 1802 data from Francisco A. Scarano and Katherine J. Curtis, "Puerto Rico's Padrones, 1779–1802" [computer file], ICPSR30262-v1 (Ann Arbor, MI: Inter-University Consortium for Political and Social Research [distributor], 2011-04-07). Data for 1828, 1854, and 1865 from Luis A. Figueroa, *Sugar, Slavery, and Freedom in Nineteenth Century Puerto Rico* (Chapel Hill, NC, 2005), Table 2.2, p. 54.

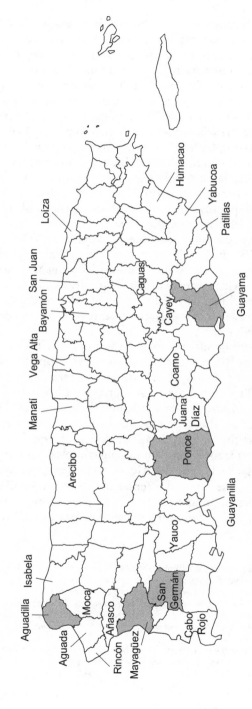

Map 5.2 Municipal Districts in Puerto Rico

Note: The boundaries depicted in this map are the current boundaries of the municipal districts of the island. There are no reliable maps which depict the municipal, or *partido*, administrative divisions during the nineteenth century. Thus, the districts depicted here only provide a general notion of their locations. It is certain that each of these was much larger in the individual years cited in Table 5.2.

of cane farming because of the lower grinding capacity than Cuban mills, and resulted in comparatively lower demand for slave labor, though there were some local exceptions where planters were able to install steam engines and other innovations. However, the failure of the island-wide sugar industry to compete in international markets during the 1850s resulted in a contraction of slavery in Puerto Rico, unlike the Cuban case, where slavery dynamically expanded during the 1850s and 1860s.

The reasons for these differences in Puerto Rican and Cuban sugar/slave development are complex and based on two fundamental factors. One was Puerto Rico's very different demographic structure; and the other the role that a potential free labor supply played in the island's development. The period from 1760 until the 1820s and beyond was characterized by unprecedented natural population growth of free people of all racial backgrounds. Puerto Rico became the most densely populated island in the Caribbean during and after the nineteenth century. There have been a number of studies which indicate that free labor played an important role as coffee and sugar estates were established during the early nineteenth century, together with a variety of ancillary activities such as food production and cattle ranching. This helps to explain Puerto Rico's reduced need for expensive slave labor.[6] The precise quantitative dimension of free labor usage is generally unknown.

The failure to modernize the industry technologically did not necessarily mean that Puerto Rican sugar estates were not profitable or highly productive.[7] Before the middle of the nineteenth century, there were highly competitive milling complexes with, however, a lower level of industrial productivity than Cuba's more mechanized *ingenios*. But the average size of slave holdings on the largest estates in Puerto Rico was considerably smaller than was the case in Cuba. In Ponce, Puerto Rico, in 1845, the average number of laborers on each milling complex was forty-five, though the largest mechanized estate had 150 workers (slave and free). In Matanzas, Cuba, during the 1850s, the center of the country's slave/sugar complex, most slaves were concentrated on plantations with more than 200 slaves each, and a significant number of estates had over 500 slaves.

---

[6] In the largest sugar-producing municipalities in Puerto Rico in 1812, Mayagüez, Ponce, and Guayama, only 11 percent of the population was enslaved. Though this increased to 23 percent in 1828, there was an abundance of free people who were workers. See Francisco Scarano, *Sugar and Slavery in Puerto Rico: The Plantation Economy of Ponce, 1800–1850* (Madison, WI, 1984), p. 30. In these same municipal districts, in 1865, about 60 percent of all workers were free, the other 40 percent enslaved. See Luis A. Figueroa, *Sugar, Slavery, and Freedom in Nineteenth-Century Puerto Rico* (Chapel Hill, NC, 2005), p. 76.

[7] Scarano found that in the major sugar zone of Ponce in 1845 only six of seventy-five mills utilized steam engines, five were driven by water, and sixty-four were powered by oxen (Scarano, *Sugar and Slavery in Puerto Rico*, p. 68).

Nothing on this scale was ever apparent in Puerto Rico's nineteenth-century sugar economy.

The other factor which impeded technical advances in the sugar industry in Puerto Rico was a historic absence of accumulated domestic capital. In the case of Cuba, paradoxically given its colonial political structures, a Cuban-born elite class led sugar's expansion after the second half of the eighteenth century. Powerful local families invested in modern milling technologies, purchased slaves, built railroads, and harnessed the resources to build the island's sugar sector. They would be challenged by Spanish immigrants during and after the 1830s, mostly Catalans. There was no domestic-born entrepreneurial elite in Puerto Rico and this explains both the smaller scale of sugar production and the reduced role of slavery in Puerto Rico's historical development. It also explains the decline of the Puerto Rican sugar industry, and slavery, after the mid nineteenth century, when the economic viability of sugar production in an age of increased international competition hinged on continued capital investment and modernization of milling operations and transportation infrastructures.

SLAVE POPULATIONS: CUBA AND PUERTO RICO

Differences in the size of slave populations were clear in 1827 when in Puerto Rico there were close to 32,000 slaves in 1827 and nearly 270,000 slaves in Cuba. In 1846, the apex of slavery in Puerto Rico, there was a total of about 51,000 slaves, while in Cuba there were 324,000. The slave population of Puerto Rico declined in the late 1850s as the sugar economy contracted, and there were about 41,000 slaves in 1860. Cuban slaves continued to increase during and after the 1850s and there were some 370,000 in 1862.

The proportion of slaves in relation to overall populations also differed dramatically. In the late eighteenth century, slaves made up about 15 percent of the population in Puerto Rico. During the nineteenth-century sugar boom, however, slaves never accounted for more than 12 percent of all people on the island. The slave population peaked in Cuba in the 1840s and in 1841 slaves made up about 43 percent of all inhabitants, an increase from about a quarter of the population in 1774 (see Table 5.3). In Puerto Rico's coastal sugar-producing districts, slaves made up larger percentages of the populations. In 1828, slaves accounted for about 21 percent of all inhabitants in Mayagüez and Ponce and 30 percent in Guayama. By 1842, after significant growth of the local sugar industry, about 41 percent of Guayama's population was enslaved. These local population data suggest demographic profiles more in line with the Cuban experience, though they could not be sustained as the sugar economy contracted after the mid-century, together with a decline in the overall slave population, locally and island-wide. Thus, Cuba – unlike Puerto Rico – was converted into a true

Table 5.3 *Slave Populations of Cuba and Puerto Rico in Selected Years and as Percentage of Total Populations*

	Cuba			Puerto Rico	
Year	No. of Slaves	% of Total Population	Year	No. of Slaves	% of Total Population
1774	44,333	25.8%	1776	6,537	8.1%
1792	84,570	31.1%	1802	13,333	8.2%
1817	199,145	36.0%	1815	18,621	8.4%
1827	286,942	40.7%	1820	21,730	9.4%
1841	436,500	43.3%	1827	31,874	10.5%
1846	323,759	36.0%	1830	34,240	10.6%
1862	370,553	26.5%	1834	41,818	11.7%
1877	199,094	13.1%	1846	51,265	11.6%
			1860	41,736	7.2%
			1867	43,348	6.6%

Source: Cuban Census Reports for each year.

slave society during the nineteenth century, though in Puerto Rico there were coastal pockets which resembled slave societies.

The expansion of slavery in both colonies was the result of both the trans-Atlantic slave trade and some reproduction among slaves, though precise rates of natural population increase are difficult to ascertain. The data for the Cuban slave trade have been regarded as reasonably accurate in describing tendencies over time. It has been estimated that nearly 780,000 slaves disembarked in Cuba over the entire history of the trade, with over 90 percent of these arriving during the nineteenth century.[8]

Estimates for Puerto Rico are more problematic because of the absence of documentation on imports, even during the period of the legal slave trade before the first Anglo-Spanish Treaty of 1817, which theoretically abolished slave trading to the Spanish colonies in 1820, and a second treaty signed in 1835. The second treaty was testimony to the ineffectiveness of the first, and it too was a dead letter despite British efforts at enforcement. Legal slave registers of imports were maintained in Havana between 1790 and 1820, but curiously no such documentation has ever been located for San Juan, most likely because of the relatively low volume of imports.

Another issue in measuring slave arrivals in Puerto Rico is the fact that at particular periods, especially during plantation growth in the 1820s and 1830s, slaves were imported from the smaller islands of the Lesser Antilles

---

[8] The data presented here are from the Trans-Atlantic Slave Trade Database at www.slavevoyages.org, which is based on more than 35,000 individual slave voyages.

Figure 5.1 Slave Trade to Cuba by Five-Year Periods, 1791–1866.

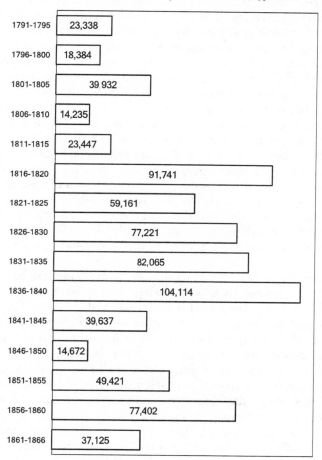

Period	Number
1791-1795	23,338
1796-1800	18,384
1801-1805	39,932
1806-1810	14,235
1811-1815	23,447
1816-1820	91,741
1821-1825	59,161
1826-1830	77,221
1831-1835	82,065
1836-1840	104,114
1841-1845	39,637
1846-1850	14,672
1851-1855	49,421
1856-1860	77,402
1861-1866	37,125

Source: Trans-Atlantic Slave Trade Database, www.slavevoyages.org.

in addition to those imported directly from Africa. For this reason, the ship manifests used to reconstruct slave exports from Africa are not useful in determining how many slaves disembarked in Puerto Rico. Historians working on this theme have estimated that no more than 50,000 slaves were imported to the island and even this estimate may be high. The strikingly lower level of imports compared with Cuba resulted from smaller comparative labor demands. This was due to the less sophisticated processing technologies used by the sugar industry, as well as to the potential availability of a free labor market.

Figure 5.1 depicts slave arrivals in Cuba by five-year periods between 1791 and 1866, when the Cuban trade was finally ended. The rhythms of the trade to Cuba were governed by a variety of factors, primarily the labor demands of a rapidly growing economy. Political variables, such as war and revolution in Europe and elsewhere, were clearly important. It is clear that the end of the Napoleonic Wars in 1815 was followed by a surge in slave trading to Cuba, coinciding both with sugar expansion and eased conditions for international shipping. As noted previously, the end of slave trading to the British colonies in 1808 and the diminishing trade to the French colonies also led to greater availability of slaves in the principal West African slave-trading ports. It is notable that during the period from 1821 to 1825, ships flying French flags carried as many slaves to Cuba as Spanish ships. After 1830, Spanish carriers, often financed with Cuban and/or Spanish capital from large plantation owners and slave merchants, carried all slaves to Cuba. The Anglo-Spanish treaties of 1817 and 1835 had little impact on the trade, with the exception of a short-term downturn in the role of Spanish shipping during the early 1820s. The largest five-year period in the history of slave imports to Cuba came just after the 1835 treaty.

The contraction of slave trading to Cuba in the 1840s may be connected to the British campaigns to end slaving. It may be, however, that the principal factor was labor-market saturation and declining sugar prices. The rebound of the slave trade during the 1850s is testimony to the modernization and expansion of the sugar industry. This also coincided with the importation of Chinese contract laborers, which began in 1847 and only ended in 1873. Some 120,000 Chinese indentured servants were brought to the island to supplement slave labor on plantations. Despite this large-scale Asian trade, the demand for African slaves continued to be very strong through the 1850s.

The Puerto Rican data on slave imports are problematic and incomplete.[9] Though clearly an undercount, the data nevertheless may be suggestive as to the timing of the trade in the nineteenth century. It has been noted previously that Puerto Rico's sugar economy developed later than was the case in Cuba and the slave trade data reflect this. While there was a clear surge in slave trading to Cuba in the 1820s, it appears that the slave trade to Puerto Rico increased significantly only in the 1830s. This corresponded to the peak decade of sugar's expansion on the island in the

---

[9] The slave trade database indicates a total of about 27,000 slaves imported to Puerto Rico and there is no question that this is well below the number actually imported. As indicated above, many slaves arriving on the islands were re-exports from the smaller islands of the Lesser Antilles. This was especially true in the period between the onset of the Haitian Revolution in 1791 and the 1820s. According to historians working on slavery in Puerto Rico, estimates of overall imports range from 45,000 to 50,000 over the entire history of the trade.

Figure 5.2 Slave Trade to Puerto Rico by Five-Year Periods, 1791–1845

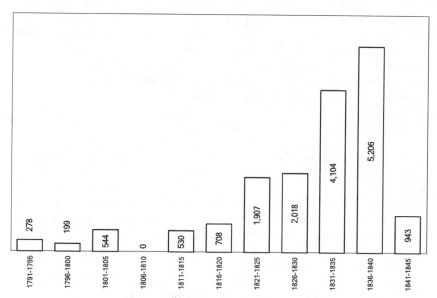

Source: Trans-Atlantic Slave Trade Database, www.slavevoyages.org/tast/index.faces.

first half of the nineteenth century. The trade fell off fairly dramatically thereafter[10] (see Figure 5.2).

Some of the demographic characteristics of the slave trade to Cuba have been well documented by a number of scholars. When the slave trade was still legal, between 1790 and 1820, about 70 percent of all slaves imported to the island were males and, though there is no surviving documentation for Puerto Rico, it is likely that a similar sex ratio prevailed among arriving slaves irrespective of whether they came directly from Africa or from neighboring islands. The Cuban census of 1827 reflected the sex imbalance of slave imports, indicating that about two-thirds of the island's slaves were male. This ratio declined somewhat by the 1846 and 1862 censuses, when about 60 percent of all Cuban slaves were males. It has also been noted that after 1820 the share of males disembarking in Cuba fell to about 60 percent in line with the male/female population ratios in 1846 and 1862.

The demography of the slave trade to Cuba changed through time, not only with respect to sex ratios, but also age distribution. During the period

[10] This slave-trade chronology is in line with Scarano's findings for the slave trade to Ponce in Scarano, *Sugar and Slavery in Puerto Rico*, p. 122. Ponce slave imports peaked during the 1830s and fell dramatically after 1845.

of the legal slave trade between 1790 and 1820, the percentage of slaves under 18 years of age increased continually. Between 1790 and 1810, roughly a third of all slaves imported to Cuba were in this younger age category. This increased to 44 percent from 1810 to 1814 and 59 percent between 1815 and 1819.[11] This may have signaled a change in the nature of markets on the African coast and the increasing prices of older slaves which pushed buyers toward the purchase of greater numbers of less-expensive children who would also be less productive in the short term. Unfortunately, the data on slave imports after 1820 are fragmentary.

Nevertheless, based on a sample of over 5,000 African-born slaves sold in Cuba between 1790 and 1880, as recorded by notaries whose records have been maintained in archival sources, only 7 percent of all transactions were for slaves younger than 15 years of age. For slaves born in Cuba, however, 34 percent of all slaves sold fell into this younger age category. Over 80 percent of African-born and 63 percent of Cuban-born slaves who were sold were between the ages of 15 and 40.[12] These data for Africans do not necessarily reflect the age structure of imports, but they are suggestive of the working-age predominance of the slave trade, a reversal of the prevailing situation prior to 1820.

The sex and age structure of the Puerto Rican slave trade were likely similar, though there has been no systematic data discovered for the nineteenth century. There are no data on the sex distribution of imported slaves to compare across time. Data for particular years, however, suggest slave population demographic structures which were very different from Cuba. One of the most important sources for the late 1820s and early 1830s is the six-volume memoir written by Pedro Tomás de Córdoba.[13] Data on Puerto Rican demography between 1824 and 1832 confirm the rapid expansion of the slave population from about 23,000 to 35,000 over these eight years. The number of people enumerated as Africans increased from 31 percent of all slaves in 1824 to 46 percent by 1832, suggesting that the upsurge in the slave population was closely linked to the slave trade.

Implicit in these data, however, is something even more important, and that is the large percentage of slaves who may have been born in Puerto Rico. The statistics from 1829 indicate very significant numbers of women

---

[11] Herbert S. Klein, *The Middle Passage: Comparative Studies in the Atlantic Slave Trade* (Princeton, NJ, 1978), p. 223.

[12] Laird W. Bergad, Fe Iglesias García, and Carmen Barcia, *The Cuban Slave Market, 1790–1880* (Cambridge, 1995), pp. 40–1. Based on a sample of over 14,000 slaves, African and Cuban-born, about 22 percent of sold slaves were between 1 and 14 years of age.

[13] Pedro Tomás de Córdoba, *Memorias geográficas históricas, económicas y estadísticas de la isla de Puerto Rico* (Puerto Rico, 1821–33). Córdoba was secretary to the Captain General of Puerto Rico between 1816 and 1836 and wrote this six-volume work with the objective of portraying Spanish colonial rule in a positive light. For 1829, he classified slaves as mothers, fathers, sons, and daughters.

and children among Puerto Rican slaves, and this is suggestive of natural reproduction. According to Cordóba's data, approximately 48 percent of all slaves in Puerto Rico were female, and an astounding 71 percent of the slave population was classified as sons or daughters with no age specificity. This does not necessarily mean they were born in Puerto Rico, as some may have been of African origin, but it is certain, at least, that a high percentage was born on the island.

To some extent, these data are consistent with statistical profiles of Ponce's slaves in 1838. The overall Ponce slave population increased between 1815 and 1846 from 1,170 to 5,152. In 1838, about 40 percent of Ponce slaves were born in Puerto Rico and another 5 percent in other areas of the Caribbean. There was an imbalance of males among African-born slaves which reflected the general 6:4 male/female ratio in African imports prevailing in the early nineteenth-century Caribbean slave trade.[14] Puerto Rican data from 1865 reveal with clarity the impact of the closing of the slave trade on sex ratios. By 1865, there was almost complete parity between male and female slaves in Mayagüez, Ponce, and Guayama, reinforcing the fact that few slaves were imported to the island after 1840.[15]

The issue of slave reproduction is difficult to examine owing to the absence of detailed data on births, deaths, fertility rates, and other demographic indicators for both Cuba and Puerto Rico. It is clear that there was a net decline in slaves, though the causes may not solely be due to changes in death rates. The slave population of Cuba in 1792 was about 85,000 slaves, but by 1862 had risen to nearly 371,000. However, over 730,000 slaves were imported over this seventy-year period. From a statistical point of view, this means an average annual net decline in slaves of about −2.2 percent between 1792 and 1862.[16] It has been recognized by historians of slavery that death rates for slaves working in sugar economies were higher than for slaves working in other economic sectors. Yet Cuban slaves were not concentrated in the sugar economy until the 1840s and 1850s. The reasons for net slave population decrease are multifaceted and include the wider prevalence of diseases in tropical environments, poor working conditions, and physical abuse by owners. It has also been recognized that among African-born slaves, susceptibility to tropical diseases was greater than among slaves born in the Americas. In slave societies with ongoing arrivals of Africans, such as Cuba, higher death rates prevailed among slave

[14] These data for Ponce are from Scarano, *Sugar and Slavery in Puerto Rico*, pp. 136–42.
[15] Figueroa, *Sugar, Slavery, and Freedom in Nineteenth-Century Puerto Rico*, p. 76.
[16] The following formula was used to calculate annual rates of slave population decline: $[((a+b)-c) \div d] \div e$; where a = the population at the start of the period; b = total slave imports between census years; c = the population at the end of the period; d = the number of years between censuses; and e = the slave population in the middle year between the two census years. Since accurate data on slave imports to Puerto Rico are lacking, it is nearly impossible to calculate these rates for the island.

populations, though the exact death rates for native-born or African-born slaves are unknown due to lack of data.

Additionally, an undetermined percentage of the Cuban slave population acquired freedom in every period through two fundamental mechanisms: manumission by masters and self-purchase or *coartación*, an institution which was widespread in Iberian colonies and absent in the British, French, and Dutch colonial possessions.[17] Voluntary manumissions by masters were pervasive within Cuban slavery and, contrary to older interpretations, it was not only aging and infirm slaves who were freed. There was a fairly even age distribution of slaves to whom masters granted freedom for all kinds of reasons, though there was a clear majority of women who acquired their freedom. There were also greater numbers of domestic slaves voluntarily manumitted by owners, as well as slaves working in urban occupations, compared with slaves living and working in rural areas. Some women may have been the mothers of children fathered by the slave-owner and many children were likely the offspring of masters, though systematic data are not available. Manumission was not confined to Cuban-born slaves – Africans were freed just as frequently.

Coartación, or self-purchase, originated in Roman law and guaranteed the right of slaves to own property, and implicitly, to possess money. This legal institution for acquiring freedom was applied to slavery in the Iberian Peninsula and then to the Americas in the regions dominated by Spain and Portugal. This institution specified the right of slaves to begin the piecemeal purchase of their freedom or the freedom of their children, spouses, or for that matter any other slave. When a "down payment" was made on freedom, the slave's legal status changed from slave to "*coartado*," and that gave them certain rights and privileges, though how these were respected or enforced is unknown. The price of freedom was frozen; the "*coartado*" could not be sold without his or her permission; a new owner was bound to the original self-purchase contract; and the "*coartado*," if rented, had the right to a percentage of the income commensurate with the percentage of value he or she had paid on his or her freedom. There is a detailed documentary record in Cuban archives on these "*coartación*" contracts.[18]

A "road" to possible freedom raises a number of questions about slavery in Cuba and Puerto Rico. First, what percentage of the slave population was able to acquire freedom and how did this contribute to net slave

---

[17] For a discussion of *coartación*, see Alejandro de la Fuente, "Slaves and the Creation of Legal Rights in Cuba: *Coartación* and *Papel*," *Hispanic American Historical Review*, 87 (2007): 659–92.

[18] In a major study of transactions involving slaves in Cuba, about 15 percent of a sample of over 23,000 slaves were "*coartados*." See Bergad *et al.*, *The Cuban Slave Market*, pp. 122–42. There are no similar kinds of systematic data for Puerto Rico. However, see Figueroa, *Sugar, Slavery, and Freedom in Nineteenth-Century Puerto Rico*, pp. 79–104 for a discussion of many cases in the sugar-producing municipality of Guayama.

population decrease? Second, how many *coartados* were able to consummate freedom after they had begun the process of self-purchase? Third,
what does the access to cash, required for self-purchase, indicate about
aspects of the slave experience? Fourth, what was the role of a large and
constantly growing free black and mulatto population within the context
of Cuban and Puerto Rican slavery? Such questions cannot be answered
because the records comprise large numbers of individual cases which may,
or may not, be typical. There was no one over-arching experience for slaves
in their daily lives other than the overwhelming absence of freedom.

RESISTANCE, MANUMISSIONS, FREE COLORED: CUBA AND PUERTO RICO

The historical record suggests ongoing forms of resistance on the part of
slaves in Cuba, Puerto Rico, and elsewhere. Rebellions and running away
were its most overt expressions. The vast majority of slaves, however,
resisted their oppression in more subtle and less visible ways by trying to
assert their basic humanity at every turn within the context of total
domination by the master class. This meant trying to protect the integrity
of their families and extended families, even with the limited means at
their disposal. The quest for *conucos* or provision grounds, small plots
where food could be grown and pigs, chickens, and other animals raised,
was important to establishing some control over food supplies. It also
meant constant attempts at negotiating the conditions of their lives, work,
and leisure time if and when this was possible.

It is difficult to generalize about the extent to which slaves had these
negotiating prerogatives. On larger plantations, striking bargains may have
been more difficult and took forms that were distinct from the possibilities
of those employed by slaves on smaller farms and ranches. The dynamics
of life and relations with masters were different for slaves in urban areas
and it is likely that slavery was more fluid and prerogatives wider. The
documentation on all of this is fragmentary and suggestive, rather than
systematic.

Slaves in Puerto Rico and Cuba lived and worked within societies with
large free black and mulatto populations. Unlike the eighteenth-century
British and French Caribbean colonies, or the nineteenth-century United
States, where free peoples of color made up no more than 10 percent of all
peoples of African descent, being black or mulatto in nineteenth-century
Cuba and especially Puerto Rico was not automatically synonymous with
slavery. Concepts of race were radically different from the black/white
dichotomy which prevailed in the United States, as mixed-race persons or
mulattos, slave and free, were conceived of quite differently by elites and all
social classes irrespective of race. In 1827, some 15 percent of the total
Cuban population was classified as "free colored," while 41 percent were

slaves. To put this another way, about 27 percent of all peoples of color in Cuba were free. Approximately 56 percent of Cuba's total population in 1827 comprised people of African descent. By 1862, free blacks and mulattos were 17 percent of the total population and 39 percent of all peoples of color. About 27 percent of all inhabitants were enslaved and 43 percent of the total Cuban population was comprised of peoples of color, slave and free (see Table 5.4).

The racial structure in Puerto Rico was in some ways similar to Cuba and in other ways completely different, especially with respect to the ratios of free peoples of color to slaves, and to the total population. Similar percentages of nineteenth-century populations were classified as white according to census data, hovering around half of the total population in each island. In Cuba, 49 percent of all people were classified as white in 1792 and 57 percent in 1862. For Puerto Rico, 48 percent were considered white in 1802 and 52 percent in 1860.

Slaves comprised only about 12 percent of the overall population of Puerto Rico at their apex in 1846 compared with 36 percent in Cuba in the same year. Free peoples of color comprised about 80 percent of all peoples of African descent in Puerto Rico throughout the nineteenth century until final abolition in 1873 (see Table 5.5). This underscores the fact that to be black or mulatto in nineteenth-century Puerto Rico could not be simply associated with slavery.

If the kinds of relations and their extensiveness between free peoples of color and slaves are not generally known, rebellions and resistance have been well documented. First and foremost, slaves ran away continuously. There was rarely an issue of the official newspapers published in Havana and San Juan where announcements for runaway slaves and rewards for their capture did not appear on the first two pages. Many slaves sought refuge in *palenques* or maroon communities where groups of runaways would coalesce to form some kind of collective existence. There were no known *palenques* in Cuba and Puerto Rico which were as large or which persisted for any significant time periods, as was the case with the vast Brazilian interior, owing to the absence of impenetrable remote areas where authorities would have had difficult access. Slave bounty hunters, *rancheadores*, were a fixture in both societies and hunted runaways for lucrative compensation. Running away was certainly an act of resistance, but few slaves were ever able to attain freedom in this way, and *cimarrones*, as slave runaways were called, were usually captured or returned to their masters voluntarily after short periods of time. Punishments were meted out as deterrents and these could be quite cruel: public whippings; binding in shackles; isolation in oppressive solitary confinement; and a whole range of other dreadful mechanisms to discourage slaves from attempting flight.

Table 5.4 *Cuban Population by Race and Legal Status, 1792–1862*

| | Whites | | Free Colored | | | Slaves | | | All People of Color | | % of Total Population |
	Population	% of Total Population	Population	% of Total Population	% of All Peoples of Color	Population	% of Total Population	% of All Peoples of Color	Population	% of Total Population	Population
1792	133,559	49.0%	54,152	19.9%	39.0%	84,590	31.1%	61.0%	138,742	51.0%	272,301
1827	311,051	44.2%	106,494	15.1%	27.1%	286,942	40.7%	72.9%	393,436	55.8%	704,487
1846	425,767	47.4%	149,226	16.6%	31.5%	323,759	36.0%	68.5%	472,985	52.6%	898,752
1862	793,484	56.8%	232,493	16.6%	38.6%	370,553	26.5%	61.4%	603,046	43.2%	1,396,530

Source: Cuban census data for corresponding years.

Table 5.5 *Puerto Rican Population by Race and Legal Status, 1802–1860*

	Whites		Free Colored			Slaves			All People of Color		Total Population
	Population	% of Total Population	Population	% of Total Population	% of All Peoples of Color	Population	% of Total Population	% of All Peoples of Color	Population	% of Total Population	Population
1802	78,281	48.0%	71,578	43.9%	84.3%	13,333	8.2%	15.7%	84,911	52.0%	163,192
1827	150,311	49.7%	120,487	39.8%	79.1%	31,874	10.5%	20.9%	152,361	50.3%	302,672
1846	216,083	48.8%	175,791	39.7%	77.4%	51,265	11.6%	22.6%	227,056	51.2%	443,139
1860	300,430	51.5%	241,015	41.3%	85.2%	41,736	7.2%	14.8%	282,751	48.5%	583,308

Source: Figueroa, *Sugar, Slavery, and Freedom in Nineteenth-Century Puerto Rico*, p. 48.

Most rebellions were spontaneous reactions against both long- and short-term abuse and degradation rather than well-organized plots with predetermined strategies and tactics. These occurred repeatedly throughout the colonial period on both islands and rarely lasted more than several days. There may have been more conspiracies which never came to fruition rather than revolts and these were discovered repeatedly by colonial authorities, often because of betrayals by other slaves who sought to curry favor with masters for privileges and prerogatives. Slave populations had extensive divisions, despite the outside image of homogeneity. There were rivalries between different ethnicities in the same way that there were within Africa. Sharp divisions existed between domestic-born and African-born slaves, and in fact when rebellions took place or conspiracies were discovered, these were usually led or organized by those born in Africa. Oftentimes, they distrusted domestic-born slaves and did not include them in planning or strategizing. Many conspiracies and plots precluded actual uprisings and were accompanied by large-scale waves of pre-emptive repression. In Cuba, the two most important were the "Aponte Conspiracy" of 1812 and the 1844 conspiracy of "La Escalera," though there were many more small-scale revolts, work stoppages, and plots.

Between the Aponte Conspiracy of 1812 and the large-scale repression launched against free blacks, mulattos, and slaves in 1844, known in Cuba as La Escalera, there were repeated slave uprisings, mostly in rural zones where sugar production was centered. Some were spontaneous reactions to repeated abuse. Others were planned rebellions. Still others, especially those in urban areas, were organized work stoppages designed to put a halt to abusive behavior by masters or extract better conditions from them. One of the conspicuous characteristics of the many acts of resistance to the oppression of slavery was the fact that they were almost always centered in areas with many African-born slaves of recent arrival. This was especially the case in the plains to the east of Havana in the province of Matanzas, where all of the great slave-based plantations were centered in the nineteenth century.

The pervasiveness of the rebellion, in the heart of the Cuban slave/sugar economy, and where enormous capital investments were being made in mill modernization and railroad construction, is important to understand if the massive repression against alleged conspirators in 1844 known as La Escalera is to be understood. The threat posed to the interests of Cuba's sugar-producing elite by the specter of slave rebellion was exacerbated by the incessant British campaign to curb the last Caribbean slave trade and to enforce the 1835 anti-slave trade treaty with Spain, which was openly flaunted by slave traders and mill owners. This was personified by the British Consul in Havana, David Turnbull – a member of the British and

Foreign Anti-Slavery Society. Turnbull was suspected of actively planning a massive slave uprising along with other antislavery British citizens working in Cuba as diplomats, merchants, and mechanics and with free blacks and mulattos on the island designed to emulate the Haitian revolt of the 1790s.

Slave rebellions and conspiracies in Puerto Rico were not as frequent or pervasive as those found in Cuba, largely owing to the comparatively smaller volume of the slave trade, the reduced presence of African-born slaves within the island's slave population, and the comparatively smaller percentage of slaves within the total population. Throughout Latin American and Caribbean slave societies, revolts were almost always associated with the arrival of African-born slaves who often exhibited little trust in slaves born in the Americas. In Puerto Rico, nearly all slave conspiracies and rebellions, spontaneous and organized, took place in districts on the southern and western coastal regions where sugar production developed intensely during the 1790s and through the 1840s.[19] None of these was on the scale of those found in Cuba.

ABOLITION

The process of slavery's abolition in the Americas was long and drawn out and began with the growth of a British antislavery movement in the second half of the eighteenth century.[20] The initial focal point of attack by activists was the slave trade. British and US legislation in 1807 which ended the slave trade to England's Caribbean colonies and to the United States was the most graphic manifestation of antislavery's successes. Yet the trade continued to Cuba, Puerto Rico, and Brazil on a significant scale. The British–Spanish anti-slaving treaties of 1817 and 1835 were dead letters and slaving to Cuba continued to 1867, the last slave trade to the Americas. While anti-slave trade sentiment increased within Spain as well as in Cuba and Puerto Rico after the middle of the nineteenth century, abolitionism would never become the political force or mass-based movements which developed in England and the United States.

The ultimate causes and timing of slavery's demise were very different in Cuba and Puerto Rico because of their distinctive political and economic histories. In the Puerto Rican case, the contraction of the sugar industry after 1850 and the availability of an extraordinarily large free black population as a potential labor market made slave labor marginal to the Puerto Rican economy, which was shifting to free-labor-based coffee production in the

[19] See Guillermo Baralt, *Esclavos Rebeldes: Conspiraciones y sublevaciones de esclavos en Puerto Rico (1795–1873)* (San Juan, 1982).
[20] See Seymour Drescher, *Abolition: A History of Slavery and Antislavery* (Cambridge, 2009).

1850s and 1860s. Capital investments in slaves were comparatively small, and while slave-owners may have been adversely affected by the end of slavery, they were a steadily shrinking sector of the Puerto Rican elite. The economic and political costs associated with abolition were relatively minor in comparative perspective and indeed abolitionism as a political force emerged in Puerto Rico in the 1840s and 1850s within key sectors of the insular dominant political and social classes. In fact, it was Puerto Rican reformists who were central to the formation of the Spanish Abolitionist Society in the mid-1860s.[21] This led Spain to proclaim the first abolition law of 1870, the *Ley Moret*, which freed the children of slave mothers born after 1868 and all slaves 60 years of age and older. The final emancipation of slaves came to Puerto Rico in 1873 – though with apprenticeship to 1876.

There was little significant abolitionist sentiment in Cuba among the island's socioeconomic and political elites. The reliance on the slave trade and slavery to sustain the island's dynamically growing sugar economy was the principal reason. The intolerance of the Spanish colonial government toward abolitionist activity was another factor accounting for the marginal spread of abolitionism on the island, since it was perceived as bound together with liberalism, anti-colonialism, and the ever-meddling British. This does not mean that there weren't important Cuban voices who spoke out against slavery or the slave trade. The framework, however, had little to do with moral repugnance or a humanistic concern for the plight of the enslaved, though this should not be entirely discounted. The real concerns that emerged during the early nineteenth century revolved around the dangers posed by the dramatic upsurge in slaving and the endemic fear of slave revolt spawned by the Haitian rebellion so close by. Cuba's elite was caught in a quandary. Its wealth rested on the sugar/slave complex; slavery could only be maintained by a vigorous ongoing slave trade; yet the growth of the slave population spawned fears of "Africanization" and "*otro Santo Domingo*."

These were the arguments used by the most visible proponents of ending the Cuban slave trade in the aftermath of the British and US closing of the trade in 1808 and the onset of the British crusade to curb it.[22] To oppose slavery would have generated little support among Cuba's elite, though raising the issue of the African slave trade had some appeal. Anti-slave trade activists made the issue of race front and center. What

[21] Christopher Schmidt-Nowara, *Empire and Antislavery: Spain, Cuba, and Puerto Rico, 1833–1874* (Pittsburgh, PA, 1999).

[22] The most famous proponents of abolishing the slave trade were Félix Varela y Morales, a Cuban Catholic priest, who was on the seminary faculty of the Diocese of San Cristóbal de la Habana, and his student José Antonio Saco. Both were exiled by the Spanish authorities because of their abolitionist views. Varela lived most of his adult life in New York City, and Saco in Paris. For brief biographies, see http://en.wikipedia.org/wiki/F%C3%A9lix_Varela and http://en.wikipedia.org/wiki/Jos%C3%A9_Antonio_Saco.

would a future Cuba "look" like if so many Africans continued to arrive as slaves? Banning the trade and encouraging white immigration could resolve both the labor issue as well as the desire to "whiten" the population on the part of elites. These ideas and efforts were doomed to failure despite the formation of various organizations in the early nineteenth century to promote European immigration as a racial counter-weight to slave imports.[23] Migrants to Cuba from Spain and elsewhere would not arrive on a significant scale until after slavery was finally abolished in 1886. And abolitionism did not gain a foothold in Cuba until the aftermath of the US Civil War in 1865 and the insurrection for Cuban independence which exploded in October 1868 and raged until 1878 – the Ten Years War.

The rebels who fought for Cuban independence eventually embraced abolition. The insurrection established control over a wide swathe of Eastern Cuba, but in regions where only about 10 percent of the island's slave population resided. The wealthy sugar districts of Western Cuba where slaves were concentrated were never threatened by the insurrection. At the beginning of the insurrection, there was ambivalence on the issue of slave emancipation on the part of the Cuban rebels because there was the hope that the wealthy sugar barons of Western Cuba would join the struggle for independence. This did not occur despite sympathy among some sectors of the planter class.

In 1869, the provisional government of *Cuba Libre* in the insurrectionary east offered freedom to all slaves who could make their way to rebel territory. The following year, slavery was abolished in areas controlled by the independence forces. Republicanism and abolitionism were formally merged and for Spain the threat to the interests of slave-owners may have been superseded by the danger to the colonial system itself. The Moret Law of 1870 was not only proclaimed for Puerto Rico, but also for Cuba, as one measure in an attempt to defuse the political pressures posed by abolitionism and insurrection. It was also recognition by Spain that international political factors had shifted decisively and that the dismantling of slavery in Cuba was inevitable. In 1868, a liberal revolution swept through Spain and resulted in the emergence of a republican government which heralded a new era of expanded freedoms guaranteed by a progressive constitution guaranteeing all kinds of new rights. The Spanish Abolitionist Society benefited from these, as its activities could be carried out openly and without fear of repression.

With mounting pressures internally in Cuba, internationally, and within sectors of the political elite on the Iberian Peninsula, an abolition

---

[23] In 1815, the Intendant and Captain-General of Cuba established the *Junta de Población Blanca* (the Council for White Population) charged with encouraging white immigration to the island to counter the increase in African slave imports.

law was proclaimed in 1880. It did not grant immediate freedom, but rather set up a system called the *patronato*, which obligated slaves to continue to labor for their former masters for a specific period of time in return for some monetary compensation. Masters were also obligated to free a portion of their slave populations each year and by 1883 about half of Cuba's slaves had been granted freedom. It was impossible to maintain the *patronato*, for with freedom realized for many, and so close for others, plantation discipline was impossible to maintain. All of Cuba's slaves were finally freed in 1886.

The fundamental factors that led to the abolition of slavery in both islands were political rather than economic. Abolitionist pressures were paramount in Puerto Rico, but these also developed within the context of a very different economic, demographic, and political environment than was the case in Cuba. Above all, the sugar industry did not modernize, despite some isolated efforts. Slave labor in Puerto Rico could not be sustained profitably without the application of new technologies to the production of sugar. Accordingly, by the 1840s, slave imports waned and slave populations declined. Slaves were never a significant portion of Puerto Rico's population, which was characterized by the existence of a large and landless free population comprising a potential labor force. Indeed, when coffee production expanded during the second half of the nineteenth century, slaves were not needed, as coffee planters tapped into this reserve pool of free labor. The relatively minor role played by slave labor in the insular economy after 1850 meant that opposition to political abolitionism was not the concerted force found in Cuba. Finally, there was no abolitionist rebellion in Puerto Rico such as the Ten Years War (1868–78), which raised the political costs of maintaining slavery in Cuba.

As the epoch of slavery drew to a close in the 1870s and 1880s, its legacy was onerous for ex-slaves and peoples of color in general. The system produced and nurtured a virulent racism on the part of dominant social classes that unfortunately became pervasive throughout the social order. Racial discrimination, endemic poverty, and reduced opportunities for social mobility were the legacies of slavery, and these extended into the twentieth and twenty-first centuries. While the dynamics of life in post-emancipation society for freedmen and freedwomen in Cuba and Puerto Rico were shaped by slavery to be sure, the fates of their descendants over the long term were determined by the way in which race relations evolved in the various historical periods which followed.

A GUIDE TO FURTHER READING

Bergad, Laird W., *Cuban Rural Society in the Nineteenth Century: The Social and Economic History of Monoculture in Matanzas* (Princeton, NJ, 1990).

Bergad, Laird W., Fe Iglesias García, and Maria Carmen Barcia, *The Cuban Slave Market, 1790–1880* (Cambridge, 1995).

Bergad, Laird W., *The Comparative Histories of Slavery in Brazil, Cuba, and the United States* (Cambridge, 2007).

Childs, Matt D., *The 1812 Aponte Rebellion in Cuba* (Chapel Hill, NC, 2006).

Figueroa, Luis A., *Sugar, Slavery, and Freedom in Nineteenth-Century Puerto Rico* (Chapel Hill, NC, 2005).

Klein, Herbert S., *Slavery in the Americas: A Comparative Study of Virginia and Cuba* (Chicago, IL, 1967).

Paquette, Robert L., *Sugar Is Made with Blood: The Conspiracy of La Escalera and the Conflict between Empires over Slavery in Cuba* (Middletown, CT, 1988).

Scarano, Francisco A., *Sugar and Slavery in Puerto Rico: The Plantation Economy of Ponce, 1800–1850* (Madison, WI, 1984).

Schmidt-Nowara, Christopher, *Empire and Antislavery: Spain, Cuba, and Puerto Rico, 1833–1874* (Pittsburgh, PA, 1999).

Scott, Rebecca J., *Slave Emancipation in Cuba: The Transition to Free Labor, 1860–1899* (Princeton, NJ, 1985).

Stark, David Martin, *Slave Families and the Hato Economy in Puerto Rico* (Gainesville, FL, 2015).

Van Norman, William C., *Shade-Grown Slavery: The Lives of Slaves on Coffee Plantations in Cuba* (Nashville, TN, 2013).

CHAPTER 6

SLAVERY IN NINETEENTH-CENTURY BRAZIL

JOÃO JOSÉ REIS

INTRODUCTION

Brazil was the largest importer of African captives in the Americas. Nearly 50 percent of the close to 11 million slaves who disembarked on the western shores of the Atlantic were carried on board Luso-Brazilian ships. The British followed with 26 percent, a distant second place. Furthermore, two of the most important ports that organized slave trade voyages were located in Brazil, namely Rio de Janeiro and Salvador da Bahia, with Liverpool occupying the third place. These numbers alone give an idea of how important African slavery was to the development of Portuguese America and, after it obtained its independence from Portugal in 1822, of Brazil as a nation. The region was the closest point in the Americas to the African continent, and Portugal pioneered the transatlantic slave trade, having established several slave-trading ports, called "factories," along the coast of Africa after the late fifteenth century. Up until the final prohibition of the transatlantic slave trade to Brazil in 1850, its slave labor force was reproduced and expanded primarily through importation of African captives.[1]

The production of sugar was the first sector of the colonial economy to employ large numbers of African slaves. Initially, they were brought from the Portuguese Atlantic Islands – where sugar plantation had been operating since the mid fifteenth century – to work in the more specialized positions in the sugar mills, while indigenous Americans made up the primary labor force in the cane fields. Between the mid sixteenth and mid seventeenth centuries, Africans gradually replaced indigenous American slaves in the cane fields. This shift has been attributed to different factors: native population decline due to Old World diseases, inexperience with and resistance to the methodical, gang labor system required by export agriculture, and Portugal's interest in promoting a most lucrative activity of the colonial system, the transatlantic slave trade. Although Brazil's

[1] All numbers for the transatlantic slave trade in this and following paragraphs come from the Transatlantic Slave Trade Database (TSTD), www.slavevoyages.org.com.

indigenous groups were still being enslaved into the mid eighteenth century in the periphery of the Portuguese colony, such as São Paulo and the Amazon region, African slaves had by then become the vast majority of the labor force. At the same time, a new class of free blacks and *mestiços* (persons of mixed racial origins) would steadily, though not completely, replace slaves in the more specialized positions on sugar plantations.[2]

For most of the nineteenth century, slavery in Brazil underwent a vigorous expansion, associated with an increase in export agriculture, the growth of cities, and the intensification of the slave trade. From the late eighteenth century, the sugar plantation economy, based primarily (though not exclusively) in the northeast, recovered from a long period of stagnation, taking advantage of an expanded international market after the debacle provoked by the 1791 slave revolution in Saint Domingue/ Haiti, the largest exporter of sugar up until then. Brazilian sugar plantations thrived, new areas of cultivation were incorporated – in Rio de Janeiro and São Paulo, for instance – and production was sustained even after the Cuban sugar boom from the 1830s onward. Sugar plantations, however, continued to be the main focus of slave labor in the northeast and some areas of the southeast of Brazil until the abolition of slavery in 1888.

Slavery also expanded in other sectors of agriculture. Cotton farming prospered in several areas of the north and northeast, mainly Maranhão, and the backlands of Pernambuco, Paraíba, Bahia, and Minas Gerais. In this latter province, despite the decline of gold and diamond mining since the boom days in the first half of the eighteenth century, the region became a phenomenon with extensive and diversified use of slave labor, not just in the emerging cultivation of coffee for export, but primarily in agriculture for local consumption, cattle ranching, small foundries, and the textile industry, in addition to the remaining mining business. The ranks of slavery were also swelled in the southernmost part of Brazil by the use of slave labor in meat-jerking production in Rio Grande do Sul, and on the tea and grain farms of Paraná and Santa Catarina. It was, nonetheless, on coffee plantations that slave labor flourished the most in nineteenth-century Brazil. Although coffee was grown in several regions of the country, beginning in the 1830s production centered heavily on the Paraíba River Valley, mainly in Rio de Janeiro, but also in São Paulo province. It soon spread to vast tracts of land in the latter's western areas, turning this region into the primary focus of the use of slave labor in the second half of the century.

---

[2] For slavery in sugar plantations in Brazil, see Stuart B. Schwartz, *Sugar Plantations in the Formation of Brazilian Society: Bahia, 1550–1835* (Cambridge, 1985); and B. J. Brickman, *A Bahian Counterpoint: Sugar, Tobacco, Cassava, and Slavery in the Recôncavo, 1780–1860* (Stanford, 1998).

Besides agriculture and mining, and usually linked to these more central activities, there developed large urban centers. Slavery represented the main form of labor in cities such as Recife, Salvador, Vila Rica (Ouro Preto), Porto Alegre, and especially Rio de Janeiro. Rio became the city with the largest slave population in the Americas, nearly 80,000 at mid-century in a total population of 206,000 souls. Around the same period, Salvador had a population of approximately 75,000 residents, about 40 percent of whom were enslaved; Vila Rica was about the same size in 1821 and had over 27,000 slaves, or 37 percent of its population. Medium-sized and smaller cities had sizable proportions of slaves: São Paulo's close to 31,000 inhabitants included 23 percent slaves in 1854, and in Porto Alegre, 30 percent of its 17,226 inhabitants were enslaved in 1856. The same was true in the far north, where urban slavery became a central reality. The urban population of Belém, capital of Pará province, included 46 percent slaves among its population of 12,471 in 1822, and in addition, another 10 percent were free persons of color. As for Recife, 31 percent of its close to 26,000 inhabitants were enslaved in 1827. In the cities, there emerged a system of slaves for hire, particularly in the transportation of goods and persons (the latter by way of sedan chairs and canoes), but also in small-scale street vending, in the manual trades, and, of course, in domestic service, a vast sector chiefly, though not exclusively, comprised of Creole (or locally born) female slaves. Over 100 occupations have been identified in which slave labor was used in the city and the countryside.

Brazilian slavery would reach its high point in the nineteenth century, nationwide as it was, extending to the various sectors of the economy, and shaping virtually all social and political institutions, and the cultural make-up of the country. But slave ownership was not confined to large slave-holding property. Both in the countryside and in the cities, there was a large number of petty slave-holders who possessed one, two, or three people working in small-scale farming, in street services, or in domestic tasks. For all of these reasons, slaves left a deep imprint on the customs, mentalities, culture, and even, through miscegenation, the very racial contours of the country's population. Since Brazil was the last nation in the hemisphere to abolish slavery (1888), it can be said that the long nineteenth century that witnessed the formation of this territorially enormous nation also marked both the peak and decline of slave society in the region.

SLAVE TRADE

In the first half of the nineteenth century, it is estimated that some 2,150,000 Africans were imported to Brazil, representing 42 percent of the region's slave imports since the sixteenth century. Much of the 1800s trade took place when it had already been prohibited as a result of British pressure, first in a series of treaties and agreements between 1815 and 1818, when Brazil was still a Portuguese dependency and the traffic was made illegal north of the equator – which included West African ports on the Bight of Benin/Slave Coast – and then after the Brazilian Parliament voted a law in 1831 that prohibited the slave trade from anywhere in Africa. Despite the 1831 ban, after some years of hesitation, the slave trade re-emerged almost unabated due to systematic toleration by low and high authorities, from the local policeman to heads of the Brazilian state. About 750,000 slaves (35 percent of the nineteenth-century total) were imported between 1831 and 1850, when a more severe law was passed.

Africans arrived in the country mainly through the port or clandestine beaches of Rio de Janeiro, without a doubt the largest point of entry for them on the Atlantic coast. According to a recent estimate, between 1790 and 1830, 697,945 slaves disembarked there, 123,590 just in the last three years of legal slave trade (1828–30). Thus, Rio imported in forty years the equivalent of almost 17 percent of all of the slaves brought into Brazil in more than 300 years.

The importation of Africans was the most common means for replenishing the enslaved labor force throughout the course of slavery in Brazil. After 1850, the slave population in general declined. It increased in the next two decades only in the most prosperous coffee-growing regions as a result of the internal slave trade, especially from the economically declining north-northeast to the southeast, but also from the south. Furthermore, there was a relocation of slaves from urban to rural sectors of the economy. In total, slaves in Brazil numbered 1,715,000 in 1864, 1,540,829 in 1874, 1,240,806 in 1884, and 723,419 in 1887, on the eve of abolition.[3]

Brazil received slaves from a diversity of peoples in various regions of the African continent. Yet each African region and broad cultural group contributed in different degrees to the formation of local populations, depending on the period, the destination in Brazil, the dynamics of competition with other slave-trading European nations, and the commercial ties between Luso/Brazilian and African slave traders. Angola, where the Portuguese had made deeper territorial inroads, was by far the major source of Brazilian slaves, 70 percent, and Brazil obtained almost half of the slaves leaving Angola to the Americas. The Bight of Benin on the African West Coast comes in a distant second, with close to 20 percent. Other points of embarkation included Upper Guinea (namely Cape Verde

---

[3] Robert Conrad, *The Destruction of Brazilian Slavery, 1850–1888* (Berkeley, CA, 1972), pp. 283, 285. On the internal slave trade to São Paulo, see José Flávio Motta, *Escravos daqui, dali e de mais além: o tráfico interno de cativos na expansão cafeeira paulista* (São Paulo, 2012). Due to the nature of this chapter, I will not specify sources to most statistical and other data presented here, for which I apologize to those who produced them.

and Guinea-Bissau) and Mozambique, the latter in the last phase of the slave trade, from the late eighteenth century through the first half of the 1800s. Major importation regions such as Rio de Janeiro, Pernambuco, and Minas Gerais bought slaves mainly from West Central Africa, chiefly Angola, through the duration of the transatlantic slave trade. Close to 1.2 million slaves disembarked in Rio de Janeiro in the nineteenth century. These slaves were the victims of well-established commercial networks in the hinterland of places such as Luanda, Benguela, Malembo, Cabinda, and other West-Central-African ports. In the seventeenth and eighteenth centuries, they were victims of wars near and in the hinterland of Angola and Congo, but from the late 1700s the dependents of local chiefs and traders were sold to Brazilian merchants in exchange for European and Brazilian products, though wars in Northern Angola also contributed in the production of captives to the transatlantic trade. Brazilian rum (*cachaça*) produced in Pernambuco or Rio de Janeiro represented the main merchandise used for buying slaves in West Central Africa (mainly Angola). However, tobacco also appeared on ships bound to the Angolan coast as did Brazilian rum on ships bound to the Bight of Benin. Besides these, European cloth, horses, cattle, beads, silverwares, earthenware, iron, gold, and sugar were exchanged for slaves in African markets.

In contrast to most regions in Brazil, the slaves who disembarked in Bahia came primarily from West Africa, from ports located along the Bight of Benin coast – especially Whydah, Porto Novo, and Lagos. In Bahia, Angola figured as the main source of captives up until the first quarter of the eighteenth century, and continued to comprise an important supplier until the 1820s. After that date, West Africa became an almost exclusive point of departure for Bahia's slaves. The leading presence of Bahian traders in the Bight of Benin explains the pattern of this trade. They offered in exchange for slaves the highly appreciated Bahian-grown tobacco rolls coated with molasses. Estimates for the last fifty years of the Brazilian slave trade (1801–51) indicate that West Africa supplied about 10 percent of the slaves imported into Brazil, but 88 percent of these captives landed in Bahia. The region was the most common destination in Brazil for captives taken in the eighteenth-century Dahomeyan wars, the Fulani jihad of the first two decades of the nineteenth century, and the devastating Yoruba wars from the late 1810s through the 1840s.

The nineteenth-century Brazilian slave trade was controlled by large merchants, often by family-run businesses that passed from fathers to sons, and sometimes included women as well, usually the widows of established slave traders. This was particularly true of traffickers based in Pernambuco, Bahia, and Rio de Janeiro. However, slave-trade voyages also incorporated investors of all sizes, including ship captains and sailors. The voyage of the slaver *Ermelinda*, for instance, which was organized in Recife bound to

Luanda, in 1841, is a case in point. The slave ship had been recently bought by a young merchant from a brother, but the main investor was their uncle, who also outfitted the ship, contracted crew, and bought provisions. The uncle controlled 32 percent of the cargo's value, the rest belonging to another thirty parties who owned as little as 0.3 percent of the merchandise. Among the petty merchants on the *Ermelinda* there were two West African freedmen, members of the crew, one of whom served as the cook. Often, slaves belonging to or rented by ship captains and owners worked as sailors. They would eventually buy one or two slaves. A survey of slave ships' crew in Brazil between 1790 and 1863 indicates that 17 percent were Africans, more than half from West Africa. Africans, both slaves and freed, participated in slave-trade voyages as sailors, interpreters (*línguas*), and petty merchants.[4]

NATIONS

African slaves usually received new ethnic identifications in the transatlantic trade. These identity terms rarely referred to specific names of a group's self-identity, but pointed instead to cultural regions or ports of embarkation, or to expressions coined by African traders for the foreign groups they enslaved, bought, and sold. However, a native African logic was not absent from the formation of a slave trade "ethnic" nomenclature, for it usually referred to broad linguistic groups, which the slaves themselves eventually embraced as their own. These newly constructed identities, called *nações*/nations, were a phenomenon developed in all New World slave societies.

In Brazil, the term Mina was an umbrella expression for West African slaves exported through Bight of Benin ports. In general, while almost everywhere in Brazil Mina continued to hold the same general meaning, in Bahia, in the first decades of the nineteenth century, more specific terms such as Jeje (for Gbe-speakers), Nagô (for Yoruba-speakers), Angola (mainly Kimbundu-speakers), and Hausas (who kept their African ethnic denominations), which appeared sporadically in an earlier period, became more prevalent. In Bahia, the ethnonym Mina gradually came to denote primarily slaves from Little and Grand Popo, or "Mina proper." This is not to say that in other areas of Brazil the more specific terms were never used. In Bahia, however, the change toward a more precise ethnic terminology for West Africans was systematic and derived from both the greater concentration of, and the need to distinguish among and control, African slaves from Dahomey, Yorubaland, Hausaland, and neighboring

---

[4] On the ship *Ermelinda*, see João Reis, Flávio Gomes, and Marcus Carvalho, *O alufá Rufino: tráfico, escravidão e liberdade no Atlântico negro, (c. 1823–c. 1853)* (São Paulo, 2010), pp. 126–45.

territories, while also reflecting the local construction of African ethnic identities in Brazil. The Nagôs stood as a general designation for those from the Yoruba-speaking peoples of Oyo, Egba, Ilesa, Ijebu, Ketu, and other kingdoms at a time when they still did not recognize themselves in Africa as Yoruba. Actually, Nagô-ness emerged in Bahia before Yoruba-ness did in Africa. As for the Jeje, they were primarily Gbe-speakers of Ewe, Adja, Fon, Mahi origin, most of whom became subjects of the kingdom of Dahomey in the course of the eighteenth century. None of the ethnonyms Nagô, Jeje, or Angola made much sense in the African context, though the term Nagô clearly derives from Anago, a small Yoruba-speaking group to the west of Dahomey. The origin of the ethnonym Jeje has not been unequivocally established.[5] In Bahia, only the numerous Hausas and smaller groups, such as the Borno, or the Fulani (locally called Fula/Fulanin/Filanin), would maintain their original African designation.

In other Brazilian locations, such as Pernambuco, Rio, São Paulo, Minas Gerais, and Rio Grande do Sul, West-Central-African slaves were more numerous. Although the vague term Angola prevailed in these places, especially for slaves embarked in and around Luanda, more specific identity labels are found from the Bantu-speaking region (main languages, Kimbundu, Kikongo, and Umbundo), such as Cabinda, Congo, Cassange, Monjolo, Rebolo, Ambaca, and Benguela, to name a few of the most common specific cultural areas, ethnonyms, or political entities mentioned in the documents. The numerous slaves from Mozambique can be added to these Bantu-speaking groups, which all together seem to have formed an umbrella identity. This Bantu-ness would manifest itself in religious expressions such as Umbanda, or in elements of street culture such as Capoeira, a martial art. The more specific notion of nation seems to have made more sense as a functional identity within the African melting pot, though the construction and dynamics of this notion did vary from region to region in Brazil depending on the ethnic demographics of the resident Africans.

African slaves referred to individuals belonging to their own nations as "relatives" to denote the formation of a symbolic kinship bond. Though this did not restore the functions of the African family disrupted by the slave trade, it at least minimized somewhat the loss. Social, economic, political, and cultural life, especially in an urban setting, was organized around the notion of nation. Its members met preferentially in specific Catholic black brotherhoods, or in Muslim and other African religious

---

[5] For Nagô, see Robin Law, "Ethnicity and the Slave Trade: 'Lucumi' and 'Nagô' as Ethnonyms in West Africa," *History in Africa*, 24 (1997): 205–19; for Jeje, see Luis Nicolau Parés, *The Formation of Candomblé: Vodun History and Ritual in Brazil* (Chapel Hill, NC, 2013), pp. 24–9.

communities. They gathered in street work groups to perform tasks such as porters and stevedores; they tended to cohabit and marry with ethnic relatives; they organized themselves in credit societies from which slaves borrowed to pay for their manumission; and they participated in revolts mobilized by ethnic leaders. This is not to say that Africans isolated themselves completely from individuals who belonged to other nations. There also existed work, friendship, amorous, and family relations that mixed members from different groups. This happened, however, in combination with strong feelings of ethnic belonging.

Despite the formation of these identities, Africans did not cease to imagine themselves as part of more specific ethnic affiliation in the realm of the nation. Out of political or social strategy, Jeje or Minas could thus identify themselves as "Dagomé" if they were Fon from Dahomey, or as Mahi, if originally enslaved in the Mahi federation north of Dahomey. By the same token, in specific contexts the Nagôs used expressions such as Nagô-Ba, Nagô-Jexá, and Nagô-Jabu to identify themselves ethnically, meaning that they were, respectively, from the Yoruba kingdoms of Egba, Ilesha, and Ijebu. Angolans could deploy more detailed appellations such as Ambaca, Cassange, Rebolo or Luanda, and Moçambicans could become Macua, Quelimane, or Inhambane. The more specific ethnic glossary emerged predominantly in conversations among members of each nation. They were for internal consumption so to speak, while more general terms such as Nagô, Jeje, Angola, and so on figured as vocabulary adopted in dealings with outsiders. African identities in Brazil were not fixed, but rather situational, contextual, a moveable strategic or political device.[6]

PROPERTY IN SLAVES

Brazilian society and the state were deeply committed to slavery and the slave trade at a time when both had either disappeared or receded considerably in regions of the Caribbean, Spanish America, and parts of North America. The force and the longevity of slavery in Brazil may be in part explained by the dissemination of property in slaves throughout the social hierarchy. Slaves did not belong only to big planters and rich merchants. They were distributed in slave-holding households that varied from one to hundreds of slaves. Poor whites, free and freed blacks, and even slaves owned slaves in Brazil. Slavery represented the best investment as long as the transatlantic slave trade remained open. Throughout the country, the majority of slave-owners were small, they owned less than ten slaves, and in

---

[6] See n 5; for West Central Africans, Mary Karasch, *Slave Life in Rio de Janeiro, 1800–1850* (Princeton, NJ, 1987), ch. 1.

some non-plantation and urban areas they owned most of the slaves. African slavery was thus disseminated with incredible vigor geographically, occupationally, and socially, demonstrating the widespread compromise of Brazilian society with the institution.

A few examples will illustrate this. In Bahia, slave holdings with between one and nineteen slaves in the Recôncavo region (tobacco, cassava, and above all sugar) represented 53.4 percent of all slaves in 1816–1817, and even in the exclusive sugar plantations their proportion was still high: 40 percent. The owners of these slaves corresponded to 83.6 percent in the Recôncavo as a whole and 76.5 percent in the sugar plantations specifically; in other words, the vast majority of slave-owners in the region were small to mid-size proprietors. In the same region, an 1835 census of a typical sugar parish, Santiago do Iguape, indicated that 46.5 percent of the slave-holders were non-whites (blacks and *mestiços*), and in the adjacent, tobacco-growing parish of São Gonçalo dos Campos, they represented 30 percent. Whites owned 84 percent of the slaves in both parishes – the mean number of slaves among them was 11.4 slaves, and 4.1 among non-whites. A similar distribution was present in the provinces of São Paulo (1829) and Minas Gerais (1833), where owners of between one and four slaves represented about 60 percent of the slave-holders, and the mean number of slaves per proprietor was seven. In some areas of São Paulo province, even after coffee became king, small farmers, who raised cattle and planted both foodstuffs and some coffee, were still numerous. In Franca, for instance, research on probate records found that owners of between one and five slaves represented 73.3 percent of the sample in 1822 to 1830, falling to 64.8 percent in 1875 to 1885 – still a high proportion.

Slave property was even more widespread in the cities. In the first half of the nineteenth century, in a sample of 395 residents of Salvador whose property appeared in probate records, only 13 percent did not have at least one slave, and 65 percent owned between one and ten slaves. Among the twenty-five freed Africans in the sample, only four did not own slaves. A mid-century census of a typical parish of Salvador found that 22 percent of the freed Africans owned slaves, the majority holding one or two. Before the ending of the slave trade in 1850, property in slaves in Rio de Janeiro was more important to middle-sized wealth holders than for the rich, who invested proportionately more in real estate, bonds, and other assets than in slaves. In 1831 to 1835, in the city of Rio de Janeiro, 70 percent of slave-holders in probate records owned less than ten slaves, even though those with ten or more owned 67.4 percent of the slaves therein listed.

That free and freed blacks sometimes became slave-owners is a phenomenon common to all slave societies of the Americas, even in the United

States, where the institution was more rigid than elsewhere regarding manumission and the upward mobility of black people. In Brazil, slaves owned slaves too. On rural estates of Pernambuco belonging to the Benedictine religious order, for instance, enslaved overseers owned slaves, one of whom had as many as eight, and in one large absentee property, in the backlands of Bahía, thirteen bondmen owned forty-four slaves. In the city of Salvador, enslaved men and women regularly took their African slaves and their Creole children to a baptismal fountain, and priests casually registered this act as an ordinary social norm. There is less evidence of this phenomenon for the southeast and the south, except for a few mentioned in primary documents or in passages in pro-slavery literature as part of an ideological discourse to praise the benign nature of Brazilian slavery as compared to other slave societies of the Americas. The slave-owning slave also emerges in the pages of *O abolicionismo* (*Abolitionism*), the famous antislavery treatise by Joaquim Nabuco, when the author mentioned *en passant* that "even slaves" owned slaves as part of his argument that the institution of slavery was difficult to combat in Brazil because it "had extended its privileges to all indiscriminately."

Slaves were the best investment for small property owners as long as the traffic existed and slaves were relatively cheap – and the larger the trade, the more slaves were bought. Again, in Salvador, most cases of slaves buying recently arrived African slaves and taking them to churches to baptize them were concentrated in the years immediately before the announced legal ending of the transatlantic trade in 1831, when slave traders intensified the importation of Africans, producing a huge supply of cheap hands all over Brazil, and therefore favoring a buyers' market. A British vicar, Robert Walsh, was in Rio in the late 1820s, where he observed that:

The black population has latterly greatly increased. As the period approached for the total abolition of the slave trade, capital has been everywhere embarked in the purchase of negroes, insomuch so, that forty-five thousand were imported during the year of 1828, into the city of Rio de Janeiro alone. It is true, that a great many of these are sent up the country; but it is also true, that a great proportion remains in the town, to supply the demands of an expanding white population, so that their increase has been beyond all ordinary calculation; my eyes really was [sic] so familiarized with black visages, that the occurrence of a white face in the streets of some parts of the town, struck me as a novelty.[7]

With the ending of the slave trade in 1850, property in slaves would become more concentrated primarily because of increasing slave prices. In the province and the city of Rio de Janeiro, for instance, slave prices tripled

---

[7] Robert Walsh, *Notices of Brazil in 1828 and 1829* (London, 1830), Vol. I, p. 465.

between the 1840s and 1860s. A good example of the ensuing slave property concentration is offered by the county of Vassouras, located in an important coffee plantation region of the Paraíba River Valley in Rio de Janeiro. Here, a combination of the coffee boom and slave price increase explains why masters of 100 plus slaves owned 23 percent of them in 1821 to 1835, a figure that more than doubled to 51 percent in 1851 to 1865. As for proprietors owning fewer than twenty slaves, the figures fell from 26.7 to 10 percent during the same period. Even though slave property did not disappear from middle- and lower-class households, their investment in slavery decreased considerably. Actually, after 1850, owners of a few slaves, particularly those residents in urban areas, would sell their human property for a good profit to coffee planters in the interior. As a result, in the county of Rio de Janeiro – which included the city and its immediate rural area – the slave population fell from 110,602, in 1849, to 48,939, in 1872. Slaves in urban occupations and on farms around Rio were now being replaced by free workers, among them European immigrants, who represented one-third of Rio's population in 1872, the vast majority being from Portugal.

SLAVES RESIST AND NEGOTIATE WITH MASTERS

The reinvigoration of slavery and its eventual demise did not occur quietly. Brazilian small and large slave-owners had to confront resistance on the part of slaves everywhere slavery existed. This resistance suggests that the nation-building project based on slave labor did not evolve without the active, if sometimes subtle, opposition from enslaved individuals and groups. Slaves struggled to improve their treatment, keep their families together, curtail the daily work load, have access to provision grounds, hire themselves out, enjoy a degree of cultural autonomy, and especially important, manumit themselves.

Although family life was precarious due, among other factors, to the high proportion of males among Africans and separation of family members by sale and inheritance partition, families persisted particularly in larger plantations. Even in these, of course, there were normally more men than women, and therefore more women than men had a chance to find a partner. However, specific plantations could display very high rates of adult (over 20 years old) slave marriages, as high as 97.5 percent in Rio Claro coffee county, in São Paulo province, albeit exceptional. In contrast, in a typical sugar plantation parish in Bahia, 100 percent of baptized slave children were illegitimate (compared with 27.7 percent among free people), in 1816.[8]

---

[8] A good summary of the literature on slave families can be found in Herbert Klein and Francisco Vidal Luna, *Slavery in Brazil* (Cambridge, 2010), ch. 8.

In general, families resulted from informal relationships rather than official marriages celebrated by a Catholic priest, but like the latter, "illegitimate" unions were meaningful enough to build and expand kinship ties, solidarity, and collective identity. Church records and, secondarily, lists of slaves in probate records have been the main source of information about slave marriages, the number of which could vary significantly, from very low in the sugar plantations of the northeast to low in the coffee plantations of the southeast. In some places, such as Vassouras, they tended to increase, gradually though steadily, through the second half of the nineteenth century. The end of the transatlantic slave trade and the resulting Creolization of the population led to a more balanced male/female ratio, which, coupled with masters' interest in natural reproduction, resulted in more slave marriages.[9] In addition, official marriages seem to have increased in this period because the slaves themselves came to value it more after an 1869 imperial decree ruled that married couples and their children younger than the age of 15 could not be sold separately. This measure was reinforced by the 1871 Free Womb Law, which ruled that legitimate families should be favored by newly created manumission schemes – though the same law also reduced the protection against sale to 12 years of age.

Historians are divided about the effect of slave families on slave control. Some argue that masters promoted families to obtain peace in the slave quarters, but others maintain that slave families produced group solidarity, implemented autonomy, and promoted the defense of acquired formal and informal rights. The slave family could actually function both ways, for while couples or parents tried not to risk family stability with acts of resistance, protecting the family from abuse could lead to sometimes explosive forms of slave resistance. The formation of symbolic kinship, such as Catholic godparenthood, also strengthened bonds among slaves and between them and freed blacks. Apparently, the decision about who married or baptized whom was frequently, but not always, made by masters, and thus could lead to disagreements or conflict, for instance when slave women refused to accept husbands chosen against their will.[10]

Access to provision gardens and the possibility of raising small or larger animals seems to have been provided preferentially to family groups. This helped slaves to better feed themselves with more than offered by masters as daily rations. Slave-run agriculture and cattle-raising helped bondmen and women accumulate resources by selling their excess production in

---

[9] Ricardo Salles, *E o vale era escravo* (Rio de Janeiro, 2008), pp. 219–25.

[10] Manolo Florentino and José Roberto Góes, *A paz das senzalas: famílias escravas e tráfico atlântico, Rio de Janeiro, c. 1790–c. 1850* (Rio de Janeiro, 1997); Robert Slenes, *Na senzala uma flor: esperanças e recordações na formação da família escrava – Brasil sudeste, século XIX* (Rio de Janeiro, 1999).

local markets. A few managed to buy their freedom with such earnings. Although land dedicated to export agriculture would compete with slave-controlled land, the manuals on slave amelioration and plantation management, both in the sugar and coffee regions, recommended the concession of provision grounds by planters. These manuals argued that such measures, besides promoting the slave family, helped prevent slave rebelliousness; however, the mere mention of these procedures as amelioration policy indicates that neither provision gardens nor the promotion of families were universal practices in Brazilian slavery, especially in the plantation world.[11]

In the countryside, but mainly in the city, slaves were often sent out on their own to contract all kinds of services and trades. The most common were to till the land, sell goods, wash clothes, or transport objects and people on foot, in canoes, boats, carts, sedan chairs, and hammocks (the last two for carrying people). A slave could acquire greater autonomy in an urban setting, in spite of the fact that the police tried to control cities like overseers controlled plantations. Urban slavery necessarily meant greater independence for the slaves-for-hire or *negros de ganho*. The hiring-out system was a typical arrangement of urban slavery, and consisted in the slaves' payment to their masters of a daily or more commonly a weekly sum previously contracted between the two parties – and everything earned exceeding this sum would belong to the slave. Very often, slaves did not even reside under the same roof as masters, whose only interest was to receive their share of the slaves' gains. Such autonomy created social and cultural benefits in the formation of a complex slave network involving family, friends, work partners, ethnic relatives, and co-religionists. In cities all over Brazil, slaves and freed people organized themselves in ethnically oriented work groups, with their own hierarchy. They divided up the urban territory into sections to better manage their access to the labor market, as well as to quell their disputes. Africans would perform many of their tasks, such as carrying heavy barrels of rum, sugar crates, and coffee sacks, singing African chants, and wearing attires and body adornments that were signs of ethnic affiliations, and can be observed in vivid paintings and drawings made by European travelers.[12]

---

[11] Miguel Calmon du Pin e Almeida, *Ensaio sobre o fabrico do assucar* (Salvador, 1834), pp. 57–66; and Francisco Peixoto de Lacerda Werneck, *Memória sobre a fundação de uma fazenda na Província do Rio de Janeiro* (Brasília, 1985 [orig. 1847, 1878]), pp. 62–5, 101–04.

[12] A sample of studies on urban slavery are: Karasch, *Slave Life in Rio de Janeiro*; Maria José Andrade, *A mão-de-obra escrava em Salvador, 1811–1888* (Salvador, 1988); Marcus J. M. de Carvalho, *Liberdade: rotinas e rupturas do escravismo no Recife, 1822–1850* (Recife, 1998); Maria Cristina Wissenbach, *Sonhos africanos, vivências ladinas: escravos e forros em São Paulo (1850–1888)* (São Paulo, 1998); Paulo Roberto S. Moreira, *Os cativos e os homens de bem: experiências negras no espaço urbano* (Porto Alegre, 2003).

The nineteenth century saw the formation or the consolidation of a strong Afro-Brazilian culture centered in great part around religion. To the West-Central African Nkisi cult, which was established in Brazil during the first century of plantation slavery, were added West African devotions to the Vodun of the Gbe-speaking peoples, the Orișa of the Yoruba, and the Islam of several Central Sudanic peoples such as the Hausa, Borno, Nupe, and, again, the Yoruba. West African religious expressions, particularly Vodun worship, were not absent in previous periods, for slaves from the Gbe area were coming in increasing numbers since the early eighteenth century to serve primarily in Bahia and Minas Gerais. But it was only in the following century that a complex religious apparatus developed, particularly in Bahia, that involved the formation of communities with groups of initiates, the consolidation of festive calendars, and the systematization of rituals and key practices such as divination and healing. By the second half of the nineteenth century, a network of Vodun and Orișa cult houses had been firmly established and Candomblé – as this religion came to be known – could claim to have penetrated beyond the frontiers of the African community. Even white folks sought services such as divination, medical treatment, the making of good luck charms, and all kinds of procedures to improve performance in life, from work to health and sex. But these activities were not the exclusive domain of spirit possession religions, or peculiar to Bahia. In Maranhão, African traditions mixed with indigenous ones to produce the Creole *Pajelança*, which particularly emphasized healing rituals. As for Islam, though it is known primarily for its involvement with slave revolts – an aspect to be explored later in this chapter – it carried out similar endeavors. Hausa Malams and Yoruba Alufas divined, produced amulets, prescribed medicine, united lovers, and promoted and cured witchcraft, and their clients came from all walks in life.[13]

Although all of these religious expressions could be found everywhere in Brazil, there were different emphases based on the source of the slave trade. While West-Central African religious beliefs were more concentrated in the southeast, West African ones thrived in Bahia. As we have seen, slaves from Angola were numerous in Bahia, and Candomblé houses headed by Angolan priests are known to have existed there. Actually, the term Candomblé is of Bantu extraction, and its first appearance detected in the archives is related to the practice of an Angolan priest in Bahia in 1807. Candomblé, however, came to be more often identified with the Jeje Vodun and the Nagô Orișa worship,

[13] João Reis, "Candomblé in Nineteenth-Century Bahia: Priests, Followers, Clients," in Kristin Mann and Edna Bay (eds.), *Rethinking the African Diaspora* (London, 2001), pp. 134–44; Gabriela dos Reis Sampaio, *Juca Rosa: um pai-de-santo na Corte Imperial* (Rio de Janeiro, 2009).

though the latter would supersede the former in the course of the nineteenth century. This was the result, in great part, of the large number of Nagôs being imported into Bahia in the last three decades of the transatlantic slave trade. From Bahia, through the internal slave trade and the migration of African freedmen and women, West African religions, including Islam, travelled both north and southward to other Brazilian provinces. Offshoots of Candomblé houses and Muslim groups are known to have existed in the provinces of Pernambuco, Rio de Janeiro, and Rio Grande do Sul, some of them with clear connections to their Bahían background.

While Afro-Brazilian religions expanded their following, Afro-Catholicism maintained its popularity. One of its most important institutions, however, the black brotherhoods (so powerful in previous times), declined. Brotherhoods represented the material and devotional basis of baroque Catholicism, which reached its heyday in the mid eighteenth century. Though they were still strong until the middle of the nineteenth century, a slow decline occurred as a result of several factors, in particular the success of Afro-Brazilian religions. But two other factors were crucial: the secularization of life in general, especially among middling groups, and – perhaps decisively – the Romanization of the Church, a victorious doctrine that strived to impose discipline among the clergy and the faithful. This included taking away the latter's control of the brotherhoods, thus dissipating their effusive, collective, and public style of celebrating patron saints with drums, dances, coronations of kings and queens, much food, and drinking. Black brotherhoods did not disappear, to be sure, and street Catholic festivals such as those dedicated to Nossa Senhora da Penha in Rio, Nosso Senhor do Bonfim (Our Lord of the Good Death) in Bahia, and the coronation of African kings in Pernambuco, Minas Gerais, and Rio de Janeiro, among other provinces, continued to be an essential part of a Creolized popular culture.

MANUMISSION AND FREED PERSONS

Candomblé, brotherhoods, and, to a lesser extent, Muslim groups depended for much of their success on the role of freedmen and women as both members and, especially, as leaders. Brazil may have been the slave society in the Americas to have manumitted the greatest numbers of slaves, in part because of its relatively easier access to African slave markets that could replace the freed slaves with new, younger ones. The cumulative process of slave manumissions and the natural reproduction of the free colored population meant that, by the mid nineteenth century, there were more free colored than enslaved in Brazil. The first national census in

1872 counted 4.2 million free blacks and *mestiços*, 3.8 million whites, and only 1.5 million slaves.[14]

Manumission was obtained either gratuitously and unconditionally; gratuitously but conditionally (one of the most common conditions was to serve masters until their deaths); or paid (more often in currency, but also in goods, such as gold in mining areas, bales of cotton, cattle, and even slaves). Of the regions for which data are available, with the exception of Rio de Janeiro, women and children were proportionately more frequently manumitted than men, and mulattos and Brazilian-born blacks (*crioulos*) more than Africans. Africans more often paid for their freedom than slaves born in Brazil, again with the exception of Rio, but here, like everywhere else, West Africans did better than West-Central Africans in the race toward freedom. The most common explanation for this difference is that West African hired-out slaves, especially women, controlled important and lucrative niches of the labor market. They were employed in the distribution of produce and the selling of cooked food either in fixed stalls or peddling through the city streets, suburban, and rural areas, including coffee and sugar plantations. The success with marketing, on the other hand, may have resulted from previous experience in African societies that, despite being basically agricultural, were also highly urbanized, mercantile, and in which women had an important role as local merchants, while men could be involved in both local and long-distance caravan trade.

Though the majority of freed persons who left slavery led a life of poverty in freedom, many managed to climb the social and economic ladder. Ex-slaves often became slave masters, and some became rich individuals according to the standards of nineteenth-century Brazil, many of whom were women, and among these most were from the Mina nation.[15] Their economic success, however, did not translate into social and political power (except within the black community), for they were discriminated against by the educated white and *mestiço* population, even those who did not get near the wealth amassed by the rich freed person. Wealthy whites would do business with freed Africans, and even slaves, but not socialize with them. The free person commonly lived and married within their own group, usually within their own nation if they were Africans. On the political front, African-born free people had no citizenship in Brazil, so they could not vote or be elected for any political office,

---

[14] For a summary of the data on manumission and the free colored population, see Klein and Luna, *Slavery in Brazil*, esp. ch. 9.

[15] For the upward mobility of Mina freedwomen in Rio, see Sheila de Castro Faria, "Damas mercadoras: as pretas minas no Rio de Janeiro," in Mariza de Carvalho Soares (ed.), *Rotas atlânticas da diáspora africana: da Baía de Benim ao Rio de Janeiro* (Rio de Janeiro, 2007), pp. 101–34; Carlos Eugênio L. Soares and Fávio Gomes, "Negras minas no Rio de Janeiro: nação e trabalho urbano no século XIX," in de Carvalho Soares (ed.), *Rotas atlânticas da diáspora africana*, pp. 191–24.

and were not allowed to be public employees; if born in Brazil, freed persons had all the civil rights a free Brazilian of any color had, but a reduced political right: they could vote in primary or parochial elections that chose the electors for provincial and national houses of representatives, but they were not allowed to be elected to any office, even membership in municipal councils. African freed persons had their mobility permanently checked by the authorities, and in some places such as Bahia, after the 1835 Malê Revolt (see below), they were no longer allowed to buy real estate, and were subjected to a head tax, among other impediments.

In spite of the difficulties of life in freedom, slaves struggled to overcome bondage, and their yearning for independence was used by masters as a tool of social control. The formulaic narrative in nearly all manumission papers tells most of the story: freedom was given out for the "good service rendered" by slaves to their masters, an expression found even in paid manumission. The ideological constraints were more potent when slaves received conditional liberty, keeping the slave in limbo frequently for many years, perhaps for life. Besides, freedom could be revoked, even when paid for, if masters alleged disloyal behavior or anything that would have harmed them physically or morally. Freedom did not mean total autonomy; it implied instead a transition from a slave-master relationship to one of patron-clientship. Actually, the legal term for the ex-master was precisely *patrono(a)*/patron(ess), meaning the one who had *patrocinado* (promoted) his or her slave's liberty. Therefore, up until the early 1870s, masters had the legal right to both manumit and to revoke manumission.

Ties of dependence became more important over the course of the nineteenth century as a mechanism to control the increasing population of free and freed blacks. In Brazil's slave society, freedom demanded protection from a former master or, in his absence, of another free person. It was dangerous for a black person to be unprotected in a society still ruled by ancient regime rules of hierarchy, where there was always someone superior. Free coloreds were often kidnapped and enslaved, particularly children, sometimes whole families. Or they were arrested on suspicion of being fugitive slaves, and could rot in prison before proving their case. At the time of their abduction, such persons had no one to vouch for them, or found themselves away from those who could.[16]

There was no law that forced masters to manumit their slaves or prevent the cancelation of manumissions given until the 1871 Free Womb Law. Besides freeing newly born slaves – though keeping them under the mother's master's tutelage until 21 years of age – this law recognized the

---

[16] Sidney Chalhoub, *A força da escravidão: ilegalidade e costume no Brasil oitocentista* (São Paulo, 2012).

slaves' property rights (*peculium*), and the right to free themselves for a price ultimately decided by a magistrate whenever there was disagreement between slaves and masters. So what until 1871 appeared as a seigniorial concession (or customary law) – both permission to own property and to use it to pay for freedom – became positive legislation. From then on, slaves were also to gain manumission if masters failed to register them for tax purposes. This law represented a strong blow to masters' paternalistic rule, for from now on the state would have the upper hand in a sensitive, crucial affair that had been since the establishment of the slave regime completely under the private control and dependent on the will of masters.

RESISTANCE

Family formation, access to provision grounds, manumission, and so on were not mere seigniorial concession, but a result of slaves' daily bargaining, which may have included subtle threats or acts more directly rebellious. Masters did not yield bargaining space gratuitously, but as a consequence of slave pressure. Whatever gains slaves acquired became customary rights that in turn were fervently defended. When such rights were threatened, slaves could retaliate, sometimes committing serious offenses such as beating, even killing masters and overseers, running away, forming maroon groups, or, in the most extreme cases, generating outright collective revolt. This is not, of course, a complete list of the possible individual and joint acts of resistance.

The statistics on slave crime in different regions of Brazil indicate that their victims were in their majority free persons, and among these a high proportion of masters and overseers. In three counties of São Paulo province, one study found the following: in Campinas, between 1830 and 1880, eighteen masters and twenty-three overseers were killed by slaves; in Taubaté, for a shorter period stretching from 1850 to 1880, six masters and eight overseers were killed by slaves; in Franca, in a period covering 1830 to 1880, 69 percent of slaves' victims were free persons, and of these 30 percent were either masters or overseers. In Juiz de Fora, Minas Gerais, between 1850 and 1888, twenty-two masters and overseers found death at the hands of slaves they owned or supervised, representing 20 percent of all victims of slave crimes against persons (as opposed to crimes against property). Toward the last years of slavery in the southeast, the killing of masters and overseers became so ordinary that newspapers avoided publishing news about it for fear of creating panic among the free. Slaves would kill and turn themselves in to the nearest police authority. They understood that a law that established the death penalty for such a crime was being systematically circumvented by the emperor's commutation to life in prison, which many slaves preferred to life in bondage.

Therefore, violence against masters and their agents represented a common mechanism of slave resistance in Brazil.

However, running away was probably the most universal form of active individual slave resistance, and it was endemic both in the countryside – where fugitives could find shelter in slave quarters, employment in farms, or hideouts in the woods and hills – and cities – where they could mix with the usually large free and freed colored population. In Recife, between 1842 and 1850, flight represented 23 percent of all slave arrests for which a cause is known. In Rio, between 1810 and 1858, the proportion of slaves arrested for running away varied immensely from one year to the other, with a low 11 percent of slave arrests in 1849 to 1850 to an extraordinarily high 75 percent in 1825 to 1830, precisely the years of the slave trade boom just before its formal prohibition in 1831, which suggests that recently arrived Africans were well represented among the runaways. This result is confirmed by a sample of 5,363 runaways listed in police records of Rio de Janeiro province (the imperial capital included), in the period between 1810 and 1830, with 73.6 percent of runaways concentrated in 1826 to 1829. In addition, for 1826 alone, 86.7 percent of all runaways advertised in Rio's newspapers were African-born, 73.2 percent of whom were between 10 and 20 years of age, reflecting the known youth of slaves, primarily from West-Central Africa, who disembarked in the region in the 1820s. That freshly disembarked Africans became runaways suggests a strong pre-existent solidarity network for which African and probably ethnic community organization was required.[17]

Slaves fled from masters for a number of reasons, besides, obviously, physical punishment or ill treatment generally. Very often, the reason was not from what, where, or whom they escaped, but to where, whom, or for what reason they did. Slaves escaped to visit lovers and family members, to participate in festivals and other divertissements, and to religious communities in order to seek advice, protection, to pray to their gods, or to perform initiation rites. They also ran away to hunt for work in more promising labor markets in cities, or to find new, and hopefully more caring, masters, willing to buy them for a discount. There were slaves who let themselves be stolen to escape oppressive masters. There were those who abandoned the service of masters to serve in the armed force, a very common conduct in times of internal or external conflict, such as the war for independence in Bahia in 1822 to 1823, and the

[17] Welington Barbosa Silva, "Entre sobrados e mocambos: fuga de escravos e ação policial no Recife oitocentista," in Flávio José Gomes and Robson Costa (eds.), História da escravidão em Pernambuco (Recife, 2012), pp. 143–68 (esp. p. 166); Flávio dos Santos Gomes, "Jogando a rede, revendo as malhas: fugas e fugitivos no Brasil," Tempo, 1 (1996): 67–93.

Paraguay (or the Triple Alliance) War in 1864 to 1870. Being slaves near international borders also represented an opportunity for a possible definitive flight, especially when beyond the border lay free soil countries. Running away became endemic – and a diplomatic issue – for instance, on the border with French Guiana at the beginning of the century, and in the far south on the border of Uruguay and Argentina, especially from the mid-1800s, for in these places slavery had been abolished (though of course, it had been restored in the French colony by Napoleon). Actually, in the Rio Grande do Sul frontier, running away to the Prata River neighboring countries had been a chronic master's headache since the 1810s at least.

The threat of being sold away was one of the most important motives to escape. Being sold meant severing social ties forged over the years, it meant leaving behind friends, lovers, relatives, and familiar territory. Sales were particularly traumatic when slaves had to move to another city or province. Some provinces were known to have a harsh slavery, such as Maranhão and Rio Grande do Sul. After the end of the transatlantic slave trade in 1850, and the intensification of the internal traffic to the southeast, disruption of slave life through sales became a daily threat. Sometimes, whole families fled together for this reason. Some of these episodes ended in tragedy, with mothers killing their children and committing suicide when slave hunters attempted to arrest them. Slaves sometimes committed suicide because they were threatened with being sold away, and suicide represented a form of flight to the afterlife – and for African-born slaves perhaps a spiritual return to their homeland.

Slaves could also escape to join or create runaway communities. Known as *quilombos* or *mocambos* in Brazil, they were located both in the forest and mountains of the hinterland or near plantation zones and small and large cities. The Amazon forest, the hilly geography of Minas Gerais, the swampy terrain of Mato Grosso and Rio Grande do Sul provinces, all served as hideouts for runaways. Slaves from *quilombos* in the Iguaçu River Valley in Rio circulated inside the imperial capital where they exchanged wood that they had felled for salt, meat, cloth, and other products hard to find near their habitat. On foot or by boat, runaways circulated through slave quarters, taverns, and markets, where they moved around with some degree of protection from local slaves, freed, and free people interested in dealing with them for different reasons, be it economic, religious, or affective. In the outskirts of large cities such as Recife, Salvador, and Rio, as well as smaller ones, such as Laranjeiras (in Sergipe province), Rio Grande, and Porto Alegre (both in Rio Grande do Sul), *quilombos* flourished in the first half of the nineteenth century, together with the intensification of the transatlantic slave trade and the expansion of slavery. In Rio, *quilombos* existed in nowadays celebrated neighborhoods, such as

Corcovado and Santa Teresa hills, Laranjeiras, and Tijuca, which at the time marked the limits between city and countryside. Of course, *quilombos* so close to urban areas were usually small and short-lived, but at times after being defeated they were to resurface somewhere else. One of the main reasons for their survival was alliances formed with outsiders.

Quilombos also prospered as a result of political and social instability. *Quilombos* defied police and slave hunters – called *capitães do mato*/bush captain – and were endemic in the vicinity of Recife, the capital of Pernambuco province, due to conflicts in 1817, 1821 to 1822, 1824, 1831, 1832 to 1835, and 1848, a cycle of predominantly free people's revolts just before, and after Brazil's independence from Portugal. External wars also weakened control over slaves, frequently promoting dangerous alliances between runaways and poor freemen. During the war against Paraguay (1864–70), *quilombos* in Mato Grosso, a province bordering on the theater of battle, swelled their ranks with runaway slaves as well as army deserters and freemen trying to evade the draft. Not until after the war did the authorities have the opportunity to unleash repression upon runaways and deserters. At the other end of Brazil, the northern province of Maranhão, the number of *quilombos* formed by slaves, criminals, and deserters increased, according to the town councilors of the village of Turiaçu in 1867. At the same time, local authorities, merchants, and farmers alleged that recruitment of national guardsmen for the war with Paraguay had hurt the ability to fight *quilombos*. This situation was reproduced in other places around the country, in Rio Grande do Sul, for instance.[18]

Quilombos sometimes evolved into fully fledged rebellions, which represented the most direct form of collective slave resistance, even though they did not always seek the destruction of the slave-holding regime or even the immediate freedom of the slaves involved. Many were simply aimed at redressing excessive oppression, reducing it to a tolerable level, demanding specific rights, the recovery of lost gains, or punishing especially cruel overseers. They were uprisings whose objective was to reform slavery, not to destroy it. Revolts became more frequent after the late eighteenth century, with the expansion of the areas devoted to export agriculture and the consequent intensification of the slave trade, which increased the size of the slave population, particularly its more rebellious African component. A high proportion of slaves in the population and, among them, a larger number of Africans from the same ethnic group, reinforced the collective identity and awareness of collective power. For instance, slave revolts and conspiracies that tormented slave-owners in Bahia in the first half of the nineteenth century – which numbered more than thirty, most

[18] See essays in João Reis and Flávio Gomes (eds.), *Liberdade por um fio: história dos quilombos no Brasil* (São Paulo, 2000).

of them in the sugar plantation region of the Recôncavo – were carried out mainly by Hausas and Nagôs. The Nagôs were especially active in the late 1820s, when the presence of captives from Yorubaland boomed just before the 1831 prohibition of the slave trade: half of the thirty-plus slave revolts in nineteenth-century Bahia happened between 1826 and 1830.

The fact that Bahia was the scene of so many slave revolts is due to the convergence there of numerous Nagôs and Hausas with recent experience in wars, some of which involved conflicts linked to the spread of Islam in their homelands. By contrast, Rio received in the same period predominantly Bantu-speaking Africans, many of them quite young, female, and inexperienced in the art of war. The Portuguese Crown installed in Rio realized the ethnic component of revolts and demanded that the governor of the captaincy of Bahia better control its slaves, forbidding them to gather for drumming and other festivities that could provide them with a chance and the spirit to foment revolt. By that time, the long cycle of Bahian slave revolts had just begun.

These early revolts were carried out mainly by the Hausas, who were later replaced by, or joined forces with, the Nagôs, whose rebellious campaign culminated in the Malê (Muslim) Revolt of 1835. Both groups, particularly the Hausas, had a substantial Muslim contingent. Because of the solid presence of Bahian slave traders on the Bight of Benin, where these slaves embarked, Bahia contained the largest African Muslim community in the Americas at the time. Muslim mentors constituted the leadership of at least the 1807 conspiracy, as well as the 1814 and 1835 rebellions. In 1835, rebels took to the streets of Salvador wearing Islamic garments and amulets containing passages from the Quran and other devotional writings as charms against the weapons of the enemy. The revolt itself was scheduled to take place at the end of the Ramadan, probably the Lailat al-Qadr, the Night of Destiny.[19]

Besides the Muslims, numerous African rebels may have also been inspired by war-like divinities, such as Orişa Ogun, the Yoruba god of war. Inside the Urubu *quilombo*, the epicenter of a rebellion in the outskirts of Salvador in 1826, there was a Candomblé cult house. Elsewhere in Brazil, Manoel Congo, the leader of a revolt in Vassouras county, in the province of Rio de Janeiro, in 1838, was called "father," probably with a religious connotation. The Campinas conspiracy of 1832 is one of the slave uprisings in which references to sorcery abound. Questioned on the matter, one suspect said that the "herbal medicine was [used] to tame the whites so that their weapons would not harm us blacks and for us to rise up boldly to slay them and all become free." The "medicine" usually

---

[19] João José Reis, *Slave Rebellion in Brazil: The 1835 Muslim Uprising in Bahia* (Baltimore, MD, 1993).

consisted of concoctions prepared and sold by Congo slaves. One of the suspects was in charge of distributing protective roots, a slave of the Rebolo nation, "Father Diogo," a title probably referring, as in the case of Manoel Congo, to his status as a religious leader.

Not only African religious messages and rituals inspired slave rebels. Though the role of Catholicism was primarily one of negotiation or even accommodation, it sometimes inspired slave rebels, and not only the African-born. In 1849, slaves of Queimado county, in the province of Espírito Santo, were convinced by their leader that a parish priest would persuade their masters to set them free on Saint Joseph's day, dedicated to the local patron saint. Cosme Chagas, a freedman and leader of slaves who joined the Balaiada liberal revolt (1838–40), in Maranhão, wrote that his men were devoted to Our Lady of the Rosary, the most revered Catholic saint among blacks in Brazil, and that his movement represented a "sacred party of that Brotherhood" of the Rosary. In 1848, in Vassouras, slaves devoted to Saint Anthony were allegedly involved in a plot scheduled to begin on the day of another saint, Saint John. Saint Anthony seems to have been an accomplice in a vast conspiracy by Bantu-speaking slaves spread over several counties of the Paraíba Valley and southern Minas Gerais. In addition to pressure from the English, this conspiracy, some historians argue, precipitated the imperial government's decision to end the transatlantic slave trade two years later. In combination with witchcraft, Saint Anthony reappeared once again as patron saint of slave conspirators in São Paulo in the final decade of slavery, when Africans had already been reduced to a minority. The rebels adhered to a syncretic faith, not unlike Umbanda, a branch of Afro-Brazilian religion particularly popular in Southeastern Brazil.

Not only African and Creole religious ideologies inspired slave rebels. The Haitian Revolution, which had an important impact on slave rebelliousness in the Caribbean and North America, had some influence on both enslaved and free blacks in Brazil. In 1805, just one year after the proclamation of Haitian independence by Jean-Jacques Dessalines, his portrait figured in medallions worn by black militiamen in Rio de Janeiro. In 1814, in Bahia, slaves spoke openly on the streets of the events in the French Antilles. During the Pernambuco Revolution of 1817, a movement against Portuguese rule led by native white planters, more radical tendencies by blacks and mulattos favored a social uprising inspired by Haitian principles. In 1824, in the city of Laranjeiras, Sergipe province, during an anti-Portuguese banquet shouts of praise by free coloreds were heard for Saint Domingue and the "King of Haiti." The same year, in neighboring Pernambuco, soldiers of a mulatto battalion handed out lampoons that hailed Christophe as "That Immortal Haitian," and invited Pernambucans to imitate the Haitians. A couple of decades later, in Recife, a protestant free black known as the "Divine Master," inspired in the Bible, taught other blacks to write using popular verses that threatened whites with a Haitian-style destruction of slavery. "Remember Haiti," he wrote in a poem entitled "The ABC of the Divine Master."[20]

Among the various political changes, it was the long abolitionist trajectory – from the laws that had banned the slave trade to those which reformed slavery and finally the campaigns of the final decade of the regime – that proved to be most important to slave agitation. Slaves participated actively in the disorganization and extinction of Brazilian slavery. Their visions of freedom constantly clashed with the gradualist perspective of conventional abolitionism. In Espírito Santo province, the anti-slave trade law of 1831 was interpreted as emancipationist by slaves in the village of Itapemirim. In Carrancas county, Minas Gerais, slaves conspired during that very year, for the same reasons, apparently encouraged by the parish priest. Following rumors of abolition two years later, in this very region, a revolt involving slaves from several farms and led by a Mina man – but, unlike in Bahia, with the input of slaves from West-Central Africa as well as Creoles – resulted in the massacre of several whites, men and women, of the same family. The 1831 law also figured in the complex web of motivations of the slaves who plotted against their masters in the coffee-growing county of Campinas, São Paulo, in 1832, for whom the emperor, as the typical "fount of justice," had abolished slavery the year before, but their masters would not obey his order. Slaves interpreted the law according to their peculiar political reading of the surrounding world. Twenty years later, again in Espírito Santo, now in the village of São Mateus, rumors circulated that the renewed abolition of the slave trade in 1850 had actually emancipated slaves. Similar episodes occurred in 1871, the year of the Law of the Free Womb, both in Espírito Santo and the sugar county of Campos, in the province of Rio de Janeiro: slaves became restless as they interpreted the discussions of that law as a sign of full emancipation.

One of the most unnerving issues for provincial authorities and slave proprietors alike was the several hundreds of thousands of Africans that had been imported after the 1831 prohibition of the slave trade, which established that they should be considered "free Africans" and wards of the imperial government. But the government did little to abide by the law, and systematically recommended judges to dismiss the so-called "liberty clauses" based on the 1831 ban, or else slavery in Brazil would simply collapse due to the countless number of people illegally enslaved. But this

[20] João Reis and Flávio Gomes, "Repercussions of the Haitian Revolution in Brazil, 1791–1850," in David Geggus and Norman Fiering (eds.), *The World of the Haitian Revolution* (Bloomington, IN, 2009), pp. 284–313.

law politicized much of the everyday slave/master relations, especially when, from the late 1870s up until abolition in 1888, militant abolitionists decided to press those cases as part of their antislavery campaign. The black poet, journalist, and attorney Luiz Gama was active in the city of São Paulo's courts between the late 1860s and the early 1880s. Unfortunately, Gama did not see what came after his premature death in 1882. The last years of slavery were marked everywhere, but especially in the coffee regions of Southeastern Brazil, by small but widespread revolts in and massive flights from plantations, and the formation of abolitionist *quilombos* in the outskirts of urban areas now almost devoid of slavery.[21]

Slave resistance in a way radicalized the abolitionist campaign, whose leaders came from a variety of social and racial backgrounds, but who were mainly based in the urban areas. In cities like Rio de Janeiro, São Paulo, Salvador, and Recife, among others, abolitionist meetings, plays, and concerts made local theaters the main stage of the anti-slavery propaganda. Street rallies were not so common, but could be huge, as would happen during Luiz Gama's funeral cortege. Though stronger in some regions than in others, abolitionism became a truly national social movement, its leaders circulating the country preaching for the cause. When Parliament voted the law and acting head of state Princess Isabel signed it on May 13, 1888, the demise of slavery had already been won in the streets and, by the hands of slaves, in the plantations.[22]

A GUIDE TO FURTHER READING

Barickman, B. J., *A Bahian Counterpoint: Sugar, Tobacco, Cassava, and Slavery in the Recôncavo, 1780–1860* (Stanford, CA, 1998).

Bergad, Laird W., *The Demographic and Economic History of Slavery in Minas Gerais, Brazil, 1720–1888* (Cambridge, 1999).

Bethell, Leslie, *The Abolition of the Brazilian Slave Trade: Britain, Brazil and the Slave Trade Question* (Cambridge, 1970).

Conrad, Robert, *Children of God's Fire: A Documentary History of Black Slavery in Brazil* (Princeton, NJ, 1983).

Dean, Warren, *Rio Claro: A Brazilian Plantation System, 1820–1920* (Stanford, CA, 1976).

Eisenberg, Peter, *The Sugar Industry in Pernambuco, 1840–1910: Modernization without Change* (Berkeley, CA, 1974).

---

[21] Beatriz Galloti Mamigonian, "O direito de ser africano livre: os escravos e as interpretações da lei de 1831," in Silvia H. Lara and Joselice Maria N. Mendonça (eds.), *Direitos e justiças no Brasil: ensaios de história social* (Campinas, 2006), pp. 129–60; Maria Helena P. T. Machado, "From Slave Rebels to Strikebreakers: The Quilombo of Jabaquara and the Problem of Citizenship in Late-Nineteenth-Century Brazil," *Hispanic American Historical Review*, 86 (2006): 247–74.

[22] Angela Alonso, *Flores, votos e bala: o movimento abolicionista brasileiro (1868–88)* (São Paulo, 2015).

Frank, Zephyr, *Dutra's World: Wealth and Family in Nineteenth-Century Rio de Janeiro* (Albuquerque, NM, 2004).

Graham, Sandra, *Caetana Says No: Women's Stories from a Brazilian Slave Society* (Cambridge, 2002).

Harding, Rachel, *A Refuge in Thunder: Candomblé and Alternative Spaces of Blackness* (Bloomington, IN, 2000).

Karasch, Mary, *Slave Life in Rio de Janeiro, 1800–1850* (Princeton, NJ, 1987).

Kiddy, Elizabeth, *Blacks of The Rosary: Memory and History in Minas Gerais, Brazil* (University Park, PA, 2005).

Klein, Herbert and Francisco Vidal Luna, *Slavery in Brazil* (Cambridge, 2010).

Parés, Luis Nicolau, *The Formation of Candomblé: Vodun History and Ritual in Brazil* (Chapel Hill, NC, 2013).

Reis, João José, *Slave Rebellion in Brazil: The Muslim Uprising of 1835 in Bahia* (Baltimore, MD, 1993).

Scott, Rebecca, Seymour Drescher, Maria Mattos Hebe de Castro, George Reid Andrews, and Robert M. Levine, *The Abolition of Slavery and the Aftermath of Emancipation in Brazil* (Durham, NC, 1991).

Stein, Stanley J., *Vassouras, a Brazilian Coffee County, 1850–1900: The Roles of Planter and Slave in a Plantation Society* (Princeton, NJ, 1985).

CHAPTER 7

US SLAVERY AND ITS AFTERMATH, 1804–2000

STANLEY L. ENGERMAN

INTRODUCTION

This chapter covers the last sixty years of US slavery, the final quarter of its existence in the thirteen colonies and the United States, and 135 years after the US abolition of slavery. In the last years of slavery, its nature differed in many important ways from the preceding years. It was not only that the success of the American Revolution and the development of the new nation under its new Constitution changed the political conditions under which slavery existed, but the formation of a federal union meant that some issues (including the legality of slavery) were left to the states and others (including the legality of the international slave trade) were left to the central government.

The Constitutional Convention had many discussions regarding slavery and the slave trade, which led to some provisions that were to have a large impact upon the nation. The Constitution provided that the new nation was not to end the slave trade for at least twenty years, at which time, in 1808, US involvement in the slave trade was legally ended. The existence of slavery, however, was left up to each state, a decision that led to the well-known North–South divide. The word "slave" does not appear in the Constitution; the euphemism used was "other people," due both to a commonly held belief that slavery would soon die of its own accord, as well as a desire by both southerners and northerners to avoid what, even then, was regarded as an odious term. For purposes of political representation, slaves were to be considered as three-fifths of a person, a boost to southern political power.

Also central to debates on slavery in the 1780s, in the aftermath of the Revolution, were the two Northwest Ordinances, which, in effect, confined slavery to the southern states. These provisions would become important some seventy years later in leading to discord over the terms of national expansion into Kansas and Nebraska.

Two other occurrences in the years between the Revolution and 1800 were to have significant impacts. First was the invention of the cotton gin by Eli Whitney and others, and its diffusion throughout the South after 1791, permitting the widespread geographic expansion of

155

short-staple cotton production to the point where the South dominated the world's cotton market. Second was the increased size and influence of the abolition movement in England and the United States after the 1780s, culminating in the British movement's first major success in 1807, with legislation ending the British slave trade. There were to be many links made between the British and the emerging American abolition movements.

SLAVERY IN THE FEDERAL PERIOD

By the eve of the Civil War, the Southern United States had the largest slave population in the Americas. This had not always been the case, since the slave population of the Caribbean colonies, even after Haitian independence, exceeded that of the South until 1850, as did the number of slaves in Brazil. It was not until the middle of the nineteenth century that the South became the New World's leading slave nation. Unlike the other slave-holding nations of the Americas, however, the growth of the US slave population was not primarily due to sustained slave imports from Africa, but rather, most unusually for any slave population, a strong rate of natural increase due, in large part, to extremely high fertility. Positive rates of natural increase had been important from the start of settlement, even when the import of slaves into the thirteen colonies was still legal.

For most other New World slave populations, the cumulated total of imports far exceeded the number of surviving slave and free black populations at the end of the slave era.[1] These other areas had relied on imports to prevent declines in their slave populations. Overall, the United States received only about 3 percent of New World slave imports from Africa, considerably below their share of New World free black and slave populations by the nineteenth century. This share was about 35 percent in 1830. Sugar was the major crop in the Caribbean, and the areas in which it was grown tended to have high mortality rates, due to their unhealthy environments as well as the intensive work routines associated with the cultivation and processing of cane. The lower fertility rates in the Caribbean were related to limitations on continuous cohabitation, longer lactation periods, more intensive labor, and a more limited diet. All parts of the slave Americas had lower fertility rates than the United States, which were unusually high by world standards.

The impact of the American Revolution led to other important legal and economic changes in US slavery. Slavery had been legal throughout the thirteen colonies. In the years from 1777 to 1804, several northern states

---

[1] Robert William Fogel, *Without Consent or Contract: The Rise and Fall of American Slavery* (New York, 1989), ch. 5.

passed legislation to end slavery, while in others emancipation was the result of court decisions. The first state to end slavery was Vermont in 1777, followed by New Hampshire, Massachusetts, Pennsylvania, Rhode Island, Connecticut, New York, and New Jersey.[2] Together, these states had about 5 percent of the slaves in the thirteen colonies in 1770. By 1810, they had 2.3 percent of the nation's slave population and about 40 percent of the nation's free black population. Unlike Brazil, where the number of free blacks and slaves were approximately equal, the share of free blacks in the US black population was quite small. And, within the slave and the black population, the United States had a much smaller share of mulattos than did Brazil.

Five of the states passed legislation with "free womb" provisions, which meant that no slaves were freed immediately, but all those born to slave mothers would be considered legally free, though subject to a term of apprenticeship – varying among states from fifteen to thirty years, and, in some cases, by gender – to the owner of the mother. While one state, New York, passed legislation in 1817 to free all slaves and apprentices by 1827, in other states there was no terminal date set, and the ending of slavery and apprenticeship was either by death, by the Civil War, or by the Thirteenth Amendment. Several states, most importantly Virginia, did, though only for a relatively short period of time, loosen the terms of manumission. Prior to the 1808 federal government's ending of the international slave trade, several states imposed restrictions on the import of slaves from Africa. Most important was South Carolina's ban, which proved to be temporary and was then followed by a large increase in legal slave imports from 1803 to 1807. While there were no state actions against the existence of slavery between 1804 and the start of the Civil War, state legislation regarding the possibility, and legal terms, of manumission did vary over this period. There were also several changes at the state level in the legal terms regarding the care and treatment of slaves.

ANTEBELLUM SLAVERY

Even with the closing of the international slave trade in 1808, the southern slave population continued its rapid growth via natural increase, based primarily on its high rate of fertility. Similarly, the southern white population grew rapidly. Following the invention and diffusion of the cotton gin, both whites and black slaves accelerated their westward movement on the basis of the expanding cotton production. The percentage of the US world cotton output increased from an estimated 0.16 percent in 1786 to 1790 to 53.14 percent in 1806 to 1810, and about 80 percent between 1836 and

[2] Arthur Zilversmit, *The First Emancipation: The Abolition of Slavery in the North* (Chicago, IL, 1967).

Table 7.1 *Distribution of Slave-Holdings, US South, 1850*

a. Percent of Slaves in Various Sizes of Slave-Holdings – 1850

	1–9	10–20	20–50	50–100	>100
Total South	26.6	22.8	29.0	13.1	8.5
Border states	35.5	27.5	27.0	7.4	2.6
Lower South	19.8	19.1	30.5	17.5	13.1

b. Percentage: Slave Population to Total Population – 1850

Total South	33.3
Border states	24.7
Lower South	45.4

c. Percentage: Slave-Holders to Free Population – 1850

Total South	30.9
Border states	26.0
Lower South	40.5

Note: Border states are Delaware, Kentucky, Maryland, Missouri, North Carolina, Tennessee, and Virginia.
Source: Lewis Cecil Gray, *History of Agriculture in the Southern United States to 1860* (Washington, DC, 1932), Vol. I, pp. 482, 530.

1860.[3] The other major slave-grown crops remained in specific locations where they had long been grown – tobacco in Maryland and Virginia, rice and Sea Island cotton in coastal areas of South Carolina and Georgia, and, eventually, sugar in Louisiana. The average holding of tobacco farms was generally about ten to twenty slaves, while rice and sugar units generally were of 50 to 100 slaves. While the optimum sizes of sugar, rice, and tobacco plantations generally fell within a narrow range, that for cotton plantations covered a larger range, most typically between 20 and 50 slaves. Farms without slaves were small, while those with only a few slaves and one white family were at the lower end of the size distribution of slave ownership. Nevertheless, the high frequency of these small farms accounted for a large share of the overall slave population (see Table 7.1).

Starting at the end of the eighteenth century, there were dramatic changes in the location and in the principal crops grown by the slave population. In 1790, almost all southern slaves were residents in states of the Old South, along the eastern seaboard, relatively few living inland within these states. The main crops grown by slaves were tobacco, mainly in Virginia and Maryland, generally on farms of less than twenty workers, and rice, grown primarily in South Carolina and Georgia, on plantations of fifty or more slaves. The "Cotton Kingdom" emerged after Eli Whitney's invention that made possible the removal of seeds from short-staple

[3] See Thomas Ellison, *The Cotton Trade of Great Britain* (London, 1886), p. 86.

cotton, which could then be profitably grown in almost all parts of the South. This led to the westward movement of southern free and slave populations, and by 1860 over 50 percent of slaves were located in the "New South," states which had been lightly settled prior to independence. Cotton became the major crop of the South. It could be grown in all states of the region, unlike tobacco, rice, sugar, and hemp. The growth of the demand for cotton in New England and in Great Britain led to the westward movement of slaves as well as the generally rising slave prices that occurred, with cyclical fluctuations, until the Civil War.

The growing European, particularly British, demand for cotton favored the lower-cost cotton produced in the United States, and the United States soon became the world's largest cotton producer, supplying 70 to 80 percent of the British demand for cotton.[4] In the decades before the Civil War, southern cotton production and exports exceeded the combined total for all other leading producers of cotton around the world – India, Turkey, Egypt, and the West Indies. A steady increase in cotton production characterized the years until the mid-1830s, when the decline in British demand for cotton and financial difficulties in England and the United States led to a major cyclical decline in both countries. This persisted for several years, leading to some defaults of American state bond issues, and sharp falls in the prices of slaves. After the early 1840s, however, the patterns of rising cotton production and slave prices were renewed, and continued up until the start of the Civil War (see Figure 7.1).

The growth of the cotton kingdom was influenced by the general expansion in the American economy. The improvements in transportation, including the introduction of canals, railroads, steamboats, and river and coastal port facilities, as well as in ocean-going transportation, led to increased movements of goods and people. The financial sector increased its efficiency in moving funds within the economy, as well as attracting funds from the nations of Western Europe. The banking system, both under the Second Bank of the United States, as well as after its demise in 1836, and the subsequent emergence of the Independent Treasury System, provided for interregional flows of funds, linking all sections of the nation. And various federal and state legal actions facilitated the emergence of a larger national market. A liberal land policy made land available at low cost, which accelerated the westward movement of the population and relatively low-income farmers becoming landowners. The geographic relocation of the slave and free population was undertaken via land and by waterway, including the use of steamboats on the Mississippi River, canals in several parts of the South, and by ship along the southern coast

[4] Ellison, *Cotton Trade*, p. 86.

Figure 7.1 New Orleans Prime Age Male Slaves Prices 1804–1861

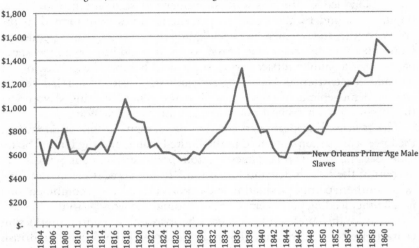

Source: Susan B. Carter, Scott Sigmund Gartner, Michael R. Haines, *et al.* (eds.), *Historical Statistics of the United States: Earliest Times to the Present* (Cambridge, 2006), Vol. 2, pp. 372–3, 381–2.

from the Atlantic Ocean to the Gulf of Mexico, often ending in Mobile or New Orleans.

Those slaves who moved by coastal shipping were recorded on coastal shipping manifests to ensure that they were not being imported from outside of the United States. This movement of the slave population, described by some as "The Second Middle Passage," continued the process of disruption of black family and community life that began with the transatlantic shipment from Africa. Some slaves moved interregionally with their masters, but even if this kept some family members together, it did mean a break-up of some extended families and communities within the slave population. Perhaps more frequent, but more often noted and commented upon by antislavery forces, were movements of only parts of a plantation, or sales involving slave traders, which involved the break-up of families and separations of mothers (and fathers) from their children, of whatever age, and from each other. Since the slave laws did not recognize marriage among slaves, family break-up, with its significant effects on slave behavior and family relations, was always possible.

These decades saw several major slave revolts in the southern states: 1800 in Virginia, 1811 in Louisiana, the Denmark Vesey uprising in South Carolina in 1822, and the Nat Turner rebellion in 1831 Virginia. There were also slave runaways, some of whom, like Frederick Douglass, reached the North and became active in the abolition movement. Yet even with the expanding antislavery movement in the North, there seemed to be no widespread expectation that slavery in the South would soon come to a halt.

The economics of the shifting pattern of crop and geographic change is one that is still not fully understood. Given differences in the knowledge required for owners and the skills needed for slave workers producing different crops, how was such a shift accomplished? Did the expanding number of cotton producers represent a movement from the production of one crop to another or were new farms and plantations created by owners who had previously not been engaged in agriculture? And were the skills and knowledge of slaves, previously important in producing tobacco, rice, and other crops, easily transferred into cotton production with little loss in productivity? Whatever the factors in the transition to cotton production, however, it seemed to have been achieved with substantial output and productivity gains within the South within a relatively short period of time.

The expansion of the cotton-growing area was also aided, in large measure, by the federal government's liberal land policy. The distribution of small southern landholdings was not too dissimilar from that in the North, with a large number of farmers owning relatively small parcels, but with, however, more large units in the South. Also important for southern growth was the development of canals and railroads, and of a national financial system. These linked the North and the South in trade, commerce, and other economic relations.[5] New York emerged as the nation's leading cotton-exporting port. And, on the basis of southern cotton, the New England textile industry expanded, aided by US tariff protection.

The principal agricultural crops of the north were grains, particularly wheat and corn, as well as the products of livestock, while those of the south were cotton, tobacco, rice, and corn. In the aftermath of the War of 1812, the North increased its rate of industrialization, first with cotton textiles, then iron and leather. Industrial development was more limited in the South. These regional differences in economic structure led to significant political differences between the regions. Northern industrialists pushed for tariffs upon industrial imports from England, as opposed to southern planters who wanted to have free trade with lower-cost imports and encouragement of exports of agricultural commodities, particularly cotton. And although the North had many who accepted the continuation of slavery in the South, an antislavery movement had emerged and continued to attract attention and support. In the South, however, the basic concern among slave-owners, and other whites, was to ensure the continuation of slavery. There was, nevertheless, little argument in favor of

[5] Douglass C. North, *The Economic Growth of the United States, 1790–1860* (Englewood Cliffs, NJ, 1961).

reopening the international slave trade. The slave trade was less needed in the US South than elsewhere in the Americas because of the high rate of natural increase of the slave population. Nor was there any large-scale movement to force northern states to reintroduce slavery, given the limited northern demand for larger numbers of slaves. This in turn stemmed from the importance of small family farms in the North, and the high price of slaves set by their greater productivity in the South.

SHIFTING ATTITUDES TO SLAVERY

There were a number of major changes that occurred outside the Southern United States in the period from 1830 to 1860 that were to have a large impact on southern slavery. Starting in 1802, with the ending of the Danish slave trade, other nations ended their slave trade from Africa. The ending of the slave trade by Britain and the United States took place in 1808. Within a quarter of a century, first the Dutch and then the French also banned the traffic. The British fleet played a role in these developments and the British Government enforced slave trade restrictions on Spanish and Portuguese governments via cash bribes. These nations, however, continued to carry slaves to Brazil, which became independent of Portugal in 1822, until the early 1850s, and to the Spanish colony of Cuba until the mid-1860s. Several decades after the ending of the slave trade, the Northern European nations – the British in 1834, the Swedes in 1847, the French and Danes in 1848, and the Dutch in 1863 – ended slavery in their own colonies. Although the Spanish colonies and Brazil did not end slavery until the 1880s, there was by then an extensive worldwide movement against slavery. Some abolitionists predicted slavery's imminent demise, but rising prices for slaves in the US South and elsewhere seemed to suggest that slave-owners thought otherwise.

The British antislavery movement expanded and paid more attention to US slavery. In the United States, there developed two opposing ideological movements. In the North, the abolition movements, black and white, led by key figures such as Frederick Douglass, William Lloyd Garrison, and Wendell Phillips, increased their numbers of political supporters, as well as their political impact.[6] In the South, in response to the increased anti-slavery argument made in the northern states, southerners developed a more vigorous pro-slavery argument, emphasizing the role of slavery as a positive good for both blacks and whites. Race, nevertheless, came to comprise a major component of the pro-slavery defense.

---

[6] Seymour Drescher, *Abolition: A History of Slavery and Antislavery* (Cambridge, 2009).

In addition to the shifting attitudes to slavery in the wider world, there were major economic changes in the North and elsewhere that were to influence beliefs about the differences between slave and free labor. Dramatic changes occurred in the world economy. While expansion westward remained based on agricultural production, in the older areas of New England and the Middle Atlantic states the economy underwent important structural changes. There was, in the aftermath of the war of 1812, a considerable expansion of manufacturing industries, particularly cotton textiles and iron, based on free white labor, both immigrant and native-born. The growth of northern industry, unlike that of southern agriculture, was influenced by tariff protection. These import taxes served to limit imports of British manufacturing production, and became a major source of political conflicts within Congress. The South did experience some manufacturing development, particularly in cotton textiles, iron, and tobacco, often with the use of slave labor, but industrial growth was more limited than in the North. The one agricultural sector of the South that was pro-tariff was the sugar producers in Louisiana, whose survival hinged on limiting sugar imports from the Caribbean and Brazil.

The westward expansion of both North and South led to further Congressional conflicts, in part due to the perceived need for maintaining equality in Congressional representation. There were two important political settlements to accomplish this end. The Missouri Compromise of 1820 admitted one free state (Maine) and one slave state (Missouri). It split the area obtained in the Louisiana Purchase at 36 degrees, 30 minutes latitude. Slavery was allowed below the line, and banned above it. The Compromise of 1850 involved California, Texas, and Washington, DC, as well as the enactment of a Fugitive Slave Law. The subsequent Kansas-Nebraska Act of 1854 left the choice regarding slavery to the residents in the territory, but led to a great deal of conflict and controversy in its aftermath. This was followed by the Supreme Court's Dred Scott decision in 1857 that stated, in effect, that slavery in the United States could not be legislated out of existence and that slaves could not be US citizens. Thus, there developed major political tensions confronting the nation, with major armed conflicts in the Kansas Territory after 1855 followed by John Brown's 1859 attempt to capture the arsenal at Harpers Ferry, then in Virginia.

THE SOUTHERN ECONOMY

The southern economy boomed from the 1820s to the mid-1830s before the collapse of 1837, which also affected the North. Cotton prices and production declined, and slave prices declined about 50 percent from their 1837 peak to 1843. Despite this sharp price decrease, there seemed little discussion at this time about slavery being doomed. When the English demand for cotton recovered and cotton production rose sharply to a peak around 1859, along with the price of slaves, there seemed no concern, on economic grounds, about the viability of slavery. The fact that the northern economic relations with the South continued as before indicates that the northern states also did not anticipate an immediate end to southern slavery.

The southern economy during this period exhibited a great degree of flexibility, with the ongoing westward movement into Texas of both plantations and small farms. There was, over time, a steady rise in cotton production, and a movement of slaves into urban and industrial pursuits when the returns from cotton production fell, with then a movement back to agriculture in times of cotton prosperity. There were also shifts over time between the production of cotton and of corn, based on relative crop prices. In general, however, the South was self-sufficient in food production, and needed to import only certain foodstuffs from the northwestern states. Southern planters were concerned with developing better seeds and sought other forms of productivity improvement, including better management techniques.[7] Southern agricultural magazines included many articles discussing the methods of improved production, with planters exchanging ideas about successful methods. The South had well-developed financial intermediaries, with most states having effective banking systems. Its transportation infrastructure grew, particularly with the extensive 1850s' growth of railroads, linking cotton-producing areas to ports for the shipment of cotton to New York or directly to England. Many planters kept detailed accounting records of their slave numbers and their prices as well as of their expenses and revenues. Thus, rather than being a backward economy with non-commercial-minded plantation owners, the South exhibited, as did the North, many characteristics of a modernizing economy with a well-developed capacity to adapt and change. The South had extensive external economic relations with the North, England, and elsewhere, though it did differ from most other modernizing societies of the time in its commitment to slavery.

Despite some constraints on the treatment of slaves due to slave-owners' interest in making profits, as well as some religious and moral reservations, slave-owners had absolute power over slaves and faced no legal limits on the cruelty they could inflict. Slaves could be bought and sold whenever owners desired, with no attention given to family arrangements among slaves or to the distances which slaves could be moved and separated from members of the slave community. Masters had the legal right to punish slaves, whether by sale or, more frequently,

[7] Alan L. Olmstead and Paul W. Rhode, *Creating Abundance: Biological Innovation and American Agricultural Abundance* (Cambridge, 2008), chs. 4–7.

by whipping, which was always a possible response to what masters believed were infractions of rules of behavior or inappropriate labor effort. The threat, and the actuality, of punishments made life in slavery a condition to be dreaded.

THE CIVIL WAR

The 1850s saw a number of important political controversies develop between North and South.[8] Some led to difficult compromises, but many seemed to lead to expectations in both regions that war over the continuation of slavery might be imminent. The decade was one of considerable prosperity for the South, with a great growth in the demand for cotton in the North and in England, leading to marked expansion in the southern cotton output, bringing it to all-time peak levels. The growth in the demand for cotton led to a movement of slaves from urban areas to rural areas, and from industrial pursuits to cotton plantations. Prices of slaves rose through at least 1859, to all-time peak levels just prior to the Civil War.

The northern states also experienced rapid economic growth in the last antebellum decade, except for a cyclical downturn in 1857, that did not affect the South. The election of 1860 was heatedly contested, with victory going to the newly formed Republican Party and its presidential nominee, Abraham Lincoln. Lincoln's proposal prior to the election, central in his 1858 Illinois debates with Stephen Douglas, was to keep slavery out of the territories, but not to interfere with slavery in the states where it already existed. He defended his position by arguing that, in the absence of technical change, an ability to move to new land due to political or economic factors, or excessive reliance on a single crop would lead eventually to declining prices for slaves, making slavery unprofitable to planters. The end of southern slavery, however, was not immediately expected by Lincoln, who forecast a hundred-year span before it would disappear. Soon after the election of Lincoln, however, war broke out. The southern states held separate conventions and these voted to approve secession.

The role of cotton was important to wartime strategy in both sections. To reduce southern exports of cotton to Europe, as well as to restrict southern imports of manufactured goods, particularly armaments, the North introduced a blockade of southern ports. While there is some disagreement, this blockade was apparently not overly successful after the expansion in the number of southern steam vessels, mainly because the

---

[8] For a still useful study of the onset of the Civil War, see David M. Potter, *The Impending Crisis: America Before the Civil War, 1848–1851* (New York, 1976).

long coastline – from the Atlantic Ocean at Virginia through Florida, and to the Gulf of Mexico ports from Florida to Texas – made tight control by the northern blockaders difficult.

The South had attempted to use the reduction in the cotton supply as a strategic tool to induce the British and French to remain neutral or to actively support their war effort. An additional reason for southerners to reduce cotton output at the start of the war was to move slave labor into greater production of foodstuffs. There were several naval conflicts involving ships carrying cotton across the Atlantic Ocean. The net outcome of the international legal battles and the British response to the "Cotton Famine" was that the British came to favor the North. The reduction in southern cotton production and exports was later to work against the South given that southern credit ultimately hinged on cotton exports.

The basic reason for the failure of the southern cotton strategy was the almost immediate response of cotton producers in other parts of the world to the decline in southern exports to the British. While these nations increased exports to England, they were never able to compensate for the decline in southern cotton exports to Britain. Major increases in cotton imports came from the East Indies, Turkey, Egypt, and Brazil (see Table 7.2). Thus, the maximum decline in British imports of cotton from 1860 to 1862 was about 70 percent, but by 1865 British imports were down only by about 40 percent. After 1865, several of these cotton-exporting nations maintained higher than pre-war levels of cotton exports, but by 1880 the South had recovered close to its pre-war share of British imports, a

Table 7.2 *European Imports of Cotton by Source Country, 1860–1870 (400 lb bales)*

	United States	Brazil	Egypt	Turkey	West Indies	East Indies	Total
1860	4,058	48	135	21	23	552	4,837
1861	3,075	46	124	36	18	949	4,248
1862	102	65	182	58	20	1,010	1,439
1863	163	67	294	127	36	1,179	1,947
1864	241	127	427	188	39	1,374	1,635
1865	522	150	549	239	84	1,231	2,775
1866	1,555	222	279	161	77	1,706	4,000
1867	1,659	220	305	129	103	1,389	3,805
1868	1,956	309	355	145	85	1,476	4,326
1869	1,583	281	353	207	92	1,578	4,094
1870	2,345	217	379	136	79	1,057	4,213

Source: Thomas Ellison, *The Cotton Trade of Great Britain* (London, 1886), p. 91.

share they basically retained into the early twentieth century. The war also saw very sharp declines in southern rice and sugar output, which took longer to recover their antebellum output levels, and in the case of rice meant a shift in the principal location of production from South Carolina to Louisiana and Texas.

The fortunes of war in the earlier years of the conflict seem to have favored the South, but after the events of 1863, the North gained the upper hand, with successful invasions in several different areas of the Confederacy. Given the pre-war expectations of limited southern military capacity, it can be argued that the South had prolonged the war far longer than most contemporaries had anticipated. The war was costly – in terms of manpower as well as resources. Recent estimates suggest about 623,036 deaths (mostly from disease), with almost 60 percent of them in the North. The number wounded equaled about three-quarters the number who died. (This was not the most costly war in this time period. Often ignored by US scholars are the estimated 20 million deaths in the Chinese Taiping Rebellion of 1850 to 1866.)

The entrance of northern troops into the South led to much instability in the southern economy and society. With some protection from northern troops, and despite the conflicts between the army and the administration in Washington about the return of slave runaways, the number of runaways who successfully left their plantations greatly increased. Large numbers joined the northern army, in segregated divisions, and fought in a number of major battles against the Confederacy. These soldiers initially were paid less than white soldiers, a source of major objection by the ex-slaves among the many complaints about how they were treated while in the northern army. The number of runaways led to the dissolution of the plantations, and freedom for some parts of the slave population. In this sense, the slaves freed themselves, though with the support and backing of the northern troops.

With the ending of the war the Thirteenth, Fourteenth, and Fifteenth Amendments meant the ending of slavery and the provision of rights to the ex-slaves. The slave-owners lost their main asset, without any compensation – the only major instance of abolition in the Americas without any payment to the slave-owners in cash, bonds, or labor time. As elsewhere, however, no payment was made to ex-slaves, nor in the United States were the freedmen given what some felt had been promised – "forty acres and a mule." The southern landowners were permitted to keep their land and livestock, but the value of land had decreased given that planters were unable to force ex-slaves back into plantation labor in significant numbers. The North created the Freedmen's Bureau to help mediate the labor arrangements between landowners and ex-slaves. As with the Stipendiary Magistrates in the British West Indies, the Freedmen's Bureau, before its demise in the 1870s, was accused of operating on behalf of the landowners to obtain labor from ex-slaves. The presence of northern troops in the

South had mixed effects on the ex-slaves in the period of Reconstruction, before it ended in 1877.[9] They did provide some limited restriction on white violence against blacks. While there were some gains for ex-slaves, these were often small, and less than the ex-slaves had hoped for and expected. And, in many cases, any gains were subsequently reversed by southern actions and legislation.

THE POSTBELLUM PERIOD

The end of the Civil War saw a marked decline in per capita southern income, of about 20 percent, after which southern income grew at roughly the same rate as that of the North for the next half-century, before converging on the northern income level by the 1980s. Declines in per capita income characterized most societies after the ending of slavery, due in large part to the reduced role of the plantation system in export crop production. While the South suffered wartime damages and disorganization due to the loss of control over the ex-slaves, the longer-term impact of tobacco the conflict came from the ending of plantation production of cotton, rice, and sugar (see Table 7.3). Cotton output returned to antebellum levels in less than two decades, and came close to regaining its share of world cotton output by 1880, a share retained until the 1910s. This, however, was with a different structure of cotton production than in antebellum times. While the planters would have preferred to return to a plantation system with coerced labor, and attempted to do so with several different methods of coercing labor, such as coerced waged labor, sharecropping, and debt bondage, such strategies were not fully successful in forcing higher labor inputs from the slaves. While most ex-slaves remained in cotton production, this was on the basis of small farms, as tenants on land rented from white landowners, or as wage workers or sharecroppers for white landowners, or else on their own land purchased after emancipation. These units, however, were less efficient in producing cotton than were the pre-war plantations. This meant that white farmers, on relatively small farms, were now able to compete with blacks in cotton production, and the share of cotton grown by white farmers increased relative to their antebellum share. The fact that whites and ex-slaves now produced the same crop had important social and political effects when the cotton market collapsed in the 1890s. Many of what had been regarded as favorable changes for ex-slaves in the previous decades were then reversed, and what was described as the "black nadir" came to characterize the next half-century.

---

[9] See Eric Foner, *Reconstruction: America's Unfinished Revolution, 1863–1877* (New York, 1988).

Table 7.3 *Changes in the Outputs of Four Major Plantation Crops of the US South prior to and after the Civil War*

	Average Output 1856–60	Average Output 1867–71	Period in Which Pre-Civil War Level Regained
Cotton (million lbs.)	1,720.2	1,323.6	1871–75
Tobacco (million lbs.)	434.2	284.3	1877–81
Rice (million lbs)	123.3	47.9	1882–86
Sugar (thousand tons)	132.4	54.4	1884–88

Source: Herbert S. Klein and Stanley L. Engerman, "The Transition from Slave to Free Labor: Notes on a Comparative Economic Model," in Manuel Moreno Fraginals, Frank Moya Pons, and Stanley L. Engerman (eds.), *Between Slavery and Free Labor: The Spanish Speaking Caribbean in the Nineteenth Century* (Baltimore, MD, 1985), pp. 225–69 (on p. 266).

A frequently commented-on form of post-emancipation coercion of black labor was convict leasing, wherein prisoners were leased to perform labor for private individuals and businesses. This lowered the costs of incarceration and provided a source of income for state governments. Such labor was often organized into gangs, and this system was frequently used in mining, agriculture, and some other industries, including the production of turpentine. The convict labor system in most southern states ended by the first decade of the twentieth century, but was followed by another system of coerced labor, chain gangs for public works, operated by state and local governments. Although neither convict leasing nor the chain gang system still exist, there remain important debates about the relative rates of black and white imprisonment, given the current higher imprisonment rate for blacks (seven times that of whites) and the extent to which it reflects racial discrimination.

After the war, women and children reduced their participation in agriculture somewhat. This often meant a shift in the type of labor performed or else a seasonal reallocation of work, rather than a complete withdrawal from the labor force. For black women, the most frequent form of employment initially, in addition to agricultural work, was as domestic servants, either as day workers or resident housekeepers. The occupational structure of blacks changed both within the South and nationally after 1915. Black males moved out of agriculture into other occupations, including industry in the South and, with the northward movement during and after the First World War, to industrial and other pursuits in urban areas. Women left domestic service at quite a rapid rate in both the North and South, moving into both industrial and service sector jobs. The labor force participation rate for black women exceeded that of white females and their wages were relatively higher compared to white women than was the case for males.

The first decades after emancipation contained many economic and physical hardships for the ex-slaves, but there were some favorable changes. Blacks were given the vote, and before 1890 more than twenty black Congressmen were elected, in addition to a larger number of state and local representatives. This was reversed within several decades with the introduction of literacy tests (arbitrarily enforced) and grandfather clauses (restricting voting to those whose grandfathers had voted). These obviously excluded black ex-slaves and served to basically disenfranchise black voters in the South.

Blacks were able to increase their ownership of land used to produce agricultural crops from virtually zero to about 20 percent by 1880.[10] Due to expenditures by blacks, white philanthropists, and various levels of government, black education increased, though expenditures per pupil were less than that for whites. Such expenditures were, however, at a higher ratio before 1890 than was to take place after 1890, and this continued to be the case until the Supreme Court decision in *Brown* v. *Topeka* in 1954. Changes after the 1890s meant the quality and magnitude of black education declined. This increased the large gap between black and white education levels, and such relative differentials in education – and consequently in employment opportunities – were to persist for many decades.[11]

Lynchings, sometimes of whites (particularly immigrants), but mostly of black males, increased in the 1880s, rising to a peak of over 100 per year in the 1890s before declining to small numbers by the 1930s and 1940s, even with the absence of any federal legislation to end this practice.

THE TWENTIETH CENTURY

From 1870 to 1915, most blacks remained in the rural South, but there was a movement from the southeast to the southwest. Generally, however, black males remained within agricultural production, mainly on cotton farms, though there was some movement into newly established industries, particularly cotton textiles in North and South Carolina and iron and steel in Alabama before 1900, and a strong oil industry in Texas after the 1920s.

Major setbacks to black Americans occurred in the decade of the 1890s, a period of cotton collapse. The Supreme Court's 1894 decision in *Plessy* v. *Ferguson* symbolized the changes in southern racial relations, providing a

---

[10] Claude F. Oubre, *Forty Acres and a Mule: The Freedmen's Bureau and Black Landownership* (Baton Rouge, LA, 1978).

[11] Robert A. Margo, *Race and Schooling in the South: 1880–1950: An Economic History* (Chicago, IL, 1990).

legal basis for racial segregation by imposing the doctrine of "separate but equal," which, however, led to more inequality and the maintenance of separate facilities. In the 1890s, blacks were prevented from voting by arbitrarily enforced devices such as literacy tests, grandfather clauses, and white primaries, in addition to violence and intimidation. These conditions were not substantially changed until a number of twentieth-century judicial and legislative decisions forced changes at the federal and state levels. It was not, however, until the Civil Rights Acts of the 1950s and 1960s that there was a major increase in black voting and political representation.

After a half-century of limited outmigration from the South, the location of the black population changed markedly after 1915. This was triggered by two important political events, which led to significant changes in international migration. Prior to the Civil War, the preferred response to increased demand for industrial labor during northern cyclical expansion was the attraction of immigrants from Western Europe. After the Civil War, immigration from Eastern and Central Europe became substantial. This meant that the North was not drawing to any great extent on the pool of black (and white) labor from the South. With the onset of the First World War in 1914, the costs and lack of availability of European immigrants made a continuation of European immigration at the earlier high amounts very expensive. The alternative for the northern employers was to attract black and white labor from the South. After the war ended, the American labor movement succeeded in its long-time goal of reducing immigration to make way for higher wages for native workers. The various immigration acts of the 1920s and 1930s meant that northern labor demands were met by black labor, with the movement from rural southern agricultural labor to urban northern industrial workers.[12] In response to northern cyclical fluctuations, the share of the black population in the North rose to approximately 50 percent, with major implications for black social and industrial life, and in the nature and success of black protest movements.

These black protest movements achieved major success after the 1940s. The most influential of the black protest movements was the National Association for the Advancement of Colored People (NAACP), founded in 1910. The NAACP was an important protest movement from the moment of its formation. Perhaps its most important contribution was its series of successful attacks leading to increased and improved black education. It played a major role in the key *Brown* v. *Topeka* decision in 1954, which reversed the 1896 *Plessy* decision, and proclaimed that separate was

[12] William J. Collins, "When the Tide Turned: Immigration and the Delay of the Great Black Migration," *Journal of Economic History*, 57 (1997): 607–32.

inherently unequal. It provided for the integration of American schools, albeit a long, drawn-out process.

The *Brown* decision was the last step in a series of attacks on discrimination in teachers' salaries and segregation of law schools, a program devised by the NAACP lawyers Thurgood Marshall and Charles Hamilton Houston.[13] Other successes, by legal and governmental measures, resulted in the ending of formal segregation of housing and the integration of the American armed forces in 1948.

The nature of the black family and the magnitude of black illegitimate births has long been an important issue. The break-up of black families under slavery and afterward was a major part of the abolitionist attack on slavery. The argument continued after emancipation, since it was argued that slavery was the cause of what some saw as the subsequent weakness of the black family. This controversy came to a peak with the controversial Moynihan Report in 1965 on the role of the legacy of slavery in creating what was described as "the pathology of the black family," at a time when the ratio of female-headed households and illegitimacy among females was about 33 percent, as it had been for about a century. Since the mid-1960s, both measures have about doubled, illegitimacy rising to about 78 percent and female-headed households to over 40 percent. The current debate is whether this change represents a legacy of slavery or is, perhaps, to be seen as a response to recent economic and social conditions, including high unemployment and low incomes.[14] This question may, of course, be raised about other aspects of the black situation today.

Since the Second World War, there has been some favorable relative improvement in measures of black vs. white income, educational attainment, and black political representation. There remain, however, substantial differences in these measures and there remain major differences in patterns of housing segregation and occupational structure. While some point to the extent of improvements in race relations over time, for others there remains great room for further improvement and more progress.

A GUIDE TO FURTHER READING

A very useful starting point is the recent collection of essays on slavery in the United States and Latin America: Robert Paquette and Mark Smith (eds.), *The Oxford Handbook of Slavery in the Americas* (New York, 2010). This contains excellent essays on many countries and topics of interest and provides a basic

[13] Richard Kluger, *Simple Justice: The History of Brown v. Board of Education and Black America's Struggle for Equality* (New York, 1975).
[14] William Julius Wilson, *When Work Disappears: The World of the New Urban Poor* (New York, 1996).

guide to both the history and historiography of slavery in the Americas. A magisterial study of slavery in world history are the four volumes by David Brion Davis, culminating in his recent *The Problem of Slavery in the Age of Emancipation* (New York, 2014). The major book on the history of blacks in America from start to date is the ninth edition of John Hope Franklin and Evelyn Brooks Higginbotham, *From Slavery to Freedom: A History of Black Americans* (New York, 2010).

Three classic works on US slavery published decades ago and demonstrating the changes in interpretation and in questions asked are: Ulrich B. Phillips, *American Negro Slavery* (New York, 1918); Kenneth Stampp, *The Peculiar Institution: Slavery in the Ante-Bellum South* (New York, 1956); and Eugene D. Genovese, *Roll, Jordan, Roll: The World the Slaves Made* (New York, 1974). Each deals with a broad range of substantive issues, including the economics of slavery.

Key writings by slaves dealing with their experiences under slavery are those by Frederick Douglass, particularly his third autobiography *Life and Times of Frederick Douglass Written by Himself* (Hartford, CT, 1882); Charles Ball, *Fifty Years in Chains or the Life of an American Slave* (New York, 1858); and Solomon Northup, *Twelve Years a Slave* (Auburn, NY, 1853). Important discussions of major topics in southern history and the history of slavery include: Lewis Cecil Gray, *History of Agriculture in the Southern United States to 1860* (Washington, DC, 1933), on southern agriculture; Douglass C. North, *The Economic Growth of the United States, 1790–1860* (Englewood Cliffs, NJ, 1961), on international and interregional trade; Claudia Dale Goldin, *Urban Slavery in the American South, 1820–1860: A Quantitative History* (Chicago, IL, 1976), on urban slavery.

The current debate on the economics of slavery begins with the classic article by Alfred H. Conrad and John R. Meyer, "The Economics of Slavery in the Ante Bellum South," *Journal of Political Economy*, 66 (1958): 95–130. A major work on various aspects of slavery as an economic institution was Robert William Fogel and Stanley L. Engerman, *Time on the Cross: The Economics of American Negro Slavery*, 2 vols. (Boston, MA, 1974), which became rather controversial and triggered numerous debates: see Paul A. David, Herbert G. Gutman, Richard Sutch, Peter Temin, and Gavin Wright, *Reckoning with Slavery: A Critical Study in the Quantitative History of American Negro Slavery* (New York, 1976); Herbert G. Gutman, *Slavery and the Numbers Game: A Critique of Time on the Cross* (Urbana, IL, 1975); and Gavin Wright, *Slavery and American Economic Development* (Baton Rouge, LA, 2006). In turn, it was defended by Robert Fogel, *Without Consent or Contract: The Rise and Fall of American Slavery* (New York, 1989).

For the end of slavery and its aftermath, see Robert Higgs, *Competition and Coercion: Blacks in the American Economy, 1865–1914* (Cambridge, 1977); and Roger L. Ransom and Richard Sutch, *One Kind of Freedom: The Economic Consequences of Emancipation* (Cambridge, 1977). For an excellent discussion of post-emancipation black economic developments, see Robert A. Margo, "Obama, Katrina and the Persistence of Racial Inequality," *Journal of Economic History*, 76 (2016): 301–41.

CHAPTER 8

SLAVERY IN AFRICA, 1804–1936

GARETH AUSTIN

For much of the twentieth century, the place of sub-Saharan Africa in the world history of slavery was commonly seen as that of victim. While sub-Saharan elites may have responded under pressure to both New and Old World demands for slaves, slavery in Africa itself tended to be seen as smaller in scale and milder and less economically exploitative in character than Euro-American and Ottoman slavery. This view was consistent with multiple interests and ideological perspectives in the early twentieth century. Chiefs and emirs sought to justify keeping their slaves as long as possible; many colonial officials wished to avoid difficult questions about the slowness with which their commitment to abolition was actually implemented; and structural-functionalist anthropologists tended to downplay conflict and exploitation in the societies they studied. Colonial-era amnesia about slavery in Africa was rarely challenged when, inspired by decolonization, research into pre-colonial history took off in the 1950s and 1960s.

The post-independence reticence about inquiries that might reveal repression and exploitation within pre-colonial African societies was definitively disrupted in the 1970s. Two pioneering collections of essays edited, respectively, by Claude Meillassoux (in French) and by Suzanne Miers and Igor Kopytoff (in English), opened the door to research which has continued to the time of writing.[1] The same decade saw the delineation of the principal axes of the debate about the motivation and other determinants of the existence, scale, and characteristics of slavery in Africa, inspired respectively by market economics, structural-functionalism (again), and Marxism; lines of argument that, revised and integrated with later theoretical influences, such as an insistence on the primacy of cultural choices, remain important today.[2] Empirical investigation has extended to the

---

[1] Claude Meillassoux (ed.), *L'esclavage en Afrique précoloniale* (Paris, 1975); Suzanne Miers and Igor Kopytoff (eds.), *Slavery in Africa: Historical and Anthropological Perspectives* (Madison, WI, 1977).

[2] Seminal early statements: A. G. Hopkins, *An Economic History of West Africa* (London, 1973), pp. 23–7; Igor Kopytoff and Suzanne Miers, "Slavery as an Institution of Marginality," in Miers and Kopytoff (eds.), *Slavery in Africa*, pp. 3–81; Emmanuel Terray, "La captivité dans le royaume Abron du Gyaman," in Meillassoux, *L'Esclavage en Afrique précoloniale*, pp. 389–453; and, for the culturalist

persistence of slavery, in many areas, well into the twentieth century, despite the abolitionist commitments of the European powers who partitioned Africa in the 1880s and 1890s. From this research, as we shall see, it is now clear that nineteenth-century Africa (even omitting Ottoman North Africa) was home to a large proportion of the world's slaves, that many of them were treated very violently, and that slaves were often a key part of the labor force. At the same time, many African slave systems differed from those in some other parts of the world in allowing for the at least partial assimilation of children of slave descent into the master's society. African slave-owners were no victims, but the circumstances under which they operated, and the strategies they used in response, were often rather different from those facing their counterparts in the Ottoman Empire or the Americas. It is the latter that has been the traditional comparator in discussions of African slavery, usually with the refrain that slavery in Africa was different from that in the Americas. This was surely true, but is of secondary importance once we place African slaveries in the context of the global history of slavery: slave systems differed to some extent over place and time within sub-Saharan Africa, and insofar as we can generalize about them, they differed from slave systems prominent in other parts of the Old World, as well as the New.

The basic achievement of the research on slavery in Africa has been to outline, and in some cases to detail, actual histories of slavery, including changes in the scale and characteristics of local forms of servitude within particular polities. This supersedes an older practice, now discredited among historians and anthropologists, of relying on colonial-period ethnography to answer, simply and ahistorically, whether or not slavery existed (as if for all time) in such and such a society (defined in primordially ethnic terms).[3] There is much we do not yet know and much we can never know. But today, the difficulty in writing a synthesizing essay is not only the remaining gaps in the gathered evidence, but also its complexity. This applies, not least, to the problem of classification. Many African languages distinguished several categories of servitude, raising the question of which ones – jurally, and in practice – fit the definition(s) usually adopted in European languages.

The definition of slavery used in this chapter integrates three essential elements: powerlessness, property, and "social death."[4] First, slaves were,

---

position, John Thornton, *Africa and Africans in the Making of the Atlantic World, 1400–1800*, 2nd edn. (Cambridge, 1998).

[3] The apotheosis of the old approach was G. P. Murdock's *Ethnographic Atlas* (Pittsburgh, PA, 1967). Regrettably, there is a current tendency among some economists to treat this as their database for pre-colonial Africa, simply because it already exists. I hope that energies will be redirected into making use of the now rich historiography of African slavery to develop a seriously historical, suitably contextualized, database.

[4] In the phrase of Orlando Patterson, *Slavery and Social Death: A Comparative Study* (Cambridge, MA, 1982).

in principle, totally subordinate to and dependent on their masters. But that does not necessarily distinguish slaves, and especially slave labor, from prison labor, for example. Second, however, the powerlessness and dependence of slaves stemmed from the status of being someone's property. This was manifested most clearly in the capacity of owners to sell slaves. In many societies, before colonial rule, this was a realistic possibility; though there were also cases in which this was unlikely, at least in practice. Third, in slavery the powerlessness of the slave, and her or his status as property, was socially and jurally grounded in being – at least originally – a social outsider. The "otherness" of slaves makes "internal slavery" an oxymoron.[5] Specifically, they were considered kinless at the moment of induction into the society as a slave. In most slave-holding societies in Africa, first-generation slaves were literally outsiders: brought into the polity (however small or large) from outside, they were thus foreign in provenance and often in language, culture, and real or assumed social characteristics. In some polities, a small minority of the first-generation slaves were indigenous: they had been reduced to slavery by judicial decision, and were regarded as having exiled themselves from the community by their criminal behavior, even though they remained physically within it.

The following discussion has five substantive sections, which respectively try to identify the major trends in slavery in the period; consider how far slave systems in Africa allowed for the social assimilation of slaves; discuss the evidence on the incidence of slavery on the eve of colonization, and on the earlier trends; tackle the question of why slavery, and why there were so many slaves in this period; and review the socially and geographically uneven decline of slavery in the early twentieth century.

DEFINING THE PERIOD: EXPANSIONIST AND ABOLITIONIST TENDENCIES, 1804–1936

Following definition, the other basic act of synthesis here is to identify the general characteristics of the period under review in the history of slavery in Africa. This will explain the chronological span of the chapter, and enable us to define what requires explanation in later sections. Two opposite, yet paradoxically connected, impulses can be identified: the expansion of slavery and slave trading, and abolitionism. In both cases, the first decade of the nineteenth century may be regarded as a starting point.

[5] Or even a contradiction in terms. See Olivier Pétré-Grenouilleau, *Qu'est-ce que l'esclavage?* (Paris, 2014).

Unlike earlier abolitions, the British withdrawal from the slave trade, in 1807, brought the abolition movement to Africa permanently. It had a major immediate effect in West Africa and at the Cape, and a cumulative impact on other Euro-American slave-trading countries, because of the diplomatic campaign that Britain launched to persuade or cajole others into doing the same. The later abolitions of slavery itself by Britain (1834), France (1848), and others had more localized impacts, important though 1834 was for the slaves and slave-owners of the Western Cape, and 1848 for their counterparts on the coast of Senegal, because the countries concerned had relatively little territory in Africa at the time. The British implemented the abolition of slavery when they took over the Gold Coast (the southern quarter or so of what is now Ghana) in 1874, having used naval power the previous year against the Sultan of Zanzibar to combat the slave trade from East Africa.

But once the Scramble for Africa got going, in 1879, the new colonial administrations tended to blend abolitionist steps into a fundamentally gradualist approach to the eradication of slavery. Usually, they announced the prohibition of slave raiding and trading very promptly, but in many areas proceeded to tolerate slave-holding for a number of years, or even decades – as elsewhere in the colonial world. 1936 may be said to symbolize the end of this period. In that year, under pressure from the League of Nations, the very staggered decline of slavery in the area that had probably had the most slaves in Africa on the eve of colonization, finally reached the point where "all persons" were "declared free" in law. This was Northern Nigeria, which included most of the former Sokoto Caliphate, plus the former kingdom of Borno. At this moment of abolition there, more than thirty years into British rule, the total number of slaves, plus former slaves and children of slaves still living in conditions approximating to slavery, approached 400,000, according to the estimate of Paul Lovejoy and Jan Hogendorn. Many were the "supposedly free daughters of slaves," taken into a form of servile concubinage.[6]

In general, though, despite the tendency for colonial tolerance of slavery, which in some places initially included returning escaped slaves to their masters, abolitionism circumscribed the last years of legal slavery. Even where slave-holding remained legal, if there were no supplies of newly imported captives to purchase, and slaves were threatening to leave their masters in expectation of emancipation, the masters had to ameliorate their harshness and negotiate, tacitly or explicitly, to try to persuade their slaves to stay.

---

[6] Paul E. Lovejoy and Jan S. Hogendorn, *Slow Death for Slavery: The Course of Abolition in Northern Nigeria, 1897–1936* (Cambridge, 1993), pp. 260, 278–83, 363.

The contrary impulse, expansion of the trading and holding of slaves, was a major feature of the "emancipatory" nineteenth century in sub-Saharan Africa. The export trades to the north and east are thought to have reached their all-time peaks during the century, with an estimated 1.2 million slaves entering the Saharan trade, and 934,000 embarked into the Red Sea and Indian Ocean trades.[7] Even the Atlantic trade, though generally in decline in West Africa from 1807, continued very strongly for several decades, especially further south, from Angola to Brazil. Overall, more than 2.8 million African slaves are estimated to have been embarked for the Americas between the coming into force of the British abolition law, on May 1, 1807, and the departure of the last ship in 1866.[8] Meanwhile, the trading and holding of slaves within the sub-continent was on the rise. Admittedly, we cannot give a figure for this, especially as we have only vague ideas about how many slaves there were at the beginning of the century. But it is clear from a string of carefully researched monographs that very large numbers of slaves were added to the population of kingdoms in tropical Africa during the century, under both Animist and Muslim regimes; albeit, the demand for slave labor was from arable and mixed farming areas much more than from pastoral ones. The year 1804, the starting date of this volume, is an appropriate marker here, not because of the achievement of Haitian independence, but because it saw the proclamation, by Uthman dan Fodio, of the jihad which created the Sokoto Caliphate. It seems clear that the Caliphate became not only the largest African-ruled state of its era, territorially and demographically, but the largest slave-owning state in sub-Saharan Africa. Slave labor was applied to produce the raw materials of the cotton cloth industry of Kano and other cities of the Caliphate, with the final products being exported over much of West Africa and beyond. This epitomized the link (to which we will return below) between the intensification of slavery and the growth of commodity production, in this case for African markets. The raiding and buying of slaves increased similarly in other states in West Africa, notably the kingdom of Asante in South Central Ghana. But the starkest increase was perhaps in the Great Lakes region of East-Central Africa, notably in the kingdom of Buganda. On the East African coast, from Somalia to Tanzania, the scale of plantation slavery increased along with the seaborne export of slaves, both being supplied from the same source,

---

[7] Paul E. Lovejoy, *Transformations in Slavery: A History of Slavery in Africa*, 3rd edn. (Cambridge, 2012), p. 138. These figures build upon the pioneering work of, in particular, Ralph Austen, starting with his "The Trans-Saharan Slave Trade: A Tentative Census," in H. A. Gemery and J. S. Hogendorn (eds.), *The Uncommon Market: Essays in the Economic History of the Atlantic Slave Trade* (New York, 1979). The figures for the Atlantic shipments are calculated from *Voyages: The Transatlantic Slave Trade Database*, www.slavevoyages.org (2008).

[8] *Voyages*.

the trade routes that Arab traders pioneered into the interior during the mid nineteenth century, which were then further developed by African slave traders and warlords. In Southern Mozambique, slavery appears to have proliferated in the Gaza kingdom from the 1860s to the 1890s, freeing Gaza men for migrant labor in South Africa. Finally, though the material base of the Ethiopian elite had long been tribute extracted from peasants, in a system comparable to, though different from, European feudalism, the southward expansion of the empire during the late nineteenth century generated very large numbers of captives, many thousands of whom were exported.[9]

Opposed as they were by definition, abolitionism and expansionism had important connections. First, the closing of the Atlantic export market for slaves obliged rulers and merchants in Western Africa to seek other commodities to fill the gap in their import-purchasing power; and slaves constituted an obvious source of labor to produce palm oil, groundnuts, or gold, as they continued to be available for purchase through the same mechanisms of war and raiding that had expanded to generate them for sale to ship captains. The fall in the price of slaves within West Africa in the aftermath of British abolition made it easier for Africans to buy them. The ironic combination of "legitimate commerce" and slave labor was reproduced later on the eastern coast, when the campaign against the seaborne trade eventually took effect there. Second, it is arguable that slaving and abolition represented different phases of the growth of the market, and indeed of capitalism; phases that overlapped in African history. The growth of commodity production, whether inspired by the European or Omani trading networks, or by intra-African regional networks such as the Hausa and Dioula ones in West Africa, or the Yao network in the Zambezi Valley, created labor demands that slavery could supply. Meanwhile, the transition to industrial capitalism was accompanied by the emergence of a new self-image of modernity, notably in Britain, within which slavery did not belong.[10]

---

[9] On the examples given in this paragraph, see Paul E. Lovejoy, *Slavery, Commerce and Production in the Sokoto Caliphate of West Africa* (Trenton, NJ, 2006); Gareth Austin, *Labour, Land and Capital in Ghana: From Slavery to Free Labour* (Rochester, NY, 2005); Richard Reid, *Political Power in Pre-Colonial Buganda: Economy, Society and Warfare in the Nineteenth Century* (Oxford, 2002); Frederick Cooper, *Plantation Slavery on the East Coast of Africa* (New Haven, CT, 1977); Patrick Harries, "Slavery, Social Incorporation and Surplus Extraction: The Nature of Free and Unfree Labour in South-East Africa," *Journal of African History*, 22 (1981): 309–30; Thomas Fernyhough, "Slavery and the Slave Trade in Southern Ethiopia in the 19th Century," in William Gervase Clarence-Smith (ed.), *The Economics of the Indian Ocean Slave Trade in the Nineteenth Century* (London, 1989), pp. 103–30.

[10] Howard Temperley, "The Ideology of Anti-Slavery," in David Eltis and James Walvin (eds.), *The Abolition of the Atlantic Slave Trade* (Madison, WI, 1981), pp. 21–35.

VARIATIONS AND CHANGE: SOCIAL INCORPORATION,
GENDER, SPATIAL DEPLOYMENT, AND HARSHNESS

The most distinctive attribute of slavery in Africa has often been seen as the tendency for slaves or, more so, their descendants to be at least partly assimilated in the slave-owning communities. Indeed, Kopytoff and Miers, in a classic essay introducing their 1977 volume, interpreted African slavery as a mechanism of social incorporation of outsiders.[11] There is an important gender dimension to this. There was also striking variation in the extent of social assimilation over time and space, which was associated to some extent with other variations, notably in the spatial concentration or dispersion of slaves, and also in the harshness of slavery with respect to work and punishment.

The European slave-holders at the Cape and on some of the islands maintained the fully hereditary pattern of slavery notorious from the New World: with no regular route to manumission or to any formal amelioration of status. Islamic scholars in West Africa taught that only non-Muslims could be enslaved, albeit with differences among themselves over the interpretation of the principle. One noted treatise dealt with the problem of opportunistic conversion, stipulating that when Muslim armies took prisoners who claimed to want to convert to Islam, and to be therefore ineligible for enslavement, this claim should be accepted only when the captives had been trying to reach territory controlled by Muslim forces, rather than fleeing in the opposite direction.[12] Once enslaved, prospects for manumission through conversion presumably depended greatly on the owner, and the situation. In the Sokoto Caliphate, for example, many slave villages or large plantations were established in which everyone, even the overseer, was a slave. It is hard to imagine how social integration into the dominant society could occur in this setting, even over several generations.

The forest kingdom of Asante, centered in South Central Ghana, is more representative of the notion of African slavery as a mechanism of social incorporation; but it also illustrates the frequent limits of such mechanisms. In nineteenth-century Asante, there was a recognized path toward a form of increasing integration which would never reach the point of equal status with free subjects. First-generation slaves were obtained overwhelmingly from outside, variously by direct capture in warfare, in annual tribute from subordinated states, or by purchase in the markets of the savanna. During most of the nineteenth century, they came mainly

[11] Kopytoff and Miers, "Slavery as an Institution of Marginality," pp. 3–81.
[12] John Ralph Willis, "Introduction: The Ideology of Enslavement in Islam" and "Jihad and the Ideology of Enslavement," in Willis (ed.), *Slaves and Slavery in Muslim Africa* (London, 1985), Vol. I, pp. 1–46.

from the savanna societies to the north, and as such were described by a highly derogatory term, underlining their otherness. However, children born to first-generation slave mothers, with Asante fathers, were described by a word literally meaning "children of the hearth," and they seem to have been at much less risk of being sold (whether within Asante or outside) than the first-generation slaves. They and their own descendants were officially regarded as members of their [free] fathers' matrilineages. Thus, they were not slaves, in the sense defined above. Moreover, their slave descent itself was concealed by a rule forbidding the revelation of anyone's social origins. Yet people of slave descent were not allowed to become chiefs, and even decades after the colonial abolition of slavery in 1908, it was not uncommon for candidates for chieftaincy to be "accused" of having a slave grandmother, and to be therefore ineligible. Nearly a century after abolition, the highest court in Ghana upheld this rule in a dispute over the succession to the second most prestigious chieftaincy in Asante.[13]

Among African slave systems which allowed for widespread assimilation in the long term, a fundamental limitation was that most excluded male slaves from initiating the process. Meillassoux argued that in the patrilineal savanna-sahelian societies in West Africa, they were strictly forbidden from sexual relations, let alone parenthood, with non-slave women.[14] It was similar in practice in the matrilineal forest case of Asante.[15] But it was not universal. In another matrilineal society, the Mang'anja of the Shire Valley in Malawi, slaves were regarded as "non-human beings," yet male slaves were given the incentive of being allowed to marry a freewoman and start a family. In Elias Mandala's phrase, marriage was "the highest form of manumission."[16]

Meanwhile, the fact that women were much more commonly incorporated in the family (in the broadest possible sense) than men is at least consistent with a plausible and often-repeated claim, that the majority of

---

[13] Strikingly, the court upheld the rule directly, instead of taking the softer option of ruling the candidate ineligible on grounds of kinship: Asante being matrilineal, by definition anyone descended from a female slave could not technically be eligible, as descent in a royal family is matrilineal. I am grateful to Dr. Kofi Baku for drawing this case to my attention. See further, Kofi Baku, "Incomplete Emancipation: The Uncertain Legal, Political and Social Status of Former Slaves and Their Descendants in the Gold Coast, 1874–1995," in Trevor Getz and Rebecca Shumway (eds.), *Slavery and Its Legacy in Ghana and the Diaspora* (London, forthcoming). On the earlier points in the paragraph, see Austin, *Labour, Land and Capital*; Akosua Perbi, *A History of Indigenous Slavery in Ghana: From the 15th to the 19th Century* (Accra, 2004).

[14] Claude Meillassoux, *The Anthropology of Slavery: The Womb of Iron and Gold*, trans. Alide Dasnois (Chicago, IL, 1991), pp. 132–3.

[15] Austin, *Labour, Land and Capital*, pp. 118, 485.

[16] Elias C. Mandala, *Work and Control in a Peasant Economy: A History of the Lower Tchiri Valley in Malawi 1859–1960* (Madison, WI, 1990), pp. 33–4 and 34, respectively.

slaves in Africa were female.[17] In any case, marriage to a slave could be a good strategic option for a freeman: minimizing marriage payments and, in matrilineal societies, enabling men to get around the problem that their children by free wives belonged to their wives' lineages, not to their own. As Emmanuel Terray commented for Asante, a son by a slave wife was "at once a son and a nephew."[18]

Slaves were deployed in contrasting forms: added in ones and twos to commoner households, with the likelihood of partial assimilation ("domestic slavery"); concentrated in large numbers to feed and otherwise serve a ruler ("court slavery"); and/or settled in distinct villages or plantations ("plantation slavery"). In the nineteenth century, states typically combined at least the first two of these, while the third was found on the Arab-Swahili-controlled east coast as well as in parts of West Africa. While domestic slavery may have tended to be the most assimilative of the three, court slavery made it easier for a tiny number of male slaves to obtain exceptional promotion within the state, to become senior administrators or even generals, and to acquire many slaves themselves.[19]

Punishment could be very harsh, including death, though in centralized states such as Asante or the Lozi kingdom (Bulozi, in what is now Zambia), the ruler reserved decisions on life and death for himself.[20] The ruling elites of certain states, such as Buganda, believed that when prominent people died, they should be accompanied to the afterlife by servants; slaves were the obvious candidates to fulfill the need. Punishment and service were combined, at least at the level of threat, in the option open to Asante masters, of sending any recalcitrant slaves to a village where slaves were kept ready for any prominent death.[21]

In domestic slavery, at least, the material life of slaves was often similar to that of free peasants, but under much greater constraints, including lack of mobility, and, often, less appetizing food and less convenient accommodation. In late-nineteenth-century Asante, only slaves ate cassava, which the rest of the population despised; in Bulozi, slaves lived in unenclosed cottages on the edge of villages; unlike all

[17] Claire C. Robertson and Martin A. Klein (eds.), *Women and Slavery in Africa* (Madison, WI, 1983), p. 1.

[18] Terray, "La captivité," p. 440.

[19] Robin Law, *The Oyo Empire c.1600–c.1836: A West African Imperialism in the Era of the Atlantic Slave Trade* (Oxford, 1977); Ivor Wilks, *Asante in the Nineteenth Century* (Cambridge, 1975), pp. 592, 671.

[20] Wilks, *Asante in the Nineteenth Century*; W. G. Clarence-Smith, "Slaves, Commoners and Landlords in Bulozi, c. 1875 to 1906," *Journal of African History*, 20 (1979): 230.

[21] As recounted by a former slave. See D. Maier-Weaver, "Autobiographical Reminiscences of an African slave, 'Mose,'" *Asante Seminar*, 3 (1975), 19–20.

other adults, they did not have their own huts.[22] Slaves tended to have to work harder than free people,[23] where they could be easily supervised. On the other hand, we will see later that masters evidently felt obliged to make certain concessions to slaves, as far as their work was concerned.

HOW MANY SLAVES? NINETEENTH-CENTURY PATTERNS AND TRENDS

It is no surprise that slaves should make up 40 percent of the population of the Cape Colony in 1808, just after the abolition of the British slave trade.[24] Historians have been skeptical, however, about claims by various European visitors that the proportion in independent African polities was of that order, or even much higher. In some cases, the visitors probably confused slaves with other non-elite subjects of the ruler. Yet on the eve of the partition of Africa there is some rather better evidence that the proportions were indeed high: not in the Sahara nor in the pastoralist economies that covered much of South Africa, but in much of tropical Africa.

The least unsystematic evidence comes from French West Africa, where the new colonial administrations carried out surveys in 1894 and 1904. The local officials responded with varying degrees of diligence. From a careful examination of this source, Martin Klein estimated that slaves comprised over 30 percent of the population in 1904, by when many slaves had left their masters on their own initiative. James Searing re-examined the parts of the surveys relating to the Wolof kingdoms of Kajor and Bawol, in Senegal. He argued that Klein's figure for 1904 was too high, because of the runaways, but estimated that in 1880 between a quarter and a third of the population of Kajor were slaves, and rather less in Bawol. The Kajor figures happen to be in line with another estimate from careful scholars, using perhaps worse data from early colonial Nigeria: Lovejoy and Hogendorn put the figure for the Sokoto Caliphate on the eve of the British conquest as "certainly in excess of 1 million and perhaps over 2.5 million people," or between a quarter and a half of the total population.[25] Among these estimates, Klein's average is particularly striking because French West Africa covered a range of different physical environments, forms of

---

[22] Austin, *Labour, Land and Capital*, pp. 66, 474; Gwyn Prins, *The Hidden Hippopotamus: Reappraisal in Zambian History: The Early Colonial Experience in Western Zambia* (Cambridge, 1980), p. 54.

[23] Mandala, *Work and Control*, p. 35.

[24] Wayne Dooling, *Slavery, Emancipation and Colonial Rule in South Africa* (Athens, OH, 2007), p. 83.

[25] Martin Klein, *Slavery and Colonial Rule in French West Africa* (Cambridge, 1998), pp. 252–6; James F. Searing, *"God Alone is King": Islam and Emancipation in Senegal. The Wolof Kingdoms of Kajoor and Bawol, 1859–1914* (Portsmouth, NH, 2002), pp. 166–72, 184–8, 191–3; Lovejoy and Hogendorn, *Slow Death for Slavery*, pp. 1, 305 (quote from p. 1).

political and social organization, and religious affiliations. It seems that, overall, the average for West Africa in the last twenty years of the nineteenth century was probably in the range from a quarter to a third.

It is likely that no other region of Africa had such a high average, unless it was West Central Africa, where the intense continuation of the Atlantic slave trade was followed by a delayed growth of "legitimate commerce," increasing motive and opportunity to keep more slaves. There was definitely an expansion of slavery in large parts of East Central Africa in the nineteenth century, taking into account the growth of slave plantations on Zanzibar and along the coast, and increased slave-holding in areas drawn into the export trades in slaves and ivory, including Unyamwezi (in what is now Western Tanzania) and Buganda, especially from the 1860s.[26] But East Africa contained not only vast areas controlled by pastoralists, but also kingdoms such as Burundi, where other forms of social, economic, and political subordination were more important than slavery. It also had politically de-centralized areas such as "Kikuyuland" where the organization of coercive capacity was perhaps insufficient for acquiring a large slave population. However, relative slave densities could be high in South Central Africa. According to Gywn Prins, oral sources (including ones documented in the 1930s, when slavery was still well in living memory) indicated that between a quarter and a third of the population were slaves during the reign of King Lewanika, who (with one brief intermission) ruled from 1878 into the early colonial period. Referring to his research in the late 1970s, Prins added that this was approximately confirmed by archaeological evidence: "Since the positions of slave houses in floodplain villages can still be roughly identified, a further check is possible. The ratio between the inner core of villages and the outer perimeter of unenclosed (slave) houses is about three to one."[27]

In general, though not necessarily in the Lozi case, the monographic evidence of large-scale importations of slaves in many parts of arable and mixed-farming Africa in the nineteenth century supports an important general thesis argued by Lovejoy, originally in 1983. Building on the earlier work of Walter Rodney on the Atlantic slave trade, Lovejoy's "transformation thesis" rejects the contention that slave/population ratios were already high when the Europeans began to trade directly with sub-Saharan Africa. Rather, slavery became much more widespread and larger scale as a result of interaction with intercontinental trade. The initial expansion was

---

[26] See François Renault, "The Structures of the Slave Trade in Central Africa in the 19th century," in William Gervase Clarence-Smith (ed.), *The Economics of the Indian Ocean Slave Trade in the Nineteenth Century* (London, 1989), pp. 146–64; Jan-Georg Deutsch, "Notes on the Rise of Slavery and Social Change in Unyamwezi c. 1860–1900," in Henri Médard and Shane Doyle (eds.), *Slavery in the Great Lakes Region of East Africa* (Oxford, 2007), pp. 76–110; Reid, *Political Power*.

[27] Prins, *Hidden Hippopotamus*, p. 73.

as a side-effect of the creation and growth of the enlarged slave-capturing and trading networks required by the external slave trades, but in the nineteenth century slavery expanded further in response to the growth of commodity production for sale outside the continent ("legitimate commerce") or, as Lovejoy emphasized in relation to the cloth production of the Sokoto Caliphate, for regional markets within Africa.[28] The post-1807 phase of the transformation thesis fits the data on the average real price of slaves on the coast of West Africa. Immediately following British abolition, prices fell: the average for 1815 to 1820 was only 30 percent of the average for the five years up to the year of abolition. But a substantial – if partial – recovery followed, such that the average for 1826 to 1830 was back to 68 percent of the figure for 1803 to 1807.[29] The recovery trend was too sustained to be explicable by exogenous fluctuations in the level of warfare. Rather, the obvious explanation is that it reflected an upward trend in effective demand for slaves as producers, whether to supply palm oil and groundnuts to European merchants, or raw cotton and indigo to the Hausa textile industry.

WHY SLAVES IN AFRICA, AND WHY THE PARTICULAR FEATURES OF AFRICAN SLAVERY?

Slavery was only the most severe of several kinds of property in people that were common in the sub-continent during the nineteenth century, and slave labor was one among a range of means used by masters or rulers to extract labor power through physical and/or moral coercion. To mention three: rulers were often considered to own their subjects in some sense, and in some cases were entitled to a share of their labor time (*corvée*); lineages might pawn their junior members as security for a loan; and husbands had rights over wives' labor power as well as their persons, often much more so than the other way around.[30] Given this, why were slaves so important, and increasingly so, in many – but not all – societies in sub-Saharan Africa in the last decades before the European partition? The literature offers basically four answers: slave labor was more profitable than the alternatives; slavery reflected a cultural choice for property in people rather than land;

---

[28] Lovejoy, *Transformations*, 1st edn. (1983), 3rd edn. (2012); Walter Rodney, "Slavery and Other Forms of Social Oppression on the Upper Guinea Coast in the Context of the Atlantic Slave Trade," *Journal of African History*, 7 (1966): 431–43. On the Sokoto Caliphate, see Paul E. Lovejoy, "Plantations in the Economy of the Sokoto Caliphate," *Journal of African History*, 19 (1978): 341–68, reprinted in Lovejoy, *Slavery, Commerce and Production*.

[29] Paul E. Lovejoy and David Richardson, "British Abolition and Its Impact on Slave Prices along the Atlantic Coast of Africa, 1783–1850," *Journal of Economic History*, 55 (1995): 113.

[30] Usually but not always: Elias Mandala offers a highly gender-equal picture of Mang'anja society in the early nineteenth century, before successive invasions. E. Mandala, "Capitalism, Kinship and Gender in the Lower Tchiri Valley of Malawi, 1860–1960," *African Economic History*, 13 (1984): 137–70.

slavery was an instrument for progressively incorporating outsiders into a society, starting at the bottom; and slavery was a ruler's/master's strategy for accumulating wealth in the face of resistance from the local and regional population. These positions are not necessarily incompatible, and this section proposes a framework which draws on all of them, in the hope of making sense of at least most of the evidence from the period. The framework has to be able to account for the expansion of slavery during the pre-colonial nineteenth century; in such a way as to also make sense of the assimilative tendency in many African slave systems, and evidence of concessions to slaves about the amount and nature of their work.

Each of the four answers has its limits. First, no economic explanation of slavery, or any other institution based on coercion, can be sufficient: the motive may have been economic, but to act on it presumes the existence of both coercive capacity and the will to use it. Second, cultural preference, as in John Thornton's claim that "Slavery was widespread in Atlantic Africa because slaves were the only form of private, revenue-producing property recognized in African law,"[31] begs the question. Third, enslaved outsiders did not enter a society at random. Hence, the uses to which slaves were put is suggestive of the motives for acquiring them, with the proviso that, as people, slaves could do things additional to the motive, or at least the main motive, for which they were obtained. All slaves were expected to do some sort of productive labor, and we have seen that female slaves of child-bearing age were also valuable for sexual and reproductive purposes. The advantages of slave wives give an extra force to Kopytoff and Miers' assimilationist interpretation of African slavery; while simultaneously per-haps narrowing it to emphasize a single gender. Finally, a Marxist-inflected emphasis on the primacy of strategies of extraction in the context of social or even class struggle[32] needs to take account of the costs of alternative strategies, in the specific economic as well as political context. In that sense, the market-economic and Marxist explanations may be compatible.

The standard approach to slavery in market economics, the Nieboer-Domar hypothesis, introduced to the study of Africa by A. G. Hopkins in 1973, was and indeed is not intended as a complete explanation for slavery.[33] Rather, it is intended to answer a narrower question: the circum-stances under which the use of slave labor, or another form of coerced labor, would be privately profitable to the slave-owner. Thus, it is of little

[31] Thornton, *Africa and Africans*, p. 74.
[32] Frederick Cooper, "The Problem of Slavery in African Studies," *Journal of African History*, 20 (1979): 103–25.
[33] H. J. Nieboer, *Slavery as an Industrial System* (The Hague, 1900; revised edn. 1910): Evsey D. Domar, "The Causes of Slavery or Serfdom: A Hypothesis," *Journal of Economic History*, 30 (1970): 18–32; Hopkins, *Economic History*, pp. 23–7.

or no relevance to the motives for using slaves in positions of authority, or as soldiers. The hypothesis is that labor coercion pays where cultivable land is abundant in relation to both capital and labor. It is assumed that no technology entailing economies of scale was available, at least not to the extent that access to that technology could make it more worthwhile to hire a laborer rather than buy a slave.

Does it fit nineteenth-century sub-Saharan Africa? There are several points to make. The most fundamental is that most of the sub-continent was indeed land-abundant and labor-scarce during most or all of the century.[34] The long-term exception was the heartland of the Ethiopian kingdom. This is consistent with the hypothesis, in that the material base of the kingdom was an agricultural surplus extracted from a peasantry tied to the land, in a relationship often compared with European feudalism, though the mode of extraction was tribute rather than serfdom.[35] As noted above, Ethiopia's large-scale involvement in slavery came in the imperial expansion southward, from which captives were exported to the Arabian Peninsula and elsewhere as slaves. For the other side of the continent, David Northrup tested the Nieboer-Domar hypothesis as far as the evidence permits for Southeast Nigeria in the nineteenth century. Comparing different areas, he found a match between relatively high incidence of slavery, and particularly exploitative forms of it, with relatively low population and relatively high participation in goods markets.[36]

Second, while capital was generally scarce, cattle are capital goods, hence the hypothesis does not predict that slavery would be profitable for pastoralists. This is consistent with the observation that the African societies with significant numbers of slaves were based on arable and mixed farming. Shaka secured first call on the labor of young men in the new Zulu kingdom not through slavery, but rather by organizing them in age regiments charged not only with military service, but also with caring for the royal herds, from which they fed themselves. Nguni-speakers, in the persons of the Gaza, adopted slavery on any sizable scale only when they left the pastures of Eastern South Africa and settled in Southern Mozambique.

Third, Nieboer was well aware that men might use their wives as cheap labor and saw the hypothesis as relevant only where household heads wanted labor on a scale beyond what (non-slave) wives and other members of the family labor force could supply. This is consistent with another

---

[34] This proposition is critically reviewed, and ultimately upheld in revised form, in Gareth Austin, "Resources, Techniques and Strategies South of the Sahara: Revising the Factor Endowments Perspective on African Economic Development, 1500–2000," *Economic History Review*, 61 (2008): 587–624.

[35] Donald Crummey, "Abyssinian Feudalism," *Past and Present*, 89 (1980): 115–38.

[36] David Northrup, "Nineteenth-Century Patterns of Slavery and Economic Growth in Southeastern Nigeria," *International Journal of African Historical Studies*, 12 (1979): 1–16.

observation for the nineteenth century, namely that the increases in the recruitment of slaves seem to have occurred where labor was required beyond the capacity of the existing household: as in to respond to market opportunities on top of their existing "subsistence" production.

Fourth, Nieboer's and Domar's versions of the hypothesis differed in that the former envisaged coerced labor as being merely cheaper than free labor, whereas Domar's model is more radical. He postulated a situation in which there was no price (wage) which it would be in the interests both of a potential employer to offer, and of a potential employee to accept: because the latter would be materially at least as well off working for him- or herself, without the encumbrance of supervision. Thus, there would be no labor market without coercion. Domar's vision fits the remark of the Scottish explorer Mungo Park, based on his travels in Senegambia and Mali in the 1790s, that "[h]ired servants, by which I mean persons of free condition, voluntarily working for pay, are unknown in Africa ..."[37] My own research suggests that this applied to Asante and much of the rest of West Africa in the nineteenth century.[38] But there were cases, the largest being in other regions of the sub-continent, where freemen in or from pre-colonial societies accepted wages: Nyamwezi caravan porters from Western Tanzania, engaged in the ivory trade from Eastern Congo to the coast, and Nguni-speakers from the Gaza state in Southern Mozambique, going to work in colonial South Africa. Evidently, the wages were enough to make wage contracts mutually beneficial. In East Africa, employers preferred waged porters to slaves because the latter tended to drop their loads and run away, while in South Africa slavery was by now illegal.[39] Thus, wage labor co-existed with slavery, though the wages were earned, directly or indirectly, from exchange with external capitalists. In both cases, slaves were acquired to take over the agricultural burdens left by the departure of men for itinerant or migrant wage work.[40]

Fifth, it is important to note that the Nieboer-Domar hypothesis does not assume that the labor is applied to commodity production. As it happens, there were major cases of the use of slave labor for colonization in the sense of bringing land under settlement. In Buganda, in the

[37] Mungo Park, *Travels into the Interior Districts of Africa* (1799; reprinted London, 1954), p. 219.
[38] Austin, *Labour, Land and Capital*, pp. 155–70, 495–8; Gareth Austin, *Markets, Slavery and States in West African History* (Cambridge, forthcoming).
[39] Stephen J. Rockel, *Carriers of Culture: Labor on the Road in Nineteenth-Century East Africa* (Portsmouth, NH, 2006); Patrick Harries, *Work, Culture and Identity: Migrant Labour in Mozambique and South Africa, c.1860–1910* (Oxford, 1994).
[40] Jan-Georg Deutsch, "Notes on the Rise of Slavery and Social Change in Unyamwezi, c.1860–1900," in Médard and Doyle (eds.), *Slavery in the Great Lakes Region*, pp. 82–4, 103; Harries, "Slavery, Social Incorporation."

eighteenth century but stretching into the nineteenth, a special class of chiefs was created who concentrated the labor of war captives in order to open the forest for cultivation. In the 1890s, in Bulozi, King Lewanika mobilized large quantities of free and slave labor in draining land in the Zambezi Valley.[41] Again, in Mang'anja society, slaves were employed for subsistence rather than to supply markets.[42]

Finally, however, slavery is the form of labor coercion most open to the market: markets deal with the transfer of ownership, and slaves are by definition property. Thus, it is not surprising that in most parts of sub-Saharan Africa, nineteenth-century expansions of slavery seem to have been responses to changes in the market: falls in the price of slaves, facilitating purchase, and rises in the demand for commodities that could be produced by slaves. That was the story, overwhelmingly, in West Africa; and in much of Eastern and Central Africa.

In my view, the Nieboer-Domar hypothesis is a valuable framework for understanding the patterns of slavery in nineteenth-century Africa. Crucially, it enables us to account for the expansion of slavery in West and East Africa during the nineteenth century, in response to the increasing demands for labor to produce commodities for sale. Where the conditions it specifies for the profitability of labor coercion applied, slavery existed or expanded. In the relatively small minority of cases where those conditions did not exist, labor relations took a different form – as the theory predicts. But while the hypothesis provides plausible motivation for the acquisition of slave labor power, and for expanding it in response to state imperatives for colonizing land, or to enable masters to respond to market opportunities, it assumes that the political and ideological conditions for slavery existed. This they clearly did. Relatively weak though states were at daily, detailed control of their subjects, the economies and the available military technologies permitted the coercion of minorities, even large minorities; and politically decentralized societies could have slaves too, though probably in lower proportions than the states. Ideologically, the exploitation of social outsiders was facilitated politically and psychically by the instrumental process of "othering" them, as non-human beings.[43]

What of the standard comparative objection to the hypothesis, namely that the physical abundance of land is irrelevant because rulers can make land artificially scarce, and use this to tie the farmers to the land, as with the spread of serfdom in Eastern Europe in the seventeenth century? Self-

[41] Holly Hanson, "Stolen People and Autonomous Chiefs in Nineteenth-Century Buganda: The Social Consequences of Non-Free Followers," in Médard and Doyle (eds.), *Slavery in the Great Lakes Region*, pp. 161–73; Prins, *Hidden Hippopotamus*, pp. 56, 60, 70.
[42] Mandala, *Work and Control*, pp. 33–4.
[43] E.g. Mandala, *Work and Control*, pp. 33–4; Clarence-Smith, "Slaves, Commoners," 230.

evident in the abstract, this argument misses the need to take account of what was possible and impossible, and the costs of the former. The low population densities made it hard to tax a population without provoking an exodus, especially where agricultural productivity was constrained by thin soils and the presence of the animal form of sleeping sickness, which precluded the availability of large animals for plowing or transport, in the forests and much of the savanna.[44] Weak states were associated with relatively strong organization at the micro level, usually on kinship lines. It made more sense for rulers and households to unite to exploit outsiders, than for the rulers to try the probably impossible, and certainly very risky, route of appropriating the land surplus in the hope of obliging indigenous households to accept servile terms in return for renewed access to land. Likewise, large-scale and sustained *corvée* was beyond the coercive and political capacity, or at least the will, of most rulers. Bulozi under Lewanika was one exception, as we have seen; another, over a much longer period, was the Merina kingdom in Madagascar.[45] The price that rulers could pay if they took on their own subjects was epitomized in the rare instances of kings and chiefs raiding their own villages for slaves. In the 1880s, the kabaka of Buganda, Mwanga, did so; thereby undermining the social contract on which his state was based, and contributing to its fatal crisis in the face of the imperialist threat.[46]

In the context of a strong economic motive for slavery, a cultural preference for property in persons rather than property in land did at least go with the grain rather than against it. Again, the hypothesis that slavery was profitable in the context of labor scarcity is consistent with the apparent preference for female slaves: the acquisition of future mothers could be a medium-term means of combatting the scarcity of subjects, taxpayers, soldiers, and followers in general.

Finally, the related combination of low population densities and weak states accounts for the fact that, cruelly as slaves could be treated, they also often obtained concessions compared to their counterparts in some other

[44] Jack Goody, *Tradition, Technology and the State in Africa* (London, 1971); Jeffrey Herbst, *States and Power in Africa* (Princeton, NJ, 2000).

[45] Gwyn Campbell, *An Economic History of Imperial Madagascar, 1750–1895: The Merina Kingdom* (Cambridge, 2005), pp. 112–33.

[46] Hanson, "Stolen People." Mwanga was at least spared the fate of a much earlier exception to the rule of not enslaving your own subjects (excepting the occasional criminal, alleged or real). The king and chiefs of the small kingdom of Akwamu, in Southern Ghana, abused the judicial process and raided villages in their own kingdom to obtain captives for sale. This led to a revolution in 1730, as a result of which they themselves were sold as slaves to their former trading partners, the Danish West Indies and Guinea Company (Ray A. Kea, "When I Die, I Shall Return to My Own Land: An 'Amina' Slave Rebellion in the Danish West Indies, 1733–1734," in John Hunwick and Nancy Lawler (eds.), *The Cloth of Many Colored Silks: Papers on History and Society, Ghanaian and Islamic, in Honor of Ivor Wilks* (Evanston, IL, 1996), pp. 159–93).

parts of the world. Partial assimilation of slaves, especially via marriage, diluted the risk of creating a hereditary caste of oppressed people with no stake in the society. Despite the tendency in some cases to work slaves extremely hard, there was a counter-vailing need to avoid provoking them into flight or, more rarely, fight. Thus in the West African savanna slaves usually had a day or two to work for themselves.[47] The plots slaves were given might be relatively remote and infertile, but they existed, and if they did manage to accumulate any property, they were entitled to keep it. Ironically, by reducing the labor time that masters obtained from slaves, the concessionary and assimilative tendencies in pre-colonial slave systems had the effect of reinforcing the incentive to acquire new slaves, thus strengthening the intra-regional slave trades.

COLONIZATION, EXPORT AGRICULTURE, AND THE SLOW DEATH OF SLAVERY

Colonization did not abolish the conditions that made labor coercion profitable for masters. In principle, it simply prohibited the primary existing form of it. There were important variations, even within the same empire in some cases. Generally, the new European administrations abolished the trading of slaves, and also suppressed the raids and warfare that were the main sources of slaves. There were qualifications, even so: African soldiers in the French army that conquered the western savanna of West Africa often returned with slave wives. According to his diary, a minor Fulani ruler in German Kamerun presided over the capture of more than 1,600 slaves between 1912 and 1920, under German and briefly French rule.[48] But the main issue was slave-holding. Colonial "men on the spot" worried that freed slaves would leave their masters, allowing production to fall while they themselves formed a criminal, discontented urban lumpenproletariat. They also noted the discrepancy between the fact that compensation had been paid to European slave-owners when their slaves were freed, including at the Cape, whereas African owners were to receive no such award (slave-owners in Zanzibar and Kenya, many of whom, incidentally, were considered Arab, were an exception). Again, British officials, in particular, wished to uphold the material base and status of the chiefs and emirs who were the tools of their policy of "indirect rule." Meanwhile, especially in plantation and settler colonies, European

---

[47] E.g. Peter M. Weil, "Slavery, Groundnuts, and European Capitalism in the Wuli Kingdom of Senegambia, 1820–1930," *Research in Economic Anthropology*, 6 (1984): 77–119.

[48] A. H. M. Kirk-Greene and James Vaughan (eds.), *The Diary of Hamman Yaji: Chronicle of a West African Muslim Ruler* (Bloomington, IN, 1996). The area is now inside the Nigerian border.

employers themselves complained that labor was scarce at the wages they were willing to pay.

Colonial administrations in different areas adopted a combination of approaches to the problem of labor recruitment in material conditions that favored coercion, but under the political constraint of having made international commitments to abolish slavery. For the governments themselves, and for European employers, one option was forced labor. There were examples of this in all the African colonies at the start, especially for transporting loads and building infrastructure. It remained general policy in the French colonies until 1945, and in the Portuguese colonies long after, though the scale varied and changed, not least under pressure from the International Labour Organization in the interwar period. In the settler economies, notably South Africa, Southern Rhodesia, and Kenya, the governments' primary strategy for forcing Africans to provide their labor was indirect. Initially, at least, they sought to force Africans to sell their labor, instead of their agricultural produce, by appropriating land for future European use, and restricting or prohibiting Africans from working on European farms as tenants or sharecroppers, rather than as pure wage laborers. As for slavery itself, where it had been "prematurely" abolished at the time of the colonial conquest, as in Southern Nigeria, the rights of employers could be strengthened by new legislation, as the British did with master and servant ordinances. But the main colonial approach to the ending of slavery was gradualism: quietly tolerating it, perhaps with some reforms, for some years or even decades. In some cases, abolition, when it occurred, was limited to ending the legal status of slavery, meaning that an owner could no longer claim the return of his runaway property. Thus, in Sierra Leone and Zanzibar, the legal status of slavery was abolished in 1896 and 1897 respectively, with the prohibition of slavery following only in 1928 and 1909. Even legal status abolition did not happen in independent Ethiopia; it finally occurred in 1942, following the British defeat of the Italian invasion. In French West Africa, slave expectations of liberation were crucial in precipitating it: from a revolt in Banamba in 1895 to mass exoduses of slaves in 1905, slaves in Mali, in particular, acted ahead of legislation, and accelerated it.

None of the colonial strategies would have surprised Nieboer and Domar. With labor still physically scarce, the wages required to persuade freemen to offer their services were relatively high. Whether slavery would actually be succeeded by un-coerced wage labor depended on whether the further growth of commodity production was sufficient to remove the economic disincentives to the use of free labor on the part of both workers and prospective employers in historically land-abundant, capital-scarce economies. The pattern of decline of slave labor, and the growth of wage labor, confirms the importance, even indispensability, of coercion for the existence of labor markets in much of Africa, until something changed which enabled masters to hire labor voluntarily. That change was the arrival or growth of markets for export products that were commercially valuable but could not be grown everywhere in Africa. This change took place particularly in the early colonial period, to 1914, facilitated by relatively high world prices for primary commodities. The geographical restriction (in some cases, maintained by government neglect of transport to remote areas) meant that people, especially men, from places un-favored by soil or transport links, might find it necessary or even attractive to migrate seasonally, to where they could get a job in the export-producing sectors, whether in mining or agriculture.

In the "peasant" colonies, as distinct from the settler colonies, prospective African employers were free to produce for the market. But when it came to recruiting labor beyond their families, they had to do this without the advantage of assistance, directly or indirectly, from the coercive power of colonial governments, such as the European settlers and planters enjoyed in other colonies. Recruitment was not necessarily a problem in the early colonial years, when African entrepreneurs could use any remaining slaves or pawns, or junior family members of partly-slave descent (though frequently masters felt obliged by the threat of abolition, and the risk that their slaves might run away, to reduce their labor demands). What happened after that depended on whether they were able to establish farms on land suited by soil and access to transport for growing one of the more lucrative export crops, such as cocoa beans in Ghana or Nigeria, and coffee near Arusha in Tanzania. In West Africa, some former slaves stayed put, often negotiating better terms. Some returned home, to where they had been captured, and made a living through a combination (as a household) of subsistence farming and migrant labor. Some managed to become cash-crop growers themselves. Meanwhile, some masters were able to make a relatively smooth transition from slave-owners to employers. In some cocoa-growing cases, in Southern Nigeria and Ashanti (Ghana), they were able to use the proceeds of farms established with slave (and pawn) labor to pay wages. But others were not so fortunate. In Southeast Nigeria, "when the slaves left, the owners wept," and had no immediate way to restore their fortunes.[49]

The death of slavery was not only slow – and incomplete, surviving successive abolition decrees in Mauretania, in particular – but uneven.[50]

---

[49] Don C. Ohadike, "'When the Slaves Left, the Owners Wept': Entrepreneurs and Emancipation among the Igbo People," in Suzanne Miers and Martin A. Klein (eds.), *Slavery and Colonial Rule in Africa* (London, 1999), pp. 189–207; Gareth Austin, "Cash Crops and Freedom: Export Agriculture and the Decline of Slavery in Colonial West Africa," *International Review of Social History*, 54 (2009): 1–37.

[50] Slavery and slave trading exist today in parts of Africa, to judge from reports of human trafficking. This is a matter for other chapters, but I would comment that an analysis of this contemporary forced

We have already seen this in geographical terms, but it was also true in gender terms. The opportunities for former slaves to get a reasonably secure foothold in the export-crop economies, whether as cash-cropping peasants or migrant laborers, fell at first mostly to men. Given that the majority of slaves in Africa were female, abolition must ultimately have improved the situation of females relative to males; but it was a long time coming.

Even so, and despite the emphasis placed in the literature on the continuities from the era of slavery, emancipation was seriously bad news for many masters in the early twentieth century, as it had been also (despite financial compensation) for Boer farmers faced with much increased labor costs once they had to pay wages to attract former slaves, who (at least for) now had real bargaining power. In the forest heartland of the former kingdom of Asante, former masters were able to capitalize on their location in an area suited for profitable cocoa production. But they had to grant increasingly good terms to the laborers who migrated from the same savanna areas from which the Asantes had formerly obtained slaves. In such cases especially, freedom mattered.

CONCLUSIONS AND REFLECTIONS

This chapter has examined the combination, and interaction, of two contrasting impulses: toward the expansion of slavery and slave trading within sub-Saharan Africa, and toward abolition. Only by the late 1930s could it be safely said that the latter tendency had prevailed, and even then, with qualifications. Historiographically, the chapter has focused on the debates over African slave systems since they became the subject of sustained historical research, in the 1970s. The literature has moved a long way since African slavery was regarded as *sui generis*, even perhaps a misnomer. While institutions of slavery in Africa, like those elsewhere, had distinctive features, they clearly belong firmly in the world history of slavery. It is encouraging to note the beginning of what should become a new strand of research, investigating nineteenth-century slavery in Africa and other slave-holding regions side by side.[51]

Analytically, it has been argued here that the most effective way to make sense of the very complex histories of slavery and emancipation in different parts of the sub-continent is to adopt a framework that combines social,

labor market belongs to the economics of crime, not the Nieboer-Domar hypothesis, which is relevant rather to cases where – in contrast to today – slavery was perfectly legal in the societies in which slaves were held.

[51] Dylan Penningroth, "The Claims of Slaves and Ex-Slaves to Family and Property: A Transatlantic Comparison," *American Historical Review*, 112 (2007): 1039–69.

cultural, economic, and political perspectives on African slavery, while emphasizing labor scarcity in a setting of land abundance as presenting the challenges to prospective employers that, in response, they often recruited slave labor to meet. The same material circumstances that made slavery profitable for masters made political centralization difficult, and thereby help to explain why slave-owners in Africa often made concessions to slaves: from time to work for themselves to partial assimilation into the community.

Inevitably, the issue arises of the long-term developmental consequences of the fact that slavery was the principal way of recruiting labor from outside the "free" household, for at least several decades, especially in the arable regions of tropical Africa. We know from comparative history that slave economies could grow, whatever the suffering of the slaves. From the Sokoto Caliphate in the west to Zanzibar in the east, there are indeed examples of apparently prosperous economies in nineteenth-century Africa. But two very damaging features are clear. First, slavery entailed inequalities as well as violence, damaging males and females alike, though often in different ways. Second, in contrast to the New World and the Ottoman Empire, in sub-Saharan Africa the original capture of slaves occurred within the same region as the slaves were put to work. The costs of the processes of capture, which included making warfare pay and encouraging raiding and the abuse of judicial process, evidently reinforced the very conditions of general labor scarcity that made slavery profitable in the first place.

A GUIDE TO FURTHER READING

1 Overviews and Collections

Lovejoy, Paul E., *Transformations in Slavery: A History of Slavery in Africa*, 3rd edn. (Cambridge, 2012). First published in 1983, but remains the fullest overview. The tables and bibliography, mainly, are updated in the later editions.

Lovejoy, Paul E. and Toyin Falola (eds.), *Pawnship, Slavery, and Colonialism in Africa* (Trenton, NJ, 2003). The major source on the history of debt bondage south of the Sahara.

Manning, Patrick, *Slavery and African Life: Occidental, Oriental, and African Slave Trades* (Cambridge, 1990). A concise overview.

Meillassoux, Claude, *The Anthropology of Slavery: The Womb of Iron and Gold*, Alide Dasnois (tr.) (Chicago, IL, 1991). A major interpretation of African slavery, including Meillassoux's thesis that slavery was the most fundamental form of private property in Africa.

Miers, Suzanne and Martin A. Klein (eds.), *Slavery and Colonial Rule in Africa* (London, 1999).

Miers, Suzanne and Kopytoff, Igor (eds.), *Slavery in Africa: Historical and Anthropological Perspectives* (Madison, WI, 1977). A collection of early studies, including an influential interpretative essay by the editors.

Miers, Suzanne and Roberts, Richard (eds.), *The End of Slavery in Africa* (Madison, WI, 1988). Together with Miers and Klein, this provides a valuable framework plus case studies on the regionally and socially uneven decline of slavery in sub-Saharan Africa.

Stilwell, S., *Slavery and Slaving in African History* (Cambridge, 2014). Recent overview.

2 Regional studies

Austin, Gareth, *Labour, Land and Capital in Ghana: From Slavery to Free Labour in Asante, 1807–1956* (Rochester, NY, 2005). The economics and political economy of the existence and growth of slavery in a major West African kingdom, and of its eventual decline in the double context of colonial rule and the adoption of export agriculture.

Cooper, Frederick, *Plantation Slavery on the East Coast of Africa* (New Haven, CT, 1977). A pioneering study, with an equally important sequel: Frederick Cooper, *From Slaves to Squatters: Plantation Labor and Agriculture in Zanzibar and Coastal Kenya 1890–1925* (New Haven, CT, 1980).

Deutsch, Jan-Georg, *Emancipation without Abolition in German East Africa c.1884–1914* (Oxford, 2006). The "slow death of slavery," German-style, in East Africa.

Dooling, Wayne, *Slavery, Emancipation and Colonial Rule in South Africa* (Athens, OH, 2007). The major analysis of abolition in the context of "European" slavery at the Cape.

Klein, Martin A., *Slavery and Colonial Rule in French West Africa* (Cambridge, 1998). A fine account of the persistence and decline of slavery under colonial rule.

Lovejoy, Paul E. and Jan S. Hogendorn, *Slow Death for Slavery: The Course of Abolition in Northern Nigeria, 1897–1936* (Cambridge, 1993). Influential monograph.

Médard, Henri and Shane Doyle (eds.), *Slavery in the Great Lakes Region of East Africa* (Oxford, 2007). Presents major research remedying the neglect of slavery in the historiography of the region.

Rossi, Benedetta, *From Slavery to Aid: Politics, Labour, and Ecology in the Nigerian Sahel, 1800–2000* (Cambridge, 2015). An incisive study of continuity and change in subsistence and recruitment on the edge of the Sahara.

CHAPTER 9

OTTOMAN SLAVERY AND ABOLITION IN THE NINETEENTH CENTURY

MICHAEL FERGUSON AND EHUD R. TOLEDANO

INTRODUCTION

The "long nineteenth century" – beginning with the reforms of Sultan Selim III in the late eighteenth century and ending with the demise of the Ottoman Empire in the First World War – constitutes the last phase of Ottoman history. It also features the height and subsequent decline of enslavement and the slave trade into the Empire, and ultimately their virtual, though not formal, abolition. The story of Ottoman enslavement and abolition is a chapter in the history of the reform movement, also known as the *Tanzimat*, which was one of the main components of the Empire's political, military, social, economic, and cultural history in the long nineteenth century.

The past three decades have witnessed major revisions in the writings about Ottoman history, disputing the reigning Decline Paradigm, rehabilitating the Ottoman record of governance in the Middle East and North Africa, and to a lesser degree also in the Balkans and Eastern Europe. Our view of the Tanzimat reforms has shifted from the classical "Westernization-Modernization" model to an interactive appropriation and assimilation one, empowering in the process the Ottoman elites, communities, and minority groups. Inter alia, the history of Ottoman enslavement too has been rewritten and significantly reinterpreted. Thus, the current chapter builds on the discussion of Ottoman enslavement in the early modern period[1] and takes it into the next and final phase of the practice.

While the study of Ottoman enslavement and slave trading in the nineteenth century has dramatically advanced since its formative period, a number of defining themes remain constant. The first is that the topic has not been properly integrated into general surveys and textbooks in Ottoman history and research on it has been conducted almost entirely independently from more general works. At the same time, historians

---

[1] Ehud R. Toledano, "Enslavement in the Ottoman Empire in the Early Modern Period," in David Eltis and Stanley L. Engerman (eds.), *Cambridge World History of Slavery*, Vol. 3 (1420–1804) (Cambridge, 2011), pp. 25–46.

working on Ottoman slavery have not always sought to relate their work to broader social, political, and economic changes. Therefore, recent and current efforts need to venture beyond this self-imposed isolation, both in thematic scope and theory, as for example, in Donald Quataert's and Ehud Toledano's work, that attempt to frame slavery as part of the larger context of economic history or patterns of forced migration and settlement, respectively.

Another major theme in the historiography of Ottoman enslavement is that much of it is based on state archival sources, most notably central and provincial archives, and various European, especially British, consular archives. State documents inevitably reflect the view of the administration, but a careful reading of them, particularly Şeriat (Arabic, Sharīʿa) and Nizami court records, can reveal enslaved voices and experience. Additionally, it appears that private papers and personal memoirs can be used to incorporate the life stories of the enslaved and enslaver, as for example in the work of Eve Troutt Powell, Hakan Erdem, Beth Baron, and Ehud R. Toledano. The regional focus of these sources has also divided the field between those studying enslavement in what now comprises modern Turkey, with sources in Istanbul and mostly in Turkish, and those working on the Levant and North Africa, with sources mostly in Arabic. The effect is to make it difficult to conceptualize the cultural diversity of Ottoman societies and their practice of enslavement in an overall sense.

Finally, with the shift in the patterns of enslavement and trafficking at the turn of the century, the field has turned its focus from enslaved East Europeans and the *kul/harem* phenomenon to domestic slavery of Africans and Circassians. Within that framework, Africans have been more extensively studied than Caucasians, perhaps also as a result of the focus of European powers on the suppression of the trade in Africans to the neglect of the Caucasian traffic and enslavement, largely due to effective Ottoman blocking efforts. Overall though, the field is growing and expanding rapidly, with an exciting range of new studies recently published and quite a number of doctoral and post-doctoral works still in the pipeline. Historians of Ottoman enslavement now analyze it in a global context, making it rightfully less unique or exceptional. New studies move away from the traditional focus on the state by working to understand the enslaved experience on its own terms, and investigate the ways in which individual slaves actively worked to ameliorate their own condition. Slavery is now seen as a type of patronage relationship formed and often maintained by coercion, but "requiring a measure of mutuality and exchange that posits a complex web of reciprocity."[2]

---

[2] Ehud R. Toledano, *As If Silent and Absent: Bonds of Enslavement in the Islamic Middle East* (New Haven, CT, 2007), pp. 5–8.

Despite the limitations of existing sources, efforts are being made to highlight this slave-centered experience. To this end, three major routes of examination have developed.[3] The first is to understand enslavement as a gendered experience. The second is the examination of how the enslaved brought with them unique cultural elements which they maintained in Ottoman lands. The third area of developing interest and controversy is the question of abolition and antislavery, where near absence of home-grown opposition to enslavement in Ottoman and other Islamic societies calls for socio-cultural explanations.

The Ottoman Empire was the last and greatest Islamic power of the modern era. In many ways, the history of the Middle East and North Africa between 1517 and 1918 is a chapter in Ottoman history, and Ottoman heritage has lingered in the southeastern Mediterranean many decades after the demise of the Empire. Some major elements of political, social, economic, and cultural life born and developed under the sultans and their government have survived well into the twentieth century, and arguably are still detectable even today. While viewed in older Western studies as the paragon of conservatism and stagnation, recent works have shown that the Ottoman Empire was through many periods of its long history a complex and fascinating entity, dynamic and adaptable, pragmatic and resilient, tolerant and accommodating.

In the long nineteenth century, the Ottoman Empire became increasingly dependent on foreign aid and trade, as it accumulated large foreign debt, and while military losses and nationalist uprisings continued to shrink its borders. While the creation of a modern, centralized state was the main intention, full implementation of the reforms was only partially accomplished, and what often resulted was a mix of previous forms of the political, social, and economic order, with "modern," Western European ones being embedded as hybrid Ottoman forms. In the midst of this transformation were two seemingly contradictory events: the slave trade reached its climax at the same time as the dawning of the age of abolition and an unprecedented amount of effort to halt it. The ongoing attempts to resolve these underlying tensions tells the story of suppression and abolition in the Ottoman Empire, which we shall follow in this chapter.

The Ottoman Empire at this time had to cope with growing European expansionism and intervention, which the Ottomans countered by

---

[3] Beth Baron, "Liberated Bodies and Saved Souls: Freed African Slave Girls and Missionaries in Egypt" in Ehud R. Toledano (ed.), *African Communities in Asia and the Mediterranean: Identities between Integration and Conflict* (Trenton, NJ, 2011), pp. 215–35; Eve Troutt Powell, *Tell This in My Memory: Stories of Enslavement from Egypt, Sudan, and the Ottoman Empire* (Stanford, CA, 2012); Ehud R. Toledano, "Abolition and Anti-slavery in the Ottoman Empire: A Case to Answer?" in W. Mulligan and M. Bric (eds.), *A Global History of Anti-Slavery Politics in the Nineteenth Century* (Basingstoke, 2013), pp. 117–36.

adopting their version of self-evolved, self-styled modernization. Through all this, however, an increasing European presence in Ottoman societies became an undeniable factor of nineteenth-century realities in the Mediterranean and beyond. Enslavement and the slave trade were among the most striking examples of the Ottoman attempt to resolve and contain European, mainly British, pressure: the traffic in Africans was prohibited in 1857 and gradually suppressed by the end of the century, whereas slavery itself remained legal.[4] British representatives in the Empire became – in the eyes of the enslaved – part and parcel of the patronage system that evolved on the ground, and those seeking protection from abuse or manumission found refuge in European consulates across the sultan's domains.

ENSLAVEMENT IN THE OTTOMAN EMPIRE: TYPES AND VOLUME

There were in fact many practices in Ottoman society that could be considered as falling broadly within the framework of "slavery" or "unfreedom," including imprisonment, indebted sharecropping, and indeed various kinds of conjugal unions. Nonetheless, this chapter will be largely limited to legal enslavement. Slavery in terms of Hanafi Islamic law, the foundation for the legal system in the Ottoman Empire, grants one person ownership over another, meaning the owner has rights to the slave's labor, property, and sexuality, and the slaves' freedoms are severely restricted. However, in practice, things were much different; the experiences of slaves in Ottoman societies varied dramatically, some rose to considerable power and prominence, whereas others labored under harsh circumstances. So much so that instead of "Ottoman slavery" it might be better to conceptualize these varieties as "Ottoman slaveries," or "modes of enslavement."[5]

The first and arguably most important way in which slaves were classified in the Ottoman Empire was between elite and non-elite slaves, or rather between military-administrative slaves and their wives and consorts, labelled *kul/harem* slaves, and domestic or menial slavery. While in no way completely at an end, *kul/harem* slavery slowly but surely came to account for a smaller segment of the entire slave population in the nineteenth century, owing largely to the demise of one of the main mechanisms of recruitment into this class, the *devşirme*, the state collection of young Christian boys by the imperial palace.

---

[4] See Ehud R. Toledano, *The Ottoman Slave Trade and Its Suppression, 1840–1890* (Princeton, NJ, 1982).

[5] For the full spectrum of Ottoman enslavement, see Ehud R. Toledano, "The Concept of Slavery in Ottoman and Other Muslim Societies: Dichotomy or Continuum?" in Miura Toru and John Edward Philips (eds.), *Slave Elites in the Middle East and Africa: A Comparative Study* (London, 2000), pp. 159–76; for gendered enslavement, see Madeline C. Zilfi, *Women and Slavery in the Late Ottoman Empire: The Design of Difference* (Cambridge, 2010), p. 104.

Slaves can also be classified along gender lines. The majority of these slaves (roughly two-thirds) were women who worked in domestic positions, though some eventually became wives or concubines in elite households. As Madeline Zilfi notes, female slaves were inherently more vulnerable in their positions, largely because they could not attain "independence" on their own, but were attached to their husband and his household. Sexual violence and the lack of control over one's reproductive abilities put female slaves in a much more precarious position than male slaves. At the same time, many of the female slaves who bore the children of their enslavers gained a special status, that of "mother of a child" (Turkish *ümmüveled*, Arabic *umm walad*), which meant they were not to be sold, and they and their children would be set free after the death of the enslaver. This is, however, only if the father recognized the child as his.

The third way to classify the enslaved in Ottoman lands is according to their origin and ethnic/racial backgrounds. Generally, African slaves were more likely to be enslaved in domestic and menial tasks, and not taken on as wives or concubines. Furthermore, their options for working their way up the socio-political ladder, whether inside or outside the household, were much more limited than, for example, slaves of Circassian or Georgian origin. Other factors shaped the Ottoman slave experience, including the class and type of employment the enslaver had and where and how they lived, whether in urban, rural, or nomadic environments. *Kul/harem* slaves in elite households in Istanbul had relatively better opportunities, social mobility, and quality of life. Domestic slaves outside of Istanbul, owned by non-elite peoples, probably had it the worst.

This chapter focuses on African and Circassian non-elite enslavement as these were the predominant types in the nineteenth century. Unlike slavery in the Americas, which consisted largely of agricultural labor and formed the backbone of the economy, slavery in the Ottoman Empire was largely domestic in nature. Scattered data and reasonable extrapolations regarding the volume of the slave trade from Africa to the Ottoman Empire yield an estimated number of approximately 16,000 to 18,000 men and women who were being transported into the Empire per annum during the peak years of the nineteenth century, i.e. the 1840s to the 1860s.[6] Ralph Austen's estimates

---

[6] The most reliable work on this is by Ralph Austen, "The 19th Century Islamic Slave Trade from East Africa (Swahili and Red Sea Coasts): A Tentative Census," in William Gervase Clarence-Smith (ed.), *The Economics of the Indian Ocean Slave Trade in the Nineteenth Century*, Special Issue of *Slavery and Abolition*, 9 (1988): 21–44; and "The Mediterranean Islamic Slave Trade Out of Africa: A Tentative Census," *Slavery and Abolition*, 13 (1992): 214–48. See also Thomas M. Rick's thorough consideration in "Slaves and Slave Traders in the Persian Gulf, 18th and 19th Centuries: An Assessment," in Clarence-Smith, *Economics of the Indian Ocean Slave Trade*, pp. 60–70. For P. E. Lovejoy's higher numbers and criticism of Austen's figures, see "Commercial Sectors in the Economy of the Nineteenth-Century Central Sudan: The Trans-Saharan Trade and the Desert-Side Salt Trade," *African Economic History*, 13 (1984): 87–95.

for the total volume of coerced migration from Africa into Ottoman territories are as follows: from Swahili coasts to the Ottoman Middle East and India – 313,000; across the Red Sea and the Gulf of Aden – 492,000; into Ottoman Egypt – 362,000; and into Ottoman North Africa (Algeria, Tunisia, and Libya) – 350,000. If we exclude the numbers going to India, a rough estimate of this mass population movement would amount to more than 1.3 million people. During the middle decades of the nineteenth century, the shrinking Atlantic traffic swelled the numbers of enslaved Africans coerced into domestic African markets, as well as into Ottoman ones. These figures should have resulted in a fairly noticeable African diaspora in both Turkey and the successor Arab states of the Middle East, North Africa, and even the Balkans.

However, if we look for persons of African descent in these regions, we can find only scattered traces of them. In Turkey, there are African agricultural communities in villages and towns in Western Anatolia, such as in Torbalı, Söke, Ödemiş, Tire, Akhisar, with a larger concentration in the province of Aydın near Izmir, and in the region of Antalya.[7] Even in the city of Izmir itself, where the largest African population in the Ottoman Empire lived at the end of the nineteenth century, a visible population still exists. Since both African-Ottomans and African-Turks were considered as Muslims and Turks, respectively, they are, in the words of one scholar, "virtually statistically non-existent in the official demographic records" of the Empire and the Republic. Hence, they are absent from standard state-produced reference sources. By comparison, in the post-Ottoman Levant, as in Saudi Arabia, the Gulf states, and North Africa, one can find higher numbers of persons of African extraction among the various Bedouin tribes in desert areas and in settled villages bordering on them. In Egypt, Africans seem to have a larger presence than elsewhere in the Middle East.

All in all, however, the impression is that only a small fraction of the descendants of enslaved Africans are still present in the post-Ottoman Mediterranean region. So where have they all gone? The most common explanation is that many enslaved persons perished because they were not

---

[7] The remainder of this section draws on: Günver Güneş, "Kölelikten Özgürlüğe: İzmir'de Zenciler ve Zenci Folkloru," *Toplumsal Tarih*, 11 (1999): 4–10 (information in this paragraph is from 4–5 and 9); Esma Durugönül, "The Invisibility of Turks of African Origin and the Construction of Turkish Cultural Identity: The Need for a New Historiography," *Journal of Black Studies*, 33 (2003): 289 (based on Güneş, "Kölelikten Özgürlüğe: İzmir'de," 4); Y. Hakan Erdem, *Slavery in the Ottoman Empire and Its Demise, 1800–1909* (New York, 1996), pp. 29–33. For the Chios case, see Philip P. Argenti, *The Massacres of Chios Described in Contemporary Diplomatic Reports* (London, 1932); Emad Helal, "Muhammad Ali's First Army: The Experiment in Building an Entirely Slave Army," in Terence Walz and Kenneth M. Cuno (eds.), *Race and Slavery in the Middle East: Histories of Trans-Saharan Africans in Nineteenth Century Egypt, Sudan and the Ottoman Empire* (Cairo, 2010), p. 35; Ehud R. Toledano, *State and Society in Mid-Nineteenth-Century Egypt* (Cambridge, 1989), pp. 56–7.

used to the colder weather and suffered from contagious pulmonary diseases. An additional factor is that Islamic law and Ottoman social norm sanctioned concubinage and subsequent absorption into the host societies. An enslaved woman impregnated by her owner could not be sold, her offspring were considered free, and she herself would be freed upon the death of her master. Thus, exogamy and the passing of several generations ensured not only the social absorption of free mixed-race children of cross-racial marriages, but also their visible disappearance from the outside observer's "gaze."

Much of this also applied to the enslaved Circassians, Georgians, Greeks, Slavs, and other non-Africans, who entered Ottoman territory either voluntarily or by force. The enslaved Circassians were mostly refugees driven out from the Caucasus by the Russians from the mid-1850s to the mid-1860s. In the Caucasus, Circassian societies comprised several tribal units, sharing related languages, cultural traditions, and social organization. Under Russian rule, the bonded class – or "caste," as Shami prefers – of agricultural workers (in Adygé Circassian, *pshitl*) was con-sidered enserfed, but in Ottoman law they were accorded the status of "slave" (Turkish, *köle*). In reality, the *pshitl* were more the clients-protégés (what in Arabic would be *tabiᶜ*) of the landlord-patron (Adygé Circassian, *pshi*; Ottoman Turkish, *bey*). This was a hereditary status, and the off-spring of free and bonded marriages inherited the status of the enslaved parent.

Other Circassians and Georgians, largely young women, were being bought into the Ottoman Empire by slave dealers for service in urban elite harems. A preference for white women prevailed among male members of the Ottoman imperial elite in the long nineteenth century, and even before. Accordingly, agents for the imperial harem and those of the leading households in the center and the provinces were instructed to recruit young women among the Circassian and Georgian populations of the Caucasus. These women were trained in the recruiting household and socialized into elite household roles. As the century drew to a close, recruitment declined under the growing restrictions imposed by the Otto-man Government on the practice, but it was still being pursued on a limited basis even by the imperial harem and some of the top-ranking officeholders. It is worth noting that despite African and Circassian domes-tic servitude being the predominant form of Ottoman enslavement in the nineteenth century, other forms also existed at certain historical conjunc-tions, for example, enslaved Sudanese men in military and agricultural work in Egypt.

The first form of note is enslavement as punishment for rebellion. However, by mid-century, the enslavement of rebels and their families as war captives seems to have all but stopped. A notable example is of Greek

Orthodox Christians from the island of Chios during the Greek War of Independence (1821–32). In legal terms, by rebelling they had broken their ties to the state and thus the protections they would normally receive under it no longer applied. In 1822, the Ottoman army proceeded to punish the island by killing most of its male inhabitants and enslaving many of the women and children. Thousands, mostly women and children, were likely enslaved as a result of this one incident. Even though Chios is the best-known example, which is still in need of further, serious research, it was probably not unique during the Greek War of Independence.

The second form of note is African military and agricultural slavery. While military and agricultural slavery had previously existed in Ottoman lands, it was not the prevailing type in the nineteenth century. The rule of Mehmed Ali (r. 1805 to 1848) and his descendants of the semi-autonomous Ottoman province of Egypt may serve as an example. From around 1815 onward, Sudanese men were enslaved and inducted into his army, and by the early 1820s, their number was estimated at 10,000. These enslaved soldiers were used to aid Egypt's expansion south into the Sudan. However, this experiment had only limited success, after which Mehmed Ali began to draft the Egyptian peasantry (Arabic, *fallahin*) into his army and moved to develop a modern, Western-style force (Turkish, *Nizam-ı Cedit*). Sudanese slaves were also used to harvest cash crops on large agricultural estates. The use of slave labor in the fields grew dramatically during spikes in demand for cotton, such as during the 1860s as a result of the American Civil War. However, enslaved agricultural laborers remained a small minority among Egypt's free cultivators, who were, nevertheless, subjected from time to time to the *corvée* for maintaining the all-important irrigation system.

WAS ENSLAVEMENT IN OTTOMAN AND OTHER ISLAMIC SOCIETIES "MILD"?

In the rhetoric that still pervades the international community, torn as it is between Huntington's "Clash of Civilizations" and Fukayama's "End of History," Muslims – as individuals and as communities – have often found themselves on the defensive. This has increased dramatically since the 9/11 terror attacks of 2001, the reaction to which has been a campaign to stop what is called "Islamophobia." Muslims had not only to offer explanations for the dismal human rights record of many Muslim-majority countries, but also to exonerate a past of enslavement and very late and often partial abolition, both anchored in Islamic scriptures and backed by conservative defenders of the faith among the *ulema*. Partly, that response is reminiscent of nineteenth-century polemic apologia deployed to counter emergent

Atlantic abolitionism and antislavery campaigns that began to target Islamic states such as the Ottoman Empire.

Islamic apologetics regarding enslavement dates back to the early European attempts to conduce the Ottoman Government to abolish slavery.[8] One may characterize the counter-arguments produced by Ottoman defenders of human bondage as denialism. Since the main points in this debate have already been discussed some three decades ago, there is no reason to repeat them in this chapter. Suffice it here to reiterate that the main thrust of the Ottoman – and by extension also the Islamic – position was that there was no comparison between the then and later pervasive model of enslavement, i.e. Atlantic plantation slavery, and bondage in Islamic societies. Although there were many exceptions to the rule, the "Atlantic model" conjured up in the minds of people an extreme image of mostly male, African, agricultural, gang-driven, unfree labor, a form of dehumanized domination of rich white men over marginalized, enslaved black persons.

Among scholars of enslavement worldwide, there is a debate between those who strongly oppose the universalization of the Atlantic model as the prototype of enslavement everywhere. Gwyn Campbell has argued for another model, the Indian Ocean World, where enslavement was quite different in terms of the populations enslaved – a small minority of Africans, with a large majority of women. Also, the tasks performed by enslaved persons were not the prevailing plantation gang enslavement allegedly characteristic of Atlantic slavery. Since Islamic societies have been a major component of the Indian Ocean World, and given the more integrative and less exclusive nature of enslavement in the Indian Ocean, some scholars have used the models' putative dichotomy to advance again the "mildness" argument for slavery in Islamic societies. However, studies of enslavement in the Indian subcontinent, for example by Indrani Chatterjee, or China can hardly support the mild nature position.

That position was as far from realities in the Muslim, Moro parts of the Philippines or in the Algero-Sahara, as it was in the Ottoman Empire. The struggle between runaway slaves and their masters in the Philippines during the US occupation, argues Michael Salman, was "inexplicable within the official colonial image of 'mild slavery.'" However, the need to keep the Muslims in the south in check while the war of conquest still

[8] Information and observations in this section draw on: Ehud R. Toledano, *Slavery and Abolition in the Ottoman Middle East* (Seattle, WA, 1997), pp. 4, 126 ff.; Ehud R. Toledano, "The Shifting Patterns of Ottoman Enslavement in the Early Modern Period: From European to African-Caucasian," in Simonetta Cavaciocchi (ed.), *Relazioni economiche tra Europa e mondo islamico, secc. XIII-XVIII: atti della "trentottesima settimana di studi" 1–5 maggio 2006* (Grasina, 2007), Vol. 2, pp. 699–718; Erdem, *Slavery in the Ottoman Empire*; Zilfi, *Women and Slavery*, pp. 97–8; Gwyn Campbell (ed.), *Abolition and Its Aftermath in Indian Ocean Africa and Asia* (New York, 2005).

continued in the north induced US officials toward a cleansed concept of Moro enslavement. Within that concept, the harsh realities of being enslaved were "screened out," or redefined as "familiar tensions within acceptable norms of hierarchy, subordination, and servitude." A midway solution for the Americans on the ground was to harbor enslaved fugitives and offer compensation to the owners for manumission. In the Ottoman Empire, too, the issue of absconding was truly revealing of the way in which enslaved persons viewed the "mildness" of bondage. Displaying also other means of resistance, violent and non-violent, enslaved Ottomans convinced the Tanzimat state to come to their rescue and ameliorate their condition through manumission and social protection.

However, on the polemics level, when Muslim writers defended enslavement in their societies, they sought to project a totally different image of the realities with which enslaved persons had to cope. They emphasized domestic, household, mainly female slavery as the predomin-ant form of bondage, and depicted that as being "part of the family," a benign mode of belonging to a patron, the head of the household, one of a number of ways that attached people to those social-political-economic units. The practice of concubinage, common in elite households, was portrayed as an intimate arrangement that enabled enslaved women to join good Muslim families and be integrated, together with their offspring, into secure and respectable households. That reality for the enslaved, far from being "mild," has been amply documented and cogently argued. However, Muslim defenders of slavery not only denied any resemblance between the Atlantic model and Islamic realities, they even rejected the use of the term "slavery" in reference to their societies. The wall they thus erected served them to repel foreign pressures as violation of the privacy and intimacy of the Muslim family. It also effectively prevented the emergence of any home-grown abolitionist movement and stifled any antislavery discourse.

In a way, this is surprising, since the debate and struggle over abolition in the Atlantic World revolved around the crucial issue of status – legal and social. The moral right of human beings to live in freedom and not be owned by another person was at the heart of it all. Yet, in Islamic societies, it seems that the issue has almost been lost, with the following questions taking center stage: the nature of bondage, i.e. how mild or harsh it is; the treatment of enslaved persons; the rescue of "uncivilized people" from paganism and delivering to them "the light of Islam"; and how much enslavement forms part of a legitimate patronage system. Although the presumption of freedom was the basic principle (Arabic, *al-asl huwwa al-hurriyya*) in scripture and law right from the early, formative days of the new religion, ways have always been too easily found to skirt and interpret it away, so that slavery would persist. To resolve that apparent incongruity, scholars of Islamic enslavement have offered several explanations, ranging from the structural to the socio-cultural and economic.

At the same time, recent scholarship has largely avoided unfocused discussions of this sort. Critical to moving beyond such polemics was the attempt to understand the enslaved within their own context, and from what has been called "a slave-centered experience." Historians working on Ottoman enslavement examine the varieties, forms, and shapes that Ottoman slaveries took, more often than not heeding John Hunwick's recommendation to look both at the commonalities imposed by Islamic law and ethics and of the differences of Arab, Berber, Turkish, Persian, and other cultural traditions, or those distinctions that are economic and political. However, we need to remember that enslavement existed in virtually all human societies of the Mediterranean basin and beyond since antiquity, lasting into the first half of the twentieth century. When attempts at abolition were launched in the second half of the nineteenth century, largely as a result of European – mainly British – pressure, Muslim societies in those regions still considered slavery as part of their natural way of life.

Ottoman enslavement was driven by two main factors: first, the desire for elites to create large households with a number of dependents, to increase their social capital as benevolent patrons; and, second, the need to fill the almost continuous labor shortage. For urban elite households, holding enslaved persons, mostly but not exclusively, African women, provided domestic service, displayed wealth, and increased social prestige. Unlike in the Americas, enslavement in the Ottoman Empire was, in general, a temporary state, with enslavers encouraged, though not specifically required, by Islamic tradition and custom to manumit their household slaves after a period of seven to ten years. Other mechanisms of manumission, such as that afforded to *ümmüveleds* or negotiated between enslaver and enslaved, ensured that the enslaved population would be continuously depleted, thereby keeping the demand at a fairly constant level and creating an active market for enslaved persons.

Enslavement was one of the ways of incorporation into patronage networks. It was the social organization of the household that facilitated the transition from enslaved to protégé. Indeed, bondage was, at its core, an important albeit involuntary means of recruiting and socializing individuals into households. The household structure was designed to benefit its head in two ways: through the prestige of managing a large number of subordinates; and as a key method of organizing their labor or military capabilities for his or her own political benefit. To the enslaved, these relationships were important as they compensated for their lack of existing biological kin relations. They were well aware of the importance of maintaining ties to the household, and only when hard-pressed would willingly break the bond, often seeking to retain their hard-earned reattachment to a patron even beyond manumission. Failure to create a post-emancipation patron–client relationship meant risking their safety and a life of destitution, especially for enslaved females. The patron, too, had a vested interest in keeping the freed person within the household and continuing to benefit from his or her labor power.

In the remaining sections of this chapter, we shall survey the two large ethnic categories of enslaved persons in the Ottoman Empire during the nineteenth century: first, we deal with the enslavement and coerced transportation of Africans and the steps taken to reduce and ultimately suppress the slave trade in Africans; and, second, we examine the practices of enslaving Circassians and Georgians and the gradual phasing out of *kul/ harem* and Caucasian concubinage.

ENSLAVEMENT OF AFRICANS IN THE OTTOMAN EMPIRE

The trade in Africans during the nineteenth century was carried out along four routes, though these were flexible and often changed and overlapped.[9] Historically, one of the main routes that brought African slaves to the Ottoman Empire was down the Nile Valley. Owing to the British influence in Egypt since the early nineteenth century, the trade there was prohibited and regulated much earlier than elsewhere in the Empire. While the flow of slaves north from Cairo to ports such as Alexandria was reduced over the century, an internal Egyptian slave trade and slavery continued regardless of regulations. Another route by which slaves were transported from sub-Saharan Africa to Ottoman lands was by the Red Sea, which served the pilgrims to Mecca and Medina. The Ottoman Empire also drew slaves from East Africa as far south as Zanzibar. Finally, in the mid nineteenth century, the trans-Saharan route to North African ports such as Benghazi and smaller ports such as Derna experienced a dramatic growth.

On all routes, African slaves were moved under gruelling conditions by land in caravans carrying from dozens to hundreds of slaves, also other cargoes such as ostrich feathers, animal hides, and canuba wax. Slaves were often sold and traded as opportunities arose at oases and other midway points. Some were destined for local clients, staying within Africa, while others were loaded onto ships in African ports bound to the northern tier of the Ottoman Empire, with docking for refuelling in Mediterranean islands. The opening of the Suez Canal in 1869 effectively connected the

---

[9] The following draws on: Toledano, *The Ottoman Slave Trade*, pp. 14–54, 57, 205, 238, 240–4; Erdem, *Slavery in the Ottoman Empire*, pp. 39–42; John Wright, *The Trans-Saharan Slave Trade* (New York, 2007), pp. 125–6.

Red Sea and Mediterranean slave trade networks. From that point onward, it was possible to load slaves onto ships along the Red Sea coast and move them north to Mediterranean port cities. There were two main slave markets for Africans in the Ottoman Empire: Istanbul and the Hijaz. As the imperial capital, Istanbul and its numerous palaces were constantly looking to replenish their slave population. The Hijaz, comprising of the Muslim holy cities of Mecca and Medina, was the site of an impressive amount of trade surrounding the annual pilgrimage (*Hajj*). Indeed, all major Ottoman cities and ports saw the arrival of slaves directly from the interior of Africa such as Cairo, Tripoli, Benghazi, Salonica, Izmir, Bursa, Beirut, and Basra.

The enslaved Africans transported across these routes were likely acquired through wars, kidnappings, purchase at internal markets, or instability in the region. Environmental factors often played a role in this instability: for example, the trans-Saharan route was dramatically affected by the unique condition of Lake Chad, which recedes to a fraction of its size annually in the hot season, and causes food scarcity and instability. Conversely, in the rainy season, it was surrounded by numerous plantation-like farms using slave labor. As noted above, the moment British anti-slave trade policing began in Ottoman lands, this trade also grew to its largest documented rate. While the reasons for this are still unclear, that rise was in large part a result of the introduction of steamships in the nineteenth century. Whereas wooden dhow-like boats were the main means of transport in Ottoman seas until this point, these ships were both more reliable and quicker. Despite the fact that many steamers were foreign owned and operated, they are known to have carried slaves whether wittingly or not.

Indeed, the Austrian Lloyd Company steamships played a critical role in the transportation of enslaved Africans to Ottoman cities in the northern tier of the Empire.[10] Alison Frank has shown how the Austro-Hungarian Empire was involved in supporting Ottoman slavery, and how this state-owned enterprise benefited from operating in a grey area around British-Ottoman Anti-Slave Trade Treaties (discussed below). When faced with accusations that their ships were complicit in the trade, the Austro-Hungarian government did not change course because it would have meant giving up their commercial position in the region, instead relying on a technicality in the legal definition to avoid "knowingly" transporting slaves. Thus, the Austro-Hungarian government was able to appear as abolitionist, while at the same time never letting such concerns interrupt their commercial traffic.

[10] Alison Frank, "The Children of the Desert and the Laws of the Sea: Austria, Great Britain, the Ottoman Empire, and the Mediterranean Slave Trade in the Nineteenth Century," *American Historical Review*, 117 (2012): 412, 426, 433–4.

PROHIBITION(S) OF THE AFRICAN SLAVE TRADE
TO THE OTTOMAN EMPIRE

Western European (chiefly British) pressure was the main force acting on the Ottoman Empire to take part in the suppression of the slave trade, after efforts to have the government abolish slavery failed in the early 1840s. After taking steps to effectively enforce anti-slaving measures for the Atlantic trade, the British and other European powers began to expand such efforts to all parts of coastal Africa, including Ottoman territory.[11] By mid-century, the economic dependence of the Ottomans on the British, French, and other European powers was such that they had no choice but to listen to British remonstrations against the slave trade. Finally bowing to pressure in 1857, the sultan issued an edict considered the first legal move to suppress the traffic in Africans into the Empire. Mechanisms were developed, documents issued, and procedures were put in place to enforce, most of the time only partially, the suppression edict.

The next major treaty was the Anglo-Ottoman Convention for the Suppression of the Black Slave Trade in 1880. The treaty accorded the British mutual rights of search and seizure of vessels suspected of trans-porting slaves in other Ottoman waters such as the Red Sea, the Persian Gulf, and parts of the coast of East Africa, but not in the Mediterranean, arguably the key linkage in moving enslaved people to Istanbul, Izmir, and other northern ports. British antislavery activities were therefore limited to Ottoman ports and not the high seas. That omission may have been intentional, as the British did not want Ottoman authorities boarding British-flagged vessels, perhaps because they suspected that their own steamers were illegally carrying slaves like the Austrian Lloyd discussed above.

Because the 1880 Anglo-Ottoman Treaty specified that slave traders were to be prosecuted under Ottoman law, the Ottoman Government had to draft new laws, in 1882 and 1883, as there were no existing legal restrictions against the slave trade or delineated punishments. However, when draft laws were submitted to Sultan Abdülhamit II for approval, none was ever given. It was only under pressure from the looming Brussels Anti-Slavery Conference in 1889 that sultanic assent was finally given, creating a clearly defined set of laws that ensured the enforcement of the prohibition against the African slave trade into the Ottoman Empire.

Doubtless, the intra-Ottoman struggle to form a coherent policy that both government functionaries and the sultan himself could agree upon

[11] The following passages draw on: Donald C. Blaisdell, *European Financial Control in the Ottoman Empire: A Study of the Establishment, Activities, and Significance of the Administration of the Ottoman Public Debt* (New York, 1929); Toledano, *As If Silent and Absent*, pp. 118–24; Erdem, *Slavery in the Ottoman Empire*, pp. 112, 150–1.

was both intense and complicated. At times, Abdülhamit II was willing to sign it, at other times he was hesitant, believing it would represent a loss of Ottoman sovereignty and tarnish his image. Ottoman reformers experienced difficulties when it came to imposing antislavery measures against the religious sanction and social acceptability that the practice enjoyed. A year later, the Ottoman Government joined the first multilateral treaty against the slave trade concluded under the General Act of the Brussels Conference. This Act was largely a repetition of the articles included in the Ottoman law signed in 1889, and thus does not represent a drastic change, but rather an international commitment to act with one key addition: that the emancipating state must act to establish places of care for rescued African slaves.

Following the prohibition of the slave trade in 1857, the nature of the traffic changed dramatically to adapt to a new set of circumstances. No longer was it possible to openly transport slaves, especially through major ports, to the markets. It thus moved "underground" and arguably added to the suffering of the enslaved themselves. There were also loopholes in the regulations for transporting slaves. For example, slave traders often acted as regular passengers aboard steamships in plain sight of authorities, flashing forged travel documents for the enslaved, who were presented as servants or members of the household. In such cases, which were all too common, authorities had little recourse. Still, the traffic was significantly reduced, so that by the turn of the twentieth century, it was only a trickle. In 1908, one of the new Young Turks' first acts was to rid the imperial palace of all of its harem slaves. The government also prohibited the sale of Circassian slaves in the Empire, and as the new Constitution was declared the same year, all citizens were granted equal rights, which ipso facto abolished the status of unfree persons.

AGENCY, RESISTANCE, AND AMELIORATION

As elsewhere, Ottoman slaves attempted to improve their condition in bondage whenever possible. This was done through a variety of techniques, some minor and within the limits of the existing system, some more drastic. Running away in any circumstance for Ottoman slaves was not done without serious risk, and would not be done unless their relationship with their owner had become unbearable.[12] Ottoman law dictated that runaway slaves were to be returned to their owners with no punishment attached; however, owners wishing to punish their slaves would often accuse them of theft in the process, something which put

---

[12] Information in the following section, mostly anecdotal for lack of appropriate statistical data, is culled from Toledano, *As If Silent and Absent*, pp. 69, 88, 104, 118–24.

them in a precarious position. The only way slaves could safely get away and stay away was if they could prove maltreatment, which was all but impossible. However, an important change occurred to the options available to slaves in post 1857. With the foreign, particularly British, consulates becoming known to slaves as sites of potential emancipation, slaves began to flee to them for protection. Indeed, extensive documentation shows many slaves did just that. If successful, slaves were cared for and helped to acquire manumission papers (Turkish: *hürriyetname* or *azatname*) from local Ottoman councils. The main reason a slave would run away was to escape abuse, whether physical or verbal in nature.

Beyond flight, slaves in the Ottoman Empire employed a variety of strategies to ameliorate their condition in bondage. One approach was to try to gain power within the household, such as trying to become the preferred concubine or wife of the head of the household. Daily sabotage was a common practice of slaves (and non-slaves alike). Another more dramatic measure was arson, both as a means to disrupt the household and perhaps cause its bankruptcy, but also as a form of social protest.

THE TANZIMAT STATE AND MANUMITTED AFRICANS

By the mid nineteenth century, a strong, centralized Ottoman state was developing mechanisms for not only halting the trade of slaves, under British pressure, but for shaping their future beyond emancipation.[13] The state's intervention in the emancipation process also occurred in tension with existing local solutions to the rising population of rescued slaves. In some instances, state intervention seemed unnecessary, but can perhaps be explained by the emerging modern state's need for a more knowable and manageable population. For example, in 1884, the British consul at Chania on Crete described to his superior in Istanbul the actions of the local Ottoman governor which, while not technically part of the British-Ottoman Convention against the slave trade, did have a positive effect on helping emancipated slaves there. It was reported that after finding suspected slaves aboard ships in the port, the Ottoman governor had them "lodged in the house of the Sheikh of the Benghazi Arabs." After a day of living under the auspices of the Sheikh's household, they declared themselves to be illegally enslaved and sought to stay on Crete. The

[13] The following is based on: Toledano, *As If Silent and Absent*, pp. 104, 118–24, 203–54; Toledano, *The Ottoman Slave Trade*, pp. 200, 203–4; Erdem, *Slavery in the Ottoman Empire*, pp. 173–6; Michael Ferguson, "Enslaved and Emancipated Africans on Crete," in Walz and Cuno (eds.), *Race and Slavery in the Middle East*, pp. 171–95; Güneş, "Kölelikten Özgürlüğe: İzmir'de," 4–10. The official documents used are: Great Britain, Parliamentary Papers, Correspondence with British Representatives and Agents Abroad and Reports from Naval Officers and the Treasury Relative to the Slave Trade. Africa. No. 1, 1885 (London, 1884–85) [C.4523]), 32, no. 53; and ibid., *Africa. No. 1, 1886*, 82–5, 87.

British consul wholeheartedly approved of these ad hoc actions by the Ottoman governor.

A year later, in the fall of 1885, the British Consul at Chania reported a similar situation, with a rather different response from the Ottoman governor. He explained to British officials there that if he were to send the slaves to the Sheikh again, he would be "exceeding his instructions" from Istanbul. After British representatives attempted to pressure the government in Istanbul to allow this local solution in Chania to continue, Ottoman officials in Istanbul issued a decree stating that only the police are capable of manumission and that they alone will issue Istanbul-approved documents to prove a person's status, demonstrating the Ottoman state's desire to be the sole actor involved in the emancipation of African slaves.

Such a state-imposed emancipation process generally occurred when slaves were found aboard ships or in Ottoman ports by the British, or when slaves ran away to foreign (usually British) consuls claiming maltreatment. In both instances, the slaves would then generally be held by the consular officials while they contacted local Ottoman authorities to obtain guarantees that they would be emancipated. If the Ottoman authorities believed their case to be legitimate, the slaves would then be granted an official court document attesting their "freedom." Granting freedom to the enslaved was traditionally done by their owners, and if necessary, endorsed by the *Sharʿi* courts. The creation of these new methods and documentation represents a clear way in which the state began to regulate the emancipation process. Nonetheless, despite being aware of the central government's new laws against the slave trade, local officials were often either unable or unwilling to rescue and emancipate the enslaved. The resulting tensions between the British and Ottoman officials are evident in many British consular reports.

With documents in hand, the rescued slaves became technically "free." However, for the Ottoman state, a new serious concern had resulted from their intervention: What should be done with these unemployed, homeless, and kinless people in a society based largely on patronage and households? To address this concern, the majority of slaves were simply placed, with British approval, in "appropriate" households as domestic servants, under the condition that they receive wages for their work and not be sold again into slavery. Once placed in a household, the slaves were then beyond the protection of British and Ottoman officials and it is very likely that many of them were re-sold and re-enslaved.

However, not all slaves were integrated back into households. Some were "freed" and simply left to their own devices. This helps to explain the emergence of poor African quarters in many cities of the late Ottoman Empire, including Izmir, Chania on Crete, and Istanbul. By the third

214 CAMBRIDGE WORLD HISTORY OF SLAVERY

quarter of the nineteenth century, the state-interventionist solution to the problem of the African slave trade had created a new problem: poor, kinless, unemployed emancipated Africans on the streets became a significant feature of the late Ottoman city. While emancipated Africans had various strategies for gaining control of their destinies and ameliorating their conditions after emancipation, some of which are discussed below, by the late 1870s, the Ottoman, Tanzimat state had developed its own solutions to that new problem by taking control of the newly manumitted slaves themselves.

THE IZMIR PLAN

The "Izmir Plan" is the best example of the way in which the Ottoman state attempted to manage the lives of manumitted Africans after their liberation. Izmir was the second largest city of the Empire, with a major Mediterranean port and productive agricultural hinterland.[14] As already mentioned above, under the 1880 and 1890 treaties, the Ottoman state was required to construct guest houses for emancipated slaves all across the Empire. They were, however, designed solely as temporary shelters until they could be transported to the main guest house in Izmir. Once in Izmir, arrangements were made to send men to vocational schools, artisan battalions, and military bands, while the women were to be placed in appropriate households as salaried domestic servants. However, state expenditures were low in the following years and the Izmir guest house never received the adequate funding to properly run and aid in the settlement of the emancipated slaves. It is known, however, that men "almost immediately found employment" upon arriving at the guest house. Just where they found employment is unclear, possibly in one of the trades that the school was associated with. Many became porters, itinerant coffee and water sellers, and small boatmen, as photographic evidence shows poor Africans working in these jobs at this time.

Another key aspect of the "Izmir Plan" took place in that city's rich agricultural hinterland. In order to further provide for the growing needs of this rapidly developing agricultural region, officials devised a plan to forcefully marry and settle emancipated Africans on that land. The state also constructed houses for them and provided some farming tools to cultivate state- and crown-owned lands. Especially when sharecropping

---

[14] This section draws mostly on the following: Izmir's rise to prominence in the nineteenth century is based on Reşat Kasaba, "Izmir," *Review* 16 (1993): 387–410; Erdem, *Slavery in the Ottoman Empire*, pp. 179, 181; Güneş, "Kölelikten Özgürlüğe: İzmir'de," 5; A. Martal, "Afrikadan Izmir'e: Izmir'de Bir Köle Misafirhanesi," *Kebikeç* 10 (2000): 176–8; and Michael Ferguson, *The African Presence in Late Ottoman Izmir and Beyond* (unpublished PhD dissertation, McGill University, 2014), pp. 41–5.

was involved, dealing with such a vulnerable population created numerous opportunities for abuse by landowners, a situation which in some ways mirrors the transition to post-slavery capitalist relations seen elsewhere. Freed African women were also sent on their own to these farming villages to work as domestic servants in the households of wealthy farmers. The legacy of that settlement project still lives on in Turkey today, as not a few villages around Izmir still include Turkish citizens of sub-Saharan African descent.

THE CALF FESTIVAL OF IZMIR

The Calf Festival of Izmir (Turkish, *Dana Bayramı*) is one of the better-known "festivals" that both enslaved and liberated Africans celebrated in Ottoman lands in this period.[15] Its existence shows that Africans brought with them cultural practices from their places of origin and sought to maintain a spiritual connection with their homeland cultures. Many aspects of this practice suggest forms of subversion, if not blatant resistance. While this particular festival described below took place in Izmir, there is enough resonance with other festivals in Istanbul, Cairo, and Chania on Crete, and in North African ports, to suggest that similar practices occurred throughout the Ottoman Empire in the period under discussion.

The annual festival, which occurred in May and lasted three weekends, took place atop a hill overlooking the city of Izmir, in what might be called the African neighborhood. On the first days of the celebration, the community dressed in white and formed a procession that wound through the streets to collect donations for the upcoming festival. Musicians playing on gourds and drums were led by the *godya/kudya* (elsewhere known as a *kolbaşı*), or the female spiritual leader of the community. The procession chanted traditional songs in African languages as they marched. The day ended with a social gathering at the highest point on the hill. The following weekend, the African community used the collected donations to buy a young calf. They then decorated the calf and paraded it through the streets, singing and dancing along the way. In some years, it is reported that different neighborhoods bought calves for themselves, and thus the festival took on a competitive dimension as well.

---

[15] Information in this section is drawn from: Güneş, "Kölelikten Özgürlüğe: İzmir'de"; Erdem, *Slavery in the Ottoman Empire*, pp. 173–6; Toledano, *As If Silent and Absent*, pp. 212–17; Ferguson, *African Presence in Late Ottoman Izmir*, pp. 139–47; Durugönül, "The Invisibility of Turks of African Origin." For studies on Zar/Bori, see: Ahmed Al-Safi, I.M. Lewis, and Sayyid Hurreiz (eds.), *Women's Medicine: The Zar-Bori Cult in Africa and Beyond* (Edinburgh, 1991); Janice Boddy, *Wombs and Alien Spirits Women, Men, and the Zar Cult in Northern Sudan* (Madison, WI, 1989).

On the Friday of the following week came the final part of the event, the actual Calf Festival. It was on this day that the celebrations reached their climax. Waking up at dawn and dressed in their best clothes, one group of Africans met in a nearby cemetery to prepare for a sacrifice, while the others once again congregated on the top of the hill to decorate the calf and parade it through the city, this time toward the cemetery. Once at the cemetery, the *godya* performed the sacrifice. The participants then each marked themselves with blood from the calf. With the ceremony completed, they cooked the calf in a large pot, along with rice and chickpeas. After the feast, there was a specialized form of dancing involving a staff, and courtship between the young people took place. The festival was a public spectacle in the late nineteenth century, as people of all backgrounds stood on rooftops, climbed up trees, and packed the streets to see the parade.

The core element of the ceremonies, parades, and festivals celebrated by the African-Ottoman communities bear the hallmarks of the *Zar/Bori* possession and healing rituals, which were "infused with Sufi rites and other localized Islamic components."[16] *Zar* (East African) and *Bori* (West African) are two names applied to the various female-led, trance-based socio-religious practices involving communication with spirits that afflict mostly women; these practices were transported to the Sudan, Egypt, and the Levant from East and West sub-Saharan Africa. Since at least the nineteenth century, these cultural effects have played an important role in the social and spiritual lives of people, particularly, but not exclusively, women, in these parts of Africa. Thus, *Zar/Bori* was a cultural component that enslaved Africans brought with them to Ottoman lands, much like the way in which core elements of Vodou were brought to Saint Domingue (Haiti) and Candomblé to Brazil and other regions to which enslaved Africans were trafficked, especially in large numbers.

The prevalence of spirit possession rituals among communities of enslaved and emancipated Africans suggests that it was not only a cultural link to their place of origin, but a critical strategy for managing the difficulties they experienced, while also creating group cohesion that enabled adaptation to the new circumstances. In addition, the Calf Festival ceremonies gave African women a major role and, thus, empowered them in a society where they were usually disempowered.

Throughout the nineteenth century, Africans celebrated the Calf Festival in Izmir unrestrained by any state officials. While perhaps striking some residents as a bit unusual or as a source of curiosity, it became part of the local fabric of the city. This changed briefly, however, when the governor

---

[16] Toledano, *As If Silent and Absent*, p. 212.

of Izmir, Hasan Fehmi Paşa, attempted and ultimately failed to prohibit the Calf Festival around 1894 to 1895. Despite its short-lived prohibition, even attempting to regulate the lives of Africans in this way represents a concrete change in the practices and attitude of those in local government, and foreshadows what happened to such practices in the twentieth century. Concerns about challenges to law and order, as about morality, particularly for women, the allure of these festivals for non-Africans, their potential as sites of sedition, and a belief among imperial elites that such practices were of barbaric nature and contravened the vision of progress, all put Africans under the watchful eye of authorities wherever they found themselves after emancipation, especially in urban spaces.

LEGACIES OF AFRICAN ENSLAVEMENT IN POST-OTTOMAN SOCIETIES

While each successor state has dealt with its heritage of African enslavement differently, the rise of the nation state in the twentieth-century Middle East and North Africa silenced manifestation and discussion of enslaved historical experiences, mostly but not exclusively of Africans. Every so often, that silence was breached and the hegemonic nationalist narrative had to face the multicultural nature of most of these societies. One such case occurred in 2005, when a Turkish marble worker named Mustafa Olpak was inspired by scholarly work on Ottoman slavery (by Toledano and Erdem) to write a biography of his family, entitled *Kenya-Girit-İstanbul: Köle Kıyısından İnsan Biyografileri* (Kenya-Crete-Istanbul: Human Biographies from the Slave Coast),[17] detailing his family history from enslavement in Africa to integration into modern Turkey during the twentieth century. One of the more poignant moments in the book is the description of the daily discrimination faced by his mother in school in the 1940s. The publication of Olpak's book opened the door to a new discussion about the history of people of African descent in Turkey, particularly those in and around Izmir, the Aegean Coast, and Istanbul, who self-identify as Afro-Turks. With the success of the book, along with support from the UNESCO Slave Route Project and the European Union, Olpak founded the Africans Culture and Solidarity Society (*Afrikalılar Kültür ve Dayanışma Derneği*) based in Izmir, which as of 2010 could boast around 1,500 members.

This attempt to raise awareness and promote an enslaved group identity was not unique to Turkey. In Jordan and in Israel, African communities of formerly enslaved and free migrants have existed for a long time among the Bedouin tribes. They are known in Arabic as *ʿAbid*, namely "slaves," have

---

[17] Mustafa Olpak, *Kenya-Girit-İstanbul: Köle Kıyısından İnsan Byografleri* (Istanbul, 2005).

been traditionally relegated to the lower rungs on the socio-economic ladder, and are beginning to talk about their discrimination and their cultural heritage. An Israeli producer created a documentary about the Bedouin *'Abid* entitled *The Film Class*. In Iran, communities of African descent have been studied by Behnaz Mirzai, who produced two documentaries about their plight and culture, entitled *Afro-Iranian Lives* and *The African-Baluchi Trance Dance*. In North African countries, there are also early signs of a rising consciousness of African identities, but they have not yet developed into actual organized movements. Throughout the Middle East and North Africa (MENA) regions, however, such activities have faced reluctant states that have viewed them as a threat to the national project, more so under attack since the uprisings associated with the Arab Spring.

CIRCASSIAN ENSLAVEMENT AND SLAVE TRADE

The term Circassian is an umbrella term, much like "African," to describe the people coming from a particular geographical region, the Caucasus and the northeastern shores of the Black Sea. The largest groups among the Circassians were the Adygé, Ubikh, and Abkhaz tribal federations, whose members engaged mostly in agriculture.[18] Considered by the Ottomans as nominally Muslim, elite circles looked down upon their "savage and uncivilized" cultural practices, and permitted their enslavement. As already mentioned, an enslaved caste existed among them, which was hereditary, so that children of free and bonded couples inherited the status of the enslaved parent. Under the Russian system, these were registered as enserfed persons, living in families and working the land under their quasi-feudal landlords. As a result of the Russian-orchestrated ethnic cleansing, it is estimated that about 350,000 people lost their lives and more than a million were forced to leave the Caucasus from the mid-1850s to the mid-1860s (Ottoman estimates are of 1.5 million people). The government resettled them often near frontier regions, such as Bulgaria, Eastern Anatolia, and the Levant, in what is a defining feature of the demographic make-up of many parts of Turkey and the Middle East today.

The enserfed population, put by the Ottomans at 150,000, was integrated into rural communities with an enslaved status, there being no legal category of enserfment in Ottoman *Sharia* law. However, as in many other

---

[18] Information in this section is drawn mostly from the following: Toledano, *As If Silent and Absent*, pp. 12, 53–4, 133–5; Toledano, *The Ottoman Slave Trade*, pp. 28, 150, 164; Erdem, *Slavery in the Ottoman Empire*, pp. 49, 46, 51; and Ryan Gingeras, *Sorrowful Shores: Violence, Ethnicity, and the End of the Ottoman Empire, 1912–1923* (Oxford, 2009), pp. 24–5.

countries of the MENA region and in African societies today, interest in understanding these experiences from within the Circassian diaspora is only beginning to emerge, though accepting and processing the enslaved past is still proving difficult. Although Circassians have organized cultural associations in Turkey and outside, they have not yet come to dealing with the history of enslavement by Ottoman, Arab, and Iranian societies. An impressive beginning of trying to show how the enslaved past still resonates with Circassian women in the present is Seteney Shami's recasting of Toledano's study about the enslaved Circassian girl named Şemsigül (mid-nineteenth-century Cairo).[19]

Enslavement of Circassians did not begin with their mass deportations from the Caucasus in the 1850s, but existed from about the last quarter of the eighteenth century, when slave-trading patterns began to shift from the Balkans, Eastern Europe, and the northern shores of the Black Sea to Circassia and Georgia. During the nineteenth century, estimates of the inflow and enslavement of people from the Caucasus into Ottoman markets revolved around 3,000 per annum. Not a few of those young Circassians – mostly, though not exclusively – were sold to slave traders by relatives, with parental consent. This was more common among the enslaved class and the poor, especially in times of desperation, such as war and poverty. But there was also sale of free-born children in an expectation that they would attain a better life in Ottoman elite harems. Kidnapping, too, was a key method of enslavement in the Caucasus, aided by the rugged mountainous terrain.

Young Circassian women were considered by elite men as particularly beautiful, often owing to their blonde hair and blue eyes; they were purchased for concubinage and domestic service in urban and rural harems. Boys and young men, while in the minority, were also recruited and socialized into the households of high officeholders, expecting to rise in the ranks of the military or the bureaucracy. Unlike Africans, it was common for Circassian women to make their way up the social ladder inside elite households. At the same time, unlike the African traffic, the Circassian slave trade was not impeded by abolitionist British pressure. The flow of human trade was channeled from the Caucasus via both land and sea. Leaving Sohum Kale and Batum, the enslaved were transported across the Black Sea to the Ottoman ports of Trabzon, Samsun, and Sinop, or directly to Istanbul and other Ottoman Mediterranean cities.

The 1857 decree against the African slave trade excluded the Circassian traffic, but signaled that proprietary rights in humans would not be automatically protected by the Tanzimat state. Indeed, as the century

---

[19] Seteney Shami, "Prehistories of Globalization: Circassian Identity in Motion," *Public Culture*, 12 (2000): 177–204.

wore on, the government began to lean increasingly on the side of the enslaved. However, overwhelmed with this refugee crisis, the government did not aggressively pursue manumission, choosing not to prosecute owners wholesale and, thereby, effectively changing Circassian social relations in a dramatic way. The second half of the nineteenth century is thus a transitional period for Ottoman management of Circassian slavery as the Tanzimat state was also faced with trying to rule and manage a people whose social structures and cultural system of meaning its administrative elites did not fully understand. By 1866 or so, whenever conflict arose between enslaver and enslaved, the state attempted to reconcile the parties and forced them to enter into a postponed manumission contract (Ottoman Turkish, *mükatebe*), which would regulate their relationship and provide for scheduled and clearly delineated manumission. While this type of contract was rooted in Islamic law, it was not often used in the Empire during the nineteenth century. In the wake of the Circassian refugee crisis, it found a new purpose.

CIRCASSIAN RESISTANCE TO ENSLAVEMENT AND OTTOMAN RESPONSE

It is clear that Circassian slaves, even agricultural slaves, thought differently of their status in Ottoman lands, hence the extensive legal challenges against their enslavement.[20] For example, in 1867, two Ottoman landowners and minor state officials brought six of their eleven Circassian slaves from their homes in Tekfurdağ to Istanbul to sell. The two Ottoman officials it seems held joint ownership over the slaves and worked the same plots of land, suggesting they were family members and Circassians of the landlords' class. The eleven slaves were also part of one extended Circassian family from the enslaved class, the Şumaf family. When the Şumafs realized they were being sold and separated from one another, they protested vigorously to their enslavers and officials in Istanbul. The court did give the enslaved litigants the opportunity to purchase their own freedom; however, they were unable to come up with the money.

Not giving up, the Şumaf family appealed to state officials and was eventually successful. Ottoman authorities intervened and offered a compromise of buying the freedom of the six slaves for them and re-settling them back in Tekfurdağ. State documents note their decision was based on the perseverance of the Şumaf family itself, and the humanitarian

---

[20] Information in the following section draws on the following studies: Toledano, *The Ottoman Slave Trade*, pp. 167–71, 175–6, 181, 184–5, 191; Toledano, "Shemsigül: A Circassian Slave in Mid-Nineteenth-Century Cairo," in Edmund Burke, III (ed.), *Struggle and Survival in the Modern Middle East* (Berkeley, CA, 1993), pp. 59–74; Toledano, *As If Silent and Absent*, pp. 97–8, 201; Erdem, *Slavery in the Ottoman Empire*, pp. 116–17, 120–4, 147–51; Troutt Powell, *Tell This in My Memory*, pp. 117, 126–7.

aspect of not wanting to break up a family. It appears that even if unwittingly, the Şumafs identified an aspect of Ottoman law that was not covered by Islamic law – the break-up of families. This gap in legal coverage – at an intersection of Circassian social norms and Islamic law – meant that cases such as this were left to the state to decide on an ad hoc basis, in this case managing to strike a balance between satisfying the enslavers, by buying the enslaved from them, and the enslaved, by helping them gain their freedom.

Collective violence was also a form of resistance by Circassian slaves in Ottoman lands. For example, in 1866, there were violent clashes between masters and their agricultural slaves in Mandıra near Edirne. The enslaved had demanded to be released from bondage, but their masters refused. This was a widespread event, with around 400 households and their slaves involved in the hostilities. When police attempted to intervene, they were denied access to the village, demonstrating how the Circassian landlords perceived this to be a domestic matter. A large police unit was eventually dispatched to the village and gained control of the situation. Though some details of what ensued remain unclear, it is likely that a resolution included the conclusion of *mükatebe* contracts, to settle and regulate enslaver– enslaved relations.

The case of Şemsigül, a young Circassian enslaved in the Caucasus and transported from Istanbul to Egypt, demonstrates the extent to which the well-being of an enslaved girl was compromised and her body violated. In 1854, she fled her captors in Cairo to the house of a neighbor to escape a forced abortion brought about by the slave trader who had likely raped her on the journey across the eastern Mediterranean. Knowing that according to the *Sharia* she would be categorized as *umm walad* and her resale prohibited, she put the case to the head of the slave dealers' guild and ultimately the police and court. Her long and complicated legal and social battle was ultimately successful, due not only to the thorough police investigation, but also to the kindness of her neighbor. Şemsigül ultimately attained her freedom, thanks to her own initiative after losing her child and suffering untold physical and sexual violence.

Such micro-historical biographies show the extent to which slavery has shaped the experiences of individuals in elite households in the late nineteenth century. Using the memoir of the prominent Egyptian nationalist and feminist Huda Shaᶜrawi (1879–1947), Eve Troutt Powell reveals how bondage affected not only Shaᶜrawi's day-to-day life experience, but also shaped her very being, identity, self-perception, and how she viewed the world. She was both the daughter of an enslaved Circassian woman, but also owned enslaved persons in her parents' and later her own household as an adult. The case of Shaᶜrawi is particularly interesting as her generation witnessed a dramatic transition in the role of women, family, and the household in Egypt. Indeed, her childhood household contained both African and Caucasian slaves.

Most crucially, however, the case demonstrates the difficult realities of Caucasian enslavement and harem life through oral history passed to Shaᶜarawi by her uncle about her mother's traumatic exit from Circassia and how she ended up enslaved in Egypt. Shaᶜarawi's investigation into her own past, brought about by her sense that the family was hiding something from her, demonstrates that her parents and uncle sought – not atypically – to obscure the history of enslavement in the family. This erasure would have worked to shield her children and her descendants from an association with an enslaved past, manifesting the long and lingering effects of enslavement. As in other societies, the shame, the stigma, and the social impediments on forming a family brought on denial, disassociation, and concealment of that past.

Ottoman involvement in managing Circassian agricultural slavery emerged from concerns about the maintenance of public order. While there may have been high-ranking officials who supported abolition, what topped their decision-making priorities was the essential need to preserve social order among Ottoman Turkish (*Hifz-ı Asayış*) in the countryside, preventing slave riots and retribution, murders, banditry, and general instability. The dismantling of Circassian social relations was certainly also meant to limit the power bases of Circassian enslaving landlords who possessed significant wealth and wielded influence outside Ottoman socio-political structures. As Erdem notes, the introduction of the *mükatebe* into Circassian slavery also worked to help regulate the trade through established state institutions, particularly preventing the flow of slaves beyond Ottoman lands, thus eroding the Empire's productive capacity and military manpower.

The fact that many Circassian agricultural slaves found themselves looking to the Tanzimat state for manumission inadvertently helped to advance one of the Empire's major concerns at the time – filling the ranks of the military. In 1882, the government developed a novel use of the *mükatebe* contract as a means to induce enslaved Circassians into the Ottoman armed forces. Male Circassian refugees were granted a twenty-five-year exemption from military service, beginning on the day they set foot in Ottoman territory. Children of those refugees born in Ottoman lands were drafted upon reaching the age of 20, like all other Ottoman subjects, despite their Circassian legal status of free or enslaved. For those enslaved Circassian men who had already farmed for twenty-five years, an unusual legal tactic was used: they were to be forced into a type of retroactive *mükatebe* with immediate manumission, followed by enlisting in the army, regardless of any debts to their previous enslavers. This innovative legal device to increase military manpower demonstrates the pragmatism of the Ottoman ways of governing the Empire.

What is notable about the Circassian slave trade in the era of global abolition is that the British put very little pressure on the Ottoman government to do anything about it. Indeed, in the 1870s, at the height of British pressure to end the African slave trade, Ottoman officials effectively stonewalled any demands about the Circassian trade. Ottoman officials were reluctant to let the British get involved in what they perceived as a domestic problem. These recalcitrant officials explained that, while it was easy to ban the trade in Africans, the Circassian traditions of the caste system were very difficult to manage and, as such, no clear policy was ever formed. In fact, the British were already spread thin when it came to both their antislavery resources and their political capital in the Ottoman Empire. Furthermore, it could be said that the British global movement against slavery, informed by their experience in the Atlantic World, shaped their view of how and where to look for slavery, which veered mostly toward African phenotypes.

It is important to bear in mind that the refugee crisis and agricultural slavery was just one aspect of Circassian slavery. The trade in young girls to Istanbul proceeded separately from this and had more long-term effects as a whole. In the eyes of the government, the crisis of agricultural slavery was mostly a question of management of elites and their property. Overall, the trade in Circassian girls to elite households began to slow down by the end of the century, when demand was confined to the dwindling harems of the imperial elites. However, as late as 1893, top Ottoman officials themselves still purchased Circassian slaves despite regulations against the trade. Fewer people could afford slaves, and there was a smaller pool of Circassians available, partly due to state abolitionist activity, and partly due to a new social order arising in the Caucasus. Also, Circassians settled in Ottoman lands wanted to keep their children for their labor on the family homestead instead of selling them into slavery.

As noted above, the legal end of the trade and enslavement of Circassians came in 1908 with the Young Turk Revolution. From 1909 onward, while not legally abolished, Ottoman enslavement and the slave trade that sustained it came gradually to an end. Enslaved persons seeking justice in this period would have had the court on their side from the beginning, and slowly but surely, all enslavers lost any legal ground to stand on.

THE BEGINNING OF MODERN SEX TRAFFICKING IN THE OTTOMAN EMPIRE?

This issue is only beginning to attract the attention of historians, and the little information currently available is tenuous and needs to be treated with caution here.[21] A terminological distinction needs to be made at the outset between Ottoman enslavement of white women, as in the Circassian and Georgian cases, and what is often referred to as "white slavery," i.e. sex trafficking in women for prostitution.

A high profile case of one young woman, who did not want to be extricated from a brothel in Istanbul and sent back to Austria-Hungary, demonstrated how complex the question of what constitutes freedom was and when governments could claim to intervene on behalf of their subjects. That proved not only embarrassing for the government, but also made all but impossible the policing of such an illicit trade with varying concepts of freedom and servitude floating within it at all times. Examining this "modern" trade is useful in that it disrupts the historiographical binary between the African and Caucasian traffic in the nineteenth-century Ottoman Empire and not only opens up an examination into a form of de facto enslavement, but causes one to consider the Empire as a site into and through which other global networks of enslavement passed.

CONCLUSION

The history of enslavement in the Ottoman Empire in the "long nineteenth century" both follows and differs from general themes in the global history of enslavement in this period. As elsewhere, suppression of the African slave trade defined the nineteenth century. Consequently, the role which the Ottoman Empire and European powers came to play in the abolition and manumission processes grew dramatically. Likewise, enslaved persons took every opportunity available to extricate themselves from bondage or at least ameliorate their condition, whether through running away, violence, or by maintaining cultural connections with their origin cultures. Suppression of the traffic and abolition of legal enslavement in the Empire also differed from other concurrent forms. The most prominent example is that the Circassian trade was dealt with almost entirely internally and through an innovative use of traditional contract slavery to – rather ingeniously – ensure manumission.

Owing to the complex and varied forms of Ottoman bondage in the period under discussion here, instead of "Ottoman slavery," they might be better understood as "Ottoman slaveries." In another sense, Ottoman societies were – on the whole, perhaps with one or two exceptions – "societies with slaves" rather than "slave societies"; they also better fit the "Indian Ocean model" rather than the "Atlantic model," if indeed we

---

[21] This and the following passages are based on Malte Fuhrmann, "Down and Out on the Quays of Izmir: 'European' Musicians, Innkeepers, and Prostitutes in the Ottoman Port-Cities," *Mediterranean Historical Review*, 24 (2009): 169–85.

accept that such models are valid. As tentatively suggested elsewhere,[22] the lack of a vibrant and forceful antislavery campaign and a late and hesitant abolitionist push in the Ottoman Empire, as in other Muslim-majority empires and countries, were more common in "societies with slaves" and the Indian Ocean World than in "slave societies" and the Atlantic World.

Ottoman forms of enslavement have left their mark on the region and still resonate today, which is rarely acknowledged by state actors. Despite this, descendants of enslaved Africans and Circassians have been sensitized, often by historical research on Ottoman slavery, to their enslaved past, and are now beginning to explore publicly that history. Among the most pressing and challenging issues awaiting thorough interrogation is the role that slavery has played in the construction of racial difference in the successor states of the Ottoman Empire, which determine the nature of communal interaction in the MENA societies even today.

A GUIDE TO FURTHER READING

Baron, Beth, "Liberated Bodies and Saved Souls: Freed African Slave Girls and Missionaries in Egypt" in Ehud R. Toledano (ed.), *African Communities in Asia and the Mediterranean: Identities between Integration and Conflict* (Trenton, NJ, 2011), pp. 215–35.

Chouki, El Hamel, *Black Morocco: A History of Slavery, Race, and Islam* (Cambridge, 2013).

Erdem, Y. Hakan, "Magic, Theft in Arson: The Life and Death of an Enslaved African Woman in Ottoman Izmit" in Terence Walz and Kenneth M. Cuno (eds.), *Race and Slavery in the Middle East: Histories of Trans-Saharan Africans in Nineteenth-Century Egypt, Sudan, and the Ottoman Mediterranean* (Cairo, 2010), pp. 125–46.

Toledano, Ehud R., *As if Silent and Absent: Bonds of Enslavement in the Islamic Middle East* (New Haven, CT, 2007).

Toledano, Ehud R., "Abolition and Anti-Slavery in the Ottoman Empire: A Case to Answer?" in W. Mulligan and M. Bric (eds.), *A Global History of Anti-Slavery Politics in the Nineteenth Century* (Basingstoke, 2013), pp. 117–36.

Troutt Powell, Eve, *Tell This in My Memory: Stories of Enslavement from Egypt, Sudan, and the Ottoman Empire* (Stanford, CA, 2012).

Zilfi, Madeline C., *Women and Slavery in the Late Ottoman Empire: The Design of Difference* (New York, 2010).

[22] See Ehud R. Toledano, "Ottoman and Islamic Societies: Were They 'Slave Societies'?" in Noel Lenski and Catherine Cameron (eds.), *What is a "Slave Society"?* (Cambridge, forthcoming).

CHAPTER 10

SLAVERY AND BONDAGE IN THE INDIAN OCEAN WORLD, NINETEENTH AND TWENTIETH CENTURIES

GWYN CAMPBELL AND ALESSANDRO STANZIANI

INTRODUCTION

Conventional slavery studies tend to make a sharp distinction between "modern" and "historical" forms of bondage, in which the latter are largely identified with either Classical Greece and Rome, or with the Atlantic slave trade and New World forms of bondage against which Western governments campaigned and which ended with formal abolition in Brazil in 1888. However, research is starting to demonstrate the existence of a large and vibrant Indian Ocean World (IOW) slave system that pre-dated, co-existed, and in some instances overlapped with the Atlantic system, and has continued in modified forms into the twenty-first century, in which concepts of "slave" and "free" derived from the Atlantic slave paradigm are often inapplicable. This chapter investigates the specific environmental context of IOW bondage, and the changes it has undergone since the nineteenth century, with reference to various IOW regions.

ENVIRONMENT AND BONDAGE IN THE IOW

Most authors consider IOW slavery to have been structurally similar to – albeit on a smaller scale – that of the Atlantic World wherein from c. 1500 to 1867 some 12.5 million slaves, mostly males from West and West-Central Africa, were shipped to the New World, chiefly to work in mines and on plantations, where they constituted the basis of a "slave mode of production." They belonged to a clearly visible black chattel class of hereditary slave status, uncivilized "outsiders," deprived of civil rights. Violence could universally be visited upon slaves by their owners who controlled the slave's productive and reproductive capacities, and could legally punish, sell, or transfer, a slave, and separate a slave mother from her children or male companion.

However, in the IOW, a macro-region running from Africa to the Far East, a significant traffic in humans started well before that of the Atlantic World, and has continued to the present day. Moreover, it was as much continental as oceanic. While the cumulative number of slaves traded across the IOW maritime space over the centuries probably well exceeded the number of African slaves landed in the Americas, the greatest IOW slave traffic was overland, notably within Africa, South Asia, and the Far East: India alone had an estimated 8 to 9 million indigenous slaves in 1841, double the number of slaves in the United States in 1865. Also, the indications are that females and children, and non-Africans, constituted the majority of humans trafficked in the IOW, and that there existed a far greater variety of forms of bondage in the IOW than in the Americas.[1]

Again, in the IOW, there was a close relationship between environment and human bondage. The core environmental feature of the IOW is the monsoons, a complex system of winds and currents governing the northern Indian Ocean, Indonesian Sea, and South and East China Seas. From April to September, the Asian continent heats up and hot air rises, producing a vacuum which sucks in air from the ocean, thereby creating the southwest monsoon. During the alternate "winter" months, the opposite occurs, creating the northeast monsoon. The monsoons largely dictate precipitation patterns across the Asian rim of the monsoon seas, critically influencing agriculture – in which, until recently, possibly 90 percent of the IOW population was engaged – and largely confining overland communications and trade to the dry (non-monsoon rain) season. The regular alternating biannual winds and currents also regulated the rhythm of trans-oceanic sailing over most of the IOW maritime zones. Hence, major disturbances to the monsoon system could induce great economic, political, and social upheaval, and propel people into human bondage.

It is in this context that other environmental factors, such as climate change, "Southern Oscillation," or "El-Niño" (ENSO), oceanic surface temperatures, and volcanism, play highly influential roles. For instance, northern hemisphere temperatures generally fell from 1770 to the early to mid nineteenth century, the period 1805 to 1818 being the coldest on record in Europe, North America, and Japan. From 1825, temperatures generally started to increase, but from 1870 to 1900 the Far East was affected by low temperatures, exceptionally cold weather hitting South China from 1876 to 1895. Moreover, between 1830 and 1900, the southern hemisphere was in the grip of a colder climate, with an advance north in the rain zone. Longer-term climatic change was complicated by shorter-term factors.

---

[1] For a full discussion of the geographical dimensions and coherence of the IOW, see Gwyn Campbell, "Introduction: Slavery and Other Forms of Unfree Labour in the Indian Ocean World," in Gwyn Campbell (ed.), *The Structure of Slavery in Indian Ocean Africa and Asia* (London, 2004), pp. vii–xxxii; and Edward Balfour, *The Encyclopædia of India and of Eastern and Southern Asia: Commercial, Industrial and Scientific, Products of the Mineral, Vegetable, and Animal Kingdoms, Useful Arts and Manufactures*, 3 vols. (London, 1885), 1: 3, 674.

Strong ENSO effects, associated with severe droughts followed in consecutive years by unusually heavy rain, were experienced from 1844 to 1846, 1876 to 1878, and 1899 to 1900. Again, a high volcanic dust veil marked the periods 1783 to 1788, 1832 to 1838, and 1884. Both the ENSO effect and high dust veil indexes correlate with crop failures, food shortages, and disease.[2]

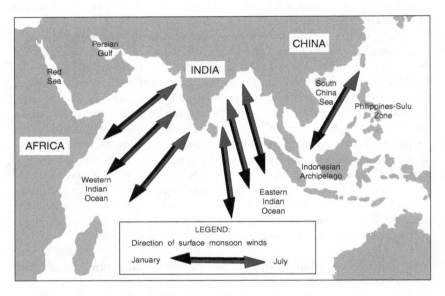

Map 10.1 The Indian Ocean World Monsoon System

It is now known from studies of historical water temperature changes in the northern Indian Ocean that the region experienced a reduction in rainfall and weaker summer monsoons from 1860 that resulted in drought and poor rice harvests, which in turn often led to famine. Moreover, weaker monsoons in the northern IOW correlated with a larger number of more powerful cyclones in the southern Indian Ocean – one of the world's seven cyclogenetic basins. Given this environmental context, it is of critical importance to identify forms of labor relations and dependence in the region.

[2] John Gribben and H. H. Lamb, "Climatic Change in Historical Times," in John Gribben (ed.), *Climatic Change* (Cambridge, 1978), p. 71; William S. Atwell, "Volcanism and Short-Term Climatic Change in East Asian and World History, c. 1200–1699," *Journal of World History*, 12 (2001): 39–40; Candace Gudmundson, "El Niño and Climate Prediction," in A. M. Babkina (ed.), *El Niño: Overview and Bibliography* (New York, 2003), pp. 5–28.

TRADITIONAL FORMS OF BONDAGE IN THE IOW

Slavery developed as a significant social institution in the centralized hierarchical polities of the Middle East, South Asia, and the Far East. These were at the core of the Neolithic Revolution wherein regimes geographically concentrated the mass of their subjects whose labor they directed into control of water and crop cultivation that together guaranteed agricultural surpluses sufficient to maintain the ruling elite, and eventually a specialized artisanal sector and a merchant class. The elite extended forced labor to the formation of armies used to expand political frontiers. Successful armies generally killed male opponents, who otherwise required physical restraint and heavy surveillance, and enslaved their women and children who additionally adapted more easily to the mores of the victor society. Slave raiding early became a major motive of such campaigns, and a class of specialist slave raiders emerged.[3]

As labor for agricultural production and public works was generally satisfied by the existing subject population, women and child captives were distributed among members of the court and army generals, or sold to those who could afford them. This is, for example, the reputed origin of bondage as a significant institution in Mesopotamia in the third millennium BCE. Records dating to the second millennium BCE indicate that probably some two-thirds of bondspeople in Babylonia were female. As their numbers grew, most thus enslaved became objects of conspicuous consumption, displayed to reflect the wealth and power of the owner. In all cases, however, given that they owed their lives to their captors, they represented indebted bodies.[4]

When conquering armies overran settled agricultural settlements without meeting resistance, they tended to maintain such communities, who were also indebted for their lives to their captors, in situ in another form of bondage that tied them to the soil. The court distributed such lands to leading supporters who thus also owned the bondspeople on it, and the product of their labor. This is most clearly seen in agrarian forms of servitude that developed in South India. However, it is reflected in forms of bondage that endured through the centuries, such as those that developed after the Persian conquest of Babylonia in 539 BCE, when Persians forced non-slave but conquered Babylonians to help construct the palace of Darius I (r. 521 to 486 BCE) in Susa. And again in Imerina (Madagascar) in the late eighteenth century, where warlords organized newly subjected peoples into 100- to 1,000-strong

---

[3] Jack Goody, "Slavery in Time and Space," in James Watson (ed.), *Asian and African Systems of Slavery* (Berkeley, CA, 1980), pp. 32–4.
[4] Gerda Lerner, "Women and Slavery," *Slavery and Abolition*, 4 (1983): 179.

territorially based units used in *fanompoana* (unremunerated forced labor) for public works.

Nevertheless, the greatest supply of servile labor in the IOW over the *longue durée* was probably more a result of impoverishment than forcible enslavement. Natural and human-induced disasters, the cost of important life rituals such as marriage and funerals, high interest rates of often 50 to 100 percent and more, and legal costs and punishments, pushed many thousands into debt. Traditionally, enslavement was legally enforced for debtors and their relatives in many IOW regions, such as pre-colonial Madagascar, Thailand, and Malaysia.[5]

Here, slavery needs to be distinguished from debt bondage with which, however, it could overlap. Enslavement for indebtedness was involuntary, whereas most people entered debt bondage voluntarily as a credit-securing strategy. Mortgaging a child, or wife, to raise a loan was common practice in the IOW from early times, and continued into the twentieth century. Certainly, by the nineteenth century, debt bondage embraced a vast range of people in the IOW, from farmers mortgaging future harvests and potential grooms borrowing a bride price, to small traders living off credit from larger merchants, the ubiquitous rural gambler of Southeast and East Asia, and opium addicts in nineteenth-century China. During catastrophes, people often entered debt bondage or slavery in return for subsistence as a survival strategy, either voluntarily, as was the case of many *dvija* caste members in India, or involuntarily, as when propelled into bondage by their kin group. Most victims appear to have been pushed into debt bondage as children. In early twentieth-century Thailand, they were rarely aged over 10 years at the time of their entry into bondage.

Those subject to debt bondage could outnumber slaves. For example, they were possibly the most numerous social category in Majapahit, in Java, while in Central Thailand in the eighteenth and nineteenth centuries, they formed up to 50 percent of the total population. Bondspeople could sometimes be exchanged, as could other servile people, as part of a marriage dowry or a monastery donation. The servitude to which those in debt bondage were subject was generally taken as paying off interest on the loan they had contracted, to which was added the cost of lodging, feeding, and clothing the debtor. Consequently, the debt in most cases increased and servitude could become permanent, even hereditary, at which point there was little to distinguish debt bondage from slavery.

[5] Anthony Reid, "Introduction," in Anthony Reid (ed.), *Slavery, Bondage and Dependency in Southeast Asia* (St Lucia, 1983), p. 10; Gwyn Campbell, *An Economic History of Imperial Madagascar, 1750–1895: The Rise and Fall of an Island Empire* (Cambridge, 2005): pp. 295–6; Bruno Lasker, *Human Bondage in Southeast Asia* (Chapel Hill, NC, 1950), pp. 147, 150.

Indeed, in nineteenth-century Thailand, where up to 50 percent of the population of the central provinces were trapped in debt bondage, if the interest owed by a debt bondsperson grew to a level exceeding the original loan, the master deemed it a bad investment and customarily sold him or her – albeit on unfavorable terms.

Here, Islam, which between the seventh and thirteenth centuries spread from its Middle Eastern heartland southwards down the East African littoral, and eastwards through South to Southeast Asia, played a major role. According to Sharia law, freeborn people could neither be pawned nor enslaved for debt. However, the distinction made in Muslim societies between indebtedness, debt bondage, and slavery was often blurred – as in the late-nineteenth- and early-twentieth-century Gulf pearl diving industry.[6]

THE INTERNATIONAL ECONOMY AND BONDAGE

The development of the international economy in the nineteenth century stimulated capital-intensive production in the northern United States and Germany, but elsewhere, including most of Western Europe, production continued to be labor-intensive. The IOW experienced greatly increased demand for labor for cash-crop cultivation, collection of forest, animal, and marine products, mineral exploitation, porterage, storage, loading and offloading vessels, and manning ships. Simultaneously, indigenous and European powers engaged in state- or empire-building projects that involved large numbers of soldiers, administrators, and workers, or industrial experiments as occurred in nineteenth-century Egypt, Madagascar, and China.

However, expansion of demand failed to stimulate growth in the supply of labor for two main reasons: uneven demographic growth, and the prevalence of systems of bonded labor. Before the eighteenth century, Asia possessed a greater population than any other continent, but while Europe's population more than doubled in the nineteenth century, from 190 to 423 million (that of Britain, Germany, and the United States increased almost fivefold in the hundred years prior to 1914), it took almost 200 years for the population of Asia to double, from around 435 to 970 million between 1700 and 1900. Thus, whereas in 1750, Asia possessed 64 percent of the global population, Europe 21 percent, and Africa 13 percent, by 1900, Asia's share of the global population had fallen to

[6] Bok-rae Kim, "Nobi: A Korean System of Slavery," in Campbell (ed.), *Structure of Slavery*, pp. 155–68; Lasker, *Human Bondage in Southeast Asia*, p. 151; Reid, "Introduction," p. 12; Matthew S. Hopper, "Debt and Slavery among Arabian Gulf Pearl Divers" in Gwyn Campbell and Alessandro Stanziani (eds.), *Bonded Labour and Debt in the Indian Ocean World* (London, 2013), pp. 103–18.

57 percent, while Europe had increased its share to 25 percent (Africa's share was then 8 percent and that of the Americas 10 percent). In addition, population growth within the IOW was uneven. China's population increased rapidly during the eighteenth century to reach about 300 million in 1795, and it climbed further to 420 million by 1850. However, the rate of growth then slowed, the total population reaching approximately 480 million by 1900. Sumit Guha has estimated that the Indian population increased by 44 million between 1600 and 1800 to reach 161 million, followed by a further 76 percent increase to reach 283.4 million by 1901. However, the rate of growth varied considerably from region to region. Population growth rates in Africa expanded significantly only from the 1920s.[7]

In this context, indigenous and European authorities, companies, and individuals competed for limited labor resources. Indigenous authorities widely employed penal labor in the harshest types of work. For instance, the Merina regime in Madagascar used convicts in road construction, mining, and foundries. More significantly, IOW regimes imposed forced labor on "free" subjects within their territories. Some, such as Korea, Thailand, and Imerina, purposefully applied selective measures of abolition, without compensation to the former masters, in order to "free" slaves formerly tied up in the private sector and made them available for state use. Europeans, thus denied access to limited sources of free labor, turned to forms of coerced labor, one of which was slaves. For instance, Robert Farquhar, first British Governor of Mauritius from 1810, delayed implementing anti-slave import measures in acknowledgment of the cheap labor requirements of local sugar planters. Others, "redeemed" pagan slaves into "Christian" settings where they worked off their redemption in situations of virtual bondage. European use of penal labor in the IOW, widespread before 1800, also increased as abolition loomed. For example, during the early nineteenth century, the English East India Company dispatched Indian convicts to Singapore, Malacca, Mauritius, and Burma.[8]

---

[7] Sumit Guha, "The Population History of South Asia from the Seventeenth to the Twentieth Centuries: An Exploration," in Cuirong Liu, Ts'ui-jung Liu, James Lee, David Sven Reher, Osamu Saito, and Wang Feng (eds.), *Asian Population History* (Oxford, 2001), p. 74; Dennis D. Cordell and Joel W. Gregory (eds.), *African Population and Capitalism: Historical Perspectives* (Boulder, CO, 1987). For Madagascar, see Gwyn Campbell, "The State and Pre-Colonial Demographic History: The Case of Nineteenth Century Madagascar," *Journal of African History*, 32 (1991): 415–45.

[8] Gwyn Campbell, "Unfree Labour and the Significance of Abolition in Madagascar, c. 1825–97," in Gwyn Campbell (ed.), *Abolition and Its Aftermath in Indian Ocean Africa and Asia* (Oxford, 2005), pp. 65–82; Martin Klein, "The Emancipation of Slaves in the Indian Ocean," in Campbell (ed.), *Abolition and Its Aftermath*, p. 206; Clare Anderson, "The Bel Ombre Rebellion: Indian Convicts in Mauritius, 1815–53," in Campbell (ed.), *Abolition and Its Aftermath*, pp. 50–65.

EUROPEAN COLONIALISM AND LABOR

Although abolition was often the most cited pretext for the imposition of European colonial rule, local exigencies obliged colonial regimes to maintain, or introduce, a number of varieties of forced labor. Abolition was declared in British colonies in 1833, in French colonies in 1848, and in the Dutch East Indies in 1860. Even when emancipated, former slaves proved remarkably reluctant to work on European-run concerns. In the Cape and Mauritius, ex-slaves were, upon abolition, declared "apprentices" and obliged to continue working for a fixed period for their old masters – although the system ended in the Cape in 1838 and in Mauritius in 1839.[9]

Moreover, some European-held territory in the IOW continued to use slave labor. In part, the reluctance to enforce abolition stemmed from the need to retain the goodwill of local slave-owning elites. Otherwise, they risked revolt, as occurred in the Muslim province of the Southern Philippines after abolition was enforced in 1904. However, such practices also reflected a lack of concern over non-African forms of bondage which, as in India, were often described by the colonial authorities as "benign." Again, European powers often declared newly conquered territories to be "protectorates" and thus avoided enforcing abolitionist measures compulsory in colonies. Indeed, complete bans on slavery in European-controlled territories occurred fitfully well into the twentieth century. In Somalia, the Italians initially permitted European settler farmers access to slave labor and even returned fugitive slaves to their owners, and in the Sudan, the British implemented effective antislavery measures only in the late 1920s. Slavery endured in Hulsawng Valley in British Burma until 1926, and in remoter regions of French Indochina and the Dutch Indies into the 1940s. In the Middle East, drawn into the British informal empire following the First World War, abolitionist pressure remained muted until after 1945.[10]

This in turn highlights the significance of indentured labor as the major non-slave workforce in the wake of abolition. Indentureship, nominally entered into voluntarily and subject to limited term (generally five-year)

---

[9] Nigel Worden, "Between Slavery and Freedom: The Apprenticeship Period, 1834 to 1838" in Nigel Worden and Clifton C. Crais (eds.), *Breaking the Chains: Slavery and Its Legacy in the Nineteenth-Century Cape Colony* (Johannesburg, 1994), pp. 25–43; Moses D. E. Nwulia, "The 'Apprenticeship' System in Mauritius: Its Character and Its Impact on Race Relations in the Immediate Post-Emancipation Period, 1839–1879," *African Studies Review*, 21 (1978): 89–101; Marina Carter, *Servants, Sirdars and Settlers. Indians in Mauritius, 1834–1874* (Delhi, 1995).

[10] William Gervase Clarence-Smith, "Islam and the Abolition of the Slave Trade in the Indian Ocean," in Campbell (ed.), *Abolition and Its Aftermath*, pp. 137–49; Indrani Chatterjee, "Abolition by Denial: The South Asian Example" in Campbell (ed.), *Abolition and Its Aftermath*, pp. 150–68. Gwyn Campbell, "Servitude and the Changing Face of Demand for Labor in the Indian Ocean World, c. 1800–1900," in Robert Harms, Bernard Freamon, and David W. Blight (eds.), *Slavery and the Slave Trades in the Indian Ocean World: Global Connections and Disconnections* (New Haven, CT, 2013), pp. 23–44.

contracts, was often, notably in the early years of the system, subject to severe abuses that led contemporary observers and subsequent historians to compare the recruitment, transport, and living and working conditions of indentured laborers to those of slaves.

Conventionally portrayed as a nineteenth- and twentieth-century phenomenon in the IOW, indentured labor had existed in eighteenth-century Cape society where it was either formalized by contracts, or imposed ad hoc by Dutch farmers in the interior on Khoi and San boy captives who were forced to work until the age of 25, by which time they were often married, often with sons subject to similar obligations. A modified indenture system arose due to the failure of the 1834 and 1848 abolitionist measures to transform ex-slaves into pliant wage laborers. Generally involving five-year contracts, it channeled manpower resources to enterprises both within the IOW and externally – as to the Fijian sugar plantations. Recruits comprised essentially poverty-stricken Indians, Chinese, Melanesians, and, for the French islands, Africans. By 1900, approximately 1 million Indian indentured laborers were employed in India; 2 million were also shipped to overseas plantations between 1834 and 1920.

Attention in the IOW has focused on indentured labor to European plantations and mines,[11] but recent research has also revealed hitherto underestimated forms of indigenous indentureship. Thus, Chinese sources indicate that from 1851 to 1901 approximately 7.7 million people sailed from China, 87 percent to Southeast Asia, mostly to meet indigenous demands for labor. Adam McKeown considers that only about 4 percent of such emigrants formed indentured labor on European estates and that even these "were still often bound to other Chinese through a variety of debt and contract schemes with widely varying levels of obligation." Indebtedness formed a central feature of indentureship. Brokers advanced money to household heads or local recruitment agents for workers who, once enlisted, were obliged to remit sums home to repay the advances. Other recruits, already in debt, signed up in order to earn money to repay their debts.

Colonial administrators also imposed various systems of forced labor. The adoption of local variations of the British Master and Servant Acts contributed to the persistence of extreme forms of dependence in labor relationships. Thus, the 1856 Master and Servant Act in Cape Province, South Africa stipulated criminal penalties for both minor and major labor offenses. The Cape legislation was a model for similar Acts in Transvaal in

---

[11] Hugh Tinker, *A New System of Slavery: The Export of Indian Labour Overseas, 1830–1920* (London, 1974); Carter, *Servants, Sirdars and Settlers*; Hubert Gerbeau, "Engagés and Coolies on Réunion Island, Slavery's Masks and Freedom's Constraints," in Pieter C. Emmer (ed.), *Colonialism and Migration: Indentured Labour before and after Slavery* (Dordrecht, 1986), pp. 209–36.

1880 and Natal in 1894. The influence of such Acts was far reaching: a 1908 report from the East African protectorate noted that children employed to herd livestock were expected to keep watch day and night, and were held responsible for the loss of animals. Again, the 5,000 slaves freed in Zanzibar between 1897 and 1907, and 6,600 emancipated in Pemba, fell under the Master and Servant Act which sought through the imposition of taxes (including forced labor) and regulation of land owner-ship to ensure adequate and controlled seasonal labor to meet both rural and urban demand. The outbreak of the First World War, which wit-nessed the mass militarization of labor in Europe, also triggered widespread imposition of *corvée* labor in the colonies.[12]

Closely following the end of the war in November 1918, the League of Nations and International Labour Organization (ILO) were founded, and with them renewed efforts to suppress slavery and the worst forms of coerced labor. The 1925 League of Nations Draft Convention directly affected the IOW – with mixed results. For instance, in the Red Sea/Persian Gulf area Britain promoted, and France rejected, a stop-and-search policy for vessels suspected of slave-running. Portugal for Mozambique and Angola, and the colonial government in South Africa, denied that local forms of forced labor constituted slavery, while the government of India pushed for parts of its territory to be excluded from the new obligations. Colonial forced labor regimes formed a core preoccupation of the ILO that, in 1935, recommended the immediate abolition of penal sanctions for labor that were written into employment contracts. Following protracted negoti-ations, a convention applicable to British territories, signed in 1939 and enforced in 1948, promoted the immediate eradication of penal sanctions for juveniles, and their progressive abolition for most other categories of labor.

There was also limited regulation of forced labor in French IOW col-onies. Initial provisions for inspection of labor conditions was restricted in applicability, but the 1926 Convention on Slavery, the 1927 Brussels Con-ference against Colonialism and Slavery, and the denunciation by André Gide of the violence and abuses in Congo led in 1927 to general regulation of colonial labor conditions. These, however, were roundly denounced by French planters and companies, and provoked mixed reactions from colonial administrators: for example, leading officials in Tonkin and Annam sup-ported the labor demands of French colonists in the north and restricted worker migration from the north to southern rubber plantations.[13]

---

[12] Frederick Cooper, *From Slaves to Squatters: Plantation Labour and Agriculture in Zanzibar and Coastal Kenya, 1890–1925* (New Haven, CT, 1980); Babacar Fall, *Le travail forcé en Afrique Occidentale française* (Paris, 1993).
[13] Marianne Boucheret, "Le pouvoir colonial et la question de la main d'œuvre en Indochine dans les années 1920," *Cahiers d'histoire*, 85 (2001): 29–55.

CORVÉE LABOR

Western abolitionist pressure prompted indigenous regimes as far apart as the Ottoman Empire, Thailand, Zanzibar, Imerina, and Ethiopia to make at least official proclamations against the slave trade and slavery. In Thailand, such measures largely ended slavery by 1900. In general, however, indigenous antislavery measures were rarely effective, or were manipulated by regimes to divert slaves from private ownership into state labor pools – as occurred in late eighteenth-century Korea, and in nineteenth-century Thailand and Madagascar. In these countries, and in Java, most productive labor was performed not by slaves, but by the nominally "free" population subject to state *corvées*, while in many states, as in Egypt under Muhammad Ali, and in imperial Madagascar, indigenous regimes used the forced labor of nominally "free" subjects to drive programs of economic modernization. Often inextricably linked with such programs were attempts, from Korea, Thailand, and Burma to Iran, Zanzibar, and Imerina to create and economically exploit "secondary empires." Critical to their success were armies comprising mostly forced labor. Indeed, in order to escape state *corvée*, which in Korea, Burma, and Thailand often claimed up to 50 percent and in imperial Madagascar up to 100 percent of the labor of "free" draftees, some slaves rejected opportunities to gain "free" status, while some non-slaves voluntarily entered slavery.[14]

In some cases, a significant number of children were drafted into forced labor units. Because of their small size, children were particularly valued in mines. Thus, bonded children were used in Chinese mines from early times until at least the mid twentieth century, and in the mica mines of India exploited from the late nineteenth century. Again, with the opening up of goldfields in Madagascar from 1883, Merina authorities summoned children from mission chapels and schools as unremunerated forced labor to mine gold. Missionaries and other state–church agents played their role in drawing up the quotas and, increasingly, in overseeing the *fanompoana* units. For example, as early as 1887 Norwegian Missionary Society churches in the northern Betsileo regions of Mananadona and Fisakana were interrupted by the recruitment of 400 gold *fanompoana* workers comprising both sexes. Child labor in the goldfields became so widespread that on December 8, 1888 the *Madagascar Times* declared:

[14] Kim, "Nobi"; B. Terwiel, "Bondage and Slavery in Early Nineteenth Century Siam," in Reid (ed.), *Slavery, Bondage and Dependency*, pp. 118–37; David Feeny, "The Decline of Property Rights in Man in Thailand, 1800–1913," *Journal of Economic History*, 49 (1989): 285–96; Anthony Reid, "Decline of Slavery in Nineteenth-Century Indonesia," in Worden and Crais (eds.), *Breaking the Chains*, pp. 64–82; Ehud R. Toledano, *State and Society in Mid-Nineteenth-Century Egypt* (Cambridge, 2003), pp. 6–7; Khaled Fahmy, *All the Pasha's Men. Mehmed Ali, His Army and the Making of Modern Egypt* (Cambridge, 1997), pp. 10, 11, 86–93, 96.

by forced labour, into which even evangelists and school children are pressed, the Prime Minister is washing for gold on his own account. It is said that more than a thousand laborers are daily employed on this work.

Child exploitation in the goldfields intensified from the late 1880s as the threat of French intervention grew. In general, the predominantly Protestant Merina officials obliged the pupils of Roman Catholic schools to undertake the heaviest gold *fanompoana*, but in 1889 the same London Missionary Society (LMS) schools in the Ambohibeloma district, where military drill was instituted by the local missionary, were being called on to supply "gold" labor, and that same year the entire "free" population of Ambositra region were summoned. Resistance to *fanompoana* was met by force. For example, in 1889, members of the church and school at Ambanimaso were seized and militarily escorted to the goldfields.

Finally, colonial regimes, burdened by metropolitan exigencies that insisted on self-sufficiency, and local realities where there were shortages of labor, also fell back on forced labor regimes. This was, for example, evident from at least the 1880s in India, where European collieries established zamindari rights over villages, and thus over the forced labor of villagers. Again, the French in Madagascar after 1895 quickly resorted to a forced labor regime that resembled, and was justified in reference to, the pre-colonial *fanompoana* practiced by the Merina.[15]

THE SECOND WORLD WAR AND DECOLONIZATION

One of the first effects of the Second World War and the British defeat of the Italian occupiers in 1941 was the abolition of slavery in Ethiopia. The heightened British naval presence also greatly restricted the import of slaves into Aden and the Gulf. However, from 1939, as had occurred in the First World War, coercion and forced labor generally increased dramatically in Europe and its Asian and African colonies. For example, in South Africa and Rhodesia, war-enhanced demand for minerals in a situation of increasing shortage of capital and labor (neighboring colonies restricted emigration) resulted in the adoption, despite criticism from British antislavery circles, of compulsory labor Acts that concerned chiefly the military, agricultural, and mining sectors.[16]

---

[15] Eric Jennings, "Forced Labour in Madagascar under Vichy, 1940–42: Autarky, Forced Labour, and Resistance on the 'Red Island,'" in Edward A. Alpers, Gwyn Campbell, and Michael Salman (eds.), *Resisting Bondage in Indian Ocean Africa and Asia* (London, 2009), p. 173.

[16] Peter Duignan and L. H. Gann (eds.), *Colonialism in Africa*, Vol. 4: *The Economics of Colonialism* (Cambridge, 1975); Francis Wilson, *Labour in the South African Gold Mines, 1911–1969* (Cambridge, 1972).

The close of the war brought increased pressure from within the colonies, from educated elites and indigenous soldiers returning from the conflict, as well as from liberal and left-wing elements in Europe, the United States, and the Soviet Union, for an end to both colonialism and slavery – which in political rhetoric were often linked. In this context, the role of the United Nations and its definition of slavery became critical. The ILO and UN slavery commission sought to include debt bondage, forced marriage, adoption, and serfdom under the general category of "slavery." In reaction, the British Foreign Office, keen to deflect international interest from the Middle East where it had major oil interests, maintained that chattel slavery had disappeared, and that other forms of constraint should be carefully qualified. In its turn, the Soviet Union qualified its Gulag system as justified penal punishment, but joined rising nationalist movements in denouncing both imperial control of land and sea, and colonial forced labor, in Africa and Asia. In Madagascar, the refusal of the local administration to ban *corvée* labor after the war was almost certainly the main cause – rather than, as is conventionally held, the nationalist movement – of the 1947 Uprising.[17]

Overall, the anti-imperialist movement proved unstoppable and in the ILO Convention of 1957, peonage, debt bondage, forced marriage, and adoption of children for purposes of exploitation were all defined as forms of slavery. International attention also focused on Saudi Arabia and the Gulf. Consequently, Qatar, Bahrein, and Kuwait abolished slavery. In 1962 to 1963, partly as result of Egyptian pressure, most slaves were freed in Saudi Arabia, and slavery was abolished in Yemen. In Oman, Britain struggled to maintain both puppet sheiks and slavery – which was only abolished in 1970 when Sheikh Bin Taimur abdicated and the British protectorate ended.[18]

In newly independent African countries, the debate centered less on conventional "chattel" slavery than slave-like conditions such as debt bondage, forced marriage, child labor, and serfdom. Some countries, including Cameroon, Ivory Coast, and Tanzania, argued that local forms of "dependence" expressed familial relationships, and insisted that independence was associated with "freedom" generally, and colonialism with "slavery." Thus, outside attempts to qualify indigenous forms of dependency as "slavery" reflected neo-colonialist tendencies. In the end, colonialism, apartheid, and "slavery-like practices" became included in

---

[17] Suzanne Miers, *Slavery in the Twentieth Century: The Evolution of a Global Problem* (Walnut Creek, CA, 2003), pp. 326–8; Gwyn Campbell, "Coffee Production in Madagascar," in William Gervase Clarence-Smith and Steven Topik (eds.), *Coffee under Colonialism and Post-Colonialism: The Global Coffee Economy in Africa, Asia, and Latin America, 1500–1989* (Cambridge, 2006), pp. 67–99.

[18] Abdel Razzak Takriti, *Monsoon Revolution. Republicans, Sultans, and Empires in Oman, 1965–1976* (Oxford, 2013).

international definitions of slavery, as – in 1968 – did prostitution, human trafficking, and the South African and Rhodesian Master and Servant Acts.

CONTEMPORARY FORMS OF SLAVERY IN THE IOW

An estimated 27 million people live in contemporary forms of human bondage, notably in the IOW. Agencies such as Anti-Slavery International (ASI), ILO, and the United Nations Children's Fund (UNICEF) have for a long time agitated for the suppression of modern forms of bondage, but governments in both the IOW and the West have to date failed to formulate effective policies. ASI and ILO highlight four main reasons for the concentration of human servitude in the IOW: poverty, illiteracy, the passivity or ineffectiveness of IOW authorities, and the disinterest of Western governments. Additional associated problems are the different definitions of bondage employed by concerned organizations and governments, and their ignorance of the historical roots of IOW servitude.[19]

The debate over servitude in the IOW changed significantly from the late 1980s with the end of the Cold War and apartheid in South Africa, and the onset of globalization. Colonialism, apartheid, and the Gulag dropped out of definitions of slavery which thereafter focused largely on child labor, prostitution, and human trafficking. Antislavery organizations stressed education and economic growth as the main tools to fight against these forms of slavery. However, it has proved hard to verify quantitative and qualitative estimates of "modern slavery," and to implement development policies designed to counter it. Indeed, while globalization has led to freer movement of goods and capital, governments have increased limitations on legal cross-border movements of labor while ignoring, or in some cases colluding in, human trafficking and oppressive forms of child labor.

Since the nineteenth century, the word "trafficking" has been invoked in connection with abolitionism. The interdiction of the slave trade turned "trade" into "trafficking" which, alongside the perpetuation of forms of slavery, has been particularly prominent in the IOW. However, a trafficked person is not necessarily a slave. Terminology covering human trafficking appeared in the 1926 and 1956 Conventions of, respectively, the League of the Nations and the United Nations. Since the expansion of globalization in the 1990s, international human trafficking and accords intended to counter it have increased, as have the tightening of border controls and publicity given to illegal immigration. Article 3 of the UN Protocol of 2000 defines trafficking as the recruitment, transportation, transfer, harbouring, or receipt of persons through coercion, or the threat

---

[19] Kevin Bales, Zoe Trodd, and Alex Kent Williamson, *Modern Slavery: The Secret World of 27 Million People* (Oxford, 2009).

thereof, or fraud, deception, and abuse of power, or the giving or receiving of payment or other benefits to achieve control over another person. However, illegal immigrants are not considered to have been "trafficked" because they are presumed to have consented to being transported. Moreover, overemphasis on "trafficking" can legitimize harsh border controls that, while restricting human trafficking, also infringe on the rights of cross-border migrants.

The US Department of State estimated that in 2012 some 26 million people were victims of human trafficking – a more than sixfold increase within a decade. Worldwide, from 2010 to 2012, there were between 6,000 and 7,000 prosecutions leading to about 4,200 to 4,700 convictions for human trafficking. Most of the countries affected lie within the IOW, including states that have not yet ratified the protocol against human trafficking, such as Thailand, Uganda, Kenya, Somalia, Eritrea, Singapore, Yemen, and Zimbabwe; and others that are signatories to the protocol, including Burma, the Philippines, India, and South Africa. The geographic range of trafficking is considerable. In Bangladesh, for example, significant numbers of women and children are trafficked into the domestic market for prostitution, while large numbers of women, men, and child victims are also trafficked abroad: most are sent first to Nepal, in order to obtain a passport, and then to the Gulf (including Iran and Iraq), the Maldives, Malaysia, Singapore, and Europe. They face particularly extreme conditions of forced labor in Bahrein and the Emirates.

Southeast Asia is another nodal point for forced labor and human trafficking. In Burma, both the army and insurgent militia recruit children, particularly orphans and children of the urban poor. Rohingyas and members of other ethnic minorities excluded from citizenship by the Burmese government are also vulnerable to trafficking, being often sold across the border to Thai fishing communities. Further afield, Burmese migrants to Southeast Asia and the Middle East are subject to forced labor and trafficking – notably into the fishing industry and construction (men) and prostitution and domestic servitude (women and children). We here focus on two salient aspects of modern human bondage: the sex slave trade and child labor.

Sex Slave Trade

The sex slave trade, a central feature of modern human trafficking, arose largely as a result of modern capitalist forces. The pre-nineteenth-century trade in slaves for sexual purposes was largely limited to a small traffic in beautiful, often highly trained girls, for elite males. The nineteenth century witnessed the rise of a recognizably modern form of sexual slavery in the IOW. This, in turn, was due to rising gender imbalance in key locations as a result of the commercial boom associated with the international economy, and military action associated mainly with European imperialism.

Thus, the labor migration that accompanied the growth of the international economy led to unprecedented concentrations of male workers in the IOW. For instance, between the 1840s and 1890s, millions of impoverished Chinese males emigrated to the new commercial centers of the Americas, Africa, and Southeast Asia. Notable concentrations formed in Hong Kong and Singapore, the population of both of which quadrupled from the 1880s. This created a huge demand for sexual services that was met by a traffic in mostly involuntary prostitutes, many of whom were girls engaged through deceit or sold by their parents. Chinese male migrant demand for females was such that in Southeast Asia the price of female slaves, traditionally about the same as that of male slaves, rose to double or even treble that of males. This was the reverse of the price structure in China. However, the price could fluctuate enormously: for example, during the 1880s drought, the purchase price of young girls in Northern China varied from $1.50 to $75, while the average sale price in Hong Kong was $45, in Singapore $350, and in San Francisco between $1,000 and $3,000.[20]

A variant system was that of the *mui tsai* in which, in exchange for payment, a girl was transferred from one family to another as an adoptee, nominally to become a domestic servant. The *mui tsai* system, which continued well into the twentieth century, involved very young girls – in Hong Kong in 1921, 69 percent of *mui tsai* were under the age of 14 – many of whom were by the late nineteenth century used as prostitutes by their new owners. By the 1920s, Chinese and Javanese females were also in high demand as concubines in Arabia. By the late nineteenth century, the traffic in females had become a multi-million-dollar, highly specialized business that linked mainly rural China, and to a lesser extent Japan, to Hong Kong, Singapore, and other overseas centers of Far Eastern male emigration. Total remittances flowing home from Chinese prostitutes abroad were considerable.

Large concentrations of soldiers led to a similar demand for females to provide sexual services, which in European colonies was often facilitated by colonial officials who feared unrest should the sexual needs of soldiers not be met. Indrani Chatterjee notes that British garrisons in India openly employed "slave" prostitutes who in the 1860s were officially taxed – a measure which, alongside fines, only served to increase the debt bondage that more often than not had "enslaved" such girls. In Natal in the late nineteenth century, some white planters controlled male workers' access to women – sometimes their wives and at other times prostitutes – to reward

[20] James Warren, "Chinese Prostitution in Singapore: Recruitment and Brothel Organisation," in Maria Jaschok and Suzanne Miers (eds.), *Women and Chinese Patriarchy: Submission, Servitude and Escape* (London, 1994), pp. 79–80, 87.

or punish indentured Indian males. Again, the Hong Kong and Singapore governments licenced brothels until the 1930s and permitted them to function in clandestine fashion until the 1950s. Again, in the Jaunsar Bawar region of India, where polygamy was a traditional practice, an increase in debt bondage in the nineteenth century, notably for bride wealth, led some husbands to mortgage their secondary wives to prostitution agents who employed them in local or distant urban brothels. Only when they had worked off the "loan" received by their husband were they allowed to return.[21]

The trafficking of people for sexual purposes boomed again with globalization from the 1980s, and is particularly active in the IOW. In India alone, an estimated 400,000 girls are trafficked each year. Again, many Cambodian women are recruited by "employment agencies" to work in Thailand, Malaysia, South Korea, Singapore, and Vietnam where, upon arrival, they have their passports seized by employers who subject them to sex work and domestic servitude. Significant numbers of Vietnamese women and children are enticed into working in brothels in Phnom Penh or (notably girls) in Cambodia. An estimated 6 million Indonesians work abroad, chiefly in Malaysia and Saudi Arabia, but also in the Emirates, Qatar, Singapore, and Hong Kong. Many trafficked sex slaves, because of a cycle of indebtedness, find it impossible to escape. Wherever war, insecurity, or poverty becomes endemic, as in the Sudan, Ethiopia, and Madagascar, sex trafficking has expanded. In South Africa, one of Africa's most dynamic yet troubled economies, internal trafficking of women and children for sexual purposes is common, as is the import of children and women from other African countries and Asia for the same purposes. In general, very little protection is offered to such females, while traditional possibilities of gaining economic independence have largely closed as the trade has fallen increasingly into the hands of male-dominated, mafia-type structures. The very high risk of contracting HIV and dying young of AIDS has further stigmatized such women, and sharply reduced their living standards and life expectancy.[22]

Child Labor

In the IOW, children – generally defined as those below the age of 18 – have always, despite the conventional academic focus on adult male slaves,

[21] See, e.g., the impact of French troops in the 1798 to 1801 French occupation of Egypt – Karin van Nieuwkerk, *A Trade Like Any Other: Female Singers and Dancers in Egypt* (Austin, TX, 1995), pp. 30–1; Chatterjee, "Abolition by Denial," pp. 150–68; see also Utsa Patnaik and Manjari Dingwaney (eds.), *Chains of Servitude: Bondage and Slavery in India* (Madras, 1985), p. 32.

[22] See, e.g., Craig McGill, *Human Traffic: Sex, Slaves and Immigration* (London, 2003).

formed the core of the trade in human beings, and the issue of child bondage is currently at the center of debates about modern slavery. Economists have long argued about whether child labor is driven by the demand or the supply side, and the significance of such factors as access to education. Recent research indicates that complex economic and social elements are at work, and that the phenomenon of child labor is often also related to rural–urban and male–female employment dynamics, and social structures – notably matriarchal versus patriarchal family units. On a more general level, economic development in the IOW is related to the rate of child involvement in the labor market.[23]

Ethiopia, for example, has one of the world's highest rates of child labor: one-half of its population of children aged from 5 to 14 years (7.5 million in total) were engaged in economic activity in 2001. Then, as now, child labor was concentrated in the agricultural sector, in the growing of coffee, cotton, bananas, sugar cane, tea, and flowers (which can include the use of dangerous pesticides), and in cattle-herding. Some children work in urban areas, as beggars, shoe-cleaners, and in shoe-making, heavy industries, and prostitution. Child trafficking for sexual and other purposes is widespread. Much child labor is related to impoverishment stemming from a mixture of population pressure, land degradation, and to unemployment and underemployment among adults and school leavers (youth). A 2001 ILO survey reported that about 90 percent of children entering the labor market worked in order to supplement family incomes. Children are un-unionized, do not demand worker rights, and are paid lower wages than adults.[24]

CONCLUSION

It is increasingly clear that in the IOW, outside European-dominated enclaves such as the Mascarene Islands, the history of human trafficking and bondage differs significantly from conventionally understood models of Atlantic slavery. There existed in the IOW a wide variety of forms of human servitude that varied according to region and time. Many traditional categories of IOW servitude and human trafficking persisted into the nineteenth and twentieth centuries. Colonial authorities tolerated many of these, notably forms of female servitude. Others, such as types of *corvée* labor, they adapted and enforced for their own purposes. In some cases, and in a few areas, they also tolerated chattel slavery – in the Middle East into the post-1945 era. The collapse of colonial empires, and the

---

[23] Gwyn Campbell, Suzanne Miers, and Joseph Miller (eds.), *Children in Slavery through the Ages* (Athens, OH, 2009).

[24] Kaushik Basu, "Child Labour: Causes, Consequences, and Cure, with Remarks on International Labour Standards," *Journal of Economic Literature*, 37 (1999): 1083–119.

Table 10.1 *Percentage of the Population of Children Aged 10–14 in the Labor Market of Three Countries, 1950–2010: Ethiopia, China, and India*

	1950	1960	1970	1980	1990	1995	2000	2010
Ethiopia	52.95	50.75	48.51	46.32	43.47	42.30	41.10	38.79
China	47.85	43.17	39.03	30.48	15.24	11.55	7.86	0.00
India	35.43	30.07	25.46	21.44	16.68	14.37	12.07	7.46

Source: ILO, *Economically Active Populations: Estimates and Projections, 1950–2010* (Geneva, 1996)

post-1945 rise of Cold War tensions and more effective international organizations, spelled the end for most forms of chattel slavery. However, the rise of the international economy, and notably of globalization from the 1980s – in the context of feeble, corrupt, or uncaring IOW governments – has encouraged a plethora of forms of human servitude and trafficking that continues to the present day and affects, in the main, the most vulnerable, notably women and children. While not a specifically IOW issue, human bondage is widespread throughout the IOW. Research into all forms of human servitude and trafficking in the modern colonial and post-colonial eras is increasingly demonstrating commonalities across regions that highlight the issue of how to define "slavery." If modern definitions of slavery, including debt bondage, are applied to the pre-colonial and pre-modern eras, conventional models of Classical and Atlantic slavery and slave societies may well need to be modified.[25]

A GUIDE TO FURTHER READING

Allen, Richard, *European Slave Trading in the Indian Ocean, 1500–1850* (Athens, OH, 2015).

Alpers, Edward, *The Indian Ocean in World History* (Oxford, 2014).

Bose, Sugata, *A Hundred Horizons. The Indian Ocean in the Age of Global Empire* (Cambridge, MA, 2006).

Campbell, Gwyn (ed.), *Abolition and Its Aftermath in the Indian Ocean Africa and Asia* (Oxford, 2005).

Campbell, Gwyn (ed.), *The Structure of Slavery in Indian Ocean Africa and Asia* (London, 2004).

---

[25] Gwyn Campbell and Alessandro Stanziani (eds.), *Debt and Slavery in the Mediterranean and Atlantic Worlds* (London, 2013); and Campbell and Stanziani (eds.), *Bonded Labour and Debt in the Indian Ocean World*; Alessandro Stanziani, *Bondage, Labor and Rights in Eurasia, 17th–20th centuries* (New York, 2014).

Campbell, Gwyn and Alessandro Stanziani (eds.), *Bonded Labour and Debt in the Indian Ocean World* (London, 2013).

Carter, Marina, *Servants, Sirdars and Settlers: Indians in Mauritius, 1834–1874* (Delhi, 1995).

Clarence-Smith, William Gervase (ed.), *The Economics of the Indian Ocean Slave Trade* (London, 1989).

Harms, Robert, Bernard Freamon, and David W. Blight (eds.). *Slavery and the Slave Trades in the Indian Ocean World: Global Connections and Disconnections* (New Haven, CT, 2013).

Miers, Suzanne, *Slavery in the Twentieth Century: The Evolution of a Global Problem* (Walnut Creek, CA, 2003).

Tinker, Hugh, *A New System of Slavery: The Export of Indian Labour Overseas, 1830–1920* (London, 1974).

Warren, James, *The Sulu Zone 1768–1898* (Singapore, 2007, 1st edn, 1981).

CHAPTER 11

SLAVERY IN INDIA

ALESSANDRO STANZIANI

INTRODUCTION

Slavery played a role in India quite different from that of slave trading and slavery in the Atlantic World. Any assessment of slavery in Indian history must first deal with the tension between Indian and non-Indian values – the latter heavily shaped by what happened in the Atlantic World. The main aim of this chapter is not to oppose the realities of slavery to the ways writers have represented them since 1800, but rather to emphasize how Indian and non-Indian values on the subject have influenced each other. We begin with a brief review of the historiography as the starting point for a critique of the sources. Such a critique will provide a base for tracing the historical dynamics of dependence in India. The chapter will also examine the legacy of pre-colonial slavery, the transformations introduced by the British conquest, and, finally, labor relationships following the formal abolition of slavery. It will endeavor to transcend the tension between two approaches: one that stresses the major break caused by the formal abolition of slavery, the other that focuses on the continuities of forms of bondage before and after abolition. The intention here is to bring out the breaks *and* the continuities as well as the possibilities available to former slaves and new immigrants (for example, in the tea plantations in Assam and in Mauritius) as they struggled to defend their legal, economic, and social rights.[1]

HISTORIOGRAPHICAL PATTERNS

Scholarship on Indian slavery is still overshadowed by the enormous literature on bondage in the Atlantic and on the British occupation of the Indian sub-continent. Some historians have argued that Indian slavery was objectively different, or even milder, compared with its counterpart in the Americas. The political repercussions of American and transatlantic

---

[1] Seymour Drescher, *Abolition: A History of Slavery and Antislavery* (Cambridge, 2009); Hugh Tinker, *A New System of Slavery: The Export of Indian Labor Overseas, 1830–1920* (London, 1974).

slavery have proved more far-reaching. Others are of the opinion that any difference is simply because there are fewer available sources in the Indian case. In fact, the few existing historiographical studies on Indian slavery are based on East India Company (EIC) records and British Parliamentary reports. These reveal official British attitudes on the subject, but there is some question as to whether they can be counted on to produce an accurate account of slavery in India. Mostly, they underscore the difference between slavery in India and what was perceived as its harsh counterpart in the Americas. According to some researchers, this approach was dictated by the converging interests of the EIC and the abolitionist movement as both sought to sharpen their criticism of the latter by demonstrating the flexibility of forms of dependence in India. More radical critiques pointed out that the colonial sources had used European categories – vassal, owner, concubine – which gave a false idea of Indian practices regarding labor and dependence. Following the recovery of sources from the Mughal dynasty and from the principalities in the Indian Peninsula, new approaches were developed, based on lexical and semantic analysis. Scholars now stressed the continuum of forms of dependence in India, as well as the fact that Indian slavery and bondage could not be separated from caste, religion, household, and military affairs. But by stressing the specificity of Indian categories, which preclude any reduction to Western notions, some authors began to echo colonial attitudes, particularly those of the "Orientalists" among the British elites and administrators. Thus, identifying Indian specificities meant achieving a clear-cut distinction between Indian slavery and American slavery; indeed, even using the term "slave" with reference to India might be problematic. This conclusion raised questions among those who thought slavery was not coterminous with chattel slavery and that, consequently, extreme forms of dependence, including slavery, were indeed present in India.[2]

SLAVERY AND COLONIAL RULE

The impact of colonialism lurks behind the issues of historical sources and the description of the specific features of Indian slavery. Just how did the British conquest affect the forms of dependence in India? While most observers are in agreement on the fact that the early colonial period contained extreme forms of dependence, opinions differ as to the methods

[2] Andrea Major, "The Slavery of East and West: Abolitionists and 'Unfree Labor' in India, 1820–1833," *Slavery and Abolition*, 31 (2010): 501–25; Indrani Chatterjee and Richard Eaton (eds.), *Slavery and South Asian History* (Bloomington, IN, 2006); Dharma Kumar, "Colonialism, Bondage, and Caste in British India," in Martin Klein (ed.), *Breaking the Chains: Slavery, Bondage, and Emancipation in Modern Africa and Asia* (Madison, WI, 1993), pp. 112–30.

and impact of the abolitionist movement. We know for certain that Britain did not adopt a decisively abolitionist attitude in India until very late – beginning in 1843 and particularly after 1860 – but transformations of the forms of labor in the various regions and sectors of the Indian subcontinent are often still unclear.

Europeans did not create slavery in India, but they transformed it and introduced new variants. War and debt were the two most common sources of enslavement and bondage in pre-colonial India. War captives were mostly outsiders, whereas debt slaves tended to be owned by local patrons, chiefs, moneylenders, or tax farmers. Slaves were present in India in the fourteenth century, as post-nomadic states emerged, but the institution probably existed earlier. The Mughal Empire (1526–1857) was created without the use of slave soldiers and the Mughals even tried to limit the extent of slavery. In particular, they managed to reduce economic slavery, the rationale being that, unlike slaves, peasants were taxpayers. At the same time, Mughal rulers actively participated in Central Asian trade and slave trading. They deported rebels and revenue defaulters and exchanged them for horses. Domestic slavery also flourished under the Mughals, as it did in the contemporary Rajput and Maratha states. Debt bondage and other forms of servitude were nevertheless extremely widespread. Famines could force people into debt bondage or slavery in return for subsistence, either voluntarily, as was the case of many *dvija* caste members in India, or as outcasts from kin groups. Those subject to debt bondage sometimes outnumbered slaves.[3]

In Bihar, *kamias* were a kind of servant of landlords, who became unfree laborers and slaves under the British. Forms of bondage were also widely found in Gujarat, especially as a consequence of advances for marriages. A *dubla* (landless person) accepted an advance from a higher caste landowner and became a *hali*, committing himself and his family to work for the master for a whole year. Further advances on grain and reduced periods of activity increased the debt.[4]

Hindu as well as Muslim families made use of domestic slaves for both household and agricultural labor. They were locally acquired, through kidnapping, debt bondage, or marriage to slaves. Males could accompany

[3] Sumit Guha, "Slavery, Society and the State in Western India, 1700–1800," in Chatterjee and Eaton (eds.), *Slavery and South Asian History*, pp. 162–86; Gwyn Campbell, "Introduction" to Gwyn Campbell (ed.), *The Structure of Slavery in the Indian Ocean, Africa, and Asia* (London, 2004), pp. i–xxxii; Gwyn Campbell and Alessandro Stanziani (eds.), *Debt and Bondage in the Indian Ocean Worlds* (London, 2013).

[4] Martin A. Klein, "Introduction: Modern European Expansion and Traditional Servitude in Africa and Asia," in Martin A. Klein (ed.), *Breaking the Chains: Slavery, Bondage and Emancipation in Modern Africa and Asia* (Madison, WI, 1993), pp. 3–36, in particular, p. 11; Utsa Patnaik and Manjari Dingwaney (eds.), *Chains of Servitude, Bondage and Slavery in India* (Hyderabad, 1985), pp. 25–6.

their masters in military campaigns, while females provided sexual services. In Rajput households, slave women could rise to prominence. They were allowed to accumulate property in the form of land, cattle, and slaves, but their position remained insecure.

Rajputs and Marathas sold, mortgaged, and rented slaves. Slaves were also highly valued gifts and were used for dowries or tributes and in strategic alliances between households. Dowries helped to expand the slave trade and markets in Rajput areas. At the same time, the offspring of concubines were not typically bought and sold; daughters in particular served as tokens of exchange in political negotiations. The sons of wet nurses were incorporated into the household as putative foster-brothers of the head.

In Hindu areas, caste origin played a role. To be sure, caste was not the rigid system described in British reports, which tended to associate slavery with low castes and translated various forms of dependence into European terms (slaves, serfs). In reality, slaves kept their caste identity and masters deliberately identified and publicized their slaves' castes. In fact, there was not only a continuum of conditions between the free and the unfree, but rituals and caste also influenced the process of enslavement and emancipation. The caste system restricted social mobility, but its rigidity should not be exaggerated. The system evolved and changed over time and new castes emerged, while others declined. Caste was correlated with occupation, but not exclusively, and the same was true for the relationship between caste and servile status. Low castes were more likely to be found in extreme forms of dependence and bondage, but not necessarily slavery. And in contrast to European perceptions, slaves did not always come from low castes. Thus, for some prisoners of war and concubines, caste did not enter into the process of enslavement. Contrary to colonial descriptions and some modern accounts, the caste system was relatively flexible and indeed changed over time. Caste was only one of many variables that played a role in Indian slavery. Most slaves did not remain locked into slavery for a lifetime. Military slavery was not conceived as a status, but as a specific career and origin, and therefore a particular relationship with the master. Slaves were integrated into the households of their masters. In the Maratha kingdom, slaves could inherit land, while others obtained manumission by purchasing a slave to act as their substitute.[5]

These forms of slavery and bondage did not disappear under the colonial rule, but they evolved in connection with it. European colonial regimes facilitated the growth of indebtedness by imposing monetary taxes, promoting commercialization, and enforcing credit contracts. At

[5] Susan Bayly, *Caste, Society, and Politics in India, from the Eighteenth Century to the Modern Age* (Cambridge, 1999).

the same time, colonial authorities maintained tight budgetary regimes that avoided funding public welfare programs and distinguished people in debt bondage from "real" slaves, whose condition they attributed solely to violent capture. As a result, enslavement through debt expanded considerably across the Indian Ocean world, affecting a wide variety of people, from farmers mortgaging future harvests and potential grooms borrowing a bride price, to small traders living off credit from larger-scale merchants. The French and British relied heavily on Indian convicts and galley slaves under the command of European officers and Indians were often forcibly recruited. Even when they were legally free, Indian sailors endured extremely harsh conditions. In the seventeenth and eighteenth centuries, Europeans exported Indian slaves to their colonies in Southeast Asia, the Mascarenes, the Cape, and elsewhere. The EIC continued slave raiding until the end of the eighteenth century, when fear of depopulation and lack of taxpayers prompted the Company to limit these practices. The 1774 Bengal Regulation Act prevented the purchase and sale of persons not already in a state of slavery. This Act was also issued in response to increasing conflicts between the Crown and the EIC, as well as between Britain and other European powers, such as the French and the Portuguese, who also took part in enslaving people in India. Holding, selling, and buying domestic slaves nevertheless remained widespread in Bombay, Madras, and Calcutta. Chattel slaves were advertised openly in the *India Gazette* and other newspapers appealed for the return of absconding slaves. Slaves acquired by the EIC in Southeast Africa were disembarked in Madras before being dispatched either to Southeast Asia or inland within India itself.[6]

In the late eighteenth and early nineteenth centuries, the EIC officially confirmed the right to possess slaves in the territories under its rule, but sought to limit the further dissemination of slavery. The rationale for this ambiguous attitude was, on the one hand, that the Company wanted to preserve its authority by allowing local slavery; on the other, it did not want peasants-taxpayers to be turned into slaves. Faced with problems enforcing the 1774 regulations, the EIC proclaimed new rules limiting the slave trade and new enslavement in Bengal (1789), Madras (1790), and Bombay (1805). These rules, too, proved difficult to enforce.

Both the English and the French made wide-scale use of violence, kidnapping, and deception to enslave people. Sepoys, ordinary migrants, and seamen discovered too late that they were not under temporary "free contract," but in fully fledged slavery. During the same period, Gujarat

---

[6] Alessandro Stanziani, *Sailors, Slaves, and Immigrants: Bondage in the Indian Ocean World, 1750–1914* (New York, 2014); Markus Vink, "'The World's Oldest Trade': Dutch Slavery and Slave Trade in the Indian Ocean in the Seventeenth Century," *Journal of World History*, 14 (2003): 131–77.

merchants were deeply involved in the slave trade from Mozambique; slaves were imported via the Portuguese enclaves of Goa, Daman, and Dui and then re-exported into the hinterland, into the homes of the Hindu or Muslim nobility. These imports accounted for about 200 to 300 slaves per year between 1770 and 1834.[7]

However, Indian powers such as the Marathas in the West, the Nayakas in the South, and the Mughals, who occupied the greatest part of India, opposed enslavement by Europeans, though they still practiced it themselves. The Maratha Confederacy extended its power in the eighteenth century before succumbing to British expansion in 1818. In the late eighteenth and early nineteenth centuries, several forms of bondage and slavery were disseminated in western India. The exaction of forced labor (*veth-begar*) by the powerful was a common occurrence in rural life. The movements of British officials and armies in the early colonial era widened the demand for this type of forced labor. Some British officials reinvented what they called "tradition" to meet the demand. The status of slavery was distinct from that of forced labor. The Arabic loan-word, "*Ghulam*," was the common term for male slaves. Several words were used to designate slave women: *dasi, batik, kunbini*. Some Maratha documents referred to a daughter (*muli*) and a slave-woman (*batik*) interchangeably. Kidnapping, tax arrears, or fines were the main sources of enslavement. Internal boundaries, such as the frontier of the Nizam's territories, Mysore, and the southern Maratha appendages, provided sites for large slave markets.

Although India did not suffer from the extreme labor shortages that provided the context for slavery in the New World, it would be a mistake to imagine that the country enjoyed an abundance of labor. In many activities, labor supply was a crucial concern for both British and indigenous powers. In the 1790s, the struggle between the EIC and Mysore, for example, considerably reduced the productive capacity and available labor force in Andhra Pradesh. Thus, the abundance of low-caste laborers without land rights did not prevent periodic labor scarcities. Francis Buchanan estimated that in South India 5 million slaves were employed in rice cultivation.[8]

In the colonial Madras Presidency, *Padiyals* were in principle free hired servants; however, their compensation for labor did not substantially differ from that of *Paraiyar* (a degraded Tamil caste), because monetary payment was still supplemented by usufructuary rights and crop shares.[9] Entry into

[7] Pedro Machado, "A Forgotten Corner of the Indian Ocean: Gujarati Merchants, Portuguese India and the Mozambique Slave Trade, c. 1730–1830," in Campbell (ed.), *The Structure of Slavery*, pp. 17–36.

[8] Francis Buchanan, *A Journey from Madras through the Countries of Mysore, Canara and Malabar* (London, 1807).

[9] Ravi Ahuja, "Labour Relations in Early Colonial Context: Madras, c. 1750–1800," *Modern Asian Studies*, 36 (2002): 793–826.

slavery could thus be a strategy for short- and even long-term survival and famines created a pool of surplus labor. In many areas of India, many landless peasants from low castes were readily available; at the same time, European and some Indian masters complained about the scarcity of labor in certain Indian areas. Agrestic slavery and forms of "wage" labor were not so much substitutes as complementary resources and solutions. The term "debt bondage" employed by the British actually included many different relationships, from short-term credit granted to independent workers to debt slavery.

Among Rajputs, given the absence of frequent fighting and the raiding economies they sustained, and a gradual squeeze on the more visible slave markets in the region through the nineteenth and early twentieth centuries, the chief households became even more reliant on reproducing servility. In particular, the custom of the bridegroom's clan providing unmarried boys equal to the number of unmarried *davris* (female domestics) included in the dowry was widespread.[10] The British authorities therefore encouraged the Jaipur court to declare those practices illegal.

The Permanent Settlement Act of 1793 (transforming tax farmers into landlords in Bihar and Bengal) did not apply to West India, particularly the southern Gujarat. There, the British found revenue management almost entirely in the hands of the Desais – originally entitled by the state to collect taxes. The British authorities decided that the Desais were unfairly exploiting the peasantry and therefore sought to introduce a system of direct tax collection, which excluded them; they also sought to bestow land ownership on the peasants. The Desais reacted by registering the peasants' lands under their own names. During the half-century-long transition from indirect to direct British rule, local peasants were used by the Desais (as temporarily entitled tax collectors), who came under increasing pressure from the British and suffered major loss of lands. Over time, the action of the British administration reduced the influence of the Desais, who were definitively relieved of their tax collector status in 1867.

The British also redefined the debt-bondage-inducing practices mentioned earlier – *kamias* in Bihar and *dublas* and *halis* in Gujarat – into their own terms, viewing them as economic transactions. They considered debtors' slaves to have outsider status in the community; in reality, the opposite was true: debt relationships were a way of expanding local communities. The debate therefore centered on whether or not the debtor had voluntarily entered into servitude: if voluntary, it was acceptable; if involuntary (according to British law), it was not. Patronage was turned into an economic relationship. Advancing funding for marriage,

---

[10] Ramya Sreenivasan, "Drudges, Dancing Girls, Concubines: Female Slaves in Rajput Polity, 1500–1850," in Chatterjee and Eaton (eds.), *Slavery and South Asian History*, pp. 136–161.

consumption, and seeding were the principal means by which patrons reduced peasants to debt bondage. The number of servants a patron had was an indication of his status. Unlike Bihar, in southern Gujarat, the British authorities did not strongly support the need to abolish these extreme forms of debt bondage. Although British memoranda from 1835 to 1836 called these relationships hereditary bondage, many other officials described them as voluntary servitude. Such ambivalence was characteristic of British engagement with dependency and bondage in India.

THE ABOLITIONIST MOVEMENT AND INDIA

When the British Parliament abolished slavery throughout the Empire in 1833, one major possession was omitted: India. Why? And how can we reconcile the universality of the abolitionist movement with this exception? The transfer of British values and institutions to India had already become a core issue in political debates and administrative governance between the 1760s and the 1810s.[11] The conquest of India was unfinished, as the wars against the Marathas and Mysore testify. Attitudes within the EIC as well as Parliament varied from caution to demands for more direct intervention to promote trade and security, and the need to abolish slavery in the Indian interior. Mixed motives and fierce resistance from Indian states and populations produced a patchwork of institutional and practical solutions that varied according to the field (law, economy, culture, lower or higher education, trade, or labor), the geographical area (Southern India, Northern India, the Malabar Coast, etc.), and, of course, the individuals concerned.

In the 1770s, Warren Hastings, the Governor-General of India, and the Provincial Council of Patna issued a declaration limiting the right of masters over their slaves to no more than one generation. Indeed, the EIC's legislation against exporting slaves from their territories was passed nearly two decades before the British prohibition of 1807. Yet, as late as March 1808, the Joint Magistrate J. Richardson denounced the continuation of slavery in India. No official action was undertaken, except to establish a register of slaves. Although the EIC emphasized its sympathy for the abolitionist movement, it also confirmed the rights of masters over their existing slave holdings. In 1817, for example, Governor-General Francis Rawdon-Hastings, the Earl of Moira, declared that a slave did not become free upon entering Company territories.[12] Many EIC officials

---

[11] Alessandro Stanziani, *Bâtisseurs d'Empires. Russie, Inde et Chine à la croisée des mondes* (Paris, 2012); and Stanziani, *Sailors, Slaves, and Immigrants*.

[12] IOL (India Office Library and records, London): BRC (Bengal Revenue Consultations) 16 August 1774, n. 442, letter from the Provincial Council at Patna to Warren Hastings, 4 August 1774; Bengal

considered political stability and preventing cross-border trade their primary concerns. Humanitarian considerations constantly ran up against
sovereignty issues, demands for profit-making, and the nature of the EIC
itself: was it a trade company or a state?

Official ambivalence had a definite impact on the Company and British
politics in the subcontinent, especially in the areas outside direct control.
Intervention in the name of freedom (abolition of slavery) was a tempta-
tion and a warning and it evolved together with tensions along the borders
between EIC possessions and the principalities. Competition with the
French also played a role: EIC interventions in French, Portuguese, and
Dutch slaving activities were couched in humanitarian language, but
strongly motivated by notions of strategic advantage. In particular, the
Mascarene Islands were of prime importance given their role as a depot
and a base for French privateers during eighteenth-century wars. The
Mascarene Islands relied upon sugar production and thus slave labor,
mostly from Madagascar, Mozambique, and the Swahili Coast, but also
India. Some 21,000 Indian slaves were exported to these islands between
1670 and 1810. Between 1791 and 1807, the British detained slave ships
heading for the Mascarene Islands. However, after acquiring Mauritius,
and in defiance of the 1807 Slave Trade Act, the British tolerated further
slave arrivals until the 1820s.

In a century characterized by rising taxation and years of famine,
"freedom" for former slave outcasts, who had deliberately been kept
destitute and barred from land ownership, meant the liberty to starve.
Some became sharecroppers, but with two-thirds of the crop paid to the
landlord, the threat to subsistence was clear. In order to survive, many
entered into debt bondage. In some areas of India, members of the most
depressed castes formed the overwhelming bulk of those in debt bondage.
The situation closely resembled slavery in that bondage could be inherited
and the vast majority of bonded people were restricted in their geographical mobility. A common argument in favor of debt bondage was that
harvest failure and famine led peasants to sell children in order to help
them survive. We now know there was indeed a strong correlation between
debt bondage and migration, on the one hand, and scarcity and famine, on
the other. Though the British colonial elites did not invent this connection, some individuals took full advantage of it, along with its rhetoric, to
perpetuate and justify slavery. The selling of family members in periods of
famine forced the EIC to find a compromise between pragmatic and
ideological imperatives. Permitting the sale of children in the face of
famine was justified by the fact that the only alternative would have been

general poor relief financed by the British. During parliamentary debates, some suggested, as a possible compromise, that a form of indenture could replace the sale of oneself or one's relatives into slavery.[13] An act to that effect was promulgated, but never implemented. Even worse, other official reports raised doubts about the connection between famine and slavery and argued that the wide dissemination of slavery stemmed from other causes (poverty, kidnapping, and violence).

Until the early 1830s, debates on slavery in India were heavily influenced by the documents issued by the EIC itself. The Company had written several reports on India and Indian slavery since the 1770s, which were virtually the sole source of information for the abolitionist movement. The 1774 declaration of the Provincial Council of Patna, under the direction of the Governor-General Warren Hastings, identified two forms of slavery: *moolzadeh* and *kahaar*. The first type referred to Muslims who were war captives, while the second identified Hindu palanquin bearers owned by their masters. The two were grouped together as slaves because both were considered unfree; however, the council found that, in practice, variations in condition could legitimate recognition of a different status. For example, if palanquin bearers could marry and work at their own discretion, then they were "free." The major arguments in debates and policy implementation were based on distinctions between different forms of slavery (debt, chattel, etc.) and eligibility criteria (whether status stemmed from inheritance, kidnapping, coercion, violence), as well as references to local Muslim and Hindu customs. In their efforts to codify, EIC officials made use of translations and "codes" such as Nathaniel Brassey Halhed's *Code of Gentoo Laws*, a translation of Hindu rules compiled with the assistance of Brahmin *pandits* in 1776. Islamic rules were translated and compiled in Charles Hamilton's *Hedaya or Guide to Arabic Books of Law*. Slave rules were in Volume 3.[14] Taken together, these collections provided the foundation of the EIC position on slavery: the respect for local rules and the easy translation in terms of property and ownership legitimated both the description of Indian slavery as "mild" and the EIC's toleration of the institution. Colonial officials generally tied it to kinship and prestige, thus separating it from its West Indian counterpart. However, not everyone shared this view.

---

[13] Utsa Patnaik, "Introduction" to Patnaik and Dingwaney (eds.), *Chains of Servitude*, pp. 29–31; Sudipta Sen, *Distant Sovereignty: National Imperialism and the Origin of British India* (London, 2002); *British Parliamentary Papers*, 1828, Sessional paper 125, p. 325.

[14] *The Digest of Hindu Law on Contracts and Successions* (London, 1801) did not distinguish servants from the slaves. This text suggests collaboration between British Orientalists and Hindu theologians in inventing a Brahmanic textual tradition as authentic Hinduism (Gyan Prakash, *Bonded Histories: Genealogies of Labor Servitude in Colonial India* (Cambridge, 1990), p. 134).

Humanitarian considerations came into play only after the mid-1830s. As is well known, within the British abolitionist movement, religious arguments and religious groups played a crucial role. Several missionaries and evangelical reports from India severely criticized local customs and EIC acceptance of them. Yet, even in Britain, some activists reproduced the EIC's attitudes and contrasted mild slavery in India with slavery in the West Indies. The criticism of Baptists was more radical, while the Anglican Church was inclined to take a more prudent view. Eventually, the horrors of slavery under the influence of Hinduism and the caste system became the real focus of all missionary condemnation, rather than Indians and slavery as such. From this perspective, slavery was one among other "abominations" such as *sati* (the immolation of widows) on which the missionaries mainly focused.

The mediation of these attitudes was hampered by the difficult interaction between the British Government of India and the Princely States. Interaction was complicated in the field by the multiplicity of agreements and rules that were binding upon Britain and those states. The complexity increased in large areas in which British and non-British territories were intermingled, with neighboring villages falling under conflicting jurisdictions.[15] In this context, lack of control was a source of anxiety for several British officials. Reports of child enslavement and kidnapping multiplied. In 1811, when the Government of Bengal passed Regulation X prohibiting the sale of slaves and their movement into British territories, the question arose as to how this regulation could be enforced with regard to the neighboring Mughal State based in Delhi, particularly in light of the imperial "Slave Trade Felony Act," also of 1811. This Act was openly at variance with required compliance with indigenous law in India and its implementation was immediately halted by the EIC. Debates continued during the following years on the tensions between local customs and British law. As for the Princely States, British relations were based on a system of subsidiary alliance, according to which Britain controlled foreign policy and in exchange guaranteed domestic sovereignty to the local powers. Thus, Britain could not intervene on the issue of slavery. Although several British governors raised the question in the 1800s and 1810s, serious debate on slavery in the Indian states did not begin until the early 1830s. The shift came about as a result of increasing evangelical influence in the higher echelons of the EIC and growing pressure from the abolitionist movement in Britain. Questions of sovereignty and political stability inhibited concrete action.

[15] Malavika Kasturi, *Embattled Identities: Rajputs Lineages and the Colonial State in Nineteenth-Century North India* (Delhi, 2002).

The British antislavery movement thus came to agitate for the abolition of slavery in India despite arguments that what existed in India was not real slavery, but merely forms of family dependence. They won the backing of the English planters in India, who claimed their enterprises were not comparable to the plantations in the West Indies. The fact that there was nothing in the subcontinent comparable to the transatlantic slave trade – the use and trade of slaves in and from India took place on land and was therefore much more difficult to quantify and control – also helped to support this view. In addition, West Indian planters had enjoyed a long-standing protection for their sugar that came under attack in the 1820s. East India interests and manufacturers alike pushed for the admission of "free labor" sugar from the East. In reaction, West India lobbies stressed the importance of slavery in India and allied themselves to those attacking the economic and political power of the EIC.

With the end of the transition period of apprenticeship of British slaves in 1838, abolitionists focused on slavery in the rest of the Americas and "disguised slavery" elsewhere. In this context, slavery in India undermined British campaigns against the institution in Spanish and Portuguese Latin America and the United States. The EIC's interests and its benevolent attitude toward slavery were also mentioned as possible causes of the exacerbation of slavery. In June 1840, the First World Anti-Slavery Convention in London adopted a series of resolutions condemning slavery in India. Evangelical agitation added to increasing criticism of the EIC's power. Abolitionism in India and the end of EIC political powers went hand in hand. The nature and future of the Empire's labor force also entered into these debates. It was no accident that the 1840 convention took place during parliamentary debates over the repeal of an 1838 ban on Indian indentured migration to Mauritius. Disguised slavery featured in both forums and India had to be seen as a source of free labor. The coolie trade was thus reopened at the same time slavery was abolished in India, in 1843.

Yet, instead of putting an end to the slavery question, this outcome raised new ones. The British sought to encourage the Indian states to embrace antislavery. Slave trading was outlawed in Jaipur in 1839 and slave status abolished in 1847. However, in the following years, British officials complained that these Acts were hardly enforced, complaints that revealed the impossibility of relating the slave trade and slavery in India to their transatlantic equivalents. In the Atlantic, the existence of a long-distance traffic in slaves gave meaning to the distinction between the abolition of the slave trade and that of slavery, whereas on the Indian subcontinent, the distinction was seldom relevant.[16] British officials contributed to the

---

[16] Indrani Chatterjee, "Abolition by Denial," in Gwyn Campbell (ed.), *Abolition and Its Aftermath in the Indian Ocean, Africa, and Asia* (Abingdon, 2005), pp. 150–68.

problem by continuing to return runaways to their masters in some areas after the official abolition of slavery in India. Antislavery policy was also compromised by the wide use of forced labor by the British themselves. The EIC employed this type of labor digging canals and on other public works projects, as well as for porterage. Abolitionists attacked these practices in the mid nineteenth century, but met resistance from engineers and other colonial personnel involved in infrastructure development. Again, government and EIC officials were divided on the topic and solutions were locally developed. The ban on forced labor was adopted in some provinces such as Sind in 1856, but it was still in use in Punjab in the 1880s. Only in 1921 was the system of forced labor officially abolished.

In addition to the attitudes of the British, we must also take into account the persistence of various forms of bondage and slavery in Portuguese India. Indeed, the British ban led to a major decline in the slave trade between Mozambique and Damao (or Diu). The Anglo-Portuguese Treaty of 1842 was supposed to put a definitive stop to this trade. Illegal trafficking continued, however, in part because the Treaty did not stipulate the abolition of slavery in Portuguese India. The Portuguese could not legally pursue runaway slaves into neighboring Karnataka, Maharashtra, or Gujarat. By the second quarter of the nineteenth century, when all the territories contiguous to Goa, Damo, and Diu were subject to British antislavery regulations, slaves escaped and Portuguese masters had little hope of recovering those who entered British territory.

POST-ABOLITION LABOR

As in all the other British dominions, the official abolition of slavery in India was followed by extremely coercive rules regarding vagrants, issued in the name of public order, and the need for economic growth as an antidote to poverty. In 1837, the commission in charge of studying the labor standards to be practiced after the abolition of slavery was divided between those wanting a modified version of the British Master and Servant Act enforced in India, and others, including T. B. Macaulay, who wanted the new labor relationships to be regulated by civil law provisions. The majority of commission members opted for the former and the draft code therefore specified criminal penalties for breach of labor contracts. Workers were qualified as servants and eventually assimilated to beggars in case they could not prove a stable employment. The new regulations governed labor recruitment and migration inside India and overseas. Forced labor for the colonial state must be differentiated from other forms of labor. Indeed, during much of the nineteenth century, the EIC and, after 1858, the British state, sought to build infrastructures, notably roads. To this end, they made use of compulsory labor, first through forced levies on local villagers. However, this proved difficult as local communities and elites resisted. There were three types of labor commonly employed in road works in the nineteenth century: *begar* (a customary form of unpaid labor demanded by dominant groups in a region), convict, and famine labor. A large percentage of the labor force employed on the Hindustan-Tibet road (1850s) was officially categorized as "unpaid" labor. A 132-mile stretch of road on the route between Kalka and Chini employed 1,164,644 workers per year, of which nearly 27 percent was "unpaid."

In the official logic, labor classified as "unpaid" was considered part of the tribute Hill States were obliged to pay for the protection they received from the colonial government. The British authorities therefore claimed that tribute labor supplied by Hill States was not like *begar*, because the Hill States were expected to give revenue remittances to those working on the roads. While convict labor was predominant in the early decades of the nineteenth century, other forms assumed greater importance later on. On the Western Road in the Madras Presidency, based on a daily average of 1,598 convicts, the total number of convict days peaked at over 40,000 during the rainy month of July. Large numbers of workers from famine-stricken regions were recruited for canal- and road-building projects in the late nineteenth century. In many areas, public works became synonymous with famine relief. The construction of irrigation works and roads proceeded most rapidly during periods of famine. Starving peasants were paid "famine wages" to build the public infrastructure that became one of the signs of modern India.[17] *Begar* on distant roads was doubly exacting because workers had no access to subsistence resources from their villages: they had to buy grain at high prices from the market.

India had multiple labor markets: the agrarian labor market; overseas migration; internal migration to plantations; recruitment for public works; labor for small-scale artisan production and cottage industries; employment in large-scale industrial sectors, railways, and mining; and urban labor including prostitution, domestic service, and municipal work.[18] Each sector had its own means to recruit and discipline workers, though they also shared modes of organization. Most importantly, the relationship between debt and labor obligation was common to all sectors: recruiters made considerable use of debt to secure workers, just as the colonial administration used taxpayers. This relationship explains the continuing imposition of criminal punishment and severe rules regarding labor

---

[17] Chitra Joshi, "Les travaux publics et la question du travail force en Inde (XIXe-début du XXe siècle)," in Alessandro Stanziani (ed.), *Le travail contraint en Asie et en Europe, XVIIe–XXe siècles* (Paris, 2010), pp. 307–26.

[18] Michael Anderson, "India 1858–1930: The Illusion of Free Labor," in Douglas Hay and Paul Craven (eds.), *Masters, Servants, and Magistrates in Britain and the Empire, 1562–1955* (Chapel Hill, NC, 2004), pp. 422–54.

mobility. Yet, absconding remained widespread and workers could always benefit from the protection of new masters and employers. Sectors were also interconnected; for example, declining emigration to Mauritius in the 1880s led to an increase in job seekers at plantations in Bengal and Assam. Jobbers who advanced funds to recruits controlled workers. Employers could either extend credit and directly control the laborers or leave jobbers in charge of them. British observers of the time, and later historians – using European terminology of labor organization – debated whether the inter-mediaries were more beneficial to the workers or to the plantation owners. Initially, the landowners thought the *sirdars* reduced their recruitment costs and then supervisory expenses, thus bringing considerable benefits. As time went by, the *sirdars* offered another advantage: first the hauliers, and then the landowners, began signing contracts with them rather than with each worker individually. Hence, workers facing problems with wages, repatriation, etc. were legally supposed to address them to the *sirdars* instead of the owners – which, for part of the 1870s, helped significantly to reduce the rate of workers' reports of abuses and, above all, publicity of their lawsuits.

Nevertheless, some plantation owners accused the *sirdars* of encouraging resistance and rioting and even the British inspectors and observers accused them of deducting excessive amounts from workers' wages. How these relationships evolved depended on the conditions specific to each sub-sector of the labor market. The cultivation of indigo in Eastern India provides an example. Most indigo was grown by small tenants of British or Indian landlords. The peasants preferred to grow other crops such as rice. One solution would have been to offer higher prices for indigo, but instead the planters engaged in a local practice: they advanced money to the peasants and afterwards made debt repayment as difficult as possible with fines for poor performance, absenteeism, etc. This *raiyati* system (as it was called) of cultivation based on advances contrasted with the *nij* system in which the planters cultivated the land using hired labor. However, in Bengal, the predominant system was *raiyati*, which was estimated to be used for about five-sixths of total cultivation in 1860.[19]

Until the 1840s, the rising price of indigo on the world market spurred planters to demand increasingly harsh rules to control laborers and tenants. In the second half of the nineteenth century, indigo exports declined precipitously as synthetic dyes quickly replaced them in the world market. *Raiyats* refused to sow and plant indigo. Incidents involving planter

---

[19] Prabhu Mohapatra, "Les contradictions des contrats. Les origines des relations du travail dans l'Inde coloniale du XIXe siècle," in Stanziani (ed.), *Le travail contraint*, pp. 5–34. Note that the *kangany* were theoretically "free" workers who emigrated from India to another Asian region. The *sardar*, a general term for an on-site recruiter and supervisor, became *sirdar* in Mauritius.

violence against *raiyats* became commonplace. In 1860, new labor contract regulations were adopted and criminal sanctions against workers were reintroduced twenty years after their abolition.

Tea production got underway in Assam in the 1840s, accelerated after 1860, and attracted considerable inland migration. Three-year contracts were the rule initially, but they were seldom enforced in the courts. The first legislation appeared in the early 1860s, in the wake of the Act of 1859 and the tea mania that developed during those years. Land prices went down thanks to the government policies and tea prices went up. At the same time, planters sought to recruit and then keep workers in place without increasing their wages. Recruitment was therefore difficult and between 1863 and 1866, 35,000 of the 85,000 workers transported to Assam died or deserted. The Bengal Council responded by adopting the Inland Emigration Act of 1859 in 1863 and then expanding it in 1865 to allow private arrests for vagrancy. Penal stipulations were reduced only in the early twentieth century (1908). While masters now seldom made use of the law to sue laborers (perhaps 5 to 6 percent of laborers per year for desertion), this was only because since 1865 planters in Assam had the private power of arrest.[20] Planters' militias controlled workers and recovered fugitives. Violence and abuses were regularly denounced. This system was gradually reformed in the early twentieth century and definitively repealed in 1915.

There were several reasons for the change: first, the humanitarian movement in Britain brought increasing pressure to bear and the Master and Servant Act was repealed in Britain itself (1875). Second, there was the quite remarkable fact that, for over seventy years until 1915, nominal wages in Assam plantations remained fixed at five rupees a month. The amount was considered the minimum wage – not to be increased for fear of encouraging "laziness" and desertion. This wage influenced all other wages in the region. The indentured system maintained low wages, encouraged labor-intensive growth, and exacerbated competition between planters and employers in general. As wages were kept at a minimum, competition for recruits pushed up the remuneration of intermediaries. Over the years, this rising cost canceled out the benefits of minimal labor costs. Moreover, low wages resulted in more illness and a higher mortality rate (4 to 5 percent per year), thus sharply reducing labor productivity. An initial solution was

[20] Prabhu Mohapatra, "Assam and the West Indies, 1860–1920: Immobilizing Plantation Labor," in Hay and Craven (eds.), *Masters, Servants, and Magistrates*, pp. 455–80; Rana Behal, *One Hundred Years of Servitude: Political Economy of Tea Plantations in Colonial Assam* (New Delhi, 2014).

proposed in 1882 with the introduction of piece-work remuneration, but the planters used this form of payment to extend workdays and therefore reduce wages per hour. At the same time, mechanization progressed, along with new managerial organization of the plantations. Financing for this process came more from British residents in India than from savings in the British homeland. Together, low remuneration and mechanization aimed to cut the cost of production at a time when stiff competition from China re-emerged. The continuing use of a coercive legal apparatus had the same purpose. The negative effects of low wages and coercion on productivity, along with humanitarian considerations, led to the abandonment of the indenture system in the early twentieth century. Between 1901 and 1915, new forms of recruitment were introduced that excluded intermediaries; labor relationships were deregulated, while the problem of reconciling low wages and poor working conditions with the possibility of a low desertion rate was solved with a new system. Immigrants were assigned small plots they could cultivate in addition to fulfilling their obligations on the plantation. Planters retained ownership of the plots and as laborers lacked the resources to cultivate them, they became increasingly dependent on the planters, with little motivation to run away and lose their plots.

INDENTURED EMIGRATION: A NEW KIND OF SLAVERY?

According to one view, the indenture contract resembled forced labor and slavery and such contracts were said to express a "legal fiction." This interpretation has an interesting history of its own: it was put forward by colonial elites in the nineteenth century and later renewed in "subaltern studies." This approach deprives the abolition of slavery of any historical significance. Other scholars have opposed this view by demonstrating that the indenture contract was not seen as a form of forced labor until the second half of the nineteenth century, whereas until then, it was considered as a contract voluntarily entered into. Indeed, indentured labor was not just disguised slavery, but an expression of what free labor actually meant at that time, i.e. a contract based on unequal rights between the master and the servant, the latter being subject to criminal prosecution to enforce the terms of the contract. Masters in the colonies exacted all their rights even though physical chastisement as a penalty fell into disuse in the British case long before the 1875 repeal of the British Masters and Servants Acts.[21]

[21] Robert Steinfeld, *The Invention of Free Labor: The Employment Relation in English and American Law and Culture, 1350–1870* (Chapel Hill, NC, 1991); Tom Brass and Marcel van der Linden (eds.), *Free and Unfree Labor: The Debate Continues* (Bern, 1997); Marina Carter, *Servants, Sirdars and Settlers: Indians in Mauritius, 1834–1874* (Delhi, 1995).

Between 1834 and 1937, over 30 million migrants from India are estimated to have gone to overseas British colonies such as Burma, Ceylon,
British Malaya, Mauritius, Fiji, the Caribbean, and East Africa. Nearly
98 percent of the total movement of migrants from India during the
colonial period consisted of laborers. The majority of these workers were
employed under indenture contracts owned by British capital. Slavery
(in the Caribbean and Mauritius) was replaced by another form of servitude: "coolie labor" under indenture and the *kangani/maistry* systems. The
growing demand in the West for raw materials and other tropical products
led to setting up modern plantations as agro-industrial enterprises by
British capital in several colonies of the British Empire, including India,
during the nineteenth and early twentieth centuries. Sugar, rubber, coffee,
and tea emerged as the most significant plantation products in the Caribbean, Fiji, Mauritius, Malaya, and Ceylon, and in Assam, Bengal, the
northern Himalayas, and southern parts of colonial India. In Mauritius,
14,000 indentured and domestic servants were prosecuted every year in the
1860s for breach of contract, absenteeism, or desertion. In contrast, masters
were seldom indicted and even more rarely convicted for breach of
contract, ill treatment, or non-payment of wages. Outside Britain, masters
inflicted corporal punishment, and could authorize the marriage of indentured servants.

In economic terms, indentured labor should not be interpreted merely
as a temporary substitute for slavery in the aftermath of its abolition.
Indentured labor began well before slavery and continued during and after
it. The first phase, from the seventeenth century to the 1830s, concerned
about 300,000 European indentured servants, mainly males, who were
intended for a wide range of occupations, most famously in Virginia
tobacco. With the rapid development of plantations, African slaves gradually supplanted servants. Lower numbers of white indentured immigrants
moved to the United States (until 1830) and Guiana and Cuba until the
late nineteenth century, responding both to push factors in Europe
(industrialization, transformation of the countryside) and to pull factors
in North America.

Unlike white settlers during the first phase of indentured immigration,
many indentured immigrants (mostly Indians) returned home during the
1850s and 1860s: one-third of the indentured migrants in Mauritius,
the Caribbean, Suriname, and Jamaica went home, but this was far from
the 70 percent repatriation rate recorded in Thailand, Malaya, and Melanesia. Distance and the cost of transport were only two of the variables
affecting repatriation; politics, concrete forms of integration, and death
from disease were also important factors.

Conditions for indentured immigrants improved over time. This was
due to several factors, not least of which was the endurance of the

immigrants themselves. They continued to report abuses, despite the difficulties they faced in so doing, and remained committed to passive resistance, as well as to absconding, forming support groups, and taking action through the courts. These approaches met with increasing "benevo-lence" on the part of colonial elites, in some instances because they firmly believed in freedom and/or the virtues of the free market, while others were responding to political pressure from Paris and London. The India Office and officials in India were doubtless inclined to protect Indian immigrants on Réunion Island not only for humanitarian reasons, but also to guarantee a labor force for British employers in India.

EVOLUTION OF LABOR RULES

Abolitionists now viewed plantation labor, many other local labor prac-tices, and indentured immigration as forms of disguised slavery. The reaction of the colonial elites depended on the location and type of activity and the situation in Assam evolved differently from that in Mauritius and Bihar. It was not until 1859, in the wake of the Sepoy rebellion, that a Workman's Breach of Contract Act was adopted. The Act was intended to give employers tighter control over workmen who absconded or refused to work after receiving advances. It was introduced at the insistence of the Calcutta Trade Association, and initially applied to the presidencies of Calcutta, Madras, and Bombay. By 1865, it was extended to all of British India. An employer who broke a contract was liable only for civil damages, whereas a laborer convicted of the same offence was subject to criminal punishment (plus civil damages). In practice, it was almost impossible for working people to sue their masters. In 1860, the Employers and Work-men (Disputes) Act specified that forced laborers (a status prohibited by general law) could be prosecuted for breach of contract under the 1859 Act. This Act was also distinctive in its emphasis on monetary advances as the main source of obligation. This Act proved to be a crucial bridge between British and local Indian practices connecting labor to credit markets. It radicalized both in a colonial context and contributed to the longevity of debt servitude in India.

Indeed, employers used the Act not only to control and fine laborers, but also to recruit them. For example, in the Assam tea plantations, 40 percent of the labor force was contracted under the Act in 1891, despite the existence of a separate labor recruitment regime in the area.[22] The Act was mainly used, together with the Indian penal code, to control and fine immigrants. Workers would usually explain to the magistrates that they

---

[22] Behal, *One Hundred Years.*

had fled because of unpaid wages, harsh conditions, insult, or physical abuse. However, the rate of conviction varied enormously from one district to another: it was very low in Punjab and extremely high in Assam, under the influence of the tea plantation lobbies.

Over the years, specific definitions of working people were consolidated by case law under the Act. Initially, all servants, artificers, laborers, etc. came under it. In 1869, it was established that domestic and personal servants did not fall into these categories. In 1904, workers who were not engaged in manual labor and performed tasks involving intellectual or managerial skills were also excluded. Thus, a kind of "working class" gradually emerged through jurisprudence definitions and hence without any connection to caste.

Indentured labor was abolished in India in 1916, putting an end to indentured emigration to Mauritius, the Indian Ocean, Africa, as well as inland migration to the Assam plantations. After the First World War, India made a series of pledges to combat forced labor as defined by the Slavery Convention of 1926 and the International Labour Organization (ILO) Convention of 1939. In 1930, the Royal Commission on Labour found that children were bonded to pay off their parents' loans in craft industries. The mortgage of labor against a loan could not always be repaid, and there were no written documents to protect the debtor. Under the 1859 Workman's Breach of Contract Act, if a workman obtained an advance of money from his employer and then refused to work, the employer could complain to the magistrate. The law was finally repealed in 1926. Nevertheless, forms of servitude persisted and some historians have argued they even increased after 1947.

LABOR IN INDIA: TWENTIETH CENTURY

In the late colonial period, the British authorities in India declared themselves to be avid supporters of free labor. The once strong belief that colonial rulers should adapt to local land customs was undermined by a growing awareness that paying landless people a non-living wage forced them to accept advances for expenses that exceeded their daily earnings. The resulting bondage allowed landowners to maintain wages at the minimum level. When the First World War ended in November 1918, the League of Nations was created in Paris; its sixth commission dealt with social issues and slavery. The Council of the League circulated a questionnaire in 1923. The British Government of India acknowledged that slavery persisted, but only in remote areas, and was dying out. In July 1923, the Government of Gujarat issued a proclamation declaring forced indenture illegal.[23]

---

[23] Jan Breman, *Labor Bondage in West India* (Oxford, 2007).

The League of Nations Draft Convention of 1925 initially excluded part of the British Raj from its stipulations in response to the Indian Government's wishes. Anti-Slavery International immediately criticized the draft and humanitarian concerns increased the British Government's doubts, particularly with reference to India and Burma. In some areas of these countries, slavery was still practiced, notably in Naga, the Lushai Hills, the Abor Tracts, and Assam in India, the Baluchi territories, and the Chin Hills and Myitkyina in Burma. Slave girls from Baluchistan were exported to Sind, while in Bihar and Orissa, the Kamiauti system of agricultural bondage bordered on slavery. Britain also made wide use of forced labor in Burma and India. Britain had further problems with the Indian Princely States where different forms of slavery were practiced. The Foreign Office supported the principle of non-intervention. The League of Nations Convention was ratified in 1926, generating considerable problems with regard to the abolition of forced labor, a core issue for the International Labour Organization. The biggest problem was finding a way to reconcile indirect rule with the suppression of forced labor. The British agreed that private enterprises and local chiefs should use only voluntary labor, but were loath to make the same requirement of the colonial state. In practice, the boundaries separating these actors were difficult to determine: the recruitment and exploitation of local labor commonly involved several intermediaries, from tribal chiefs to the state via private companies. Even worse, to assuage British concerns about indirect rule, non-British colonial governments agreed they could delegate their authority to recruit forced labor to subordinate authorities.

The ILO Committee of Experts on Native Labour finalized its report in 1935. It recommended the immediate abolition of criminal sanctions to enforce labor contracts whether written or verbal, now seen as a legacy of the period immediately following the abolition of slavery. But the Colonial Office was often unable to impose amendments to colonial legislation. It therefore required that the abolition be limited to written contracts only. The Convention signed in 1939 allowed criminal sanctions to be abolished gradually and required their immediate suppression only for juveniles and certain offences. Criminal penalties were retained for drunkenness, lack of diligence, failure to perform one's duties, desertion, damages to the employer's property, and abusive or insulting language. The Convention finally came into effect only in 1948.[24]

---

[24] BNA (British National Archives), CO 318/423/6 Vernon minutes, 24 April 1936; M. K. Banton, "The Colonial Office, 1820–1955: Constantly the Subject of Small Struggles," in Hay and Craven (eds.), *Masters, Servants, and Magistrates*, pp. 251–302.

BONDAGE AFTER 1947

After independence, Indian planners established both minimum and max-imum limits on land ownership, envisaging an agrarian society in which owners cultivated their own lands. They called for the state to ban various forms of debt-based bonded labor, for example, bonded laborers should be released from debts incurred more than five years previously and be allocated uncultivated land. Unfortunately, the promise was not fulfilled; only half of the land worked by tenant farmers changed owners, usually for the benefit of high-caste farmers.[25]

Today, forms of debt-bonded labor, wherein freedom of choice, wages, and bargaining power are "significantly restricted," are still central features of labor systems throughout the Indian Ocean world, though often hidden from the eyes of authorities and therefore missing from official statistics. Even now, in Tamil Nadu, despite the 1976 Abolition of Bonded Labour Act, impoverished villagers can fall into debt bondage. The mechanization of agriculture and urban development have changed the picture. Lured by wage advances, thousands of peasants migrate to work in distant brick-works and rice and sugar cane plantations where the rate of pay is so low that most either return, still impoverished or indebted, while some fall into even greater debt obliging them to work for their hirer, bonded to the workplace as virtual slaves. Moreover, this process is not accidental. Employers, while fully subscribing to the tenets of classical economics that in theory reject bonded labor, in practice use whichever form of labor most maximizes profits. In the case of the three industries in Tamil Nadu studied by Isabelle Guérin, local capitalists encourage debt bondage because it helps them to discipline, control, and reduce the cost of local manpower. There are deep connections to traditional forms of exploitation given that upper castes dominate ownership, while *Paraiyar*, former untouchables (in the brick and sugar cane industries) and *Irulars*, a "tribal" group (in rice drying) – historically the bulwark of local servile labor – form the majority of the workforce. Furthermore, the workforce comprises entire families – men, women, and children.

It can also be argued that exploitation of these traditionally servile groups has increased, rather than diminished, with globalization. The processes of mechanization and vertical integration in an increasingly competitive global market have created business structures that survive through cost-cutting, thereby leaving certain sectors highly dependent on cheap servile labor. Like conventional forms of bondage in pre-colonial and colonial Gujarat, contemporary forms of bondage rely on debt. By contrast, modern limitations on mobility imposed upon migrant workers

---

[25] Alice Thorner and Daniel Thorner, *Land and Labor in India* (Bombay, 1962), pp. 61–4.

are not for life and do not involve their families. The jobber pays earnest money for the wives and children, depending on their productive capacity. There are no longer patron-masters who surround themselves with clients, but rather capitalist entrepreneurs who satisfy their time-bound demand for labor by recruiting workers in the rural hinterland.[26] The bonded laborers in sharecropping in lower Sind, known as *haris*, are minority Hindus and Bhills. As they are not registered as tenants, they are vulnerable, unable to claim any rights and in a worse bargaining position than Muslim sharecroppers in other regions such as southern Punjab.

Contemporary overviews indicate the scope of the problem. The first exhaustive survey of bonded labor, carried out by the Gandhi Peace Foundation and the National Labour Institute in 1978 to 1979, estimated the total number of bonded laborers in agriculture in ten states of India at 2.62 million. Some 87 percent of bonded laborers were members of Scheduled Castes or Scheduled Tribe communities. Similar percentages were estimated in a more recent report of 2009. In 1995, Antislavery International (ASI) claimed that, despite the legal prohibition adopted in India in 1970, some 10,000 children were dedicated annually to a god or goddess under the Davadasi system. The girls were married to the local god and any female children born to her were in hereditary bondage. However, evidence was hard to obtain and these figures appear to be exaggerated. According to the US Trafficking in Persons Report of 2013, in India, the estimated number of those in forced labor due to debt bondage ranges from 20 to 65 million. The India Exclusion Report of 2014 offered a detailed analysis of persisting forms of bondage. Laborers are kept in bondage through the use of violence. While agricultural bondage is still the most prevalent form, the non-agricultural sector makes increasing use of bonded labor (brick kiln workers, migrants, building workers, fishermen, carpet weavers, potters, etc.).[27]

Although men make up the majority of bonded laborers, women and children play an important role in occupations such as floriculture, silk production, and *bidi* (cigarettes) making, not to mention domestic services and the sex trade. According to Human Rights Watch, in 2003, in the three states of Karnataka, Uttar Pradesh, and Tamil Nadu alone, about

---

[26] Isabelle Guérin, "The Political Economy of Debt Bondage in Contemporary South India," in Gwyn Campbell and Alessandro Stanziani (eds.), *Bonded Labour and Debt in the Indian Ocean World* (London, 2013), pp. 119–34.

[27] Gandhi Peace Foundation and the National Labour Institute, *National Survey on the Incidence of Bonded Labour: Preliminary Report* (Delhi, 1979); Socio-Economic and Educational Development Society, *Report on Bonded Labour Rehabilitation Scheme under Centrally Sponsored Bonded Labour System Act, 1976* (Delhi, 2009), p. 17; Suzanne Miers, *Slavery in the Twentieth Century* (Walnut Creek, CA, 2003), p. 436; US Department of State, "US Trafficking in Persons Report 2013: Country Narratives – India," www.state.gov/j/tip/rls/tiprpt/2013.

350,000 children were recruited in the silk industry as bonded labor, while the total number of bonded children was estimated at 15 million.[28] Caste and economic forces work together to encourage bondage: while the overwhelming majority of bonded laborers come from lower castes, land-holding and credit mechanisms can pull the illiterate, the indebted, and the nutritionally insecure into servile status.

<h3>CONCLUSION</h3>

The difficulties historians encounter in attempting to grasp the reality of slavery in India stem from the fragmentation of the sources, the wide variety of institutions involved, and the heavy burden of the colonial legacy. The endless debate over categories (Was it real slavery? How should it be categorized? etc.) reflects precisely those tensions. Slavery and extreme forms of dependence were widespread well before the colonial era, though there were important regional differences across the Indian subcontinent. Soldier-slaves, concubines, debt slaves, and agricultural slaves played different roles in different regions. These differences continued during the colonial period. The British colonial administration was divided as to the proper attitude to adopt toward Indian forms of slavery and dependence. Their diverging views were partly linked to different representations, with some British administrators inclined to side with "Orientalists" and others, on the contrary, with "Europeanists." At the same time, their disagreements were compounded by pragmatic questions, namely: What forms of sovereignty should be adopted in the various Indian regions? Attitudes differed not only in space, but also in time, in response to changing views in Great Britain with regard to labor, slavery, and institutions (notably, how much autonomy should be given to the EIC), and to colonial frictions with Indian elites and the Principalities.

This ideological, intellectual, and pragmatic complexity helps to explain the variety and contradictions among the solutions adopted on the ground. In particular, the slow decline of local military slavery – practiced by most of the Indian territorial powers and condemned by the British – did not keep the latter from conducting forced recruitment, especially for the Navy. Similarly, the new monetary mechanisms linked to rising trade and the British presence, along with British forms of taxation, interacted with established forms of bondage and debt slavery, transforming the latter into relationships rooted at once in caste and economic inequalities. It is precisely this embeddedness between local and imperial forms of dependence, between local economic channels, imperial structures, and global

---

[28] Human Rights Watch, *Small Change: Bonded Child Labor in India's Silk Industry* (New York, 2003), pp. 2, 18.

capitalist dynamics, that helps to account for the very long-term persistence of extreme forms of dependence in India even today. For example, debt bondage practiced in most regions of India prior to the colonial era was transformed and continued through forms of taxation imposed by the British, by their own notions of "debt," and also by the integration of local Indian communities into broader economies. In other words, in the case of India, the abolitionist ideal – already expressed in very different forms depending on the period and the British authorities involved – was confronted by complex issues of sovereignty not only in relationships with local powers (direct and indirect rule), but also in relationships between Britain's central institutions and the EIC. In addition, of course, local societies appropriated and helped shape the impact of imperial initiatives in matters of credit, land ownership, and legal institutions.

We have shown that these tensions were revived after 1947 and continue to this day. It is noteworthy that international organizations continue to produce somewhat conflicting figures on current forms of extreme dependence in India. Indian and Western economists also hesitate over how to respond to the persistence of extreme forms of dependence and bondage in India, despite the country's major economic growth in recent decades. According to some, this persistence derives from the dynamics of global capitalism itself, which has embraced bonded labor in South Asia, especially the Southeast. While some advocate adopting a coordinated set of measures aimed at ensuring both growth and a certain degree of equality, others remain skeptical about such solutions and instead favor local solutions grounded in microeconomic behavioral analyses.

A GUIDE TO FURTHER READING

Ahuja, Ravi, "Labour Relations in Early Colonial Context: Madras, c. 1750–1800," *Modern Asian Studies*, 36 (2002): 793–826.

Bayly, Susan, *Caste, Society, and Politics in India, from the Eighteenth Century to the Modern Age* (Cambridge, 1999).

Behal, Rana, *One Hundred Years of Servitude. Political Economy of Tea Plantations in Colonial Assam* (New Delhi, 2014).

Breman, Jan, *Labor Bondage in West India* (Oxford, 2007).

Chatterjee, Indrani and Richard Eaton (eds.), *Slavery and South Asian History* (Bloomington, IN, 2006).

Hay, Douglas and Paul Craven, *Masters, Servants, and Magistrates in Britain and the Empire, 1562–1955* (Chapel Hill, NC, 2004).

Kasturi, Malavika, *Embattled Identities: Rajputs Lineages and the Colonial State in Nineteenth-Century North India* (Delhi, 2002).

Major, Andrea, *Slavery, Abolitionism and Empire in India, 1772–1843* (Liverpool, 2002).

Mander, Harsh (ed.), *India Exclusion Report* (Bangalore, 2014).

Patnaik, Utsa and Manjari Dingwaney (eds.), *Chains of Servitude, Bondage and Slavery in India* (Hyderabad, 1985).

Prakash, Gyan, *Bonded Histories. Genealogies of Labor Servitude in Colonial India* (Cambridge, 1990).

Sen, Sudipta. *Distant Sovereignty: National Imperialism and the Origin of British India* (London, 2002).

Stanziani, Alessandro, *Sailors, Slaves, and Immigrants. Bondage in the Indian Ocean World, 1750–1914* (New York, 2014).

CHAPTER 12

SLAVE RESISTANCE

ROBERT L. PAQUETTE

Slavery defines a relation of extreme domination. Since war and other acts of violence stand as the most conspicuous means of mass enslavement in history, slavery has connoted, as the sociologist Orlando Patterson has argued, the idea of deracination or disembeddedness from society as well as ritualized dishonorableness. Although debate continues as to what sticks in the metaphorical bundle of property rights set the slave apart from other extreme forms of dependency, slavery resides at the far end of a lengthy continuum of servitudes because of the especially burdensome ignominy attached to the status. The slave-owner holds socially recognized, enforceable claims so extensive and expansive that a human body, including usually its reproductive capacity, falls under a kind of allodial tenure. Plato imagined the ideal slave as a perfect extension of his master's will; Aristotle envisioned him as a "living tool." The problem of slave resistance, as the Baron de Montesquieu brilliantly explored in *Persian Letters* (1721), stems from the inability of any master, at ground level, to exercise absolute dominion so as to reduce the will of his slave to total subservience.

Slaves resisted wherever slavery existed. They resisted as individuals and in groups. They resisted passively and violently. They organized acts of collective resistance that were essentially their own. They resisted as elements in larger movements that contained restive people from other vulnerable, low-status groups, like Indians, free persons of color, and poor whites, who, on other occasions, might well serve officialdom as agents of slave repression. Although opportunities for slave collective resistance at any point in time enlarged or diminished depending on how slaves were used and the changing nature of the balance of forces arrayed against them, the threat always loomed that the individual slave, the very someone who was supposed to have become an extension of his master's will, could respond to his caprices with resistance that nullified the relation itself, naked will to naked will, by suicide or murder. Willful slaves, however, only rarely took those extremes.

Remaining in heart and spirit quintessentially social beings, they sought to live – not merely survive – by redeeming themselves, whether incrementally or abruptly, from the theory and practice of social death. Like every other human being in history, individual slaves existed as congeries or bundles of different identities. A common oppression may have acted infrequently to bring slaves of diverse types together into some sort of collective action. But more often than not, identities forged by origin, status, occupation, gender, color, and residence meant slaves differentiated among themselves in ways that undercut class consciousness or collective solidarity. Slaves fought among themselves. They also married, raised children, formed families and communities, produced for their own use goods and services which they exchanged for profit, hired out their skills to others, erected mutual support societies, gathered together for worship, engaged in a wide variety of other cultural activities that bore marks of their own aesthetics and ingenuity, committed very human acts of vengeance, and rose up, albeit infrequently, in mass, bloody rebellion. Eunuchs, "the ultimate slave," the last one of whom belonging to the Chinese imperial court died in 1996, created fictive kin in attempting to assert a very human claim to life after death.[1]

By far the richest source of information for the study of collective slave resistance comes from the zones of commercialized agriculture in the Americas. But the prevalence of field hands on plantations should not divert attention from the wide variety of occupations filled by slaves in history, from antiquity to modernity. Slave eunuchs administered empires for rulers in the Middle East and China. In the Muslim world, where certain regions retained legal slavery well into the twentieth century, slaves performed military service for imperial rulers. Russian slaves managed estates populated by hundreds of serfs. African slaves supervised the labor of indigenous miners in Central Mexico. Slave governors acted as the surrogates for kings in certain parts of West Africa. In 1943, the protectorate of Aden experienced a most unusual slave revolt: dozens of privileged royal slaves belonging to sultans outside the port city rose up to resist British attempts to emancipate them.[2]

Given the limitations imposed by the intellectual and moral horizons of any particular culture and period, rebellious slaves typically did not have grand designs of ending servitude everywhere, but to qualify terms of their own bondage or to elevate themselves out of slavery by degrees into a different dependent status. In part, this evolution explains how quickly sharp theoretical distinctions between slavery and other unfree statuses break down in reality. Over time, such a process of adaptation, assertion, and concession could evolve slavery into dependencies of different kinds, more

---

[1] On eunuchs and the meaning of slavery, see Orlando Patterson, *Slavery and Social Death: A Comparative Study* (Cambridge, MA, 1982), esp. pp. 299–333.
[2] Suzanne Miers, "Slave Rebellion and Resistance in the Aden Protectorate in the Mid-Twentieth Century," *Slavery and Abolition*, 25 (2004): 80–9.

like serfdom or peonage with an implicit, yet fluid, set of reciprocal, ethically informed customary obligations that rulers in advanced states might eventually codify into law. The enlarged sphere of freedom associated with individualism, a modern concept, would have appeared foolish and dangerous in tradition-bound societies in which some notion of dependency would have informed the very understanding of what it meant to be human. Pro-slavery apologists in the antebellum South, for example, claimed that nowhere in the civilized world did pure or abstract slavery exist. Instead, their slaves qualified as "servants" because they had acquired by custom and positive law certain recognized protections characteristic of personhood.

The most daring and imaginative leaders of resistance movements, whether comprised of slaves or some other aggrieved group, have recruited followers through traditional idioms that claim to re-establish or restore what at one time had been considered fair and just. The word "revolution" itself, it should be recalled, first acquired political content in late seventeenth-century England as an act of restoration reminiscent of the circular movement of planetary bodies. The French Revolution linked the modern meaning with the idea of social transformation, a world turned upside down. Depending on the definition of revolution, the messianic *imperium in imperio* forged by the Zanj (slaves of East African origin) within the Abassid Caliphate for more than a decade, beginning in 869, the overthrow of the Ayyubid dynasty in Egypt during the mid thirteenth century by military slaves (*Mamlūks*), recruited primarily from Central Asia; or the temporary capture of the Danish Virgin Island of Saint John by Akan-speaking slaves (Minas) from the Gold Coast in 1733 might look revolutionary. But none of these upheavals captures what Edmund Burke had in mind when reflecting on revolutionary France or what Thomas Jefferson or Napoleon had in mind when interpreting events in Saint Domingue/Haiti.

Thus, while resistance to enslavement can be seen as a universal phenomenon, visible to greater or lesser degrees in any given society depending on a wide range of factors that included the effectiveness of the forces of control, popular resistance to slavery as a social system, that is as a condition unfit for anyone, anywhere, emerged as something new under the sun. It is one thing to play Spartacus and mount resistance to slavery as a good for a person or group of persons who are attempting to escape their bondage, quite possibly to reach a place, say, a homeland where the legitimacy of human bondage obtained. One crosses a qualitatively different threshold, however, when freedom from bondage is asserted as a universal or natural right of impersonal individuals shorn of the particularistic identifying marks impressed on them by the conventions of discrete societies and when nation states arise that assert as one of their primary missions deliberative political contriving to improve the life of "citizens."

This transformation of mind under the impact of science and rationalism, as Alexis de Tocqueville observed with respect to the French Revolution, meant that an existing state of subordination, "patiently endured ... comes to appear intolerable once the possibility of removing it crosses men's minds. For the mere fact that certain abuses have been remedied draws attention to the others and they now appear more galling; people may suffer less, but their sensibility is exacerbated."[3] In the West, an age of democratic revolution had humbled and deposed kings and aristocrats on a scale heretofore unimagined. With plain folk impelled to the streets or manor house by one or another vision of human betterment, personal liberation, and earthly happiness, slave resistance in the modern world would inevitably be shaped in both the minds of some insurgents and, perhaps even more importantly, in the minds of many incumbents with new content and potentiality. Because the Haitian Revolution intertwined with the French Revolution, a slave insurrection that broke out in 1791 in the North Province of the sugar-producing heartland of the French colony of Saint Domingue metastasized into a historically unique social revolution with repercussions on slaves and slave-holders throughout the hemisphere.

More than 3 million ethnically diverse enslaved Africans arrived in the Americas during the first half of the nineteenth century, about 30 percent of the total volume of the Atlantic slave trade and a decline from the peak numbers posted during the last half of the eighteenth century. British anti-slave-trade policies after 1807 had an impact on how the traffic was conducted. Slaves rebelled aboard slaving vessels usually before they had embarked on the Middle Passage while anchored off the coast of West Africa in parking areas. To date, nearly 600 cases of shipboard rebellion have been documented for the transatlantic slave trade. Their frequency varied by coastal supplying region. Greater attention to preparedness with armaments and restraining devices, better trained crews, and established protocols appear to have substantially decreased the proportion of shipboard rebellions during the nineteenth century. More formalized instructions to slave-trading captains warned them to be on their guard for trouble with an especially volatile freight of densely packed young males. The celebrated capture by mutinous slaves of the schooner *Amistad* (1839) happened after recently imported Mande-speaking slaves, having been sold at auction in Havana, had boarded a coastal vessel for transit eastward to a lesser Cuban port.

In the Americas during the nineteenth century, major slave plots and insurrections rarely lacked an urban component, especially a port city, in which slaves had greater elbow-room to assemble, communicate, and plan

---

[3] Alexis de Tocqueville, *The Old Régime and the French Revolution*, trans. Stuart Gilbert (New York, 1955), p. 177.

collective resistance. Increasing the chances of success meant, however, mustering support in the countryside where legions of slaves under close supervision tilled plantations. The most serious eruptions of collective slave violence broke out in sugar-producing regions where, as in the North Province of Saint Domingue in 1791, slave supermajorities, in some cases more than 90 percent of the total population, worked on clusters of estates with an average in excess of 100 slaves per unit. Nineteenth-century Cuban slave insurrections concentrated in the western part of the island in a sugar-planting zone densely packed with slaves and connected to the ports of Havana, Matanzas, and Cárdenas. Puerto Rican history shows few signs of significant collective slave restiveness until the expansion of sugar cultivation during the first half of the nineteenth century in coastal districts like Ponce in the south, though even in this case the actual insurrections proved small and infrequent, and were outnumbered by alleged slave plots. In the history of the United States, the largest slave insurrection, involving several hundred slaves, erupted upriver from New Orleans in 1811 in the country's first major sugar-producing region, in a stretch of bottomland along the east bank of the Mississippi River with an unusually high ratio of slaves to whites.[4]

Because of the continued flow of African slaves into certain regions like northeastern Brazil and western Cuba, slave insurrections with a distinctly African ethnic flavor and restorationist outlook continued to break out during the first half of the nineteenth century. In the fifty-year period from 1800 to 1850, when colonial Cuba imported most of its African slaves, the majority of the more than 500,000 arrivals came from the Bight of Benin and Bight of Biafra. These so-called Lucumí and Carabalí slaves, separately and together, initiated an unusual spate of African ethnic uprisings that rocked the Cuban countryside from 1825 to 1844. The largest, in 1825, 1833, and 1843, embraced several hundred slaves each. Leaders of these and other acts of collective resistance may have had quite limited aims, unaffected by an age of democratic revolution. If the Muslim leaders of the slave insurrection in Salvador, Brazil, in 1835, one of the largest urban-based slave insurrections of the nineteenth century, had somehow managed to make it back to their homeland in the vicinity of the Bight of Benin, they would have found a collapsing Oyo Empire in which endemic warfare was producing mass enslavements. Similarly, communities of maroons in Jamaica, Suriname, and Cuba, having carved out settlements with infrastructure inherited from Africa and reaching agreements with white authorities, quite literally made peace with slavery. Part of the price for the maintenance of a relatively autonomous existence entailed that they

---

[4] Robert L. Paquette, "A 'Horde of Brigands'? The Great Louisiana Slave Revolt of 1811 Reconsidered," *Historical Reflections*, 35 (2009): 72–96.

help track down and capture runaway slaves so that they could be returned to their masters. In 1832, Jamaican maroons helped suppress the largest slave revolt in the history of the British Caribbean.

As an age of revolution beginning in the last quarter of the eighteenth century ushered in an age of ideology, new understandings of liberty and equality, of self and society, increasingly put slavery – an evil, a sin, a violation of natural right, a sign of regressiveness and moral turpitude, an impediment to human progress – beyond the pale. By no means, however, did the process generate slave resistance evenly and uniformly as some kind of eruptive innovation, innocent as a newborn of the past. By no means did African ethnic rebellions disappear. By no means did the leaders and soldiers of slave insurrections envision the future the same way. But the impact of transatlantic political, military, and ideological currents surfaced in the shibboleths, emblems and symbols, manifestos, testimony, correspondence, and constitutions of rebellious slaves. Several hundred runaway slaves, for example, formed what probably was the largest community of maroons in the history of the North American mainland. They ensconced themselves in Spanish Florida on the Apalachicola River during the War of 1812 under British auspices in a fort in which they claimed the status of free citizens under the Union Jack. When hundreds of slaves erupted into violence in the French colony of Martinique in 1831, rebellious slaves announced their affinity with the French revolutionaries who had risen the previous year and wrote "Liberty or Death" on a French Tricolore that was hoisted in the main square in the port city of Saint-Pierre.[5]

Secular motivations for slave rebellion hardly excluded religious ones, which could run concurrently in complex movements. Prophetic and religious influences informed and shaped numerous conspicuous acts of slave resistance after 1804. African religious practices and the use of sorcery, fetishes, and charms to ward off evil and steel participants for battle show up after 1804 in numerous significant acts of collective slave resistance, stretching from low-country South Carolina, through the Caribbean, to northeastern Brazil. Denmark Vesey joined a Presbyterian church before he became a class leader of Charleston's African Methodist Episcopal Church. Nat Turner fancied himself as a prophet with a millenarian vision informed by Matthew 19:30: "But many that are first shall be last; and the last shall be first." Sam "Daddy" Sharpe, the slave credited by Jamaican authorities with masterminding the great slave insurrection of 1831, which lasted for months, cost the lives of hundreds of slaves, and resulted in the destruction of hundreds of estates, was a Baptist minister. Islamic religious leaders mobilized the predominantly non-Muslim slaves who fought

[5] Bernard Moitt, *Women and Slavery in the French Antilles, 1635–1848* (Bloomington, IN, 2001), pp. 130–2.

Brazilian authorities in the city of Salvador in 1835. In the Denmark Vesey plot, Gullah Jack handed out fetishes, Denmark Vesey quoted from the Bible, and at least some of his lieutenants spoke of the natural-rights promise of the Declaration of Independence.

Because the slave's voice is only faintly heard, if at all, in existing sources on slave resistance, the resulting scholarship drawn from these sources tends to paint slave rebels with more temperament than mind. During the US presidential election of 1800, officials in Richmond, Virginia, uncovered the most sophisticated plot hatched by slaves against slavery since the creation of the United States. Some observers, particularly Federalist partisans, discerned unmistakable evidence in the affair of the explosive potentiality of what was called the Gallican doctrine of universal liberty and equality. Several non-Federalists, acute observers in Richmond at the time and with access to slave testimony, commented on the rebels' uncommon spirit, that they sought freedom not merely as a good, but as a "right."[6] A literate slave blacksmith named Gabriel with alleged ties to radical French-speaking whites had enlisted rebellious slaves into undertaking a coordinated march of slave soldiers in a three-pronged attack on Richmond. Gabriel, it was charged, planned to strike on a Saturday night, when many slaves had free time to assemble. They intended to move in columns, set diversionary fires, and, according to one recruit, slaughter whites in the streets, sparing only "Quakers, Methodists, and Frenchmen." Governor James Monroe would be taken hostage; and the rebels, once holding the upper hand, would attempt to negotiate an end to slavery.

Embroiled in one of the most bitterly contested presidential elections in US history, Jefferson solicited intelligence from Monroe, asking for "something of the excitements, the expectations & extent of this negro conspiracy." He had no wish to exaggerate the scope of the plot or its revolutionary potential to Jefferson or anyone else, but called Gabriel's pre-empted movement "unquestionably the most serious and formidable conspiracy we have ever known of the kind." The rebels, however, would have enjoyed only "momentary" successes, for, as he reassured his old friend, "in point of numbers, in the knowledge and use of arms," and in "every other species of knowledge" whites had a gross advantage over blacks.[7] Still, as slave-holders would remind themselves from Jefferson's presidency to that of Jefferson Davis, it takes only a single incendiary to ignite an explosion in a powder magazine.

---

[6] George Tucker, *Letter to a Member of the General Assembly of Virginia, on the Subject of the Late Conspiracy of the Slaves; with a Proposal for Their Colonization* (Baltimore, MD, 1801), p. 7.
[7] Philip J. Schwarz (ed.), *Gabriel's Conspiracy: A Documentary History* (Charlottesville, VA, 2012), esp. pp. 64–5.

The Haitian Revolution would drive home to southerners and other slave-holders in the Americas the necessity for greater precaution, vigilance, and regulation in handling their enslaved laborers. Existence proves possibility. Part of the profits from the profitable use of slave labor went into bolstering defenses and sharpening management techniques. The notion of "total war" had not yet entered the vocabulary, but colonial wars with racial overtones as was the case in Saint Domingue suggested to contemporary observers a qualitative leap in the magnitude of struggle. Chroniclers of antiquity, thinking especially of Rome's experience with the First Sicilian Slave War (137–132 BC), Second Sicilian Slave War (104–100 BC), and Spartacus Revolt (73–71 BC), three of the largest slave insurrections in history, involving tens of thousands of slaves, noted that "servile war" represented the fiercest and bloodiest of all wars. Nat Turner had envisioned such a war in racialist terms in his millennialist dreams. Few references to the term "servile war" entered the transatlantic press before 1800. After the creation of Haiti, however, the idea circulated widely, connoting in the antebellum South and elsewhere the extermination of one race by another. Not by coincidence did southern newspapers gradually diminish their references to slave insurrections anywhere after 1800. When General Thomas Pinckney published in November 1822 for the benefit of his fellow South Carolinians reflections on what caused the plot masterminded by Denmark Vesey, a literate, multilingual, religious artisan, possibly of African birth from the Gold Coast who had once worked as a slave in Saint Domingue, he listed as the first three, "The example of St. Domingo"; the infiltration into southern towns and plantations of the discourse of "universal liberty"; and the ability of literate slaves, especially privileged domestic slaves in southern households, to access revolutionary doctrine.[8]

In both the 1811 slave insurrection near New Orleans and the 1822 Vesey plot in Charleston, the rebels appear to have been attempting a breakout to Haiti, whose 1816 revised constitution offered a kind of free-soil asylum to those slaves who could get there. During official investigations into Cuba's Conspiracy of Aponte (1812), alleged to be revolutionary, island-wide, and combining slave soldiers with an African-oriented, free-colored leadership, several of the arrested coadjutors had proclamations from Haiti in their possession. In an 1814 uprising of enslaved fisherman in Bahia, Brazil, merchants on the scene claimed to government officials that the rebels had spoken openly about Haiti. In Barbados in 1816, during one of the three largest slave insurrections in the history of the British Caribbean, a rebellious domestic female slave encouraged her fellow slaves to set fires,

---

[8] Thomas Pinckney, *Reflections, Occasioned by the Late Disturbances in Charleston* (Charleston, SC, 1822), pp. 6–7.

"as that was the way they did in Saint Domingo."[9] In 1822, more than fifty slaves forced to rake salt in the Turks and Caicos Islands hijacked a ship in group flight to Haiti. Whatever the romanticization of the political and economic situation in revolutionary and post-revolutionary Haiti by American slaves and their abolitionist supporters, evidence exists throughout the principal slave-holding regions of the Americas that Haiti had become at the very least a powerful symbol of black pride and source of ecumenical antislavery energy. Runaway slave William Wells Brown, writing in 1855, placed Toussaint above George Washington in a pantheon of greatness because, he argued, Toussaint's political and military leadership had done more to advance the cause of "universal" liberty.[10]

Even without the specter of the replication of the Haitian example hanging over their heads, slave-holders had long recognized the troublesomeness of slaves in carrying out the master's will. Persistent rebels might be rare, but they could turn up in problematic numbers from one place to another. Runaway slave advertisements for certain antebellum southern states disclose a significant percentage of slaves, above 10 percent, described as having flogging scars on their backs. Pablo Gangá, a slave coachman and mastermind in 1825 of one of the largest slave insurrections in Cuban history, escaped to the bush, mobilized others, survived there for more than a decade, and then reappeared as a sorcerer/leader inculpated in the infamous Conspiracy of La Escalera uncovered in 1843. Cuban officials suspected that some of the slaves involved in the 1825 revolt had arrived from Charleston in 1822 as a result of the punishment there of guilty ones sentenced to transportation out of the country for involvement in the Denmark Vesey conspiracy.

No ruling elite in history has ever made relentless suffering of subordinates a proper end of society, and legitimacy, an essential ingredient of maturing political authority, cannot obtain without consent, without recognition by the master of the slave's subjective self. Although most persistently violent slaves had predictably abridged lifespans, in every country in which the master-slave relation was woven into the fabric of social life, many masters learned that a better way to manage slaves might be to shelve the lash for emergency use and recognize the agency that was denied slaves in theory by attempting to direct their behavior through incentives, to obtain, for instance, increased productivity, sexual favors, or children by offering rewards, privileges, and even cash payments.

[9] As quoted in David Brion Davis, *Inhuman Bondage: The Rise and Fall of Slavery in the New World* (New York, 2006), p. 169.

[10] William Wells Brown, *St. Domingo: Its Revolutions and Its Patriots. A Lecture, Delivered before the Metropolitan Athenaeum, London, May 16, and at St. Thomas' Church, Philadelphia, December 20, 1854* (Boston, MA, 1855), p. 37.

Quantitative evidence, drawn from the narratives of slaves in the United States, indicates that slave stealing (taking) occurred far more on plantations with masters who were Scrooge-like in their provisioning than on those who doled out generously in accordance with the paternalistic ideal. The promotion of slave families and the distribution of provision grounds for cultivation by slaves on their own time often resulted from a conjunction of interest of the two principals in the relation.

Modern scholarship on slave resistance has flourished in part because of the attempt to describe the essence of the master–slave relation and to put selective lessons learned in service to current ideological purposes. It is hard to imagine a social group more disadvantaged in premeditating or pre-planning rebellion than slaves. Insurrectionary leaders had to work in great secrecy and with considerable ingenuity to mobilize followers and to steel them for what was to come. Some chieftains ultimately relied on gathering strength from plantation to plantation while on the march, using terror to get reluctant slaves to join in. Few persons in the antebellum United States had studied the history of slave rebellion more than Thomas Wentworth Higginson, a Unitarian minister who supported John Brown's attack on Harpers Ferry and led black troops into battle during the Civil War. When he asked "the ablest men" under his command "why there had been so few slave insurrections, they always made the same answer – that they had neither the knowledge, nor the weapons, nor the mutual confidence to make any such attempt successful."[11] For these and other reasons, slave insurrections with more than 1,000 warriors have proved quite rare in history. After 1804, the largest slave insurrection in the Americas erupted in Jamaica in December 1831 and at its peak had tens of thousands of slaves under arms.

The Jamaican insurrection lasted several months. Most major insurrections in the Americas, those with at least a hundred slaves, rarely lasted only a few days in the face of counter-attack by masters and their auxiliary forces. Given the quick and gruesome end of such movements, with summary justice dispensed fervidly, deciphering the goals of slave insurrectionaries becomes difficult. In certain cases, one cannot even jump to the conclusion that release from bondage rather than the qualification of its terms was the primary goal. Nor should one expect homogenous goals extending through the ranks of insurrectionaries from the officers to the rank-and-file. Individual slaves could have more than one motive for rebelling: personal liberation, plunder, vengeance, return to homeland, and creation of a new society. Tension and conflict between conjoined actors in any resistance movement who differed by gender, occupation,

---

[11] Thomas Wentworth Higginson, "The First Black Regiment," *Outlook*, 59 (1898): 527–8.

color, and origin can help explain why acts of collective slave resistance were betrayed, aborted, or destroyed. The insurrection in lower Louisiana in 1811 embraced men and women, privileged slaves and field hands, blacks and mulattos, Creole slaves and African-born slaves. Mixed-race slave drivers led them on a march to New Orleans. Some of the rebels clearly aimed at vengeance for mistreatment; others looked to plunder; still others may have thought of seizing a ship in New Orleans and setting sail for Haiti. When a Kongo slave was interrogated as to why he joined the movement, he curtly replied: "to kill whites."[12] Numbers of rebels wildly fluctuated during insurrections. As was often the case in major slave insurrections, unknown numbers of slave recruits melted away from the main body during ferocious counter-attacks by a diverse array of forces that usually included regular troops and militia.

If power demands numbers, violence demands weapons. In the Americas, laws were passed in every major slave-holding region to prevent slaves from carrying guns, knives, clubs, and other threatening objects. Close monitoring by masters and their surrogates acted as a check on the stockpiling of weapons. At the time of the Denmark Vesey plot, authorities turned up a few weapons but no cache, which they suspected had been secreted somewhere in a slave burial ground. Few slave insurrections in the history of the western hemisphere began with stockpiled weapons, for a rash of thefts to amass them would have alerted authorities. Slaves in open violent revolt armed themselves initially with makeshift weapons – axes, cane knives, spears – and weapons quickly liberated from places – stores, armories, household deposits – where slaves knew stockpiles to be.

Many observers have described, in error, outbursts of collective slave violence as spontaneous. In no uprising, slave or other, does the idea of rebelliousness germinate in the minds of participants all at the same time. Certain individuals rise to the fore and lead; they practice politics: men (and women) moving men (and women). Here, the "hidden transcripts" of the oppressed, another way of saying the matrix of untaught feelings, inscribed prejudices, and repressed passions, can react under certain stimuli, perhaps a charismatic leader, to quickly form a deliberative salient that rouses others to follow along at quickstep toward desperate battle with objectives imposed. Although violent, collective slave revolt of any serious magnitude happened infrequently in history, its significance for scholars derives from the very rupture of the surface calm so as to reveal the swirling undercurrents within society, the surprising ascent of heretofore hidden actors, and political enactments fueled by blazing emotions, but largely concealed during periods of deceiving normality. Slave-holders also reveal a

[12] Saint Charles Parish Courthouse, Hahnville, Louisiana, Original Acts, Book 4, 1811, no. 17, (microfilm, Burke Library, Hamilton College).

good deal about themselves and their own mind in how they respond to the challenge. Indeed, in explaining how slave restlessness can metastasize into serious slave insurrection, how incumbents respond to collective resistance must be considered as carefully as what insurgents are trying to do. Neither slaves nor masters in their conscious being had homogenous or unambiguous minds. The analyst of slave resistance must try to connect the recorded unusual event to the causes that sorted out one possible response from another and the forces that allowed it to gather momentum.

Aside from the occasional driver or other privileged slave, slaves lacked pocket watches with which to coordinate movements at different locations. Yet, thought went into the timing of attacks nonetheless. Rebellious slaves liked to begin concerted activity under the cover of darkness. Maroon attacks in Brazil and elsewhere usually took place at night. After the 1835 revolt in Salvador, which broke out at night, authorities in Brazil complained that masters had been too permissive in allowing their slaves to ramble about after dark. At unsettled moments in various slave-holding societies, rumors circulated wildly about slaves' night plotting. One notable South Carolina planter, who would become governor of the state, confessed that he liked to punish his disobedient slaves in the stocks at night because "the slave anticipates the approach of night with the liveliest emotions. To him it is the period when he can freely indulge in the various inclinations of the mind."[13]

In Christian slave-holding countries, masters learned not to relax too much on Sundays and Christmas, for slaves had a long history of using heightened moments of white distraction to resist. Indeed, the very first major revolt of African slaves in the Western Hemisphere erupted around Christmas 1521 on a sugar plantation in Hispaniola owned by the eldest son of Christopher Columbus. In 1805, British authorities executed a handful of slaves for attempting to launch an insurrection at Christmas in Trinidad. The Jamaican insurrection of 1831 is often called the "Christmas Rebellion." In 1843, the uncovered slave plot that snowballed into Cuba's Conspiracy of La Escalera had targeted Christmas for the time of uprisings on various plantations. Masters also saw Sunday as a time of relative indiscipline for slaves and, with reason, took measures to be on their guard against trouble. At least some of them knew that the first blows in the slave insurrection that became a revolution in Saint Domingue had been plotted by a gathering of privileged slaves on Sunday. Barbadian rebels in 1816 chose Easter Sunday to begin their work.

Laws in every slave society restricted slave movement and assemblage. Curfews and required tags, passes, licenses, and tickets curtailed slaves from

---

[13] Whitemarsh B. Seabrook, *Essay on the Management of Slaves, and Especially of Their Religious Instruction* (Charleston, SC, 1834), p. 11.

moving about off estates. Maturing slave societies passed laws to ensure that large slave-holdings had a sufficient number of supervisory personnel to prevent resistance. The "Twenty-Nigger Law," passed by the Confederacy during the Civil War, a source of no small resentment by enlisted poor whites, drew on antebellum experience in various slave-holding states as to the minimum number of slaves to require at least one adult white male supervisor, though in South Carolina and Louisiana the minimum number was set at thirty. Slave codes prohibited or restricted the use of horses by slaves; authorities regarded cavalry, a troop of light horse, as one of the best ways of quelling disturbances by breaking the ranks of rebels. Slave codes had similar prohibitions on slave ownership of dogs. Cuba, by reputation, bred the best bloodhounds in the Americas for hunting down runaway slaves, and the US Army purchased some in attempting to subdue allied Indians and runaway slaves in the Second Seminole War (1835–42). Indians, poor whites, free persons of color, and slaves filled roles as slave hunters in the southern United States, Cuba, Suriname, and Brazil. Typically, they went to work with trained dogs they had bred and raised themselves. According to a British official in Cuba, during the suppression of the 1825 insurrection, which involved hundreds of African-born slaves, many "were taken or destroyed by the Country people with their formidable dogs, in some woods where they sought refuge."[14]

Housing of slaves on the most advanced sugar plantations in Cuba by the mid nineteenth century resembled a halfway house to the modern penitentiary, with guard dogs, watchmen, sealed barracks-like, masonry compounds, locked iron gates, grated windows, and watch towers. Many plantations in Africa and America contained special places of detention where unruly slaves endured solitary confinement. The very word "torture" in its origin has a link to Ancient Greece and the punishment of slaves. Although reforms in the nineteenth century attempted to outlaw mutilations, burnings, brandings, breakings on the wheel, excessive whippings, and any number of other brutal punishments, they continued to take their toll on slaves.

Rebellious male slaves generally received more lashes than rebellious female slaves for the same misdeed. Capital punishment remained standard fare for slaves convicted of involvement in arson, poisonings, murder, and insurrection. In Florida in 1828, law required that for felony convictions on lesser counts, slaves would have their hands burned or ears nailed to a post. Not until 1833 did South Carolina and the French Caribbean outlaw the use of branding in punishing slaves. At about the same time, officials in Brazil, witnessing a swelling number of insurrections, primarily from

---

[14] Henry Kilbee to Joseph Planta, July 6, 1825, British National Archives, FO 72/304.

recently imported African slaves, moved to remove punishment of slaves from the public square, where most slave societies preferred it as a deterrent, to the private sphere so as to not antagonize other slaves. One of the most effective ways that masters pre-empted concerted movements was to offer rewards and freedom to those slaves who betrayed others. One of the slaves who betrayed the Vesey plot in 1822 stood out in the 1850s as a prosperous free person of color who, unlike others of his class, did not have to pay taxes. For minor acts of insubordination, slaves might be locked up in the stocks, lose free time, have their provisions cut, be redeployed in more exacting labor, and be threatened with sale away from their families. Masters could also socialize punishments, depriving all for the acts of one so as to create internal pressure in the quarters against resistance.

In the tension-filled, conflict-ridden, negotiated relation that was slavery, a dialectical process of resistance and accommodation generated the reality of both the former yielding the latter and the latter yielding the former, depending on the circumstances. The push and pull of masters and slaves, their informal bargaining, could center on such issues as property versus possession, stealing versus taking, privilege versus entitlement, customary practice versus innovative regimen. No few outbreaks of violent slave resistance occurred when one overseer was replaced by a hard-charging successor. Reciprocal obligations, no matter how unequal, imply something to be lived up to on both sides of the relationship so that the bluntness of force can retreat into a darkened background.

Seeing resistance and accommodation as opposing, exclusivistic behaviors denies the dynamic of their interaction, both within individuals and between slaves and masters. Masters liked to extrapolate from the family metaphor to justify and rationalize their dominion over slaves. But paternalism, a much debated – and misunderstood – concept in the literature on resistance, operated as a two-way street, defined by slaves as well as by masters. Paternalistic masters could always be blindsided by a violent individual act of slave resistance as seemingly obedient slaves turned into savage and ingenious killers. The more serious concern, however, was preventing one violent disposition from infecting groups of slaves. Collective resistance implies ties of commonality – race, religion, class – that overcome divide-and-rule techniques. Group identity strengthens around the identification of an enemy. Hence, masters used paternalism as a kind of disconnect to weaken collective solidarity by binding slaves as individuals to the master. Paternalism offered not so much generosity as a better way to control and discipline slaves. Since slaves had wills of their own, they took what was given to them and turned it as best they could to their own purposes, whether in trying to hold paternalistic masters to account on provisioning standards or in receiving extras for labor beyond what was considered normative.

Despotic power, that intoxicating substance for which the world's sages have issued abundant warnings, could fatally cloud masters' judgment with chronic bouts of self-deception about their slaves' loyalty and terms of unwritten or tacit agreements in a larger moral economy. When investigating and recording collective acts of slave rebellion, masters did not always understand what they saw, preferring to credit outside agitators for the disruption rather than the intelligence and agency of their own slaves. Out of paternalistic practice by a benign master might come the needed space for more ambitious projects of rebellion; slaves who accommodated to power could put themselves in a better position to resist. In his first autobiography, Frederick Douglass confirmed his manhood by pummeling the slave breaker Edward Covey. In reflecting on his experience as a slave, he stressed, "whenever my condition was improved, instead of its increasing my contentment, it only increased my desire to be free, and set me to thinking of plans to gain my freedom."[15] That many of the most significant slave insurrections in the history of the Americas had privileged slaves – foremen, artisans, and domestics – at the forefront suggests the crucial distinction between accommodation to bondage and its acceptance. But privileged slaves, to gain additional rewards, perhaps even manumission, also frequently betrayed the rebellious designs of their fellow slaves to masters. In the history of slave rebellion in the Americas, more conspiracies were betrayed than ever got off the ground into open violence.

Divide-and-rule practices could backfire on masters by creating space for the ascent of home-grown leaders who had the respect and ability among their fellow slaves to organize resistance when opportunities presented themselves or to counsel against rash acts that might be destructive of alternative strategies of resistance. Slave drivers figured prominently in many of the largest slave insurrections in the sugar-planting regions of the Americas, but in studies of runaway slaves, they seem to be a disproportionately small number among the categories of slaves for whom occupations are known. Solomon Northup, in his autobiography, spoke of his involvement in a conversation about insurrection while working as a slave driver on a Louisiana sugar plantation in the 1840s. "[W]hen the subject has been discussed," he said, "there have been times when a word from me would have placed hundreds of my fellow-bondsmen in an attitude of defiance. Without arms or ammunition, or even with them I saw such a step would result in a certain defeat, disaster and death, and always raised my voice against it."[16]

---

[15] Frederick Douglass, *Narrative of the Life of Frederick Douglass, an American Slave* (Boston, MA, 1849), p. 99.
[16] Solomon Northup, *Twelve Years a Slave*, Sue Eakin and Joseph Logsdon (eds.) (Baton Rouge, LA, 1968), p. 190.

Students of slave resistance have distinguished violent from passive resistance. Day-to-day resistance implies a wide variety of indirect, masked, and passive acts by which enslaved individuals or groups of individuals protested their condition and countered their master's will. Acts of day-to-day resistance may be explained by the specifics of enslavement, but they might also speak to timeless human and sociological phenomena that transcend slavery per se. From antiquity to modernity, slaves have feigned stupidity and sickness, misdirected and prevaricated to their superiors, secretively pilfered or destroyed their master's goods, committed abortion and infanticide, malingered and dragged their feet, mutilated or immolated their own bodies, and deserted their posts. Such behavior fed pejorative stereotyping of slaves in ways that resemble how the upper orders have been characterizing the lower orders from time immemorial. Samuel Cartwright, an antebellum southern physician, discerned running away and rascality by slaves in such abundance that he invented two "Negro diseases," drapetomania (chronic "absconding from service") and dysaethesia aethiopica (chronic mischief-making caused by "hebetude of the mind").

In the United States, the experience of the Second World War and the exposure of Nazi atrocities shaped scholarly discussions of slave culture and, by extension, day-to-day resistance. Despite rearguard action by such African American scholars as Carter Woodson and W. E. B. Du Bois, the racialist views of U. B. Phillips, a Georgia-born historian and pioneer in the use of plantation records and census data to understand slavery in the Old South, held sway during the first half of the century. Phillips emphasized the benignity of the institution and the contentedness and docility of slaves. A changing post-war climate of opinion, however, spurred investigation into whether slavery was so oppressive that slaves had little capacity to resist, or whether slaves within the oppressive confines of bondage acted like a bunch of agile and secretive saboteurs reminiscent of a wartime underground. Fresh scholarship built on the work in Woodson's *The Journal of Negro History*, founded in 1916, which published numerous essays on slave initiatives, accomplishment, and resistance. Du Bois' dear friend, the Communist historian Herbert Aptheker, published *American Negro Slave Revolts* (1943), a volume that not only includes a chapter on "Individual Acts of Slave Resistance," but remains, whatever its exaggerations and special pleadings, an essential starting point for understanding the history of slave rebelliousness in the United States. "The fundamental factor provoking rebellion against slavery," he memorably concluded, was slavery itself, "the degradation, exploitation, oppression, and brutality which it created, and with which, indeed, it was synonymous."[17] Yet, for

---

[17] Herbert Aptheker, *American Negro Slave Revolts* (New York, 1943), p. 139.

all of Aptheker's ingenuity in mining sources to reveal acts of individual and collective slave resistance, the fact remains that actual slave insurrections in the United States proved infrequent and of a lesser magnitude than what was visible in Cuba, Jamaica, and Brazil at similar stages of economic development. If one wants to call "major" Nat Turner's force of less than 100, no major slave insurrection, precisely defined as an armed, violent open rising against established authority, occurred in the United States after 1831. Although some regions in the United States like low-country South Carolina and lower Louisiana had Caribbean-like proportions of slaves, only two southern states in the United States in 1860, South Carolina and Mississippi, had a slave majority in their populations. Resident masters in the United States also held their slaves on average in much smaller units than the sugar planters of, say, Jamaica, Cuba, or Bahia.

While Kenneth Stampp's *The Peculiar Institution* (1956) reversed the essentials of Phillips' interpretation of slavery in a way that accorded more with the sensibilities of a post-war public, Stanley Elkins' *Slavery: A Problem in American Institutional and Intellectual Life* (1959) had a significant heuristic impact on the study of slave resistance in two ways. First, he linked the Sambo stereotype of slave docility not to planter paternalism, but to a system of oppression that was so stifling and oppressive that it resembled a concentration camp. Second, to understand better the peculiarities of slavery in the Old South, he adopted the comparative method, finding slavery in North America harsher and more brutal than its counterpart in Latin America. Although subsequent scholarship dealt fatal blows to much of what Elkins had to say, the book had an undeniable heuristic value for the study of slave resistance. Scholars searched countries like Cuba, Brazil, and Jamaica for an explanation as to why slave insurrections in the United States were relatively small and infrequent. The Sambo stereotype, which Elkins thought unique to the United States, appeared, as it turned out, in other slave and non-slave societies as well.

In the United States, the emergence of the stereotype itself attended the rise in the antebellum South of a more comprehensive, articulate pro-slavery defense in the face of a first-of-its-kind transatlantic antislavery crusade. Colonial masters in the eighteenth-century Americas had regarded liberty as something that beat naturally in the human breast and consequently looked upon their slaves more as the "domestic enemy" rather than as "perpetual children." Masters expected their slaves to rebel and responded to insurrection with ferocious repression, executions, and public displays of mutilated bodies to leave no doubt in the minds of slaves that violent resistance was tantamount to suicide. Studies of human psychology have rejected the Sambo-Nat Turner dichotomy as simplistic; the two types could be aspects of the same personality, as so many slave-holders discovered when evidence inculpated their most trusted slaves as leaders of plots, insurrections, and mass desertions of estates.

If one regards resistance as a natural by-product of any social organization, not to mention an inscription in our genetic code by natural selection, day-to-day resistance can be seen as a predictable, if variable, cost of doing business, in most cases of no threat to the larger social order. The economic historians Robert Fogel and Stanley Engerman tackled the related problem of how to square the abundant evidence of day-to-day resistance with high rates of slave productivity on plantations, showing how the gang system of labor and studied management techniques compensated for the costs of slave resistance. Fogel credited the historian Eugene Genovese with a more sophisticated view of resistance that replaced the untenability of slaves' "perpetual sabotage" with one of amelioration of slavery through the achievement of limited goals, even if it meant bowing to the master's monopoly of force in extracting from slaves regular, intensive labor.[18]

Whatever the lost work days as a result of slaves' day-to-day resistance, a meaningful generalization requires a proper standard of comparison. Studies of the antebellum South in the 1850s place the number of lost days at a lower rate than that for certain categories of twentieth-century wage-earners working in factories. That certain acts of slave resistance may have extracted from masters concessions that made bondage more durable suggests problems with writings that tend to glorify all acts of violence from below as somehow liberating and progressive. Masters who successfully translated power into authority could not stab the wind of perfect subordination, but they did tend to get much of what they wanted from their slaves as evidenced by sustained profits derived from the selling of crops cultivated by tightly supervised labor in plantation zones. Resistance to slavery raised the costs of production, but not necessarily to the point where the generalized use of slave labor for commercial purposes lost its allure.

Sex ratios factor into the question of slave resistance. Young male slaves made up the majority of the runaways in various slave-holding regions of the Americas and elsewhere. Creolization of slaves in the United States and elsewhere decreased the number of group flights. A database compiled for antebellum Florida indicates that in acts of slave theft, the whites who did the recording identified male slaves 97 percent of the time, though this figure may well reflect eyes fogged by gender bias in much the same way that masters tended to ignore slave women in

[18] Robert William Fogel, *Without Consent or Contract: The Rise and Fall of American Slavery* (New York, 1989), p. 60.

investigating the perpetrators of insurrection.[19] Slave women took advantage of such "invisibility" to contribute to collective acts of resistance. Male slaves themselves, however, may have chosen to exclude slave women from plotting perhaps less because violence was an essentially masculine undertaking than because women as child-bearers represented the survival of the group if the worst occurred during rebellion. During the 1811 uprising in the Territory of Orleans, evidence indicates that women initially joined the disciplined march down the Mississippi toward New Orleans, but had mysteriously disappeared during the decisive battle against white and free-colored militiamen. Slave women figured prominently in internal marketing networks in most slave societies. In 1831 in Antigua, troops had to be called out to restore order because a crowd of angry female slaves were demonstrating against prohibitory regulations. "Sunday was their own day," the women said, and they intended not to abandon "the right of selling on that day."[20]

Where mass enslavements have endured, scholars interested in the genesis of slave sub-cultures have sometimes expanded the concept of day-to-day resistance so far as to be virtually congruent with any behavior that helped slaves to carve out from the raw materials of existence a viable pattern of life. While all such acts challenged abstract slavery and asserted the slaves' humanity, separating the personal from the political in such quotidian behavior can prove difficult to say the least. Slave flight may not indicate a dramatic rejection of accommodation, for most acts of running away or marronage were of the *petit* variety, that is, temporary, with slaves returning to their masters' household after a brief hiatus. Moreover, even if the explicitly political dimension of an individual slave act can be definitively established, its effectiveness for group politics remains another matter. The suicide of a respected slave leader may lead to a worsening of conditions for other slaves. Destruction of the master's mill may result in debt and the break-up by sale of slave families. The poisoning of one master may lead to his replacement by a far more brutal one. Little wonder that within slave quarters one slave might contest another over a course of action. An able leader with a vision of life for his people outside the house of bondage might worry that cumulative suicidal or nihilistic acts of violence under the pressure of slavery could do more to degrade a people than to elevate it with the moral values necessary to bind a community together into collective strength. For slaves or, for that matter, any other oppressed group, the fact of oppression could not

---

[19] Larry Eugene Rivers, *Rebels and Runaways: Slave Resistance in 19th-Century Florida* (Urbana, IL, 2012), p. 21.
[20] "Disturbances in Antigua," *Philadelphia Inquirer*, April 28, 1831.

readily justify a violent response because it may well have made matters worse for the vast majority of other slaves.

Estimates of numbers of slaves during slave insurrections present problems of precise calculation. Rebel units grown fast to a peak in the heat of the moment can dwindle rapidly later on by attrition because at least some of the less-than-enthusiastic recruits fly from the ranks when learning that a deadly and usually overwhelming force is heading against them. As was the case in Nat Turner's bloody revolt in Southampton County, Virginia, in 1831, generalized repression unleashed after a crushed insurgency rolled back hard-won incremental gains attained by slaves elsewhere in the South. Black preachers in the late antebellum South hardly presented the prophet Nat as a role model for their flocks to emulate. On the one hand, any slave might smile at the resistance of a fellow slave who had the courage to be a disrupter of the status quo; on the other hand, the best slave leaders had to worry about the good of more than one in contemplating frontal assaults. Insurrectionary leaders might clash on the most effective strategy of resistance. That many slaves remained loyal to masters during times of slave insurrection does not equate to a posture of abject submissiveness. Individual and collective slave violence, usually suffocated within a short period of time with a display of didactic brutality by the powers that be, drove home the grim consequences of failure. Post-1804, piked heads and other gruesome displays of mutilated corpses dotted the landscape after many failed slave insurrections. Official records in Cuba for rebellious slaves sentenced to death during the first half of the nineteenth century frequently ended with a formulaic expression that severed heads would remain on public display "until time consumed them."[21]

Although scholars have not always been precise in distinguishing between forms of collective slave resistance, slaves have mounted protests and demonstrations, hatched conspiracies, rioted, attempted mass breakouts or desertions, ganged together into banditry, engaged in work stoppages and slowdowns as well as raised themselves into insurgency with any number of goals in mind. That slaves joined other low-status groups in various kinds of rebellion in history also complicates the description of what is essentially collective slave resistance and what may be a much more complex phenomenon that consists of a conjunction of disaffected groups. Slave conspiracies outnumbered slave insurrections by far and present special problems of analysis. Given the frequency of torture to extract evidence and the fact that the uncovered plot never reached the stage of open violence, the actual existence of slave plots, much less the goals of the

---

[21] *Colección de los fallos pronunciados por una sección de la Comisión Militar establecida en la ciudad de Matanzas, para conocer de la causa de conspiración de la gente de color* (Matanzas, Cuba, 1844).

rebels, cannot always be established beyond peradventure. Influenced by literary theory, scholars have re-examined texts of trial records on conspiratorial slaves in Antigua (1736), Cuba (1812), South Carolina (1822), and Mississippi (1835) to cast doubt on the reality of conspiratorial behavior or, at least, its seriousness and magnitude, in order to emphasize how the knowledge of the "truth" of plot is contrived or manufactured unwittingly by officials in charge. A more traditional approach might, like a courtroom, analyze all the available evidence to reach a conclusion about likelihood and probability of guilt. During the presidential elections in the United States of 1856 and 1860, charges of abolitionist-instigated slave plotting swept the antebellum South in state after state. Of those cases closely examined by scholars, few hold up under scrutiny of the available evidence, despite signs that the white panic about the possibility of an antislavery Republican president had indeed stirred up some slaves.

A list of factors that favored collective slave resistance, weighted by findings for slave societies in the Americas, might include the following: high concentrations of slaves, especially those with high proportions of young males; households, plantations, and other units in which masters were largely absentees; sudden and sharp reversals in living conditions that resulted in serious violations by the master or his surrogates of the customary guidelines or moral economy that governed relations of production and exchange; real or perceived perceptions by slaves of internal divisions within a ruling class or between rival elite groups; the existence nearby of favorable terrain into which slaves might escape and fend off enemies; sufficient space within slavery for a strong cadre of leaders to emerge; shifts in policing agents – troops, militiamen, patrols, vigilant associations – that led to a real or perceived weakening of the forces of control; readily available avenues of communication – waterways, ports, crossroads – to transmit information and facilitate the recruitment and mobilization of slaves into battle; sharp ethnic distinctiveness between slaves and the master class, coupled with weak or ineffective processes of acculturation; and traditions of militancy, which might be culturally specific to the enslaved outsiders or generated over time by a persistent rash of slave rebelliousness over many years in the same region.

Various studies have pinpointed the bruiting about of rumors, especially of a decreed emancipation that was somehow thwarted or denied by local authorities, as one of the most recurring precipitants of slave insurrection in the Americas. The three largest slave insurrections in the history of the British Caribbean, Barbados (1816), Demerara (1823), and Jamaica (1831), reveal this spark in raising in each case thousands in revolt. At least several of the most formidable slave insurrections in the history of the Americas – in Saint Domingue (1791) and in Barbados (1816), for example – offered few clues in the preceding history, which had been for the most part quiescent for decades. Outside of the discovery of several alleged plots and a problem of marronage after the onset of Barbados' sugar boom in the mid seventeenth century and the implication of slaves in the burning of buildings in the port of Bridgetown in 1701, Barbados remained relatively quiet until an African-born head driver named Bussa on the Bayley Estate, relying on drivers from other plantations, mobilized more than a thousand mostly Creole slaves to rebel.

More research needs to be done on slave resistance during times of epidemic disease and natural disasters. More than 300 Lucumí (Yoruba) slaves rose up in 1833 on one of the largest coffee plantations in Cuba during a serious cholera epidemic. A prevailing sickness of some kind caused whites to leave Alexandria, Louisiana, in abundance in 1837 and their absence supposedly led to slave plotting there. But slaves often suffered more than whites at such moments and thus unless the disease or disaster dramatically weakened the forces of control, slaves remained preoccupied with their own survival and sought help from their masters, their families and neighbors, and the authorities. The entrance in Norfolk, Virginia, of yellow fever in 1800 appears to have had no connection to Gabriel's plot in Richmond.

Slaves certainly took advantage of imperial rivalries to advance individual and collective interests, but not always through resistance. In times of emergency, masters armed slaves, in some cases dangling the prospect of freedom as an incentive to fight. French Enlightenment intellectuals thought republics far more susceptible to slave rebellions than monarchies and despotisms since the constant presence of freemen in a republic would make slaves more aware of their beastly status and to chafe bearing it. A variant of this kind of thinking, especially after the Haitian Revolution, which was often seen by slave-holders throughout the Americas as initiated by the agitations of free persons of color, made them a prime target of concern. Even when discovered to be marginal or non-existent in slave plots and rebellions, they often found themselves subjected to repression after the event. Slave-holding southerners fretted about slave insurrection throughout the Civil War, particularly after the Emancipation Proclamation. Outside of a few plots of questionable validity, plantation slaves remained rather quiet within the armed camp that was the Confederacy until the intrusions of Yankee troops deep into the southern heartland made mass desertions, often led by drivers, a more acceptable risk. A "moment of truth" had arrived, and much to their masters' surprise, the "ungrateful" slaves often decamped en masse from their estates.[22]

[22] Eugene D. Genovese, *Roll, Jordan, Roll: The World the Slaves Made* (New York, 1974), pp. 97–112.

Predictably, societies that have featured slavery at the core of larger social formations and have large numbers of slaves gathered together for fieldwork, construction projects, and other large-scale purposes have yielded the most impressive examples of slave collective violence. Current research in Arabic sources will undoubtedly uncover more serious instances of slave revolt given the pioneering role of Muslim traders in the long-distance trade in West African slaves. Beside the revolt of the Zanj in what is today Iraq, the largest slave insurrection from the time of Spartacus to the Haitian Revolution, and the *Mamlūks'* overthrow of the Ayyubid dynasty in Egypt, a number of slave uprisings in nineteenth-century Africa related to Islamic expansionism and commercialized agriculture on Muslim-owned plantations occurred. As slave prices within Africa declined with the winding down of the Atlantic slave trade during the first half of the nineteenth century, large-scale production of agricultural commodities by slaves increased. The Sokoto Caliphate in Central Sudan may have had more slaves in 1860 than did the United States or Brazil. Slaves rose up in support of the jihad that created the caliphate. Slaves of different ethnicities in and around the Niger River also rose up in protest against the caliphate's consolidating power in the mid nineteenth century. At about the same time, scores of non-Muslim slaves working in plantation agriculture under Muslim masters in Zanzibar and other areas of East Africa revolted and, on the mainland near Mombasa, even formed maroon enclaves. In contrast, to the south, in the slave society fashioned by Dutch settlers in Cape Colony, the majority of white farmers in the late eighteenth and early nineteenth centuries owned one or more slaves, who in aggregate may have reached 40 percent of the total population. Several hundred slaves marched on Cape Town to demand emancipation in 1808 and a smaller-scale disturbance broke out in 1825.

Gradual emancipation or delayed implementation of emancipation triggered serious collective resistance. In the French colonies of Saint Martin and Martinique in 1848 slaves who had heard about legislated emancipation from the metropolis revolted because colonial officials appeared to be dragging their feet in implementing it. Slaves in the nearby Dutch colony of Saint Eustatius rose up in 1848 when they heard about events in Saint Martin, part of an island that had a Dutch half. In Cuba and Brazil, slave resistance speeded up a prior process of gradual emancipation as slaves protested on and deserted plantations in large numbers. Cuban slavery unraveled in the context of a thirty-year anti-colonial rebellion against Spanish rule during which both sides enlisted slave soldiers with the promise of freedom. Brazil's Golden Law (1888), which ended slavery, essentially ratified an existing fact to which the mass desertions of Brazilian slaves from plantations had contributed.

A GUIDE TO FURTHER READING

Aptheker, Herbert, *American Negro Slave Revolts* (New York, 1943).

Baralt, Guillermo A., *Esclavos rebeldes: conspiraciones y sublevaciones de esclavos en Puerto Rico (1795–1873)* (Rio Piedras, Puerto Rico, 1982).

Barcia, Manuel, *Seeds of Insurrection: Domination and Resistance on Western Cuban Plantations, 1808–1848* (Baton Rouge, LA, 2008).

Blanchard, Peter, *Under the Flags of Freedom: Slave Soldiers and the Wars of Independence in Spanish South America* (Pittsburgh, PA, 2008).

Breen, Patrick H., *The Land Shall Be Deluged in Blood: A New History of the Nat Turner Revolt* (New York, 2016).

Camp, Stephanie, *Closer to Freedom: Enslaved Women and Everyday Resistance in the Plantation South* (Chapel Hill, NC, 2004).

Childs, Matt D., *The 1812 Aponte Rebellion in Cuba and the Struggle against Atlantic Slavery* (Chapel Hill, NC, 2008).

Craton, Michael, *Testing the Chains: Resistance to Slavery in the British West Indies* (Ithaca, NY, 1982).

da Costa, Emilia Viotti, *Crowns of Glory, Tears of Blood: The Demerara Slave Rebellion of 1823* (New York, 1994).

Egerton, Douglas R. and Robert L. Paquette (eds.), *The Denmark Vesey Affair: A Documentary History* (Gainesville, FL, 2017).

Finch, Aisha K., *Rethinking Slave Rebellion in Cuba: La Escalera and the Insurgencies of 1841–1844* (Chapel Hill, NC, 2015).

Gaspar, David Barry and Geggus, David Patrick (eds.), *A Turbulent Time: The French Revolution and the Greater Caribbean* (Bloomington, IN, 1997).

Geggus, David Patrick, *The Impact of the Haitian Revolution in the Atlantic World* (Columbia, SC, 2001).

Genovese, Eugene D., *From Rebellion to Revolution: Afro-American Slave Revolts in the Making of the Modern World* (Baton Rouge, LA, 1979).

Millett, Nathaniel, *The Maroons of Prospect Bluff and Their Quest for Freedom in the Atlantic World* (Gainesville, FL, 2013).

Okihiro, Gary Y. (ed.), *In Resistance: Studies in African, Caribbean, and Afro-American History* (Amherst, MA, 1986).

Paquette, Robert L., *Sugar Is Made with Blood: The Conspiracy of La Escalera and the Conflict between Empires over Slavery in Cuba* (Middletown, CT, 1988).

Reis, João José, *Slave Rebellion in Brazil: The Muslim Uprising of 1835 in Bahia* (Baltimore, MD, 1993).

Richardson, David, "Shipboard Revolts, African Coastal Violence, and the Structure of the Atlantic Slave Trade," *William and Mary Quarterly*, 58 (2001): 69–92.

Slavery and Abolition: A Journal of Slave and Post-Slave Studies. Special Issue: Slavery and Resistance in Africa and Asia, 25 (2004).

CHAPTER 13

BLACK CULTURAL PRODUCTION IN THE NINETEENTH CENTURY

ALEX BORUCKI AND JESSICA MILLWARD

This chapter discusses the elements of enslaved culture and religion in three nations: the United States, Cuba, and Brazil. Though the dates of abolition of the slave trade and slavery in these three countries differed, the ways in which enslaved people worshipped and the cultures they formed, share similarities across time and space. This chapter analyzes some of these elements while at the same time discussing how divergent patterns of place, colonial systems, and gender shaped distinctive histories for the United States and Latin America. It discusses instances where enslaved culture and expression are still evident, be it in the language patterns among the Gullah of South Carolina, the rhythms of Cuba, or the practices of Candomblé in Brazil. We also put forward some reflections on black culture and constructions of race in relationship to national narratives across the Americas.

Enslaved people in the Americas produced a culture that was adaptive, innovative, distinctive, multi-variant, and, in addition, was clearly reflected in the broader cultures of many nation-states that emerged in the Americas after 1804. As social actors, enslaved people retained elements of their African culture even as they tried to develop a new existence. What then counts as cultural expression? This chapter is particularly focused on how spiritual and religious practices shaped cultural expression both within and beyond enslaved black communities in the western hemisphere. Sources examined include the historical, such as legal petitions; the anthropological, in the case of songs and rituals; and the political, such as newspaper accounts, as well as contemporary descriptions of public celebrations.

We focus on religious practices and culture of the enslaved in the United States, Cuba, and Brazil because of the wealth of research available on this topic in each country, but we do recognize that our generalizations do not necessarily apply to other countries including those with black majorities (much of the non-Hispanic Caribbean), as well as those with black minorities (many of the Spanish-speaking countries of the mainland Americas, from Mexico to Argentina). The cases of Cuba and Brazil do not shape a Latin American pattern, just as the United States' case does not provide the pattern for all former English-speaking colonies.

Comparisons within the Americas point to slave cultures taking quite divergent paths in the United States on the one hand and Cuba and Brazil, on the other, based partly on their different demographic history. In these three countries, enslaved populations grew throughout the nineteenth century, with almost 4 million enslaved people living in the United States by 1860, more than 1.5 million in Brazil by 1872, and nearly 400,000 in Cuba by 1862.[1] The growth of enslaved populations in the United States after 1808 was the result of natural reproduction, and their geographical distribution was influenced by a very active internal slave trade from the Old South (Maryland, Virginia, the Carolinas, and Georgia) to the New South (Alabama and to the West). This internal traffic to the new states west of Georgia had the unintended effect of blending "African" cultural markers into regional slave cultures across the expanding US South during the nineteenth century. In specific places such as the Carolina Sea Islands, the enslaved retained stronger elements of their African cultures. By contrast, the transatlantic slave trade sustained the increase of African populations in Cuba and Brazil. The continuance of this traffic brought peoples who created new associations and rituals in nineteenth-century Havana, Salvador, and Rio de Janeiro. Thereafter, selected elements of African cultural production became central to the construction of the national culture in the following century. In Cuba and Brazil, this is most visible in the forms in which African-based drumming and dancing underpinned the rhythms in the music of popular celebrations such as Carnival. Certainly, slave culture was evident in the United States as manifested in the call and response patterns of the Baptist and Methodist churches, yet it was rarely adopted into the national narrative, and no US national holidays are centered on the legacies of slave culture. The US holiday known as Memorial Day, for example, initially had particular meaning for African Americans following the Civil War; Charlestonians, many of whom had been enslaved, found it important to honor those who died in the war. Now, however, many simply associate Memorial Day with white war veterans. As this example suggests, how and why slave culture and by extension black culture was adopted into national rituals is less obvious in the US context than it is in the rest of the Americas.[2]

Freedmen and freedwomen were far more numerous in Brazil and Cuba than in the United States during the last century of slavery. This has resulted in a seemingly paradoxical emphasis on the importance of free people of African ancestry in the making of slave culture in Latin America.

---

[1] Laird W. Bergard, *The Comparative Histories of Slavery in Brazil, Cuba, and the United States* (New York, 2007), pp. 118–29.

[2] David Blight, *Race and Reunion: The Civil War in American History* (Cambridge, MA, 2001), pp. 64–95.

By the early 1800s, nearly 37 percent of the total Brazilian population was enslaved, whereas free people of African ancestry made up 30 percent of the total population. In Cuba, by the same decade, free people of color were 19 percent of the total population, while enslaved people accounted for 35 percent of the total population. In contrast, free blacks were only 10 percent of the total black population in the Chesapeake and Upper South regions (and even these mostly lived in Delaware and Maryland) and just 2 percent in the Lower South by 1810. They were also significant in the urban centers of Baltimore, Charleston, and New Orleans. Free black populations were significant in northern states, like New York, New Jersey, and Pennsylvania, where slavery underwent a slow death in the early nineteenth century. But nowhere did free populations of African ancestry approach the ratios apparent in Cuba and Brazil.[3]

Religious and spiritual practices sustained enslaved people even as the enslaved transformed forms of worship. In the United States, former slaves founded their own churches. In Latin America, the enslaved and free blacks developed multiple types of public and secret societies that functioned as religious associations. Thus, the relationship between enslaved and freed was never severed. Interaction between the two was a key aspect of the black experience and fostered a very active cultural life.

Religion also reveals the ways in which gender shaped enslaved culture and vice versa. Women often functioned as the carriers of culture. They passed traditions down through the generations whether via oral narrative, root work (folk medicine based on African knowledge), or communal practices. Despite their crucial roles, women do not often appear in the records of religious associations and churches, black women's activism in antislavery societies in the United States being an exception. In Cuba and Brazil, men initially led nineteenth-century black associations, but women eventually achieved a certain degree of leadership in most groups, though clearly not in the all-male *Abakuá* societies of Cuba.

The diversity of Latin American and Caribbean societies makes any attempt at generalization about slave cultures difficult. First, Haiti freed itself from the transatlantic slave trade and slavery during its own process of independence, completed by 1804. Then, one at a time, the entire group of mainland new Spanish-American nations, from Mexico to Argentina, abolished the slave trade and slavery itself in little more than four decades after 1810. Meanwhile, British and the final French abolition of slavery impacted on the British and French Caribbean in the 1830s and 1840s. Nevertheless, Latin America remained the major destination of new African slaves during the nineteenth century – the overwhelming majority

[3] George Reid Andrews, *Afro-Latin America, 1800–2000* (Oxford, 2004), p. 41; Ira Berlin, *Generations of Captivity: A History of African-American Slaves* (Cambridge, MA, 2013), Table 2.

disembarking in Brazil until 1851 and Cuba until 1867. These new arrivals met long-established slave cultures in Rio de Janeiro, Salvador, and Havana, where people of African ancestry in both the city and the countryside had built slave communities for centuries.

The long history of local slave communities as well as the centrality of slavery in representations of both national literature and history explains our focus on Cuba and Brazil. As the slave trade continued in these two countries into the mid nineteenth century (Cuba was still a Spanish colony), we may ask how the new African arrivals not only accommodated themselves to already existing slave cultures, but also how they shaped these cultures. To what degree was slave culture and religion different as a result of the influx; specifically, how did new African developments such as wars and religious change impact slave cultures in Brazil and Cuba? Candomblé emerged in the last century of slavery in Brazil through the increase and diversification of African-based associations. *Umbanda* presents a more challenging case, given that it emerged after abolition. In early twentieth-century Rio de Janeiro, African-based religions met European-style *spiritism,* which together became the cradle of Umbanda. While born in Brazil, this religion became very popular in regions ranging from Buenos Aires to Miami in the late twentieth century. In the case of Cuba, religions with links to three separate African regions emerged. One was inspired, though not exclusively, by the Yoruba pantheon (*Santería*); a second concerned the Abakuá secret societies, which adapted the rituals of the Ekpe (or Leopard) Society of the Efik people in the Old Calabar region; and a third was the *Palo Monte* or *Palo Mayombe,* a religion linked to practices of West-Central Africa.

African-based religions not only flourished in Cuba and Brazil, their influence extended beyond the black community. This is observable in the widespread white attendance at the Day of Kings (*Día de Reyes*) of January 6, or Epiphany, celebrated in commemoration of the adoration of the three Magi to Jesus. As one of the kings was represented as black, most commonly Saint Balthazar, Africans and their descendants attached their own meanings to this festivity. From Havana to Buenos Aires, black associations came to celebrate the Day of Kings as a way of honoring their leaders and their African homelands. This was the main black festivity, and was inscribed in the calendar of Catholic celebrations from Christmas in December to Carnival, the pre-Lenten celebration in mid February. Slaves and free people of African ancestry increasingly participated in Carnival as well. Black musicians and performers (sometimes professional performers who earned a living by reproducing European music and theatre) produced a mix of instruments, rhythms, and styles that would be seen as the precursors of national popular music and dance by twentieth-century audiences. Examples are *Lundú, Maxixe,* and samba in Brazil and *Son* and *Danzón* in Cuba. While the Day of Kings declined in importance during the nineteenth century, black participation in Carnival and the larger popular culture became central. Different segments of the urban population intermingled in these celebrations, and scholars have observed that elites at first contested this new popular culture, with its obvious black component, promoting instead a *whitening* project that stressed the centrality of European culture and immigration to national representation. By the mid twentieth century, however, they embraced an official policy of co-option. Governmental cultural projects began portraying Cuban and Brazilian culture as a mixture of African and European elements.

As slave populations grew to unprecedented levels in the United States in the nineteenth century, slave culture, associations, and worship took a very different path than in Latin America. African arrivals in what became the United States accounted for less that 4 percent of the total transatlantic slave trade to the New World. Africans mostly arrived in the eighteenth century, with a peak of slave arrivals in the four years before the ban on this traffic to the United States in 1808. Nonetheless, a wide range of ethnic groups forged a distinctive cultural hybridity which was evident in architectural spaces, oral tradition, worship practices, hair adornment, written work, music patterns, and foodways, to name a few. Cultural expression blended elements of the past with the lived reality of the present. In some local areas, cultural production was highly distinctive – for example, the language spoken by the Gullah people of the Carolina Sea Islands. In others, African, indigenous, and European beliefs merged as in the case of burial practices in Louisiana. By the early nineteenth century, enslaved people had created a distinctive Afro-American culture which blended disparate forms of expression. Of all the mainstream art forms, music is recognized as the one most influenced by the shift from slavery to freedom. African visions of freedom fused with Christian doctrine to create Negro Spirituals. Musical instruments were created by Africans in the cabins and fields and led to the blues, gospel, and jazz. Jazz, ironically, has been co-opted as an art form and is now exclusively associated with the United States. Cultural markers from the enslaved past are clear enough despite the long history of white supremacy that inhibited African cultural ways from becoming mainstream in the United States. Elements of enslaved spirituality and religion continue to form the basis of modern African American identity.

African beliefs, formalized religion, and Christian activism offered sites of spiritual freedom for slaves and free blacks alike in the United States. African world-views were adjusted in the wake of the experiences of the enslaved. Church membership allowed free African Americans to develop a politically active community. Spiritual freedom and religious experiences empowered many blacks. Some chose to serve as missionaries at home and abroad. African descendants used elements of traditional African belief systems as well as Christianity to sustain them in slavery. When they became free, their churches became vehicles for promoting and protecting black community life.

ASSOCIATIONS, SPIRITUALITY, AND WORSHIP

The proliferation of urban black associations, mostly led by freed rather than enslaved Africans, was probably the key feature of nineteenth-century slave culture in Cuba and Brazil. These associations enabled African-based culture and religion to not only bridge the slave-free divide among blacks, but also ensured their festive events would continue into the following century. The first documented African-based associations in colonial Latin America were the Catholic black lay-brotherhoods or confraternities (*cofradías* in Spanish and *irmandades* in Portuguese). After 1800, they evolved into societies separated from the Church, such as the Cuban *cabildos*, the *salas de nación* in Buenos Aires and Montevideo, the Brazilian *terreiros* (sites of meeting for Afro-Brazilian religion, most commonly associated with Candomblé), and by the end of the century, the Cuban *Casas de Santo* (associated with Santería). Debate continues over the degree to which these groups were different from each other, whether Catholic and non-Catholic groups overlapped, and the respective influence of European and/or African cultures and religions. Black confraternities had existed in the Iberian Peninsula before contact with the New World, given the early presence of Africans and their descendants in Seville and Lisbon. Africans and their descendants performed as the defeated "Moors" in the Corpus Christi processions in these cities. This festivity typically allowed non-Europeans such as Africans to express an officially unrecognized "otherness" under a Catholic umbrella, though not intended as a means of self-affirmation. Indeed, their dances were supposed to be non-Christian or pagan, often to an exaggerated degree, as a prelude to the "body of Christ's" victory over idolatry. In the Iberian Peninsula, black confraternities mediated between the larger society and the black communities. As already mentioned, secret and not-so-secret societies existed in the African homelands of slaves too, such as the Ogboni society for the Yoruba of the Bight of Benin, the Ekpe society in the Bight of Biafra, and the Kimpasi society in West-Central Africa. These reflected and represented both religious and material interests of members. African-based societies in Cuba and Brazil drew on organizational patterns and traditions from both Africa and Europe.

In colonial Latin America, freed Africans petitioned the Church in order to form a confraternity. This allowed them to collect money to adorn the altar of a saint (for example, Saint Benedict of Palermo or the Virgin of the

Rosary), as well as to organize an annual procession. The official function of these confraternities was Catholic devotion. But these groups offered broader services such as organizing funerals for their members and holding meetings on Sundays and holy days to celebrate and socialize. They also assisted their members to achieve freedom, borrow money, and obtain support in cases of judicial litigation, effectively channeling community solidarity in addition to recreating African cultures in dance, music, and clothing.

In villages and small towns, most Africans and their descendants, both free and enslaved, were part of a single confraternity that would be known as "the" black brotherhood of the town by the larger population, but in the larger hubs of the slave trade such as Havana, Salvador, and Rio de Janeiro, an African sense of ethnicity was one of the main features defining membership. Most black brotherhoods did not replicate African ethnic groups in a strict sense. Rather, they formed groups based on "meta-ethnic" shared cultural similarities. While some of them appropriated the nomenclature of the slave trade, such as Angola, Congo, and Mina, others provided quite specific descriptors of African homelands. New scholarship shows that African kingship and leadership also delineated who was "in" and "out" of these groups by stressing links of loyalty to either an ideology or to a specific leader within the community.[4] In other words, an African was a member of a black confraternity because he followed leaders who recreated forms of kingship and ideas of sovereignty based on African beliefs. Sharing similar slave-trading routes as shipmates in slave vessels also bonded Africans together in these "meta-ethnic" associations. Membership constituted a sense of social belonging based on how they thought about their African homelands, their shared experience in the slave trade, and the emerging leaderships of African communities in the New World. Examples of kingship and ideologies of sovereignty in nineteenth-century Cuba range from the Oyo-oriented religion focused on Xangó, as recreated by some Yoruba cabildos, to the various forms of "macro-organizations" coordinating various groups under the "King of Congo."[5]

The decline of Catholic black confraternities as well as the emergence and multiplication of new groups independent of the Church, such as the Cuban cabildos and the Bahian terreiros, are important defining social aspects of nineteenth-century black culture in Cuba and Brazil.

[4] Mariza de Carvalho Soares, *People of Faith: Slavery and African Catholics in Eighteenth-Century Rio de Janeiro* (Durham, NC, 2011), pp. 67–11 and 223–39; Luis Nicolau Parés, *The Formation of Candomblé: Vodun History and Ritual in Brazil* (Chapel Hill, NC, 2014), pp. 1–67.

[5] María del Carmen Barcia, Andrés Rodríguez, and Milagros Niebla, *Del cabildo de "nación" a la casa de santo* (Havana, 2012), pp. 11–54. On the ceremonies in Brazil inspired by the Congo court, see Cécile Fromont, "Dancing for the King of Congo from Early Modern Central Africa to Slavery-Era Brazil," *Colonial Latin American Review*, 22 (2013): 184–208.

In Salvador do Bahia, an increasing level of complexity characterized organizational structures and rituals over time. In the eighteenth century, we can see African-based religious practices at the individual and familial level, particularly associated with burials and healing. These practices continued in the following century, but the formation of a network of extra-familial institutions led to new developments of slave culture. Isolated instances of African-based religions already existed in eighteenth-century Brazil. However, associations such as the terreiros, with their elaborate and complex organization, including initiation rituals, emerged only in the nineteenth century.[6] While Catholic black confraternities did not disappear, the newer groups marked the urban spaces with their public and private rituals, most times facing strong police repression. 80 percent of the free blacks who left a will in Bahia between 1790 and 1830 were members of Catholic confraternities. As a mark of the diminishing status of confraternities, only 9 percent of the free black men and women who left a will in Bahia from 1850 to 1890 were members of confraternities.[7] The newer organizations reached a critical mass in the nineteenth century, as the slave trade brought fresh waves of transatlantic arrivals to both Brazil and Cuba. Slave culture and religion were re-Africanized there, unlike in the United States.

In Cuba, a web of associations independent of Catholic black confraternities emerged in the nineteenth century. Sources not only reveal the rapid expansion of cabildos, but also the increasing number of followers of Yoruba gods turned into saints (and vice versa). Clearly, the new arrivals were reshaping an already existing slave culture. Cuban Santería melded the Yoruba pantheon of gods with Catholic saints, but it also drew on non-Yoruba African elements from a range of belief systems spanning Gbe-speaking Bight of Benin to the West-Central African religions that inspired the Cuban Palo Monte. For instance, Xangó (Changó, Shango, or Sangó) was an Orisha (god) of thunder supporting the political legitimacy of the Oyo Kingdom in what is today Southwest Nigeria. In Cuba, this Orisha was linked to Santa Barbara. As a result of the wars leading to the destruction of Oyo after 1815, an influx of slaves shipped from the Bight of Benin contributed to the emergence of Oyo-inspired rituals and made Sango of central importance. Modern-day *Regla de Ocha* (Orisha) as well as *Ifa* divinatory practices became central to slave culture and religion around this time. Thus, Henry Lovejoy demonstrates that while the syncretism of Santa Barbara/Sango took place before the main wave of Oyo captives

[6] Parés, *The Formation of Candomblé*, pp. 84–5.
[7] Richard Graham, *Feeding the City: From Street Market to Liberal Reform in Salvador, Brazil 1780–1860* (Austin, TX, 2010), p. 26.

arrived, the new arrivals did reshape this belief.[8] However, Oyo-Yoruba rituals and practices had been in dialogue with both non-Oyo and non-Yoruba beliefs both in the Bight of Benin and Cuba long before this development.

African ethnicities that evolved into larger "meta-ethnic groups" (like Santería and Candomblé) were less evident in the case of Palo Monte and Palo Mayombe in Cuba, even though this religion clearly incorporates elements of Kikongo-speaking cultures of West-Central Africa, as analysis of Kikongo ritual language demonstrates.[9] Rather than establishing shrines summoning a complex pantheon of African gods, Palo Monte sought contacts with forces of nature and spirits. It is difficult to link Palo Monte with specific events in the nineteenth century (in contrast to Santería), and it has thus received less scholarly attention than it should. Abakuá societies also became visible in nineteenth-century Cuba, inspired by the Ekpe Society. Illustrations of the time depict Abakuá dancers performing at the public Day of Kings. Nevertheless, the meaning of this public ritual (ñañigos, called diablitos or little devils in Spanish) is difficult to assess. Scholars have relied on oral sources to investigate such groups. Abakuá societies began in the 1830s in the town of Regla and spread to Havana and other ports. Different from all other African-based religions in the Americas, the Abakuá were male secret societies. But, as with other slave religions, they began accepting white initiates in the late nineteenth century.

In Brazil, the nineteenth-century trend toward more institutionalized religions is best represented by Candomblé. Priests and priestesses were initially African-born and only later Afro-Brazilians and, later again, whites. As in Cuba, values and practices were derived from religions located in the Bight of Benin (Gbe and Yoruba), as well as Angola. Every Candomblé group rented or owned a house of prayer or temple dedicated to the adoration of multiple gods through dance, music, and rituals of possession and divination. While some scholars argue that this mixing of different African gods with Catholic saints illustrates Creolization, others point to the impact of Catholicism itself as the core around which African-based religions developed. Yet another interpretation points to the significance of Vodun rituals (from Gbe-speaking people) that incorporated multiple gods into a singular temple, rather than just one god per temple, as the core of Candomblé.[10] While at the beginning of the nineteenth

---

[8] Henry B. Lovejoy, "Old Oyo Influences on the Transformation of Lucumí Identity in Colonial Cuba" (unpublished PhD thesis, University of California Los Angeles, 2012), p. 212.

[9] Armin Schwegler, "El vocabulario (ritual) bantú de Cuba" in Norma Díaz, Ralph Ludwig, and Stefan Pfänder (eds.), La Romania Americana. Procesos lingüísticos en situaciones de contacto (Madrid, 2002), pp. 97–194.

[10] On the historiography, see Parés, The Formation of Candomblé, pp. 208–9.

century each Candomblé house (*terreiro*) organized around a particular African ethnicity (even though actual membership was multi-ethnic from the outset), later in the century Candomblé fostered such a strong sense of belonging that even nominal associations with a specific ethnicity faded. In other words, while ethnic self-identification initially shaped membership, later on the broad membership of these groups, which included native-born Brazilians both white and black, meant that ethnicity had a merely liturgical role.

The role of freed Africans was central for the nineteenth-century development of both Brazilian Candomblé and Cuban Santería. While the followers were mostly enslaved, leaders were almost exclusively free, which seems paradoxical given the African-oriented basis of religions within slave cultures. However, the fact that, in comparative terms, Africans could attain freedom more easily in Latin America than in the United States points to one of the reasons for the more visible recreation of African-inspired religions in Cuba and Brazil. As we have seen, free people of color had always led Cuban black confraternities. Colonial law, at least in Cuba, actually prohibited slaves from leading these groups. The vital role of freed Africans, with their superior mobility and resources, complicates the analysis of African-oriented religions as part of slave culture. Freed Africans, and later Afro-Cubans and Afro-Brazilians, also kept alive the transnational aspect of African-oriented religions in the New World by maintaining contacts with the Bight of Benin. As African returnees populated the Brazilian and Cuban quarters in the ports of Ouidah and Lagos from the mid-1830s, religious leaders from Cuba and Brazil promoted the circulation of peoples and ideas across the Atlantic. Such links perhaps explain the tendency of African-based associations in Cuba and Brazil to stress aspects of Yoruba over non-Yoruba religions, especially after abolition.

Biographies of nineteenth-century figures integral to the making of these new societies reveal strong transnational and transcultural features. Thus, Rufino, a man born in the kingdom of Oyo, was sent as a slave to Brazil in the early nineteenth century. Once free, he worked as a cook on slave ships connecting Recife to Angola. He eventually landed in Sierra Leone, where a British naval vessel deposited him along with other crewmen and all the slaves belonging to a captured slave ship. Rufino attended madrassas and the mosque in Freetown. On returning to Brazil, Rufino established a following in Recife and became an *alufá*, or Islamic teacher. His Creolized form of Islam not only involved amulets and divination, common in West Africa, but also Catholic rituals as practiced in Recife. Here, the trans-local construction of slave religion was based on Islam rather than on a Yoruba, Gbe, or Catholic set of beliefs and rituals. From the mid to late nineteenth century, Muslim communities of ex-slaves formed in Rio de Janeiro, Salvador, and Pernambuco and communicated with each other. As with other African-oriented religions, these groups survived because they attracted clients who were not Muslims. Cosmopolitan leaders like Rufino influenced many lives, including the lives of white Brazilians.[11]

While nineteenth-century African-based Islam disappeared from Brazil, Candomblé became the main vehicle of Afro-Brazilian religion. African-born religious leaders, and later, Afro-Brazilians, not only provided services to the members of their terreiros, but they also had a large clientele of both men and women of full and mixed African and European ancestry, regardless of social standing. Candomblé and Santería were spaces of social inclusion from the beginning and were able to survive despite strong police repression.[12] In the late nineteenth and early twentieth centuries, ruling elites considered African-based religions as barbaric relics that prevented the modernization of their countries. However, patron–client alliances with local police and politicians provided some relief from such repression.

In nineteenth-century Cuba and Brazil, the culture of slaves and former slaves eventually became part of the larger urban popular culture. Sometimes, white intellectuals, such as those in Pernambuco and Santiago de Cuba, claimed African-based folkways as part of their own regional cultures. In Havana and Rio de Janeiro, in particular, the wider popular culture drew in African elements into their emerging conception of the nation. In a surprising development, African-based aspects of slave culture that were severely harassed by the police as well as condemned by white (and sometimes black) intellectuals became celebrated in mid-twentieth-century representations of the nation-state. While we will not delve into the twentieth-century, national, and selective appropriation of black culture here, we can indicate how the Day of Kings and Carnival celebrations in Brazil and Cuba began this process in the late nineteenth century.

Catholic processions involving black, white, and Amerindian people, as well as those of mixed ancestry, who performed street dancing were common in colonial Latin America. While black Catholic confraternities conducted the procession of the saint of their choice, they also participated in the annual Epiphany Day celebration, which became the main black festivity of the nineteenth century – the Day of Kings. But black societies outside the Catholic Church, such as the Cuban cabildos, were also involved. During the Day of Kings, the members of black confraternities elected their new officers and celebrated with a mass, as well as with street

[11] João Reis, Flávio Gomes, and Marcus J. M. Carvalho, *O Alufá Rufino: Tráfico, escravidão e liberdade no Atlântico Negro (c. 1822–c. 1853)* (São Paulo, 2010), pp. 305–19, 337–54.
[12] Parés, *The Formation of Candomblé*, p. 87.

dances. Most commonly, European travellers rather than white Cubans reported these festivities, highlighting the African character of clothing, music, dancing, and singing. These were not secret celebrations, but very public performances that sometimes involved the colonial authorities, as in the case of the visit of the leaders of Havana's cabildos to show respect to the Captain General of Cuba. The Day of Kings became the main urban celebration of the city, and one that white audiences witnessed and sometimes attended.

But just as black Catholic confraternities faded from public space, making way for both cabildos and terreiros in the nineteenth century, so the Day of Kings also lost significance. The pattern was first apparent in Rio de Janeiro in the mid century. Then, in Cuba, the colonial government forbade the cabildos from joining the Day of Kings celebration in 1884, with the intention of assimilating all African displays in the years leading to abolition, and also attempting to assert control over black associations. African-based dance and music traditions continued through the bands of black performers and musicians during Carnival. In Havana, each band represented a neighborhood – black bands being from black parts of town, and with most of the neighborhood following "their" group during the parade, a massive multiracial street celebration evolved. These groups, most commonly known as *comparsas* and sometimes, as in Santiago de Cuba, called *congas*, were banned from the Havana Carnival in the early 1910s. This provoked a debate and they were reinstated in 1937. However, congas continued in Santiago de Cuba throughout this period, giving continuity to Eastern Cuban celebrations and connecting this region with both Haiti and Jamaica.

In a very different story, Rio de Janeiro's Carnival was originally modeled on its Venetian counterpart – merrymaking for the rich. Increasingly, Carnival parades added Afro-Brazilian music and dance, as people from Salvador (such as the famous *Tia Ciata* who merged Candomblé and Epiphany celebrations) gained prominence in the late nineteenth century. With the turn of the century, black participation in street Carnival increased and incorporated troupes of musicians and performers previously associated with the Day of Kings of Salvador – the homeland of Candomblé. Afro-Brazilians began to appear in the early-twentieth-century Carnival, which now became a popular celebration. Black artists were thus central to the emergence of twentieth-century music and dance in both Brazil and Cuba.[13] The social world

[13] John C. Chasteen, *National Rhythms, African Roots: The Deep History of Latin American Popular Dance* (Albuquerque, NM, 2004), pp. 39–44. On how race, black culture, and popular culture intersected in nineteenth-century Cuba, see Jill Lane, *Blackface Cuba, 1840–1895* (Philadelphia, PA, 2005).

of Carnival troupes generated a variety of rhythms and dances, but Brazilian samba and Cuban son were the two that mid-century cultural policymakers catapulted into becoming national symbols.

In the US South, religion, spirituality, and belief in a higher being were consistent sources of power for countless African Americans, whether slave or free. There is considerable debate, however, regarding the type of religious practices embraced by Africans and their descendants in the colonial era. Michael Gomez, for example, suggests that "the vast majority of African-born slaves and their progeny continued to practice various African religions until well into the 19th century."[14] Gomez cites examples of meditation, hoodoo, and the ring shout as indications that African descendants maintained elements of African worship. Indeed, African world views and spiritual practices enabled many slaves to withstand the terror of their new environment.

Nevertheless, the spiritual life of the enslaved in what became the United States exhibited fewer visible markers of African religious practices than its counterpart in Latin America. This was due in a large part to the spread of Baptist and Methodist faiths among US slave-holders in the late eighteenth and early nineteenth centuries, as well as the comparatively earlier ending (relative to Brazil and Cuba) of the transatlantic slave trade, which prevented significant numbers of new African arrivals in the United States after 1808.[15] The Baptist faith allowed followers to become exhorters, which appealed to enslaved and free blacks alike. But, as in Cuba and Brazil, one cannot claim that African religious practices vanished in the antebellum South. Language and worship are where African-based traditions are most likely to be found. The Gullah derived their name either from "Angola" or from the Gola of the Windward coast. They maintain distinct language patterns down to the present. Complicating the narrative that all Gullah were from Angola, anthropologists have traced certain of their songs to the Mende in present-day Sierra Leone.[16] It is also important to look at the material evidence of the enslaved past. Students of black religion need to go beyond documentary sources. Archeological work in Annapolis, Maryland has revealed the complex belief systems of enslaved

[14] Michael Gomez, *Exchanging Our Country Marks: The Transformation of African Identities in the Colonial and Antebellum South* (Chapel Hill, NC, 1998), p. 247, for the examples, see p. 288; see also Sterling Stuckey, *Slave Culture: Nationalist Theory and the Foundations of Black America* (New York, 1987).
[15] While twenty-eight slave vessels arrived directly from Africa to the United States from 1808 to 1860, at least 4,138 slave ships arrived in Brazil between 1808 and 1856, and at least 1,782 arrived in Cuba from 1808 to 1866. See *Voyages: The Transatlantic Slave Trade Database*, www.slavevoyages.org. These figures do not include slave trading happening within the Americas, e.g. from the Caribbean to post-1836 Texas.
[16] Walter Rucker, *The River Flows On: Black Resistance, Culture, and Identity Formation in Early America* (Baton Rouge, LA, 2006).

people. Spiritual caches discovered under the floorboards at Slayton House comprised a collection of ordinary objects such as pins, buttons, and strings. By themselves the items were trivial, but viewed together they had strong spiritual significance. The caches were placed on an east-to-west or north-to-south axis at the center of one room. Collectively, they comprise a cosmogram, which for some African ethnicities guaranteed protection over long periods of time. Aspects of Ife religions have come to light in the form of artifacts that might have made an altar or shrine to the Orisha Shango.[17] These objects of worship escaped the written record, but were of particular importance to enslaved women who used them to establish contact with the deities and with their ancestors.

African-based religions nevertheless struggled to survive in the North American environment. Islam competed with Christianity prior to the nineteenth century, but both the first Great Awakening in the late eighteenth century and the second during the antebellum period eroded its influence. The vitality of the religion and the dedication of its followers was not enough to guarantee its survival. Pressure on family structures of the enslaved severely restricted inter-generational transfers of belief systems.

Funerals and rituals surrounding death were central to the enslaved everywhere in the Americas. Survivors often placed objects such as medicine bottles on the graves of loved ones. These marked the deceased as an object of reverence worthy of special care and ritual observance, as well as linking the living with supernatural power and influence. Excavations from the Slave Burial project in New York prove that grave decorations were not confined to the antebellum South.

Religious practices of the enslaved may not have left as visible a legacy in the United States as in the rest of the Americas, but oral transmission of knowledge was exceptionally strong. Enslaved preachers interpreted the Bible and also produced divined visions and prayed for their followers. Formerly enslaved blacks went on to form their own churches. When manumitted, Richard Allen formed the African Methodist Episcopal church in Philadelphia; likewise, former slave Daniel Coker became a prominent preacher in Baltimore. Originally traveling with her owner as he moved west with a Mormon wagon train, slave Biddy Mason walked from Mississippi to Utah. Her owner manumitted her, and Mason pushed on to found the First African Methodist church in what became Los Angeles, California.

Owners assumed that conversion to Christianity obliterated any "heathen" practices among the enslaved. In reality, the enslaved meshed their

---

[17] Mark P. Leone, *The Archaeology of Liberty in an American Capital: Excavations in Annapolis* (Berkeley, CA, 2005).

beliefs with Christianity. Water immersion rights in Africa informed the
Christian conversion of slaves in plantation North America.[18] The enslaved
embraced baptism into Baptist and Methodist faiths throughout the Deep
South because some of the practices, specifically baptism by water, paralleled Congo rituals. There are no parallels to this in Latin America, where
the Catholic Church monopolized baptismal procedures. In terms of
Catholicism, the hybrid nature of ritual and practice is much more visible
in the blending of European and indigenous practices as evidenced in
Mardi Gras in New Orleans.

African Americans also joined secret societies because they believed in
the organizations' guiding principles – the Prince Hall Freemasons, being a
prime example. Barred from participating in white Masonic groups, Prince
Hall established the Prince Hall Masonry in the late eighteenth century.
Born free in Boston, Hall was a tireless abolitionist, supporter of education
for blacks, and even championed back-to-Africa movements. Within the
Prince Hall Masonry and later freemason organizations, skilled black
tradesmen found a place of fraternity. Freemasonry was a distinctive
African American self-help society that, in the minds of its early members,
had strong links with Africa. Conversion to Christianity did not diminish
the power of secret societies. As with African American Christianity, the
Prince Hall masons serve as another example of a non-African institution
being adapted and modified to serve the interests of (at least a portion of)
the black community.

GENDER AND COMMUNITIES

While enslaved men outnumbered female slaves in the Latin American
countryside, enslaved women outnumbered male slaves in almost every
city of nineteenth-century Cuba and Brazil. The gender imbalance of slave
populations in urban areas is explained by the close association of women
with domestic service throughout Latin American history. Freedwomen
probably formed the majority of the newly freed people in nineteenth-
century Cuba and Brazil prior to formal abolition. Partly, this was because
masters were more likely to manumit women than men, but also because
women saved money to free themselves. When manumission became an
issue for slave families, women were manumitted first, because their
children would then be born into freedom rather than slavery. Furthermore, female slaves born in Latin America and women of mixed ancestry
had greater probability of obtaining freedom than African-born women
and they were heavily over-represented among the free black population.

[18] Jason R. Young, *Rituals of Resistance: African Atlantic Religion in Kongo and the Lowcountry South in the Era of Slavery* (Baton Rouge, LA, 2007), pp. 78–9.

Free women of color were central for provisioning street markets in cities such as Salvador, and they often owned modest amounts of property, including provision stores and taverns. Paradoxically, even though women of African ancestry were very active in the urban economy and (in comparison to men) more successful in purchasing freedom, the new nineteenth-century African-based associations were mostly led by men.

While the records of the Spanish and Portuguese Inquisitions in the Americas are filled with cases of enslaved and free women of color accused of witchcraft and healing in the earlier periods, the early nineteenth-century leadership of the new types of associations was mainly African and male. In the case of Salvador, most leaders were African-born in the first half of the nineteenth century, with Afro-Brazilians replacing them after 1850. The gender counterpoint is that very few women led associations in the first half of the nineteenth century, something that became more common after 1850. This is in stark contrast with the conceptions of "matriarchy" dominating twentieth-century Candomblé, which seems almost modern by comparison. Luis Nicolau Parés draws the contrast between the mainly female participants in Candomblé ceremonies and the mostly male leadership. The African character of this religion, more pronounced in the early nineteenth century, probably determined distinctive gender roles, though it should be noted that when two or three leaders shared control, at least one could be a woman. Most probably, when Africans gave way to Afro-Brazilians, in the second half of the nineteenth century, women became better represented in the leadership, reflecting their majority presence in the freed population, as well as in Candomblé membership. This is one of the reasons why Parés asserts that Creolization and race mixing dominated the history of Candomblé in the late nineteenth century, a feature that helped secure its survival.[19]

Magic, conjure, and healing was another realm of religion practiced throughout the Diaspora. The mystical powers held by conjurers made them both revered and feared by enslaved Africans and their descendants in the United States. The role of conjurer was not gender specific. Some men and women were believed to possess these magical powers, but the identity of the conjurer was often not widely known. Planters attempted to subdue any practices of root work, Voodoo, or "Hoodoo." Nonetheless, the enslaved sought out the conjurers for their powers to both heal and harm, indicating their consistent belief in the effectiveness of non-Christian powers. The enslaved visited neighboring plantations in search of a particular conjurer. Likewise, a conjurer might travel to a particular individual as the situation warranted.

[19] Parés, *The Formation of Candomblé*, pp. 96–9.

If the identity of a conjurer was often concealed and not gender specific, midwifery was the opposite. Midwives were exclusively women. They derived their knowledge of herbs and roots from traditions passed on from other women and, in some cases, from their mothers. Midwives, like conjurers, were revered in the slave community. They were also respected and feared by whites, who despite their anxiety, counted on them to deliver enslaved children. Enslaved women in the United States as throughout the Diaspora were carriers of tradition. They possessed the crucial oral knowledge to pass on to descendants. It is important to note that no matter how secretive these black women were or how secretive they were forced to become in engaging with the outside world, they did not live in isolation. Their connections to other women in the enslaved community were strong, and this helped deflect the pain and trauma associated with gendered violence.

It should not be assumed, however, that enslaved women shirked from a public religious life. Enslaved and free black women were very active in free black churches, mutual aid societies, and women's auxiliaries. The participation of free black women as Oblate Sisters of the Catholic Church is one such example. Moreover, free black and formerly enslaved women such as Jarena Lee, Maria Stewart, and Sojourner Truth preached and advocated for the abolition of slavery in the United States.

AUTOBIOGRAPHIES, PRINT CULTURE, AND THE MULTIPLE MEANINGS OF FREEDOM

Nineteenth-century Latin America offers a wealth of sources for students of slave cultures and religions. Beyond parish records and accounts produced by the colonial state and the new nations, there were newspapers and the narratives of foreigners traveling to Latin America. The British records (and their Brazilian and Cuban counterparts) of suppression of the slave trade generated registers of Liberated Africans arriving in Havana and Rio de Janeiro after 1825, which allow for analysis of individual lives of those sent from Africa to the Americas, some of whom went back to Africa. Studies based on identifying the names of these Africans and their regions of African provenance illustrate how these men and women were enslaved, their identities while in transit from Africa to Cuba and Brazil, and who they became as they transitioned from freedom to slavery and then back to freedom. Newspapers, novels, and short stories produced in Cuba and Brazil offer materials for further research. Scholars are still seeking to add to the limited number of autobiographical narratives of the slave experience in Latin America. Juan Francisco Manzano in 1830s Cuba wrote the only known autobiography by an enslaved person in Latin America. Narratives written by Jacinto Molina (1766–1841) in Uruguay and Candelario Obeso (1849–84) in Colombia may provide useful and, as yet, unexplored windows to slave culture.

The paucity of nineteenth-century Afro-Latin American authors, compared with the rich genre of slave narratives in the United States, both before and after the Civil War, probably originates from the more active abolitionist campaign in the latter, where autobiographies of former captives were central to the fight against slavery. Abolitionism in Cuba and Brazil, as other chapters in this volume attest, took a different path. A further factor is the more materially abundant North American print culture and higher literacy rates compared to Cuba and Brazil. Thus, in the case of Manzano's work, white Cuban abolitionist Domingo del Monte sponsored the writing of his autobiography. It was first published in English in the United Kingdom in 1840, because writings on slavery and abolition were censored in Cuba. In fact, the first Spanish language edition based on the original manuscript was only published in 1937, a century after Manzano wrote it. Martín Morúa Delgado, who was of mixed ancestry, wrote two anti-slavery novels in nineteenth-century Cuba, but these works were published only after abolition. Esteban Montejo's autobiography, transmitted through white scholar Miguel Barnet, narrates his life as a runaway slave in the last decades of slavery in Cuba, but it was taken down in the 1960s, when Montejo was approximately 100 years old.[20]

Brazil had even fewer nineteenth-century writers of African ancestry. Maria Firmina dos Reis published the abolitionist novel *Úrsula* (1859), which is deemed the first novel by an Afro-Brazilian author. One of the few autobiographies of an African who crossed the Atlantic as a slave, Mahommah Gardo Baquaqua, partially describes his life under slavery during two years in Brazil. He later escaped and lived in the United States, Haiti, and Canada. White author Samuel Moore put his account into biographical form (1854). Afro-Brazilian writers of mixed ancestry such as Luiz Gama, José do Patrocínio, and André Rebouças entered the lettered world during the last thirty years of slavery in Brazil, and fervently campaigned for abolition.

Some of the new national novels in Cuba and Brazil reveal how depictions of slave culture and religion shaped the nascent Latin American literature. Nineteenth-century works such as *Cecilia Valdes* (1839) by white Cuban author Cirilo Villaverde, as well as *As vítimas-algozes* (1869) and *O feiticeiro* (1922), by white Brazilian authors Joaquim Manuel de Macedo and Xavier Marques, respectively, provide the white elites' gaze on slave

[20] See the introduction on Afro-Latin American autobiography in Ricardo Batrell and Mark A. Sanders, *A Black Soldier's Story: The Narrative of Ricardo Batrell and the Cuban War of Independence* (Minneapolis, MN, 2010).

culture. Newspapers and pamphlets produced in the emerging print culture, sometimes by associations of people of African ancestry, constitute additional material for scholars studying how Afro-descendants saw slave culture.

In the United States, the impact of religion and spirituality on the African American written word is most evident in the nineteenth century. African American published work followed one of two dominant genres. The first was the writing of autobiographies by former slaves infused with conversion narratives. For example, Sojourner Truth, the itinerant preacher and anti-slavery advocate, published her own autobiography (1850). Conversion moments are found in the *Narrative of Frederick Douglass* (1845) and in the autobiography of Reverend James W. C. Pennington (1849), both fugitive slaves from Maryland. Autobiographies laced with Christian undertones are a particular feature of the writings of former slaves in the United States. Without question, the volume of autobiographies produced by formerly enslaved people is far greater in the United States than in other parts of the Diaspora.

The second genre produced by African Americans was in the call for abolition, by means of petitions, tracts, and statements against slavery, such as David Walker's *Appeal* (1829), which were also infused with references to Christianity. Walker's *Appeal* was widely read in the northern states as well as the South. Southerners feared the spread of Walker's message of liberty for the enslaved and banned his work. Slaves like Nat Turner in Virginia heard Walker's message. Turner believed himself to be a Prophet sent to avenge the evils of slave-holding, and he and his associates killed fifty-five people in Southampton, Virginia during August of 1831. Turner was eventually caught and hung, but he allegedly gave an interview where he spoke of reading signs and symbols as he planned the rebellion. This shows how religion also played a key role in some of the major slave revolts of the nineteenth century. Yet, this intersection of religious vision and access to print culture was not limited to enslaved men. Formerly enslaved women such as Sojourner Truth and Harriet Tubman claimed to receive prophetic visions in their written accounts of their experience. Though the works produced by enslaved people or on behalf of enslaved people were varied, the collective voice of African American narratives was almost overwhelmingly preoccupied with ending slavery.

Individually, freedom petitions represented the initiatives of individuals as they negotiated the legal terrain in the United States, as well as demonstrating how gender and lettered culture intersected for slaves. Enslaved people, often women, engaged an attorney, eventually went to court, and laid claim to their freedom. The pattern in the United States was similar to that in Cuba discussed by Camillia Cowling. Cowling suggests that black women making legal claims forced the court and, by extension, lawmakers to view the enslaved as people and view black women as women. There were gendered values assigned to freedom, but for black women in particular, the ability to gain entry to the legal record and the physical space of a courtroom called into question the very practices of law which placed them outside discussions of liberty, independence, and freedom.[21] Legal action embodied the evolution from human property to personhood across the African Diaspora.

Freedom for US blacks came about in a context that was both evangelical and racist, and had no parallel in Cuba or Brazil. There is no better example than the case of free and enslaved blacks who migrated to Liberia under the auspices of the Protestant-based American Colonization Society in the nineteenth century. Christian-sponsored resettlement campaigns promised free blacks a better life and enslaved blacks freedom, provided they relocated to Liberia. The American Colonization Society (ACS) and the Maryland State Colonization Society (MSCS) were responsible for resettling one-quarter of emigrants to Liberia in the four decades leading up to the American Civil War. Indeed, manumitted blacks from the Chesapeake constituted the largest proportion of emigrants to Liberia. Proponents championed African American civil rights and retained a basic assumption about blacks' capacity to become productive citizens – though only in Africa.[22] In pursuing and exploiting emancipation for the purpose of emigrating, African Americans accepted but also questioned the inherent contradictions of Christian uplift. During the nineteenth-century slave manumissions, the Christian missionary enterprise and African colonization became synonymous with one another. The Christian mission to "civilize," "colonize," and "proselytize" Africans on the continent had the explicit aim of resettlement campaigns such as those endorsed by the ACS and smaller state colonization societies. Free blacks, once expatriated, were believed to be fine representatives of democracy, Christianity, and civilization.[23] By agreeing to participate in relocation schemes, former bondspeople exploited opportunities provided by agencies such as the ACS in order to visualize and attempt to actualize what they saw as the potential of

[21] Camillia Cowling, "Negotiating Freedom: Women of Colour and the Transition to Free Labour in Cuba, 1870–1886," *Slavery and Abolition*, 26 (2005): 377–91, 378.

[22] Eugene Van Sickle, "The Missionary Presences and Influences in Maryland and in Liberia, 1834–1842" (unpublished MA thesis, West Virginia University, 2000), p. 38; Marie Tyler-McGraw, *An African Republic: Black and White Virginians in the Making of Liberia* (Chapel Hill, NC, 2007); Michele Mitchell, *Righteous Propagation: African Americans and the Politics of Racial Destiny after Reconstruction* (Chapel Hill, NC, 2004), p. 21.

[23] Eric Burin, *Slavery and the Peculiar Solution: A History of the American Colonization Society* (Gainesville, FL, 2005); R. J. M. Blackett, *Beating against the Barriers: Biographical Essays in Nineteenth Century Afro-American History* (Baton Rouge, LA, 1986); Penelope Campbell, *Maryland in Africa: The Maryland State Colonization Society, 1831–1857* (Urbana, IL, 1971).

a new life. In Liberia, the formal mechanisms of citizenship worked as their own form of entitlement as "Americans" in Africa.[24] Colonization was not, however, widely supported by black churches. Nonetheless, it demonstrates how some US free blacks had an alternative to being woven into the public narrative of their nation that was not available in Latin America.

CONCLUSIONS: SLAVE CULTURE IN NATIONAL AND TRANS-NATIONAL PERSPECTIVES

While this chapter has focused on the United States, Cuba, and Brazil, the movement of people of African ancestry within the Americas brought about new variations of locally developed slave culture and religions. Forced relocation from (and sometimes to) Africa, as well as migrations within the Americas, shaped the diffusion and intersection of religious practices as their practitioners crossed the Caribbean, as well as traveled from Brazil to other South American nations. Intra-Caribbean migrations brought Haitian Vodun and Jamaican Obeah (African-based religions not discussed here) to Cuba, the Dominican Republic, Central America, Colombia, and Venezuela. In turn, migrations from the time of the Saint Domingue rebellion to the twentieth century brought all Afro-Caribbean religions to the United States. In South America, Afro-Brazilian Candomblé and Umbanda attracted practitioners in neighboring areas, particularly in the Río de la Plata. This highlights the hemispheric aspect of the African Diasporas in the Americas.

From funeral rites and healing practices, the most explicit manifestations of African culture influences throughout the Americas, to the creation of complex webs of societies in Cuba and Brazil and African American churches in the United States, black associations were central to the evolution of slave culture. Religion became much more formalized under new organizational umbrellas, a key feature of the nineteenth century's slave cultures. In the case of the United States, where print culture was richer than in Latin America, slave narratives and autobiographies provide an access point for understanding the influence of slave culture on the present.

Any aspect of culture once implanted in a new context is subject to adaptations, transformations, and appropriations by other groups. We may wonder to what degree the participation of white members of late-nineteenth-century African-based religious ceremonies in Cuba and Brazil anticipated the incorporation of elements of slave culture in the national

---

[24] Anne McClintock, *Imperial Leather: Race, Gender and Sexuality in the Colonial Contest* (New York, 2005), esp. ch. 1; John Saillant, "The Black Body Erotic and the Republican Body Politic, 1790–1820," *Journal of the History of Sexuality* 43 (1995): 403–28, see esp. 418–19.

culture in the following century. In the mid twentieth century, white Cuban and Brazilian intellectuals began studying African-inspired cultures and religions when looking at folklore with a nationalist eye. In the second half of the century, Cuban and Brazilian repertories of national culture included aspects of African-based culture developed earlier in slave communities. This did not mean that the broader society was free of racism and discrimination, but it does underscore how official policy appropriated certain aspects of popular culture that had been embedded in the black experience. Another post-abolition feature, the Jim Crow era, largely prevented, or at least delayed, this movement of cultural appropriation in the United States.

A GUIDE TO FURTHER READING

Acree, William G., "Jacinto Ventura de Molina: A Black 'Letrado' in a White World of Letters, 1766–1841," *Latin American Research Review*, 44 (2009): 37–58.

"African Origins," http://african-origins.org/

Baker, Cecily and Tekia Ali Johnson (eds.), *Africana Legacy: Diasporic Studies in the Americas* (Wyomissing, PA, 2006).

Blight, David, *Race and Reunion: The Civil War in American History* (Cambridge, MA, 2001).

Clegg, Claude, *The Price of Liberty: African Americans and the Making of Liberia* (Chapel Hill, NC, 2004).

Falola, Toyin and Matt D. Childs, *The Yoruba Diaspora in the Atlantic World* (Bloomington, IN, 2004).

Genovese, Eugene, *Roll Jordan Roll: The World the Slaves Made* (New York, 1974).

Hahn, Steve, *A Nation under Our Feet: Black Political Struggles in the Rural South from Slavery to the Great Migration* (Cambridge, MA, 2003).

Higginbotham, Evelyn Brooks, *Righteous Discontent: The Women's Movement in the Black Baptist Church: 1880–1920* (Cambridge, MA, 1993).

Konadu, Kwasi, *The Akan Diaspora in the Americas* (Oxford, 2010).

Law, Robin and Paul Lovejoy, *The Biography of Mahommah Gardo Baquaqua: His Passage from Slavery to Freedom in Africa and America* (Princeton, NJ, 2003).

Lemelle, Sidney and Robin Kelley, *Imagining Home: Class, Culture, and Nationalism in the African Diaspora* (New York, 1995).

Lum, Kenneth, *Praising His Name in the Dance: Spirit Possession in the Spiritual Baptist Faith and Orisha Work in Trinidad, West Indies* (New York, 2000).

Morrow, Diane, *Persons of Color and Religious at the Same Time: The Oblate Sisters of Providence, 1828–1860* (Chapel Hill, NC, 2002).

Ogundiran, Akinwumi and Toyin Falola (eds.), *Archaeology of Atlantic Africa and the African Diaspora* (Bloomington, IN, 2007).

Palmié, Stephan, *The Cooking of History: How Not to Study Afro-Cuban Religion* (Chicago, IL, 2013).

Parés, Luis Nicolau and Roger Sansi-Roca, *Sorcery in the Black Atlantic* (Chicago, IL, 2011).

Raboteau, Albert J., *Slave Religion: The "Invisible Institution" in the Antebellum South* (New York, 1978).

Reis, Maria Firmina dos, *Úrsula: Romance* (Belo Horizonte, 2004).

Rucker, Walter, *The River Flows On: Black Resistance, Culture, and Identity Formation in Early America* (Baton Rouge, LA, 2006).

Washington, Margaret, *Sojourner Truth's America* (Urbana, IL, 2009).

PART III

ABOLITION

CHAPTER 14

SLAVERY AND THE HAITIAN REVOLUTION

DAVID GEGGUS

The revolution of 1789 to 1803 that transformed the prosperous French colony of Saint Domingue into the independent black state of Haiti occupies a special position in the history of slavery. The slave uprising of 1791 to 1793 that was the revolution's central event was by far the largest in the history of the Americas and it brought about the first abolition of slavery in a major slave-owning society. The prominence of slavery as a political issue in the revolution and of enslaved people among its protagonists sets the Haitian Revolution apart from the other anti-colonial struggles of the period and from the French Revolution, with which it was closely connected. Yet, it was never just a slave revolution. Like its counterpart in France, the revolution in Saint Domingue was socially and politically complex; the colony's white and free colored populations each waged separate struggles of their own that interacted with that of the slaves. The development and outcome of the Haitian Revolution was thus shaped by three overlapping conflicts with mutually hostile agendas.

From these different struggles emerged a series of landmark achievements: colonial representation in an imperial legislature (1789); racial equality (1792); slave emancipation (1793); and colonial independence (1803). The Haitian Revolution is an event of global significance, partly because of the precedents it set and partly because of where it took place. Saint Domingue was arguably the most valuable colony of its time. It represented the apogee of the European imperial expansion initiated in the fifteenth century.

PRE-REVOLUTIONARY SAINT DOMINGUE

In the second half of the eighteenth century, when France supplied tropical produce to most of Europe, Saint Domingue was the world's major exporter of sugar, coffee, and, for a while, indigo as well. These were not yet the cheap bulk commodities they later became, but valuable staples, the lifeblood of international trade. Though no larger than Massachusetts, Saint Domingue, with fewer than 600,000 inhabitants, was exporting on the eve of the French Revolution more than Brazil and

Mexico combined, more than the United States, and close to twice as much as the British West Indies. It did not generate the tax revenue of a Bengal or a Mexico, but it accounted for a large proportion of France's overseas trade, which was the most dynamic sector of the Old Regime economy. Its commerce kept a small navy in business and provided employment for hundreds of thousands of French people.

This wealth derived from the labor of an enslaved workforce that numbered at its height more than half a million; it was the third largest slave population in the Americas, where in 1790 one in four slaves lived in a French colony. With a white population of some 30,000 and a free colored middle sector rapidly approaching that size, Saint Domingue's social structure broadly resembled that of most other Caribbean colonies, but it was among the most unbalanced in its population between black and white, and between slave and free, in the Americas.

The enslaved population was very heterogeneous. Split up between 7,000 plantations, working sun-up to sundown six days per week, it was divided not only by location, but by differences in culture and class. About one in three adults was born locally and grew up in slavery speaking the local Creole language. From their ranks were chosen many of the domestic servants, artisan craftsmen, and slave drivers who made up the slave elite. Field hands were generally Africans, who had crossed the Atlantic beneath the deck of a slave ship. Africans formed just over half of the slave population in the late 1780s, rather fewer than historians usually suppose. The largest sub-group were "Congos" from West-Central Africa; they were especially prominent in the mountains, but constituted no more than one in four slaves overall. On a typical sugar plantation of 200 workers, there might be speakers of a dozen or more different languages, all at different stages of assimilation into colonial society. Long accustomed to growing their own food and marketing the surplus, the Creoles tended to be wealthier than the Africans, and more likely to live in families and to have children. Coffee and indigo plantations were considerably smaller than sugar estates, but, with close to fifty slaves on average, they were still much larger than most US cotton farms. Plantations were like small villages where elements of African cultures were preserved or blended.

As elsewhere in the Americas, working conditions were at their worst on the lowland sugar estates, where slaves toiled all day and part of the night during the grueling harvest season. These estates often belonged to absentee owners and were run by managers whose incentive was to maximize output at whatever cost. Overwork, underfeeding, and infectious disease were less prevalent on the mountain coffee plantations, though heinous acts of cruelty were no rarer there and as likely to go unpunished. Writers often claim that Saint Domingue slavery was uniquely harsh, but this is unproven, and also improbable, given that only one-third of the slaves lived on sugar estates. In the Northern Plain, however, where the 1791 slave uprising began, the fertility of female slaves was exceptionally low and workloads do seem to have been high compared to the rest of the colony and to the Caribbean in general.

In sharp contrast to neighboring Jamaica, Saint Domingue experienced only a few, small slave rebellions prior to 1791. Maroonage, or escaping from slavery, perhaps proved a more attractive option, especially escape across the frontier into the sparsely populated Spanish colony of Santo Domingo. Plantations' rates of loss were not unusually high, however, and most absenteeism was short-term. After 1776, an extradition treaty between Saint Domingue and Santo Domingo made life more difficult for maroons. Though communities of a few hundred fugitives grew up in some frontier zones and clashed with settlers and militia, they had largely disappeared by the 1780s, after the expansion of coffee cultivation had cleared much of the mountain forests. The longest-lived of these communities was the Maniel, who lived on Spanish territory in the southeast. Having shrunk to fewer than 150 residents, they signed a peace treaty in 1785, which the French government eventually rejected. Poisoning scares gripped the colony in the middle decades of the century, but they also sharply declined, probably as colonists adopted a more scientific attitude toward disease. On the other hand, the subversive potential of the syncretic religious practices colonists called *Vaudoux* no doubt increased with time. Ethnically-based religions were divisive, but the umbrella structure of Vodou brought disparate groups together on common ground. Solidarity was also expressed in work strikes; little is currently known about them, but they were quite common in the Northern Plain in the 1780s.

The significance of slave resistance for the coming of the Haitian Revolution remains controversial. Some interpret maroonage and Vodou as a training ground for violent rebellion; others see them as safety valves that released anomic tensions in slave society. The claim that they supplied many political leaders of the 1790s is greatly exaggerated, but not without foundation. To what degree Vodou had coalesced into a unifying force before the revolution is unclear, but colonists certainly feared the influence wielded by magico-religious specialists; some earlier figures like Macandal and Dom Pedro, both African sorcerers, had already achieved mythical status. Slaves ran away less often than soldiers in the colonial garrison deserted, and with much less success. The total number of fugitives in Saint Domingue went on increasing, albeit no faster than the population in general. It is possible that declining prospects for maroonage made organized revolt more likely.

The slave population certainly grew at a precipitous rate, but so did the free population. More than 220,000 Africans arrived in the years 1784 to 1790, when Saint Domingue rivaled Brazil as the largest single market for the Atlantic slave trade. The new arrivals included more young males than ever before; and many, as prisoners of war, presumably had military experience. This mounting influx of recently enslaved Africans was not quite as significant as might be thought, because the 1791 slave uprising was not only led by locally-born Creoles, but broke out in the most Creolized region of the colony, whereas the regions with the most African slaves were among the slowest to be drawn into the Haitian Revolution. Nonetheless, the number of slaves in Saint Domingue did dramatically increase relative to the number of troops, who were the ultimate enforcers of the status quo. Slaves thus may have had increasing reason to believe that rebellion might be met with success.

Pre-revolutionary trends in social control, slave resistance, and the conditions of slave life may have made Saint Domingue less stable, but the evidence is far from clear-cut. It is unlikely that there would have been a Haitian Revolution without the French Revolution of 1789.

THE FREE POPULATION AND THE FRENCH REVOLUTION, 1789 TO 1791

When France's absolute monarchy went bankrupt in 1788 and was forced to call an Estates-General to discuss wide-ranging reforms, few imagined that the country's distant colonies either belonged on the agenda or had any right to participate. The planter elite of Saint Domingue nonetheless seized the opportunity and set in motion a political process that successively pulled in all the other sectors of colonial society. The Haitian Revolution began as a bid for free trade and limited self-government by wealthy planters, merchants, and lawyers. When their initially secret activities became public in the course of 1789, they were challenged by middle- and lower-class whites, who quickly succeeded in establishing a broad democratic franchise for white men in the colony. After winning representation for France's colonies in the National Assembly in Paris, and continuing to ignore royal officials, whites in Saint Domingue elected their own local assemblies that in May 1790 drew up a highly contentious colonial constitution.

Much less successful was the colony's free colored middle class. Almost as numerous as the white population, it was unusual in the Americas for including a substantial number of prosperous middling planters, but it was subject to the same discriminatory laws and extra-legal harassment typical of colonial societies. Apart from a large free black minority that lived closer to the enslaved masses, most free coloreds were of mixed racial descent. Encouraged by the Declaration of the Rights of Man (August 26, 1789), which the National Assembly had passed without any thought for the colonies, they called for civil equality with their white counterparts, both in Paris, where they founded a political club, and in several parts of Saint Domingue, where they drew up local petitions.

Though white activists quickly gained much of what they wanted from the revolution, they got more than they had bargained for. Colonists in Paris were shocked to find racial discrimination and slavery, the pillars of their colonial world, suddenly under attack. Several of the leading figures in the National Assembly were members of the Friends of the Blacks, a recently founded antislavery society. Its immediate aim was to abolish the slave trade, but, in the fall of 1789, it also took up the cause of colonial free coloreds. At a time when centuries-old privileges were being swept away in a torrent of reforming zeal, it seemed for a while that it might succeed. Fear of Revolutionary France strengthened autonomist, and later secessionist, currents among whites in Saint Domingue, but the colonial lobby in Paris was forced into a defensive stance. Dropping its demands for free trade, it made an alliance with metropolitan merchants and managed to convince a majority of politicians that any change in the status quo would jeopardize the colonial trade on which France depended. News that arrived in December of a small slave rebellion in Martinique helped make their case. As a result, the National Assembly refused to even discuss the slave trade during its two years' existence, and for eighteen months it stonewalled the freemen of color. Though they and their allies emphasized the freemen's merits as tax-paying property owners and militia men, their common interest in preserving slavery, and their shared European ancestry, liberal politicians in Paris responded with an embarrassed evasiveness. In Saint Domingue, free colored protests met with a series of murders, executions, stand-offs, and property seizures. The collecting of severed heads as trophies – a tactic that all sides in the Haitian Revolution would come to use – seems to have begun at this time.

Several members of the colonial elite were willing to make minor concessions to wealthy light-complexioned *gens de couleur*, but the new egalitarian ideology made such co-optation difficult, and the advent of voting rights greatly raised the stakes. Racial equality previously meant just access to jobs and the removal of humiliating distinctions; now it would mean political power. An additional obstacle was the new political influence of the poor whites, the most racist segment of Saint Domingue society. Above all, the men of color had difficulty separating their cause from that of the enslaved. Colonizers had long claimed racial discrimination to be an essential bulwark of the slave regime. The Friends of the Blacks replied that continued mistreatment of free coloreds might drive them to combine with the slaves in revolt. Most free coloreds were slave-owners and not abolitionists, but the abolitionists clearly saw racial equality as a first step toward an eventual slave emancipation.

Prominent among the free colored activists in Paris was Vincent Ogé, one of Saint Domingue's few non-white merchants. Frustrated by his lack of progress, he returned to the colony in October 1790 and gathered

300 armed men in the mountains of the north. Confident in the justice of his cause, he hoped he could impose terms from a position of strength, but the rebellion was swiftly and brutally suppressed by government forces. Ogé did not die entirely in vain, however. After a lengthy and fractious debate in May 1791, the National Assembly was shamed into granting equal rights to a small minority of free coloreds, men (who could prove they were) born to two free parents. Even this compromise measure created such a storm of protest from colonists on both sides of the Atlantic that the decree was withdrawn four months later. By then, however, it had helped to set off two large-scale uprisings that would change Saint Domingue forever. Exasperated by colonial intransigence and encouraged perhaps by changing opinion in France, freemen of color launched a rebellion in August in the West and South provinces in the regions where they were most numerous. At the same time, a massive slave revolt broke out in the colony's Northern Plain. Although simultaneous, the two rebellions were not connected. They had quite different goals, but, by forcing the whites to fight a war on two fronts, each was a major factor in the success of the other.

THE SLAVE UPRISING, 1791 TO 1793

Despite the importance of the slavery question to the politics of whites and free coloreds, the slaves themselves had kept a low profile during the first two years of the revolution. In the fall of 1789, news of the popular revolution in Paris caused unspecified disturbances on certain plantations; probably generated by false rumors of slavery's abolition, they were quickly suppressed. White conservatives and radicals on occasion also spread rumors of maroon activity or slave conspiracy as an excuse to mobilize or to undermine their opponents. But until the summer of 1791, the slaves primarily looked on as tensions mounted between whites and free coloreds, and divisions deepened within the white population. In the aftermath of the Ogé rebellion, whites in some districts had disarmed free colored men (who formed an important part of the militia and rural police), thus weakening control of the slave population. Several free blacks who had escaped capture after Ogé's defeat and later became minor leaders in the slave uprising constitute a more direct link with the northern rebellion. The colonists' rejection of the May 15 decree on racial equality also appears to have fueled more rumors among slaves about the cover-up of an abolition law. A mobilizing factor in the Martinique rebellion of 1789, such rumors would feature in more than twenty slave revolts and conspiracies over the next forty years. Whether the product of genuine confusion or manipulation by astute leaders, the rumors obviously echoed the growth of the international antislavery movement. In Saint Domingue's case, they appear to have blended with news that arrived in early August 1791 that King Louis XVI had turned against the French Revolution and, after attempting to flee from Paris, was being held prisoner.

This helps to explain why the slaves who took up arms in late August usually claimed to be fighting in the king's name and that they were seizing a freedom that the king had granted them. Sometimes it was only a partial freedom, "three free days" per week, which was another rumor that had been circulating in the Caribbean for some time. The insurgents' rationale was presumably that "my enemy's enemy is my friend," since the white colonial militants opposed the royalist administration. It no doubt seemed plausible, because in the 1780s the government had sought to implement a limited reform of slavery and to punish atrocities committed by planters. The rebels may also have heard about the early American Revolution in Virginia, where Governor Dunmore (who visited the Northern Plain in 1789) had freed slaves who would fight for the crown against rebellious colonists. Colonial radicals came to believe that white royalists were in fact behind the slave uprising, and some historians still favor this interpretation, failing to appreciate how the rebels consciously propagated this idea so as to divide their opponents. They also wished to appeal to the conservative Spaniards of neighboring Santo Domingo. Finally, for Africans, as for Europeans, royalism was a familiar, traditional ideology. Although conservatives claimed that the slaves had been led astray by the Rights of Man, the insurgents usually deployed a traditionalist church and king rhetoric and rarely used the new language of rights.

The ideological influence of the French Revolution on the slaves is therefore unclear, but its political influence, undermining authority and dividing the free population, is obvious. The Northern Plain rebellion broke out amid discussion of secession and counter-revolution and with civil war brewing between free coloreds and whites. One of the colony's two regiments had been deported three months earlier, after it mutinied. As a new Colonial Assembly was gathering in the city of Cap Français (Le Cap), the insurgents apparently aimed to eliminate all the colonial politicians in one bold stroke. On the night of August 22/23, they began killing and burning on a scale never seen in any other slave revolt. The urban component of the plot was stifled, but the rebels quickly overran half of the densely settled Northern Plain. With Le Cap under siege, they began to penetrate the surrounding mountains, usually with the complicity or collaboration of the local free coloreds, and by the end of the year they controlled most of the eastern half of the North Province. Well over 100,000 slaves lived in this region. Not all were insurgents; many fled the fighting or had to continue working for the rebels, and a few defended their plantations against them. Yet, in magnitude, duration, or outcome there would be nothing remotely similar in the history of modern slave rebellions.

The uprising was planned and led by locally born "elite" slaves (coachmen, slave drivers, domestics), but Africans made up a large proportion of the insurgents and grassroots leaders. African-derived religious practices formed part of their preparation for revolt, and belief in the protective power of amulets or in post-mortem return to Africa helped mobilize resistance. The popular idea that they elected "kings" as leaders, however, seems mistaken; the insurgents quickly adopted European military ranks. Their goals are difficult to discern and no doubt varied between participants and through time. The earliest demand they articulated was that the whites leave the colony. Yet, some spoke of only modifying slavery, such as allowing extra "free" days or dismissing estate managers. The most militant leaders, Boukman and Jeannot, were killed early in the uprising. Jean-François and Biassou, who became the supreme leaders, were less radical. Twice, in December 1791 and September 1792, they sought to negotiate a peace that would have freed their immediate entourages but returned most of their followers to slavery. As these approaches came in response to the imminent arrival of troops from France, they might be interpreted as pragmatically flexible rather than callous betrayals. But at no point did these men espouse freedom as a universal right, and on occasion they rounded up women and children on the plantations for sale to their Spanish neighbors, trading slaves for munitions.[1]

Because the leaders could not compel their followers' surrender and the colonists, in any event, refused to negotiate, the insurrection continued. A cordon of posts in the mountains, constant patroling, and merciless reprisals by planters kept it from spreading into the northwest or southward into the West Province, but neither side could defeat the other. Colonists' fear of leaving Cap Français vulnerable to an urban revolt had early on hampered the deployment of forces and so allowed the rebellion to snowball to overwhelming proportions. France sent 12,000 soldiers to Saint Domingue in the course of 1792, but they succumbed rapidly to tropical fevers, as was common in Caribbean wars, and as crises multiplied, they were dispersed to all parts of the colony. Since many enslaved Africans had been prisoners of war and few

---

[1] For an interpretation that stresses the influence of republican, libertarian ideas among the insurgents, see Laurent Dubois, *A Colony of Citizens: Revolution and Slave Emancipation in the French Caribbean, 1787–1804* (Chapel Hill, NC, 2004). Contemporary sources are collected in Jeremy D. Popkin, *You Are All Free: The Haitian Revolution and the Abolition of Slavery* (Cambridge, 2010); David Geggus, *The Haitian Revolution: A Documentary History* (Indianapolis, IN, 2014).

French troops in 1791 had previously seen combat, it is possible that the slaves had more battlefield experience than the garrison. They compensated for their lack of firearms with ambushes, psychological warfare, and hit-and-run tactics, and they proved an elusive enemy in mountainous and forested terrain. They also benefited from the proximity of the Santo Domingo frontier, which prevented their being attacked from all sides and facilitated trade with the neighboring Spanish. The insurgents suffered heavy losses, however, when fighting in open countryside and lacking adequate artillery, they were unable to capture towns.

The simultaneous revolt of the freemen of color in the west and south provinces denied the northern whites the assistance they would otherwise have expected. The free coloreds were familiar with the terrain and climate, and proved to be accurate marksmen, probably because they carried hunting rifles instead of muskets. Wearing straw hats and mounted on mules and ponies, they also formed a rag-tag but effective cavalry. They quickly persuaded white planters of the need to make concessions. The wavering of the National Assembly in Paris, however, and the strident racism of urban poor whites, kept the conflict going through the fall and into the spring of 1792. Port-au-Prince, Jacmel, and Léogane were besieged. Massacre, torture, and the mutilation of corpses were widely practiced, as in the north. The large free colored communities of the west and south found new strength in alliance, while those of the north remained fragmented. The free coloreds of Cap Français and the northwest region joined with their white counterparts in combating the slave uprising. In the zone of insurrection, however, groups of free colored landowners, notably in the northeast, formed a temporary alliance with the insurgent slaves, and about one-fiftieth of the insurgent army itself consisted of freemen, among whom free blacks were quite prominent as camp commanders.

The interaction of free and enslaved was even more complex in the west and south. The region witnessed a half-dozen slave rebellions in 1792 and early 1793, of which several were apparently promoted by free coloreds to put pressure on their white opponents. They were short-lived and localized and ended with the freeing of small numbers of insurgents, who then became rural police. A longer insurrection, in the mountains between Léogane and Jacmel, was led by a free colored shaman, known as Romaine la Prophétesse, but was eventually supressed by free colored and white forces. Both whites and free coloreds also began to arm small groups of slaves as mercenaries – a trend that would grow in the following years. Out of these diverse developments, several autonomous groups of slave insurgents emerged in mountainous zones. Though these local revolts were dwarfed by the conflict that remained unchecked in the north, they make up nearly half of only fourteen or fifteen American slave rebellions that involved more than 1,000 participants.[2] Overall, however, the plantation regime remained largely intact across the west and south provinces. Though work slowed or stopped where whites fled the countryside, there was relatively little destruction of property, and most slaves remained living on their estates. The colonists' fear of weakening slavery further in this region was a powerful disincentive to offering concessions to the northern insurgents. The ability of local free coloreds to control the countryside was probably the main reason these two provinces avoided the north's fate.

Even the most prejudiced colonists had to recognize that they could not defeat the slaves without the military assistance of the freemen of color. Recognition of this fact, and the ascendance of the liberal Girondin faction in Paris, led to the groundbreaking decree of April 4, 1792 that finally abolished racial discrimination in all French colonies. Most colonial whites grudgingly had to accept it. Those considered hostile were deported by civil commissioners who arrived from Paris in September 1792, just as France became a republic. Léger-Félicité Sonthonax and Etienne Polverel were radical idealists armed with dictatorial powers. After spending several months purging the white population of potential opponents, they turned their attention to suppressing the increasingly assertive slaves. Campaigns launched in the north and south early in 1793 made unprecedented headway and, for a moment, it seemed as though they might succeed.

The rapid spread of war in Europe, however, following the execution of the French king, suddenly tipped the balance of power against the French Republic and reshaped the struggle for Saint Domingue. Spain and Britain saw the upheaval in the colony not so much as a threat at this time, but as an opportunity to seize a valuable possession. War with its colonial rivals meant that France could no longer safely send troops across the Atlantic, and it exposed Saint Domingue to imminent invasion. The prospect of foreign intervention also encouraged white colonists to resist the autocratic commissioners. Above all, the French and Spanish governments each took the extraordinary decision to recruit the insurgent slaves as soldiers, and in the ensuing competition it was the Spanish who succeeded. They offered freedom and land to Jean-François and Biassou's followers, along with guns, uniforms, and cash. To outbid the Spanish, defeat the treasonous colonists, and raise forces to resist a British invasion, Sonthonax took the desperate gamble of proclaiming slavery abolished and called on all the black population to defend the new regime of liberty. Contemporaries compared the news to an electric shock. Sonthonax had no authorization to take such a step, and the 28-year-old official would not have dared do so without the prospect of France losing Saint Domingue. It is significant,

---

[2] David Geggus, "Slave Rebellion During the Age of Revolution," in Wim Klooster and Gert Oostindie (eds.), *Curaçao in the Age of Revolution, 1795–1800* (Leiden, 2011), pp. 23–56.

however, that he was a closet abolitionist, one of the few radicals to have (anonymously) advocated slave emancipation early in the French Revolution. It was perhaps also important that, though antislavery remained a weak force in France, the issue had been gaining support in Paris since the beginning of the year, and Sonthonax doubtless drew encouragement from this. The landmark emancipation proclamation of August 29, 1793 thus grew out of local and metropolitan developments, and it had three essential causes: the undefeated slave insurrection, the outbreak of war, and the fortuitous presence of a radical abolitionist in charge of the colony.

A new era began. After three centuries of unchecked growth, slavery was proscribed precisely where it had most flourished. Amid the rubble of Cap Français, which was burned in June and from which thousands of colonists fled abroad, Sonthonax gathered around him a small group of free colored and white radicals who began to construct a largely black army. The challenge for Sonthonax was how to preserve without slave labor the plantation regime that fueled the export economy. His solution was a sort of revenue-sharing serfdom. Most former slaves were to be paid, but were to remain tied to their old estates. As many preferred to become independent peasant farmers, the policy did not prove popular and set up a conflict that would last for decades. In those parts of Saint Domingue where the plantations remained intact, white and free colored slave-owners rejected emancipation and surrendered great swathes of the west and south provinces to British and Spanish invaders.

WAR AND THE RISE OF TOUSSAINT LOUVERTURE, 1793 TO 1798

The next five years of international war and foreign occupation helped forge a new egalitarian and multiracial polity in Saint Domingue under the aegis of the French Republic. With the planter class eclipsed, the influence of the *anciens libres*[3] briefly peaked then progressively declined, as former slaves rose to power. At first, Sonthonax's emancipation policy attracted very few of the insurgents. They continued fighting the French as "Auxiliary Troops of Carlos IV" and, with a smaller number of Spanish soldiers, occupied much of the north and west provinces. Planters welcomed British forces into much of the west and south. In September 1793, after the first multiracial election in a French colony, held in Le Cap, Sonthonax sent a multiracial deputation to explain his actions to the legislature in Paris. Inspired by a mixture of ideological fervor and eagerness to use slave emancipation to destabilize the British Caribbean, the National Convention responded to the commissar's fait accompli by abolishing slavery in all

---

[3] "Formerly free," as free coloreds were henceforth called now that ex-slaves were known as "newly free."

of its colonies. The decree of February 4, 1794 not only freed slaves, but declared them to be citizens. It was one of the most radical acts of the French Revolution and occurred at its radical high point with the Jacobins in power and the Reign of Terror in full swing. Even radical Jacobins, however, soon had misgivings about how disruptive the decree might prove. In Saint Domingue, most former slaves remained subject to forced labor, as Sonthonax envisioned, and few were able to exercise any political rights. Officials in Guadeloupe and Guyane applied the decree with even greater restrictions, and colonists in France's Indian Ocean colonies rejected it outright. Nonetheless, the decree freed more than 600,000 people[4] and proved to be a fearsome weapon of war. French agents used it to galvanize black resistance in several British colonies, and in Saint Domingue it helped encourage some of the insurgents who had joined the Spanish to switch sides and rally to the French Republic. By far the most important of these was Toussaint Louverture, the most talented of the auxiliaries' commanders.

Toussaint was a black freedman, born in the mid-1740s to African parents, who had been free for at least twenty years. Much about his early life is obscure. Because he lived on the plantation where his family were still slaves, many thought he was a slave himself. So did historians until the 1970s, when it was discovered that he had owned and rented land and slaves on a small scale. He seems to have joined in the 1791 slave uprising belatedly, after waiting several months, but it is possible that he was in fact its organizer, as he later let people think. He first appears as a public figure in December 1791 as an advisor to Jean-François and Biassou advocating the ending of the rebellion and return of most of the insurgents to slavery. Yet, though he could have profited from the amnesty offered to free insurgents, he remained fighting on the side of the slaves as a second-rank commander and, unlike his superiors, he did not sell captives. Like them, he swore allegiance in May 1793 to the Spanish, whose aim was to restore the slave regime, but the following August, when Sonthonax was preparing his emancipation proclamation, he adopted the evocative sou-briquet "L'Ouverture" (the opening) and claimed in certain letters to have always supported the cause of freedom for all. His actions did not change, however, and he continued to reject overtures from the French. Toussaint probably found monarchism more appealing than republicanism, and with the French Republic struggling for survival, Spain certainly looked more like a winning side.

Toussaint's *volte-face* in the spring of 1794 was motivated by a number of factors: friction with his rivals in the black auxiliaries, France's

---

[4] In Saint Domingue, Guadeloupe, and Guyane. The decree was not promulgated in Martinique, which was occupied by British forces.

improving fortunes in Europe and Saint Domingue, and the return of hundreds of refugee colonists who were impatient to reclaim their slaves. News of the February emancipation decree sealed the change of allegiance. It was a turning point in the revolution, because it unambiguously united for the first time the forces of black self-liberation, antislavery idealism, and the resources of a modern state. The effect was dramatic. Toussaint quickly seized for the Republic most of the land he had conquered for Spain and, in the fall, he drove the Spanish from several of their frontier towns, permanently redrawing the map of Hispaniola. Defeated in Europe and Saint Domingue, Spain made peace in summer 1795. It also surrendered Santo Domingo to France, though the French opted to delay the transfer. Jean-François, Biassou, and 800 followers went into pensioned exile in different parts of the Spanish Empire. The British, meanwhile, remained entrenched in most of the West Province and the Grande Anse region at the tip of the southern peninsula. Decimated by tropical fevers, they increasingly recruited slaves as soldiers, and with diminishing success they struggled to maintain slavery and the export economy. During four years of constant warfare, Toussaint's ragged forces died by the hundreds trying to drive southward to the capital, Port-au-Prince.

In the process, he forged a formidable army. "As naked as earthworms," as he once described them, most of the rank and file were Africans; the officer corps included many mulattos and a few whites, but was dominated by black Creoles like himself. Prominent among them was Moyse, who was his wife's nephew, and the stern Jean-Jacques Dessalines, a former slave of his son-in-law. Since capturing the port of Gonaïves in December 1793, Toussaint was able to trade coffee from the mountain zone he controled for munitions. With General Laveaux, the beleaguered French governor, he established a close relationship built on mutual respect, commitment to slave emancipation, and growing rivalry with the *anciens libres*. Men of mixed race led by goldsmith André Rigaud were ascendant in most of the southern peninsula, where they were waging their own struggle against the British/slave-owner alliance. In the north, local *ancien libre* commanders also ran their districts as independent fiefs and resented both the rising power of the ex-slaves and Laveaux's attempts at centralization. When the commandant of Cap Français, General Jean-Louis Villatte, tried to overthrow Laveaux in April 1796, Toussaint and other black officers foiled the coup. In gratitude and recognition of the shifting balance of power, Laveaux named the ex-slave lieutenant-governor of the colony.

This was a year of crisis for the new republican regime in Saint Domingue. The British threat was at its height. Plantation workers revolted against military conscription and at rumors of the return of slavery. Remnants of the black auxiliaries fought on in the northeast in the king's name. There were more rebellions by disgruntled *anciens libres*, and a rift developed between Rigaud's southern enclave and the French administration in the north, where Sonthonax was again in charge, after a two-year absence. Localized massacres of surviving colonists continued, as they would throughout the revolution. French rule was preserved only at the cost of increasing dependence on one black general. In May 1797, Sonthonax named Louverture commander-in-chief of the colonial army, but then was deported by him three months later on trumped-up charges. Sonthonax's successor, General Hédouville, received similar treatment the following year. Though acting as a loyal servant of the Republic, Toussaint negotiated the withdrawal of British forces in 1798 as an independent ruler. The remaining 60,000 or 70,000 slaves in Saint Domingue were freed; more whites went into exile, and Toussaint doubled the area under his control.

THE GOVERNMENT OF TOUSSAINT LOUVERTURE, 1798 TO 1801

To keep open the trade routes on which Saint Domingue's economy, and therefore the black army, depended, Toussaint quickly concluded trade treaties and non-aggression pacts with Britain and the United States, despite the fact that France was still at war with both countries. He also expelled French privateers from the colony, amnestied colonists who had allied with France's enemies, and secretly informed the British in Jamaica of a French plot to incite a slave revolt there – an ironic clash between the Haitian and French revolutions. The black governor thus pursued a policy of de facto independence that put Saint Domingue's needs ahead of the Republic's war effort and the interests of its merchants. He was also wary of the conservative trend of French politics in the late 1790s. Many have thought he was preparing an outright break with France, but this is very unlikely. De jure independence would have brought no advantages and would probably have provoked retaliation by the slave-owning British and Americans, as well as the French.

Five years of international war greatly weakened the plantation economy, destroying buildings, livestock, and crops, and turning thousands of former slaves into combatants in a war of liberation. To maintain or revive exports, both the British and Republicans had sequestrated and leased out the property of absentees, whose numbers ballooned during the revolution. In the Republican zone, Toussaint continued Sonthonax's system of remunerated forced labor. It was an improvement on slavery, but it still allowed for corporal punishment of workers, and it clashed with their aspirations to become independent smallholders or start a new life in the towns. Moreover, a new generation had grown up during the revolution that had never done field labor. In remote regions, the ex-slaves drifted toward a peasant lifestyle that concentrated on the production of foodstuffs for subsistence and local markets. Faced with popular recalcitrance, Louverture used the army to impose control. As Inspector of Agriculture, Dessalines suppressed protests with beatings and summary executions. Estates leased to military officers proved the most productive. There thus grew up alongside the *anciens libres* a new black landholding elite with a military background.

Toussaint also encouraged white colonists to return and resume direction of their plantations. Some think his motive was to accumulate hostages so as to discourage a future French attack, but most believe he valued whites' technical and managerial skills and that he wanted a multiracial, egalitarian future for Saint Domingue. Relations with the *anciens libres*, however, dramatically declined. Toussaint and Rigaud soon came to blows after the expulsion of the British, their common foe. The War of the South (June 1799 to July 1800) began as a boundary dispute between rivals and was at bottom a regional power struggle, but it was also shaped by class conflict and used the language of race in its propaganda. Each of the leaders had an African mother and claimed to be defending slave emancipation and the French Republic. On each side, the armies consisted overwhelmingly of former slaves. But Toussaint, the son of slaves, and Rigaud, freeborn with a white father, represented the classes in which they were raised, and so did their officers. In the region under Toussaint's command, hundreds of *anciens libres* were arrested and killed, accused of favoring Rigaud. Dessalines led an invasion of the south that was marked by fierce resistance and mass executions. Rigaud and dozens of other leaders fled to France. By August 1800, Toussaint Louverture controlled the entire colony. In January 1801, he annexed neighboring Santo Domingo, and in July he promulgated a constitution that made Saint Domingue a colony in name only. Dictatorial in structure, the constitution named him governor for life, with the power to name his successor. It declared slave emancipation inviolable, but preserved the forced labor regime and allowed the purchase of Africans from slave ships to replenish the workforce.

Louverture's critics called him a hypocrite, outwardly pious and moralizing, yet ruthlessly ambitious. In their eyes, his regime was a ramshackle tyranny that allowed senior officers to amass fortunes while their unpaid troops preyed on the rural masses. The general's admirers saw a brave new world in the making. It combined the French Republic's awkward compromise between slavery and freedom with a hybrid blend of colonial status and independence that he himself pioneered. Admirers described a multiracial, egalitarian experiment defended by a citizen army, in which the birth rate was rising and racial prejudice was fast disappearing. The regime's success in reviving agriculture remains uncertain. Official figures from 1801 show sugar production some 90 percent below pre-revolutionary levels and coffee down by about half.

Toussaint's struggle to find a middle ground that would conciliate free labor with export agriculture, and colonial status with political autonomy, met with serious resistance in Saint Domingue and insuperable opposition in France. In October 1801, a rebellion of plantation workers in the north killed more than 300 white colonists before Louverture crushed it. It was apparently instigated by Toussaint's own nephew, Moyse, whom some historians credit with wanting to divide up the plantations. Although it is more likely he wanted them run by black officers rather than Europeans, Moyse's rebellion revealed deep fissures in post-slavery society and the difficulty of Toussaint's balancing act. Meanwhile, in France, preparations were already under way to reassert metropolitan dominance in the colony. When Napoleon Bonaparte came to power in 1799, he hoped to revive France's colonial empire, but he hesitated at how to deal with Saint Domingue. Toussaint's annexation of Santo Domingo, contrary to Bonaparte's personal directive, settled the matter. Bonaparte decided to remove the governor and dismantle the black army, and later to reimpose slavery.[5]

THE STRUGGLE FOR STATEHOOD, 1802 TO 1820

Unlike his French, British, and Spanish predecessors, Bonaparte managed to send a large and experienced army to Saint Domingue during the healthy months of the year. The Leclerc expedition sailed with the approval of Britain and the United States, which had by then made peace with France and preferred to see Europeans rather than ex-slaves in control of Saint Domingue. The expedition also received Spanish and Dutch assistance, and later, hunting dogs from Cuba. It therefore had the appearance of a Euro-American crusade, though it also included many *anciens libres*, eager to avenge the War of the South. After three months of desperate fighting, Toussaint and Dessalines surrendered in May 1802. Much of the army and of the rural population had offered no resistance at all in the face of French assurances that military officers would keep their jobs and that slavery would never be restored.

In the course of the summer, however, it became clear that Bonaparte's intention was to re-establish both slavery and racial discrimination. Toussaint was deported and died in a French prison. Most of the French army died of disease. Resistance snowballed, beginning with the rural masses

---

[5] Two classic studies of Toussaint, written from left- and right-wing perspectives, are: C. L. R. James, *The Black Jacobins: Toussaint L'Ouverture and the San Domingo Revolution* (New York, 1963); and Pierre Pluchon, *Toussaint Louverture: un révolutionnaire noir d'Ancien régime* (Paris, 1989).

who balked at being disarmed. By October, both the *anciens libres* who had accompanied the expedition from France and the black generals that had collaborated with the French since May had gone into rebellion. Led by Rigaud's successor, Alexandre Pétion, the *anciens libres* accepted their former enemy Dessalines as supreme commander. Unity was needed to expel the French, and independence was necessary to preserve racial equality and slave emancipation, though it was not articulated as a goal for many months. Atrocities were widespread throughout the Haitian Revolution, but the War of Independence was especially brutal. The French military adopted a quasi-genocidal strategy. The Indigenous Army (as it now called itself) massacred civilians and used scorched earth tactics. Fighting continued until November 1803.

In January 1804, Jean-Jacques Dessalines declared the independence of the "State of Haiti." By resurrecting the island's pre-Columbian Indian name, he symbolically erased the European colonial past and claimed an American identity for a population of primarily African descent, of which roughly a quarter was African-born. The Declaration of Independence was only the third in world history. It proclaimed that secession had been necessary to avoid re-enslavement, but it did not use the word "rights." Much of the document called in blistering prose for the extirpation of all things French. During the following few months, most of the remaining colonists perished in a series of organized massacres. Dessalines publicly justified the killing as retribution for past treatment, as an act of national reconciliation to reunite former slaves and *anciens libres*, and as a warning against future attempts at reconquest. White people were thereafter banned from owning property. The new state was a military autocracy; though many have called it a republic, it made no such pretensions. In 1805, Dessalines took the title "emperor." A republic was declared in 1806, when *anciens libres*, ascendant in the west and south, assassinated him, but the country then split along these regional and class lines. Down to 1820, the ex-slave general Henry Christophe ruled a breakaway northern state that became a monarchy.

Haiti's independence was achieved amid apocalyptic destruction. The colonial population fell by at least one-third during the revolution, a decrease of at least 180,000 people, and it cost the lives of about 70,000 European troops and many thousands of sailors. With plantations and towns in ruins, much of its working-age population killed, and most of its literate minority eliminated, the new state was able to export barely a quarter of its pre-revolutionary output. All the early post-independence regimes sought to maintain the plantation economy, but while Haiti remained an important coffee producer, it inexorably became a country of peasant smallholders, unique in the Americas. The aspirations of its formerly enslaved masses were, at enormous cost, eventually realized.

At a time when colonial rule was almost unchallenged, and slavery and racial discrimination were normative in the Americas, the emergence of a black independent state became an object of inspiration and subdued pride for people of African descent, but was widely regarded as dangerous by governments and colonial elites, though the declaration of independence included an assurance that Haiti would not try to export its revolution. President Thomas Jefferson later imposed an embargo on US trade with Haiti that lasted four years, and Haitian ships were banned from British colonies until the 1840s, but the country was never commercially isolated. No other state accorded it diplomatic recognition, however, until France did so in 1825, at the price of a large indemnity. The United States and the Vatican did not establish official relations until the 1860s.

REPERCUSSIONS OF THE REVOLUTION

An inspiration for some, a nightmare for others, the Haitian Revolution seized international attention from its earliest days. It excited fear, greed, and admiration. At the first arrival of news of the 1791 slave revolt, slaves in neighboring Jamaica celebrated; the British stock market fell, while the Cuban planter Francisco Arango and the London *Times* each welcomed a lucrative opportunity for their nations. By the time Toussaint Louverture died in April 1803, biographies of him, both scurrilous and flattering, had appeared or were in press in eight different countries. Black militiamen in Rio de Janeiro donned cameo portraits of the former slave Dessalines only months after he had been crowned emperor. The international impact of the revolution was wide-ranging and diverse, but in many ways ambiguous and contradictory. It is therefore controversial.

Though it abruptly closed what had briefly become the largest single market for the Atlantic slave trade, the trade's volume scarcely declined in the 1790s from its all-time peak in the previous decade. The revolution liberated one-third of the Caribbean slave population definitively, and more than 40 percent if we include those temporarily freed in Guadeloupe and Guyane: in total, at least one in five American slaves. Yet, by a cruel irony, it also stimulated the growth of slavery elsewhere. By driving up the price of tropical products, and creating a diaspora of French colonists with slaves and capital, the destruction of Saint Domingue's plantations encouraged the spread of slavery to new frontiers, as well as reviving older slave economies. In the case of sugar, this effect did not last long; increasing world demand soon took over as the driver of expanding output, but Saint Domingue had so dominated the coffee market that its recovery took about two decades. The resulting crisis helped launch coffee production in Brazil, and the implantation of French exiles in eastern Cuba and the mountains of Jamaica was critical to the crop's take-off there.

In Cuba and especially Louisiana, black and white refugees also bequeathed durable cultural legacies, both French and French Creole. Francophone influences in nineteenth-century Trinidad and Puerto Rico, however, owed more to migrants from the Windward Isles than from Saint Domingue. More ephemeral in their presence and impact were the thousands of refugees who crowded into the seaboard cities of the eastern United States. Everywhere, however, the sight of the once wealthy reduced to destitution, and the stories told by them and their slaves, gave immediacy to newspaper accounts of the revolution. Governments feared the influence of black immigrants from French colonies and often tried to exclude them, usually without success. Alarmed by the French Revolution, Spain restricted immigration as early as May 1790.

The Haitian Revolution was a costly imperial disaster for France, Spain, and Britain, and it temporarily ended France's standing as a major colonial power. Their losses were, however, only a small part of those they suffered during the Revolutionary and Napoleonic Wars, and there were several other chapters in France's imperial decline during the century after 1715. Because the loss of Saint Domingue removed the rationale for France's recent re-acquisition of Louisiana, the revolution also helped bring about the Louisiana Purchase of 1803, which doubled the size of the United States, though it is highly uncertain if France could have kept the colony anyway in the face of British and US opposition.

Whether the Haitian Revolution helped change ideas about racial difference, or merely reinforced existing preconceptions, is not easy to determine. The revolution occurred at a critical juncture in European thought, when humanitarianism was gaining ground, but the beginnings of biological science were preparing the way for the so-called "scientific racism" of the nineteenth century. The epic struggle for Saint Domingue fed both sides of this debate. The spectacle of a people freeing itself from bondage, defeating the armies of three colonial powers, and establishing an independent state inspired many existing opponents of slavery and racial discrimination. Many more admired the abilities of Toussaint Louverture. Other commentators, however, found it easy to rationalize the successes of the Haitians, and a selective reporting of the revolution's numerous atrocities provided vivid propaganda for diatribes about civilization and barbarism. Moreover, the sharp divergence in mortality rates suffered by white and black soldiers in the tropics, which was highlighted by the conflict, may also have encouraged people to think in terms of immutable racial differences.

Similarly unclear is the Haitian Revolution's influence on subsequent changes in race relations. The abolition of institutionalized racial discrimination in most American colonies and the independent states of Latin America during the thirty years following Haitian independence might appear to owe something to the French precedent set in 1792, but there is little evidence of this; local circumstances amply explain each case. In contrast, the worsening position of free blacks in the Spanish Caribbean, especially the growing hostility to the black militia that emerged in the 1790s, doubtless owed something to Haitian-inspired fears, though it could also be explained simply by the expansion of the slave economy in these decades, especially as comparable developments had occurred in French and British colonies a century earlier. Even in Santo Domingo, where the Haitian Revolution had its most direct impact, the revolution's influence remains uncertain. Some attribute to massacres perpetrated by Haitian invaders in 1802 and 1805 a major role in generating the much-publicized antipathy between the two nations of Hispaniola. Some evidence, however, suggests this hostility was a later development. For Simón Bolívar, Haiti became a byword for anarchy. It evidently shaped his fear of *pardocracia* that caused him to execute his mixed-race comrades, Piar and Padilla, and it left him pessimistic about the likelihood of a race war in South America. Thomas Jefferson reacted similarly, though his pessimism clearly pre-dated the revolution. Through the nineteenth century, memories of the Haitian Revolution encouraged the development of black political activism, but also a pervasive fear among whites that caused intense resistance to it. Antonio Rebouças in Brazil, G. W. Gordon in Jamaica, and Antonio Maceo in Cuba were all frivolously accused of links with Haiti by their enemies; Bolívar called the mixed-race Mexican president Vicente Guerrero "a new Dessalines."

In the history of American slave resistance, the 1790s stand out as the decade of peak intensity, and over the next half-century rebellions and conspiracies were unusually numerous and large. This clustering was the product of several factors: the still massive influx of Africans; shrinking white populations; the unsettling influence of abolitionism; and the various revolutionary movements of the age. Several connections to the Haitian Revolution can be established, though they have often been exaggerated. As its ex-slave leaders opted for "a revolution in one country," which they announced in the declaration of independence, the revolution's contribution to slave rebellion elsewhere was very rarely a matter of direct assistance. An attempt by south-coast privateers to raise a rebellion in Maracaibo in 1799 was the chief exception. Far more common were revolts and conspiracies where insurgents drew inspiration from the revolution or from later events like the coronation of King Christophe in 1811. The most remarkable case was the conspiracy, begun soon after the coronation, in Havana by the free black woodworker José Antonio Aponte. He drew pictures of battle scenes and revolutionary leaders as a consciousness-raising exercise and also promised his followers help from Haiti. Such (spurious) promises featured in a half-dozen other plots and revolts, including a large rebellion on Curaçao in 1795, whose leader adopted the name of André Rigaud. A still larger category is that of conspiracies and rebellions that involved Francophone slaves or men of color, known or presumed to have come from Saint Domingue or Haiti. The 1811 insurrection in Louisiana led by the slave driver Charles Deslondes, which was the largest in North American history, is perhaps the best example.

Scholars who have claimed that the Haitian Revolution inspired Gabriel's conspiracy in Virginia (1800), the Christmas Rebellion in Jamaica (1831), and the Malê rising in Rio de Janeiro (1835), or the multi-class revolt in Grenada led by Julien Fédon (1795–96), have imagined the linkage rather than demonstrated its existence. This raises a question of methodology and epistemology. Since it is highly likely that participants in most of these events would have known at least something about the Haitian Revolution, some may feel it beyond question that the unprecedented success of black rebels in the French colony must have played a significant role in motivating resistance elsewhere. The historical record, however, reveals that there were other causal factors in these specific cases.

A similar issue arises with respect to the Haitian Revolution's impact on the abolition of slavery and the slave trade elsewhere. Before 1791, the antislavery movement in Europe had made next to no progress, and the only places in the Americas where slavery had been abolished were a few states in New England where it had been insignificant. A popular approach has therefore been to emphasize the Haitian Revolution's primordial position in the narrative of slavery's extirpation and to imply that its influence inevitably hovered over all subsequent developments, whether or not this can be demonstrated. The destruction of Saint Domingue, it is argued, showed the extreme danger of holding slaves and of importing more from Africa. Abolition and emancipation were necessary to avoid "another Haiti." Every new slave rebellion was a reminder of 1791 that progressively tarnished the image of slave-holders and caused governments to lose patience with them. In addition, the military successes of the Saint-Dominguan slaves inspired abolitionists and enhanced respect for blacks in general, so increasing the appeal of antislavery.[6]

Pro-slavery forces, too, however, used the Haitian Revolution in their propaganda. As noted above, it is moot whether white opinion was more impressed by the heroics of the black struggle than by its violence; it also turned slave-owners into sympathetic victims. Above all, the fact that most parts of the Americas increased their importation of enslaved Africans without any significant decline in slave prices during the revolution renders implausible the argument that attributes abolition to a sense of imminent

---

[6] Robin Blackburn, *The American Crucible: Slavery, Emancipation and Human Rights* (London, 2011), pp. 171–274.

peril. Yet, there is much to discuss. In the British case, the abolitionists' first, and short-lived, advance came in 1792 following a parliamentary debate in which the Saint Domingue uprising featured prominently. The antislavery movement then fell dormant for a dozen years, victim of a conservative reaction that the Haitian Revolution also helped stimulate. The revival of the movement in 1804 clearly owed something to the public alarm that accompanied Haitian independence. Yet, this alarm soon dissipated and seems to have played little part in the eventual abolition of the British slave trade in 1807. At the Cortes of Cádiz in 1811, and more generally in the Hispanic world, the perceived dangers of the Haitian example were commonly cited as reasons to end the slave trade and not to end slavery.[7]

In all, there were two important ways in which the Haitian Revolution made critical, if indirect, contributions to antislavery successes. First, by destroying France's status as a major colonial power, the revolution acted as an enabling factor in the voting of British abolition in 1807. It is hard to imagine Parliament ending the slave trade, if France had remained both a commercial and political rival, able to profit from Britain's losses. The same reasoning also applies, albeit with less force, to the British Emancipation Act of 1833, and perhaps also to the House of Commons vote in April 1792. The second important contribution concerns Simón Bolívar. During his long struggle to end Spanish colonial rule, Bolívar twice had to seek refuge in Haiti, where he received supplies, guns, and soldiers. In return, his host, President Alexandre Pétion, asked him to add slave emancipation to his political agenda. When Bolívar later began the dismantling of slavery in Venezuela, he certainly also had local reasons for doing so. Yet, without Haitian help, he might never have made a successful return to South America. Haiti thus made a major contribution to the decolonization of Spanish America, as well to ending slavery there.

However, if Haiti promoted decolonization on the mainland – and it additionally gave support to Francisco de Miranda's 1806 expedition and Francisco Mina's in 1816 – it also hindered it in the Spanish West Indies. One of the reasons Bolívar gave for refusing to attack Cuba was his fear of creating "another Haiti." As this view was widely shared by the Cuban elite, it goes far in explaining their grudging acceptance of Spanish rule for another half-century. The Dominican Republic constitutes a different sort of case. In 1821, the Republic of Haiti annexed its Spanish-speaking neighbor and abolished slavery there, as well as the national independence its inhabitants had declared a few weeks before, ironically as Haití Español.

---

[7] For diverse viewpoints, see Seymour Drescher and Pieter C. Emmer (eds.), *Who Abolished Slavery? Slave Revolts and Abolitionism: A Debate with João Pedro Marques* (New York, 2010); and David Geggus (ed.), *The Impact of the Haitian Revolution in the Atlantic World* (Columbia, SC, 2001).

Finally, the revolution inspired a good deal of imaginative literature; the first plays, poems, and novels about it were produced while it was still in progress. Most of these early pieces were inconsequential, but a few were by notable writers. Victor Hugo's first published work, *Bug-Jargal* (1820) and Heinrich von Kleist's *Verlobung in St. Domingo* (1811) were rather superficial, but William Wordsworth's fine sonnet "To Toussaint L'Ouverture" managed to capture the depth of its subject.

A GUIDE TO FURTHER READING

Dubois, Laurent, *Avengers of the New World* (Cambridge, MA, 2004).

Gaffield, Julia (ed.), *The Haitian Declaration of Independence* (Charlottesville, VA, 2015).

Garrigus, John, *Before Haiti: Race and Citizenship in French Saint-Domingue* (New York, 2006).

Geggus, David, *Haitian Revolutionary Studies* (Bloomington, IN, 2002).

Geggus, David and Norman Fiering (eds.), *The World of the Haitian Revolution* (Bloomington, IN, 2009).

Girard, Philippe R., *The Slaves Who Defeated Napoleon: Toussaint L'Ouverture and the Haitian War of Independence, 1801–1804* (Tuscaloosa, AL, 2011).

Gómez, Alejandro, *Le Spectre de la révolution noire: L'impact de la Révolution haïtienne dans le monde atlantique, 1790–1886* (Rennes, 2013).

Piquet, Jean-Daniel, *L'Emancipation des Noirs dans la Révolution française (1789–1795)* (Paris, 2002).

Popkin, Jeremy, *"You Are All Free": The Haitian Revolution and the Abolition of Slavery* (Cambridge, 2010).

CHAPTER 15

SLAVERY AND ABOLITION IN ISLAMIC AFRICA,
1776–1905

RUDOLPH T. WARE III

INTRODUCTION: IRONIES OF SLAVERY AND ABOLITION

One of the terrible ironies of the nineteenth century is that the formal abolition of the European slave trade *out of* Africa led to the dramatic expansion of slavery *within* Africa. As Steven Feierman noted in a seminal essay a generation ago, this outcome was paradoxical on multiple levels:

The extension of the slave trade as a result of abolition is an irony in two senses: as the Oxford English Dictionary defines it, *irony*, is "a contradictory outcome of events as if in mockery of the promise and fitness of things"; it is also a drama whose inner meaning – for those who look back on events – is quite different from the outer meaning it had for those who were immediately concerned. We have not yet reached the bottom of the irony, in either sense of the term, because the "legitimate trade" that abolitionists wanted to substitute for the slave trade was usually a commerce in the products of slave labor ... many prominent abolitionists were quite conscious that they were asking for the local use of slaves who had previously been exported.[1]

"Legitimate commerce" was the preferred term of British imperialists to name the trades in African agricultural products that would replace – after American and British abolition of the North Atlantic slave trade in 1807 – the now illegitimate trade in human beings. England had dominated the slave trade during the eighteenth century, carrying at least 2.5 million slaves across the ocean. Over the course of the nineteenth century, other nations followed with successive abolitions of the slave trades and slavery, with Brazil and Cuba finally abolishing the institution only in the 1880s.

Yet, as efforts to end the slave trade accelerated in the early 1800s, many Europeans knew that African agriculture would only grow to meet new markets by utilizing slave labor more intensively than ever before. After centuries of providing slaves for export, many African political economies

---

[1] Steven Feierman, "A Century of Ironies in East Africa," in Philip Curtin, Steven Feierman, Leonard Thompson, and Jan Vansina, *African History from Earliest Times to Independence* (London, 1995), p. 353. Many thanks to Steven Feierman and Amir Syed for reading and providing feedback on earlier versions of this chapter.

centered on enslavement and had come to employ slaves domestically in increasingly significant ways. The decline and ultimate demise of external demand for enslaved Africans did not lead to the reduction of slavery within Africa.[2] Instead, as slaves became cheaper almost everywhere in Africa, more intensive and extensive uses of enslaved labor expanded. Slave plantations much like those in the areas around the Atlantic and Indian Oceans came to abound in sub-Saharan Africa, including in Islamic Africa.

In this chapter I reprise Feierman's framing of the ironies of slavery and abolition to explore the *history* of slavery in Islamic Africa over the course of the long nineteenth century. I also hope to shed light on the contested *historiography* of the period; metropolitan politicians, colonial administrators, and missionaries had important stakes in narrating slavery and abolition in Africa during the nineteenth century, especially among Muslims. They crafted facile stereotypes about "cruel Arab slavers" ravaging the continent, and imagined the oppression stretching into the endless future without the "civilizing" intervention of Christian Europe. Ending slavery in Muslim Africa played a special role in the imperial invectives of the nineteenth century, shaping how the "white man" imagined his "burden" of civilizing the darker races through colonization.[3]

There were dissenters. Some Europeans dared to remind their brethren that in ending the African slave trade, they were merely undoing their own handiwork. Others defended Islam against the charge of complicity with slaving: in 1884, orientalist G. W. Leitner countered British claims – used to justify colonial conquests in Africa – that slavery was "the inevitable consequence of Mohammedan government." His response bears repeating:

This is as great a libel on that religion as the assertion would be on Christianity, that it was in favour of slavery because Christ, although confronted by one of its cruellest [sic] forms in the Roman Empire, did not attempt to legislate, as Muhammad did, for its eventual abolition in this world, but merely promised spiritual freedom to the repentant servants of sin, whether bond or free.[4]

But these were the exceptions that proved the rule. Most European intellectuals wove Africa, Islam, and slavery together in a tightly bound rhetoric justifying colonial expansion.

Few modern historians are imperial apologists, but subtle echoes of these older discourses can still be heard in the literature on slavery in

[2] This is the basic thesis of the best synthetic treatment of the history of slavery in Africa, Paul Lovejoy's *Transformations in Slavery: A History of Slavery in Africa* (Cambridge, 2000), which builds sound empirical arguments on the theoretical base of two very different Marxist scholars, Walter Rodney and Claude Meillassoux.

[3] Ann E. McDougall, "Discourse and Distortion: Critical Reflections on the Historiography of the Saharan Slave Trade," *Revue d'Histoire Outre-Mer*, 336–7 (2002): 195–227.

[4] G. W. Leitner, *Muhammadanism* (Woking, 1889), p. 16.

Islamic Africa, and distorted images of slavery in nineteenth-century Islamic Africa have been projected anachronistically into the distant past. But these nineteenth-century dynamics were novel and distinct from earlier patterns of slavery, and reading history backward can lead to serious misperceptions. As we shall see, histories of slavery and abolition in America and Africa were not merely analogous; they were interconnected. The end of slavery in the United States led directly to massive slaving in the Nilotic Sudan and the development of slave-worked cotton plantations in Egypt. As I noted in a chapter for Volume III of this series, the high-volume slave trade in the Nile Corridor was largely a product of the nineteenth century, reaching as many as perhaps 5,000 sub-Saharan African slaves per year by the 1840s and 1850s. The collapse of US cotton exports during the Civil War created a huge market opportunity for Egyptian producers, and Ottoman slavers responded by pillaging the Sudan on an unprecedented scale, importing as many as 25,000 to 30,000 slaves per year in the early 1860s.[5] Nineteenth- and twentieth-century political struggles have led to a heavily racialized portrayal of a timeless and intensive slave trade between the Sudan and Egypt; however, this was largely an artifact of the very recent past, one tied, ironically, to the US Emancipation Proclamation.

People remember the last thing they see. Relatively recent nineteenth-century patterns of American slavery have deeply colored our perceptions of the institution as a whole. This was also the case in Africa, as the political struggles and social dynamics of slavery in the nineteenth century have overwhelmed what came before. Largely in response to the abolition of external slave trades, slavery within Africa expanded and acquired a distinctly modern and capitalist character. Plantation complexes, powerful discourses of race, and rigid social distinctions between slave and free became commonplace. This wholly modern phenomenon was the "traditional African" or "Islamic" slavery which colonialists sought – with varying levels of sincerity – to supplant.

In Islamic Africa, new slaveries were justified with ancient texts. African Muslims – like Muslims elsewhere – usually accepted the enslavement of some categories of non-Muslims, as well as the practice of keeping their descendants in slavery even after they converted to Islam. But in some parts of Islamic Africa – and this is a story forgotten in the self-congratulatory narratives of emancipatory Europe – Islamic ideals were used to *struggle against slavery* rather than to defend it. Throughout Islamic Africa, subalterns who sought to improve their lot, and some religious scholars, invoked the numerous calls to manumission and the fair and

---

[5] Kenneth M. Cuno, "African Slaves in 19th Century Rural Egypt," *International Journal of Middle East Studies*, 41 (2009): 186.

moral treatment of slaves in the Quran and the normative practice of the Prophet and his companions (*sunna*). But some forward-thinking scholars in West Africa had more radical readings of the Quran and *sunna*, challenging the slave trade and slavery itself as early as the 1770s. Indeed, it can be counted among the ironies of the period that African Muslims have been left out of the genealogies of modern abolitionism – glossed as white, European, and Christian – for as we shall see, some of the founders of the modern European abolitionist movements were aware of (and inspired by) their African counterparts.

The complex history of slavery in a region as vast as Islamic sub-Saharan Africa could never be adequately surveyed in a chapter of this length. Islamic Africa was a space that expanded dramatically over the course of the nineteenth century. In 1776, Islam was already the dominant religion over truly vast areas of sub-Saharan Africa: throughout much of the Sahel and Savanna regions of West Africa, the Nilotic Sudan, along the Red Sea and Indian Ocean coasts, and in the Comoros Islands. It was also the religion of a significant minority in many parts of equatorial Africa, as well as at the Cape of Good Hope. By the beginning of the twentieth century, Islam was virtually everywhere; it was present in every state of what was now a divided and colonized continent. What follows is a survey of the major historical dynamics in three distinct regions: Western Africa, East Africa, and, finally, the enslaved Muslim community in South Africa. North Africa and the Nilotic Sudan are treated in other chapters in this volume. For debates over the status of slavery in Islamic law, as well as patterns of female slavery, eunuchs, military slavery, some summary history of racial thought in Islam, and other questions about the institution of slavery and its historical evolution in Muslim African societies, I refer readers to my chapter in Volume III of the *Cambridge World History of Africa*, "Slavery in Islamic Africa, 1400–1800." Indeed, this present chapter should be seen largely as a companion piece to that earlier chapter, in that it carries forward into the nineteenth century much of the analysis, as well as updating and amplifying some its conclusions.

WESTERN AFRICA

As the eighteenth century came to a close, the Atlantic World was awash in slaves like no other time in its history, though still a small part of the global population of just under 1 billion. At least 6.5 million enslaved people, more than half the total volume of the Euro-American Slave Trade, were shipped across the Atlantic during the eighteenth century. Modernity was born. Atlantic societies, whether in Europe, the Americas, or Africa, grappled with the political, ethical, and religious implications of the world the slave trade had made. By the last quarter of the eighteenth century, a

signal issue had come to crystallize struggles over slavery, political authority, and religious legitimacy in Islamic Africa, as well as the widespread
enslavement of Muslims by Muslims. Although dominant interpretations
of Islamic law saw slavery as permissible, all agreed that Muslims were
forbidden from enslaving free Muslims. Since the late 1500s, however,
temporal authorities had flaunted the law as the Atlantic economy
expanded and the demand for consumer goods and slaves reached deep
into the Muslim societies of West Africa. Kings who called themselves
Muslims frequently captured and sold free Muslims – sometimes their
own subjects – in exchange for textiles, guns, tobacco, and rum. Resistance
to the enslavement of Muslims became an important avenue for expressing
a broader societal critique of the Atlantic political economy and the African
monarchs who supplied it with Muslim captives. The enslavement of
clerics in particular, people who had memorized and in a sense embodied
the Quran, often served to focus that socio-political unrest, contributing in
important ways to the development of powerful homegrown clerical
revolutionary movements from the Senegambian Coast to Lake Chad.[6]
Unfortunately, the chief irony of the period is that clerics' efforts to end
the enslavement of Muslims had unintended consequences too; quite
often, they led to more Muslims than ever being enslaved within Africa.

Islamic West Africa in the Age of Revolutions

These nineteenth-century movements, known collectively in the Africanist
historiography as the "West African Jihads," were the most significant
socio-political phenomena across the sub-region in the period. These were
revolutionary movements led by Muslim scholars, along with their disciples
and clients, which overthrew monarchical political authorities and replaced
them with distinct forms of clerical rule. In all of the major movements
there was a Fulbe (Fula-speaking or Fulani) ethnic element to the revolutions. The most famous was led by 'Uthman dan Fodio (d. 1817), which
led to the establishment of the so-called Sokoto Caliphate (in modern
Niger and Nigeria) at the beginning of the nineteenth century. In the
middle of the nineteenth century, al-Hajj 'Umar Tal (d. 1864) led a similar
movement, which profoundly affected much of modern Mali and Eastern
Senegal. For two generations, the historiography of these (and related)
movements have portrayed them as driven by progressive advances in the
"orthodoxy" of supposedly syncretistic African Muslims. As Africans came
to better understand Islam, we are told, they became increasingly militant

---

[6] The problem of the enslavement of Muslims and particularly clerics as people embodying the
book is addressed most fully in chapter 3 of my *The Walking Qur'an: Islamic Education, Embodied
Knowledge, and History in West Africa* (Chapel Hill, NC, 2014).

and eventually rose up to overthrow rulers who were guilty of religious mixing. Sometimes, Fulbe ethnic characteristics are used to explain a supposedly puritanical focus on religious orthodoxy, since British and French colonial administrators alike often classed Fula speakers (some of whom are relatively light-skinned) as "hamites" rather than "negroes" and attributed their alleged militancy and martial prowess to racial characteristics. They have also portrayed both movements as slaving movements, sometimes insinuating (and sometimes directly stating) that the jihads were little more than thinly veiled pretexts to wage war with the primary purpose of acquiring slaves. The first of these clerical movements has been the least well documented. This history is now being revised as a new generation of researchers works on the intellectual contents of Islamic movements in West Africa. Research into its dynamics help cast subsequent movements in quite a different light, revealing important antislavery characteristics common to each.[7]

Muslim Liberation Theologies

From 1776 until his death in 1806, Abdul-Qadir Kan led a revolution in the Senegal River Valley state of Fuuta Toro, seeking to end the Atlantic slave trade and to effectively end slavery as a social institution within the lands he controlled. This African abolition appears to have been largely successful during Kan's lifetime, though his rivals and political successors undid his revolution in the 1810s and 1820s, fully re-establishing and even extending the institution of slavery in Fuuta. Several of the larger revolutionary movements share elements of this trajectory: early leaders showed a deep concern with the illegal enslavement of Muslims, but the movements they authored soon developed contradictory dynamics. Ironically, they all ended up expanding rather than curtailing slavery. Indeed, as we shall see, the political economy of West Africa in the nineteenth century may have made it impossible to construct a durable political order without slaving. Ultimately, the revolutionary movements created states so central to the slaving economies of the region that by the end of the nineteenth century the idea that they had once contained abolitionist elements was all but unthinkable.

But Muslim liberation theologies were possible. Nineteenth-century scholars carefully pondered the legality and morality of slavery just as had some of their predecessors. Shaykh Muusa Kamara, a scholar from Fuuta Toro and moral inheritor of the abolitionist tradition of Abdul-Qadir Kan, was one example. He considered that the strong calls to

[7] See Paul E. Lovejoy, "Islam, Slavery, and Political Transformations in West Africa: Constraints on the Trans-Atlantic Slave Trade," *Revue d'Histoire Outre-Mer*, 336–7 (2002): 247–82.

manumission in the Quran and the *sunna* of the Prophet amounted to a de facto abolition: "I say that the Prophet ... had manumitted all the slaves whom he possessed. He did not die (God bless him and grant him peace) owning a single slave. He inspired a desire among the people to manumit slaves to the point where some would say that he was forcing them, that he was compelling them to do so. He would have a slave manumitted for a single hit or slap from his master."

Kamara was so convinced of the inherently abolitionist nature of the Quranic call and the Prophetic example that he saw the colonial abolition of slavery not only as the fulfillment of God's will, but also of the Prophet's wishes. The latter, he argued, avoided a direct abolition only out of forbearance: "I also say that the French have turned people away from sins with respect to God for that which concerns the rights of slaves as they have manumitted all the slaves found in their empires. No one any longer has property rights over another. All are equal in liberty ... [Freeing the slaves was his wish] but the intensity of his desire to be tolerant to the people prevented him from it."[8] Kamara was certainly influenced by European abolitionism, but the roots of such thinking ran deep in Senegambia.

Fuuta Toro and Senegambia

Around 1770, Sulayman Baal, a scholar, began a popular movement preaching against the hereditary rulers in Fuuta Toro, the *saltigis*, rulers who were selling their own subjects to Europeans and Saharans and allowing them to raid Fuuta for slaves. The proximate cause for Baal's discontent was a series of episodes where Quran reciters had been sold as slaves. Baal's movement eventually became a revolution as a multi-ethnic and international coalition of clerical lineages that had been politically marginal sought control of the state. The movement was progressively radicalized by the enslavement and assassination of clerics in Fuuta and in neighboring Wolof country. The clerics garnered many disciples of peasant and low-status origins, including the unfree *ceddo* military caste.

By 1775, the British governor of Senegal, Charles O'Hara, incited the Saharan slavers in massive warfare against the clerics, devastating the region and enslaving many thousands of Fuuta's Muslims within the span of a few months. Sulayman Baal, the father of this revolution, died in one of these battles and the revolution seemed doomed until Abdul-Qadir Kan, a

---

[8] Constance Hilliard, "Zuhur al-Basatin and Ta'rikh al-Turubbe: Some Legal and Ethical Aspects of Slavery in the Sudan as Seen in the Works of Shaykh Musa Kamara," in J. R. Willis (ed.), *Slaves and Slavery in Muslim Africa* (London, 1985), Vol. I, pp. 179–80. The translation is slightly amended for clarity.

Quran teacher and legal scholar living in a remote village in the far eastern portion of Fuuta, assumed leadership of the movement as its first *imam* (*Almaami* in the Fula dialect of the region). Almaami Abdul-Qadir Kan instituted a number of bold military moves – likely including an offer of freedom to the slaves of his enemies – and turned the tide against the Saharan slavers and the *saltigis*. This action had ancient precedent in Islamic religious practice; the Prophet offered freedom to the slaves of his enemies during the siege of Ta'if, and his example was likely imitated here.[9] Kan then forbade passage of European slavers through his territories on the Senegal River and overland. Finally, according to a number of contemporary sources, he offered liberty to any former slave who would recite a single verse of the Quran! Rather than using Muslim identity as a sword to enslave non-Muslims, this scholar of Islamic law instead used it as a shield to protect anyone against enslavement who would formally claim Muslim identity.

By the 1780s, details of this remarkable religiously inspired abolition reached Europe. The founder of the London Society for the Abolition of the Slave Trade, the Reverend Thomas Clarkson, in a 1789 publication sang the praises of the African Muslim ruler:

To the sovereigns of Europe the wise and virtuous Almammy sets ... [an] illustrious example in extirpating the commerce in the human race; and when we consider this amiable man as having been trained up in a land of slavery, and as having had in the introduction of such a revolution all the prejudices of education and custom to oppose; when we consider him again as sacrificing a part of his own revenue; as refusing the presents of Europeans; and as exposing himself in consequence of it to the vindictive ravages of the agents of the latter, he is certainly more to be respected than any of the sovereigns of Europe, inasmuch as he has made a much nobler sacrifice than they, and has done more for the causes of humanity, justice, liberty, and religion.[10]

Clarkson was not alone in acknowledging the antislavery content of the movement; the Almaami's stance against slavery was well known. It was documented by slave-ship captains, merchants, slavers, colonial administrators, European explorers, and others. Antoine Pruneau de Pommegorge, to name only one, confirmed that the Almaami had "forbidden pillages and the taking of any captives at all throughout his country, and finally, by other political (and at heart very humane) means, he has been able to repopulate his vast kingdom, attracting many peoples there, where they find security ... Thus here is a man who gives a lesson in humanity to other civilized peoples by forbidding in all of his states captivity and

---

[9] Martin Lings, *Muhammad: His Life Based on the Earliest Sources* (Rochester, NY, 1983), p. 320.
[10] Thomas Clarkson, *Letters on the Slave Trade, and the State of the Natives in Those Parts of Africa, Which Are Contiguous to Fort St. Lewis and Goree* (London, 1791), p. 80.

oppression."[11] In Kan's Fuuta Toro, according to the testimony of slavers, there were no slaves for purchase. Instead, primary agricultural products were traded and Fuuta's merchants paid with cash for the goods they desired.[12] Indeed, the final British Lieutenant Governor of Senegambia mentioned that after the British abolition of the slave trade in 1807, relations with the people of Fuuta Toro had improved dramatically: "It may be here necessary to remark that there has been greater facility in negociating [sic] with Almamy and less probability of again having disputes with him in consequence of the abolition of the Slave Trade, *a commerce which that Prince always opposed as being contrary to the Laws of his Religion*, and the means through which several of his subjects, followers of the Prophet, were led into captivity."[13]

Unfortunately, Kan's abolition was short-lived. The combined forces of the Atlantic slave trade made war against him. A coalition of Muslim clerics, deposed *saltigis*, French slavers, and non-Muslim Bambara ended the Almaami's rule. He was assassinated in 1806, and his revolution died with him. No Almaami ruled for more than two consecutive years thereafter, and within a generation the clerical class of Fuuta Toro (known collectively as Tooroɓɓe) became a slave-owning aristocracy ruling decentralized fiefdoms. Previously, anyone who memorized the Quran and studied the sciences could become a cleric; hereafter the Tooroɓɓe frequently denied Islamic education to members of other lineages in order to maintain social supremacy. Though this clerisy emerged as a social group largely by taking a position against slavery, a generation later they retreated to the commonly held position endorsing the legality of enslaving non-Muslims, and keeping Muslims in bondage as long as they had been bought or captured before converting. Worse still, now that clerics were in positions of political authority in Fuuta Toro, few independent clerics remained who were capable of formulating autonomous critiques of state power, one of the basic social functions of clerics for centuries in West Africa.

The situation in Fuuta Jallon (another Fulbe polity in modern Guinea) was similar to the situation in the Senegal River Valley after the assassination of the Almaami. The Imams of Fuuta Jallon (who had never experimented with abolition) had reacted to British abolition negatively, claiming that the Quran guaranteed them the right to keep slaves and that if the British abolition of slavery in their colony of Sierra Leone proceeded

[11] Antoine Pruneau Pommegorge, *Description de la Nigritie* (Amsterdam, 1789), p. 74.
[12] Pierre-Raymond de Brisson, *Relation des voyages de Saugnier à la côte d'Afrique, à Maroc, au Sénégal, à Gorée, à Galam* (Paris, 1799), p. 264.
[13] British National Archives, Kew (hereafter BNA), CO 267/29, January 1, 1811: "Answers to the Questions Proposed to the Lieutenant Colonel Maxwell," Answer 36.

that it would do irreparable social and spiritual harm to their society.[14] Sierra Leone, and its capital, Freetown, which had been founded by Diaspora Africans in the 1780s, became a Crown Colony in 1808 and played an important role in the British effort to police the slave trade. It was the site for repatriating the so-called "recaptive" Africans who were confiscated from slaving vessels. Sierra Leone served as a beacon drawing enslaved persons away from bondage in neighboring African societies and the Imams of Fuuta Jallon were concerned that the proximity of such a site would undermine their social control. They also feared the collapse of their whole economic system, since Fuuta Jallon had relied on selling non-Muslim slaves to the Europeans (or putting them to work at home) as the basis of its economy for the whole of the eighteenth century.

Sokoto and the Central Sudan

Fifteen hundred miles to the east, another Fulbe community initiated dramatic changes affecting populations much larger than those in Senegambia. By 1780, the Atlantic slave trade had become a major factor in the Yoruba and Hausa regions of what is now Northern Nigeria and Niger. Many Hausa Muslims were enslaved and sold on the Atlantic coast and, like the *ceddo* in Senegambia, the Yoruba warlords brokering coastal trade retained some as a military caste. 'Uthman dan Fodio – a scholar of Fulbe origin and a Sufi of the Qadiriyya order – began preaching against the Hausa nobility in the late 1780s. From the clerical village of Degel, neighboring the Hausa sultanate of Gobir, he openly criticized the religious laxity of the Hausa rulers who were selling free Muslims for Atlantic trade goods. Shaykh 'Uthman's critique swelled the size of his community, and skirmishes eventually broke out in the 1790s. The Shaykh declared his jihad only after the sultan of Gobir sold 300 Quran reciters as slaves instead of ransoming them. Here, again, the enslavement of Muslims (and clerics in particular) served as the proximate cause for transformative political upheaval.

The subsequent revolution, beginning in 1804, transformed the region as beleaguered peasants and many Fulbe flocked to Dan Fodio's party. To develop the legal justification for what he considered to be a jihad, Dan Fodio, a consummate scholar of the Islamic religious sciences, drew on the puritanical writings of a radical (and somewhat marginal) fifteenth-century North African scholar, Abdul-Karim al-Maghili.[15] Adapting al-Maghili's arguments allowed Dan Fodio to justify his claims of "jihad" against Hausa

[14] BNA, CO 268/8, Letters from the Imam of Foota Jalloo (1810).
[15] See John O. Hunwick, *Sharī'a in Songhay: The Replies of al-Maghīlī to the Questions of Askia al-Ḥtjj Muḥammad* (Oxford, 1985) for a translation of some of Maghili's writings.

rulers. The latter, he claimed, had put themselves beyond the fold of Islam, making them a group of organized apostates. Though Dan Fodio had been openly critical of the Hausa rulers selling Muslims, this juridical choice made all Hausa Muslims who supported the royalty targets for captivity and enslavement.

While spirit possession cults known as *bori* were present in Hausaland, virtually all Hausa had professed Islam since the sixteenth century if not before. They had been recognized by the sixteenth-century scholar Ahmad Baba as a Muslim people against whom jihad and enslavement were forbidden. Sokoto held that they were enemies of the religion and enslavable, but Shaykh 'Uthman – like Almaami Abdul-Qadir – offered freedom to the slaves of his enemies. This stratagem has drawn little attention from historians, but the appeal must have been obvious to the slaves of Hausaland: if the revolution was successful, low-status individuals who fled the Hausa sultanates to join Dan Fodio might even become owners of their erstwhile masters. This was likely an important reason for the momentum of the revolution quickly becoming irresistible. This was a revolution in the fullest sense of the word; a total inversion of the social order was being made possible. Gobir was toppled in short order and the Sokoto eventually subsumed even the older, larger, and more populous Hausa states of Kano and Katsina. One of 'Uthman's sons and principal generals, Muhammad Bello, established the state's new capital at Sokoto in 1809.

There was an ethnic element as well: unlettered Fulani participated avidly (and avariciously) in the conquests and subsequent enslavements. Shaykh 'Uthman himself strongly criticized this, but proved powerless to stop it. In one of his jihad-era Hausa poems he writes: "And one who enslaves a freeman, he shall suffer chastisement/The Fire will enslave him be sure of that ... When we conquer a town, and commit injustice/Then truly there is no good in us/Some there are among us who do it constantly."[16] Scholars of Bornu, an ancient Islamic polity in the Lake Chad region, roundly criticized the slaving excesses. Though the people of Bornu were likely responsible for spreading Islam to Hausaland in the first place, they nonetheless became a target of the Sokoto "jihad" in 1808 to 1809. Bornu organized an effective defense, but many Muslim and non-Muslim polities were not so fortunate. The Sokoto conquests produced unprecedented numbers of captives, transforming the region. All of the Hausa city-states had significant slave populations by the last quarter of the nineteenth century.

[16] Mervyn Hiskett translates this in "Enslavement, Slavery and Attitudes Towards the Legally Enslavable in Hausa Islamic Literature," in Willis (ed.), *Slaves and Slavery*, Vol. I, p. 121.

Asma' bint 'Uthman b. Fudi (1793–1864), or Nana Asma'u, was one of the Shaykh's daughters and one of Sokoto's most important intellectuals. She was a principal architect of the new moral order. Asma'u authored scores of original works and translations in Arabic, Hausa, Fula, and Tamasheq. She was an unusually gifted poet, capable of using all the traditional Arabic meters, as well as those of the African languages of the region, to communicate artfully. She was also an engaged scholar, forming cadres of female teachers known as *jajis* who extended Islamic education in Sokoto.[17] Her social and scholarly accomplishments speak for themselves, but Asma'u also played a major role in justifying the Sokoto state and the role of slavery within it. Asma'u's *jajis* targeted enslaved or recently freed Hausa women, many of whom had been distributed as spoils of war to the soldiers who fought to establish the Sokoto state. Her writings and teachings sought to draw them away from *bori* cults that were (and remain) common to many of the Muslim societies of Africa and the Middle East. Asma'u embodies the successes and contradictions of Islam and slavery in Sokoto. Women found avenues to Islamic education and social dignity through following her teachings and her inspiring example, yet few other intellectuals were more central to justifying a political hierarchy that reduced tens (and perhaps hundreds) of thousands of freemen and freewomen to slavery over the course of the nineteenth century.

Al-Hajj 'Umar and the Greater Niger Bend

'Umar Tal was a son of Fuuta Toro and an heir to the revolutionary tradition of Sokoto. His story links together both of these revolutionary movements in time and space, and like his predecessors, Tal's movement had antislavery elements at its outset, but ironically ended up producing Muslim slaves in significant numbers. Tal was born in the small village of Halwar in Fuuta Toro in 1797 during the rule of Abdul-Qadir Kan. His childhood encompassed the final years of the Almaami's reign and the first years after his assassination. Fuuta became a weak and divided state thereafter, and Fuuta's Muslims were nearly as vulnerable to enslavement as they had been before the revolution. Bambara slavers frequently raided Fuuta Toro, especially its eastern regions. The nineteenth-century history of Fuuta abounds especially with stories of women who were victims of kidnappings by Saharans and Bambara. Tal's formative years were marked by insecurity and upheaval. In oral history, he is sometimes represented as a spiritual successor to Kan and the protector of Fuuta's Muslims, and Tal may have framed some of his own political and religious aspirations in

---

[17] For a more thorough (and favorable) view of Asma'u's impact, see Beverly Mack and Jean Boyd, *One Woman's Jihad: Nana Asma'u, Scholar and Scribe* (Bloomington, IN, 2000).

these terms. Like most members of the clerical class in the region, Tal memorized the Quran early in life and began advanced study of the traditional religious sciences, including law, theology, Sufism, rhetoric, and logic, as well as Arabic grammar and morphology. Like many West Africans of the pre-colonial period, he pursued knowledge through peripatetic circles in West Africa, and then moved beyond them to combine itinerant study with pilgrimage to the holy cities of Islam.[18]

En route to Mecca in the 1820s, he passed through Sokoto and found the conflict smoldering between Sokoto and Bornu. In his writings, he sharply condemned political violence between Muslims and he hoped to help resolve the conflict, but his haste to complete his pilgrimage prevented him from doing so. When he returned in the 1830s, he had been made caliph of the Tijaniyya Sufi order for all of sub-Saharan Africa by one of the founder's first disciples. Armed with significant intellectual and spiritual authority, Tal took up residence in Sokoto for an extended period under the patronage of Muhammad Bello, ultimately marrying one of Bello's daughters. It was during this time that Tal gathered a great deal of wealth, political clients, and some slaves. It appears that he was considered a potential political heir to Muhammad Bello before the rigidly hereditary nature of the Sokoto political class became firm. Tal also claims – and there is little contemporary reason to doubt it – that he initiated Muhammad Bello into the Tijaniyya Sufi order during his time in Sokoto. The Sokoto elite would ultimately deny that Bello ever "converted" to the Tijaniyya as they made Qadiri identity a key component of belonging in the Sokoto state over the course of the nineteenth century when inter-Sufi polemics increased in importance.

Al-Hajj 'Umar was one of the main reasons that bitter disputes between Qadiris and Tijanis marked much of the nineteenth-century history of the region. Wherever Tal travelled, he spread the Tijaniyya *tariqa*, or Sufi way. For Tal, and most scholars in the Tijaniyya, initiation into the order precluded following any other Sufi paths. This was a novel position in West Africa, where scholars routinely received initiations into multiple Sufi orders in order to strive for spiritual perfection. Tal spread the order and its doctrines of exclusivity from Sokoto in the east to Fuuta Jallon in the south, and finally to his homeland of Fuuta Toro from the 1830s until his death in 1864. In the 1840s, Tal began building a small polity in Dinguiray, a village in what is now Northern Guinea. At this stage, it could hardly be qualified as a state, being composed mainly of Tal's disciples, clients, and, it seems, some slaves. It appears that Tal was critical of the Fulbe elite in Fuuta Jallon

---

[18] This section draws on Amir Syed's doctoral dissertation: "al-Hajj Umar Tal and the Realm of the Written: Mastery, Mobility, and Materiality in 19th Century Islam" (University of Michigan, Interdisciplinary Program in Anthropology and History, forthcoming).

in this period for selling slaves to Christians, and he built his clerical community in the interstices of the established Fulbe and Mandingo states in the region. By the mid-1850s, Tal may have been positioning himself to become the Almaami of his homeland in Fuuta Toro. Much of what happened in this period remains unclear. After enjoying good relations with the French, it is said that he ultimately ran afoul of the newly expansionist French colonial state based at the mouth of the Senegal River. Ultimately, Tal called on the population of Fuuta Toro to migrate away from the coast and follow him to the interior as he constructed a new Islamic polity away from French hegemony.

To achieve his vision of a new political order, Tal targeted the traditional enemies of the Fuutanke, the non-Muslim Bambara kingdoms of Kaarta and later Segu, which lay to the east. Many heeded his call for migration and jihad, perhaps motivated by the prospect of open war against a traditional enemy that had raided Fuuta for slaves for generations.[19] As in the expansion of Sokoto, some pastoral Fulbe seem to have participated mainly to take slaves and booty. Though Tal was at pains to explain his newfound interest in statecraft after many of his early writings stressed traditional Sufi themes of pious distance from power, he likely expected his war against the Bambara to be uncontroversial for most of the region's Muslim intelligentsia. He was wrong. The Jakhanke, a set of pacifist clerical lineages with predominantly Soninke and Mandingo origins, were openly critical of what must have looked to them like naked Fulbe political ambition, and many chose to migrate from the region. For centuries, Jakhanke clerics were welcome even in non-Muslim polities due to their reputation for religious tolerance and their strict abstinence from explicitly political matters.

But the greater resistance to 'Umar's political activities came from a Fulbe state in the Masina (a western floodplain of the Niger) led by Ahmadu Lobbo III. The Diina state, with its capital at Hamdullahi, had been founded in the early years of the nineteenth century by Fulbe-speaking Muslims, but when Tal declared war against Kaarta and Segu, Ahmadu Lobbo claimed these kingdoms as his protectorates. Tal outlined his perspective on the conflict in a detailed treatise, and slavery played an important role in his argument: it was impossible, he argued, that a Muslim state could be the political ally of a non-Muslim state when the latter was involved in enslaving Muslims.[20] Some of the scholars of the

---

[19] On the migration and its aftermath, see John H. Hanson, *Migration, Jihad, and Muslim Authority in West Africa: The Futanke Colonies in Karta* (Bloomington, IN, 1996).

[20] See Sidi Mohamed Mahibou and Jean Louis Triaud (trans. and eds.), *Voila ce qui est arrive: Bayân mâ waqa'a d'al-Hâgg 'Umar al-Fûtî: plaidoyer pour une guerre sainte en Afrique de l'Ouest au XIXe siècle* (Paris, 1983).

Masina sought to make peace with Tal, but a prominent Qadiri from Timbuktu fanned the flames. Ahmad al-Bakkay, a scholar claiming Arab descent, referred to Tal as a heretic in polemical assaults against Tijani doctrines. He also sought to position himself as the racial superior of both Lobbo and Tal, referring to the latter as "an ignorant black," and suggesting that the former should accede to his own superior religious knowledge. Al-Bakkay assured Ahmadu Lobbo that if he allowed 'Umar to conquer Segu, then Masina would be next, and then Timbuktu. Masina chose instead to fight. The ensuing conflict tore apart the region of the inland Niger Delta in the mid nineteenth century and produced many captives on both sides, many of whom were enslaved and sold locally or into the Saharan trade.

As with all of conflicts arising from jihads across West Africa, the most powerful arm was the weapon of *takfir*, or excommunication. Literally meaning "to accuse of unbelief," takfir has been generally discouraged throughout Muslim history, in part due to many reported sayings of the Prophet which are best paraphrased as follows: "if a Muslim calls his brother an unbeliever it is true of one of them." In other words, indulging in accusations of unbelief is itself a form of unbelief. Whatever the spiritual risks of condemning practicing Muslims, the tactic was used in virtually all of the intra-Muslim conflicts in nineteenth-century West Africa. It was much less common in earlier eras when religious scholars like Ahmad Baba and others tended to craft capacious definitions of Muslim identity to protect free Muslims from victimizing one another with political violence and enslavement. The widespread use of takfir in the nineteenth century has an intellectual history to be sure, but stepping back from the individual cases and their intellectual justifications, the overall pattern is clear. Accusing political rivals of unbelief, using the dominant interpretations of Islamic law of the time, made their persons and property (including women and children) licit as booty of war. When Muslim parties clashed militarily without the formal denunciation of takfir, enslavement and confiscation of goods were forbidden on both sides. Captives could only be taken among the combatants, and they were to be ransomed rather than sold. The new economic logic of the nineteenth century, where local slavery was expanding everywhere within Africa, fueled such conflicts. Guns, horses, slave laborers; all of these things could be acquired cheaply and easily through slaving and slave-trading. Takfir transformed Muslim enemies into saleable assets. All of this unfolded against the backdrop of the Euro-American slave trade in the Atlantic. By the early nineteenth century, the slave trade had eroded long-established political entities, creating a host of unstable client states. The end of the external demand created a fractured political situation which opened West Africa up to chaos. Muslim clerics – among others – tried to create stability and order in a very unstable world. Here, as elsewhere in Africa, their actions produced so many unexpected, ironic outcomes precisely because the world they lived in had been turned upside down rapidly.

After the "Jihads"

A number of smaller "jihad" movements convulsed West Africa in the second half of the nineteenth century, so many that they could not be adequately summarized here. But nearly all of them involved mutual takfir, which made the taking of slaves licit according to conservative interpretations. The very ubiquity of jihad both reflected and augmented the increasing tendency toward slave exploitation in nineteenth-century Islamic West Africa. More than cash value, slavery had inestimable political value during this period. It was all but impossible to acquire a military apparatus (soldiers, guns, horses, ammunition, and a secure food source for a standing army) without expansive slaving. As Martin Klein has noted, the automatic weapons revolution in Europe in the second half of the nineteenth century meant that many rifles flooded African markets:

With the new weapons, military units with no social bases could dominate large areas, and those with a social base could build empires ... [but] unlike muskets which could be charged with any projectile, the new weapons used bullets and shells tooled to fit ... [Those] who competed for power had little choice but to seek superior weapons and learn how to use them. In areas close to the coast, cash crops [sometimes cultivated with slave labor] facilitated rearmament. In the interior, however, that option was often not available ... State builders like Umar [Tal] ... could always sell slaves and use the revenue to pay for new weapons. As a result, the new state builders all became proficient slavers, more proficient than any eighteenth-century slaving state.[21]

Abolition and military modernization came together to lead to escalating violence in West Africa. Offshoots of the main movements, as well as other independent "jihads," evolved into significant military movements, which, in many places, enabled armed African resistance to European imperialism. This pattern first appeared in the battles between 'Umar Tal and the French in the 1850s, and as the pace of mainland European colonization quickened in the 1880s, jihadi states often provided the military resistance to occupation. The Hausa emirates of Sokoto offered significant military resistance to the establishment of the British colonial state in Nigeria, but as the inevitability of conquest became clear, some of the Muslim elite

---

[21] Martin Klein, *Slavery and Colonial Rule in French West Africa* (Cambridge, 1998), p. 43.

migrated to the Sudan and to the Arabian Peninsula. Most of the Sokoto elite, however, was incorporated into the colonial state as the model of "native administration." Under Frederick Lugard, Sokoto famously became the laboratory for the British policy of "indirect rule" through African elites in the early twentieth century. Rule through the Hausa and Fulani elite proved so expedient that it was extended to areas that had never been part of Sokoto; for example, the British completed Sokoto's century-old failed conquest of Bornu when they annexed the region.

Colonial rule set into motion two contradictory tendencies with respect to so-called "Muslim slavery." The first was the formal legal abolition of slavery that colonial states were all but required to implement as the fulfillment of their *civilizing mission* in Africa. But the second was that colonial states in West Africa (whether British, French, or Portuguese) depended heavily on local hierarchies, which had never before been so closely tied to slavery. This generated tension, contradiction, and irony in colonial administrations. There were, at different times, tangible metropolitan incentives to downplay or exaggerate the importance of slavery in West Africa's Muslim societies. Colonial census data, collected with wholly unscientific methods and in politically charged contexts, often gave wild, speculative estimates of slave populations that amounted to one-third, one-half, or sometimes three-quarters of the population. It is all but impossible to assess the accuracy of such claims. But it is clear that by the end of the nineteenth century, there were many enslaved persons in the densely populated Muslim areas from Senegal to Nigeria. As abolition was effected in the early years of the twentieth century, they almost always focused primarily (or exclusively) on visible practices of slaving and slave-trading, leaving slavery itself largely unchallenged.

But even this half-hearted commitment to emancipation created a space within which the enslaved could make claims. Many sought fuller participation in Muslim institutions in part as a way to have their dignity and humanity acknowledged by the societies that held them in bondage, but also because quite often the enslaved – though perhaps ethnically other – came from Muslim backgrounds to begin with. This was a gendered phenomenon. In Sokoto and its hinterland, where female seclusion was more common than elsewhere in West Africa, low-status women increasingly chose veiling and seclusion in part to have their femininity and virtue acknowledged in local terms.[22] Demand for Quran schooling and other forms of Islamic education soared in the last years of the nineteenth century and into the twentieth, especially, perhaps,

---

[22] See Barbara Cooper, "Reflections on Slavery, Female Seclusion, and Female Labor in the Maradi Region of Niger in the Nineteenth and Twentieth Centuries," *Journal of African History*, 35 (1994): 61–78.

among girls of low-status and slave backgrounds.[23] Some – though certainly not all – Sufi movements now gave new expression to clerical ambivalence about slavery and sought to "democratize" access to Islam and Islamic knowledge. In the last years of the nineteenth century and the first years of the twentieth, this group certainly included several branches of the Tijaniyya Sufi order, including the communities of al-Hajj Malik Sy and al-Hajj Abdullahi Niasse in Senegal and the communities of Shaykh Hamallah in Nioro and Yacouba Sylla in Mali, Southern Mauritania, and Ivory Coast.

The Muridiyya Sufi movement in Senegal also exemplified this new tendency to emphasize the equality of believers before God, and the refutation of the legacy of "jihad." As a young man, a decade before founding the Muridiyya, Ahmadu Bamba Mbacké expressed clear dismay at a series of political conflicts in Senegambia in the 1870s that pitted Muslims against one another and resulted in the enslavement of free people. Apparently, the ironies of wars of liberation ending in increased slavery were not lost on Bamba. He developed a positive philosophy of non-violence and radical disengagement from the political sphere, but he also condemned slavery itself. According to the oral tradition, a zealous disciple once came offering the gift of a slave to consecrate his submission to Bamba's spiritual authority. The response attributed to Bamba highlights the prominent (though not dominant) strand of theologically inspired antislavery thought that ran through West Africa in the long nineteenth century: "If you own him, then you own me, because he and I have the same Master."

EASTERN AFRICA

In the last quarter of the eighteenth century, the dramatic expansion in the international trade in African slaves stimulated the development of a slaving economy in East Africa. Before this, slavery seems to have been generally marginal to the economic, social, and political life of the Swahili coast. It also may have been largely a fluid social institution that allowed for relatively free mobility from slave to client status. In the interior, few social institutions akin to slavery existed at all. For centuries, the Bantu-speaking peoples of the coast (who adopted Islam as early as the eighth century CE) had enjoyed relatively peaceful relations with their non-Muslim neighbors in the hinterland away from the coast. Those Swahili fishing towns and trading cities did have slavery before the nineteenth century, but few of their slaves were from the East African interior. Two

---

[23] See Rudolph Ware, *The Walking Qur'an*, esp. chs 3 and 4, for the full articulation of this argument.

relatively small (and interrelated) slave trades had existed on the East African coast before the late eighteenth century, and they now began to expand to meet unprecedented international demand for slaves: the first was the Swahili and Comorian-operated trade which brought Malagasy slaves from Central Madagascar to markets in the Comoros Islands and the Arabian Peninsula. The second was a Portuguese-operated trade in Mozambique that dealt in Malagasy slaves, but also acquired slaves through slaving and trading on the East African mainland. Some of these slaves were kept in East Africa, others were sold into the Atlantic trade, and still others were sold in the Indian Ocean Islands to feed the burgeoning plantation economy developing in the Mascarene Islands (especially Maur- itius and Réunion) during the eighteenth century.[24]

The tremendous growth in the Caribbean-style plantation economy of these islands (here, too, sugar was the main crop) had profound effects on the Swahili coast at the end of the eighteenth century and into the nineteenth century. Cut off from the merchant transactions with Shona gold producers in Southern Africa by the expanding Portuguese colony of Mozambique, Swahili in the southernmost city-states (especially Kilwa) began to seek alternative trade goods, especially ivory in the last quarter of the eighteenth century. At roughly the same time, the French began to import increasingly large numbers of slaves to work plantations in the Mascarene Islands, and Kilwa became an important source. Kilwa's rulers promised 1,000 slaves a year in a 1776 treaty with France. To meet this new demand, Malagasy slaves were not enough, and it appears that the ancestors of the Yao people of Kilwa's hinterland began to take captives as well as tusks on their forays in search of elephants. The techniques and technologies of hunting men mirrored those needed to hunt beasts and a relatively robust trade developed fairly quickly. Concomitantly, local slavery began to develop at Kilwa so that perhaps 40 percent of Kilwa's workforce may have been slaves by the end of the nineteenth century.

Cloves and Slaves

These developments were just the light rain preceding the deluge. Over the course of the nineteenth century, older patterns of Swahili Islam, mercantilism, and slavery would undergo dramatic changes due to the emergence of a slave plantation complex directed by Omani Arabs and centered on the city of Zanzibar. The land of the "Zanj" or the land of the blacks was to become the center for the Oman economy in the

---

[24] See Thomas Vernet, "Slave Trade and Slavery on the Swahili Coast (1500–1750)," in B. A. Mirzai, I. M. Montana, and P. Lovejoy (eds.), *Slavery, Islam and Diaspora* (Trenton, NJ, 2009), pp. 37–76.

nineteenth century. By the 1770s, Omani Arabs and some Swahili speakers had significant numbers of slaves who were used mainly in grain cultivation at Zanzibar and also on Pemba Island to the north.[25] The introduction of cloves at Zanzibar in the first decades of the nineteenth century transformed this essentially non-capitalist slave system into a Caribbean-style plantation complex. Once a closely guarded agricultural secret grown only in Eastern Indonesia, clove seeds were introduced into the Mascarene Islands in the last quarter of the eighteenth century and in the early years of the nineteenth century they were brought to Zanzibar.

Omani Arabs observed the French plantation complex in the Mascarenes directly and sought to reproduce it in Zanzibar, experimenting first with sugar and other cash crops in the first decades of the nineteenth century. But ironically it was the sharp drop in slave prices following successive stages of abolition that made slave plantations producing cloves profitable. The Treaty of 1822 abolished the slave trade from Omani-controlled East Africa to any European lands, including the Mascarenes, and slave prices dropped in cash value to half of what they had been in the 1780s. This led directly to the dramatic expansion of slavery in Zanzibar and all Omani-controlled regions. The Sultan of Oman, Seyyid Sa'îd, appropriated and purchased the plantations of some of the first Omani clove planters and made himself the largest stakeholder in the coast's slave-based economy. The commerce became so central to the Omani political economy that the Sultan moved his capital to East Africa in the 1840s. A later, 1847 treaty forbade the overseas export of slaves altogether and this led to another collapse in the price of slaves and a concomitant expansion in the use of slave labor in Zanzibar. While the Omani sultanate was heavily involved in this clove-exporting slave economy, Omani and Swahili merchants also owned plantations with hundreds, and sometimes over a thousand, slaves each. After about 1850, slaves came to be used more intensively on the mainland as well as on coastal islands, and were increasingly put to work in grain farming rather than just in cash-crop cultivation. In the 1870s, the slave trade across the Indian Ocean was abolished and, predictably, slave prices collapsed again, but this time clove prices collapsed as well, casting the economy into a crisis for much of the next two decades. The slave population at the island of Zanzibar swelled steadily from about 15,000 in 1820 to over 100,000 in 1870. The island needed a constant supply of slaves as both mortality and desertion rates were high.

---

[25] See Thomas Vernet, "East Africa: Slave Migrations," in Immanuel Ness (ed.), *The Encyclopedia of Global Human Migration* (Malden, 2013), Vol. 3, pp. 1283–90.

Struggles over Belonging: Slave Life at the Coast

The fundamental struggle for the enslaved individuals who survived life at the coast was how to move from belonging to a coastal family to belonging *in* a coastal family. This was a kind of social mobility that could not be accomplished without first accepting Islam and attempting to acquire the rudiments of Muslim education. As in West Africa, Islamic education and Sufi orders became primary avenues for former slaves to claim full participation in coastal society. Here, the Qadiriyya was particularly important in this respect. Socially and religiously, the Arab presence at the coast was not homogeneous. The Omanis occupied a dominant political position vis-à-vis the Swahili, but also in relation to other Arabs. Often, immigrants from the Hadramawt region in Yemen, and other Yemeni Arabs, came to the coast as porters or day laborers. Their social identities as Arabs and Muslims positioned them well for social mobility in coastal society, but did not guarantee it. Especially among the Hadramis, there were those who came from socially recognized Muslim clerical lineages (some were *shurafa* claiming descent from the Prophet) and developed their esteem largely as scholars and saints rather than as merchants. In the early twentieth century, some of these Ba 'Alawi Sufis were instrumental in responding to societal demand for Islamic education. They did not dissolve social distinctions as such – certainly, they believed that their status as shurafa marked them as distinct from formerly enslaved Africans – however, most had no significant investment in the Omani (and Ibadi) ruling class or its social hierarchies.[26]

The rapidly expanding power of a foreign, slave-owning class that saw itself as politically, religiously, and racially distinct from coastal African Muslims had profound long-term effects. Arab genealogies and cultural mores were conflated with Islam itself more than had ever previously been the case at the coast. And why not, since being "black" (*zanj* or *washenzi*) had come to mean slave, barbarian, and non-Muslim? *Waungwana* – the urbane civilizational ideal of Swahili Muslim society since perhaps the eleventh century CE – gave way, in the nineteenth century, to *ustaraabu*, being Arab. In previous centuries, slaves who converted to Islam were rarely (if ever) emancipated simply for having adopted the religion of their masters. However, slaves who became practicing Muslims were able to stake claims for participation in Muslim society, especially when they bore children for their owners or were successful in petty commerce. Some were ultimately able to achieve legal emancipation and a measure of autonomy, if not for themselves, then for their

---

[26] See Anne Bang, *Sufis and Scholars of the Sea: Family Networks in East Africa, 1860–1925* (London, 2003).

descendants. It was precisely this fluidity that allowed for the tensions within Swahili society to be transcended from time to time in earlier centuries. This became much more difficult in the nineteenth century. The new market-driven slavery produced one of the most pronounced forms of anti-black racism to exist in sub-Saharan Africa before the European colonialism of the late nineteenth century. Here, slavery was obviously not an "incorporative" institution which allowed for significant social mobility.[27]

One of the many indications of this is the presence of communities of escaped slaves that dotted the East African mainland serving as the hinterland to the Swahili coast. These communities, which paralleled Cimarròn, or Maroon, communities in the Americas, challenged slavery with flight, but reinforced it as well, insofar as the former slaves who founded such communities sometimes owned slaves themselves. Under the right circumstances, a non-Muslim from the mainland could accept Islam, learn Kiswahili, and, if successful in commerce, become an accepted member of coastal society. But for each one who did so, there may have been a hundred who died, overworked and penniless, far away from their homelands. For every woman who bore a child for her master and acquired a modicum of stability for herself and her child, there were many more who died childless after suffering sexual abuse, syphilis, and overwork. A native Swahili Muslim might develop advanced Arabic literacy, acquire wealth, and ultimately have their claims to Arab or Persian genealogies recognized by the broader society, or they might not. As in many other modern, race-based slave societies, money had the power to "whiten," but within limits.

The Extension of the Zanzibari Economy throughout East Africa

Over the course of the nineteenth century, the whole coastal plantation complex spilled over onto the African mainland. The Zanzibari trade spread inland with astonishing speed, bringing societies which had engaged in regional trade into international trading circuits in the most violent ways possible. From the 1850s until the 1890s, the East African interior, which had been essentially untouched by the slave trade, underwent in a few short decades the violent political transformations that West Africans had experienced over a span of several centuries. Societies that were raided one day became raiders the next. The pace of change was dizzying and its extent was staggering. The slaving and mercantile networks centered on Zanzibar reached into each and every East African

---

[27] That some earlier African slaveries were essentially incorporative was the basic argument of the classic volume edited by Suzanne Miers and Igor Kopytoff, *Slavery in Africa: Historical and Anthropological Perspectives* (Madison, WI, 1977).

society from the Horn of Africa to the Congo Basin. In the largely decentralized societies of the greater Congo Basin, the profound social dislocation of mainland societies may have made Islam an attractive option, even if it was the religion of the conquering slavers who destabilized society in the first place. Indeed, along with the prestige of the trade goods that may have given Islam a certain instrumental appeal, it was also associated with rapidly transforming consumption patterns in the East African interior. No single individual more embodied the dramatic transformation than Tippu Tip, a Swahili slave trader based at Zanzibar who may have owned as many as 10,000 slaves by the mid-1890s. In his heyday, his armed, mobile retainers carved out what is perhaps best described as a personal fiefdom of many thousands of square miles along the caravan routes that stretched from Zanzibar all the way into what is today the Democratic Republic of Congo.

In Buganda (in modern Uganda), traditional rulers experimented in mid-century with the development of an indigenous Muslim scholarly class and weighed the intellectual and practical benefits of receiving Swahili merchants and clerics or Protestant missionaries. Ultimately, they settled on the latter, though not before the economic and religious imprint of Muslim coastal society had left its mark on the region. In the Horn of Africa, dynamics of abolition and the development of the slaving complex also had important effects. Russian colonization of the Caucasus region in the early nineteenth century, combined with the Tsar's earlier abolitions of slavery, cut off a major source of slaves to the Ottoman region, leading to an increased importance of African slaves in the Empire's last decades. After the 1847 British treaty with Zanzibar, the highland Christian kingdom of Ethiopia became an important alternative source of slaves and demand increased there because slaves could be smuggled fairly easily across the Red Sea into the Arabian Peninsula and beyond.[28] While this was not a slave trade in Islamic Africa, the main markets for the slaves exported from the Christian kingdom were Muslim markets, and some of the slaves were produced via warfare and raiding conducted by the Muslim armies that dominated in the low-country hinterland of the Ethiopian kingdom. Among Somali speakers, slaving, slave trading, and slavery all expanded dramatically over the course of the nineteenth century as this region became a somewhat important secondary market for slaves. Slavery is not well documented in Somali society before the nineteenth century and seems to have been a minor social institution if and when it was present. Tens of thousands of enslaved East Africans were brought into Somali society over the course of the nineteenth century and they were

---

[28] Feierman, "A Century of Ironies," p. 353.

often exploited for agricultural production in a society that was making a transition from a largely pastoralist economy to one that incorporated more agriculture, including cash crops.

SOUTH AFRICA

In some ways, South Africa's history is quite different from the other regions, but in many ways the dynamics of slavery and abolition at the Cape of Good Hope at the beginning of the nineteenth century presaged developments on the rest of the continent at its end. In 1652, the Dutch East India Company (VOC) established a permanent settlement at the Cape, and the first slaves, including Ibrahim van Batavia, a Muslim brought from what is now Indonesia, arrived a year later. In the second half of the seventeenth century and over the course of the eighteenth, the Muslim community at the Cape expanded significantly. Unlike the other European slaving powers, Dutch imperialism looked east to the Indian Ocean rather than west to the Atlantic. Roughly a quarter of the enslaved were brought from South Asia, another quarter from the Malaysian/ Indonesian Archipelago, and a similar number from Madagascar and the Mascarenes. The remaining slaves were brought from sub-Saharan Africa, especially Portuguese Mozambique and West Africa. Islam was present in each of these regions and was the dominant religion in many parts of South Asia and the Archipelago. It is unsurprising then, that a significant, if unknown, minority of the enslaved population were Muslims. A number of prominent political exiles from the Archipelago and South Asia were sent to the Cape and were housed at Robben Island, among other places. Still larger numbers of Muslims were among the so-called *bandietten* or convicts who were captured and coerced into hard labor at the Cape, but had the advantage of acquiring freedom after serving their terms.

Racial thinking was obviously central to Dutch (and later British) imperialism at the Cape. The ancestors of today's Afrikaaner population sometimes framed their genocidal conflicts with the indigenous populations of South Africa as more than merely a religious and civilizational divide; often enough they referred to themselves as *mense*, men, and the people of color who surrounded them as *skepsels* or creatures. It is deeply ironic, then, that the first time that the Afrikaans language was written – as distinct from Dutch – it was written in the Arabic script by enslaved people of color at the Cape. Along with Afrikaans, Malay was an important language for the Muslim community at the Cape. Indeed, a vibrant vernacular tradition of Islamic instruction, and Arabic, Afrikaans, and Malay literacies were overlaid in the Cape's Muslim community. These vigorous communities of religious instruction in the late eighteenth and nineteenth centuries – in spite of serious obstacles – sit in sharp contrast to the frontier *trekboer* population among whom clergy, schools, and literacy were rare.

Muslims at the Cape were not only drawn from Indian Ocean regions: some were West African. Indeed, another of the hidden ironies of abolition is that the British policing of the international slave trade helped swell the Muslim community at the Cape. We have already seen that Freetown, Sierra Leone – which so dismayed the slave-owning Muslim aristocracy of Fuuta Jallon – was one of the places where African "recaptives" were settled. The Cape Colony was another. Here, however, Africans who were "recaptured" by the British were known as "Prize Negroes." In spite of obstacles of language and origin, these Muslims seem to have developed an *esprit de corps* and their own ethics regarding slavery. One Cape Imam, Ackmat, described the religious and ethical principles of Muslim slave ownership to a British 1824 to 1825 commission of inquiry in the following terms, which recall views held by some West African clerics:

No Mahometan can or ought to sell a Mahometan as a slave. If he buys a slave from a Christian, and that slave becomes a Mahometan, he is entitled to sit down as an equal in the family, and cannot afterwards be sold. He is allowed to sit down as an equal in the family if he chooses, or he remains connected with the family of the original owner. There may be persons calling themselves Mahometans who act in violation of this principle, but they are not acknowledged by us, and they forfeit their title to be considered Mahometan ... If a slave wished to be sold or to redeem his freedom and separate from his owner, he would be allowed to go out to earn the means of redeeming his freedom and separate from his owner ... but for the purchaser to sell the slave against his will would be considered a crime, as I have stated, and forfeit his title to be received as a Mahometan.[29]

At the Cape, as in many New World contexts, Islam provided a powerful oppositional identity to juxtapose to that of the slave-owning classes.[30] Certain Muslim institutions, especially schools, clearly played a major role in shaping that identity. After abolition in the 1830s, Sufi orders played critical roles as well, though more research is needed on their role during slavery.

---

[29] Papers relative to the condition and treatment of the native inhabitants of southern African within the Colony of Good Hope or beyond the frontier of that colony (issued March 18, 1835), p. 210, cited in Shamil Jeppie, "Leadership and Loyalties: The Imams of Nineteenth Century Colonial Cape Town, South Africa," *Journal of Religion in Africa*, 26 (1996): 153.

[30] This section draws primarily from John E. Mason, "'A Faith for Ourselves': Slavery, Sufism, and Conversion to Islam at the Cape," *South African Historical Journal*, 46 (2002): 3–24 and Robert Shell's "Islam in Southern Africa, 1652–1998," in Nehemia Levtzion and Randall Pouwels (eds.), *History of Islam in Africa* (Athens, OH, 2000).

CONCLUSION: THE LONG SHADOWS OF THE LONG
NINETEENTH CENTURY

The slave exodus of 1905 from Banamba, a town in the Middle Niger Valley, marks the end of the period under study here. In West Africa, this was the date when many thousands of formerly enslaved peoples left the societies that had held them in bondage and tried to return to their lost homelands. Similar, if less dramatic, repatriations occurred across Africa in the first years of the twentieth century as slavery's legal end came to be enforced. But most of the enslaved could not or did not go back to lives that had been taken away from them or their ancestors. Most struggled instead to salvage their dignity in the societies that had held them as slaves. As it had been at the Cape of Good Hope, Islam became a powerful framework for meaning and identity for many oppressed and formerly enslaved people. Throughout Muslim Africa, Islamic know-ledge and piety served as potential avenues for social dignity during the term of legal slavery, so it is no surprise that this dynamic continued after abolition. Indeed, one might argue that the extension of Islam in sub-Saharan Africa during the colonial period (long acknowledged as one of the ironies of colonialism) owed as much to the dynamics of abolition itself as it did to explicit colonial policies. Already at the end of the nineteenth century, signs of the role that Islam and Muslim institutions (especially Quran schools and Sufi orders) would ultimately play were becoming visible. In societies as disparate as Senegal and Kenya, Sufi movements began to provide new frameworks for Muslim identity for many formerly enslaved people.

Yet, this struggle for dignity was complex, and the colonial abolitions that freed the slaves strengthened other sorts of fetters. When Europeans arrived in Africa and the Middle East as rulers in the late nineteenth century, they privileged free, "noble," male interlocutors, who pretended that they had inalienable customary or Islamic legal rights to forms of social control that had always been the subject of intense struggle. Colonial governments, bolstered by burgeoning orientalist and anthropological scholarship, invested the claims of such aristocrats about Sharia and customary law with the unprecedented military power of the conquerors. They were only too happy to do so, since this confirmed their sense of the Eastern or African backwardness and gave them courts and chiefs who could institute repressive mechanisms of social control at little cost (indeed often at a profit) to the state. This is what was known in Africa as "Indirect Rule." The African auxiliaries of colonial states worked hard to erase earlier legacies of struggles and extend repressive ideologies and mechanisms of social control. Colonial states usually underwrote these forms of oppres-sion, as long as they were not explicitly described as slavery.

Among the most troubling legacies of the intensive slavery of the nineteenth century in Africa is the tenacity of its afterlives. As in most slave societies, former slaves and their descendants have found slave status difficult to transcend. Ideologies attaching an indelible taint to the descendants of slaves, rather than merely echoing archaic prejudices, probably became more important during the twentieth century precisely because augmenting the slave population through slaving became all but impossible. Less physical control meant more ideological control. Though it is difficult to document, the social stigmas attached to slavery likely became more virulent because sanctioned violence against the descendants of slaves and direct coercive control of their labor were restricted by the formal illegality of slavery. Eventually, even illegal slave trading became impractical on any kind of large scale, even in Mauritania, Sudan, Senegal, and other places where it can be documented well into the twentieth century.

The ubiquity and profundity of slavery and its attendant ideologies were artifacts of the nineteenth century, but for a wide range of reasons they were represented in nineteenth- and twentieth-century discourse as timeless. In the twenty-first century, Christian NGOs, South Sudanese politicians, and antislavery activists in Mauritania and elsewhere have tended to elaborate on some racial and religious tropes with clear roots in nineteenth-century abolitionism, evangelization, and imperialism. That Muslim societies accepted and justified slavery through racial and religious ideologies is patent. But throughout the Muslim world – in the nineteenth century and before – there were also critics of slavery, racism, and the increasingly obvious conjunction of the two. Such critiques were rooted in normative Islamic notions of ethical behavior. The nineteenth-century Moroccan historian Ahmad al-Nasiri (1835–97) can serve as but one example. Though Nasiri projects deep into the past the nineteenth-century dynamics which equated the people of the lands of the blacks (Sudan) with slaves, he, like many of his contemporaries, rejected the association and affirmed human liberty as the basic condition of the children of Adam.

Since antiquity they [the blacks] have been among the most admirable of the Islamic peoples. Their race is pious. Most of them are lovers of knowledge and the acquisition of knowledge. This fact pertains to the majority of their empires neighboring Morocco as you know. And this is what must be considered when you recognize the wrong that has generally been done to these people since antiquity. The country of Morocco has enslaved the people of the Sudan who ever they may be. They obtained many every year and they were sold in the markets of the city of the desert peoples of Morocco. They would have their brokers selling them in the market, acting as though they were brokers for wild animals and there were even more atrocities ... *This by the everlasting existence of God, becomes a part of the most detestable of all things, the most odious and most serious from a religious point of view.* For the people of the Sudan are a Muslim people. They have the same rights and duties as we ... *the nature of humankind is the state of liberty, exempt from slavery. Those who presume the contrary of liberty, presume the contrary of that which is natural law.*[31]

As we have seen, slavery abounds in the history of Islamic Africa in the nineteenth century, but historiographies that allege Islam's uncomplicated association with the will of slavers inevitably conceal the long history of Islam's role as a faith that could be used to bring freedom and justice to the slave. It is worth recalling that Bilal, an African and the Prophet Muhammad's *muezzin* (i.e. the person who makes the call to prayer in a Muslim community), accepted the religion as a slave. He was perhaps the second adult male to accept it after Abu Bakr, who would eventually become the first caliph. When the Prophet learned of Bilal's steadfast commitment to the worship of One God even in the face of torture from his owner, he asked Abu Bakr to redeem him. Many years later when the Muslims returned to Mecca from Medina, Bilal made the call to prayer from the top of the Ka'ba, recognized as the House of God by the monotheists and polytheists alike. It is reported that this scandalized the aristocracy of Mecca. Perhaps this sight, a black former slave standing atop the House of God, more than announcing the victory of the new religion, shook them because it heralded the inversion of social roles possible with Islam. Over the course of the long nineteenth century, even as slavery ironically took firmer root than ever before in Africa, some Muslims from the Cape to Cairo and from Senegal to Somalia found inspiration in these egalitarian dimensions of Islamic thought and practice, even as others sought to find in the Book of God ways to keep the naturally free children of Adam in bondage.

A GUIDE TO FURTHER READING

Feierman, Steven, "A Century of Ironies in East Africa," in Philip Curtin, Steven Feierman, Leonard Thompson, and Jan Vansina (eds.), *African History from Earliest Times to Independence* (London, 1995).
Glassman, Jonathon, *Feasts and Riot: Revelry, Rebellion, and Popular Consciousness on the Swahili Coast, 1856–1888* (Portsmouth, NH, 1885).
Hall, Bruce, *A History of Race in Muslim West Africa, 1600–1960*. Cambridge, 2011.
Hilliard, Constance, "Zuhur al-Basatin and Ta'rikh al-Turubbe: Some Legal and Ethical Aspects of Slavery in the Sudan as Seen in the Works of Shaykh Musa Kamara," in J. R. Willis (ed.), *Slaves and Slavery in Muslim Africa* (London, 1985), Vol. I, pp. 161–80.
Klein, Martin, *Slavery and Colonial Rule in French West Africa* (Cambridge, 1998).

[31] Hilliard, "Zuhur," p. 178. Emphasis added.

Mason, John E., "'A Faith for Ourselves': Slavery, Sufism, and Conversion to Islam at the Cape," *South African Historical Journal* 46 (2002): 3–24.

McDougall, E. Ann, "Discourse and Distortion: Critical Reflections on the Historiography of the Saharan Slave Trade," *Revue Française d'Histoire d'Outre-Mer*, 336–7 (2002): 195–227.

Vernet, Thomas, "East Africa: Slave Migrations," in Immanuel Ness (ed.), *The Encyclopedia of Global Human Migration* (Malden, MA, 2013), Vol. 3, pp. 1283–90.

Ware, Rudolph T., III, *The Walking Qur'an: Islamic Education, Embodied Knowledge, and History in West Africa* (Chapel Hill, 2014) (chapter III, "The Book in Chains: Slavery and Revolution in Senegambia, 1770–1890" and chapter IV, "Bodies of Knowledge: Schooling, Sufism, and Social Change in Colonial Senegal, 1890–1945").

CHAPTER 16

EUROPEAN ANTISLAVERY: FROM EMPIRES OF SLAVERY TO GLOBAL PROHIBITION

SEYMOUR DRESCHER

PROLOGUE

In the first volume of *The Cambridge History of World Slavery*, on the ancient world, "abolitionism" is indexed as "absence of." In the third volume (1420–1804), the index points readers to references regarding a few assaults on slavery in late eighteenth-century transatlantic revolutions. As late as the eve of the American Revolution, Adam Smith cautioned his students that slavery was likely to last for ages to come, if not forever. During two subsequent centuries, what had seemed for millennia to be an inevitable feature of human existence was globally transformed into an unconscionable crime against humanity. Without attention to abolitionism as historically constructed intellectual, social, and political movements, the transformation of a global institution into a crime against humanity remains unintelligible.

From an economic perspective, the transatlantic slave system was reaching an all-time peak in the last quarter of the eighteenth century. Absent the intervention of antislavery, this transatlantic system would have continued to expand in response to the accelerating pace of economic globalization and industrialization. In contrast to previous empires with slaves, however, northwestern European empires offered an anomalous contrast.

While many of their colonies had accumulated proportions of slaves to non-slaves unparalleled in history, slavery was not legally sanctioned in their European domains and their judicial traditions proclaimed that the air of their kingdoms was too free for a slave to breathe. In this situation, masters returning to Europe with slaves in tow became sources of contention and catalysts for critiques of slavery overseas.

THE EMERGENCE OF AN ABOLITIONIST PROJECT

In the Portuguese and Spanish Empires, there was less discontinuity between metropolitan and colonial variants of the institution. At the frontier of interreligious enslavement in the Mediterranean, patterns of predation and victimization remained firmly entrenched. The Portuguese

373

pioneers of the sub-Saharan African slave trade presented their activities as an extension of the religiously "just war principle," traditionally sanctioned by the Papacy with regard to the Muslim world. Quite early, however, in the Iberian expansions into the Americas and the inauguration of the transatlantic slave trade, Spanish and Portuguese protests emerged against the inhumanity entailed in the processes of enslavement and discipline. Beginning with Dominicans like Bartolomé de las Casas, a long line of clerics condemned the treatment inflicted upon Native Americans. In the late seventeenth century, some even petitioned the Papal Curia to endorse the view of critics of African slaving and American slavery. Nevertheless, both secular and religious authorities remained dismissive of any radical attempt to undermine the system. Over the course of three centuries, fundamental denunciations of slavery remained both rare and ineffectual. Certainly, there were no wide-ranging popular debates in favor of altering the slave system.

Similarly isolated instances of hostility to slavery and protests against the slave trade also appeared in northwestern Europe when they began to launch their overseas ventures. Especially during the period of the English Revolution, radical religious reformers framed their challenge in terms of a struggle between liberty and slavery. The Massachusetts Bay Colony prohibited "bond slavery" in order to avoid the Caribbean and Chesapeake practice in making bondservants of their co-religionists. The founders of Rhode Island, calling attention to the developing English practice "to buy Negers . . . to have them for service or slaves forever," limited all terms of service, black or white, to a maximum of ten years. By the end of the century, however, New England legislation began to accept the acquisition of black slaves. Their initial example was not widely remarked upon as a precedent by their late-eighteenth-century successors.[1]

ABOLITIONIST TRAJECTORIES

More frequent signs of antagonism to the inhumanity of slavery appeared in northwestern Europe during the third quarter of the eighteenth century, but sentiments began to coalesce into political action only in the wake of the American Revolution. In the 1780s, political antislavery crystallized almost simultaneously in the United States, Great Britain, and France. Nevertheless, despite its transnational origins and initial cosmopolitan perspective, antislavery followed very different trajectories toward the abolition of the transatlantic slave trade and slave emancipation. Both the American Declaration of Independence (1776) and the

[1] John Donoghue, "'Out of the Land of Bondage: The English Revolution and the Atlantic Origins of Abolition," *American Historical Review*, 115 (2010): 943–74 (quote on 964).

French Declaration of the Rights of Man and Citizen (1789) affirmed the universality of human rights to liberty and equality, but neither of their first national constitutions explicitly committed their nations to either immediate or gradual abolition of slavery. The formation of the Federal Union entailed leaving the issue of emancipation in the hands of the individual states. Nor, for more than a generation after the ratification of the constitution, was there any attempt to mobilize civil society for a nationwide attack on the expansion of slavery. The United States would experience a relatively long time lapse between its first states' actions against the slave trade and national slave emancipation. It would also require the deadliest military conflict in the Americas to bring the institution to an end.

British abolition took a different turn. Beginning in 1787, it quickly developed a durable pattern of mass popular mobilizations, national petitioning, legislative investigations, and debates. From the very outset, in 1788, the first abolitionist campaign against the slave trade accounted for more than half of the petitions reaching Parliament in that year. For the next half-century, abolitionist agitation absorbed the attention of the public sphere to an extent that was never replicated anywhere else in Europe. The defeat of the first slave trade abolition Bill in 1791 produced a redoubled mobilization effort. The number of abolitionist petitions in 1792 increased fivefold by 1788; the number of signatories, sevenfold. Women, deemed ineligible to sign, joined a pioneering consumer movement to boycott sugar. The "anti-saccarite" appeal extended to children in order to attach them to the cause.

The degree to which the British depended upon successive civil society mobilizations was made clear during the decade after 1792. An abolition bill successfully passed in the House of Commons, but the Lords postponed a decision. War with revolutionary France and slave revolutions in the Caribbean intervened. Further abolitionist mobilization was vulnerable to the general reaction against popular radicalism. British military forces, directed against French revolutionary threats on both sides of the Atlantic, permitted the expansion of British slavery more rapidly in the two decades after French slave emancipation in 1794 than at any previous point in its history. Conversely, Napoleon's restoration of French colonial slavery in 1802, after its ending in 1794, and renewal of war with Britain reopened the door to a British abolitionist revival against the slave trade. The combined French military disasters in Saint Domingue (1804) and Trafalgar (1805) provided abolitionists with sufficient leeway to revive civil mobilization, and a government coalition sufficient to secure the abolition of the British transatlantic slave trade (1806–07).

By the time that the British acted, in 1807, the French Empire had gone through a cycle from slavery to emancipation to slavery. Before 1791, the small French abolitionist *Société des amis des noirs* had lost the battle to place antislavery on the constitutional and legislative agendas, and the slave Caribbean remained the most productive zone of the French Empire. The handful of slave insurgencies in the slave colonies paled in comparison with thousands of ongoing insurrectionary episodes in the French metropole. The contrast between the booming prosperity of overseas slavery and economic crisis at home allowed the pro-slavery interest to identify French abolitionists as visionary anti-patriotic imitators of the British. Two years later, the initial popular response to the massive Saint Domingue slave revolution in France underscored the contrasting salience of abolitionism in the two societies. In the winter of 1792, the British petition and sugar boycott campaigns were at their peak. Sugar prices in Europe were rising to levels not recorded in generations. In Britain, there were nationwide calls for finding "sugar-free" alternatives. Across the Channel, Parisian crowds sacked sugar warehouses in the traditional form of a *taxation populaire*. At the radical Jacobin Club, not a single speaker linked the soaring price of sugar to the slave revolution or even noted that their sugar had been the product of slave labor.

By 1793, it was overseas events that forced emancipation onto the French metropolitan agenda. The government's agents in Saint Domingue concluded that between the successful slave insurgency and the looming threat of British invasion, the only means of retaining the colony was to align the slaves with France by decreeing general emancipation. The French Government ratified and expanded the decree to all French colonies in February 1794. Exigencies of revolutionary warfare severely disrupted the development of civil society on both sides of the French Atlantic. In the Caribbean, Toussaint Louverture's constitution for the colony in 1801 prohibited basic elements of civil society: the right to public assembly; the right to association; and, above all, the free movement of inhabitants from the plantations, now under military supervision. Despite emancipation, Toussaint Louverture and his successor, Jean-Jacques Dessalines, attempted to revive the plantation system. Liberated slaves were subjected to extended periods of compulsory plantation labor. In France, too, Napoleon's restoration of French colonial slavery coincided with severe constraints on civil society, including the end of French antislavery associations.[2] Antislavery in post-revolutionary France was thus also severely thwarted by the course of revolutionary upheaval and suppression.

Napoleon Bonaparte's momentous military defeat in the Caribbean meant that newly independent Haiti (1804) became the first nation in

---

[2] David Patrick Geggus and Norman Fiering (eds.), *The World of the Haitian Revolution* (Bloomington IN, 2009); Miranda Frances Spieler, "The Legal Structure of Colonial Rule during the French Revolution," *William and Mary Quarterly*, 66 (April 2009): 365–408.

the western hemisphere to prohibit slavery everywhere within its borders. Elsewhere, in 1802, Napoleon's victories in some colonies resulted in the re-enslavement of tens of thousands of overseas French citizens in 1802. As a result, there remained nearly as many slaves in the rest of the French colonies as remained free in independent Haiti. The Franco-Caribbean revolutions gave a powerful new meaning to the threat of the enslaved to the institution of slavery. The Haitian Revolution encouraged some slaves to take advantage of the long revolutionary wars of independence that created most of the new nations in Spanish America. By 1825, most mainland new states had abolished their slave trades, liberated slaves in arms, and enacted gradual emancipation ("Free Womb") laws, freeing the children of slaves at birth. Spanish American slave trade abolitions and emancipation initiatives came in the wake of brutal military and civil conflicts, again accompanied by breakdowns in civil society.

The long-term impact of the Haitian Revolution has been addressed at greater length elsewhere in this volume. In Europe, it had the effect of polarizing the debate over emancipation, sometimes inhibiting even abolitionists. In 1806 to 1807, British abolitionists explicitly decoupled slave trade abolition from any project of slave emancipation. They insisted that action against the slave trade would act to diminish the danger of violence, noting that during the entire period in which the slave trade had been under parliamentary discussion, there had been no slave-inspired revolt in the British colonies. The immediate impact of the Saint Domingue revolution on the Netherlands was still more cautionary. In the Batavian Republic, established by revolutionary France only a year after the French emancipation decree, the Dutch National Constituent Assembly declined to support a motion for overseas slave emancipation on grounds that any such action "might very well lead to a violent insurrection as bad as anything in Saint-Domingue," and "was bound to bring ruin to many virtuous and patriotic burghers."[3]

INTERNATIONALIZING SLAVE TRADE ABOLITION

The gap between British and continental antislavery remained wide for a generation after British slave trade abolition. Until British colonial slave emancipation in 1834, the only abolitionist group in mainland Europe was a committee of the French Society of Christian Morality, formed at the instigation of a visiting English Quaker. During the Napoleonic Wars, Britain established itself as the principal political agent operating against the transatlantic slave trade. Diplomatically, three successive

---

[3] Seymour Drescher, *From Slavery to Freedom: Comparative Studies in the Rise and Fall of Atlantic Slavery* (New York, 1999), quotation on pp. 211–12.

British governments unsuccessfully suggested opening negotiations with Napoleon for a mutual termination of the slave trade. At the war's end, Sweden, Denmark, and the Netherlands had to pledge to continue the wartime termination of their slave trades in order to regain their former tropical colonies.

When the British Government allowed the restored Bourbon monarch five more years to "stock up" its returned slave colonies, the British public intervened. Up to one-third of the nation's nearly 4 million eligible petitioners successfully pressured their government to renegotiate the concession. The Bourbon monarch refused, but Napoleon Bonaparte had taken due note. One of his first acts after reoccupying Paris in March 1815 gestured to British public opinion with a decree abolishing the French slave trade. Following Waterloo, the British-restored monarch was induced not to rescind the decree. However, the association of abolitionism with repeated French humiliations by both Haitians and Britons encouraged opponents of abolition to label the decree as a symbol of French capitulation. During the next fifteen years, unofficial toleration allowed the French slave trade to become the largest in Europe. Full suppression came only after another French Revolution, in 1830.

Britain's popular mobilization also induced its government to internationalize abolitionism. Its first achievement was the Congress of Vienna's moral declaration against the slave trade. The treaty's only article directed toward the world beyond Europe declared that "the slave trade has been considered by just and enlightened men in all ages, as repugnant to the principles of humanity and universal morality." This formulation allowed the Congress to invent a new "European" tradition. In effect, the signers pretended to have held from time immemorial what they had just been induced to accept. Clearly, no international legal obligations were incurred by the article at a time when even British courts acknowledged that the slave trade was sanctioned by "the law of nations." The Congress also credited "the public voice, in all civilized countries" with "calling aloud" for slave trade suppression at a moment when British abolitionists could barely find few scattered voices of support in Paris, Amsterdam, Madrid, or Lisbon. However, condemnation of the slave trade, now officially adopted by the international Congress, allowed British governments to invoke a European consensus on the immorality of the trade and the desirability of its termination. The only article in the treaty touching on the world beyond Europe underwrote Britain's subsequent project to involve every "civilized" country in bilateral treaties against the trade. They were designed to prevent their flags from being used by slavers on the oceans of the world. They also allowed Britain to create a network of international (actually bilateral) courts, to adjudicate the disposition of slaves captured in the wake of seizures.

IMPERIAL EMANCIPATIONS

In the 1820s, British abolitionists extended their commitment to ending their own imperial slave system. At the domestic level, this meant deepening their own reservoir of active supporters. During the generation after the great petition campaign of 1814, the sources of active membership expanded in a number of directions. Their institutional base of religious support shifted more definitively toward non-conformity. Methodists, Baptists, and Congregationalists experienced their most rapid rate of expansion in the decades before 1840. Irish support, including both Protestants and Catholics, was added to the ranks in the 1830s. Gender boundaries were decisively breached. In mass petitioning, British women abolitionists came into their own in the 1820s and 1830s. Their most dramatic entrance into public consciousness was in the form of an 1833 petition roll loaded with more than 180,000 names. It was the most widely publicized petition delivered to the legislature in the history of British antislavery. In the final popular campaign of 1837 to 1838, women may have outnumbered men as signers of petitions to Parliament and addresses to the monarch.

In the run-up to slave emancipation, British working class adherents also became more visible and vocal supporters of emancipation at electoral and petition rallies. Perhaps the most surprising addition of laborers to the British abolitionist mobilization were the Caribbean slaves themselves. They could not form associations or circulate petitions, but their entry into the British public sphere came in the form of uprisings. Although no mass slave insurgencies had occurred in the British colonies during the earlier agitation for transatlantic trade abolition, massive post-war uprisings occurred as a counterpoint to the shift of British attention to colonial slavery. All major slave insurrections (Barbados in 1816; Demerara in 1823; Jamaica in 1831) came in the wake of metropolitan initiatives to increase the surveillance of masters or to ameliorate the conditions of slavery.

British slave interventions contrasted with the pattern of the earlier uprisings in the French Caribbean. The total death toll of both whites and black insurgents in the British colonies did not equal a fraction of those who died in the Saint Domingue revolution alone. Especially beginning with the Demerara uprising, insurgent slaves took care to preserve the lives of those whom they took into custody. When encountering the forces of suppression, they presented documents from their captives testifying to their good treatment. The most striking novelty of the uprising was the metropolitan abolitionists' ability to compare the slaves' insurgency to English workers' actions and to contrast the behavior of the self-disciplined black laborers with the "barbaric" behavior of the forces of order. In particular, those in Demerara and Jamaica produced more demands for immediate emancipation than calls for retrenchment. The catalyst for immediate parliamentary action required a final massive petition campaign in 1833, and metropolitan and overseas agitations were aligned as never before.

After another popular mobilization in 1838 to terminate the "apprenticeship system," British antislavery stood at the height of its influence as a popular movement. Abolitionism had been enshrined as a national policy entailing a commitment to continue Britain's role as the vanguard in the campaign against the slave trade and slavery itself. The British abolitionists crowned their imperial victory by assembling a world antislavery convention in London in 1840. Though the conference was overwhelmingly an Anglo-American affair, all of Europe's slave empires were canvassed as prospects for abolition in Africa, Asia, and the Americas. In retrospect, the newly launched British and Foreign Anti-Slavery Society would be identified as the world's oldest, continuous human rights organization.

More immediately, the British abolitionists' achievement was signaled by the fact that the anniversary of British emancipation on August 1, 1834 was celebrated across the Atlantic in Haiti and in the northern United States. As the first European empire to formally endow its ex-slaves with metropolitan civil rights, it was also honored as the first society to implement emancipation in a plantation slave system with minimal deadly violence. As one French abolitionist summarized the process, 800,000 slaves had been liberated on the same day and hour without a tenth of the disorder that might result from agitation over the most minor political question in contemporary "civilized" Europe.[4]

As British popular abolitionist agitation ebbed in the late 1840s and 1850s, its Anti-Slavery Society settled into its position as a lobbying organization monitoring the antislavery policy of its government, acting through diplomatic, consular, and military agents abroad. The Society also disseminated information about slavery and abolition throughout the world. It sponsored agents, propaganda, organizational counseling, and even subsidies to encourage foreign lobbying and campaigns. Even without popular agitation, abolitionists could raise slavery-related issues in Parliament far more frequently than they were raised in any other legislature in Europe. In globalizing the issues of slavery and the slave trade, British abolitionists internationalized the moral basis of their appeal to "humanity and justice." Even before the European revolutions of 1848, the British Society casually invoked the themes of "inalienable rights" and "rights of humanity." They created a narrative of two generations of European and

[4] Alexis de Tocqueville, "The Emancipation of Slaves," in *Writings on Empire and Slavery*, Jennifer Pitts (tr.) (Baltimore, MD, 2003), pp. 199–226.

transatlantic sympathizers who had been brought to regard personal freedom as the "inalienable right of every man, without distinction of race,
clime, or colour."[5]

French antislavery remained profoundly marked by the twin revolutionary upheavals at the outset of its own antislavery process. At the beginning
of the Bourbon restoration, British abolitionists could only identify a
handful of allies in France, none linked to the returning dynasty. The
French political elite viewed the Caribbean revolutionary experience
largely through the lens of repatriated colonists and defeated veterans.
Their tales of personal suffering offered far more detailed descriptions of
atrocities endured than those that had been inflicted on their former slaves.
For decades, the Haitian Revolution was virtually a taboo subject in the
French legislature – too horrific to warrant discussion.

The formation of the French Society for the Abolition of Slavery in
1834 was explicitly created for the purpose of following the British
example of non-violent emancipation. Its members developed an antislavery narrative that distanced France from the revolutionary uprising of
Saint Domingue. The members were dedicated to compensating the
slave-owners and imposing constraints upon the liberated slaves sufficient to ensure the continuity of the plantation system. They were not,
however, inclined to imitate the British agitational model of extra-
parliamentary mass mobilization. By French law, associated activities
were far more sharply constricted than they were in Britain. Even more
than the Haitian Revolution, memories and fears of revolutionary potential in France itself made abolitionists hesitate to take the route of large
public meetings and mass petitioning.

Despite cordial relations between British and French abolitionists,
severe foreign policy clashes between their two nations complicated
cross-Channel relations. The only joint Anglo-French antislavery public
meeting, scheduled by the French Abolition Society in Paris, was aborted
by the government in the wake of a hostile French press. The French
Society never attempted to repeat this initiative. Unlike their British
counterparts, French abolitionists also never succeeded in linking the
metropolitan political reform agenda to colonial emancipation. The
second French slave emancipation in 1848, like the first, came in the form
of a revolutionary decree. In its wake, France's antislavery society also
quietly dispersed. A second Napoleonic empire took a second step backward. It sanctioned an indentured immigration system entailing the purchase and liberation of African slaves, subjecting them to fourteen years of
military service or involuntary labor in compensation for their "liberation."

[5] See *The Anti-Slavery Reporter*, July 1846; November 1846; June 1847; January 1848; July 1848;
December 1849; May 1851; June 1851; and October 1851.

For three generations of European antislavery after the 1780s, European abolitionism on the continent remained confined to small intermittent interventions. Limited metropolitan-representative political and civil institutions also inhibited attention to overseas slavery. In two Scandinavian nations with slave colonies civil society antislavery mobilization was miniscule. The small Swedish abolition society explicitly rejected public petitioning in favor of private appeals to the king. Emancipation quietly came to Swedish Saint Barthélemy in 1847. Denmark opted for gradual (free womb) emancipation in 1847, a process that was precipitously terminated by immediate emancipation by a slave uprising the following year. In the Netherlands, with its somewhat larger stake in slave labor, Dutch antislavery remained modest and cautious. In 1863, the Dutch became the last Northwestern European state to abolish slavery, on the British model.

Central and Eastern European polities not directly involved in slavery never initiated overseas abolitionist interventions. The rulers of Russia, Prussia, and the Habsburg Empire easily subscribed to the moral condemnation of the slave trade in the Treaty of Vienna. They also entered into the subsequent British-inspired bilateral treaty network, allowing for naval searches of suspected slavers sailing under their respective national flags. Central European religious missionary movements in Africa had neither the power nor the metropolitan-backed incentive to intervene in the question of slavery before the European Scramble for Africa in the last quarter of the nineteenth century.

For the rulers and nobilities of Eastern Europe, the problem of Western slavery was insignificant compared to servile peasant labor issues. Their preoccupations were with the social and economic consequences of the ending of serfdom. Most European serf emancipations were made in anticipation of or response to military threat or defeat: Austria in 1791 to 1848; Poland in 1794 to 1807; Prussia in 1807 to 1848; and Russia in 1816 to 1861. Even Russia's serfs, with the largest servile population in any European jurisdiction, did not occupy a prominent place in Western antislavery discourse. The Crimean War, however, increased speculation that the conflict between the Anglo-French West and Russia might serve the "cause of civilization" by accelerating servile liberation throughout Eurasia. In the wake of Russia's defeat, Tsar Alexander II was convinced that Russia's international and internal security were crucially dependent on the rapid elimination of serfdom. Planning was initiated behind closed doors, intended to minimize the disruptive impact to the existing social order. The Tsar was concerned that any forces unleashed by emancipation might generate reactions beyond his ability to manage. Therefore, the transition to civil equality was hedged with constraints that endured for generations.

Of the small nations of Western Europe, Spain and Portugal had by far the weakest metropolitan antislavery movements of the major European overseas empires before the 1860s. Portugal's loss of Brazil in the 1820s did not diminish its interest in the African slave trade to both Brazil and Cuba or its appetite for "New Brazils" in its African empire. Long after the passage of a gradual emancipation law in 1858, Portuguese traders continued to sponsor one of the most coercive systems of labor recruitment in the European colonial system.

In Spain, abolition first became a political issue following Napoleon's displacement of the Bourbon monarch and his occupation of the country. Proposals to consider slave trade abolition and emancipation were met by strong opposition from Cuban delegates who blocked further movement on the motion. During the second third of the nineteenth century, the Spanish Empire presided over the most dynamic and wealthiest of Europe's remaining slave colonies. Cuba's economy was also one of the engines of Spain's industrial growth. Despite intermittent abolitionist proposals during several constitutional crises, Spanish policy remained committed to both the slave trade and slavery. As late as 1855, the Spanish Cortes unanimously affirmed its conviction that slavery was indispensable to the maintenance of landed property in Cuba. The Cortes vowed never to meddle with the system.

NAVIGATING ABOLITION

If humans were no longer to be allowed to be subject to ownership and involuntary domination, there remained fundamental questions to be answered. How were prohibitions of slaving and slave emancipation to be reconciled with the sanctity of individual property enshrined in centuries of legal and customary guarantees? How was the process to be reconciled with all of the economic networks and capital created by colonials, metropolitans, and international investors? How far were those who were neither slaves nor slave-owners to be held responsible for bearing the costs of the disruptive path to abolition and emancipation? To what extent were slaves to be expected to bear some of the costs of their liberation?

Labor-time and money were conceived of as the major ways to bridge the gap between abolitionist insistence on a new conception of rights and the slave-owners vested claims on other persons. Compensated emancipation constituted an economic solution to a moral conundrum. Abolitionists held that human beings were not and could never be property. Yet, from the perspective of merchants and slave-owners, they had operated under the same sanctity of private property as was offered to any other legal enterprise. Indeed, they had often received more positive affirmation of their enterprises in the form of subsidies and market protection than

individuals involved in many other economic activities. In return for
abolition, slave-owners and their creditors might expect compensation in
loans, market protection, or alternative labor supplies, and such measures
rationalized by legislatures as the means to ease the transition to freedom
and by abolitionists to prevent the disruption that might injure both ex-
masters and ex-slaves.[6]

For slave-owners and their creditors, the same concessions could be
rationalized. Anticipatory compensation was proposed for the potential
depreciation of their property or disruption of their enterprises. In public
debates, bureaucratic planning and parliamentary investigations of the
distribution of costs and risks of change were usually discussed before,
during, and after each stage of legislation. At some point in the discussions,
abolitionists and anti-abolitionists usually acknowledged that to some
degree moral responsibility had to be borne by the entire society that
had acquiesced in, acquired, and profited from slavery.[7]

Abolition could be eased for slave-holders by legislating a transition
period for ending the institution through gradual emancipation. Societies with weak or moderate abolitionist movements could acquiesce in
the choice of "free womb" compensation. This process allowed slave-
owners to retain lifetime control over currently held slaves and over the
labor of all future children of slaves until an age when they would have
paid for the full costs of their rearing. Another mode of using labor-
time as a form of compensation to slave-holders was to provide for a
period in which newly freed slaves would owe their ex-owners by
remaining bound to a certain proportion of unpaid labor per day for
a prescribed period of time.

Abolitionists occasionally asserted that if any indemnity was due, it
should go to the slaves rather than slave-owners. In no case, however,
was compensation ever voted for such a purpose. The slave-owners of
Great Britain (and their metropolitan creditors) received the largest lump-
sum indemnity. The compensation package cost the British taxpayers £20
million, plus the annual costs of the anti-slaving naval patrol and the cost
of a protected market for "free labor" sugar for a time following emancipation. Compensating owners for more than twice as many slaves as all other
European colonial slave empires combined, the British also paid more than
twice the price.

---

[6] Frédérique Beauvois, *Indemniser les planteurs pour abolir l'esclavage? Entre économie, éthique et politique: une étude des débats parlementaries britanniques et francais (1788–1848) dans une perspective comparée* (Paris, 2013), chs. 3–5. See also Stanley L. Engerman, *Slavery, Emancipation and Freedom: Comparative Perspectives* (Baton Rouge, LA, 2007).
[7] See Martti Koskenniemi, *The Gentle Civilizer of Nations: The Rise and Fall of International Law 1870–1960* (Cambridge, 2001); and Bardo Fassbender and Anne Peter (eds.), *The Oxford Handbook of the History of International Law* (Oxford, 2012), esp. chs. 5, 8, 24, 37, and 38.

Haiti, in exchange for French recognition of its independence and trade expansion, agreed to pay compensation in 1825, to be distributed to former masters. The agreed sum was large enough to make the compensation charge for each Haitian more than four times as large as the analogous cost to each British taxpayer. Moreover, even French legislators who refused to condemn Haitians as responsible for the violent destruction of the Saint Domingue revolution made no attempt to oppose the burden imposed on the ex-slaves of their former colony.

THE SECOND WAVE: THE 1860S TO THE 1920S

By the 1850s, Britain's age of mass mobilization and dramatic governmental and military initiatives ebbed. After British naval action precipitated Brazil's termination of its slave trade in 1850, the last remaining opening for African slave importation still remained beyond Britain's unilateral power to alter. The US Government prevented any repetition of a blockade against the Cuban trade. Neither its slave trade nor its slave system was declining. In 1860, there were more slaves toiling in the Americas than ever before. Europeans envisioning the institutions' duration were still reckoning its probable demise in terms of generations. The dynamism of the slave plantation zone seemed to transgress the axiom that the march of civilization entailed slavery's inevitable decrepitude.

The American Civil War transformed the situation. The combination of American slave emancipation at one edge of the Western world, Russian serf emancipation at the other, and final British closure of the Atlantic slave trade between the two hemispheres acted as a catalyst for abolitionism. With the cautious liberalization of the empire, organized antislavery revived in France. The aborted Parisian international antislavery meeting of 1842 finally came to fruition in 1867. It was sponsored by the French, British, American, Spanish, and Dutch Anti-Slavery Societies and was attended by delegates and speakers from West Africa, and all major areas of the Americas, including both former slaves and abolitionists. It sponsored addresses to the rulers of Spain, Portugal, Brazil, the Ottoman Empire, Zanzibar, Transvaal, and the Papacy requesting their adherence and participation in the global movement for the elimination of the slave trade and slavery. Though carefully monitored by French police agents, it gave William Lloyd Garrison leeway to spontaneously close the proceedings with an unscripted declaration of "Liberty, Equality, Fraternity!" Only the Franco-Prussian War in 1870 and another Parisian revolution in 1871 interrupted the activity of French antislavery.

By then, the clock had been ticking rapidly on the last slave societies in the Americas. The American Civil War transformed the situation of antislavery in the Spanish Empire, even before Lincoln's Emancipation

Proclamation. As Union victory became more certain, opportunities opened up for the formation of a Spanish abolitionist movement within a burgeoning civil society in Spain. As in France, antislavery was linked to demands for political democratization. Founded in 1865, the Spanish Abolitionist Society agitated in a manner closer to the British model of the social movement than any other in Europe. However, as in the United States, the movement was challenged by anti-abolitionist mobilizations both in Spain and Cuba. As a result, the Spanish colonial abolition process was once more disrupted by the military mobilizations that had played a large role in earlier conflicts in South America.

The generation of 1860 in Europe took another major step in internationalizing antislavery. In the arena of law, the impetus toward Western slave emancipation accelerated a change in the international law regarding the slave trade and slavery. Ever since the establishment of the Roman Empire, the tradition of its civil code had been formed to justify the legitimacy of slavery as part of the *jus gentium*, or the law of nations. As late as mid-century, lawyers and statesmen routinely echoed the judgment of English and American high courts to the effect that the slave trade might be contrary to the law of nature, but not to the law of nations. As the last European empires of slavery were legislating its termination, members of the first international law association began to insist that the legal status of the slave trade and slavery should not be inferred from prior cultural habits or historical traditions, but directly from "nature." The Congress of Vienna's declaration that the slave trade had been declared an affront to humanity and incrementally rendered illegal by the network of (bilateral) treaties was acclaimed the true measure of moral progress and of the evolving moral conscience of European nations. Branding it as a "crime against humanity" seemed to be on the verge of achieving international consensus.[8]

THE NEW LINE: ANTISLAVERY EMPIRES AND CIVILIZATION

The 1860s and 1870s therefore marked a moment of consolidation of European antislavery as a whole. Emancipation, both gradual and immediate, had been legislated for their overseas colonies. The transatlantic slave trade was successfully ended. The locus of British anti-slave-trade treaty-making shifted unobtrusively from the Atlantic into the Indian and Pacific

---

[8] See Robin Law, "Abolition and Imperialism: International Law and the British Suppression of the Atlantic Slave Trade," in Derek R. Peterson (ed.), *Abolition and Imperialism in Britain; Africa, and the Atlantic* (Athens, OH, 2010), pp. 150–74; Howard Temperley, "The Delegalization of Slavery in British India," in Howard Temperley (ed.), *After Slavery: Emancipation and Its Discontents* (London, 2000), pp. 169–87; Suzanne Miers, "Slavery to Freedom in Sub-Saharan Africa: Expectations and Reality," in Temperley (ed.), *After Slavery*, pp. 237–64.

Oceans. By 1860, trading, kidnapping, and abduction in India for purposes of slaving were now punishable by terms of imprisonment. Substantive change, however, still depended upon impoverished servants being able to find alternative employment.

In Africa, the definitive ending of the transatlantic trade in the mid-1860s coincided with costly and inconclusive conflicts on the Gold Coast and Gambia. The British Anti-Slavery Society and other organizations voiced opposition to further colonial expansion. They urged that most West African colonies be abandoned on the grounds that British rule "had brought chiefly injustice and misgovernment." Moreover, since the laws of Britain and France prohibited slavery anywhere within their colonies, both governments were reluctant to assume the responsibility for repeating the costly experiments of compensated slave emancipation entailed in any expansion of colonial sovereignty.

Antislavery advocates and government agents also had to come to terms with differences between the institution that they had abolished in the Americas and those that prevailed in the eastern hemisphere. Old World slaves were officials, eunuchs, soldiers, artisans, and marriage partners, as well as workers and servants. Some forms of concubinage routinely provided for the exit of offspring from their mother's initial status. Moreover, the authority of European agents who might be asked to govern vast new densely populated areas usually depended on the cooperation of their native slave-holding elites.

In many areas, Europeans faced the additional problem of sustaining and enlarging a labor force in order to create the industries and infrastructure needed for capitalist development. Finally, from a metropolitan moral perspective, the prior existence of indigenous slave systems engendered a less urgent sense of imperial responsibility than those that had been deliberately nurtured by European abolitionists. More diverse paths to abolition seemed appropriate in addressing the complex relationships encountered by European missionaries, merchants, and magistrates in Afro-Asia.

In one respect, the alternative approach to Old World abolition had already been worked out in India well before the imperialist surge of the last third of the nineteenth century. At the height of their domestic political influence, British abolitionists had been able to pressure their government to legislate against slavery in India. In 1843, slavery was delegalized. Courts were forbidden to sanction the sale of persons or to enforce practices that deprived individuals of their right to leave the service of others, unless they had contracted to work for a specific time period or until repayment of debt. This precedent, which has been termed the "Indian" model of abolition, was actually suggested by Lord Mansfield's formula in resolving the Somerset case, which in 1772 had declared British colonial slave law as not binding in England. As in the Somerset precedent, slaves could leave their masters. Without a general exodus from the status, there would be no social or economic discontinuity to bridge. No special apprenticeship period was required. Slaves would liberate themselves one by one, as opportunity and desire arose. No compensation was necessary for either masters or slaves. The government provided no special shelters, magistrates, or civil society agencies to act as networks of protection and publicity. Delegalization would guarantee a slow death for slavery without economic or social disruption.[9]

Moreover, the antislavery project could now rationalize the expansion of European domination throughout the Eastern Hemisphere. Even the universalist demands of antislavery and other advocates did not preclude their active acquiescence in European domination and imperial tutelage. Under the aegis of a civilizational ideology, European empires of New World slavery consensually became empires of Old World antislavery. As in the earlier case of transatlantic slavery, enslavement and the slave trade were easily identified as the fundamental source of slavery's persistence and expansion. The slave trade tended to be identified as the most horrific aspect of a barbaric institution. The extreme level of murderous brutality, physical uprooting, and family and community devastation placed it within a separate sphere of moral depravity and abolitionist urgency. The need for action was intensified by reports of the accelerated expansion of slave raiding as a consequence of the mid-nineteenth-century European weapons revolution, including the spread of the field artillery which doomed traditional defensive strategies in Africa. The flood of new armaments allowed slavers to become more proficient and deadly than their earlier counterparts.

As had occurred at the end of the eighteenth century, slaving became the focal point for a revival of European popular mobilization and civil society organization. By the 1880s, antislavery could also be framed in an entirely new historical perspective. Most eighteenth-century Europeans could refer to the "civilized nations" of the Ancient World as casually as they did to their own. Every major Western European maritime society then possessed or coveted slave colonies. By the 1880s, every Western society identified itself, its empires, and its standing in the civilized world in terms of antislavery. The absence of slavery not only provided an empirically verifiable line between the civilized and the non-civilized, but offered an explicit rationale for defining the relationship between the two. The perspective of a world sharply divided between benefactors and beneficiaries allowed contributors to the *Anti-Slavery Reporter* to refer as

---

[9] Richard Huzzey, *Freedom Burning: Anti-Slavery and Empire in Victorian Britain* (Ithaca, NY, 2012).

casually to "inferior races" as did other contemporaries. Regarding slavery, their priorities remained intact. The claim of all human beings to natural and civil liberty could justify civilized intervention. In this perspective, intervention against the slave trade was the most incontestable motive for undertaking an imperial tutelage of the uncivilized in the interest of humanity. The slave trade was, prima facie, a case of savage inhumanity.

The global hegemony of this formula could be observed even in newly emergent Japan. The Meiji Restoration established Japan's antislavery and civilizational bona fides via a legal decision as early as 1872 in a case concerning the involuntary transit of Chinese coolies to Peru. When the ship stopped en route in Yokohama, a passenger jumped overboard and swam to a British warship. When a second passenger also sought asylum, the British captain's report and a British consular intervention prompted the Japanese Government to conduct a formal hearing. The Japanese, still bound to unequal extraterritorial treaties with European states, sought to ensure the recognition of their jurisprudence as a modern legal system. At the hearing, a British judge joined the presiding Japanese magistrate on the bench. The captain of the transport ship also sought out a British lawyer to represent him. Most of the proceedings were conducted in English. By coincidence, the judgment was rendered almost exactly 100 years after the Somerset decision in London. Hardly by coincidence, the Japanese magistrate replicated the fundamental premise of Lord Mansfield: Slavery "was so repugnant to all sense of natural justice that it has ever been held that it can exist or be recognized *only* by force of express law, and which there is no obligation on the part of a sovereign state either in law or comity of nations to in any manner assist or countenance" (emphasis added). The judgment achieved its aim. The Anglo-American press praised the judgment as evidence of the remarkable "civilizing progress" being made by the Japanese in favor of freedom. In a single sentence, the Japanese magistrate had established his country's credentials as an antislavery, sovereign, and civilized nation.[10]

Antislavery was certainly not the principal motive for the dramatic expansion of European imperial domination in the 1880s known as the "Scramble for Africa." Both European governments and abolitionists received reports of dramatic extensions of slaving in Central and Eastern Africa for decades before attempting to initiate serious political or military interventions. As late as the European Berlin Congress of 1878, the British Anti-Slavery Society singularly failed to persuade its own government even to place an abolitionist declaration on the conference's agenda. The Society's appeal to other diplomats to raise the issue was equally unfruitful.

[10] David V. Botsman, "Freedom without Slavery? 'Coolies', Prostitutes and Outcasts in Meiji Japan's 'Emancipation Movement,'" *American Historical Review*, 116 (2011): 1323–47.

Other delegations declined to intervene on grounds that it was up to England to take the lead. For continental governments, the slave trade and slavery were still primarily an "English" concern. Even the Berlin Congress of 1884, convened specifically to create ground rules for dividing up Africa, was very tangentially concerned with the issue of slavery. At the last moment, the British government decided to garner some distinction by proposing an article branding the slave trade as analogous to piracy. Almost every other delegation objected to adopting such an extreme form of criminalization. In the end, the initial declaration only bound the signatories, acting independently as sovereign nations, to help suppress "slavery and especially the slave trade." This Congress's declaration, like its predecessor at Vienna, limited itself to a moral exhortation.

Only three years later did an international civil society movement aim at bringing antislavery front and center in Europe's relation to Africa. Contrary to previous mobilizations, it did not emerge from the usual social networks. During the first century of political abolitionism, antislavery was predominantly recruited from the ranks of Protestants, liberals, and radical secularists. In 1888, as the last antislavery mobilization in the Americas neared victory in Brazil, Pope Leo XIII issued a striking epistle of congratulations to its bishops. Looking beyond Brazil, the Pope referred to "new roads" and "new commercial enterprises undertaken in lands of Africa," where "apostolic men could endeavor to ... secure the safety and liberty of slaves." For more than a decade, a French cardinal in Africa had been hoping to launch a "great crusade of faith and humanity" in order to convert and liberate the continent's slaves. Cardinal Lavigerie suggested that the Catholic Church had long been attacked as refractory to modern progress and civilization. Since antislavery was now emblematic of civilization, the Church could now place itself in advance of its former detractors. Rather than fearing popular mobilizations, the Church should embrace and lead antislavery by offering anew the path to the Faith through humanity.

Lavigerie launched his "new crusade" at a church in Paris in July 1888. He succeeded in arousing interest throughout western and central Europe. New antislavery societies were formed in Belgium, Germany, Switzerland, Italy, Spain, Portugal, Austria-Hungary, and Haiti. Lavigerie's message also aroused skepticism and suspicion. His clear intention was to ensure Catholic, and particularly papal, domination of the movement, placing the Pope "at the forefront of progress and civilization" in order to fulfill "Saint Peter's initial aim to defend human dignity and purify a stain on Europe." The scars of a century still showed. The Cardinal's radical republican critics noted that the Papacy appeared to have sanctioned the antislavery crusade only after the last Catholic slave-holding society formally emancipated its slaves.

The militant republican press of the Left greeted the call with silence. Lavigerie declined to attend an antislavery banquet where Victor Schoelcher, the octogenarian secularist republican hero of French emancipation in 1848, was to preside. In Switzerland and Germany, antislavery Protestants with a deep stake in their own African missions were suspicious of the Cardinal's attempt to ensure papal leadership of the movement. In some German cities, an exclusively Catholic antislavery association was founded to support Catholic missions in Africa.

Mutual suspicions mounted. Lavigerie called for an international public meeting of the antislavery societies. He rejected Paris as the place for the meeting because of its approaching celebration of the centenary of the French Revolution. When the site was switched to Lucerne, Switzerland, Lavigerie aborted it at the last moment. He feared that the prospect of an insufficient turnout of southern Europeans would allow Protestants to disrupt his project with political and religious divisions. Nationally, the Swiss and German representations would dominate the conference. When the postponed meeting convened a year later, one of its major resolutions specified that each antislavery society would act upon slavery within its own national and imperial sphere. This was unacceptable to the British Society, which accepted no limits to its long global agenda.

The international mobilization opened up a final fault line in antislavery. Taking advantage of the fact that the West's last Christian nation had ended its slave system, Lavigerie insisted on a religious as well as civilizational line of demarcation dividing slave and antislavery societies. His program emphasized the dominance of Arab slaving in Africa. He was perceived as presenting his crusade as another chapter in the millennial conflict between Christianity and Islam. This immediately led to a rigorous polemical response from the Ottoman minister at Brussels. Noting that his own ruler had condemned and prohibited the slave trade a generation earlier, the diplomat denounced the Cardinal's inference that Islam offered Muslims a religious right to enslave black idolaters. Although Lavigerie and the movement reframed the argument and appealed to Muslims to join in suppressing the slave trade, the campaign became the catalyst for Muslim intellectual responses extending well into the twentieth century.[11]

By the time Lavigerie's meeting finally convened in 1890, it had been outflanked. Brushing aside Lavigerie's calls for the revival of a holy order of

[11] Francois Renault, *Lavigerie, l'esclavage Africain et l'Europe, 1868–1892* (Paris, 1971), pp. 363–83; Avril A. Powell, "Indian Muslim Modernists and the Issue of Slavery in Islam," in Indrani Chatterjee and Richard M. Eaton (eds.), *Slavery and South Asian History* (Bloomington, IN, 2006), pp. 262–86.

knightly crusaders to stamp out the slave trade, the British government decided that the enthusiastic public response to Lavigerie's appeal offered them a popular domestic opportunity to open another attack on the slave trade at the intergovernmental level. In order to avoid arousing concerns about the role of British imperial interests, King Leopold of Belgium was requested to convoke the conference in Brussels. The broad diplomatic response indicated the widening interest in the project. Every Western nation from the Baltic to the Mediterranean and from the United States to Russia were invited. However, the inclusive perspective of the Paris Civil Society Conference of 1867 was absent. Due recognition was accorded to the imperial activists in Africa. Minor "powers" from Europe and Latin America were not invited, presumably to prevent the meeting from becoming unwieldy. The Ottoman and Persian Empires, Leopold's Kingdom of the Congo, and Zanzibar were invited in recognition of the need for their cooperation in destroying the long-distance networks of the African trade. The demarcation line between European and African states was clear. Ethiopia and Liberia, Africa's two recognized independent nations, were not invited, nor were any of the native rulers of the still unoccupied areas of Africa.[12]

The Brussels Act of 1890 was the most extensive international document yet produced for the repression of the slave trade. Representing the culmination of a century of treaty-making, it carefully avoided committing signatories to specific steps toward ending slavery itself. Nor did it address other forms of conscripted labor or the acquisition and domination of women and children. Nevertheless, large-scale raiding and trading diminished as Europeans brought new areas under their effective control. By 1900, the slow death of slavery through the march of Western civilization appeared to be inexorable.

There were no further European-wide mobilizations, but dedicated groups of civilians and non-governmental organizations (NGOs) enhanced the network of publicity. The British Anti-Slavery Society remained the most consequential of these NGOs. It could still effectively demand antislavery action, especially against large-scale atrocities committed by weaker states like Portugal and Leopold's Congo. The early twentieth century witnessed one of the largest resurgences of any British antislavery protest since British slave emancipation of the 1830s. The 1906 British Parliamentary election became British non-conformity's last major humanitarian political mobilization against coerced labor atrocities in the Congo.

---

[12] David Brion Davis, *Slavery and Human Progress* (New York, 1984), quotation on p. 311. See also Suzanne Miers, *Slavery in the Twentieth Century: The Evolution of a Global Problem* (Lanham, MD, 2003), chs. 5–9.

Ideologically, antislavery was now firmly wedded to the linkage between the world's "stage" of civilized life and the West's expansion. The older evangelical emphasis on religious conversion aligned with social reform increasingly competed with more secular appeals to human rights against economic exploitation, but both struggled with reflexive commitments to European domination as a necessary precondition of native transformation. While antislavery advocates could leverage their governments to bring pressure to bear on the horrific abuses in the Congo or Angola, antislavery advocates came to terms with "intermediate" forms of coercion in the name of the civilizing process. Not unlike the older tutelary educational forms of indentured labor and apprenticeship, these were rationalized as devices to habituate less advanced peoples to the ethic of free labor in civilized societies.

WORLD WARS AND THEIR CONSEQUENCES

The outcome of the First World War and the establishment of the European-dominated League of Nations offered another venue for international cooperation against slavery. The British Anti-Slavery Society publicized the persistence of slavery and used its governmental contacts to initiate a League call to organize against "slavery in all its forms." British antislavery again asserted a leading role in stimulating negotiations in Geneva. This time, however, the British Society also acted to limit the participation of other humanitarian activists – both Continental European and African. Responding to the League's call for information in 1922, colonial powers carefully hedged the process by reservations for national and imperial sovereignty. Information would be received and distributed only from governments. Only two petitions reached the League's Slavery Commission, and none came from the colonized populations. The inquiry proceeded in stately fashion examining, through testimony from invited experts and governmental reports, a broad range of conditions, from the slave trade to forms of chattel slavery, debt bondage, and forced labor. Humanitarian criticism and commentary on the drafting still remained largely British. French antislavery remained politically polarized.

The resulting Slavery Convention of 1926 defined slavery as "the status or condition of a person over whom any or all of the powers attaching to the right of ownership are exercised." It was to remain the core definition in the Supplementary Convention of 1956. Adhering nations undertook to prevent and suppress the slave trade and to bring about, as soon as possible, the complete abolition of slavery in all its forms. A broad vision of slavery in world perspective had emerged by the 1920s. The League's Western-led consensus designated slavery as a "remnant," confined to less civilized corners of the world. The process of abolition could be imagined as congruent with the European-sponsored history of moral progress. The separate existence of the International Labour Organization, attending to labor practices in self-governing areas, institutionalized the difference between modern and backward peoples at the level of laborers and continued to rationalize the intermediary status of coerced, even if remunerated, non-slave labor as "appropriate for colonized peoples."

The 1926 Convention allowed forced labor as a public practice, but disallowed the removal of laborers from their habitual residence. By the late 1920s, the assumption that slavery was on a path to rapid extinction was pervasive. The Convention of 1926 was as commemorative as it was anticipatory. The French Government harkened back to its emancipation decree of 1848, leaving the Saint Domingue uprising of 1791 and the consequent metropolitan emancipation decree of 1794 in a common shadow. The Portuguese pioneers of Europe's transatlantic slave complex re-imagined their overseas enterprise as a 500-year-old civilizing policy of "Christian brotherhood with native peoples."

Before the Second World War, the British Anti-Slavery Society kept its eyes firmly fixed on the coerced laborers still toiling in their Afro-Asian area of concern. They imagined that the League henceforth endowed them an institution through which they could more easily gain the collective attention of sovereign governments than through the arduous system of parliamentary interventions and appeals to public opinion. A consensual interstate system aligned against the remnants of the institution appeared to ensure the progressive disappearance of the slave trade and slavery. During the generation after the Convention of 1926, however, the history of slavery and antislavery took unanticipated turns along the entire Eurasian landmass. With the rise of Fascism and Communism, traditional antislavery perspectives were disrupted. Italy justified its conquest of Ethiopia by claiming to outlaw slavery in all occupied territories. Some British prominent antislavery figures suggested that the sooner Italian rule was established, the better it would be for the elimination of slavery. Looking further eastward, a deep divide developed between those who viewed the Soviet agricultural and industrial revolution of the 1930s as another great experiment in human development and those who identified it as a new form of slavery.

As a global humanitarian movement, antislavery was totally disoriented and fragmented by the early 1940s. Networks of coerced laborers in the tens of millions were mobilized in Eurasia for war-related projects from the Atlantic to the Pacific. Within Nazi Germany alone, between 1939 and 1944, approximately 13.5 million foreigners were working within the boundaries of the German Reich, 12 million involuntarily. They filled the gap created by an equal number of German soldiers under arms from

Norway to North Africa and from the English Channel to the Soviet Union. In 1944, there were more slaves and "less-than-slaves" in the heart of Europe than in all of the Americas a century earlier. "Less-than-slaves" denotes those individuals whose captors deliberately intended to work them to destruction. They were more valued for their immediate short-term labor than for their potential for long-term servitude. The system was ended only by the most massive military mobilization in world history, which destroyed the labor system, together with the state and institutions that had incarcerated them.

In the wake of the unprecedented evidence of death, devastation, and inhumanity that lay all around them, the victors determined to put the principal perpetrators of the conflict on trial before military tribunals. The decision to hold state and civilian actors responsible for their conduct in courts of criminal law expanded the scope of international law in dealing with atrocities. Slavery was included among the list of charges. In the tradition of antislavery, the enslavement and deportation of civilians were included under the count of "crimes against humanity." Both perpetrators and victims had referred to the analogy between historical forms of slavery and slavery during the war. The tribunals were able to use the abundance of documents created by the Nazi hierarchies as evidence of the practice of slavery. The leader of the *Schutzstaffel* (SS, or Protection Squad) had himself told his senior officers: "If we do not fill our camps with slaves – in this room I mean to say things very clearly – with worker slaves, who will build our cities, our villages, our farms ..."[13]

As the trials moved beyond SS members charged with the operation of concentration camps, other defendants sought to distance themselves from responsibility for, or participation in, enslavement. Industrialists who had contracted to rent workers for specific sums per diem entered various pleas to exculpate themselves from responsibility for the formalities and conditions of their laborers. The lawyers for the defense disputed the charge that the Nazis' use of slave labor, especially Jewish labor, was embedded in a process of annihilation in which "extermination through work" had been one element alongside more direct acts of murder. At its extreme, even the notorious selections on the train ramp at Auschwitz, where disembarking captives were sorted into separate columns for work camps or gas chambers, were reconceptualized in terms of the oldest positive rationale for enslavement: "Without the exemption from execution of those capable of work the entire transport would have been exterminated." The defense

---

[13] Adam Tooze, *The Wages of Destruction: The Making and Breaking of the Nazi Economy* (New York, 2007), quotation on p. 473; Kim C. Priemel and Alexa Stiller (eds.), *Reassessing the Nuremburg Military Tribunals: Transitional Justice, Trial Narratives and Historiography* (New York, 2012).

argued that selection itself meant that more persons were preserved from being instantly murdered than was actually the case. The employment of those selected as capable of labor was a classic argument in defense of the slave trade as reducing human sacrifice in Africa. Coerced labor was a form of rescue. Trials for enslavement could become venues for allowing employers to distance themselves from both the enslavers and the enslaved. Only decades later would a new generation of Germans insist upon collective self-examination of the full range of crimes against humanity and insist upon the broad participation of German industrialists in the implementation of enslavement.[14]

Nonetheless, the categories of genocide and crimes against humanity were not only brought into the international courtroom, but made their way into international law as one of the last pieces of "imperial" justice – a parting shot expanding the definition of slavery to include debt bondage, serfdom, servile marriage, and human trafficking. The Soviet Union threw its international support behind the emerging extra-European states during the discussion leading up to the 1956 Supplementary Convention. The anti-colonial bloc demanded the immediate, not "progressive," elimination of all forms of servitude applied to all colonies. In terms of priority, when the Universal Declaration of Human Rights was proclaimed by the United Nations in 1948, slavery, servitude, and the slave trade were the first specific practices designated as violations of human rights.

By the time the 1956 Supplementary Convention was adopted, almost all member nations had legally prohibited slavery. It marked a definitive end of European imperial control of the agenda of antislavery and an attempt to extend slavery to a wide variety of related institutions and practices. It also signaled the diminution of the Anti-Slavery Society's role as the world's vanguard antislavery NGO. By the early twenty-first century, in addition to a number of regional UN bodies and specialized agencies, there was a plethora of human rights movements located in countries around the globe.

During the last generation, there has been an unprecedented upsurge in human rights activities, including the proliferation of treaties, institutions, and NGOs. The antislavery agenda has also undergone a rapid expansion of demands for governmental apologies and compensation. Perhaps appropriately, the most extensive commemoration thus far has been the bicentenary of the abolition of the British slave trade in 2007.

---

[14] See Devin O. Pendas, "The Fate of Nuremberg: The Legacy and Impact of the Subsequent Nuremberg Trials in Postwar Germany," in Priemel and Stiller (eds.), *Reassessing the Nuremberg Military Tribunals*, pp. 249–75; Stuart Eizenstat, *Imperfect Justice: Looted Assets, Slave Labor and the Unfinished Business of World War II* (New York, 2003).

Demands for compensation increased as well. Attention has shifted dramatically, from the indemnification of slave-owners to reparations to the enslaved. At the end of the twentieth century, Europeans again appeared to take the lead when Germany undertook to ensure compensation to 1.5 million living survivors of the Nazi regime's slave and forced labor programs.

CONCLUSION

During the past two and a half centuries, there has been a transformation in attitudes toward slavery. A millennial pattern of human relations with a myriad of variations was converted into a crime against humanity, condemned by all nations and punishable under international law. Antislavery was a process driven by popular support in some areas, and imposed in the absence of public support (and even opposed violently in others). Antislavery did not arise everywhere spontaneously or simultaneously. Historically, popular mobilization in Britain played a crucial role in both its initial emergence and its global extension. Antislavery also was bound up with a European imperialism that both undermined and strengthened other hierarchies. Emerging as a symbol of one solvable form of human domination, antislavery became a model for popular mobilizations, attacking newly designated forms of coercion and degradation. As European imperial hegemony dissipated, a plethora of sub-national formations emerged to ambitiously monitor an expanding list of human rights and violations. Sub-national organizations of coercion have sustained aspects of slavery that were once communally, and internationally, sanctioned.

In another respect, the history of antislavery has undergone a dramatic change. For a century and a half, the history of abolition was presented as the inevitable and heroic extension of Europe's freedom principle to global dominance. Whether in its non-violent or violent forms, the principal agents of change comprised a small vanguard of religious, cultural, and political leaders. From the last quarter of the twentieth century and continuing into the twenty-first, new frames of reference intruded on this master narrative. The massive migration of descendants of slaves into Europe merged with the entangled history of antislavery and imperialism. Complex networks of European and non-European interaction both to fight slavery and to extend European domination became integral to the story of antislavery. Neglected histories of popular mobilization, both slave and free, were retrieved. The long history of non-European slavery was brought into the complex story of an institution transformed from an existential fact of human relationships into a crime against humanity.

A GUIDE TO FURTHER READING

Brown, Christopher Leslie, *Moral Capital: Foundations of British Abolitionism* (Chapel Hill, NC, 2006).

Davis, David Brion, *The Problem of Slavery in the Age of Revolution* (Ithaca, NY, 1975).

Dorigny, Marcel (ed.), *The Abolitions of Slavery from Léger-Félicité Sonthonax to Victor Schoelcher, 1793, 1794, 1848* (New York, 2003).

Drescher, Seymour, *Capitalism and Antislavery: British Mobilization in Comparative Perspective* (Oxford, 1986).

Etemad, Bouda, Thomas David, and J. M. Schaufelbuehl, *La Suisse et l'esclavage des noirs* (Lausanne, 2005).

Grant, Kevin, *A Civilized Savagery: Britain and the New Slaveries in Africa, 1884–1926* (New York, 2005).

Huzzey, Richard, *Freedom Burning: Anti-Slavery and Empire in Victorian Britain* (Ithaca, NY, 2012).

Janse, Maartje, "'Holland as a Little England?' British Anti-Slavery Missionaries and Continental Abolitionist Movements in the Mid-Nineteenth Century," *Past and Present*, 229 (2016): 123–60.

Jennings, Lawrence C., *French Anti-Slavery: The Movement for the Abolition of Slavery in France, 1802–1848* (Cambridge, 2006).

Marques, João Pedro, *The Sounds of Silence: Nineteenth-Century Portugal and the Abolition of the Slave Trade* (New York, 2006).

Miers, Suzanne, *Britain and the Ending of the Slave Trade* (New York, 1975).

Nowara, Christopher-Schmidt, *Empire and Antislavery: Spain, Cuba and Puerto Rico* (Pittsburgh, PA, 1999).

Oldfield, J. R., *Popular Politics and British Antislavery: The Mobilization of British Public Opinion against the Slave Trade, 1787–1807* (London, 1998).

Temperley, Howard, *British Antislavery: 1830–1870* (London, 1972).

CHAPTER 17

ANTISLAVERY AND ABOLITIONISM IN THE UNITED STATES, 1776–1870

JAMES BREWER STEWART

For more than a millennium, people all over the world remained untroubled by slavery. It seemed perfectly normal to treat human beings as possessions as well as persons and to define the enslaved as debased inferiors as well as children of God. Starting in the later eighteenth century, abolitionists in Great Britain, France, and the United States began challenging these assumptions, demanding that their fellow citizens condemn slavery as a moral abomination and a heinous crime.[1] This revolution in moral perspective ultimately precipitated an enormous Civil War that emancipated 4 million African Americans and killed as many as 750,000 men at arms.

Three powerful ideological forces inspiring the American Revolution gave rise to unprecedented attacks on slavery – Enlightenment rationalism, evangelical Protestantism, and transatlantic Quaker activism. The first, political ideas of the European Enlightenment led influential patriots to justify their Revolution as an expression of "natural laws" by which rational human beings could act decisively to eradicate tyranny and promote social progress. As demonstrated by Thomas Jefferson's lifelong refusals to free slaves in the United States, Enlightenment ideas did not automatically lead to antislavery conclusions. Yet, when patriots insisted that the dictates of "reason" compelled their own struggles for freedom, the subjugation of the enslaved became ever more difficult to justify in the minds of leaders such as John Adams, Thomas Paine, Alexander Hamilton, Benjamin Rush, and Benjamin Franklin.

For ordinary Americans, the second source of antislavery ideology was evangelical religion. Well before the Revolution, common people began expressing deeply emotional religious feelings that could lead to antislavery conclusions. During the 1730s and 1740s, pious souls throughout the

---

[1] For comprehensive explanations of this fundamental transformation, see: David Brion Davis, *The Problem of Slavery in Western Culture* (Ithaca, NY, 1966); David Brion Davis, *The Problem of Slavery in the Age of Revolution* (Ithaca, NY, 1975); David Brion Davis, *The Problem of Slavery in the Age of Emancipation* (New York, 2014); and Seymour Drescher, *Abolition: A History of Slavery and Antislavery* (New York, 2009).

colonies, black no less than white, participated in what was called the "Great Awakening," a mass upheaval stressing that sinners save themselves through a sudden communion with God that also committed them to lives of Christian engagement. A God who granted everyone the choice of salvation placed little value on race or status. White evangelicals hoped to bring spiritual redemption to the enslaved, not physical liberation from their masters. But for those enslaved, the Great Awakening called forth powerful preachers whose messages of hope set enduring precedents for the African American abolitionists who succeeded them.[2]

Quakers supplied the third significant source of early antislavery ideology. Beginning in the 1670s, the religion's founder Englishman George Fox concluded that slave-holding defied God's basic precepts. Thereafter, abolitionist Quakers continually challenged their slave-holding co-religionists to take responsibility for the "oppressed African." Having embraced pacifism, such Quakers shuddered at the prospect of slave insurrection and the horrors of the "Middle Passage" and, by the 1750s, Pennsylvanians John Woolman and Anthony Benezet were openly confronting wealthy Quakers in Philadelphia and Rhode Island who profited handsomely from the African slave trade. In 1758, these two men succeeded in committing Philadelphia's Yearly Meeting to oppose slavery. Meanwhile, in England, likeminded Quakers launched their own assault on slave trading in the British West Indies. No group more fully typified the rising tempo of transatlantic commercial capitalism or placed higher value on principles of social efficiency, economic progress, moral benevolence, and civic-mindedness, all vital aspects of God's broader plan for human progress. Oppressed slaves would be transformed into pious workers. Indolent masters would learn sobriety, thrift, and moral probity.

As relations with England dissolved into warfare, patriots of all persuasions linked antislavery ever more closely with their cause. Patrick Henry, John Adams, Albert Gallatin, Alexander Hamilton, Thomas Paine, and Benjamin Franklin became active in manumission efforts. Above all, it was the unprecedented actions of the enslaved and of free blacks that turned the Revolution toward emancipation. The British Royal Governor of Virginia, Lord Dunmore, in 1776, promised freedom to all slaves who deserted their rebellious masters and served in the king's army. By the end of the Revolution, an estimated 20,000 slaves were fighting in the British cause. Difficulties in obtaining white volunteers led revolutionary legislatures to grant freedom to as many as 5,000 slaves who were fighting in

---

[2] Works bearing on the above two paragraphs include: Timothy D. Hall, *Contested Boundaries: Itinerancy and the Reshaping of the Colonial American Religious World* (Durham, NC, 1994); Mechal Sobel, *The World They Made Together: Black and White Values in Eighteenth Century Virginia* (Charlottesville, VA, 1989).

their militias. In the southern countryside, several thousand enslaved people escaped to Spanish or French settlements, made their way to Indian villages, or fled to the North. Never before in the history of North America had so many enslaved so forcefully seized the moment to secure their freedom.

African Americans all over the North also made the most of these turbulent circumstances. Bostonians Prince Hall and Crispus Attucks became celebrated war heroes, while others less famous also claimed leadership among the nation's black Founding Fathers. Young James Forten, a teenaged Philadelphian, escaped from a British prison ship in 1779 and became a dedicated Patriot. Two decades later, he numbered among his city's wealthiest businessmen and most active abolitionists. Born enslaved, the purchaser of his own freedom and self-educated, Richard Allen embraced Methodism during the Revolution. By 1794, he had founded the Free African Society to assist the formerly enslaved as well as the African Methodist Episcopal Church, soon to become the nation's leading black denomination. Masonic lodges and faith-centered groups assisted escapees from slavery. Churches, temperance societies, and private schools proliferated. With black and white antislavery and national patriotism now so fully entwined, slavery itself slowly unraveled across the North.[3]

Since the enslaved in the North were too few to threaten white supremacy, white antislavery leaders felt confident that emancipation would enhance social harmony, not dislocation. In 1783, the Massachusetts Supreme Court outlawed the institution and by 1804 every Northern state had enacted gradual emancipation laws, thereby creating permanent distinctions between "North" and "South." In the Revolutionary South, by contrast, abolition made no headway whatsoever.[4]

Southern planters became even more preoccupied with preserving their authority as the enslaved fled, fought, and petitioned for their freedom. Whatever their moral misgivings, the slave-holders' financial and psychological dependence on "their property" remained as complete as ever. Within the Upper South, extended criticisms of slavery by genuinely antislavery Baptists and Quakers only reinforced slave-holders' defensiveness. Instead of abolishing the institution, they attempted to humanize it by reducing barbaric punishments and easing restrictions on private manumissions. But by trying to reform slavery, the planters only added

---

[3] Arthur Zilversmit, *The First Emancipation: The Abolition of Slavery in the North* (Chicago, IL, 1967); Richard S. Newman, *The Transformation of American Abolitionism: Fighting Slavery in the New Republic* (Chapel Hill, NC, 2002).

[4] Joanne Pope Melish, *Disowning Slavery: Gradual Emancipation and "Race" in New England* (Ithaca, NY, 1998).

to their problems. Private emancipations in the Upper South rapidly expanded the free black population, while falling slave and tobacco prices made Upper South planters all the more defensive. In the Deep South, however, slave labor remained enormously profitable and had reconfirmed itself as the cornerstone of the economy. In contrast to the Upper South, there were no private manumissions or proposals for emancipation.[5]

But with slave-holders' increased confidence came new insecurities. Rapidly emerging free states now crowded their northern borders. Critics everywhere, their own bondspeople included, openly condemned their way of life. Hence, when slave-holding delegates approached the 1787 Constitutional Convention, convened to create a strong Federal Union, they constituted a bloc capable of destroying the proceedings if they felt their interests were threatened.

To the nationalistic Founding Fathers, this was a result to be avoided at any cost and so was any attack on the sanctity of private property, human property included. Consequently, they wove unassailable guarantees for the planters throughout their Constitution. To be sure, the Founders registered their distaste for the "peculiar institution" by avoiding the words "slave" and "slavery" in their document and by delaying the suspension of the African slave trade until 1807 and terminating it after 1808. Otherwise, slave-holding delegates got what they wanted.

Article Four affirmed the master's right to recover escaped slaves from the free states, but Article One granted the most substantial concession. It provided that three-fifths of the slave population was to be counted for purposes of taxation, for apportioning representation in the House of Representatives, and for determining the number of delegates from each state to the Electoral College. In this manner, the Constitution guaranteed slave-holders political power that far exceeded the actual numbers of whites and recognized their authority over their "chattel" as the supreme law of the land.

Though it is clear that the Founders' document protected slavery, it also contained many ambiguities that opened it to explosively conflicting interpretations. Such disagreements were destined to become limitless, angry, and finally irreconcilable. But for the moment, with nationhood achieved, the white-inspired antislavery impulse of the Revolution dissipated. Conflict generated by African American activism, however, most certainly did not.

[5] Robert McColley, *Slavery in Jefferson's Virginia* (Urbana, IL, 1964); Robert Olwell, *Masters, Slaves and Subjects: The Culture of Power in the South Carolina Low Country, 1740–1790* (Ithaca, NY, 1998); Barbara J. Fields, *Slavery and Freedom on the Middle Ground: Maryland During the Nineteenth Century* (New Haven, CT, 1984); Stephanie McCurry, *Masters of Small Worlds: Gender Relations and Political Culture in the Antebellum South* (Chapel Hill, NC, 1997).

As the new century opened, free African Americans continued demanding equal citizenship by organizing their own militia brigades and rallying to commemorate patriotic occasions. Their frequent petitions to Congress provoked objections from slave-holding politicians, as did their increasingly successful efforts to protect escapees from slavery in defiance of the Slave Law of 1793. Meanwhile, slavery itself expanded rapidly. Waves of white settlers poured into newly opened territories that quickly organized themselves as the new slave states of Kentucky (1793), Tennessee (1796), Louisiana (1812), Mississippi (1817), and Alabama (1819). From 1793 to 1819, slavery's territorial reach within the Federal Union had more than doubled and its dominance in the nation's economy was becoming obvious. Eli Whitney's new cotton gin created vast opportunities to adapt enslaved labor to an extraordinarily profitable commodity, short-staple cotton, and the rich soils of these newly forming states promised its limitless cultivation. By 1840, slavery constituted the nation's second largest capital asset, exceeded only by investment in real estate itself.

But as slavery's influence magnified, the boundaries of the free North also expanded. In accordance with the Northwest Ordinance (1787), new northern states entered the Union with antislavery constitutions: Ohio (1803), Indiana (1814), Illinois (1818), and Michigan (1837). However, each of these states also legislated stringently against African Americans by denying them suffrage, abridging their legal rights, including the right of public education, and limiting their ability to immigrate.[6]

The American Colonization Society, founded in 1816, offered a respectable outlet for some of this white bigotry, and also for the feelings of those genuinely troubled by slavery. Copying a British example, the Society proposed to resettle free blacks in the West African colony of Liberia, while encouraging "enlightened" slave-holders to implement piecemeal emancipations. Here, it was hoped, was also a way to allay misgivings that widespread manumission would saddle the nation with an intolerably large and volatile free black population, or worse, stimulate insurrections. The idea of eradicating slavery at a glacial pace by transporting unwilling blacks was patently impossible. Nevertheless, several thousand African Americans actually did emigrate in the decades before 1860, believing that white racial hatred guaranteed their unrelieved misery if they remained in the United States. But soon after the Society's formation, black leaders rejected it as a racist plot, a position that nearly all serious abolitionists maintained before the Civil War.

---

[6] Leon Litwack, *North of Slavery: The Negro in the Slave States* (Chicago, IL, 1960).

Despite these grave weaknesses, colonization gained influential supporters during the 1820s. Respected ministers and nationally prominent
slave-holding politicians such as Henry Clay, James Monroe, and John
Marshall held national offices in the American Colonization Society,
which conducted ambitious campaigns in England and the United
States. At least they were doing *something* about slavery, colonizationists
insisted, by urging masters to practice charity, not brutality, and to
prepare their slaves for manumission. But by appealing to sincere reformers, the American Colonization Society also generated unexpected consequences. Its publications honestly reported some of the most gruesome
aspects of slavery and idealistic young northerners such as William Lloyd
Garrison found such information disturbing. Soon enough, radicals such
as he would issue militant demands for the institution's immediate
abolition and condemn colonization as a program that actually protected
slavery by offering racist palliatives.[7]

In 1819 to 1820, Congress demonstrated just how volatile the issue of
slavery could be when, over stringent northern protests, Congress admitted
Missouri to the Union as a slave state. Northern congressmen protested
that slavery should never expand into newly forming western states at the
expense of northern "free labor." Southern politicians responded that no
territorial limitations should be placed on the growth of their "peculiar
institution" and some even threatened secession. The issue of slavery's role
in westward expansion had suddenly awakened deeply conflicting visions
of the Republic's future, but also an urgent desire for a Union-preserving
compromise. To sustain the equal balance between North and South,
Congress admitted Maine as a free state along with the slave state Missouri,
while formally excluding slavery from Louisiana Purchase lands north of 36
degrees, 30 minutes. But this settlement left a no less ambiguous legacy
regarding slavery's status than had the US Constitution. Congress had
clearly legislated slavery's explicit prohibition by excluding it from some of
the Louisiana Purchase territories. Was that a precedent, slave-holders
worried, upon which future Congresses might build still further
restrictions?

For the moment, however, the crisis had been averted, and relieved
politicians took pains to repress any further contention over slavery. While
electing slave-holder Andrew Jackson as President in 1828, the newly
created Democratic Party explicitly campaigned on a platform that upheld

---

[7] The three preceding paragraphs draw on: Osmane K. Poer-Green, *Against Wind and Tide: The
African American Struggle against the Colonization Movement* (New York, 2014): Eric Burin, *Slavery and
the Peculiar Solution: A History of the American Colonization Society* (Gainesville, FL, 2005): Marie
Tyler-McGraw, *An African Republic: Black and White Virginians and the Making of Liberia* (Chapel
Hill, NC, 2004); Beverley C. Tomek, *Colonization and Its Discontents: Emancipation, Emigration and
Antislavery in Pennsylvania* (New York, 2011).

slavery in the South and white supremacy everywhere. When anti-Jacksonian dissidents coalesced into the Whig Party in the early 1830s, they relied on similar strategies. In the North, moreover, rapidly compounding racial tensions were developing throughout the 1820s that reshaped the political culture into a system of white racial tyranny.[8]

Urban life in the North rapidly grew increasingly complicated in the 1820s and conflict between people of differing skin colors became ever more volatile. Industrialization fostered a rapid transition from artisan work to wage labor, which, in turn, attracted immigrants from all over the British Isles, particularly Ireland. These newly arrived workers compensated for their economic and cultural insecurities by claiming to be "white" and then asserting their "superiority" by abusing their free black neighbors. Elite white lawyers, ministers, and businessmen in the meantime convinced themselves that free African Americans, an incorrigibly "degraded" people, were causing these frictions even as a rising generation of talented African Americans launched an unprecedented assault against slavery and white supremacy by casting ballots, organizing militia units, and rallying on August 1, the date marking Great Britain's ending of West Indian slavery.[9]

In response, white northern mobs visited a reign of terror on African Americans. Race riots erupted in Philadelphia, New York City, Hartford, and Boston. In Cincinnati, in 1829, armed mobs returned for three successive nights to lay siege to black neighborhoods, leaving homes and churches in rubble, several dead, and more than 600 traumatized people contemplating exile in Lower Canada. Politicians in Ohio, Indiana, Illinois, Pennsylvania, New York, and Connecticut approved constitutions based on universal white manhood suffrage, while stripping free blacks of their voting rights.

Given these circumstances, committed abolitionists remained few, isolated, and unorganized. Quaker newspaper editors Benjamin Lundy and Elihu Embree worked on the fringes of the Upper South and were all but ignored. *Freedom's Journal*, the nation's first newspaper owned and operated by African Americans, appeared in 1827 and disappeared in 1828. But at the same time, forces were at work that would lead in the early 1830s to the sudden emergence of an abolitionist movement of unparalleled scope led by idealistic white New Englanders and militant African Americans. Inspired by Christian egalitarianism and a profound sense of personal

---

[8] Richard D. Brown, "Slavery, the Missouri Crisis and the Politics of Jacksonianism," *South Atlantic Quarterly*, 17 (1966): 15–28; Donald J. Ratcliffe, "The Decline of Antislavery Politics, 1815–1840," in Matthew Mason and John Craig Hammond (eds.), *Contesting Slavery: The Politics of Bondage and Freedom in the New Nation* (Charlottesville, VA, 2012), pp. 267–91.

[9] James Brewer Stewart, "The Emergence of Racial Modernity and the Rise of the White North, 1790–1840," *Journal of the Early American Republic*, 19 (1998): 181–217.

responsibility, young men and women of both races were soon to launch an unprecedented effort to convince their fellow citizens that slavery was a terrible sin, that it must be immediately eliminated, and that racial prejudice was a war with Christianity. Just as the nation's political system and social order were closing ranks in defense of slavery, radical activists in the North took up the cause of "immediate, unconditional emancipation." It is difficult to imagine more dangerous or, if one prefers, a more perfectly timed and necessary moment for launching a radical crusade against slavery.

Historians cite January 1, 1831 as the moment when "immediate abolitionism" exploded into the public's consciousness. On that date, a young Bostonian, William Lloyd Garrison, launched his remarkable newspaper, *The Liberator*, with this equally remarkable promise:

I *will be* harsh as truth and as uncompromising as justice. On this subject I do not wish to think, or speak, or write with moderation No! no! Tell a man whose house is on fire to give a moderate alarm; tell him to moderately rescue his wife from the hands of the ravisher; tell the mother to gradually extricate her babe from the fire into which it has fallen; – but urge me not to moderation in a cause like the present. I am in earnest – I will not equivocate – I will not excuse – I will not retreat a single inch and I WILL BE HEARD.[10]

Reflected in this vibrant outburst was a religious vision rooted in evangelical Protestant religious revivals known as "the Second Great Awakening" that swept across New York and New England in the 1820s. This mass religious outpouring, like its pre-Revolution predecessor, emphasized the individual's choice to embrace "moral revolution" that freed a person to renounce sin and strive for personal holiness. Once "saved," the individual should bring God's truth to the unredeemed and combat the evils that sin inevitably perpetuated – drunkenness, impiety, sexual license, and the exploitation of the defenseless. To the ears of the initial white leaders of radical abolitionism, Congregational brothers Lewis and Arthur Tappan, Gerrit Smith, Theodore Dwight Weld, and Elizur Wright Jr., Baptists such as Garrison, and radical Quakers such as Lucretia Mott, Arnold Buffum, and John Greenleaf Whittier – these doctrines confirmed that slavery was the most God-defying sin of all.[11]

Their solution became "immediate emancipation," pressed earnestly on the consciences of all American citizens, slave-holders and non-slave-holders alike. Calling their strategy "moral suasion," abolitionists

[10] Emphasis in the original.
[11] The three preceding paragraphs are based on: James Brewer Stewart, *Holy Warriors: The Abolitionists and American Slavery* (New York, 1996); and David Brion Davis, "The Emergence of Immediatism in British and American Antislavery Thought," *Mississippi Valley Historical Review*, 49 (1962): 41–59. The famous Garrison quotation is from the initial issue of the *Liberator*, January 1, 1831.

believed that theirs was a message of healing and reconciliation. With appeals to conscience they would inspire masters to release their slaves, thereby advancing the nation toward a peaceful end to all racial and political conflict. But by adopting Christian pacifism and presenting themselves as peacemakers, these idealistic immediatists woefully misjudged the forces opposing them, for as we have seen, by 1831, slavery and white supremacy had secured unprecedented dominion over American politics and society. Compounding the dangers inherent in this situation were three additional 1831 events, each immensely divisive, that guaranteed the rejection of "immediate emancipation."

The first event, the Nullification Crisis in South Carolina (1828–31), revealed how enraged slave-holders were to become in response to the abolitionists' appeals. Even before the appearance of the *Liberator*, extremist planters were threatening secession in order to protect slavery from perceived external threats from the Federal Government over tariff rates. The second event brought forward militant African American pamphleteer David Walker, who in 1829 published his widely circulated *Appeal to the Colored Citizens of the World*, which eloquently excoriated whites for their bigotry and free blacks for their apathy, and called in extreme circumstances for the slaves to rise in violent revolution. Then, in late 1831, Southampton County enslaved insurrectionist Nat Turner led an uprising that took the lives of fifty-five whites and a far greater number of blacks.[12]

As racial crises multiplied, immediate abolitionists became cyclones of agitation, founding dozens of antislavery societies, numerous newspapers, and blizzards of pamphlets and petitions. In collaboration with free black activists, they founded schools, churches, and voluntary associations where people of both races and genders associated freely. "Promiscuous assemblies" was what their increasingly hostile detractors called them. By 1835, abolitionists were flooding the US Postal Service with pleas addressed directly to slave-holders to repent and emancipate. The following year, they inaugurated their "Great Petition Campaign" by sending to the US House of Representatives an unprecedented flood of citizens' demands for Federal legislation against slavery. Never before in the history of the Republic had the subject of human bondage so dominated public discussion.

The impact of this unending agitation vastly exceeded the immediatists' modest numbers. More importantly, it also ended in unqualified disaster. Elected officials from President Jackson on down joined with civic leaders

---

[12] The three preceding paragraphs draw on: William W. Freehling, *Prelude to Civil War: The Nullification Crisis in South Carolina* (New York, 1966); Peter Hinks, *To Awake My Afflicted Brethren: David Walker and the Problem of Antebellum Slave Resistance* (University Park, PA, 1997); and Kenneth Greenberg, *Nat Turner: A Slave Rebellion in History and Memory* (New York, 2003).

of every sort and ordinary whites in a harrowing barrage of repression. In the South, mobs ransacked post offices and burned abolitionist mailings, while state legislatures voted cash bounties for capturing leading abolitionists. Suspected abolitionist "sympathizers" faced hot tar and feathers, the whip, and extended incarceration. Mayhem erupted in Northern cities and towns as mob assaults on black communities and abolitionist meetings exploded in Boston, Philadelphia, Utica, Rochester, Pittsburgh, Syracuse, New Haven, and Cincinnati (again), as well as in innumerable smaller communities. Finally, in 1837, in Alton, Illinois, an embattled abolitionist editor who rejected non-violence, Elijah Lovejoy, seized his rifle, confronted the mob, and was cut down in a fusillade of gunfire.

Severely shocked but hardly defeated, immediatists opened debate over how to proceed given the bald fact that "moral suasion" had failed. By 1840, three quarreling factions had developed conflicting responses that irreparably split the movement. One, led by Garrison, the formidable orator Wendell Phillips, and the grand dame of Boston abolitionism, Maria Weston Chapman, argued that the nation's values had been exposed as being so irredeemably corrupted that abolitionists must flee from established religious denominations, boycott all elections, repudiate the Federal Union, and demand northern secession. The pro-slavery US Constitution, they proclaimed, was "A Covenant With Death – An Agreement With Hell!" A second, headed by businessman Lewis Tappan and minister Amos Phelps, insisted that the movement remain true to its programs of evangelization. The third faction, led by clergyman Joshua Leavitt, mathematics professor Elizur Wright Jr., and slave-holder-turned-abolitionist James Gillespie Birney now argued that the US Constitution was actually an antislavery document that compelled abolitionists to organize an emancipationist political party, the Liberty Party, that would compete against the Whigs and Democrats in the elections of 1840 and 1844.[13]

Abolitionists advocating these positions spent the years between 1837 and 1840 in acrimonious debate, at the end of which abolitionist unity was permanently shattered. But as they debated with one another the abolitionists were also making themselves into powerful competitors in the nation's "marketplace of ideas," infusing it with highly egalitarian visions and vocabulary. Thanks to their efforts and theirs alone, slavery and white supremacy were now subjects that Americans could no longer avoid.

Immediatists also extended the "marketplace of ideas" to the British Isles and Western Europe. From the early 1830s onward, Garrisonian

[13] Stewart, *Holy Warriors*, pp. 75–97; Aileen Kraditor, *Means and Ends in American Abolitionism: Garrison and His Critics on Strategy and Tactics* (New York, 1969); Ronald Walters, *The Antislavery Appeal: Abolitionism after 1830* (Baltimore, MD, 1980).

abolitionists in particular found themselves ever more deeply enmeshed in rich transatlantic networks of reformers and revolutionaries that joined abolitionism with the closely related issues of women's rights, Chartism, the working man's rights, and struggles to overturn monarchical rule throughout Europe. Black abolitionists such as Frederick Douglass, Sarah Forten, Harriet Jacobs, and Charles and Sarah Parker Remond traveled abroad while "building an antislavery wall" against the "global reach" of plantation slavery.[14]

The wave of repression against them did yield the abolitionists one highly significant gain when northerners began objecting to the idea of defending slavery by suppressing people's rights of free speech, free assembly, and freedom to petition the government. By the later 1830s, they were coming to believe that an aggressive "slave-power conspiracy" existed, aimed at depriving northerners of their basic civil rights. Sensing this shift, immediatists drew sharp distinctions between their own uncompromising egalitarianism and the views of those who expressed concern about their personal liberties, but who cared nothing for the enslaved. "Antislavery," they insist, must never be confused with "abolitionism."

This distinction, while useful, can also be misleading. Militant slaveholders never bothered making such a fine discrimination. Moreover, immediatists understood their mission to be one of liberating the entire nation from slavery, not just the South, a view that spoke of their own deep-seated concern for the Free States' civil liberties. Most importantly, many evangelical Protestants in the North never distinguished precisely between "abolition" and "antislavery." Like the abolitionists, their religious values taught them that material and moral progress as well as their personal liberties were the antithesis of those of the slave South. Much like the abolitionists, these deeply pious Protestants saw the planters as unleashing their lusts in gambling halls and racetracks, on dueling grounds, and especially against defenseless women in the slave quarters. For them, Christian duty demanded at least opposing slavery's westward expansion and its stranglehold on politics if not openly condemning the institution. Though never making many "whole-souled" converts, immediatists were now attracting ever greater numbers of sympathizers.

Abolitionists quickly channeled the fears of this emerging constituency into the political process by inundating the US House of Representatives

[14] Caleb McDaniel, *The Problem of Democracy in the Age of Slavery: Garrisonian Abolitionists and Transatlantic Reform* (Baton Rouge, LA, 2013); Richard J. M. Blackett, *Building an Antislavery Wall: Black Americans in the Atlantic Abolitionist Movement, 1830–1860* (Baton Rouge, LA, 1983); Kathryn Kish Sklar and James Brewer Stewart (eds.), *Women's Rights and Transatlantic Antislavery in the Era of Emancipation* (New Haven, CT, 2007).

with antislavery petitions. Politically driven abolitionists such as Joshua
Leavitt, Elizur Wright Jr., Theodore Dwight Weld, and Gamaliel Bailey
took the lead in lobbying antislavery-minded Congressmen to advocate for
these memorials. The petitions themselves were designed so that anyone
suspicious of the "slave power," not just dyed-in-the wool immediatists,
could sign them by demanding restricted measures such as ending slavery
in the District of Columbia and the interstate slave trade and banning the
admission of new slave states to the Federal Union. The very act of signing
such petitions allowed large numbers of previously uninvolved people a
safe yet politically potent way to express their hostility to the slave South.
The fact that the petitions were passed door to door by local volunteers,
most of them women, explains why the campaign rapidly spread new
networks of anti-Southern activism.[15]

The clear predominance of women in the petition campaign also marks
the abolitionist movement as the originator of the American Women's
Rights movement. By circulating and signing petitions, organizing
fundraisers, developing boycotts of slavery-produced products, and leading
their local antislavery societies, women by the thousands obliterated the
widespread belief that the two genders must operate in "separate spheres."
During the later 1830s, forceful leaders such as Angelina and Sarah Grimke,
Lucretia Mott, Abby Kelly Foster, and Maria Chapman Weston
announced the emergence of abolitionist feminism when objecting to
the "slavery of sex" as well as to slavery on the plantation. Though a
substantial portion of the male abolitionist leadership recoiled at this
"heresy," William Lloyd Garrison and close associates such as Wendell
Phillips, Parker Pillsbury, and Henry C. Wright embraced it, as did black
abolitionist Frederick Douglass. They likewise warmly applauded when, in
1848, the Seneca Falls (New York) Convention marked the official
founding of the Women's Rights Movement.[16]

The first fruits of female empowerment became evident as early as 1836,
when Congressmen found themselves facing over 30,000 antislavery petitions, the majority bearing the signatures of women. In 1837, that number
jumped to close to 100,000 and by May of 1838 the American Anti-Slavery
Society's "Great Petition Campaign" had generated an extraordinary
415,000 petitions. Thus, deluged, the Congress, in 1836, enacted its highly
controversial "gag rule," which stipulated that antislavery petitions could
not be debated, but must instead be automatically tabled.

[15] James Brewer Stewart, *Joshua R. Giddings and the Tactics of Radical Politics* (Cleveland, OH, 1969), pp. 37–102.
[16] Blanche G. Hirsch, *The Slavery of Sex: Feminist Abolitionists in America* (New York, 1976); Stacey Robertson, *Hearts Beating for Liberty: Women Abolitionists in the Old Northwest* (Chapel Hill, NC, 2010); Susan Zaske, *Signatures of Citizenship: Antislavery and Women's Political Identity* (Chapel Hill, NC, 2003).

This blunt curtailment of a citizen's constitutional right of petition only spurred further controversy. In early 1837, President John Quincy Adams, now a Whig Congressman from Massachusetts, defended civil liberties by constantly presenting antislavery petitions in defiance of the gag rule and by forcing antislavery subjects into debates as confrontationally as possible. Since Adams enjoyed unshakeable constituent support, he became the recipient of antislavery petitions from all over the North. However, by 1838, other antislavery Whig Representatives had joined him, notably Joshua Giddings from northeastern Ohio.

The accelerating counterpoint between abolitionist agitation and pro-slavery suppression was now creating concentrations of northern voters who were not immediatists, but who insisted that their Representatives express their opposition to the "slave power." In total contravention of the politicians' pro-slavery consensus, these voters supplied their Representatives with stern mandates to address slavery questions openly and often. And as sectional crisis deepened during the 1840s and 1850s over slavery's further extension into western territories, early insurgents such as Adams and Giddings were to be joined by talented office seekers who made opposition to slavery the vehicle for realizing their political ambitions. Some were insurgent Democrats, such as Senators John Parker Hale of New Hampshire and Salmon P. Chase of Ohio. Others claimed Whig allegiances, such as Representatives George W. Julian, from Indiana, Thaddeus Stevens of Pennsylvania, and Illinois' Abraham Lincoln along with Senators Charles Sumner and Henry Wilson (Massachusetts), and William Seward (New York State). Together, they stood foursquare for "free soil, free labor and free men" and in adamant opposition to the "slave power conspiracy." Each had personal relationships with immediate abolitionists and each became a prominent Republican Party leader on the eve of the Civil War.

As these momentous shifts reshaped the white abolitionist movement, African American activists also reordered their assumptions and approaches while pushing their white associates ever further away from pacifism and closer to acts of open resistance. From the beginning, many black activists had gravely doubted the white "immediatists'" assumptions that southern planters would embrace "moral suasion." Their bitter trials by fire with racial tyranny hardly fostered such optimism. Nevertheless, they initially responded with great enthusiasm to the white crusade for "moral suasion."

One such incentive was the white abolitionists' hostility to the American Colonization Society and their eagerness to challenge segregation. Northern black activists were heartened by the sudden appearance of whites who took their views seriously and published their thoughts respectfully. Black and white abolitionists also discovered that they shared many of the same values of piety, thrift, sobriety, and self-improvement. Black leaders had long been advocating these qualities when exhorting their communities to "uplift" themselves. Thus united, black and white abolitionists together moved decisively during the early 1830s to establish academies, colleges, and libraries, and to underwrite temperance societies, debating societies, literary clubs, and "juvenile associations." One monument to this brief crescendo of interracial creativity endures to this day, Oberlin College, founded in 1835 as the nation's first institution of higher learning open to students of both genders and of all complexions. But on every other front, as we have seen, the abolitionists' unprecedented efforts to face down "color phobia" backfired in the face of mob rule and legislative repression.[17]

Black activists, like their white counterparts, developed new approaches in response to the racial tyranny of the 1830s. Most white immediatists abandoned hope of converting the planter class and instead began denouncing slavery's northern supporters. Black activists continued to seek the "uplifting" of their communities, but only as part of campaigns to face down bigots, demand the rights of citizenship, and assist individual slaves in escaping their masters. A new generation of talented African American leaders moved abolitionism in that direction. Some, like James McCune Smith, Martin Delany, and James W. C. Pennington had northern roots and abolitionist educations, while others, notably Frederick Douglass, Samuel Ringgold Ward, Sojourner Truth, and Henry Highland Garnet were survivors of slavery. Whatever their backgrounds, they seldom flinched when confronted by northern bigotry and when involving whites in protracted struggles to overturn segregation and black disenfranchisement.

It was black David Ruggles, for example, who first refused in 1841 to sit in the "colored-only" sections of steamboats and railway cars operating in Massachusetts. After being physically ejected from several of these conveyances, he filed anti-discrimination lawsuits and invited leading white abolitionists such as William Lloyd Garrison and Wendell Phillips to join him. Soon they and another young black militant, Frederick Douglass, were mounting campaigns against segregated transport. These involved as many as forty protesters, spread rapidly throughout New England, led to the integration of public conveyances. Soon thereafter and again allied with white abolitionists the protesters expanded their protests to address segregation in the public schools.

---

[17] The two preceding paragraphs draw on: Donald Yacovone, "The Transformation of Black Temperance, 1827–1854, an Interpretation," *Journal of the Early Republic*, 9 (1988): 131–62; Stewart, "The Emergence of Racial Modernity"; Newman, *Transformation of American Abolitionism*.

In small Massachusetts towns all over the state such boycotts proved successful, as did another led by Frederick Douglass in Rochester, New York. The most significant struggle, however, took place in Boston, led by previously obscure local blacks and supported by some of the North's most prominent whites. Black abolitionists William C. Nell and John T. Hilton began an anti-segregation petition campaign in 1846 to the Boston School Committee, and when their petitions were rejected they launched boycotts and rallied parents in mass demonstrations to prevent students from registering for segregated classes. Next, black and white activists merged assets and expertise to force desegregation by bringing expensive lawsuits. In 1849, the North's first fully credentialed African American attorney, Robert Morris, and white, Harvard-educated Charles Sumner (soon to be elected US Senator) brought a suit against the Boston School Committee on behalf of Benjamin Roberts, whose 5-year-old daughter walked each day past five "all-white" elementary schools before arriving at the grossly inferior "colored school" to which she had been assigned. Though their lawsuits initially failed, continuing agitation finally resulted in victory, when, in 1855, the Massachusetts Legislature voted to outlaw segregation in public schools across the state.[18]

But when black abolitionists attempted to regain their voting rights by plunging into politics, the results were much less satisfying. During the 1840s, black abolitionist Henry Highland Garnet led a campaign to force the repeal of New York State's $200 property qualification required of all black voters. Assisting him were white leaders of the Liberty Party such as Henry Brewster Stanton, Joshua Leavitt, and Alvin Stewart. But a state-wide referendum in 1846 to repeal the restriction was rejected by a nearly 2 to 1 margin. In Pennsylvania, white opinion stymied a similar effort before it ever reached the voters. In this respect, the free and the slave states remained tightly united by ties of white supremacy. By the same token, however, two decades before the attempt to reconstruct the defeated South as a bi-racial democracy, black and white abolitionists sought precisely this goal when struggling to secure the franchise in the North.

Dedicated abolitionists did hit on a much more effective political tactic – aiding enslaved people who sought refuge in the North. African Americans involved in the "Underground Railroad" such as Harriet Tubman and William Still relied on one another, but also depended on whites' involvement. Some, like Quaker Levi Coffin, specialized in harboring refugees from the South once they had reached the Free States. A few venturesome

---

[18] James Brewer Stewart and George Price, "The Roberts Case, the Easton Family and the Dynamics of the Abolitionist Movement in Boston, 1776–1870," *Massachusetts Historical Review*, 4 (2002): 89–116; Bruce Laurie, *Beyond Garrison: Antislavery and Social Reform* (New York, 2007).

souls actually moved south, assisted escapees, and were heavily punished once apprehended – Charles T. Torrey, for one. Torrey, from Massachusetts, stood high in the abolitionist Liberty Party before moving to Baltimore in 1844 to engineer slave escapes. Caught, convicted, and sentenced in 1845, he died in the Maryland penitentiary from tuberculosis the following year. In 1836, Garrisonian sea captain Jonathan Walker shipped out of New Bedford, Massachusetts for Pensacola, Florida where he assisted fugitives until arrested in 1844, branded with the letters SS (for slave stealer) and imprisoned for a year. The punishment for the Reverend Calvin Fairbank was far harsher in 1844, fifteen years' hard labor for abetting numerous slaves escape in and around Lexington, Kentucky. William Chaplin, another prominent immediatist, proved the most ambitious "slave stealer" of all when he visited Washington, DC in 1848, hired two seafaring adventurers and their transport ship, and laid plans to ferry seventy-seven fugitives to the Free States. Since the plot was betrayed just as the ship left port, a pursuing steamer captured it. The angry masters (some influential members of Congress) sold most of the escapees and made sure that the adventurers received harsh sentences. Drayton and Sayres both languished in prison for several years while Chaplin, who evaded prosecution, was later convicted for abetting fugitive slaves in Maryland.

Increasing numbers of militant northerners began practicing "hands-on" emancipation. Throughout the 1840s and 1850s, the borders separating Maryland, Virginia, Kentucky, and Missouri from New Jersey, Pennsylvania, Ohio, Indiana, and Illinois witnessed increasing levels of low-intensity warfare between emancipation-minded abolitionists who operated inside the slave states and slave-holders bent on suppressing them. Well before John Brown's raid on Harpers Ferry, these abolitionists initiated numerous emancipatory forays, some successful and others violently aborted by vigilant Southern whites. And well before the Kansas "border wars" of the late 1850s, abolitionists and defenders of slavery engaged directly in armed conflict.[19]

What prompted the Yankees' defiance were the same general concerns that had so troubled so many white northerners about the pro-slavery mobs: the assault on civil liberties, the "gag rule," and the threat of slavery's expansion into western territories, that is, the planter's seemingly unstoppable determination to undermine the freedom of all Americans, not just those whom they enslaved. Seeking every possible means to push back against the "slave power," northern state legislatures began

---

[19] The three preceding paragraphs draw on: Stanley Harrold, *Border Wars: Fighting over Slavery before the Civil War* (Chapel Hill, NC, 2012); and E. Fuller Torrey, *The Martyrdom of Charles Torrey* (Baton Rouge, LA, 2014).

enacting "personal liberty laws" that relieved judges and law enforcement officials from the obligation to enforce the 1793 Fugitive Slave Law within their particular state's borders.

When Boston authorities seized fugitive George Latimer in 1842, anti-slavery Bostonians' angry response captured perfectly why state legislatures felt compelled to enact such laws. They convened an enormous protest meeting, invited militant abolitionists such as Wendell Phillips and William Lloyd Garrison to address them, and demanded the passage of a personal liberty law. Obviously, most Massachusetts voters agreed. The following year, the legislature met this demand by prohibiting Massachusetts justices from acting under the 1793 Fugitive Slave Law and barring state officials from arresting presumed escapees. By the mid-1840s, several other state legislatures had done likewise. Black activists in major cities who had long before established vigilance committees of their own to protect runaways now found their work shielded from interference on the state level.[20]

Southern politicians, for their part, now felt quite certain that the law of the land in the Free States legitimized "slave stealing." Meeting this threat, they decided, required stringent new measures on the part of the federal government. These they secured as part of a comprehensive legislative compromise designed by Congress in 1850 to resolve compounding sectional disagreements over slavery's expansion into territories conquered during the Mexican War (1846–48). The treaty ending that war of conquest added to the enormous slave state, Texas, admitted in 1845, still vaster expanses into which slavery might well be extended. This conquered territory eventually was to make up all or parts of the states of Arizona, New Mexico, California, Nevada, Utah, and Oklahoma.

In 1819 to 1820, disagreement over slavery's extension into Missouri had raised the dangerous prospect of southern secession in response to northern demands that western territories be exclusively reserved for "free labor." By 1850, those disagreements erupted even more intensively, dividing the Congress and both major political parties, the Whigs and the Democrats, along stark sectional lines. Northern politicians united in demanding that slavery be prohibited in the territory taken from Mexico, while making it clear that they had no interest in abolishing slavery. Their intent was to protect the interests of white settlers moving west, not to interfere with slavery in the South.

[20] The two paragraphs immediately above are referenced by: Thomas D. Morris, *Free Men All: The Personal Liberty Laws of the North, 1780–1861* (Baltimore, MD, 1970); Stanley Campbell, *The Slavecatchers: The Enforcement of the Fugitive Slave Law* (Chapel Hill, NC, 1970); and Paul Finkleman, *An Imperfect Union: Slavery, Federalism and Comity* (Chapel Hill, NC, 1991).

Southern Congressmen responded with ultimatums that slavery be permitted in every new territory. As secession seemed an increasing possibility, it was clear that the "territory question" generated deep political objections to slavery that had little in common with the formally organized abolitionist movement.

As in the resolution of the Missouri Crisis, Congress devised complicated compromises that equally balanced slavery with "free soil" in the territories; it also sweetened the bargain for the slave-holders by giving them what they wanted with respect to runaway slaves. As part of the compromise, Congress enacted an extraordinarily harsh new Fugitive Slave Law that authorized federal commissioners, not state judges, to process escapees, and obliged every citizen to assist in their capture. Those who protected fugitives risked severe penalties and the fugitives themselves were stripped of the right to trial by jury and the opportunity to testify. Free blacks found themselves in jeopardy of summarily being claimed as escapees, seized, and shipped south without so much as a hearing. The conflict over slavery's future in western territories, not over fugitive slaves, ultimately propelled the nation into civil war: this repressive new law inspired abolitionists to gradually abandon their pacifist convictions in favor of direct confrontation.

Abolitionists hungered for confrontation as the 1850 compromises unraveled following the Kansas–Nebraska Act (1854). This legislation reignited the entire controversy over slavery and westward expansion by making it possible for slavery to be established where the Missouri Compromise had explicitly forbidden it, that is, above 36 degrees 30 minutes. What drove their insurgent spirit all the more were the violent Kansas border wars that erupted between pro- and antislavery settlers (1855–57), the brutal assault by a slave state Congressman, Preston Brooks, on Massachusetts Senator Charles Sumner (1855), and the (theoretical) nationalization of slavery decreed in the Supreme Court's Dred Scott Decision (1857). For abolitionists, these events documented beyond all question slavery's unconditional control over the nation's affairs. They also found little reassurance in the collapse of the Whig and Democratic Parties and the rise of a new antislavery party, the Republican Party, dedicated though it was to halting the westward march of slavery. Granted, it appealed to far more northern voters than had any previous political organization opposed to the "slave power." But at the same time, the vast majority of Republicans openly scorned the abolitionists, appealed unabashedly to white supremacists, and made clear that they opposed only slavery's territorial expansion, not its continued existence. All but a small minority of the new party rejected immediate emancipation and were perfectly willing to enforce the Fugitive Slave Law. To increasing numbers of abolitionists, the only recourse was direct confrontation with Federal authority through unflinching defiance of the Fugitive Slave Law.[21]

Resistance sometimes turned violent, as in Christiana, Pennsylvania, where in 1851 an abolitionist shot a slave-holder, and in Boston, in 1854, when an attempt to free a fugitive by storming the court house and overpowering his guards led to a fatality. And even when physical violence did not result, oratorical militants such as Wendell Phillips, Theodore Parker, and Frederick Douglass increasingly urged their audiences to physically obstruct Federal "slave catchers" if more peaceable methods failed. On several occasions, well-organized groups of abolitionists overwhelmed the marshals and spirited fugitives to safety. On others, they stored weapons, planned harassing maneuvers, and massed as intimidating mobs. For African American activists, these appeals to arms represented nothing new, since they built on militant traditions that traced back at least to David Walker's *Appeal*. Leaders such as Frederick Douglass, Samuel Ringgold Ward, and Henry Highland Garnet were hardly innovators when declaring in the 1850s that the killing of tyrants was obedience to God. Neither were the black insurgents in Detroit who drove away Federal Marshals with volleys of paving stones. For white abolitionists, by contrast, the journey away from peaceful "moral suasion" was full of ambivalence. From one perspective, "moral suasion" had yielded so little that more extreme measures seemed justifiable. More than two decades of peacefully preaching against the sin of slavery had yielded not emancipation, but numerous new slave states and an increase of over a million held in bondage, trends that seemingly secured a death-grip by the "slave power" on all aspects of American life.

Yet from another perspective, the white abolitionists' commitment to pacifism continued to have deep appeal. It upheld their movement's high religious vision at a time when settlers slaughtered each other in Kansas and Senator Charles Sumner recuperated from that near-fatal assault. Then, too, "non-resistance" had always registered the immediatists' sincere abhorrence of black insurrection. To jettison that conviction now was, perhaps, to embrace the prospect of servile revolt. That, however, is precisely what some white abolitionists began to do, a few quite consciously, but most through a hesitant process of rationalization that left them without defenses when they found themselves in the overpowering presence of formidable John Brown.

[21] Authoritative studies of the political crisis of the 1850s include: Eric Foner, *Free Soil, Free Labor, Free Men: The Ideology of the Republican Party before the Civil War* (New York, 1970); Richard H. Sewell, *Ballots for Freedom: Antislavery Politics in the United States, 1837–1860* (New York, 1976); William W. Freehling, *The Road to Disunion: Secessionists at Bay, 1776–1854* (New York, 1990); idem, *The Road to Secession: Secessionists Triumphant* (New York, 2007); and Michael F. Holt, *The Political Crisis of the 1850s* (New York, 1992).

"Old Brown" was a truly complex and dangerous man, endowed with a personality of immense authority. His magnetism, his skill at manipulating others, and his prophetic vision of Godly retribution helped him to draw frustrated immediatists to support his cause of capturing the federal arsenal in Harpers Ferry, Virginia, arming the slaves, and inciting insurrection. He made a familiar figure of himself at abolitionist meetings during the 1850s where he came to know many leading immediatists. All were well aware that Brown possessed a killer's instinct. It had been widely documented that he had butchered six unarmed settlers during the Kansas wars in 1857 and that leading abolitionists had given him money to purchase rifles and pikes. Now, as Brown laid plans for fomenting slave insurrection, immediatists again gave him cash and asked few questions. Some black activists such as Harriet Tubman and Jermain Louguen generally knew that Brown plotted insurrection, but not where, when, or how. And then there were the most violence-prone abolitionists of all, those who knew all that Brown would tell them in exchange for financing his attack – Liberty Party leaders Gerrit Smith and Frederick Douglass and four strong Bostonians in the struggle against the Fugitive Slave Law – Thomas Wentworth Higginson, George Luther Sterns, Franklin L. Sanborn, and Samuel Gridley Howe.[22]

Brown satisfied these men's desires to engage in conspiracy and their yearnings for a dramatic example of direct action that would shatter slavery. After many weeks of preparation, he and his band of eighteen descended on Harpers Ferry, seized the arsenal, and were quickly routed by troops commanded by Colonel Robert E. Lee. As abolitionists everywhere rushed to embrace his insurrectionary deeds, Brown was arraigned, tried, sentenced, and hanged by Virginia authorities in December 1859. His raid can perhaps be best understood less as Brown's supreme act of will and more as the predictable result of the abolitionists' frustrating struggles in the unremitting cause of resistance, their ambivalent feelings about the Republican Party, and their mounting desires for a morally definitive confrontation with slavery.

In the aftermath, several significant abolitionists such as Lydia Maria Child, Samuel May, and Lewis Tappan forthrightly condemned Brown's recourse to violence. Others, equally significant, rushed to embrace Brown's insurrectionary deed, though some, like Garrison, attempted to separate their belief in the slaves' inherent right to rebel from Brown's act of terrorism. Wendell Phillips captured feelings of the insurrectionist's

[22] The most authoritative biographies of John Brown are: Steven Oates, *To Purge this Land with Blood: A Biography of John Brown* (New York, 1976); and Tony Horowitz, *Midnight Rising: John Brown and the Raid that Sparked the Civil War* (New York, 2012). See also Jeffrey Rossbach, *The Secret Six and a Theory of Slave Violence* (Philadelphia, PA, 1982).

admirers unusually well when proclaiming to an enormous audience in Boston's Faneuil Hall that Brown had "twice as much right to hang Governor Wise [of Virginia] as Governor Wise has to hang him." Brown's deeds, Phillips emphasized, in no way led to social chaos. Instead, Brown had sought to destroy a turbulent, anarchic society of slavery that had tormented the nation for nearly a century. The South was in chronic insurrection against Christian morality, not John Brown. Brown at Harpers Ferry according to a significant number of abolitionists upheld the law, enlightened governance, human rights, and religious morality. He embodied justice, not insurrection.[23]

With Abraham Lincoln's election as President in 1860, the full political significance of the abolitionist movement's extended pilgrimage from "moral suasion" to resistance and (finally) to insurrection at last became clear. Long observation of the abolitionists' behavior had convinced the slave-holders that the North, not the South, had collapsed into anarchy. Race mixers, law breakers, and armed insurrectionists had now overrun the Free States. Despite their reassurances about never meddling with slavery where it presently existed and about their fidelity to white supremacy, Abraham Lincoln and his party were, in the opinion of most planters, actually "black Republicans," no different than Frederick Douglass or William Lloyd Garrison. Fully alienated, slave-holders elected secession and, next, armed conflict. In this respect, the abolitionists played a role greatly disproportionate to their meager numbers by leading the planters to a final reckoning with slavery.

As hostilities opened, the long-divided abolitionist movement reunited around the demand that the war must destroy slavery, not simply restore the Union. Lincoln and most Republicans initially insisted just the opposite, holding no brief for either the military expropriation of the slave-holders' "property" or for racial equality. In 1862, Lincoln, still embracing colonization, succinctly summarized his party's majority view when explaining that "What I do about slavery and the colored race I do because it helps to save the Union and what I forebear, I forebear because I do not believe it would help to save the Union." But as the war's appalling brutality unfolded, so did the logic of abolishing slavery as the best way to ensure Union victory. Giving force to this argument was the fact that the abolitionists themselves were now being hailed by the northern public as vindicated prophets whose warnings about the evils of slavery were proving true. Sharing this view was the Republican Party's small but rapidly emerging radical wing, led in Congress by the same emancipation-minded Senators and Representatives who had developed

---

[23] James Brewer Stewart, *Liberty's Hero: Wendell Phillips* (Baton Rouge, LA, 1986), pp. 177–208.

close relationships with abolitionists well before the Civil War, most notably Charles Sumner and Henry Wilson (Massachusetts), Benjamin Wade and Salmon P. Chase (Ohio), Thaddeus Stevens (Pennsylvania), Owen Lovejoy (Illinois), and George W. Julian (Indiana).[24]

Abolitionists labored mightily to convince the public to embrace emancipation out of moral conviction, not military necessity, by returning to the tactics of the 1830s. They founded Emancipation Leagues, organized mass rallies, and sponsored massive petition campaigns. Northern blacks meanwhile demanded to enlist in the Union Army and, once accepted, they fought with great distinction, adding greatly to the abolitionist appeal. Most important of all were the actions of the enslaved when deserting their masters en masse, seeking Federal protection and raising thorny questions that argued for emancipation: should Federal authorities return escapees to the enemy? Or should they be treated as spoils of war, people enslaved to Yankees instead of Confederates? Or were they in fact men and women who deserved legal protection and civil rights?

Responding to these pressures, President Lincoln in September 1862 issued a Preliminary Emancipation Proclamation, made permanent on January 1, 1863, which was limited in scope, but nevertheless transformed the war into a struggle to exterminate slavery. Though some abolitionists led by Frederick Douglass and Wendell Phillips harshly criticized its (and Lincoln's) limitations, others, following William Lloyd Garrison, stoutly defended the President. Abolitionists were dividing once more, this time over whether or not to merge their efforts with those of the Republican Party. The presidential election of 1864 saw Garrison ardently supporting Lincoln, while Phillips and Douglass joined in an abortive attempt to supplant the President with a presumably more radical candidate, war hero John C. Fremont. The following year saw the Confederacy's surrender, Lincoln's assassination, and volcanic discord among abolitionists as to whether or not to declare victory and formally disband their movement. Some, led by Garrison and Maria Weston Chapman, decided that the ratification of the Thirteenth Amendment outlawing slavery was reason enough to end their long crusade. Others, led by Phillips, Douglass, and abolitionist-feminists such as Elizabeth Cady Stanton and Charlotte Forten insisted that the struggle be extended with demands for full citizenship for the 4 million who were no longer enslaved, but who were as yet in no sense truly equal.

[24] For Lincoln's evolving views on slavery and abolition, see Eric Foner, *The Fiery Trial: Abraham Lincoln and Slavery* (New York, 2011); for the Republican Party's views on these issues, see: James Oakes, *Freedom National: The Destruction of Slavery, 1861–1865* (New York, 2014); and Hans L. Trefousse, *The Radical Republicans: Lincoln's Vanguard for Racial Justice* (New York, 1974).

This faction sustained the American Anti-Slavery Society as an eloquent voice for racial equality throughout the political struggles of Radical Reconstruction that led to the military occupation of the former slave states, the impeachment and trial of President Andrew Johnson, and the extension of full citizenship to African Americans by means of the Fourteenth and Fifteenth Amendments. When the latter of those amendments was ratified, in 1870, the formally organized abolitionist movement came to an end. Several of its most charismatic leaders, however, figures such as Douglass, Phillips, Stanton, and Harriet Jacobs, continued to speak out forcefully on behalf of people of color and also in defense of women's suffrage and the rights of the working class. Meanwhile, by the 1880s, it had become clear to all that Reconstruction had failed and that southern whites had succeeded in recreating slavery by "another name," debt peonage, and convict chain-gang labor enforced through political disenfranchisement and lynch law. It was no accident that prominent among those convening in 1909 to establish the National Association for the Advancement of Colored People were the children and grandchildren of abolitionists.

A GUIDE TO FURTHER READING

Davis, David Brion, *The Problem of Slavery in the Age of Revolution* (Ithaca, NY, 1976).

Davis, David Brion, *The Problem of Slavery in the Age of Emancipation* (New York, 2014).

Foner, Eric, *Free Soil, Free Labor, Free Men: The Ideology of the Republican Party before the Civil War* (New York, 1970).

Harrold, Stanley, *Border Wars: Fighting over Slavery before the Civil War* (Chapel Hill, NC, 2012).

Horton, James O. and Lois E. Horton, *In Hope of Liberty: Culture, Community and Protest among Northern Blacks* (New York, 1997).

McPherson, James M., *The Struggle for Equality: The Abolitionists and the Negro during the Civil War and Reconstruction* (Princeton, NJ, 1965).

Oakes, James, *The Scorpion's Sting: Antislavery and the Coming of the Civil War* (New York, 2014).

Richards, Leonard L., *The Slave Power: The Free North and Southern Domination* (Baton Rouge, LA, 2000).

Robertson, Stacey, *Hearts Beating for Liberty: Women Abolitionists in the Old Northwest* (Chapel Hill, NC, 2010).

Stewart, James Brewer, *Holy Warriors: The Abolitionists and American Slavery* (New York, 1996).

CHAPTER 18

THE EMANCIPATION OF THE SERFS IN EUROPE

SHANE O'ROURKE

The emancipation of the serfs was an epochal event in the history of Europe. Spanning an eighty-year period from the last quarter of the eighteenth century into the second half of the nineteenth century, emancipation brought an end to serfdom in all European states. Emancipation represented the enactment of the belief that no human being should have property rights in another, a belief that at the start of this period was seen as impossibly utopian. An institution that had existed in one form or another for a millennium and a half disappeared within a relatively short period. However, it would be a mistake to conclude from this that serfdom was moribund or in decline by the end of the eighteenth century. It remained vigorous, expanding continuously and tenaciously defended by those who profited from it. Only a commensurately epochal crisis could have ended such an entrenched institution so quickly. That crisis came with the French Revolution and the revolutionary wars. Revolution and war were to be an essential part of the process of emancipation either directly or indirectly. The resulting political crisis offered two forms of emancipation: one initiated from below by the peasantry; and one initiated from above by the state. Whether it was by popular action or by the action of the state, emancipation was a political act consciously aimed at the destruction of serfdom. Serfdom demonstrated a surprising capacity to resist abolition and frequently a second or even third major crisis was required to bring it to completion. Nevertheless, by the mid-1860s, serfdom no longer existed in Europe.

THE ORIGINS OF SERFDOM

Arising in conjunction with the waning of the Roman Empire, serfdom had expanded into Western and Central Europe by the early medieval period. It had begun as a contractual relationship in which land and security had been exchanged for labor and fealty. This simple arrangement developed over the centuries into a system of bewildering complexity and density. Legal, ecclesiastical, political, and economic powers were inextricably tangled in serfdom. The state in Western and Central Europe developed on top of this basic relationship and functioned as part of it. Serfdom, like slavery, was a protean institution, forever adapting to changing times and circumstances. It was embedded in a wider system of privileges and responsibilities in which the lord or seigneur, as well as compelling labor service from the peasant, exercised an array of judicial, social, and physical power over the peasant. The original exchange of labor had expanded into obligations to supply produce to the lord, to use his mill, to buy beer at his tavern, to ask for permission for his children to marry and pay for the privilege, to pay to transfer his tenancy to the next generation, and so on. Sometimes the bondage was vested in the land tilled by the peasant and sometimes it was in his person, or it could be a mixture of the two. The serf was subject to the jurisdiction of his lord's court and he could be fined, beaten, or imprisoned on the order of the court. There was no single system of serfdom, nor one formed centrally by the state. Serfdom existed in myriad forms in Europe ranging from vestigial demands to onerous labor and financial obligations. Everywhere, even where it was only residual, serfdom and the wider system of which it was a part was deeply resented by the peasantry.

Custom, law, and local circumstance determined the extent of the lord's power over serfs. The preponderance of power was always on the lord's side given the financial and institutional resources that he controlled. The serf, however, at least in Western Europe, was never defenseless against the caprices of the lord. Most crucially, and very different from slavery, serfs existed within the law. They had legal rights that individual or communally could be enforced, though often with considerable difficulty, through the courts. Critically, too, the serfs had an occasional ally in the crown, which sometimes acknowledged a wider state interest than the interests of the noble class. But the state was a latecomer to this relationship and found itself dealing with an entrenched and resilient system. Attempts to reform it would prove extremely difficult.

In Eastern Europe, serfdom had arisen much later, roughly at the same time that slavery had developed in the New World. An expanding international grain market had led to the enserfment of a formally free peasantry in Prussia, parts of the Austrian Empire, and the Polish-Lithuanian Commonwealth. In Russia, too, serfdom had developed, but this had more to do with the military needs of the Muscovite and Imperial states than with the international grain market. This second serfdom, as it has been called, was much harsher and more exploitative of the peasantry than the Western European version. The further east one went the harsher it became. In Prussia and the Austrian Empire, the serfs still had the protection of the law and the occasional attempts by the crown to limit the levels of exploitation. In the Polish-Lithuanian Commonwealth and in Russia, the peasantry was subjected to excessive exploitation, backed up by a ferocious array of powers to ensure compliance. The peasants here, like slaves, existed outside the protection of the law. These serfdoms were much closer to chattel slavery than to the serfdoms of Western Europe. Peasants could be bought, transferred from place to place, and their families broken on the whim of the lord. Not surprisingly, serfs' revolts in Eastern Europe had levels of savagery far in excess of those in Western Europe. The revolts of Bogdan Khmelnitskii in what is today Ukraine in 1648, of Stepan Razin in 1672, and of Emelian Pugachev in 1772 in Russia had levels of violence far closer to the Haitian Revolution than the peasant revolts in Bohemia in 1775 or in Transylvania in 1784.

Serfdom was sanctified by tradition, the law, and the Church. For most of its existence, it was viewed as part of the natural order of things. The only protests came from the peasantry and these usually did not involve violent challenges, but less extreme forms of protest. Even peasant revolts rarely sought the overthrow of the system as a whole. They were more concerned with rectifying local grievances and specific complaints. In addition, levels of violence were usually relatively restrained, particularly in Western Europe. In Eastern Europe, there was no such restraint either by the peasants in revolting against serfdom or by the state in repressing them. Bereft of allies in the wider society, peasant revolts had little chance of achieving their aims. Usually the best they could hope for was an amelioration of their conditions. As long as the elites of Europe shared a consensus about the legitimacy of serfdom, its future was secure.

THE ENLIGHTENMENT CHALLENGE

That consensus began to disintegrate rapidly in the eighteenth century as Enlightenment thought increasingly challenged the assumptions on which the old order was based. Many of the most illustrious figures of the Enlightenment such as Kant, Voltaire, and Adam Smith attacked serfdom on a variety of grounds. It was an affront to natural law according to Kant, economically wasteful according to Smith, and an outrage to human dignity in Voltaire's account. Voltaire in his famous campaign for the liberation of the serfs in Franche-Comté in 1770 demanded "l'entiere abolition de cette derniere trace des siècles barbarie."[1] Alexander Radishchev, deeply influenced by Abbe Raynal's *History of the Two Indies*, argued that Russian serfdom was comparable only to the slavery of the Americas. In his *A Journey from St. Petersburg to Moscow*, he wrote:

---

[1] Voltaire, *Extrait d'un mémoire pour l'entière abolition de la servitude en France* in *Oeuvres Complètes de Voltaire* (Paris, 1817), Vol. VI, p. 204.

For I remembered that in Russia many agriculturists were not working for themselves, and that thus the abundance of the earth in many districts of Russia bears witness only to the heavy lot of its inhabitants. My satisfaction was transformed into indignation such as I feel that when in summer time I walk down the customs pier and look at the ships that bring us the surplus of America and its precious products, such as coffee, dyes and other things, not yet dry from the sweat, tears, and blood that bathed them in their production.[2]

These were part of the same attacks that undermined the legitimacy of slavery. It was the cumulative nature of them beginning in the seventeenth century and intensifying in the eighteenth that destroyed the legitimacy of serfdom. This was a development of immense significance, eating away at one of the main props of serfdom. There was no remotely comparable intellectual defense of the legitimacy of serfdom. An institution that had been the bedrock of the social order since the ending of the Roman Empire was deprived of moral and intellectual legitimacy in a remarkably short time. Indeed, so effective was the campaign that serfdom became emblematic for all of the evils of the Ancien Régime in Europe.

By the second half of the eighteenth century, the rulers of the great serf states in Europe had accepted the case against serfdom and recognized, in theory at least, the need for abolition. Frederick the Great in Prussia, Empress Maria Teresa and her son, Emperor Joseph II, in the Austrian Empire, and Catherine the Great in Russia were all converts to emancipation at some future point. The state had always recognized that its interests were not identical with those of the nobility and that unlimited exploitation of the peasantry harmed the fiscal, military, and economic interests of the state. Various palliatives were introduced to limit the excesses of the nobility. Frederick the Great in Prussia, for example, in 1772 banned the sale of serfs without land. Attempts were also made to restrict the number of labor days that a lord could demand from his serfs. Catherine the Great considered herself an enlightened monarch. She toyed with the idea of curbing some of the excesses of serfdom in Russia. The reaction of the nobility to these gentle hints convinced Catherine that the security of her throne depended on dropping any attempt to interfere with serfdom. In fact, under Catherine, the serf system reached its apogee and she herself gave over a million serfs to various favorites at court. Although all of these rulers had accepted the intellectual and moral case against serfdom, in terms of practical politics emancipation remained a utopian project. Against the opposition of the nobility and the sheer complexity of the task of emancipating the serfs, the intellectual and moral case against serfdom counted for little. Only in the Austrian Empire was there a

---

[2] A. Radishchev, *A Journey from St. Petersburg to Moscow*, L. Weiner (tr.) (Cambridge, MA, 1958), p. 157.

determined effort under Empress Maria Teresa and Emperor Joseph II to confront the problem of emancipation head on.

Empress Maria Teresa's son, Joseph II, from the mid eighteenth century until his death in 1790, made prolonged efforts to reform the agrarian system in the empire, hoping eventually to abolish serfdom. Both mother and son were motived by a mixture of the fiscal and military needs of the state, a desire to curb the nobility, and humanitarian concern for the peasantry. A series of decrees attempted to define and limit the amount of labor the lords could extract from the peasantry, to remove restrictions on the peasant's right to move, and to limit the power of the lord's court, culminating in 1789 in a decree that would have abolished serfdom. No other rulers in Europe had confronted so directly and so persistently the problem of serfdom as Maria Teresa and Joseph II. On paper, their achievements were impressive. Yet, the reality fell far short of what the decrees promised. Opposition from the nobility, ensconced within their provincial parliaments and diets, prevented the implementation of much of the legislation. It also threatened the state with outright rebellion in Hungary, Bohemia, and other parts of the empire. Dangers came from the peasants as they willfully misinterpreted legislation or staged risings to carry out a more complete abolition of serfdom. By the end of his reign, Joseph was in despair and repealed many of the reforms. His successor, Leopold, recognizing the danger to the state, quietly dropped the whole reform program. The empire had been so scarred by the experience that serfdom was not finally abolished until the 1848 revolutions.

The attempts of Maria Teresa and Joseph to reform and ultimately abolish serfdom were unprecedented in that they were not preceded by an existential crisis, externally or internally. They also demonstrated the limits of what was politically feasible in normal circumstances. Rational and humanitarian motives lay behind mother and son's attempts to abolish serfdom. Yet, against the self-interest of the noble class, its willingness, and its ability to threaten the empire, the reform effort stalled and, despite some achievements, ultimately failed. Rationalism and humanitarianism ground to a halt against much less elevated sentiments. The self-evident wrongs of serfdom and its increasing delegitimization were insufficient to drive through emancipation on their own. By 1789, Joseph's failure was complete and the outlook for emancipation anywhere in Europe seemed bleak.

The failure of reform in the Austrian Empire revealed how tenacious the system was. The serf system had successfully resisted determined and prolonged challenges from above and below. Even when attempts by the state and peasant rebellion coincided as in Bohemia in 1775, serfdom emerged unscathed. The deadlock that was produced defeated Joseph. To break that deadlock would require something of extraordinary significance, something that would galvanize sufficient political will to run the risks of emancipation and to overcome all opposition. Even war, however, in the eighteenth century did not threaten the political or social system. Defeats and victories in the wars between eighteenth-century absolute monarchs occurred without ever provoking an existential crisis. The wars did not seek to alter fundamentally or permanently the balance of power between the great states of Europe. In this context, even exogenous shocks to the system were limited and easily dealt with. The French Revolution and subsequent revolutionary and Napoleonic Wars changed this context. Ideologically, the revolution laid down an explicit challenge to the old order of which serfdom was the embodiment. The revolution also changed the nature of warfare. Now at stake were not small slithers of frontier territories, but the very existence of the empires as independent powers. Military defeat, economic collapse, and the obvious inability to withstand revolutionary and Napoleonic France provided the impetus to break the deadlock that had thwarted all previous attempts at reform.

THE FRENCH REVOLUTION AND REVOLUTIONARY WARS

Table 18.1 summarizes the ending of serfdom across Continental Europe. The first major initiative was in the largest country in Western Europe. A series of bad harvests in the 1780s, culminating in the threat of a catastrophic failure in 1788, caused widespread peasant uprisings. These risings were very similar to other peasant rebellions that had taken place in the seventeenth and eighteenth centuries. They expressed peasant grievances over taxes, the high price of bread, the seigniorial regime, and above all the continued existence of serfdom. There still existed about 1 million serfs in France on the eve of the Revolution. What distinguished this rebellion from numerous others that had preceded it was a political crisis of unprecedented depth and scope. The summoning of the Estates General and its call for a register of grievances transformed a traditional peasant jacquerie with limited and specific grievances into a comprehensive assault on seigniorial privilege. For the first time, the peasants could count on allies in the center of political power who articulated peasant desires into comprehensive assault on the old order. For radicals in Paris, serfdom in particular and seigniorial privilege in general were essential in mobilizing opinion in favor of an ever more radical revolution. The Great Fear, beginning in the Franche-Compté, the heartland of French serfdom, swept over France in the spring and summer of 1789. It radicalized opinion against the Old Regime in the countryside and in the town and gave an emotional charge to the more intellectual criticisms of serfdom and privilege.

Table 18.1 *The Major Emancipations of Serfs in Europe*

State	Year of Emancipation	State	Year of Emancipation
Savoy	1771	Saxony	1832
Baden	1783	Brunswick	1832
Denmark	1788	Schaumburg-Lippe	1845
France	1789	Schwarzburg-Sonderhausen	1848
Switzerland	1798	Reuss (older line)	1845
Schleswig-Holstein	1804	Saxe-Weimar	1848
Poland	1807	Austria	1848
Prussia	1807	Saxe-Gotha	1848
Bavaria	1808	Anhalt-Dessau-Kothen	1848
Nassau	1812	Saxe-Coburg-Gotha	1848
Estonia	1816	Oldenburg	1849
Courland	1817	Schwarzburg-Rudolstadt	1849
Wurttemberg	1817	Anhalt-Bernburg	1849
Livonia	1819	Lippe	1849
Mecklenburg	1820	Saxe-Meiningen	1850
Grand Duchy of Hesse	1820	Reuss (younger line)	1852
Hannover	1831	Hungary	1853
Electoral Hesse	1831	Russia	1861
Saxe-Altenburg	1831	Romania	1864

Source: Jerome Blum, *The End of the Old Order in Rural Europe* (Princeton, NJ, 1978), p. 356.

Growing radicalism, and the obvious inability of the state to suppress it, stimulated the more astute members of the nobility to recognize the dangers that this posed to their entire way of life. Peasant attacks had expanded from specific grievances related to serfdom and seigniorial privilege to attacks on the property of the nobility in general. Piecemeal concessions to the peasantry were no longer able to defuse the crisis. The depth of the crisis in the countryside prompted the extraordinary session of the National Assembly on August 4, 1789. In a highly charged emotional atmosphere, noble deputies proposed the abolition of the entire feudal system. The result was a decree remarkable both for being sponsored by the prime beneficiaries of the system and its destruction in a few short sentences of the seigniorial system, beginning with the abolition of serfdom. The first article of the decree declared:[3]

The National Assembly completely destroys the feudal regime. It decrees that, in rights and duties, both feudal and *censuel*, deriving from real or personal mortmain, and personal servitude, and those who represent them, are abolished without compensation; all others are declared redeemable, and the price and manner of the

[3] Peter McPhee, *The French Revolution 1789–1799* (Oxford, 2002), p. 58.

redemption will be set by the National Assembly. Those of the said rights that are not abolished by this decree will continue nonetheless to be collected until settlement.

Subsequent articles suppressed manorial courts, hunting privileges, and the collection of tithes, all without compensation. The scope of the reform was breathtaking, as was its terse and seemingly unambiguous language. That vast, dense tangle of feudal privilege of which serfdom was the heart, whose very complexity had thwarted previous attempts at reform, was cut off at its roots. The abolition of serfdom was immediate, unconditional, and without compensation. The concision and clarity of the decree could be grasped by even the most uneducated. Those three basic principles were fixed immediately in the minds of the peasants and became the basis of their attitudes to subsequent elaborations of the principles of the decree of August 4. The decree provided the model against which all future emancipations would be measured and had resonances far beyond France. What had happened in France spilled across its borders rapidly.

The Decree of August 4 established the principles on which subsequent emancipation legislation would be worked out in the National Assembly. The debates in the Assembly and the legislation demonstrated again the tenacity of serfdom and the feudal system. A very effective rearguard action managed to salvage a great deal of what had seemingly been abolished by the Decree. Noble representatives had been particularly effective in arguing that many of the dues that the peasant paid had not been rooted in serfdom, but were rents owed to lords for property or other services. The legislation that emerged reflected this much more conservative interpretation of the decree of August 4. However, the peasantry was not to be mollified by half measures. They were helped by the clarity and simplicity of the original decree that provided a justification for resistance to the subsequent salvage operation carried out by the nobility. From 1790, a new wave of uprisings swept through the countryside, coinciding with new outbreaks of radicalism in Paris. By August 1792, the Assembly hurriedly passed new legislation that effectively put the principles of August 4 into law.

The emancipation of the serfs in France came about as part of a much wider attack on the Old Regime. It was the revolutionary circumstances of 1789 that enabled emancipation of the remaining serfs to take place. Peasant revolt from 1788 had helped create the revolutionary situation in France that climaxed, in peasant eyes at least, with the decree of August 4. Peasant protest and national politics fed off each other in a spiral of increasing radicalization. It was the combination of action from below together with political radicalism at the national level that enabled serfdom to be abolished. Joseph II could not and would not embrace peasant revolt as a lever to force emancipation against the wishes of the nobility. This left peasants bereft of leadership and support at the national level, condemning their revolts to failure along with Joseph's attempts to abolish serfdom. In France, revolutionary action solved the conundrum of how to abolish serfdom.

Events in France would have been disturbing enough for the states east of the Rhine in any context. The serfdoms of Prussia and of the Austrian and Russian Empires were more onerous and extensive than the French. What made abolition in France so threatening was the universalism of the revolution and the manner in which emancipation had been carried out. The language of liberation and emancipation summoned people of all countries to follow the French example, explicitly challenging the serf systems that existed across Europe. That challenge was answered in 1792 with the first attempt to suppress the revolution from outside. The War of the First Coalition began the era of revolutionary wars and opened the way for a much more extensive emancipation of serfs.

Paradoxically, the first effect of the revolution was a decisive setback to the cause of emancipation. The destabilizing effects of the revolution were experienced very quickly on the states bordering France. Peasant revolts broke out in the Rhineland states and in Saxony. These were suppressed without much difficulty, but they added to the already profound anxiety of the ruling elites. Every criticism of the existing system now had associations with Jacobinism. In Austria, whatever remained of the reform spirit dissipated in the much more conservative climate with the Emperor Leopold VII abandoning the reform program of his deceased brother. In Russia, Catherine the Great swiftly dropped her initial support of the revolution and vigorously persecuted anyone suspected of revolutionary sympathies. Alexander Radishchev, the author of the celebrated attack on Russian serfdom, was arrested and sentenced to death, a sentence later commuted to banishment for life. Even in Britain, the campaign against the slave trade suffered in the fearful atmosphere of the 1790s.

Such setbacks were only temporary, however. Between 1792 and 1815, serfdom was abolished by French forces or their proxies in the Rhineland states, Switzerland, the Grand Duchy of Warsaw, the Hanseatic States, and Württemberg. France imposed emancipation on these states with little cost to itself, but Prussia and the Austrian and Russian Empires were a different matter. Despite the repeated defeats inflicted by the French on these three states, they made no attempt to encourage serf revolt as a means of further undermining their opponents. Even in Russia, in 1812, when emancipation could have altered the outcome of the campaign, Napoleon did not consider it. French policy, particularly under Napoleon, was to reduce the empires to satellite status under French dominion, but not to cause chaos by sponsoring peasant revolt. Even so, emancipation now no longer depended solely on French intentions.

No state was more affected by the revolutionary wars than Prussia. Defeats in the Battles of Jena and Auerstedt in 1806 were so complete that the continued existence of Prussia was dependent on Napoleon's whim. The Treaty of Tilsit (1807) left Prussia reduced to a satellite, but still intact as an entity. This reprieve provided the opportunity for a wholesale reconstruction of the state. The scale of such an overwhelming defeat made previously unthinkable actions not only thinkable, but demanded their implementation as a vital state interest. King Frederick William II of Prussia summed up the new mood post-Jena: "The abolition of serfdom has been my goal since the beginning of the reign. I desired to attain it gradually, but the disasters which have now befallen the country now justify, and indeed require, speedier action."[4] Serfdom was widely seen as a major cause of the failure of the Prussian state to resist the onslaught of the French. It was the starting point of the whole reform program that was devised and implemented with astonishing speed. A decree in 1807 effectively abolished serfdom, freeing the serfs from dependence on their lords and making them proprietors of their holdings. The swiftness and radical nature of the decree reflected the shock that the Prussian kingdom had suffered. What was not made clear by the decree was what degree of compensation the lords would have for loss of their land. Later Acts in 1811 and 1816 made redemption difficult and complicated, reflecting the receding shock of the early period. However, the emancipation of the serfs was irreversible.

The abolition of serfdom in Prussia was irrefutably the result of military catastrophe. Recognition that serfdom needed to be abolished had existed for at least half a century, but nothing justified the risks of such a drastic measure. Only an existential crisis mobilized sufficient political determination to bring about emancipation. The King, supported by a small group of enlightened bureaucrats, set about renovating the state. The keystone of that renovation was the abolition of serfdom. Other measures would follow, but emancipation was the precondition for all other reforms. The Prussian path to emancipation offered an alternative to the model offered by France in 1789 or the one imposed by French arms afterwards. The Prussian way, as explained by one of the architects of the reform, was "a revolution from above." By initiating and controlling the process, the state ensured that its interests were secured first and foremost. The basic terms of emancipation were dictated by the state and, though there was some negotiation, those terms remained unchanged. Not surprisingly, both peasants and nobles felt deeply cheated by the outcome. Nevertheless, the Prussian experience now provided an alternative model to that of the French Revolution, and an obviously much more congenial one for ruling elites.

The ending of the revolutionary era in 1815 ushered in a profoundly conservative mood in Europe. The desire for a return to stability and an

---

[4] C. Clark, *The Iron Kingdom: The Rise and Downfall of Prussia 1600–1947* (London, 2006), p. 327.

end to social upheaval brought a halt to the emancipations that had begun in 1789. The sense of urgency and crisis that had driven emancipation diminished rapidly and there were no new emancipations after 1815. In Württemberg, serfdom was even reimposed. The Prussian emancipation took a decidedly more conservative turn, reflected in the Decree of 1816, which gave much more attention to noble interests. In Russia, too, the early reforming zeal of Alexander I fizzled out and little came of his many attempts to emancipate the serfs. The Austrian Empire, after its Josephite experience, had not made any attempts to abolish serfdom during the war and had even less reason to pursue this course after the war ended. Even so, the change in Europe in 1815 was astonishing. In Western and Central Europe, serfdom had all but disappeared. Echoes of it would linger on, but the institution itself had been destroyed during the revolutionary era. Serfdom remained in the Austrian Empire and vestiges lingered on in Prussia. Both states recognized the necessity and inevitability of abolition, but without an existential crisis, they lacked the political will to abolish serfdom. The 1848 Revolution provided the necessary crisis, and emancipations followed in both the Austrian Empire and Prussia by 1850.

EMANCIPATION IN RUSSIA

By mid-century, serfdom had effectively disappeared from all of Western and Central Europe. It had taken sixty years to eliminate serfdom, but it happened. Only in Eastern Europe did it survive, above all in the Russian Empire. Here, millions of people remained in bondage. There were approximately 48 million serfs in Russia on the eve of the emancipation: roughly 22.5 million belonged to private landlords, 23.5 million to the state and almost 2 million to the crown. Together, they made up more than 80 percent of the population.[5] Russian serfdom was not vestigial nor an irksome reminder of a lower social status. Serfdom in Russia was a form of chattel slavery in which the serf could be bought and sold, separated from his family, exiled to Siberia or conscripted into the army, and beaten with birches or flogged with the fearsome knout, which could easily kill a person. Labor services were heavy, varying from three to six days a week, and the tendency in the nineteenth century was for these to rise. In areas where agriculture was poor, cash payments replaced labor services. Most serf-owners, like slave-owners, recognized that a balance had be struck between their theoretically unlimited powers and what was practically possible to extract from their serfs. But that balance was weighted very much in the interests of the serf-owners. The serf-owner's power extended

    [5] F. W. Wcislo, *Reforming Rural Russia: State, Local Society, and National Politics 1855–1914* (Princeton, NJ, 1990), pp. 7–8.

far beyond his ability to extract labor through force. Many owners of serfs used that power to exploit the female serfs under their control. Lev Tolstoy, himself a scion of a wealthy serf-owning family, wrote "serfdom is an evil, but a very pleasant one," referring to his life as a young man when he had used this power liberally.[6]

Like a slave, a Russian serf existed outside the law. The law afforded him no protection from the whims of his master. Serfs in France and the Prussian and Austrian Empires had a venerable tradition of appealing to royal courts to defend their rights. They sometimes found in their favor. A Russian serf had no legal rights and Catherine the Great removed the last remaining recourse of the serf, the right of direct appeal to the emperor. The major difference from slavery was that Russian serfs were required to pledge allegiance to the tsar and had the dubious privileges of paying taxes and serving in the national army, both deeply detested. Peter the Great had abolished formal slavery in Russia in 1723 because too many serfs were selling themselves into slavery and thereby avoiding taxes and military service. This says much about the nature of Russian serfdom. The levels of exploitation and the degree of debasement generated fierce resentments among the serfs and deep fear and suspicion among the nobles. This was not a theoretical fear. The Pugachev Revolt (1773–75) had far more in common with the Haitian Revolution in terms of violence than it did with the serf revolts of Western and Central Europe. Nobles who fell into rebel hands were murdered indiscriminately. The almost contemporary peasant revolts in the Austrian Empire – in Bohemia and Transylvania – were also violent, but on both sides the violence was more restrained, and primarily directed against real estate rather than people. Executions were restricted to the leaders of the revolt. In Russia, the specter of Pugachev remained within living memory well into the nineteenth century and haunted the nobility until 1917. Few Russian nobles were under much illusion about the real feelings of their serfs toward them.

The delegitimization of serfdom had advanced steadily in Russia in parallel with that in Europe. Nearly all of the Empire's elite recognized the abusive and corrupting power of serfdom. The attempts that were made to delegitimize serfdom in ideological terms were lame and unconvincing, possessing none of the power of the pro-slavery ideologies of the southern United States. From Catherine the Great onward, all the emperors believed that Russian serfdom was harmful for the Empire economically, politically, and, above all, morally. Often, the emperors used the word slave (*rab*) or slavery (*rabstvo*) to describe the peasantry rather than the more technical term serf (*krepostnoi*) or serfdom

---

[6] S. Tolstoy, *The Diaries of Sofia Tolstoy*, C. Porter (tr.) (Richmond, 2009), p. xii.

(*krepostnichestvo*). In 1834, for example, Nicholas I wrote: "Since the time I came to the throne, I have gathered all the papers which relate to the legal process which I want to lead against slavery when the time comes to free the peasantry in all the empire."[7] But as with his predecessors, the time never came for Nicholas to do this. The practical problems of freeing tens of millions of serfs were overwhelming. The state was built on serfdom and a real fear existed within the ruling elite that emancipation would lead to the collapse of the state. Even attempts to limit some of the worst abuses of serfdom provoked such hostility from the nobility that they were hurriedly abandoned. Nicholas I set up no fewer than nine secret commissions to look at ways of reforming or abolishing serfdom. Each time, the commissions concluded that serfdom needed to be abolished, but not at that moment, which was hardly surprising since the commissions were dominated by some of the largest serf owners in Russia. The one commission that made a serious attempt to limit the abuses of serfdom, led by Count Kiselev, one of the most able ministers of the nineteenth century and a personal friend of Nicholas, was abandoned by Nicholas at the critical moment. Within the bureaucracy by mid-century, there was a small group, as in Prussia, which, though comprising nobles, was committed to abolition in the interests of the state. Yet, these were relatively junior officials who had no influence on this most sensitive of matters.

All over Europe, the French Revolution and revolutionary wars had stimulated emancipations. The humiliation of defeat and fears for national survival had galvanized the political will to abolish serfdom. Russia, however, had emerged triumphant from the wars in 1815. Victory over Napoleon demonstrated the effectiveness of the serf system, if not its legitimacy. Alexander I had thought much about abolishing serfdom and, in 1815, at the height of his prestige, he had sufficient political capital to at least attempt emancipation. Yet, the crushing victory of the Empire removed the stimulus of reform and Alexander opted for stability rather than a new upheaval. His successor, Nicholas I, the embodiment of what an autocrat should be, neither had sufficient nerve to push reform through nor faced a crisis of sufficient magnitude to force him. From 1815 to 1853, Russian prestige and power dominated the continent. In such circumstances, the political will to take on the task of emancipation was always lacking. All initiatives failed in the end.

The only major emancipation before 1861 had been in the Baltic states, a peripheral area of the Empire. But this was widely recognized to have been a disaster. The peasantry were freed there, but without land, creating an impoverished rural proletariat in which class hatreds mingled with ethnic

[7] A. P. Zablotskii-Desiatovksii, *Graf P. D. Kiselev e ero vremia: materialy dlia istorii Imperatorov Aleksandra I, Nikolaia I n Aleksandra II* (St. Petersburg, 1882), Vol. 2, p. 210.

ones in a particularly poisonous mix. The reform in the Baltic states provided a model of how not to emancipate the serfs. What was singularly lacking was a model of how to do this. The problems were immense and no state had ever attempted such a large emancipation. In France, Prussia, and the Austrian Empire, the emancipations had been traumatic, but serfdom in these places involved much smaller numbers and was embedded in a much more diverse social structure. In Russia, the serfs were an absolute majority of the population and they existed in a social structure that was starkly binary in nature. Russia was a servile society in the full meaning of the word rather than a society with serfs. Serfdom in Russia ground on through inertia in the first half of the nineteenth century and, until something sufficiently traumatic occurred, there was little prospect that this would change.

The Crimean War of 1853 to 1856, in which Russia lost to Britain, France, and the Ottoman Empire, provided sufficient trauma to the Russian political system to convulse it out of the stasis that Nicholas had attempted to impose on it. Defeat on Russian soil, the death of the Emperor Nicholas I in 1855, and the realization that the Empire's status as a great power was at stake shook the political elite out of its complacency, not least the new Emperor Alexander II. The only reform that matched the gravity of the situation was the emancipation of the serfs. It was widely believed within the elite that without emancipation Russia would fall further and further behind the Western powers. For the first time in a generation, emancipation moved to the center of the political agenda. Emancipation would be dependent on many factors, but first and foremost would be the attitude of Alexander. Without his support, there was no possibility of emancipation. Alexander revealed his intentions, in a typically ambiguous way, in a speech to representatives of the Moscow nobility in 1856.

I have learned, gentlemen, that rumours have spread among you of my intention to abolish serfdom. To refute any groundless gossip on so important a subject I consider it necessary to inform you that I have no intention of doing so immediately. But, of course, and you yourselves realize it, the existing system of serf ownership cannot remain unchanged. It is better to begin abolishing serfdom from above than to wait for it to abolish itself from below. I ask you, gentlemen, to think of ways of doing this. Pass on my words to the nobles for consideration.[8]

Alexander's model, insofar as he had one, was the Prussian one, as his reference to reform from above indicated. But beyond that, he had no clear idea.

---

[8] S. F. Platonov, *Aleksandr II Vremia Velikikh Reform: Kratkii Obzor Vremeni Imperatora Aleksandra II i Velikh Reform* (Moscow, 2013), p. 69.

Alexander was committed to reform from the end of the Crimean War. As an emperor with unlimited powers, unburdened with assemblies, and responsible only to his conscience and God, he was free to introduce whatever measure he wished. However, on this matter his position was much less secure than it seemed. He was opposed by most of his family, the court, the bureaucratic elite, and the provincial nobility. His grandfather and great-grandfather had been murdered because they had offended the great nobility. Within his family, only his brother, Grand Duke Konstantine, and his aunt, Grand Duchess Elena Pavlovna, unequivocally supported him. Small groups of committed abolitionists were concentrated in the Ministry of the Interior and the Naval Ministry, but these were middle-ranking officials, far removed from setting policy on the serf question. Emancipation would be a political battle waged within the elite, first over whether or not to emancipate and second over the terms of emancipation. Popular or economic reasons were secondary in this battle.

Alexander's intention was to follow the Prussian model by introducing reform from above. On his summer vacation in 1857, he discussed emancipation with Prussian experts. The problem for Alexander was that the Prussian model was useful only in a very general sense. The Russian context was very different in its scale and intensity. Finding a solution that was politically feasible and satisfied both the nobility and the peasantry was to prove difficult. The overwhelming majority of the nobility were opposed to emancipation in principle and even more so when it threatened to deprive them of access to land. The peasantry anticipated being emancipated with the land they worked and without compensation to the nobility. Seeking to resolve this dilemma, Alexander turned to the bureaucracy as his father had done so many times before. True to form, the bureaucratic committee debated for eighteen months and then informed the emperor that there was little that could be done. After nearly two years of work, Alexander found himself no further forward.

The year 1857 provided a critical juncture in the emancipation process. The bureaucracy delivered its verdict that the time was not right, the initial shock of defeat in the Crimea was diminishing, and the Empire was peaceful. There was no imminent threat to the serf system outside the political elite and it could have continued under its own inertia for decades more. Everything was tending toward the discreet dropping of the emancipation project, but it was at this point that Alexander decisively intervened in the process. He publicly called for the nobility to submit reform projects, thereby taking the issue of emancipation out of the hands of the bureaucracy and openly committing the state to some form of emancipation. The battle now shifted to what type of emancipation would be enacted and who would enact it. The failure of the bureaucracy to deliver any sort of reform led Alexander to set up a commission under one of the few men that enjoyed his complete trust, General Iakov Rostovtsev. This was an ad hoc commission outside the normal bureaucratic chain of command and answerable only to the emperor. Rostovtsev was allowed to choose the members of his commission and, critically, he selected them overwhelmingly from the younger bureaucrats who were committed to emancipation. He also selected several experts on the question from outside the bureaucracy who shared the same general commitment to emancipation. This commission's task was to draft the emancipation decree, subject to revision at the highest level.

Three basic principles were established: immediate freedom of the serf from the lord, emancipation with land which would be communally owned, and compensation for the landlords for the loss of their property. These principles reflected awareness of the calamitous emancipation in the Baltic states in 1819. What was at stake in 1857 was how much land the peasantry would receive and what levels of compensation would be offered to the nobility.

These were technical issues that the experts could work out, but it was also an intensely political process in which opponents of emancipation sought by every means to discredit the Commission in the eyes of the emperor and to convince him to abandon it. The emperor was subject to constant pressure from the court, senior bureaucrats, and his entourage to bring the emancipation project to an end. This type of politics helps explain the longevity of serfdom across Europe, where reforming monarchs confronted at every turn opponents of emancipation. This was a battle fought not in ministries or committee rooms, but in soirées, balls, and hunting parties. The informal side of autocratic politics was particularly dangerous for the supporters of emancipation since, with the exception of Rostovtsev, they were excluded from this battle as they were rarely in the presence of the emperor. It was widely feared that Alexander would give way under such pressure, as he was not known for his strength of character. Yet Alexander showed unsuspected steel and, ably supported by his brother Grand Duke Konstantine Nikolaevich and his aunt Grand Duchess Elena Pavlovna, remained steadfast in his support for the Commission, intervening openly at critical junctures to support it. The Committee was able to complete its work and produce draft legislation that for its time and place was extremely radical.

The proposals of the Commission, which became law with only minor modifications in 1861, embodied the principles of peasant freedom from the lord's authority, emancipation with land, and redemption payments to the lords for that land. The government was to pay the redemption fees and the peasantry would repay the government over the next fifty years. By this Act, 22 million people were emancipated from serfdom. A transitional period of two years was established, but serfdom as an institution and as the foundation of the Russian state was gone. Two years later, a similar Act freed the remaining state serfs.

The Emancipation Act has been subjected to withering criticism over the decades. Its failure to satisfy either the nobility or the peasantry was obvious from the start. It has been blamed for many of the subsequent disasters in Russian history. Yet, the criticism seems unfair to say the least. The achievements of the emancipation were staggering. Twenty-two million people were emancipated, virtually without violence, from a form of slavery. A similar Act two years later freed another 23 million people. The contrast with the United States undergoing its own traumatic emancipation process at the same time is striking. The Emancipation Act was the foundation stone of a modern state, giving the Empire the possibility of developing into a state based on law and citizens rather than despotism and bondsmen.

THE AFTERMATH OF SERFDOM

Serfdom had been abolished, but its malevolent legacy lived on for decades. The peasantry was bitterly disappointed with the terms of emancipation, since it had expected to receive the land it worked without paying any compensation. In their eyes, the land had already been paid for several times over by the sweat and blood of their ancestors. The moral outrage of the peasants endured until the 1917 Revolution, when they finally imposed their version of a just settlement on the countryside, the so-called Black Repartition (the seizure and redistribution of all non-peasant lands).

The long-term goal of the emancipators had been to create citizens out of serfs. They had recognized that this would be the work of at least two generations and that formal emancipation had only been the beginning of the process. Transforming serfs into citizens would require further reforms to the legal system, the provision of universal education, and economic development. However, none of these hopes was to be realized, or at least realized in ways sufficient to make peasants into citizens. The last two tsars, Alexander III and Nicholas II, proved to be more interested in imposing the state on the peasants than integrating them into it. The peasants remained apart from the state with little but mutual hostility connecting them. Very rapid population increase in the decades after the emancipation created unprecedented pressure on the land. In these circumstances, grievances over the emancipation settlement grew rather than diminished over the decades. Resentment at the continuing presence of the nobility in the countryside remained as strong as ever. Riots in Poltava Province in 1902 shocked the government by the ferocity of peasant violence and the depth of peasant alienation from the regime. Yet, nothing was done to address peasant grievances and the bankruptcy of government policy toward the peasantry was revealed in all its clarity in the 1905 Revolution. Russian defeat in the Russo-Japanese War in 1903 to 1904 gave the peasantry the opportunity to solve the peasant question from below. Revolution swept the countryside as peasants burned manor houses and seized the land and property of nobles. Brutal repression in 1906 restored the authority of the government, but did nothing to address the fundamental grievances of the peasantry. The Stolypin Reforms attempted to create a new basis of support for the regime in the countryside by establishing a class of independent small peasant proprietors who would support the government. However, the First World War cut short this final attempt to solve the peasant question by the imperial regime.

CONCLUSION

By the second half of the 1860s, serfdom had disappeared from Europe. A cycle that began with the emancipation of the French peasantry in 1789 closed with the emancipation of state peasants in Russia in 1863. An institution that had existed in various forms in Europe for a millennium and a half disappeared within the space of about eighty years. The process of emancipation was rooted in the delegitimization of serfdom that began with the Enlightenment thinkers in the eighteenth century. Remarkably rapidly, the moral case for serfdom was undermined and from then on the institution was defended purely on pragmatic grounds. But the moral case on its own was incapable of mobilizing sufficient political will to destroy such a deep-rooted institution. Its defenders were numerous, articulate, and located at the very heart of power. Even the most powerful monarchs, such as Catherine the Great and Frederick the Great, accepted that they had little power in this respect. Only Joseph II in the Austrian Empire sought to take on the vested interests that supported serfdom and abolish it. Joseph made a determined and prolonged attempt to emancipate the serfs, yet in the end he failed and serfdom survived in the Austrian Empire until the 1848 revolutions. Joseph's failure revealed the limits of reform, however rational and moral the reform was. Until the broader political context changed, no emancipation was possible in any major state.

The wider political context changed in the most radical way just as Joseph was accepting defeat in his attempt to abolish serfdom. The French Revolution and the responses to it opened the way to emancipation at a very rapid pace. The Revolution provided the two basic models of emancipation. The peasants in France emancipated themselves through a series of risings from 1788 to 1792. This emancipation from below was supported and recognized, albeit belatedly, by the central authority in ways which would have been impossible under the Old Regime. Prussia provided the alternative model of emancipation. This was an emancipation initiated from above and framed to take account above all of the interests of the state. Crushing military defeat allowed the monarch, with the support of a few enlightened officials, to emancipate the peasantry regardless of the risks involved. Only a crisis that threatened the existence of the state could mobilize sufficient political will to carry out emancipation. The Austrian and Russian Empires survived the crisis of the Revolutionary and Napoleonic eras with serfdom intact. Existential crises transformed the situation in Austria in 1848 and in Russia in 1853 to 1856. Both states responded with emancipation projects that definitively ended serfdom. The emancipation of the serfs in Europe was rooted in the long term in serfdom's loss of intellectual legitimacy after the Enlightenment and in the short term by acute political crises arising from revolution and war.

A GUIDE TO FURTHER READING

Beales, Derek, *Joseph II*, 2 vols. (Cambridge, 1987, and 2009).
Blum, Jerome, *The End of the Old Order in Rural Europe* (Princeton, NJ, 1978).
Clark, Christopher, *Iron Kingdom: The Rise and Downfall of Prussia 1600–1947* (London, 2006).
Eddie, S. A., *Freedom's Price: Serfdom, Subjection and Reform in Prussia 1648–1848* (Cambridge, 2013).
Field, Daniel, *The End of Serfdom: Nobility and Bureaucracy in Russia, 1855–1861* (Cambridge, MA, 1976).
Jones, Peter M., *The French Peasantry in the French Revolution* (Cambridge, 1988).
Link, Edith M., *The Emancipation of the Austrian Peasant 1740–1798* (New York, 1949).
Markoff, John, *The Abolition of Feudalism: Peasants, Lords and Legislators in the French Revolution* (Pittsburgh, PA, 1996).
McPhee, Peter, *The French Revolution 1789–1799* (Oxford, 2002).
Moon, David, *The Abolition of Serfdom in Russia, 1762–1907* (Harlow, 2001).
Wcislo, Francis W., *Reforming Rural Russia: State, Local Society and National Politics 1855–1914* (Princeton, NJ, 1990).

CHAPTER 19

BRITISH ABOLITIONISM FROM THE VANTAGE OF PRE-COLONIAL SOUTH ASIAN REGIMES

INDRANI CHATTERJEE

What did British Parliamentary abolition of the slave trade in 1807 and delegalization of slavery in 1833 to 1843 mean for the British colony in India? This chapter answers by foregrounding pre-colonial Hindu, Buddhist, Turko-Afghan, Rajput, and Mughal regimes of "wealth-in-people" in the Indian subcontinent. These regimes, which treated slaves as "property," also ensured basic provisions and protections for them. The English East India Company re-engineered these property regimes as "antislavery" measures. Earlier scholarship on British abolition did not take pre-colonial regimes of slave wealth into account. This chapter addresses these regimes of property in the first part, before surveying the effects of delegalization on the lives of both owners as well as of the owned in the subsequent years.

PROPERTY AS A THEOLOGICAL CATEGORY

Four distinct aspects of property in pre-colonial South Asia set the treatment of slaves-as-property apart from the terms in which property came to be discussed in British-made law in the nineteenth century. First, as Michael Aung-Thwin had suggested in his study of classical Burmese laws, property was always discussed in terms of its owners. The question was not whether a person was a slave, but "To whom are you bonded and for what purpose?"[1] Thus, when historians studied the nature of "slavery" in the subcontinent's past, they were required to ask themselves about the property-holding institution *before* they could ask about the transfers or treatment of such property. This was because from the outset, the subcontinent was home to a plethora of contemporary Vedic Hindu, Upanishadic Buddhist, and Jaina philosophical and epistemic traditions, all of which pronounced upon "property" in terms of its owners. For instance, as modern scholars of the Dharmasastra (Hindu jurisprudence) have found, the ideal owner was the "extended family" (*kula*) that performed rituals of

---

[1] M. Aung-Thwin, "Athi, Kyun-Taw, Hpaya-Kyun: Varieties of Commendation and Dependence in Pre-Colonial Burma," in Anthony Reid (ed.), *Slavery, Bondage and Dependency in Southeast Asia* (New York, 1983), pp. 64–89.

birth and death.² These jurists, acknowledging that all property was socially constructed, had therefore placed both the definition of property and ownership within the same ontological terrain. As Donald Davis puts it, that a certain something was property and certain person(s) its owner(s) also rested on concurrent or "practical observation" or cognition by several people, including the owner(s). This had procedural implications; witnessing and personalized knowledge were established in order to first determine the "title" and then the integrity of all transactions in property.

Broadly, all property was categorized as either mobile (*jangama*) or immobile (*asthavara*). The former included cattle, coin, and slaves; the latter included houses, lands, ponds, and orchards. Since the locus of ownership lay in the wider "family," jurists went to great lengths to protect co-ownership rights in property. For instance, codes such as the *Arthasastra* (written between the third and the eighth century AD) tried to balance such multiple proprietary rights of owners to their slaves along with the usufructuary rights of those who hired them or took them on loan from the owners. In the context of discussing pledged slaves, the text warns the creditor not to make the pledged work at unclean tasks (such as cleaning dung). It also alerted the creditor that "giving corporal punishment to them, and dishonoring them shall result in the loss of the capital and result in the freedom" of the pledged female – whether domestic servant or sharecropping cultivator.³

Contemporary Buddhist codes (*Mulasarvastivadin vinaya*), written for the guidance of ordained men by other monks, also preserved the proprietory rights over such slaves as belonged to laymen living in the communities around the monasteries. These codes thus forbade monks from luring laymen's property into monasteries, and then buying or selling them. Gregory Schopen argues that by prohibiting the ordination of such slaves, many of whom were female, these codes preserved ordination as a purely male free person's privilege. However, since such slaves-as-property could be received as gifts by monks, or as a monk's inheritance, the availability of dedicated laborers was assured to each such gift-receiving monastery and teaching lineage. A Vinaya text even had the Buddha direct that slaves inherited by the monastic order (*sangha*) by the provisions of a will be held as "property in common."⁴

Monastic lineages acquired property in people under a particular form of government that I call "monastic governmentality." Such holding of

² Donald R. Davis, *The Spirit of Law* (Cambridge, 2010), pp. 89–107.
³ *The Kautiliya Arthasastra*, trans. R. P. Kangle (Delhi, 1972), 3.13: 9–11.
⁴ Gregory Schopen, *Buddhist Monks and Business Matters: Still More Papers in Monastic Buddhism in India* (Honolulu, HI, 2004), pp. 118, 193–218. For his discussion of gender and slavery, see Gregory Schopen, "On Some Who Are Not Allowed to Become Buddhist Monks or Nuns: An Old List of Types of Slaves or Unfree Laborers," *Journal of American Oriental Society*, 130 (2010): 225–34.

property in common was particular to far-flung monastic governments of all schools of Hindus and Buddhists in the first half of the millennium. Sometimes this meant the attachment of entire families in "gift" to a monastic corporation. Such gifts of attached lay workers to favored teachers constituted a particular kind of monastic self-denial by means of a permanent gift of people since the earliest centuries. This practice of donation was the hallmark of generosity. Such laborers were especially valuable for monastic lineages which frowned on monks continuing to cultivate, or to manufacture goods for sale or trade. The subsistence of such monastic lineages depended on the lay cultivators, craftsmen, artisans, and traders who were attached to these lineages. Sometimes such laborers were "gifted" to individual monks or temples by lay followers. In Southern India between the tenth and fourteenth centuries, individual devotees gave "gifts" of especially favored female slaves, to Hindu and Jain (non-Buddhist) monks, deities, and temples. These females were the *tevaratiyal* (Tamil for "devotee"; other terms used were "daughter of god" and "temple-servant"). To make such gifts was to shelter them from use and abuse at the hands of *lay* human actors: to be thus the "slave of a god," a deity, or a teacher was to occupy a protected and privileged status.

Second, the model of attaching individuals and families to either a monastic teacher or to a lay military commander rested on an implicit recognition that the person(s) thus attached were provided for by their owners, and kept whatever income made by this attachment. The *Arthasastra* assured the slaves that they were entitled to enjoy not only whatever they earned without prejudice to their master's work, but also the inheritance received from their fathers.[5] Such a provision allowed male slaves in the twelfth century to work for visiting Syrian Jewish merchants, and even to travel abroad as their appointed agents. Such provisions also allowed medieval Tamil temple women (the *tevaratiyal*) to use their acquired rights in property to transact with the managers of the temples to secure regular support from them in the form of food and the right to perform particular kinds of ritual functions. Clearly, slave-agents and freedmen alike held and managed property.

Third, both claims of slaves to support and claims to serve in particular capacities were in turn heritable. This was premised on the ability of slaves to earn and keep their income, and therefore to bequeath it to, and inherit it from, kinsmen and women. Classical legal codes, such as the *Arthasastra*, promised that the property of slaves shall pass into the hands of their kinsmen; only in the absence of any kinsman was a master to take it. In a situation where the demands of kinship were emphatically upheld in property law and inheritance, the emphasis lay in classifying each slave according to his or her identity in both birth-based households (*kula*) as well as in socially assigned working groups (*jati*).

Fourth, all lay and ecclesiastical governors, by virtue of maintaining social order, were involved in safeguarding the procedural aspects of transactions in property, such as sale, hire, lease, and mortgage of slaves. Hence, documents from the thirteenth century show deeds of transfers of slaves that had to be fully witnessed by a minimum of five men of significance, or heads of different professions in the neighborhood of the city (*panchamukhanagara*).

Most of these four aspects of slavery-as-property regimes were absorbed into the practices of Central and West Asian (Persian, Turkic, Afghan, and Mongol-Mughal) governors who settled in the subcontinent from the thirteenth century. Many of the Muslim mystic brotherhoods (Sufi lineages) shared with the Buddhists and Jains two common characteristics: first, a direct ritualized relationship between a teacher and a disciple, and, through this basic dyad, a series of adherences and associations between the disciple's household and kingroup, and the teacher's intellectual and social lineages; and, second, it established a material economy of "gifts" that disciples made to their teachers. These gifts often took the shape of landed estates, herds, tolls of lucrative markets, and trades.

Though earlier tenants, cultivators, and traders living on such lands may have continued other aspects of their lives, there are no records of entire clusters of laborers given to any single entity that can be found in the Turkish or Persian languages for this period. A great deal more is known about slaves purchased by lay military commanders and soldiers and trained in their households. Such slaves lived in a regime in which males brought up since childhood in the household-establishment of a military commander or Sultan could also expect to graduate to positions of authority over time, including the government of provinces on behalf of the Sultan or master. In studying these groups of slaves, Sunil Kumar has referred to a dialectic, and not a binary opposition, of *bandagi* and *naukari* in early modern northern India.[6] According to Kumar, the term *bandagi* arose from the term *banda* ("slave" singular), which summed up a political relationship originating in a soldier's household that involved the training of loyal personnel as the backbone of particular military-administrative corps. On the other hand, *naukari* (from *nokor*, singular) represented a

    [6] Sunil Kumar, "Bandagi and Naukari: Studying Transitions in Political Culture and Service Under the North Indian Sultanates, 13th–16th Centuries," in Samira Sheikh and Francesca Orsini (eds.), *After Timur Left: Culture and Circulation in Fifteenth-Century North India* (Delhi, 2014), pp. 60–110; idem, "Service, Status and Military Slavery in the Delhi Sultanate: Thirteenth and Fourteenth Centuries," in Indrani Chatterjee and Richard M Eaton (eds.), *Slavery and South Asian History* (Bloomington, IN, 2006), pp. 83–114.

cluster of relationships – such as that of personal retainer, loyal friend, comrade in arms, and bodyguard – that could be enacted between the same military commander and his non-slave companions. The latter came very close to the category of "favored slave" (*banda-i-khass*) known from the Persian chronicles of the Sultanate. Such specially privileged slaves are also known from epigraphs on monuments of that period that identified the favored slave with the title, "al-Sultani" (of or belonging to the Sultan).

These monumental buildings are crucial testimony to the twofold success of such patterns of proprietorship in slaves by both groups of owners. While access to bricks, stones, and mortar (rare in a period when most residential buildings were of timber, mud, and thatch) spoke of the slave's worldly successes, the purpose to which such buildings were put indicated the slave-sponsor's command of courtly etiquette (*adab*), as well as an Islamicate ethical and legal learning. In 1242, for example, a mosque was built in Bihar by "the slave (*'abd*) of the sultan (al-sultani) Tughril Tughan Khan. This slave-of-a-slave-Sultan was Mubarak, the treasurer (*al-khazan*)."[7] Such evidence establishes a smooth continuity with older regimes of property-holding both in slaves and by slaves (the second principle outlined above). Mosque-building by slaves thus made visible their worldly success as well as their good standing as Muslims, especially when their epigraphs used the oft-cited *hadith* that those who built a mosque (Arabic, singular, *masjid*; plural *masajid*) for "Allah would be guaranteed a place in paradise." Epigraphs from buildings such as mosques, monastic residential lodges (*khanqahs*), and repair of tombs are significant for this reason. Such dedications spoke of the unimpeachable status that Islamic legal learning (*'ilm*) had already attained among slaves in both lay and Sufi Muslim households by the end of the fourteenth century.

Furthermore, the tone of humility taken in these slaves' epigraphs displayed the cultivation of courtly manners (*adab*). Take, for instance, the epigraph of one "Majd of Kabul," the favored slave (*bandah-i-khas*) of very powerful lay governors.[8] In 1267, this slave presided over the construction of a tomb commemorating one of his masters, Sultan Shah, who had died two years earlier; he also inscribed in this building a sign of his gratitude for the masters' kindnesses (*'abdaha ma al-mamnun wa naimataha*"). A self-representation of modesty and humility was discernible in those dedications in which slave-builders identified themselves as "weak" or "humble" (*al-'abd al-zaif*), regardless of their wealth and power at the time of their sponsorship. This persisted even when slaves were not

[7] Qeyamuddin Ahmad, *Corpus of Arabic and Persian Inscriptions of Bihar, A.D. 640–1200* (Patna: K. P. Jayaswal Research Institute, 1973), Inscription 1 and p. 5.
[8] Ahmad, *Corpus*, Inscription 2 and pp. 6–9.

deracinated, and could still remember their father's name, such as the slave called "Bahram bin Haji" (Bahram the son of Haji) in a fourteenth-century epigraph. Wealthy enough to sponsor mosque construction, this man's reasons for doing so were signaled in terms of a larger pious vocabulary. Thus, the epigraph highlighted his trust in Allah (*al 'abd al-wāsiq bi-Allah*), hope for His mercy, and prayers for the pardon of his parents. It was also possible that such humility in self-presentation corresponded with the humbler stations at which such slaves worked. Even if such a slave was appointed to the office of a news courier (*barīd*) for an entire provincial administrative unit (*khitta*) in the mid fourteenth century – a very influential position – his profile on such public construction remained meek as a claim on *civitas*.[9]

Though there are fewer epigraphic traces of female slaves as sponsors of devotional buildings in Eastern India, Islamic jurists appeared to have provided incentive to the production of loyalty when they divorced the reproduction of the jural status of the slave (Persian term *banda,* Arabic *'abd*) from that of the physical reproduction of persons in households containing slave women. It is significant that in the thirteenth century, an Islamic jurist Ziya al-Din Barani counted the famous courtier-poet Amir Khusraw, who was also a co-disciple of a famous Chishti Sufi shaykh, as a *freedman*, not a slave. Amir Khusraw was the child of a Muslim slave father and a Hindu slave's daughter; even in the eyes of an orthodox jurist, he was a freedman-client (*maulazada*) and not a slave (*banda*).[10] The famous Sufi mystic, Sharafuddin Maneri, also had a son with a slave girl (*kanizak yek pesar shud*); the genealogy treats the son as just another heir of the father. This predisposition toward freedman status of infants born of a slave mother and a non-slave father in Islamic law favored not only the infants born of slave mothers, but also the slave mothers themselves, who acquired the elevated status of *umm-i-walad* as a result of such labor. The children born of such mothers in a layman's household were often referred to as *khanah-zada* (born in the household) and treated as persons with substantial claims upon their erstwhile masters and employers.

In this, as in other norms taken over from classical societies of the subcontinent into societies living under Islamic law after the thirteenth century, much remained unchanged. What shifted was the unit of ownership of a slave. Islamic legal theory of property did not allow an entire family to own a slave, only one person at a time could. This singularity of proprietorship could protect the slave from being used or abused by those who were *not* her owners. Thus, Maneri advised, "As long as all his [slave's]

[9] Ahmad, *Corpus,* 5–6: 16; Shamsuddin Ahmed, *Inscriptions of Bengal* (Rajshahi, 1960), Vol. 4, Inscription 11 and p. 30; Inscription 15 and pp. 42–3.
[10] Kumar, "Bandagi," p. 75.

qualities of service are devoted to the Lord, he cannot become the slave of anyone or anything but the Lord."

There were, however, two ways in which slaves could be, and were, transferred by lay owners to religious estates such as those governed by Sufi mystics. One was as a permanent endowment, by means of a deed called *waqfnama*. By definition, a *waqf* is a formally codified endowment of property in perpetuity to Allah according to which any prior legal claim of the owner is negated. Under Sunni Hanafi law, only immovable property (*ushr* and *kharaj* land) could be objects of *waqf*: but it allowed exceptions in the case of moveable property that followed immoveable property. Slaves fell in the former category, along with cattle, tools, and other machinery of a landed estate. Therefore, a *waqfnamah* that listed slaves-as-moveable property effectively and permanently removed them from the possession of the founder of the *waqf*, and simultaneously ensured the singularity of the authority of the saint over that slave-as-endowed property.

Both Sufi (Muslim mystics) teachers and lay Sultans presided over territorial estates (*vilayat*) administered by particular courts. In the subcontinent, the Persian term *dargah* (literally a threshold of a court) was associated from the thirteenth century with a shrine built over the grave of a revered religious leader. By the fourteenth to fifteenth centuries, many such *dargah* were residential-cum-learning complexes, made up of a school (*madrassa*) and an assembly hall, as well as a lodge or hostel (*khanqah*), which could also in turn act as a hospice when necessary. Proclaiming one's slavery to a *dargah* was thus equal to proclaiming one's devotion to a saint. It was also close to the status of the temple-owned slaves referred to earlier. In both temple and *dargah*, such servant-slaves shared in the sanctity of the revered saint and the power of the deity to whom the estate was dedicated. Slavery to, and services performed for, the "saintly" teachers (*khidmat-i darveshan*) was often analogized with keeping the company of angels. Such claims distinguished the slaves of such Sufi teachers from those who were non-slave lay followers and disciples of the same teachers. This paralleled the greater power and value of the slave, slave-born, and freedman-client over non-slaves in the administration of the lay Sultans. The same values shaped the exalted status of the "slave of the dargah," master to favored disciple, who succeeded his teacher as a chief administrator. By the sixteenth century, even lay military warlords proclaimed their devotion to a Sufi shaykh as a form of bonded enslavement, as for instance one non-slave proclaimed his attachment to the Madari Sufi teacher at the head of a lineage originating from Syria and settled in Patna (*bandagi-i-hazrat-i Miran Sayyid Jumman Madari*).[11]

---

[11] Ahmad, *Corpus*, 56: 131–4.

By the early sixteenth century, as the evidence above reveals, the two distinct loci of proprietorship – one monastic, the other lay – had begun to merge into one. Yet, tensions remained between the two. One of the reasons for this tension was precisely to do with the inheritance of wealth from those who were both "slave" of the lay Sultans and "slaves of the shrines." The death of a lay Muslim master did not automatically manumit his or her slaves. They remained inheritable parts of the estate, and laymen's heirs could sell each part of their share of an inheritance to whoever paid the best price. When such dead men had themselves been slaves in the service of a Sultan, the latter could technically claim to inherit the slaves of his dead servant. Such governors developed very high stakes in monitoring civil transactions (sales, inheritance, mortgage) in slaves. Living as they did among people among whom transfers of "wealth-in-people" occurred for both pious and temporal ends, lay Sultans became as invested in issues of succession and transfer of property as monastic administrators in other estates.

Among their non-Muslim subjects, corporate sharing or partnership in proprietorship was permissible. This allowed devout lay and monastic Hindus and Buddhists alike to give gifts from their "wealth-in-people" in ways that shared the profit of such a gift. For instance, an overlord was often included as an indirect beneficiary of a lay person's gift of people to a deity, as when lay local military commanders-cum-tax collectors (called *nayaka*) "donated" a corps of cowherds to a temple, but took care to include both the immediate superior and their common overlord, a king, as gaining spiritual "merit" from such a gift.[12] Their mention in such grants reveals an awareness of the high value of such personnel to the lay governors, who after all were just as determined to expand their own access to skilled labor as their subordinates.

But Islamic jurists of the same period appeared unwilling to dilute principles of individual proprietorship of a slave in order to allow access to third parties. Even a man's bride could not encroach on the husband's property in a slave girl without his permission. The wife's right to transact in her husband's property had to be expressly written into her marriage agreement. For example, one wife secured four guarantees from the husband: that he would not take a second wife; nor beat his wife; nor abandon her without food and maintenance without her consent; and, finally, that if he took a slave girl as his concubine, his wife would be "entitled to sell that slave girl and take the proceeds in lieu of her marriage-dower (*mihr*), and if she so desires make that slave girl forbidden (*haram*)

[12] Noboru Karashima (ed.), *A Concise History of South India: Issues and Interpretations* (Delhi, 2014), p. 197.

to the said husband by manumitting her or by marrying her off or by giving her in gift."[13]

Given this stand-off between lay and monastic administrations, and the simultaneous tussle between the Islamic law's individual proprietary authority and non-Islamic practices of corporate property, it was not surprising that an incipient regime, such as that of the early Mughal administration of Akbar, should seek to resolve the multiple tensions in one inspired stroke – by placing Akbar's authority in a continuum of Sufi practice and doctrine. This placed the person of the Mughal emperor in that of a revered teacher, both *guru* (to the majority "Hindu" subjects in the subcontinent) and *pir* (to the minority Muslim subjects). And since Sufi teachers were expected to be learned in the law, the Sufi chronicler, Abul Fazl Allami, also represented Akbar as anxious about the numbers of slaves held by his own imperial household as a violation of Quranic injunctions on rightfully held slave property.

From Akbar's tenure as emperor (1556–1605), the Hindustani term for a disciple (*chela*) of a revered teacher came to be used for all first-generation slaves by Mughal emperors. The term *chela* resonated both with Hindus and with Muslims. It conjured up the fusion of dedicated service and disciplined followership to individual leaders that characterized the novitiates and ordained members of Vaisnava and Saiva "Hindu" *gosain* lineages.[14] Since a great deal of both ethical teaching as well as craft production and cultivation was organized by such Buddhist, Hindu, and Sufi teachers' lodges (*matha, vihara,* and *khanqah*), using the term *chela* for well-trained slaves and servants also made it possible for the disappearance of boundaries between the slave soldier and the non-slave but equally well-trained official to work under a common discipleship of a teacher-emperor. At the same time, positioning the Mughal emperor as both revered teacher and lay judge enabled the Mughal government to also manipulate the instruments of inheritance and succession laws that impinged on other kinds of mobile and immobile "property" of subjects they considered to be their "loyal" subjects, and members of an inner coterie of "companions."

This resolution, however, heightened Mughal administrative vigilance toward the just transfer of proprietary rights in people. Jurists often encountered the transfers of slaves in post-mortem disputes over immoveable and moveable property. For instance, in Surat, male slaves-as-agents of merchants had taken possession of their dead master's effects, including his

[13] Documents 1 and 2, dated between 1637 and 1639, in Shireen Moosvi, *People, Taxation and Trade in Mughal India* (Delhi, 2008), pp. 281–2.

[14] Irfan Habib, "Akbar's Social Views – A study of their Evolution," *Indian History Congress, 53rd Session* (Warangal, 1992–93), pp. 219–36; for Gosains, see William R. Pinch, "The Slave Guru: Masters, Commanders and Disciples in Early Modern South Asia," in Jacob Copeman and Aya Ikegame (eds.), *The Guru in South Asia: New Interdisciplinary Perspectives* (London, 2012), pp. 64–79.

widow and daughter. Though articulated as inheritance or dower claims, such investigations also showed the potential for many well-placed intimate slaves to exercise "mastery" over property, even as they remained legal property of others.

Such a regime had to ensure that transfers of all property, and especially of slaves, was evidenced by either documents or personal witnesses. In 1632, a Mughal emperor, Shahjahan, would not allow Portuguese navies to "steal" people from lands the Mughals claimed as their own. He sent a Mughal navy to recover such "stolen" wealth from the Portuguese and Indo-Portuguese populations settled at Hugli, a port-town on the River Ganges. The Jesuit priest, Cabral (b. 1599), who acted as an intermediary in the negotiations between the Mughal commander and the Portuguese of the town, observed quite acutely that the Portuguese navies had "bought up Bengali prisoners," but "could not show the smallest scrap of a document in support" of these purchases.[15] On these grounds alone, the Portuguese owners were deprived of a fair number of their slaves. Yet, it is hard to estimate the demographic or social impact of such a Mughal-style official "liberation" since there is no consensus about the numbers. More important to note, however, is that the Mughal dispossession of the Portuguese property-owners was based on a very strict interpretation of lawful trade: it did not halt all trading in slaves. While the Portuguese lost their monopoly in supplying slaves to the Arakanese in these years, their place was filled by the Dutch.

The efforts of Mughal regimes to maintain authorized legal standards remained. In the mid seventeenth century, yet another Mughal emperor, an orthodox Sunni Muslim, heard that a Persian (Shi'a) embassy had bought up large numbers of free Indians and was taking them away as slaves; he ordered his officials at the border to dispossess the ambassadors of their goods. The possibility of theft or embezzlement of especially trained slaves remained high in the early eighteenth century. Recognizing their use to European slave-holders in Mughal India, an English governor of the East India Company upheld and extended to Europeans in India the "judicious precautions established by the ancient law of the country (which requires that no slave shall be sold without a cawbowla or deed attested by the Cauzee signifying place of the child's abode) if in the first purchase, (its parents' names, the names of the seller and purchaser, and a minute description of the persons of both) . . ."[16]

[15] John Cabral, November 12, 1633, in *Travels of Fray Sebastian Manrique 1629–1643*, Vol. 59 of Hakluyt Society, 2nd series (Oxford, 1927), pp. 395–400; also Sanjay Subrahmanyam, "Slaves and Tyrants: Dutch Tribulation in Seventeenth-Century Mrauk-U," *Journal of Early Modern History*, 1 (1977): 201–53.
[16] Minute on Regulations of 1774, in *House of Commons, Parliamentary Papers, Slavery in India: Return to an Address dated 13th April 1826*, (Sessional paper no. 125), 1828, 3.

The avoidance of wrongful transfers of property also motivated devout but lay Hindus, who assiduously recorded their gifts of wealth-in-people to particular deities and monks. When Hindu Rajput officers, working for the Mughal administration, sought to extend cultivation in the Brahma-putra River Valley, they did so by dedicating vast numbers of people to deities living on what was until then inviolably sacred estates. These gifts of households to monastic estates deserve discussion because few people have understood that as the property of the gods, they were exempt from use and abuse by powerful laity. Hence, it is critical to note the predominantly non-Brahmanic caste status of such dedicated households. While the majority of the households gifted in 1683 were likely prisoners of war from 1667 to 1668 (Bengali-speakers called *goriya*), the greater majority of the households gifted by 1735 were identified as oblates (*bhakats*), with a tiny minority of the same groups identified as workers (*paiks*).

By 1738, the group that was called *sudra paiks* clustered together a vast range of occupations and statuses. Some among this cluster were skilled workers, literate and numerate (called *kayastha* and *bhandar-kayeth*, respectively). Others carried the emblems of authority – the umbrella, the stave, and the trident (*chhatra-dhara*, *danda-dhara*, *trishul-dhara*) – significant in displays of dignity of the deity. Included among this group were those who worked with waste products (hair, skin, blood, excreta), such as the barber (*napit*), the cobbler (*chamar*), and the sweeper (collect-ively enumerated as *chandal*). The significance of such detailed lists of the "caste" status of such oblates was that they all shared in the exemption from taxation that the monastic estate or the deity enjoyed within the boundaries of the lands in which they lived. Thus, even those workers with the lowest of ritual rank – the so-called untouchables – remained exempt from paying labor services or cash dues to third parties when attached to monastic or religious estates. As in adjacent Buddhist regimes of Burma, Nepal, and Tibet, these attached workers also remained exempt from the lay militia commander's demands for military labor service – a significant life-preserving privilege available only to slaves of the monas-teries (*hpaya-kyun*). In Eastern India, too, therefore, becoming the slaves of gods exempted cultivators, artisans, and merchants from being des-troyed by war.

For these reasons, documenting the transfers of people remained a viable activity even in the later eighteenth century, when erudite Hindu Brahman lawyers codified and translated their legal traditions into Eng-lish. In the compendium that resulted, a clause spoke directly to a wrongful transfer of property-in-a-slave. The Hindu code asserts that enslavement by violence was illegitimate: "If a thief having stolen the child of any person, sells it to another, or a man by absolute violence, forces another to be a slave, the magistrate shall restore such person to his freedom."[17] It appeared that at least in the eyes of the late Mughal officials, the enslavement of a non-slave by means of treachery or force – once outlawed in the *Arthasastra* – remained illegitimate as a source for slaves.

So absolute was the Mughal official guarantee of property-rights-in-people that they were prepared to secure them for *all* groups regardless of the religious identity of the masters. This was most visibly on display when various European (and Christian) slave-owners in Mughal domains requested Mughal authorities to either catch fugitive slaves, or ensure that the religious status of such fugitives would not be changed by the Mughal officials. Even as late as 1786, the Mughal official who administered local policing in Hugli accepted the petition of slave-owning Portuguese Catholics resident in that port-town.

Lay Mughal owners of property-in-slaves in the late eighteenth century were completely conversant with both the slave's status as "property" and his or her simultaneous ability to administer and extend the property of his master or mistress. Furthermore, lay owners, having relied on governors to ensure property rights, expected the same patterns to be followed by the English East India Company's government. An aristocratic Mughal mistress informed the Company's Governor-General that the intersex (referred to as either castrated or as an androgynous being) slave-steward of her household, Daulat Afzun, having been "brought up from his childhood at her household," had been her husband's "agent and cashier, managed all his affairs and signed documents for him."[18] Yet, when this house-bred one (Persian and Islamic legal category of slave) went astray, the mistress minced no words in asking for his punishment: "in Sharia," she said, "a slave is the property of his master and his ungrateful behavior towards him is unlawful." For the moment, putting aside the accuracy of her legal pronouncement, let us note that this simultaneity of property-as-manager-of-property was historically acceptable to Warren Hastings, the English Governor-in-General in Calcutta to whom the mistress complained. So, when Daulat Afzun took the cash, jewels, and other articles entrusted to him and retired from his mistress's household, the Governor-General instructed the local governor of the latter town to apprehend the absconding slave.[19] But twenty years later, the break with this Mughal past became dramatic, and absolute.

---

[17] Nathaniel Brassey Halhed, *A Code of Gentoo Laws* (London, 1776), ch. 8, p. 160. Clauses regarding slaves were re-transcribed versions of older clauses in *Naradasmriti* and *Arthasastra*.

[18] *Calendar of Persian Correspondence* (hereafter, *CPC*) 5: 884 (1776, reprint Calcutta, 1930), pp. 140–1.

[19] *CPC*, 5: 1621 (1779), 371.

COMPARING MUGHAL AND ENGLISH AMELIORATION IN THE LATE
EIGHTEENTH CENTURY

The timing of the break was important. Since the early eighteenth century, the English East India Company had competed with other European companies for control of lucrative trade routes and markets all over the Indian Ocean world. Captains of British boats had thus fixed prices at which they would buy slaves from ports of East Africa for transport to English settlements elsewhere.[20] Only in the late eighteenth century did the break with Mughal property regimes in the Indian subcontinent begin. After 1776 revealed the power of settler-colonists, British ruling regimes became mindful of the political repercussions of inter-racial sexual relationships in the case of ambitious middle-class British officers and soldiers serving in India. These men had often hired or bought Indian female servants to labor in their households, and then established some of them as concubines. These female servants also often came from Muslim households. In aristocratic Muslim and Hindu households of pre-colonial vintage, slave-consorts and concubines had wielded significant influence. If they had borne children to their male owners, they were elevated to the status of *umm-i-walad*, and expected their children to receive maintenance and, sometimes, even to inherit portions of their erstwhile owner's wealth or income. Sometimes, as in the ruling houses of late Mughal Bengal, sons of such women succeeded to their fathers' offices and titles, as did Najm-al-daulah, the son of the slave-entertainer and consort of Mir Jafar, Munni Begam. Such females were the earliest to feel the impact of official British decrees on inheritance and property in Company-administered parts of South Asia. British legal documents after the 1790s shifted the very grounds from under the feet of such slave-born sons and daughters. British law considered wedlock to be the only source of succession; therefore, concubine-born sons were deemed "natural," a euphemism for bastardy.[21]

The related shifting away from Mughal jurisprudence was structural. Already by 1782, learned English Orientalists, such as William Jones, had expressed their disdain for the Muslim and Hindu textualists who served in the older Mughal judiciaries.[22] The latter sought to maintain the physical

[20] See "Terms of Trade at Madagascar" of 1736 to 1753, OIOC, London, Home Miscellaneous 628, pp. 503–13; for subcontracting for the same slaves with "bakshis" of Indian ships, see Press List of Ancient Records of Government of India, Public Department, Vol. 4, pp. 43–4.
[21] For details of these changes, see Indrani Chatterjee, *Gender, Slavery and Law in Colonial India* (Delhi, 1999); idem, "Colouring Subalternity: Slaves, Concubines and Social Orphans under the East India Company," in Gautam Bhadra, Gyan Prakash, and Susie Tharu (eds.), *Subaltern Studies* (New Delhi, 1999), Vol. 10; for Englishmen's slave-concubines in eighteenth-century Bengal Presidency, see Durba Ghosh, *Sex and the Family in Colonial India* (Cambridge, 2006).
[22] William Jones, *The Mahomedan Law of Succession to the Property of Intestates, in Arabick, Engraved on Copper Plates from an Ancient Ms with a Verbal Translation and Explanatory Notes* (London, 1782), Preface.

integrity of slaves, especially against their employers, who were often third parties. From 1790, disputes involving slaves and bondsmen became the special provenance of British criminal law alone, not Muslim criminal law, in courts established by the government of the East India Company. In these cases, the Company-appointed European judges were released from the compulsion to follow Hindu and Muslim *property* laws and practices. By 1793, Mughal judicial interpretations were resolutely subordinated to the superiority of British officers in the localities and in the central judiciary established by the Company. The immediate fallout of this judicial restructuring was that European judges bypassed those very provisions by which both slaves and owners had been compensated when *third parties* physically maimed or destroyed them. In their place, colonial European judges, including William Jones, pleaded on behalf of Europeans' "right to punish" (even unto death) the children and females they had bought, hired, or kept as pledges. Though many local Indian slave-owners and kinsmen of slaves tried to seek compensation from Europeans who had mutilated or killed slaves, after 1793 such claims always failed. No European man ever paid compensation for slaves belonging to an Indian owner or corporation.

The shift became stark after the outbreak of the French Revolution in 1789. Since the French East India Company (and other Catholic powers such as the Portuguese) held substantial colonies in India, the Company's Governor-General in India, Earl Cornwallis, sought to destroy the possibility that rival European militias and navies could be increased by recruiting Indian laborers. He wrote up a law addressed specifically to "Europeans" who hired non-slave persons and then sold them or took them away for sale elsewhere. He required these leases to be executed on paper and signed by both the local district judge and *qazi*. Envisioning the hire-lease contract as a fixed-term contract, Cornwallis devised a clause that would have allowed the hireling to either stay or leave after the expiry of the term; most importantly, it was supposed to protect the hireling from being sold as a slave. So, the Proclamation warned the slave auctioneers at Calcutta and other towns that they were not to sell *ajirs* as slaves. The protection of a pawned person from sale was very old. Yet, the same Mughal officer who had been a staunch ally until then, Muhammad Reza Khan, objected strongly to this legislation.[23] It appeared that the clauses of the Cornwallis Proclamation were not half as protective of the slaves as the Mughal (and Muslim) officer desired.

In the course of Napoleonic warfare, when the British took over coastal Ceylon (named Sri Lanka from 1971) from the Dutch, the Company's

---

[23] *CPC*, 8: 1325 (1788), 570–2.

hunger for African naval manpower grew manifold. From 1801, the British governor of the island authorized the secret purchase of Africans being landed at the Indian ports of Bombay and the Portuguese-held Goa, Daman, and Diu all along the west coast.[24] An expense statement from 1804 shows that the British governor of the island had spent a substantial 20,219 Rix Dollars to buy seventy-nine grown African men and nineteen African boys capable of bearing arms, as well as two women, and in transporting them all to Colombo. Therefore, it is not wrong to suspect that the parliamentary order to stop trading in slaves from 1807 actually benefited manpower-hungry British militias in the colonies. At least in the Indian Ocean, parliamentary abolition permitted British naval patrols of both Crown and Company to take valuable crew off others' boats and ships, and to do so without paying compensation to the owners.[25] This was more or less admitted by the governor of Sri Lanka in 1805 to 1811 when he commented on the 500-to-600-member "Negro Regiment" that "they had scraped together out of Prize vessels."[26] In that sense, and regardless of what the morality or intentions of British middle classes may have been, the effects of the parliamentary law of 1807 were amenable to the physical and structural extension of colonial armies.

EVANGELICAL ROOTS OF BRITISH ABOLITIONISM

In domestic politics within the subcontinent, a similar process unfolded in 1813 to 1856. Company-led measures transformed the Hindu, Buddhist, and Muslim codes and practices of slaves-as-property. The imprint of evangelical Christianity is obvious in these transformations. From the late eighteenth century, many of the European judges who presided over both civil and criminal courts in Company-administered parts of India belonged to a growing minority of devout evangelical Christians. From 1794, with an evangelical Governor-General at the helm of the Company, the temple- and mosque-attached laborers began to lose their protections, as did the monastic traders and bankers themselves.[27] Fairly significant portions of their once-exempt lands were appropriated for taxes levied by the Company.

The effects on South Asian populations of the attached estates were clear. Both pious Hindu and Muslim non-slave donors protested the Company's appropriation of funds because it impinged on their mandated sacraments including *dana* (gift) and *zakat* (charity) respectively. However,

---

[24] Shihan de Silva Jayasuriya, "Recruiting Africans to the British Regiments in Ceylon: Spillover Effects of Abolition in the Atlantic," *African and Asian Studies*, 10 (2011): 15–31.

[25] Indrani Chatterjee, "Abolition by Denial: the South Asian Example," in Gwyn Campbell (ed.), *The Aftermath of Abolition in Indian Ocean Africa and Asia* (London, 2005), pp. 150–68.

[26] Cited in Jayasuriya, "Recruiting Africans," 21.   [27] *CPC*, 11: 624 (1794–95), 147–8.

the denial of funds more directly adversely affected those ordained and novitiate figures who depended on the temple-centered economies in the subcontinent.

Identical effects were experienced by the Muslim slave managers such as Daulat Afzun, who lost the deposited jewels against which he had raised loans on behalf of his master.[28] It was especially revealing that their Muslim master had earlier received income from shops and markets under Mughal imperial seals (*altamgha*). These shops and markets were comprehended under canonically recognized institutions, such as the *waqf*, which permitted less aristocratic donors to assign revenue to endow particular public institutions. In these decades occurred also the direct destruction of the wealth of intersex slaves such as Almas Ali Khan, one of the two principal tax-farmers (*amils*) in the domains of the independent princely regime at Awadh. By 1798, this capable and influential slave manager too had been coerced to give up farms he held in the Gangetic Doab to the amount of 49 lacks of rupees.[29]

The rapid re-calibration of the wealth of the *chela*-run and slave-managed economies suggests that, at least where the Company officials were concerned, political and religious inspiration converged in policy. These officials, both in India and in the House of Commons in Britain, supported evangelical causes. Charles Grant, for instance, who served as the Company's Commercial Resident in Malda in the 1780s, authored the *Observations on the State of Society among Asiatic Subjects of Great Britain* in 1792, and was then elected to the Court of Directors in 1794. He was a director when the Court approved the annexation of Almas Ali Khan's estates by Governor-General Shore (1793–98). He was a Director when the trading gosains from Malda lost their trade privileges.

By virtue of their influence on the Court of Directors, both Shore and Grant ensured a cross-class collaboration with middle- and working-class members in the evangelical churches of early-nineteenth-century Britain. For instance, they secured for a Baptist missionary, William Carey, then working in Bengal as a manager of an indigo-growing plantation owned by a member of the Company's Supreme Council of government (James Udny), the office of teacher of Bengali and Sanskrit in the colonial Fort William College in 1801. Reverend Claudius Buchanan was the Vice Provost of the same college.

These years were critical in consolidating the scope of Evangelicalism in British India. The British and Foreign Bible Society, the first large-scale

[28] *CPC*, II: 203; 323 (1794–95), 52, 81.
[29] Extract of Political Letter from Court of Directors to Bengal, 15 May 1799, in *Minute of the Governor General of Bengal, 13 January 1798 with Papers Therein Referred to and Copy of the Treaty with the Vizier Saadut Ally*, Minutes, Papers of the House of Commons, 1799, para. 41, p. 28.

experiment in uniting evangelicals of various stripes in a gigantic publishing venture to cover the globe with Bibles, began in 1804. John Shore was its first President: and Carey's mission press, operating out of Serampore, was its first and favored instrument from 1806, when Buchanan transferred all translation projects to this press. A war of evangelical polemics began under the aegis of the Foreign Bible Society in Bengal in 1806 to 1807, especially when Carey's mission press began publishing scurrilous pamphlets about Muhammad and Krishna. When challenged by a Mughal jurist, this Baptist missionary refused to acknowledge that he had been abusive, or had lied.

The growing strength of Evangelicalism in Company administration as well as in the House of Commons in 1807 amalgamated the economic goals of British Whigs – freedom to trade with India – with the attempts of evangelicals to make the Company disgorge the wealth it acquired from its officials managing the temple economies. By 1813, the triumph of Evangelicalism was complete when the Charter Act of that year gave evangelical missionaries the formal right to preach against Muslim and Hindu monastic governments and laws in all parts of Company-governed lands in the subcontinent.

The results were practical as well as ideological. The practical results showed in the worsening conditions of laborers in those regions newly annexed by the Company. For instance, after defeating (Saiva Hindu) Gurkha-ruled armies in 1814 to 1816, the Company annexed the hill states of Western Himalaya. In the charters (*sanads*) issued in 1816 to 1817, the Company fixed that each hill state would provide unpaid laborers (*begar*) to the Company's government. Under the Gurkha, such unpaid labor could be extracted during war. Furthermore, those who provided labor services (generally called *jhara*; among these a special form used for transporting mail and baggage in relays of runners was *hulak*) were exempt from other taxes.[30] But under Company government, such laborers were conscripted in peacetime. Moreover, British military and political officers seeking to extract such labor from hill-based "coolies" did not pause to consider whether the laborers they sought to conscript were committed to monastic estates alone, and therefore exempt from service to the lay (British officer).[31] By 1830, tax-paying cultivators were conscripted to carry the bags of British travelers to the hills every summer

---

[30] For exemption of hulaki porters from other labor services, see Order of Girvanyuddha, April 1804, in *Regmi Research Series* (henceforth *RRS*), 4(4), 1972, 69–70; by 1816, when the kingdom was at war with the Company, all males between the age of 15 and 60 were liable to conscripted labor for wartime, for which see *RRS*, 4(5) (1972): 81–2.

[31] For whipping unwilling laborers in a field next to a temple of a goddess, see James B. Fraser, *The Himala Mountains* (New Delhi, repr. 1982 [original 1820]), p. 195.

and British political officers were refusing any remuneration to such laborers.[32]

The ideological gains were that identical results in other lately annexed regions were defended as the extension of virtue, not as the wrongful denial of protection to the vulnerable. This occurred in the newly annexed Assam (in the 1830s) when Baptist missionaries called for the liberation of the 800-odd disciples (*bhaktas/bhokots*) of a Vaisnava abbot (*mahanta*). This demand for liberation persisted even though missionaries knew that, unlike the African slaves they were used to describing, these monastic servants did not work round the clock, but only when the monastic lords required their services. This system, the missionary declared, was made possible by the structure of endowed lands. Such lands had to be taken away from the lords.

Some evangelical missionaries as well as lay colonial officers understood the significance of lay donations of people to shrines and monastic estates. For instance, an American Baptist missionary passing through Company-governed Akyab and Arakan in 1836 noted that the 150 families attached to a monastery comprised "slaves of the pagoda" Shwedagon and they had become such, "chiefly by being given to some pagoda by a great man, as a meritorious offering. Sometimes they are malefactors whose punishment is thus commuted. More generally they are unoffending inhabitants of some district, whose prince or ruler, for any cause, chooses to make such a donation."[33] Such observers understood that monastic oblation preserved the lives of criminals: by their permanent "attachment" to a local monastery, such people lived out a life of service instead. But they considered this immoral on theological grounds.

British military officers, on the other hand, wished to control the same labor pools in order to raise cash taxes from the people or to redirect the labor of these populations toward colonial armies. From the 1830s, British officers demanded that monastic servants, hitherto exempted from labor to third parties, work for British armies and auxiliary corps. In Assam, for instance, colonial officers compelled old Vaisnava abbots to contribute military contingents of 100 men or so from among their attached subjects and tenants. Many of these monastic governors were unwilling. They were obliged to commute with a cash payment of 1,800 rupees per year to the Company. Despite this, old Vaisnava abbots would not give up their protected "servants" and disciples to be destroyed in war. Seizures of

[32] Aniket Alam, "The Conquests of Mahasu Devata: Legends and Folklore as Sources for Himalayan History," *Journal of the Asiatic Society*, 47 (2003): 64–87.

[33] (Rev.) Howard Malcolm, *Travels in South-Eastern Asia Embracing Hindustan, Malaya, Siam, and China, with Notices of Numerous Missionary Stations and a Full Account of the Burman Empire* (London, 1839), pp. 80 and 274.

monastic property-in-people by the Company constituted the sum of "abolition" in the case of monastic estates in the subcontinent.

This process became more competitive after 1833, when the East India Company lost its charter of trade and private English traders and industrialists began to access the same lands and resources in regions annexed by British Indian armies. These lands were turned over to commercial crops – such as indigo (in Gangetic Awadh), cotton and opium (in Western and Central India), and tea (in eastern Himalayan terrain). As documents dated 1837 CE show, private British planters also sought bonded laborers and bought slaves, but on conditions much more hostile to the bonded than pre-colonial and local deeds had earlier been.[34]

Under these pressures, native Hindu and Muslim concepts of claims and privileges were reversed by British commercial capitalism. Native masters' ability to protect their own properties from being destroyed or damaged by third parties also dissolved in the colonial courts. The final ignominy came when neither monastic owners nor lay governors could sustain either their own exemption from labor nor extend such exemptions to old or favored slaves. Nor, due to the drive by colonial and private British interests, could erstwhile patrons stand to benefit in any way from emancipating their slaves and turning the relationship into that of patron–client.

From the 1840s, this policy was extended to all regions annexed by the Company. The two-clause Act V of 1843 could afford to be brief: its task was a post-facto legitimation of colonial seizures of people. One of its clauses prohibited any slave from judicially claiming the status of being a slave – and masters from claiming property in slaves. This consolidated the inability of both "slaves of the gods" (the women, children, and men attached to various monastic and temple estates), as well as their masters – the monks and the temple-administrators – from seeking protection from deployment by third parties. Nor could erstwhile masters offer protection to such beings nor seek indemnification from other employers or masters. As Company Subsidary Alliances dispossessed the lay Muslim lordships, they also despoiled the wealth of the intersexed Mughal stewards (*khwajaserais*). For instance, in households of the Shi'a who governed Awadh and Murshidabad in the early nineteenth century, many old-established *khwajaserai* (such as Almas Ali Khan, Darab Ali Khan) had accumulated huge estates. Their wills left some parts of their estates in *waqf*; the rest of their estates were claimed by the male Nawabs who were direct descendants of the original manumitters of such men. Sharia provisions of *wala* (the mutual obligations of manumitter and manumitted) made pious Islamic

---

[34] D. Liston, "Translation of a Servitude-Bond Granted by a Cultivator over His Family and of a Deed of Sale of Two Slaves," *Journal of Asiatic Society of Bengal*, 6 (1837): 950–2.

emancipators appear as hindrances to the smooth operation of British private capitalists keen to establish indigo, tea, and coffee plantations in such estate-held lands. A clause in Act V of 1843 prohibited any master from claiming anything from another person on the grounds that he or she had been a slave. This clause was directed at those Muslim masters, or mistresses, who had held *wala*. Thus, when the Nawab of Surat died in 1842, it was found that he had left behind a daughter born of his former slave-concubine; he had emancipated the concubine the day before he had married her ritually. In 1857, this widow had died, leaving two grand-daughters. The dead man's niece (brother's daughter) claimed the cash and immoveable property, over and above the claim of the granddaughters, on the grounds of *wala*. The Judge of Surat argued that Act V of 1843 rendered the plaintiff's claim inadmissible. The High Court of Bombay upheld this position. By 1879, so did the Privy Council, holding that the operation of Islamic legal institutions (such as *wala*) constituted a "disability" in the lives of descendants of freedmen.[35]

"LIBERATION" AND THE PROLETARIANIZATION OF THE ERSTWHILE PROTECTED GROUPS

The kind of liberation dealt to monastic tenants and subjects inland was extended to the seas at the same time, especially in the western Indian Ocean world in the 1830s. Abolitionism enabled British navies to secure the domination of the seas sufficient to stop and search all European ships suspected of carrying slaves. The pattern of "secret" purchases stopped. African freedmen or clients, who worked as crew for Arab or East African owners, were absorbed into laboring groups in British-controlled work-shops. For instance, in 1835 to 1836, seventy young African boys and girls (between 6 and 15 years old) were forcibly taken off the Arab-commanded dhows sailing between Porbandar, a port in Gujarat, and Bombay. Instead of the secretarial and treasury work that such African children had had open to them earlier, these African and Muslim boys were now either sent directly to work on the boats of the British Indian navy or handed over as private servants to British naval officers. Yet others were given to British police constables and army officers and clerks in the British Indian bur-eaucracy. The girls were put to domestic service in establishments man-aged by individual British and Portuguese functionaries in Bombay. Their new employers contracted "to feed, clothe and protect them," and above all, bring them up as Christians. It did not matter which church: even the

---

[35] ILR.3 Bom 422, Privy Council 17 March 1879, Sayad Mir Ujimuddin Khan vs. Zia-ul-Nisa Begam and Rahim-ul-Nisa Begam, Appeals from the High Court of Bombay.

Catholic Vicar-General of the Apostolic Mission received a free gift of seven African servants in this general distribution of gifts.

"Liberation" of such African children was another word for Christian evangelizing. Such Christianization, it might be remembered, was completely contrary to the old Mughal official's guarantee that the Portuguese Catholics' slaves would *not* be forced to convert. In the 1830s, however, even though seventeen of the young African Muslim boys and eleven of the girls taken off these boats in these years "refused to serve Christians,"[36] they were sent off with Portuguese (Catholic) gentlemen of the locality. Many of these young Muslims resisted ("were wayward" says the note). Their reluctance was overcome by putting them directly in a British-run school, "saying nothing about religion," but shaping them indirectly to a regime of work. Only the most stubborn of such resisters, usually young boys, could evade a mandatory Christianization, and secure a lodging arrangement in the houses of local Muslims.

Finally, such "liberation" policies – first of missionary antislavery and then of colonial governments authorized by British Parliament – also suggest the extent to which abolitionist non-recognition of Hindu, Muslim, and Buddhist monastic properties reversed the prevailing laws respecting the transfer of "property." Until then, the laws regarding a third party's property in people (see *Mulasarvastivada* above) had been scrupulously maintained in the subcontinent. Hindu rulers like the Rao of Kutch (Maharao Sri Dayasinhji) had given shelter to six African Muslim slaves when they complained at the capital Bhuj that they had been starved by the captain of an Arabian Sea vessel passing through Mandavi.[37] The Rao had allowed these slaves to live as members of his household. But when the navigator of the vessel proved to the Rao that the slaves belonged to a "near relation" of the Shia Imam of Muscat, the Rao immediately restored them to their rightful owners. This was not, however, the way in which British officers, after the demolition of the Charter of the East India Company (in 1833), treated either their African Muslim subjects or the property of the Hindu Vania mercantile agents of a distant (Shia) Imam of Muscat.[38] Take for instance the fate of the ten Siddi slaves – four boys, six girls aged 10 to 16 years old – sent by the Imam's relations to their Bania commercial agent in India (at Rajkot, a man called Madhoji) by means of a Turkish

---

[36] NAI, FPC. See entries of February 19, 1836, enclosure 37: 23; February 1836, enclosure 40; see also Edward Alpers, "On Becoming a British Lake: Piracy, Slaving and British Imperialism in the Indian Ocean During the First Half of the Nineteenth Century," in Robert Harms, Bernard K. Freamon, and David W. Blight (eds.) *Indian Ocean Slavery in the Age of Abolition* (New Haven, CT, 2013), pp. 45–58.

[37] Asst. Resident Bhuj to Secretary to Governor of Bombay, February 11, 1836, in NAI: FPC, February 23, 1836, enclosure 64.

[38] Extract Poll Progs. Governor Bombay, November 16, 1836, in NAI, FPC, enclosures 1–12; February 6, 1837, enclosure 7.

middleman. All were simply taken over by the Company's officers, and brought up by a private Christian orphanage run by a Doctor Wilson.

"Freeing" such children without any written contract constituted an inexpensive procurement of labor for colonial navies and plantations at the same time that they also completely reversed older laws of property. Partly due to the ongoing dispossession of indigenous courtly systems by colonial administration, new generations of Afrasians could not find ready employment in Mughal-era courtly regimes. So, in the 1840s to 1850s, as many freedmen and young naval crew on boats plying between Aden, Karachi, and Bombay were taken off their boats, they found themselves subject to a completely different discipline of missionary education and industrial clock-time.[39] Such redirection of skilled laborers did not merely affect Afrasian sailors, but also extended to erstwhile members of indigenous courts. When the Mughal Shi'a potentate in Awadh (Wajid Ali Shah) had his kingdom annexed to British India in 1856, all fifty-four males in his household who were of African descent were "liberated." But twenty-nine of these, between the ages of 15 and 35, were then re-employed by the local colonial administration as sweepers and jail wardens. Thus, such men went from positions of intimacy with a prince to the status of petty cogs in a colonial wheel.[40]

CONCLUSION: ABOLITIONISM AS COLONIAL AND POST-COLONIAL TRIUMPHALISM

The overwhelming historiographical consensus that has shaped the study of abolition is that of its triumph and the place of such triumph in establishing the legitimacy of British imperialism in the later nineteenth century. As this chapter has argued, such triumphalism often ignores the destruction of a more capacious understanding of rights and privileges in the subcontinent that had been articulated by pre-colonial Buddhist, Hindu, and Mughal Muslim jurists. From the late eighteenth century, older laws governing property-in-people shifted against slaves when native Arab, Indian, and African owners lost their ability to protect their own properties from being destroyed or damaged by third parties. In the second phase that began after 1833 and continued until the end of formal indenture in 1917, the practices of Company courts were consolidated and extended with the cooperation of many Indian participants. Abolition by means of colonial legislation as well as by judicial decisions changed both

[39] For Nasib the *khalasi*, see correspondence in OIOC, F/4/2066/94848; for Mubarak the Hyderabadi sailor rescued as "Abyssinian slave," see OIOC F/4/2157/103848.
[40] Sec. to Government of North West Provinces and Oudh to Sec. to GOI, Foreign, April 5, 1878, NAI, Foreign General B, May 1878, nos. 169–71.

Hindu and Muslim laws as they operated between families of patrons and clients. They also dramatically laicized "freedom."

If this was not obvious to earlier historians of abolition, it was because such "liberation" went hand in hand with laicization of erstwhile monastic property – of both lands and laborers – seen in Eastern India. Such laicization brought a great deal of hitherto "sequestered" land onto the domestic market at the same time. Those Indians who managed to acquire lands on this market thus became staunch supporters of the new laws and regulations, both bulwarks for and embodiments of Anglicized notions of "freedom" and of refashioned norms of gender and family formation. For instance, in the 1840s, the laicization of land-holding was extended to the wet rice-growing river valleys of Tamil Nadu, in the southern peninsula, where temples had organized labor and cultivation hitherto. By 1857, when the great revolt against British rule occurred in the subcontinent, the lay Muslim households, the intersex Mughal stewards, the Sufi, Vaisnava, and Saiva monastic lords alike had all been dispossessed of their wealth, both in lands and in people. After the Revolt of 1857, when all of the government of Indian provinces was taken over by British Crown and Parliament, older regimes of "attachment" no longer needed British initiative to be dismantled. From the 1870s, the new Indian members of the colonial regime took the lead.

Colonial abolitionism consolidated its gains through the late nineteenth and early twentieth centuries. The marital and adoption strategies among all the older Mughal-Rajput regimes and societies between the late eighteenth and the end of the nineteenth centuries changed as all groups, Muslim and Hindu alike, learned new doctrines of "illegitimacy" wherever children born of a slave mother existed.[41] In the later 1860s to 1870s, the project of reconstituting "legitimate" lineages was extended across the Indian Ocean littoral, to include the Hindu (Vaisnava) and Jain allies of various Arab and African potentates as well. British abolitionist officers set about reconstituting Gujarati Bania households with African servants along racialized lines, and attempted to drive African Muslims out of their favored statuses along the Arab-Persian-Sindh (Pakistan) littoral.[42] By the late nineteenth century, such efforts came together in an officially choreographed disruption of geo-political as well as affinal and devotional networks that had enmeshed many households and regions across the Indian Ocean. Spies working on behalf of British naval patrols and residents at

[41] Andrea Major, "Enslaved Spaces: Domestic Slavery and the Spatial, Ideological and Practical Limits of Colonial Control in the Nineteenth-Century Rajput and Maratha States," *IESHR*, 46 (2009): 315–42; also Andrea Major, *Slavery, Abolitionism and Empire in India, 1772–1843* (Liverpool, 2012).

[42] For descriptions of Africans in Kachchhi households in Zanzibar, see British Consul to Actng Ch. Secy GBy, January 22, 1869, NAI, Delhi, FPP, A, July 1869, no. 229.

Aden reported that a pious Hafiz Abdul Qayum had set sail from Mecca to Bhopal with four women who had been slaves in various parts of the Arabian Peninsula. The man was caught and put on trial. Though all the members of the Bhopal household gave evidence that what looked like a purchase was an act of emancipation valued in Islamic law, their pleas did not prevent the Hafiz from being imprisoned. Furthermore, colonial officials took this opportunity to condemn the Hafiz's patron, a man of eminent Sayyid ancestry and considerable immersion in Arabic and Quranic exegesis, Muhammad Siddiq Hasan Khan, of being a "low seditious scoundrel."[43] Suspecting him of being a Wahhabi and of sending envoys to Mecca in order to secure support for a claim as a spiritual leader in British Bhopal, the British Government of India deposed this man from the administration of Bhopal by 1885. The fact that he was the husband of the ruling begum provided him no protection at all.[44]

The result of the elevation of Puritanical norms of conjugality and sexuality was as malignant for the hosts of the salon cultures of the past as they were for the skilled performers who made up the corps of "temple women" in the southern peninsula. The moralizing anti-nautch (or anti-*Devadasi*) movement of evangelical missionaries of the late eighteenth and nineteenth centuries marked a triumph also in enabling the annexation of the lands on which such temples had subsisted. From the late nineteenth century, English-educated middle classes of a variety of caste backgrounds expressed their partnership in this colonial project by means of the same anti-nautch stances.[45] At the same time, many among the educated non-Brahman groups benefited from the colonial laicization of properties and freedoms. Since protection was no longer to be claimed on the basis of whose slave or client a family was, many groups united in a common claim of being an underclass.[46]

The epistemological, political, and economic triumph of British abolitionism was best marked in a twenty-first-century independent South Asian and Anglophone historiography of both slavery and abolition that erased the complex histories of property regimes in the pre-colonial South Asian past. Neither pre-colonial Asian histories of property nor the world views of pre-colonial Asian poet-musicians and performers who once sung of themselves

[43] Note by H[enry] M[ortimer] D[urand], dated 14-8-82, k.w. no. 1, NAI, Delhi, FPP, A-I, July 1883, nos. 14–23.
[44] Saeedullah, *The Life and Works of Siddiq Hasan Khan, Nawab of Bhopal 1832–1890* (Lahore, 1973), pp. 54–80.
[45] Devesh Soneji, *Unfinished Gestures: Devadasis, Memory and Modernity in South India* (Chicago, IL, 2013); Lucinda Ramberg, *Given to the Goddess: South Indian Devadasis and the Sexuality of Religion* (Raleigh, NC, 2015).
[46] Rupa Viswanath, *The Pariah Problem: Caste, Religion and the Social in Modern India* (New York, 2014).

as slaves of the *dargah* and as "slaves of the Sultan" could find a dignified place in this historiography. In convincing educated South Asians of post-colonial nations that alternative modes of attachment and value were either "immoral" or "feudal" and therefore best left unstudied, the Liberal and Evangelical worlds of British abolitionism secured their ultimate triumph.

A GUIDE TO FURTHER READING

Adam, William, *The Law and Custom of Slavery in British India: In a Series of Letters to Thomas F. Buxton, Esq.* (Boston, MA, 1840).

Chanana, Dev Raj, *Slavery in Ancient India: As Depicted in Pali and Sanskrit Texts* (Delhi, 1960).

Chatterjee, Indrani, *Gender, Slavery and Law in Colonial India*, (Delhi, 1999).

Chatterjee, Indrani and Richard M. Eaton (eds.), *Slavery and South Asian History* (Bloomington, IN, 2006).

Chattopadhyay, Amal K., *Slavery in India* (Calcutta, 1959).

Dange, Shripad Amrit, *India from Primitive Communism to Slavery: A Marxist Study of Ancient History in Outline* (New Delhi, 1972).

Mohan, Sanal P., *Modernity of Slavery: Struggles against Caste-Inequality in Colonial Kerala* (New Delhi, 2014).

Patnaik, Utsa and Manjari Dingwaney (eds.), *Chains of Servitude: Bondage and Slavery in India* (Madras, 1985).

Pinto, Jeanette, *Slavery in Portuguese India 1510–1842* (Bombay, 1992).

Robbins, Kenneth X. and John McLeod (eds.), *African Elites in India: Habshi Amarat* (Ocean Township, NJ, 2006).

CHAPTER 20

THE TRANSITION FROM SLAVERY TO FREEDOM IN THE AMERICAS AFTER 1804

CHRISTOPHER SCHMIDT-NOWARA

There is no consensus on the consequences of the transition from slavery to freedom in the Americas, unsurprising given the large number of places and periods studied and the different methodological approaches employed. Some historians have measured the economies of societies soon after emancipation and have sketched a gloomy portrait, emphasizing "emancipation and its discontents." In the words of Stanley Engerman: "The recent historiography on emancipation has greatly tended to emphasize its failures, particularly the disappointments experienced at the time by those newly freed but by others too."[1] These scholars point to the decline of plantation economies and the generally negative effects that decline had on living standards for ex-slaves. Wealth and security plummeted and the flight from the estates in places such as the British West Indies and the Paraíba Valley of Brazil left freed people vulnerable in the new labor markets. Thus, not only slavery but also emancipation handicapped the freed population and disrupted economies on a massive scale, which had dire consequences for society as a whole and the newly freed in particular: "the slave plantations produced for the market, even for the world market, but had for centuries shielded their workers from the impact of those market forces which they would have needed to understand and exploit if they were to improve their lives as freedmen."[2]

There are two differing arguments that emphasize how the legacies of slavery and emancipation, especially in plantation economies, limited people in the transition to freedom and try to show how enslaved people carved out new economic and political roles for themselves after the end of slavery. First, drawing upon the arguments of Sidney Mintz, scholars have argued that conditions in plantation societies paradoxically prepared slaves for the transition to freedom. Efforts to reduce costs and to defuse tensions

---

[1] Stanley Engerman, "Comparative Approaches to the Ending of Slavery," *Slavery and Abolition*, special issue on "Emancipation and Its Discontent," 21 (2000): 297.

[2] Howard Temperley, "Introduction," *Slavery and Abolition*, special issue, ibid., 1–10; quote is from Engerman, "Comparative Approaches to the Ending of Slavery," 297; Pieter Emmer, "'A Spirit of Independence' or Lack of Education for the Market? Freedmen and Asian Indentured Labourers in the Post-Emancipation Caribbean, 1834–1917," *Slavery and Abolition*, 21 (2000): 165.

led planters in numerous places to allow slaves access to provision grounds and to market the surplus. In the transition to freedom, freed people could draw upon these skills, customary rights, networks, and some access to land to establish themselves as peasants and vendors who could negotiate with planters even if they could not always completely abandon work on the plantations. As free people, they could more effectively control the use of their time and labor.[3]

Second, recent scholarship has paid more attention to the struggle over political rights and political equality during the transition from slavery to freedom, conceptualizing emancipation as a lengthy process that persisted beyond immediate post-slavery economic restructuring. Studies of citizenship and its complexities in post-emancipation societies have become a primary area of research. The efforts of ex-slaves in Haiti and in French Guiana to defend themselves against re-enslavement by the French, the slaves' demands for freedom in exchange for military service and involvement in political parties in much of independent Spanish America, and their cross-racial alliances that sought civil equality and political democracy in Cuba and Puerto Rico after slavery are clear. These efforts helped the transition from slavery to freedom, and transformed states and societies not only in the struggles to reorganize economies, but also in the long-term conflicts over rights and enfranchisement that have shaped American nations and colonies since emancipation.

EMANCIPATIONS IN THE NINETEENTH CENTURY

If the consequences of emancipation are still debated, its causes are coming into clearer focus. War was the motive force of emancipation through much of the Americas between the Haitian Revolution and the abolition of Brazilian slavery. Legislation and abolitionist agitation were also key factors, most centrally in the British Empire. In most slave societies, war undid the discipline and order upon which slavery relied, allowing enslaved people to make new demands for freedom to which imperial, national, and emergent states had to respond even in the face of fierce defiance from slave-holders. The most well-documented history of the role of war in setting emancipation in motion is the US Civil War. Yet, the findings and conclusions of historians concerning the United States are parallel to those of scholars working on Caribbean and Latin American

---

[3] Sidney Mintz, *Caribbean Transformations* (New York, 1974); Dale Tomich, "*Une petite guinée*: Provision Ground and Plantation in Martinique, 1830–1848," *Slavery and Abolition*, 12 (1991): 68–91. Urban slaves were often tightly integrated into the economic fabric of their cities and played a major role in markets and skilled trades, as did freed people. See, e.g., studies of Rio de Janeiro, including Mary Karasch, *Slave Life in Rio de Janeiro, 1808–1850* (Princeton, NJ, 1987); and Zephyr Frank, *Dutra's World: Wealth and Family in Nineteenth-Century Rio de Janeiro* (Albuquerque, NM, 2004).

slave societies. There were two major periods of warfare that transformed New World slavery: first, during the anti-colonial revolts from the later eighteenth century until the 1820s and, second, the crisis of the 1860s when the three largest slave systems were either destroyed or subverted.

In both the American and the Haitian Revolutions, enslaved people took up arms to gain their freedom, as in the case of the slaves who fled to the British army in Virginia, or else to directly challenge slavery as a system, as in the case of Saint Domingue/Haiti, where rebellion forced the declaration of abolition in 1793 to 1794 (first in the colony and then ratified in the metropolitan legislature). Freed slaves then defended their emancipation against the French expeditionary force sent to return them to bondage in 1802. The struggle to end slavery in Saint Domingue also led to the destruction of colonialism, as Haiti declared its independence from France in 1804. In contrast, the struggle against colonial rule in British North America led to independence and the resurgence of slavery after 1783, in spite of the social instability caused by the revolution. In continental Spanish America, the independence wars of the 1810s and 1820s undermined slavery and initiated the emancipation processes across two continents.

In the mid nineteenth century, the largest plantation societies of the "second slavery" came under military, legal, and political attacks. The trigger was the US Civil War and emancipation, which had far-reaching consequences in Cuba and Brazil. In the United States, the Civil War produced widespread challenges to slavery from enslaved people, abolitionists, and the Union army before the Emancipation Proclamation on January 1, 1863. Cuba, economically firmly in the US orbit because of the island's increased reliance on the North American market for its sugar, felt the impact immediately and soon experienced an uprising for independence (the Ten Years War, 1868–1878) that would set the stage for abolition and emancipation. Finally, in Brazil, the Paraguayan War (1864–70) threw the elite's commitment to slavery, bedrock of the independent state since 1822, into crisis; while planters in the Paraíba Valley remained committed until the bitter end of slavery in 1888. Several Brazilians came to argue that the Brazilian state and its economy could only be modernized by abolishing slavery.[4]

After 1804, the revolutionary linking of anti-colonialism and antislavery remained vibrant in the Spanish colonies. No outright suppression of slavery took place immediately, but across two continents during the Spanish American revolutions, slavery was weakened by the need that

___

[4] See the special issue on "The Politics of the Second Slavery," *Review: A Journal of the Fernand Braudel Center*, forthcoming; and Don H. Doyle (ed.), *American Civil Wars: The United States, Latin America, Europe and the Crisis of the 1860s* (Chapel Hill, NC, 2017).

both royalist and patriot forces had for manpower. Both sides recruited enslaved men and women to take part in the struggles in a number of different roles. The end result was that in the next decades the independent republics of Spanish America passed laws abolishing slavery once they had separated from Spain – some emancipations being immediate and some deferred via the law of the free womb. Under British pressure, they also banned the slave trade. In some marginal slave-holding societies, such as Chile and Mexico, abolition was immediate (though in Mexico, the law was effectively suspended in Texas), but where the institution figured more centrally in the economy, such as Venezuela, Colombia, Peru, and the states of the River Plate region, abolition was gradual and protracted until the 1850s.[5] The sparsely populated countryside of the new republics made it possible for freed people to carve out autonomous lives for themselves by making use of various kinds of now unclaimed lands (for example, lands that had belonged to the Spanish crown during the colonial era). In cities such as Lima, free people melded into the heterogeneous urban plebian culture as they sought to escape the rigors of servitude. Ex-slaves could take part in the partisan political life of the new republics and help place final abolition firmly on the liberal agenda, as in Colombia, where the Liberal Party made much of its efforts to free those still in slavery through emancipation funds and by ultimately adopting abolition as a popular cause in the 1850s.[6]

In Cuba, commitment to slavery and the slave trade had led the colonial elite to maintain its loyalty to Spain in the 1810s and 1820s, and slavery continued to flourish on the island until the 1860s. Then, increasing division about the colony's economic and political future led to the outbreak of a separatist war that had striking parallels to the earlier Spanish American revolutions. Slaves were able to make use of the crisis to pursue new avenues to freedom and to help place the issue of abolition on the agenda, within the insurgency, the Spanish administration, and metropolitan political life. What made this combination of national revolution and antislavery distinctive from earlier Spanish-American challenges was its convergence with the crisis of the second slavery in the Americas. Planters and merchants in Cuba, Southeastern Brazil, and the southern United States had combined large enslaved populations, access to vast hinterlands,

---

[5] On the persistent commitment to slavery in Spanish America even as it declined during and after the revolutionary era, see Juan Carlos Garavaglia, "The Economic Role of Slavery in a Non-Slave Society: The River Plate, 1750–1850," in Josep M. Fradera and Christopher Schmidt-Nowara (eds.), *Slavery and Antislavery in Spain's Atlantic Empire* (New York, 2013), pp. 74–100; and Peter Blanchard, "An Institution Defended: Slavery and the English Invasions of Buenos Aires in 1806 and 1807," *Slavery and Abolition*, 35 (2014): 253–72.

[6] See Andrews, *Afro-Latin America*, chs. 2 and 3; Peter Blanchard, *Under the Flags of Freedom: Slave Soldiers and the Wars of Independence in Spanish South America* (Pittsburgh, PA, 2008).

advanced technologies of production and transport, and booming consumer markets for their goods to construct plantation regimes of unprecedented size and productivity. Though politically stable for several decades, these regimes entered into crisis at mid-century. The US Civil War was the detonator because the US Government had provided indirect diplomatic and military cover for Brazil and Spanish Cuba. Freedom for slaves there resounded through these regimes, partly because there was a new abolitionist power in the north, partly because the Brazilian and Spanish states were enmeshed in wars that, even if not on the scale of the North American conflict, threw slavery and territorial sovereignty into question.

Nonetheless, while the connection between war and emancipation was common in the Americas, warfare was far from the cause of freeing all slaves – politics and legislation were also crucial. Several colonial regimes freed their enslaved populations through laws passed by metropolitan legislatures in the mid nineteenth century, including Denmark, the Netherlands, and France. The most important example of a legislated emancipation was Britain's "mighty experiment," when more than 700,000 slaves in the colonies were emancipated gradually between 1834 and 1838 by the metropolitan parliament under pressure from a large antislavery movement and slave uprisings in colonies such as Demerara and Jamaica.

Even in those slave societies affected directly by war, emancipation was frequently channeled through laws and political conflict. The tortuous route to emancipation in Cuba and Puerto Rico between 1868 and 1886 illustrates the unevenness of slavery's ending and the transition to freedom. The year 1868 was a momentous one in Spain and its last American colonies. A democratic revolution overthrew the Bourbon monarch Isabella II in the September Revolution (1868–74). Quickly thereafter, anti-colonial revolts broke out in Puerto Rico and Cuba. The colonial state suppressed the Puerto Rican rebellion within days, but in Cuba the insurgency took root in the vast eastern region of the island and would challenge Spanish rule until 1878. In Spain, abolitionists held key roles in the revolutionary governments and in the Cortes, though pro-slavery forces were deeply entrenched and defiant. In Cuba, the rebellion's leaders soon decided to declare slavery abolished, in part as a response to the flight of slaves to the insurgent army. That decision polarized metropolitan attitudes: abolitionists insisted that only immediate abolition would bring the colonial war to an end, while conservatives, in cooperation with the powerful economic interests in Havana, resisted any change to the colonial system through the mobilization of publicity, lobbying groups, petitions, and military forces.

Madrid's revolutionary government tried to compromise by passing a gradual emancipation law in the summer of 1870, the Moret Law, which took its name from the Minister of Overseas Colonies, Segismundo Moret y Prendergast, a whole-hearted economic liberal, moderate abolitionist, and reluctant democrat. The Moret Law was extremely cautious given the need to assuage conservative opinion and vested interests on both sides of the Atlantic, but it did free several categories of enslaved people and it also sought to ban the use of the whip and the break-up of families through sale. Articles 1 and 2 freed those born to slave mothers since the triumph of the revolutionary regime in the peninsula (September 17, 1868); Article 3 freed those who had served the Spanish flag against the insurgency in some capacity or who had been freed by the decision of the Captain General of Cuba, with indemnification for owners who had remained loyal to Spain; Article 4 emancipated those who were 60 years of age at the time of the law's publication and those who reached the age of 60 thereafter; and Article 5 declared free all slaves who belonged to the state, primarily the so-called *emancipados* taken from the illegal slave trade after the 1817 treaty banning the trade went into effect. Finally, Article 19 would free all slaves who were not inscribed in the censuses to be carried out at the end of the year, a matter of contention between Madrid and planters on the ground.

However, there were caveats to these articles, some written into the Moret Law, others arising from circumstances in the colonies. Articles 6 though 11 spelled out that those born free (*libertos*) to enslaved mothers would remain under the tutelage of their mother's owner (their *patrono*) until the age of 22 or, in case of marriage, until the age of 14 for women and 18 for men. Freed parents could buy the freedom of their children from the patrono through indemnification. Labor was uncompensated until the age of 18, at which time the liberto would be paid half a day's wages, receiving only one-half of that amount, the other half being held as a *peculium*, to which the liberto was entitled upon reaching the age of 22. The spirit and the letter of Article 5 were repeatedly broken, as the Spanish Abolitionist Society would point out in detail given that the state began acquiring slaves during the Cuban insurgency as it confiscated the property of all insurgents, including slave property. Moreover, additional articles gave patronos and the government leeway in enforcing the rights of former owners to the labor of now freed people. Finally, the Moret Law called for the drafting of rules (*reglamento*) to make the law operational and called for a future definitive law, measures that gave slave-owners plenty of opportunities for delay and obstruction.

The Moret Law immediately received criticism from all sides, with Cuban slave-holders and their allies in particular effectively blocking the actualization of some of its measures for two years. Moret's abolitionist colleagues were also critical because they felt that the law was too timid politically and morally. Emilio Castelar, a republican and abolitionist who was one of Moret's mentors at the University of Madrid, asked why consideration was given to slave-holders, and not to the slaves themselves. Rafael María de Labra, the pre-eminent abolitionist of the era, writing in retrospect, caustically called the Moret Law "the practical joke of 1870" and bemoaned its betrayal of the September Revolution's promise and ideals:[7]

The preparatory law for the abolition of slavery in Cuba and Puerto Rico of 4 July 1870 would have been a measure of extraordinary effect and immense reach during another era. Without denying its importance, one must recognize that the circumspection of its precepts and the reduction of the emancipatory work to the *extinction of slavery* through the liberty of the newborn and of the sexagenarian blacks was not the most appropriate for a democratic situation created by the [September] Revolution, which had ... declared the natural rights of man and universal suffrage. There were many who considered the law (hard to understand, badly applied, and bastardized in Cuba by the dominant reactionary and proslavery elements) to have given a breath of life, with good will but with excessive fear, to the proslavery interests that had been almost overwhelmed by the revolutionary wave.

In contrast to Labra's harsh judgment, written eleven years after the final disappearance of Cuban slavery, the findings of historians since the 1980s have shown the Moret Law's corrosive effect on slavery in spite of the staunch resistance of planters and their political, military, and business allies, since the enslaved people themselves, in cooperation with other elements of society, were able to take advantage of provisions of the law to free themselves and family members and to force the hand of local and metropolitan rulers.[8]

There is no doubt that, as Labra recounted, implementation of the Moret Law ran into effective opposition in Cuba, though in Puerto Rico its effects came more quickly. Publication in Cuba of the Moret Law was delayed for several months, while its measures requiring the formation of courts of appeal (*Juntas Protectoras de Libertos*) that would oversee enforcement of the law's provisions were not put into effect until 1872. Moreover, clever parliamentary maneuvers by Antonio Cánovas del Castillo, the leader of peninsular conservatism and a stalwart ally of the planter class, further weakened the law's impact by adding the requirement that no definitive law of abolition could be passed until Cuban deputies took their seat in the metropolitan Cortes, which measure was put on hold for the

---

[7] Christopher Schmidt-Nowara, *Empire and Antislavery: Spain, Cuba, and Puerto Rico, 1833–1874* (Pittsburgh, PA, 1999), p. 138. See also Rafael María de Labra, *La república y las libertades de Ultramar. Estudio histórico-político* (Madrid, 1897), pp. 31, 80 (emphasis in the original).

[8] Rebecca J. Scott, *Slave Emancipation in Cuba: The Transition to Free Labor, 1860–1899* (Princeton, NJ, 1985); Astrid Cubano-Iguina, "Freedom in the Making: The Slaves of Hacienda La Esperanza, Manatí, Puerto Rico, on the Eve of Abolition, 1868–76," *Social History* 36 (2011): 280–93.

duration of the war in Cuba: "Art. 21. The Government will present to the Cortes, when the Deputies from Cuba have been admitted, the proposal for a law of indemnified emancipation of those who remain in servitude after the present."[9] For that reason, blocking elections in Cuba became part of the pro-slavery strategy in Madrid and Havana, while abolitionists during the September Revolution would struggle for elections and to have a definitive emancipation law passed. The abolitionists were successful in passing such a law for Puerto Rico in 1873 during the most radical phase of the Spanish Revolution, but anti-abolitionists resisted a new law for Cuban slavery until 1880, when Cuban deputies did finally join the Cortes, and one that was still gradualist in nature. In other words, there can be no doubt that Cuban and Spanish defenders were largely successful in maintaining control over the vital core of slave labor for almost twenty years after the September Revolution and the outbreak of the colonial insurrection.

At the same time, the Moret Law appears to have effectively chipped away at slavery, to a degree greater than Moret and most abolitionists expected. The numbers are revealing. In the rich plantation zone of Matanzas, the slave population in 1877 was 70,390, down from 89,643 in 1862. Overall, the slave population in Cuba seems to have declined from 287,653, according to the census carried out in 1871, to 235,710 in 1877, though several historians express skepticism about these figures. Many factors went into that decline, including the suppression of the slave trade, manumissions and *coartación* (legally regulated self-purchase), and the negative natural rate of growth among the slave population. However, the Moret Law also had an impact by freeing the elderly (21,032), those not counted in the census (9,611), slaves owned by the state (1,046), and those who provided service to the flag (658). Moreover, some 61,766 children born to enslaved mothers were also technically born as free people between those years, though, as we have seen, they were not to be completely liberated until they reached the age of 22.

Others who were to be held in servitude managed to escape their condition as shown by the numerous stories of how the Moret Law affected those seeking freedom. If the 1870 law included articles that strengthened the slave-owner's hand, it also included measures, especially Article 10, that a slave, a freed person with an enslaved family member, an abolitionist, or a sympathetic lawyer could use against the patrono. The patrono's rights could be brought to an end in individual cases: by marriage of the liberto, if the patrono abused his rights or failed in his duties to maintain the liberto, and if the patrono encouraged prostitution.

---

[9] *Gaceta de Madrid*, July 6, 1870, 2. Constitutional and representative government had been suspended in Cuba since 1837.

Moreover, the presence of the Juntas Protectoras de Libertos provided some counterweight to the habitual predominance of the master class, even if planters tried to co-opt them. A consequence of this new institutional presence in Cuba was a spike in the number of petitions for *coartación* and change of owner.[10]

Recent studies have demonstrated that such initiatives reflected not only slave agency, but also the willingness of sympathetic members of free society to inform enslaved people about the new tools that the law put at their disposal and to help them make use of them. For example, in Manatí on the north coast of Puerto Rico, liberals and abolitionists who controlled the municipal government and staffed the Junta Protectora were eager to undermine their arch-enemy, the Marques de la Esperanza, who was the leading figure of the colony's pro-slavery Spanish Party and the island's biggest slave-owner. They urged slaves to press cases against him and his overseers for violating the provisions of Article 10 and by disrupting his plantation, the Hacienda La Esperanza, with their investigations. In Havana, mothers of libertos were especially active in bringing cases to the attention of authorities as the free womb law had placed them at the nexus of slavery and freedom. Often with the help of free neighbors or lawyers with abolitionist sympathies, they petitioned against masters who were illegally selling the slaves' children, moving them against their will, or ignoring the terms of *coartación*. Even if they were not always successful, their suits made the Juntas Protectoras and the island's Consejo de Administración pay close attention to the provisions and implications of the Moret Law in spite of the aggressive mobilization of planters and their allies against the law and the Madrid regime that implemented it.

In Puerto Rico, the alliances against planters like the Marques de la Esperanza persisted into the early years of emancipation, though they were vulnerable to counter-revolutionary responses. The Spanish Cortes, in the most radical moment of the metropolitan revolution (the First Republic of 1873), passed a law abolishing Puerto Rican slavery in the spring of 1873. A concession to conservatives who still took part in the Cortes was the requirement that the newly emancipated slaves sign mandatory three-year labor contracts. However, under the administration of the Republic and the momentary predominance of progressive forces in the colony, many ex-slaves fled their former owners and signed contracts with free people whom they found more sympathetic and lenient. In the case of Manatí and the Hacienda La Esperanza, abolitionists encouraged the libertos to sign contracts with them rather than with the Marques and his overseer, essentially freeing them from the onerous contracts and at the same time

[10] Scott, *Slave Emancipation in Cuba*, pp. 76–7.

reducing the productivity of La Esperanza. The overthrow of the First Republic brought this moment of social and political euphoria to a close and the restored regime in Madrid and San Juan tried to undo the initiatives of libertos and abolitionists. However, it was too late to turn back the clock for major enterprises like La Esperanza. A fraction of the pre-emancipation workforce was returned to the hacienda, which now suffered an acute crisis, so that by 1889 its owners had abandoned sugar planting and turned it into a cattle ranch. Several factors contributed to this decline, including the low price of sugar on the global market, a disease that damaged sugar cane around the island, and planter indebtedness. To these factors must be added the inability to retain control over the workers, who now exercised their freedom of movement and contract to escape from the hacienda, its owner, and its overseer. Emancipation in Puerto Rico thus hastened the decline of sugar on the island and the ascent of crops like coffee that relied on free workers.[11]

The situation in Cuba was quite different. The size of the slave population and the size of the sugar plantations were always much greater than in Puerto Rico. Spain's First Republic and the Cuban insurgency were unable to abolish slavery in the island as planters and their military and political supporters effectively held abolitionism at bay and continued to rely on a strong core of enslaved workers through the 1870s. The situation began to change with the end of the insurgency in 1878 and the subsequent incorporation of the colony into the metropolitan constitution, a measure that led to the election of Cuban deputies to the Spanish Cortes and therefore the enactment of a new, definitive emancipation law. This was referred to as the *patronato*, which was passed in 1880 and affected the almost 200,000 people who remained enslaved. However, while more decisive than the Moret Law, the patronato, despite the bold claim of the first article that "the state of slavery ceases in the Island of Cuba according to the prescriptions of the present law," still sought to delay emancipation until 1888. Under these new provisions, all enslaved people were now called *patrocinados*. They continued to be bound to their patronos, who maintained important slave-holder prerogatives, including the use of corporal punishment and the ability to transfer a patrocinado to another patrono. However, there were also more assertive methods for hastening slavery's demise, including a quota of enslaved people to be freed on a yearly basis beginning in 1884, more effective oversight of the law by newly constituted bodies that could free patrocinados whose rights were violated, and enhanced

[11] Schmidt-Nowara, *Empire and Antislavery*, pp. 153–5; Cubano-Iguina, "Freedom in the Making," 291–2. On the fate of sugar in Puerto Rico, see Andrés Ramos-Mattei, *La Hacienda azucarera: su crecimento y crisis en Puerto Rico (siglo XIX)* (San Juan, 1981); and Luis Figueroa, *Sugar, Slavery and Freedom in Nineteenth Century Puerto Rico* (Chapel Hill, NC, 2005).

ability to purchase freedom. In the event, the patrocinados pursued emancipation by denouncing abusive patronos and overseers, by purchasing freedom, or by negotiating new arrangements with individual masters, processes that had started under the Moret Law. These, coupled with the mandatory emancipations spelled out in Article 8 of the law, expedited the end of this final stage of slavery. The government decreed slavery completely abolished on October 7, 1886.

EXCEPTIONS TO EMANCIPATION IN THE NINETEENTH CENTURY

But emancipation was not the end of the story of slavery. I will explore the struggles over freedom, work, and citizenship that took place in post-emancipation societies in the next section. Here, I would like to introduce scholarship on the widespread phenomenon of re-enslavement in New World slave societies that has complicated the understanding of the transition from slavery to freedom. Many people across the hemisphere who had reason to consider themselves freed had to fight to defend their liberty against those who would make them slaves again. Not all of them were successful. Moreover, hundreds of thousands of enslaved people were legally free in Brazil and Cuba, though they were generally held in ignorance of their true legal status.

What created this exceptional situation in which so many people found themselves in limbo between slavery and freedom or, in some cases, were returned to slavery after emancipation? The uneven geopolitics of slavery and abolition in the nineteenth century were a decisive factor. Just as some societies, such as the French Caribbean colonies in the 1790s, experienced emancipation, neighbors like Cuba sought to maintain variants of slavery and slave trafficking, imperiling recently freed people who found themselves in those places where slavery continued to thrive. British attempts to suppress the transatlantic slave trade after 1807 in the face of resurgent trafficking to Brazil and Cuba also created anomalous legal conditions in which many slaves were supposed to be free and some freed people were treated as slaves.

The abolition of slavery in the French colonial empire in the 1790s and then the re-enslavement of emancipated people in 1802 is the most notorious example of this broader phenomenon. In Saint Domingue, armed resistance to re-enslavement was successful and led to the 1804 declaration of Haitian independence from a French metropole still committed to slavery and eager to rebuild and expand plantation economies in its remaining Caribbean colonies. The expeditionary force sent to Saint Domingue to re-enslave freed people was not an anomaly; French support for emancipation and freedom was always equivocal. For example, in French Guiana in the 1790s, the local governors manipulated the revolution's suppression of slavery and the slave trade to raid and plunder passing slave vessels destined for other plantation societies. The French nominally freed the captives taken from those vessels and landed in Guiana, but, in fact, the colonial government treated them as slaves, leasing them out as laborers to planters and other employers. Perversely, French abolition led to a spike in the number of unfree workers in this part of the Caribbean. Even the people of revolutionary Haiti sometimes found themselves in legal limbo despite the fact that emancipation there was unambiguous. Many former slaves or free people of color had fled the colony/nation during the conflicts of the 1790s and 1800s, sometimes individually, sometimes as members of a household. In the passage between Saint Domingue and the slaving port of Santiago de Cuba, people who had been free for a decade suddenly found themselves returned to the status of slaves because of the connivance of Spanish colonial officials with former French owners who knew that the Spanish government was more likely to favor their interests than those of people freed by a revolutionary insurgency.[12]

These unpredictable twists in the road to freedom in the French Caribbean were a precursor to similar developments over the course of the nineteenth century, especially in the wake of the British abolition of the slave trade to its colonies in 1807 and the government's policy of suppressing the transatlantic trade through naval patrols, mixed courts, and bilateral treaties with slaving powers such as Spain, Portugal, and Brazil. According to these treaties, several of which were amended over the years, the signatories agreed to ban the traffic and to create mechanisms by which to police and punish illegal slavers. These measures were largely ineffective, however, as the slave trade to Brazil and Cuba swelled to immense proportions through the 1820s and 1830s, but they did provide the Royal Navy with some enforcement tools, such as a limited right of search (greatly hindered by the US refusal to permit the search of ships flying its flag) and the ability to adjudicate suspected slavers in mixed-commission courts located around the Atlantic, including in key slaving nodes such as Havana and Rio de Janeiro. In the one-fifth of cases in which slavers were caught red handed, the captives on their condemned ships were emancipated. What emancipation meant was unclear. If the captives had the misfortune to be liberated in Rio or Havana, they became known as *emancipados* (in both Spanish and Portuguese) under the protection of the local government, but living and working in conditions difficult to distinguish from slavery. The tension between British

---

[12] See Miranda Frances Spieler, "The Destruction of Liberty in French Guiana: Law, Identity, and the Meaning of Legal Space, 1794–1830," *Social History*, 36 (2011): 260–79; and Rebecca J. Scott and Jean M. Hébrard, *Freedom Papers: An Atlantic Odyssey in the Age of Emancipation* (Cambridge, MA, 2012), ch. 3.

antislavery and the resurgence of slavery in some parts of the Americas thus unintentionally created a class of men, women, and children nominally free, but often treated as though they were indeed slaves.[13]

There were even more complex situations that arose from the military, legal, and diplomatic struggles over the transatlantic slave trade. All slaves introduced into Brazil and Cuba after a certain date – 1820 in Cuba and 1831 in Brazil – were legally free people who had been kidnapped because they had been brought to these slave societies after the legal abolition of the slave trade by the Spanish and Brazilian Governments in treaty with the British. These decades did see hundreds of thousands of Africans brought to Cuban and Brazilian shores in carefully orchestrated and well-financed operations that provided labor to the booming sugar and coffee plantations. Luiz Felipe de Alencastro has recently shown the lengths to which Brazilian governments, planters, and slavers went to preserve a thin veneer of legality over the illegal kidnapping and enslavement of hundreds of thousands of people after 1831:

... during the 1850s, the [Brazilian] Empire regularly granted amnesty to slave-holders guilty of kidnapping, and it allowed the correlated crime of enslaving free people to go on. Indeed, the 760,000 Africans brought to Brazil up to 1856, as well as all their descendants, went on as slaves until 1888. It was necessary to enact an over-arching collusion, a pact favoring the violation of anti-slavery laws so as to avoid slave rebellions, as well as rebellions of people who were illegally enslaved. This collusion ensured that slave-owners (i.e. kidnappers), as well as their partners and creditors need not be overly concerned that the country might collapse.[14]

A very similar situation was unfolding in Cuba, where the Spanish colonial regime worked in cahoots with planters, slavers, and financiers to ensure the flow of enslaved workers to the island's plantations until the final suppression of the trade in 1867. Occasional rumors that the administration would capitulate to the British and enforce the slave trade ban, or even free those captives illegally brought to the colony, would throw planters into a temporary panic, but their interests were always respected.

ECONOMIES AND POLITICS AFTER EMANCIPATION

What happened when slavery and the status of laborers between slavery and freedom were abolished? Responses varied across the Americas and

---

[13] On the fate of captives freed by the Royal Navy and the mixed courts, see Robert E. Conrad, "Neither Slave Nor Free: The *Emancipados* of Brazil, 1818–1868," *Hispanic American Historical Review*, 53 (1973): 50–70; David R. Murray, *Odious Commerce: Britain, Spain and the Abolition of the Cuban Slave Trade* (Cambridge, 1980).

[14] Luiz Felipe de Alencastro, "Affirmative Action: An Opinion Submitted to the Brazilian Supreme Court in the Case ADPF/186," *Translating the Americas*, 1 (2013): 99.

across the decades. Emancipation led to a crisis of the plantation economies in several American societies. In Haiti, after several years of trying to maintain compulsory labor on state-owned plantations in the northern tier of the country, the government under Alexandre Petión broke up the estates and oversaw the spread of peasant ownership across the country. In the British West Indies, Seymour Drescher has argued that the government and the abolitionists committed "econocide" by lowering the labor supply of thriving and expanding sugar economies, especially in relatively underdeveloped territories such as Trinidad and Guiana. The transition to free labor was rocky in several colonies, as the apprentices, those freed from slavery but bound to labor for their former masters for up to 45 hours per week, protested their intermediate condition. Nonetheless, given the continued access to a bonded labor force, planters were able to maintain levels of production during the apprenticeship period. Once the government ended this system in 1838, however, two years before scheduled for agricultural workers, there was significant disruption in the relations between planters and freed workers. In the first months after emancipation, several plantation societies experienced widespread flight of workers from their former estates, especially in those larger colonies with uncultivated spaces such as Jamaica or Guiana. Even though some workers then returned to plantation labor by necessity, there was hard bargaining over wages, access to provision grounds, and ownership of houses. Planters had to make major concessions and the profitability of their estates, already pressed by the rise of more productive rivals in Cuba, declined over the next generation.[15]

Historians who have sought to understand how freed slaves responded to their new legal, economic, and political situations have called attention to the customs and expectations forged during slavery itself, a view at the core of Sidney Mintz's influential works on this topic. Mintz argues that in several post-emancipation Caribbean societies such as Jamaica, Haiti, and Puerto Rico, freed slaves sought to retain access to land that would allow them to remain somewhat autonomous from the plantation economy. That quest for autonomy as a free peasantry had roots deep in the slave economies: "the subsequent adaptation to a peasant style of life was worked out by people while they were still enslaved."[16]

In Martinique in the first half of the nineteenth century, amid efforts to revive the island's flagging sugar economy, planters sought to place the

[15] Seymour Drescher, *Econocide: British Slavery in the Era of Abolition*, 2nd edn. (Chapel Hill, NC, 2010). On post-emancipaton responses, see Douglas Hall, "The Flight from the Estates Reconsidered: The British West Indies, 1838–42," *Journal of Caribbean History*, 10 (1978): 7–24.

[16] Mintz, *Caribbean Transformations*, p. 151. cf. Emmer, "Freedmen and Asian Indentured Labourers," 150–68.

responsibility for provisioning upon their enslaved workers, rather than accepting the time and expense of supplying them with clothing and food themselves as they were obliged to do by the Code Noir. Passing on the burden of provisioning meant supplying slaves with land for the cultivation of animals and crops, from which they would provide their own support. This quickly evolved into a mix of autonomy and freedom even under slavery and became a source of tension between masters and slaves:

Instead of separating the direct producers from the means of subsistence, slavery provided them with the means of producing a livelihood. While slaves gained access to the use of property and had the opportunity to improve their material conditions of life, the price of subsistence was work beyond that required for sugar production. With these developments, the time devoted to the slaves' maintenance became separate from commodity production and a de facto distinction between time belonging to the master and time belonging to the slave was created.[17]

After emancipation, the experience of working in a peasant economy supplied freed slaves with expectations of controlling their time and labor, a development that was at odds with planters' desires to keep them at work on the plantations:

These activities played an important role in helping the former slaves to resist the new encroachments of plantation agriculture and shape a new relation between labour and capital ... For the great majority of freed slaves the existence of provision-ground cultivation and marketing networks enabled them to struggle effectively over the conditions of their labour. The skills, resources and associations formed through these activities during slavery were decisive in enabling freed people to secure control over their own conditions of reproduction and to establish an independent bargaining postion *vis-à-vis* the planters after slavery.[18]

The quest for autonomy, if not complete escape, from the plantation was one of several crucial factors in the decline of British and French plantations after emancipation. However, freed peoples' efforts to evade the plantation and to drive a hard bargain with planters when they did return to plantation work captured the attention of planters and government officials who increasingly placed the blame for economic decline on the culture and customs of the ex-slaves, whom they deemed racially incapable of rational behavior in a market society. In the British Empire, one of their counter-measures was to promote the flow of indentured laborers to the West Indies, primarily from India, but also from China, Africa, and the Portuguese islands. Asian migration to the Caribbean in the long nineteenth century was a small portion of vast overseas movements

---

[17] Tomich, "Provision Ground and Plantation in Martinique," 84.
[18] Tomich, "Provision Ground and Plantation in Martinique," 87–8.

from India and China. Nonetheless, it was significant enough to have an impact in certain post-emancipation plantation societies, such as Trinidad and Guiana. For planters, the advantage of indentured labor was its predictability, at least during the five- to ten-year term of the contract that bound workers to the estates. Unable to entice ex-slaves with higher wages or to coerce them with the meager resources of the colonial state, planters found a temporary reprieve in the stream of indentured workers, though even this new traffic in unfree workers could not stop the decline of most West Indian sugar islands.[19]

In Brazil and Cuba, the transition to freedom had a quite different economic outcome, as the major staple crops experienced no major decline. Brazilian coffee and Cuban sugar expanded dramatically at the end of the nineteenth century, though there was turnover of landownership and spatial and technological shifts in production. One reason for this expansion was reliance on free European immigration to the plantation belts of Brazil and Cuba after the final abolition of slavery. In Brazil, the old core of the coffee economy, which had always relied on slave labor, did experience declines in output. In contrast, on the expanding western frontier in São Paulo state, Italian immigrants became the main labor force and coffee production flourished. Their transatlantic transportation was directly subsidized by the state government of São Paulo, which created an impressive infrastructure for recruiting, transporting, and receiving the immigrants, part of a deliberate policy of avoiding dependence on freed workers, many of whom had already fled from São Paulo plantations before emancipation in 1888. In Cuba, Spanish migrants were essential to the restructuring of the post-emancipation sugar economy, working on estates alongside ex-slaves and gaining access to land as colonists who supplied their cane directly to the new *centrales*, mills with huge capacity for processing cane, which quickly displaced the old haciendas that had relied on slave labor. With these new arrangements, Cuban sugar production actually increased by over 25 percent five years after emancipation, a stark contrast to other post-emancipation sugar-producing regions such as Haiti, where output declined by 98.3 percent, Louisiana, Northeastern Brazil, and Suriname (with declines of 75.2, 32.8, and 38.2 percent respectively).[20]

In neither case did the state – the new Brazilian Republic (1889) and the Spanish colonial state in Cuba – impose formal segregation as the United States did after the ending of Reconstruction. Segregation and discrimination were, however, part of the economic and social reality and affected

---

[19] See Emmer, "Freedmen and Asian Indentured Labourers"; and Engerman, "Comparative Approaches," 288–92. There was also a large traffic in Chinese indentured workers to Cuba as a complement to slavery between the 1840s and the 1870s.

[20] Figures on sugar output are from Engerman, "Comparative Approaches," 287.

the opportunities of freed people. The São Paulo Government's policies of promoting and subsidizing mass European immigration after emancipation had divisive and discriminatory consequences:

This was intervention seemingly devoid of any racist content, but in fact, by choosing to invest funds in European workers and refusing to make comparable investment in Brazilians, the province's planters, and the state apparatus which they controlled, had made their ethnic and racial preferences in workers crystal clear.[21]

European immigrants filled the highest paying jobs in the still vibrant coffee economy, as well as in urban trades, while blacks and mulattos found themselves shoved to the margins of the rural and urban job markets. In turn, the marginalized mobilized to demand equality. In São Paulo, organized labor sought to overcome the efforts of the state and business leaders and to demand equality of access to employment, but with only minimal success.

In Cuba, the transition to freedom from slavery had converged with the struggle to achieve national independence (the Ten Years War, 1868–1878). Wide sectors of the colonial population were strongly politicized from their participation in the anti-colonial revolt, including enslaved people and libertos, many of whom rose to positions of prominence in the insurgency, a process parallel to what had happened in the Spanish American revolutions in the 1810s and 1820s. One of the outcomes of the linkage between antislavery and anti-colonialism and the broad social participation in the independence movement was the articulation of an anti-racist, egalitarian nationalist political image. Many Cubans came to believe that the war against Spanish rule was also a struggle against the legacies of slavery and racism, so that national independence would be the setting for a society grounded in political equality.[22]

In Puerto Rico, there was also a "complicated story of alliances and negotiation among people of colour, white creoles, and Spanish authorities" around questions of citizenship, political rights, and social mobility, though largely within the framework of legally recognized, rather than revolutionary, politics.[23] As in Cuba, the setting in which these conflicts and convergences took place shifted significantly in the final decades of the

[21] George Reid Andrews, "Black and White Workers: São Paulo, Brazil, 1888–1928," *Hispanic American Historical Review*, 68 (1988): 491–524, quote is on p. 89.
[22] Aline Helg, *Our Rightful Share: The Afro-Cuban Struggle for Equality, 1886–1912* (Chapel Hill, NC, 1994); Ada Ferrer, *Insurgent Cuba: Race, Nation, and Revolution, 1868–1898* (Chapel Hill, NC, 1999); Fernando Martínez Heredia, Rebecca J. Scott, and Orlando F. García Martínez (eds.), *Espacios, silencios y los sentidos de la libertad: Cuba entre 1878 y 1912* (Havana, 2001); Alejandro de la Fuente, *A Nation for All: Race, Politics, and Inequality in Twentieth-Century Cuba* (Chapel Hill, NC, 2001).
[23] Jesse Hoffnung-Garskof, "To Abolish the Law of Castes: Merit, Manhood and the Problem of Colour in the Puerto Rican Liberal Movement, 1873–1892," *Social History*, 36 (2011): 313.

nineteenth century. During Spain's September Revolution, Puerto Rico enjoyed extensive if not complete liberalization under the auspices of the metropole's 1869 constitution. This was unlike Cuba, which was ruled through exceptional measures in response to the anti-colonial insurgency. Greater freedoms of the press and association, the Moret Law, municipal self-government, and elections to the Spanish Cortes as of 1871 were among the new freedoms that enabled political organizations and demands for a host of reforms, including the immediate abolition of slavery. The liberal political party that represented Creole interests against the conservative Spanish Party brought together various factions of society, including skilled workers, many of whom were free people of color. They were interested not only in abolition, but also in removing the legal and social barriers that had shaped colonial life over the centuries.

The overthrow of Spain's revolution in 1874 led to temporary conservative retrenchment, but by the end of the decade many of the constitutional protections, though now more constricted under the 1876 constitution of the restored monarchy, were extended to the colonies. In Puerto Rico, this period was marked by the growth of the Autonomist Party, which sought devolution of political and fiscal control to the island, greater male political rights, and modernization of the colonial economy and society. Once again, the coalition supporting autonomy crossed class and racial boundaries, though these could be reasserted in moments of conflict. For example, in 1887, the Spanish Government made widespread arrests of those artisans and laborers known to support the Autonomist movement in response. The paramilitary force in charge of the repression, the notorious Civil Guard, resorted to torture and public humiliation, as it singled out the popular supporters of the party. Colored artisans and political leaders like the printer Pachín Marín demanded that the Autonomists respond to force with force and organized protests, challenged opponents to duels, and no doubt engaged in informal violence, which was met in kind by the Spanish Party. The Autonomist Party leadership, largely from the Creole landed class and urban professions, sought to control its popular supporters, urging docility and gratitude for the white leadership's efforts to abolish slavery and to promote democratic reforms. This divergence of perspectives eventually led Marín to leave the island and to seek out more radical and potentially egalitarian political movements, such as the Cuban Revolutionary Party, which he and other Puerto Ricans of color supported from exile in New York City.[24]

---

[24] Astrid Cubano-Iguina, "Political Culture and Male Mass-Party Formation in Late-Nineteenth-Century Puerto Rico," *Hispanic American Historical Review*, 78 (1998): 631–2; and Ileana Rodríguez-Silva, "Abolition, Race, and the Politics of Gratitude in Late-Nineteenth-Century Puerto Rico," *Hispanic American Historical Review*, 93 (2013): 621–57.

Marín and other Puerto Rican supporters of revolution threw themselves into the Cuban struggle because the uprisings in Puerto Rico were
quickly stifled in the 1890s. But in Cuba, the outbreak of war in 1895, nine
years after the abolition of slavery, precipitated the end of Spanish rule and
the birth of a new republic that so many sectors of Cuban society had
hoped for since 1868. Now the legacies of slavery and racial discrimination
would be overcome, though many were quick to note that old forms of
inequality were difficult to eliminate. In 1912, one black veteran lamented
that the possibility of equality and mobility that he had experienced during
the war against Spain was being set aside in favor of old racial hierarchies;
Cubans were forgetting the heroism and sacrifice of people of color. The
Independent Party of Color staged an uprising in Eastern Cuba, which the
national government suppressed with much violence targeted against men
of color, evoking the political violence of the colonial era when the Spanish
Government responded to revolts and conspiracies among the enslaved
and the free colored population with reigns of terror.[25]

The efforts to change society from within were even more complex
because they were compounded by the challenge of confronting the
United States, a country that had rejected racial democracy after slavery.
The US military defeat of Spain in 1898 and occupation of Cuba and
Puerto Rico threw a wrench into the works for democratic forces in both
islands. Mass mobilization to defend and to advance democracy by effectively organized political parties, in Cuba by the rebel army, caught the new
imperialists by surprise. The North American occupiers expected to dictate
laws, constitutions, and social norms, including aspects of Jim Crow, to
people whom they believed they would hold in tutelage indefinitely. They
would find instead that the long fight to expand political freedom during
the transition from slavery that commenced in 1868 in both islands forged
a strong commitment to racial equality, which, if often honored in the
breach and the repression directed against the Independent Party of Color
would indicate, nonetheless differed significantly from the formalized
racial segregation and political disenfranchisement that Yankee conquista-
dors believed was the proper way to organize a post-emancipation society.

CONCLUSION

The political and cultural clash among Cubans, Puerto Ricans, and Americans over citizenship, sovereignty, race, and equality tells us much about
the transition from slavery to freedom and the ways in which historians

---

[25] See the differing interpretations of the causes and consequences of the 1912 revolt and state terror
in Helg, *Our Rightful Share*; and de la Fuente, *A Nation for All*. It has been estimated by Helg (p. 225)
that 5,000 to 6,000 were killed, 99 percent of whom were Afro-Cubans.

approach its study. Shifts in what is considered to be important have recently led historians to emphasize the political, legal, and military dimensions of slave emancipation. Earlier generations of historians and anthropologists delineated the structural features of slavery and post-slavery societies. Now what concerns scholars is not only the economic situation of post-emancipation societies – including living standards, relations between workers and planters, conflict over land, and levels of agricultural output – but also the ability of ex-slaves to achieve autonomy from the former master classes and the states, national and colonial, that generally favored the interests of white property owners. The growing emphasis on the political struggle for rights and citizenship has thus encompassed a variety of social groups and political interests going beyond the master–slave relation. Second, historians have become more attuned to the temporal and spatial unevenness of slavery, emancipation, and freedom. Far from a linear history that moved from Saint Domingue to Brazil over the course of a century, American emancipations were punctuated by spikes in the slave trade and the surge of slavery in regions such as western Cuba, southeastern Brazil, and the southern United States, where slavery was dismantled through protracted warfare, legislation, and civil disobedience that pitted distinctive regional societies against one another.

A GUIDE TO FURTHER READING

Andrews, George Reid, *Afro-Latin America, 1800–2000* (Oxford, 2004).

Cooper, Frederick, Thomas C. Holt, and Rebecca Scott, *Beyond Slavery: Explorations of Race, Labor, and Citizenship in Postemancipation Societies* (Chapel Hill, NC, 2000).

Figuero, Luis, *Sugar, Slavery, and Freedom in Nineteenth Century Puerto Rico* (Chapel Hill, NC, 2005).

Fradera, Josep M. and Christopher Schmidt-Nowara (eds.), *Slavery and Antislavery in Spain's Atlantic Empire* (New York, 2013).

Helg, Aline, *Our Rightful Share: The Afro-Cuban Struggle for Equality, 1886–1912* (Chapel Hill, NC, 1994).

Schmidt-Nowara, Christopher, *Empire and Antislavery: Spain, Cuba, and Puerto Rico, 1833–1874* (Pittsburgh, PA, 1999).

Scott, Rebecca, *Slave Emancipation in Cuba: The Transition to Free Labor, 1860–1899* (Princeton, NJ, 1985).

CHAPTER 21

ABOLITION AND ITS AFTERMATH IN BRAZIL

CELSO THOMAS CASTILHO

INTRODUCTION

The abolition of African slavery in 1888 resulted from a legislative process steeped in two decades of social, political, and legal struggles. Broad segments of the population participated in this extended period of political ferment. Slaves, politicians, women, raftsmen, law students, theater artists, and newspaper editors formed part of the surprisingly wide range of people behind the interracial abolitionist mobilizations, the first national social movement. This movement crystallized even as the institution of slavery remained economically vital in some regions, and was essential to the social and political order across the whole country. Most notably, it emerged from within areas where slave-holders wielded extraordinary power. It is unique in this respect given that such public contestations were not evidenced on this scale, and under these political circumstances, in other parts of the Atlantic World. This contrasted with the political realities of the US South or the British Caribbean, where such levels of popular, interracial political activism within important slave-holding regions were unimaginable.

In response, large coffee and sugar slave-owners, politicians, newspaper editors, and merchants coalesced to dispute the pace and terms of aboli-tion. Theirs, too, was an interracial political formation, though comprised from a much narrower, elite stratum of society; women, for example, played virtually no role in this public activism. In large measure, the abolitionist and slave-holders' mobilizations clashed over control of the political process, as previous legislation had set the nation on a course toward ending slavery. The 1850 prohibition of the Atlantic slave trade was followed by the 1871 Gradual Abolition Law, which established a "free-womb" pathway to extinguishing slavery by freeing all newborn slaves. Cumulatively, these laws provide a context from which to situate the unprecedented levels of political activity spanning from the mid-1860s through the late 1880s.

The existence of these laws should not imply that Brazilian abolition was a foregone conclusion, or that it evolved in linear fashion.

486

Theoretically, immediate abolition could have occurred in 1871, or at any one of many points in the early 1880s. Or, as abolitionists cautioned, slavery could have also remained in place through the early decades of the twentieth century, per the framework of the 1871 law. Slavery endured as long as it did because of slave-holders' political influence, its economic importance, and because, historically, slavery did not contradict Brazilian ideals of national belonging.

The abolition decree of May 13, 1888 freed upwards of half a million people. It officially began a new chapter in Brazilian history, though historically high rates of manumission had fed the expansion of free populations of color that numbered in the millions, signifying that freed-people and the reluctant political elite had also been long disputing the meanings of freedom and citizenship. In part, the social and political struggles between former slaves and their former owners that surfaced in the aftermath of abolition were not entirely unfamiliar; yet, to properly situate them, it is crucial to account for how the political agitation surrounding the abolition of slavery itself changed the terms through which people enacted citizenship in the post-emancipation era.

This chapter explores the contentious history of Brazilian abolition, focusing on the integral role of the mass, interracial abolitionist mobilizations that hastened the end of slavery and expanded the boundaries of public politics. As we will see, these posited a fundamentally different model of citizenship, one rooted in the ideals of slave emancipation and broad political participation. This conception of political belonging, to be sure, built on, and in some cases reproduced, aspects of gendered, class, and racial prejudices. It was a social movement, like all social movements, fraught with internal contradictions and divisions. Emerging from slaves' pursuits for freedom, abolitionism sparked profound debates about Brazil's political future – so much so that the former slave-holders' post-emancipation political agenda entailed erasing all vestiges of mass politics. To them, greater black political participation embodied the most threatening consequences of abolitionism. Public discussions of race and citizenship changed perceptibly from the struggle for abolition to Afro-Brazilian activism in particular.

Structured chronologically to properly convey the political contingencies of the time, this chapter utilizes three entry points – c. 1871, c. 1881, and c. 1887 – to analyze the ebbs and flows of abolitionist politics over time, including the lingering controversies over slave emancipation that extended into the post-abolition period. The conclusion briefly surveys the more recent effects that reckoning with the slave past has had on political practice and on Brazilian formulations of citizenship in the late twentieth and early twenty-first centuries. Furthermore, it also points to the continuing relevance of modern slavery in Brazil, an issue that gained wide

visibility most recently during the 2014 World Cup. Brilliantly, the editor-
ial page of the nation's largest newspaper – *Folha de São Paulo* – ignored
the successful opening match of the World Cup, played in São Paulo's
sparkling new arena, which featured a Brazilian victory over Croatia, to
instead support a constitutional amendment that proposed harsher penalties against contemporary enslavement. Neither the city nor the nation had
ever staged an event of this magnitude, yet the billions of people worldwide eager to read about local reactions to the match were treated to a
scathing denunciation of the persistence of slave-labor practices.

SLAVERY AND NATION-BUILDING

Prior to delving into that first moment of collective activism in the late
1860s, I will briefly situate the political legitimacy and public role of slavery
in early Brazilian citizenship formations. This context makes more apparent the broader contestatory features of abolitionism. Brazil's founding
charter deliberately promoted the idea of an inclusive and integrated
nation, while also preserving and enabling the expansion of slavery. The
1824 constitution sanctioned slave-holding, if through the euphemistic
principle of honoring private property, and the state was complicit in the
marked spike in the African slave trade in the decades following
independence (1822).

Yet, Brazilian legislators envisioned that rather ample constructs of
nationality would ease social tensions around slavery. They derived such
"lessons" from the recent conflicts in the French, Spanish, and Portuguese
Empires. Birthright citizenship, regardless of race, defined the broad terms
of Brazilian nationality, and integrationist narratives of nationhood
stressed Brazil's multiracial heritage. Even Brazilian-born freedpeople
acquired citizenship status.

Meanwhile, structural and cultural features enforced hierarchies within
the free population. The differentiated distribution of electoral rights, for
example, created varied levels of voting participation. Brazil's indirect
system of representation, borrowed from the French model, divided voters
into "passive" and "active" categories. Voting privileges were distributed by
gender, age, and income specifications, and until the passage of a restrictive
electoral law in 1881, a considerable number of men voted; roughly
50 percent of eligible voters went to the polls in the 1870s. Voting, to be
clear, represented only one of many different and equally important forms
of demonstrating citizenship.

Public participation was imperative to fulfilling citizenship status, either
in the form of joining associations, engaging through the press, or signing
petitions. These public dimensions of citizenship had their own unequal
structure, as issues of race, class, gender, age, and geography influenced

who gained access to such platforms. For much of the nineteenth century, nevertheless, people enacted their "free" and "citizen" status identities on the backs, literally and figuratively, of the enslaved. Citizens owned slaves as part of reaffirming their "free" status. Whites became "whiter," in part, through owning more slaves. People of color also solidified their free status through owning slaves.

The legal equality underlining Brazilianness notwithstanding, free people of color were more vulnerable than whites to the vagaries of the slave system. The possibility of being illegally enslaved was real, especially prior to the 1871 Gradual Abolition Law. People of color joined associations to affirm respectability and to shed the stigmas of blackness. Therefore, citizens' public reputation and the state's political, economic, and legal apparatus evolved in relation to, and without really challenging, the edifice of slavery. Brazil came of age as a slave nation, which is why the abolitionist model of citizenship, predicated on slave emancipation and broad political participation, represented as much a threat to the ruling political order as it did to the labor system.[1]

CIRCA 1871: ABOLITIONIST FORMATIONS

The making of an abolitionist public in the late 1860s drew from a confluence of political activities occurring across the social spectrum; from the emperor's public proclamations for gradual abolition to an enslaved person's petition for freedom; from the free and freedpeople who dealt with slaves to the law students who defended them in court and publicized such cases in the press to the newspaper editors, who increasingly judged the institution of slavery; from the new associational rituals that included staged manumission ceremonies to the production of theatrical dramas centering on the problem of slavery. These varied facets of public activism became interconnected as never before in Brazilian history. The abolitionist movement fostered opinion, and made the issue of abolition a national problem, challenging slave-owners' historical rights over control of the manumission process.

From the mid-1860s through the mid-1870s, abolitionist politics sparked a profound debate over the political future of the country. The 1871 Gradual Emancipation Law signaled the eventual end to slavery, but as we shall see, abolitionist activism continued into the mid-1870s. Slaves, associations, and journalists employed the "rights" inscribed in the 1871 law to weaken the legal and social power of slave-owners. This process instigated public reactions from slave-owners, who were placed in the bewildering

---

[1] Christopher Schmidt-Nowara, *Slavery, Freedom, and Abolition in Latin America and the Atlantic World* (Albuquerque, NM, 2011), pp. 137–43.

position of having to defend their own "rights." The 1870s political contestations over the implications of the 1871 law reignited a larger abolition debate that the gradual abolition law was presumed to have ended.

The politicization of abolition occurred mostly in cities – in plazas, theaters, in front of newspaper buildings, and around courtrooms. Quantitative surveys of associational activism during this era can offer only a small glimpse of this phenomenon, as they have been compiled from a limited number of local case studies. The most comprehensive estimate catalogs the existence of twenty-three associations within the 1867 to 1871 period, which were active in nine of the twenty provinces in Brazil, including the capital city of Rio de Janeiro. Associations were formed in the far northern provinces of Maranhão and Amazonas, in northeastern Ceará, Pernambuco, and Bahia, and in southeastern and southern São Paulo, Rio de Janeiro, and Rio Grande do Sul, respectively.

The geographical breadth of this activism indicates slavery's national importance. It also suggests that, within the provincial capital cities where most of these emerged, the associations were bound up with a host of other associational and political issues. These were not self-contained spaces of activism, and those in abolitionist societies oftentimes also joined republican or liberal associations, forcing partisan associations to position themselves on this matter. Activists also formed religious brotherhoods, literary associations, and mutual-aid societies. There was wide intermingling across associations, and the presence of even a few abolitionist societies in a given place is suggestive of much broader engagement of abolition.

The fact that at least eight of Brazil's twenty provinces created provincial emancipation funds by 1870 demonstrates that the local state, in response to proposals introduced by local politicians, broached the issue of abolition prior to the 1871 law. Pernambuco, Piauí, Ceará, São Paulo, Amazonas, Santa Catarina, Espírito Santo, and Minas Gerais, of the provinces that we know of, passed legislation to end slavery. Granted, the gendered frameworks sustaining these laws still observed the slave-owner's "right" to not participate in these manumission campaigns, and relied on discretionary allotments from the provincial budgets to compensate the owners. Therefore, the actual impact of reducing the slave population was, at best, symbolic.

Nevertheless, the local and national press reported on these laws, and in light of the national government's opposition to abolition, the political implications of emancipation funds did not go unnoticed. It was not unusual to read in the Pernambucan press, for example, articles pressuring the local government to adopt an emancipation fund because other provinces had already done so, or to read in newspapers from Ceará that it was imperative to actually implement these funds, as the implementation had already occurred in other parts of the country. These initiatives, for however modest they were in numbers of slaves freed, iterate the national dealings with abolition before the 1871 law. Provincial legislation also provides a tangible reference point from which to assess the comparative successes of the 1871 law in terms of strengthening a slave's legal right to seek manumission.

These associational and legislative activities evolved from a series of interlocking local, national, and international developments that surfaced in the mid-1860s. Together, they sparked an unprecedented reckoning with Brazil's own problem of slavery. More specifically, the freeing of the "liberated Africans" in 1864, the US Civil War, and Brazil's own war against Paraguay (1864–70) produced a context from which a wide range of people, including the emperor, increasingly imagined a Brazil without slavery. The successive and overlapping nature of these different events reinforced such ideas, and catalyzed the heightened levels of activism in the late 1860s.

The controversies surrounding the plight of the "liberated Africans" provided a starting point for activists to denounce the government's role in keeping "free" people in unfree conditions, and for being complicit in the "illegal slave trade" that thrived from 1831 to 1850. The "liberated Africans" referred to those people that the state had seized from ships involved in the illegal slave trade. Between the 1831 law and the actual closure of the trade in 1850, over 700,000 Africans were forcibly brought to Brazil; British and Brazilian authorities rescued about 11,000 persons, designating them "liberated Africans." The government then implemented a scheme that allowed them to petition for full freedom, but only after having served apprenticeships for up to fourteen years. The legal processes to gain independence were cumbersome, and were roundly criticized in the press during the early 1860s.

The liberated Africans' predicaments shed greater light on the status of the other 700,000 Africans, whose "illegal" enslavement the state sanctioned by not enforcing the 1831 law. But as the 1831 law remained on the books, abolitionist leaders like the mulatto Luiz Gama successfully spurred some 300 freedom lawsuits through the courts in São Paulo. Gama had earlier worked as a police clerk, performing tasks like handling liberated Africans' petitions for freedom, which helped him form deeper connections with illegally enslaved Africans. The interracial group of people in his circles included law students, masons, journalists, and freedpeople. From repudiating these matters, activists pivoted to the institution of slavery itself. Not coincidently, abolitionist orators in São Paulo pressed for the abolition of slavery in the late 1860s based on the fact that at least half of the country's 1.5 million slaves had been smuggled illegally. This issue gained momentum over the 1860s as public reactions to the US Civil War and Brazil's Paraguayan War generated more antislavery sentiment.

The US Civil War signaled a turning point in the hemispheric history of African slavery, triggering abolition discussions in Spain and Spanish Cuba. In Brazil, it had a deep impact on the emperor. In 1864, with a Union victory in sight, Emperor Pedro II instructed the prime minister to devise a framework for emancipation. Three years later, he opened the parliamentary session with a powerful speech about the need to end slavery. His opinion certainly received more attention than that of ordinary citizens, and in 1871 he selected a prime minister intent on passing abolition legislation. The US Civil War was invoked across Brazil by slave-owners and abolitionists alike. The former pointed to the potential devastation associated with too direct an approach to abolition; the latter similarly pointed to the carnage of war as a warning of what happens when nations fail to deal with emancipation through legislative channels.

Brazil's own war with Paraguay significantly stoked concurrent abolitionist activism. In part, the running themes of "liberation," "freedom," and "civilization" that Brazilian nationalists used to rally behind the war also lent themselves to foment growing domestic concerns with slavery. How was Brazil to liberate Paraguayans from their despotic leader while it maintained millions of enslaved, asked journalists? Along similar lines, abolitionists seized on the fact that in 1869, with a military victory assured, Brazil imposed the abolition of slavery in Paraguay as part of its state-building initiatives abroad. The war required vast military mobilizations, and the fact that as many as 7,000 freedpeople fought for the nation posed tremendous problems for Brazil's image domestically and internationally.

The press magnified such circumstances by highlighting the frequent instances whereupon returning home, these freed veterans used their pensions to manumit their families. They, and not the military generals, were depicted as the heroes of the nation. The war's victory commemorations became platforms from which to confront the realities of Brazilian slavery; orators implored crowds to show the same patriotism that they initially showed for the war toward the liberation of Brazil's own enslaved people.

It was from this politicized context of the mid-to-late 1860s that associations and provincial legislatures across the country inflamed the abolition debate. Patriotic and other associations began incorporating manumission ceremonies into their public repertoire in the late 1860s; theatrical productions of abolitionist dramas created public spaces where people imagined and participated in the dramas of abolitionism. In one famous 1867 play, *Gonzaga, ou a revolução de Minas*, the Bahian playwright and law student Antônio de Castro Alves returned to a famous late-eighteenth-century colonial conspiracy against the Portuguese, and inserted an important antislavery storyline to this quest for independence. Slavery, then, was presented as a contradiction of the nation's founding ideals.

Presented in Recife, Salvador, and São Paulo, and discussed in Rio's newspapers, *Gonzaga* exemplified an innovative form of politicizing the abolition debate. Freedom lawsuits, while certainly not new, were portrayed as an attack on the nation's laws, and thus drew wider interest. The combined publicity afforded freedom lawsuits, associational manumission ceremonies, provincial emancipation funds, and abolitionist theater in the late 1860s generated many times over the public interest that had existed in abolition only a few years prior. On the eve of the legislative session that passed the 1871 Gradual Abolition Law, abolitionism was a palpable political current.

Parliament approved the 1871 law despite entrenched opposition. It was the first time in three years that a prime minister even permitted discussion on the matter. After the Paraguayan War had ended, the new prime minister was compelled, by both mounting popular opinion and the emperor's insistence, to mobilize reformist coalitions from the far north, northeast, and the far south to overcome the resistance of southeastern coffee planters. Slavery was more integral to the coffee economy than it was to other regional economies, but it remained a political problem throughout all of Brazil. It endured in eighteen of Brazil's twenty provinces until the final abolition law due to the landed elite's political interest. Slavery was more than just a labor issue; it structured an entire social order.

The 1871 law dwarfed the provincial emancipation laws of recent years, as it freed every child born after September 28, 1871. These *ingenuos*, as they were called, remained under the owner's care until they turned 8, whereupon the owners then had the choice to free them outright and receive "maintenance" compensation from the government, or to keep them until they turned 21 and forego any remuneration. Overwhelmingly – over 95 percent of the time – the owners kept the *ingenuos*, reinforcing relations of power and exploiting their labor. The new law, however, made freeing the newborns obligatory.

The 1871 law also introduced a national emancipation fund that created freedom opportunities for the currently enslaved, as opposed to the provincial measures that mostly centered on newborns. This fund produced paltry results, however, freeing less than 1 percent of the enslaved population in its first decade – although it did create mechanisms through which slaves could press for freedom. If owners did not register slaves on the national slave census, for example, the slaves had the opportunity to sue for liberty. These suits exposed the owner's illegal maneuvers, damaging their honor before their peers and their authority over other slaves.

Over time, the national fund created ceilings on a slave's worth, causing a depreciation of the owner's assets. Lastly, the new law guaranteed a slave's right to freedom if he or she could indemnify the owner. Within the provincial emancipation frameworks, owners maintained the final say over who "deserved" freedom, but the 1871 law undercut their authority in this regard, and prohibited the practice of revoking manumissions, which they had previously preserved for instances where the newly freed failed to display proper "gratitude." The law brought the state to mediate the processes of manumission in novel ways, and rendered slave-owners' historically wide-ranging power less unassailable. In the end, it was the enslaved and their allies who utilized it, and shaped its implications.

Abolitionist activism in the aftermath of the 1871 law further polarized the abolition debate. The abolitionism movement was not linear, so there may well have been less political activity in 1875 than, say, 1870, but that does not diminish its continued importance. This is especially true because much of the ongoing activism occurred through the courts, initiated in large part by urban slaves, especially enslaved women. In major cities, enslaved women, by virtue of comprising large segments or majorities of urban slave populations (men's labor was preferred in agricultural work), struggled for themselves and their children's rights to freedom. These pursuits represented the conflicts over autonomy that former slaves also faced after 1888. Their initiatives brought new generations of law students and journalists into the quotidian realm of slavery.

Through the mid-1870s, articles commonly appeared in the largest dailies about irregularities with the slave registration process, cases of slave-owners illegally separating slave families, and instances of the owners misrepresenting the birthdates of *ingenuos*. The logistical delays in the execution of the national emancipation fund, which was not implemented until 1876, also led to the impression that this had become another law (like the 1831 unenforced prohibition of the slave trade) that the state did not prioritize. These portrayals were only partially true. The 1871 law maintained a focus on the politics of emancipation, but in terms of manumission and the defense of slaves' rights to the legal arena, the law fundamentally altered the ways in which slaves and their owners resolved conflicts.

In the post-1871 era, associational activism remained important in cities like Recife, Fortaleza, Salvador, Porto Alegre, and São Paulo. New republican associations in Recife and Fortaleza already decried the slow pace of gradual abolition as early as 1873. These associations launched newspapers that demanded immediate abolition. In the mid-1870s, the publication of the antislavery novel *A escrava Isaura* gained national attention. Similarly, the theatrical production of *Uncle Tom's Cabin* in the late 1870s captivated audiences in the national capital. It was performed on scores of occasions, and then circulated around the country. Much more research is still needed on abolitionism in the 1870s, when most of the "major" leaders of the movement first encountered and immersed themselves in abolitionist activities. A more contextualized understanding of these experiences would shed light on the processes of political radicalization.

The rise of slave-owners' public politics in the 1870s was a key factor of reinvigorating the abolition debate post-1871. In 1870, coffee barons from Rio de Janeiro and Minas Gerais created activist organizations to petition parliament to extend the period of labor control. In 1872, sugar planters in Pernambuco followed suit. Known as "agricultural clubs," these were unambiguously motivated to contest the perceived affront on their power, as represented by the 1871 law and abolitionist activism. In both regions, these respective sectors remained active throughout the 1870s, and organized major agricultural conferences in 1878. A testament of their visibility was the attendance of the prime minister at the conference in Rio and the presence of imperial representatives in Recife. At both conferences, slave-owners expressed deep anxieties about the fact that the *ingenuos* born in 1871 would be eligible for freedom in 1879, and discussed ways to ensure their labor. In the end, slave-owners did precisely this, opting to not free the *ingenuos* until they turned 21. Predictions about the end of slavery started to become less certain, and the struggle over emancipation remained as fraught as it had been into the late 1870s.

CIRCA 1881: TURNING POINTS

January 1881 marked both a material and a symbolic turning point for Brazilian abolitionism. Freedpeople and raftsmen, in conjunction with the merchants and journalists of the leading abolitionist society in Fortaleza (Ceará), accomplished the boldest abolitionist feat yet: they refused to load enslaved people onto slave ships, thus closing the provincial port to the domestic slave trade. Locally, the movement in Ceará aspired to free the whole province, and two years later, the interior municipality of Acarapé became Brazil's first "free soil" territory. By May 1883, the municipal campaigns had circled back to Fortaleza and freed the provincial capital.

The implications of these rapidly moving developments were as straightforward as they were alarming, at least from the perspective of slave-owners: the local mobilizations, and not the legal mechanisms of the 1871 law, were controlling the pace and terms of emancipation. And these were not isolated happenings. Abolitionist leaders followed and participated in these events. Through their involvement with Ceará, these leaders – José do Patrocínio, Joaquim Nabuco, André Rebouças, Rui Barbosa, Eduardo Carigé, João Ramos, and João Cordeiro – solidified the movement's national framework.

The intensification of abolitionist politics in the early 1880s arose as one prime minister after another from 1878 to 1883 refused to support further emancipation reforms. It arose amid a context where politicians' attempts to introduce abolitionist legislation proved disastrous and debilitating to their re-election prospects. It arose amid a context where a new electoral law in 1881 excluded the "illiterate" from the polls. Abolitionism peaked as slave-owners reactivated "agricultural clubs" across the country. Despite the constricting of abolition debate in parliament and the new restrictions to the ballot box, the movement, invigorated by the actions of those who refused to board slaves from the port of Fortaleza, became the principal means of political participation for tens of thousands of Brazilians.

Associational activism peaked at the turn of the 1880s. The number of abolitionist societies grew on a national level from twenty in the late 1860s to roughly 150 within this period. Not surprisingly, most of these were concentrated in provinces where abolitionism had earlier flourished, like Rio de Janeiro, São Paulo, Bahia, Pernambuco, and Ceará. The socio-economic profile of associations also widened to include more groups comprised of "middle sectors" as opposed to "elites." Women's abolitionist associations also increased during this era, fueling the mobilizations from Fortaleza and Recife, to São Paulo and Ouro Preto, to Porto Alegre. The Aves Libertas society in Recife was the most important of these nationally, as it drew on gendered expectations about charity to raise more money and free more slaves than all male associations combined in Recife during the height of associational activism. The fundamental dynamics of these newer associations remained similar in that they interacted extensively with enslaved and freedpeople.

Abolitionist societies in early 1880s Rio provided the movement with a presence in the capital city that it had previously lacked. These groups gained prominence due to a combination of factors, including the visibility of capital-city political organizing, ties with national networks, and prox-imity to parliamentary affairs. Joaquim Nabuco founded the all-important Brazilian Anti-Slavery Society in 1880. Its newspaper, *O abolicionista*, circulated nationally, delivering information on new abolitionist societies and political breakthroughs and controversies to a wide audience. Its pages drew the interest of city newspapers across Brazil; in Recife, for example, local papers commented on the fact that a national journal had mentioned the creation of two new abolitionist societies in Pernambuco.

The Brazilian Anti-Slavery Society was also interracial. Its white presi-dent Joaquim Nabuco, who was widely recognized as the leader of the movement, deliberated politics and strategies with the most renowned Afro-Brazilian abolitionists, such as Luiz Gama, José do Patrocínio, and André Rebouças. Nabuco, like Gama, represented a link to the activism of the late 1860s. Nabuco, the son of a Brazilian senator, and Gama, son of a freed African woman, both agitated through the courts and associations in São Paulo; Nabuco also participated in legal and political abolitionism in his native Recife in 1870.

Gama died in 1882, but his role in the abolitionist movement inspired future strains of radical activism, especially in rural São Paulo. The

Brazilian Anti-Slavery Society's treasurer, André Rebouças, played an active role in politicizing students and professors at the famous Engineering Polytechnical School in Rio. And Rebouças, the son of a prominent statesman, also enjoyed close access to the emperor. It would be Rebouças, according to historian Jeffrey Needell, who persuaded the government on the final terms of the abolition decree that specified an immediate and non-compensated end to slavery. Patrocínio's imprint on abolitionism, meanwhile, was established in the press via the several dailies that he edited in the 1880s. He also founded an abolitionist society of freedpeople in the capital city, and made two visits to Ceará (1878 and 1882) that helped bridge the two mobilizations.[2]

The Brazilian Anti-Slavery Society arose amid two important developments in Rio de Janeiro. The first was local in scope and pertained to a wider wave of popular political activism fueled by protests over tramway fares, which brought to the surface simmering urban tensions. The public and contentious practices of abolitionist societies in the national capital, therefore, should be seen as feeding and reflecting existing types of political resistance. Rather than just being regarded as inherently more radical than other abolitionist groups around the country, it is just as important to analyze Rio-based abolitionist societies as these related to other contemporary activities. The second key point pertains to the fact that Nabuco's impetus to form the Brazilian Anti-Slavery Society resulted in large part from his frustrated efforts to pass legislative reform on emancipation.[3]

Nabuco and a small group of national deputies devised a bill in 1880 to establish a terminal date to slavery: January 1, 1890. Nabuco was cognizant of, and no doubt inspired by, the fact that a similar law passed in Cuba in 1880 to establish 1888 as the end date for slavery on the island. His bill provided greater rights to slaves on the one hand, stating that when they saved 75 percent of their value, the government would then pay the remaining sum for their manumission. On the other hand, it also stipulated that slaves who fled their owners prior to 1890 would not receive the benefits of the abolition law (which were not specified), and that they would have to serve their owners for double the time they remained fugitives. From the vantage point of the ruling Liberal cabinet, it was seen as a thoroughly excessive and unnecessary bill. The 1871 law had solved the issue of abolition, the cabinet argued. The project was not even put to a vote, and soon thereafter, Nabuco spearheaded the founding of the

[2] Jeffrey Needell, "Brazilian Abolitionism, Its Historiography, and the Uses of Political History," *Journal for Latin American Studies*, 50 (2010): 231–61, here 257–8.
[3] Sandra Lauderdale Graham, "The Vintem Riot and Political Culture: Rio de Janeiro, 1880," *Hispanic American Historical Review*, 60 (1980): 431–49.

Brazilian Anti-Slavery Society. He and five other deputies who supported the legislation subsequently lost their re-election bids.

The constitution of dynamic abolitionist publics in the early 1880s went far beyond the founding of associations; they centered on a range of repertoires that appealed to a wide cross-section of society. Across the country, these gatherings occurred in plazas and theaters, and included plays, musical performances, manumission ceremonies, and dramatic oratory. Ordinary people, of different races and backgrounds, developed a connection with a movement through these events. Abolitionist publics flourished. "Abolitionist concerts," as they have been called, changed people's views about Brazilian nationalism, the urgency of abolitionism, and the practices of citizenship. Dozens upon dozens of these concerts were staged regularly in the early 1880s. In Rio de Janeiro, André Rebouças played a leading role in organizing over forty events in 1880 and 1881 alone. In Fortaleza, the raftsmen and freedpeople who closed the port to slave traders also formed part of such happenings in theaters and plazas. In Recife, Salvador, Ouro Preto, Porto Alegre, São Paulo, and a host of other important cities, abolitionist opinion swelled through these processes.[4]

The movement gained a cultural place in people's lives that other surging political issues – like republicanism – could not. At abolitionist bazaars, for example, people proudly consumed "abolitionist" products, such as coffee, wine, and beer. The bazaars, as with the other events, created local activists and local abolitionist narratives, and challenged the most basic ideas about where and when political formations occurred.

This spate of public abolitionism hardened the resolve of parliamentary leaders and slave-owners. One prime minister, for example, infamously declared himself a "slavocrat" in 1882. In the southeast and northeast, the "agricultural clubs" that surfaced in the 1870s reappeared, and with greater intensity. These represented a response to the abolitionist mobilizations, and, curiously, employed some of the same approaches to win over public opinion, including forming associations, printing petitions, and publicizing through the press. Mostly, they decried having lost control of the political process. They resented the ongoing legal challenges based on the 1871 law, and slaves' awareness of the growing opportunities for manumissions through abolitionist societies. Despite parliamentary backing, they recognized that they were losing political ground.

In large part, the ongoing municipality-by-municipality freedom campaigns sweeping Ceará in 1882 and 1883 legitimized the notion that local

---

[4] Angela Alonso, "Flores, votos e balas: o movimento pela abolição da escravidão no Brasil" (Tese de livre-docência [thesis]: Universidade de São Paulo, 2012), pp. 8, 114, 139–41; Celso Castilho, "Performing Abolitionism, Enacting Citizenship: The Social Construction of Political Rights in 1880s Recife, Brazil," *Hispanic American Historical Review*, 93 (2013): 377–409.

governments could (and should) press the issue of abolition even when parliament resisted. By mid-July, seventeen of Ceará's fifty-six municipalities pronounced themselves free. The important border city of Mossoró in neighboring Rio Grande do Norte also declared freedom in September 1883, and in other places, like Recife, campaigns to free provincial capitals were launched, if ultimately stymied. By the year's end, the movement in Ceará pressured the provincial government into an "indirect" abolition law that, via an exorbitant tax, led owners to free their remaining slaves. Mass celebrations on March 25, 1884 marked the feat in Fortaleza and across the country, and the raftsmen became national heroes. In Rio, the recently formed Abolition Federation, comprised of over fifteen abolitionist societies, organized the week-long commemorations. The Federation, headed by men intimately familiar with the Ceará movement like Patrocínio and João Clapp, modeled themselves on the abolitionist confederation in Ceará.[5] The outpouring of some 10,000 people led to the formation of neighborhood freedom campaigns as had occurred in Fortaleza. Within months, the northern province of Amazonas also abolished slavery, mainly through a provincial emancipation fund. And the southern provincial capital of Porto Alegre also pronounced itself a "free" city. There, the state mediated by creating conditional manumissions where the freed were obliged to provide up to seven years of labor to their former owners.[6]

The making of these "free" territories all across Brazil had wide ramifications on the framing of the abolition debate going forward. Only a few thousand, at most, of the 1 million or so still enslaved as of 1884 gained freedom through these campaigns, but cumulatively these actions signaled that Brazil was no longer totally a slave nation.

Parliamentary politics also took a drastic turn in 1884, and for the first time since 1871, a prime minister took power with an interest in hastening abolition. The rise of Bahian Senator Manoel Pinto de Souza Dantas, a member of a Bahian abolitionist society in the early 1870s, generated immediate controversy. Days into his mandate, his son, Rodolfo Dantas, introduced a bill calling for the immediate and uncompensated emancipation of all slaves over the age of 60. A political crisis ensued, as this project undermined the economic foundations of Brazilian slavery. Even though it affected less than 20 percent of the overall enslaved population, the implications of a government-sponsored abolition reform not based on indemnization shocked the system. Opponents from both Dantas' own

[5] *Relatorio do Estado e das Operações da Confederação Abolicionista Apresentado à Assembléa Geral Annual de Seus Membros em 12 de maio de 1884 Por Seu Presidente João F. Clapp* (Rio de Janeiro, 1884), pp. 3–4.

[6] Roger A. Kittleson, "'Campaign All of Peace and Charity': Gender and the Politics of Abolitionism in Porto Alegre, Brazil, 1879–1888," *Slavery and Abolition*, 22 (2001): 83–108.

Liberal Party and the Conservatives mustered joint support for a vote of "no confidence." Faced with replacing Dantas or dissolving the chamber of deputies as a way to resolve the impasse, the emperor initially chose the latter.

Not surprisingly, the elections for the new deputies shone more, not less, light on abolitionism. A host of candidates, intent on reasserting an abolitionist presence in parliament, ran on "abolitionist" tickets, including the famed Joaquim Nabuco, who after his previous defeat in 1881, had spent three years in London on a self-imposed exile. While in exile, he published a political tract entitled *Abolitionism*, where he placed emancipation as but one of several transformative changes the movement espoused, including land, education, and political reforms.

The inclusion of "abolitionist candidates" in Recife, Fortaleza, Salvador, São Paulo, and Porto Alegre made the issue of political representation central to local campaigns, even though the vast majority of those turning out for the public meetings and signing petitions could not vote under the terms of the new electoral law. Their engagement forced opposing candidates to position themselves on abolition reform, and, through their appropriation of public spaces, they prompted new debates about political belonging and participation.

In a sign of slave-holders' enduring political strength, however, only a few abolitionist candidates won their electoral battles. Just as importantly, the continuing gridlock in parliament led to the dismissal of the Dantas cabinet. In September 1885, under a decidedly anti-abolitionist administration, the new abolition reform finally passed, though under very different terms. Crucially for the slave-owners, the government adhered to the principle of indemnification. Only the enslaved aged 65 and over gained their immediate freedom. The 1885 law did officially ban the domestic slave trade, which while it had stopped flows to the main coffee provinces in 1880 and 1881, had continued in the northern and northeastern parts of the country.

The ebbing and flowing that characterized abolitionist politics since the late 1860s persisted into the late 1880s. The political tide had once again turned in 1885. The state's repressive apparatus dampened public agitation, and as of early 1886, slave-owners still held a strong political position. Nevertheless, abolitionist activism continued to evolve.

CIRCA 1887: REACTION, ABOLITION, AND POST-ABOLITIONISM REACTION

The hard anti-abolitionist line put forth by the new Cotegipe administration (Baron of Cotegipe, 1885–1888) sparked unseen levels of slave resistance and renewed imperial involvement in the political process. Both the overwhelming spike in slave flight and violence and the influential political role that Princess Regent Isabel exercised in the final year of slavery had much to do with the broad public support for abolition cultivated through associational activism.

It is impossible to isolate one single factor as the impetus for the final abolition of slavery, as the political actions of these ostensibly separate "influences" – slaves, associations, and the monarchy – had evolved in a mutually influential manner. Their interactions iterate the cross class, race, and regional dimensions of Brazilian abolitionism. Abolitionist groups took a radical turn in the late 1880s because of slaves' relentless pressure; the enslaved's decisions to escape bondage were inspired by the creation of "free" territories and the havens that they offered. The Princess Regent's position on abolition intensified as a result of participating in imperial emancipation funds; she had a perceptible feel for public opinion. These varied social pressures accelerated the passage of the abolition law and initiated the types of conflicts and struggles over autonomy that became more apparent in the post-emancipation era. From this view, the abolition of slavery appears as a fluid process rather than as a division between two discrete periods – one ending on May 13 and the other beginning on May 14.

Between 1884 and early 1888, the national slave population decreased by 50 percent, going from slightly over 1 million to about half a million on the eve of emancipation. Most (80 percent) of the enslaved lived in the southeastern provinces of São Paulo, Minas Gerais, and Rio de Janeiro. Yet, slavery remained a national institution, as it was politically and socially vital across all regions. The election of pro-Cotegipe/anti-abolitionist deputies to parliament in 1886 attests to this dynamic. The creation of fugitive slave communities (*quilombos*) and "free soil" territories across the country also reflects slavery's nationwide presence. Slaves changed the tenor of the political debate in the mid-1880s through fleeing, often en masse.

The government responded by passing the 1885 Sexagenarian Law, which included harsh measures against those aiding fugitive slaves. Large communities of freedpeople developed in the environs of Porto Alegre, Fortaleza, Ouro Preto, and Rio de Janeiro (Leblon). In the northeast, the city of Cachoeira in the Bahian hinterland became a place of refuge, if not officially a "free" city. And, from Pernambuco, some 3,000 people escaped to Ceará via a maritime freedom route, which had been organized by a popular abolitionist society. People from other surrounding provinces probably escaped to Ceará as well, though this topic demands further research.

The enslaved's mass flight from the São Paulo coffee fields to "free" communities in the port city of Santos had an extraordinary effect on national politics. Traces of this phenomenon were evident in the late 1870s and early 1880s, but it intensified markedly during the mid-1880s. Enslaved people created the "Pai Felipe" (Father Felipe) community in Vila Matias and also settled in the more famous Jabaquara, which was owned by abolitionists.

These initiatives exemplified the mounting pressures on the coffee planters, as they could ensure neither their labor force nor their own authority.[7] The army famously refused to pursue slave runaways in 1887. Meanwhile, the coffee planters lobbied the São Paulo provincial government – comprised largely of planters – to finance schemes for immigration as a replacement for enslaved labor. Once secured, argues Thomas Holloway, planters turned in late 1887 and early 1888 to accepting mass conditional manumissions as a compromise to keep people working in the fields.[8]

Through such arrangements, the formerly enslaved and the former slave-owners began dealing with struggles over autonomy and people's changing sense of rights. By February 1888, the capital city of São Paulo became one of fifteen "free" municipalities in the province. These sudden turns of events, which seemed unlikely in early 1886, severely weakened the prime minister's anti-abolitionist governing coalition.

Similarly, Princess Regent Isabel participated in isolating and, ultimately, removing the embattled prime minister. This marked the third time (1871–72, 1877–78, and 1887–88) that she presided over the nation's affairs in her father's absence. It is often forgotten that it was Isabel who had signed the 1871 law into effect. In the mid-1880s, Isabel publicly and controversially supported the Rio de Janeiro's municipal emancipation funds. She appeared at freedom ceremonies, distributed letters of manumission, and connected the throne to an abolitionist milieu that the prime minister and his coterie otherwise decried.[9] In early 1888, she demanded an abolition project from Cotegipe, which he refused. His legitimacy in shreds, the prime minister resigned a few months later.

Intent on producing an abolition law, Isabel quickly turned to Pernambucan Senator João Alfredo Correia de Oliveira. The new prime minister, who had been part of the cabinet that passed the 1871 law, accepted the charge. The terms of the law remained unclear as late as March 1888. It could have included compensation, a period of "apprenticeship," or some combination of both. The prime minister, after all, had inherited the same chamber of deputies that, for the previous two years, had steadfastly supported Cotegipe's anti-abolitionist agenda. Ultimately,

---

[7] Maria Helena Machado, *O plano e o pânico: os movimentos sociais na década da abolição* (São Paulo, 1994); Robert Toplin, *The Abolition of Slavery in Brazil* (New York, 1972).

[8] Thomas Holloway, "Immigration and Abolition: The Transition from Slave to Free Labor in the São Paulo Coffee Zone," in Dauril Alden and Warren Dean (eds.), *Essays Concerning the Socio-Economic History of Brazil and Portuguese India* (Gainesville, FL, 1977), pp. 150–77.

[9] Camillia Cowling, *Conceiving Freedom: Women of Color, Gender, and the Abolition of Slavery in Havana and Rio de Janeiro* (Chapel Hill, NC, 2013), pp. 159–73.

it included neither, and the law's conciseness belied the country's long history of slavery.

The Brazilian abolition law of May 13, 1888 ended slavery immediately and without monetary compensation. It was roundly celebrated across the country. Newspapers suspended publication for three days because their workers wanted to participate in the festivities. The street commemorations eclipsed any other social happening in Brazilian history – even the nation's own independence. These celebrations became a first instance where people crafted narratives of abolition, of its "heroes" and "history," a process through which people claimed their space within the new, "free" national imaginary.

To many, abolition signified national redemption. Afro-Brazilians and the newly freed, of course, partook in making this narrative of Brazilian fulfillment. In poetry and song, the idea that abolition occurred from collective action validated the idea of popular political participation. Of course, to others, particularly former slave-owners, abolition represented an affront to their own and to what they argued were "national" interests. This sentiment fueled their need to reclaim their political power.

The differing, and sometimes competing, perceptions of how slavery ended shaped contestations over citizenship in the post-abolition era. The vast mobilizations that were critical to abolishing slavery unleashed fears that went beyond the labor issue; on a grand scale, they struck at the entire political order.

In the months following abolition, the former slave-owners aimed to re-establish their authority over both the formerly enslaved and the political process. The newly freed asserted themselves in large and small ways, and the public reactions can only be seen as a reflection of freedpeople's persistence to reset the terms of their relations with the wider society.

In the aftermath of abolition, few, if any, influential slave-holders spoke publicly of re-enslavement, but a national indemnification campaign quickly emerged that put the issue of compensation back on the parliamentary agenda. Within two weeks of May 13, two separate bills reached the chambers and the senate, respectively. Both were submitted by men of northeastern roots; the first by a deputy from Piauí who maintained ties with the agricultural clubs headed by Pernambuco's sugar planters, and the second by the baron of Cotegipe, the recently deposed anti-abolitionist prime minister. Neither stood much chance and did not even reach the floor for discussion. Yet, these initiatives fostered a collective sense of victimization among the landed elite. Conservative newspapers fanned their objectives, printing and reprinting articles about other historical examples of emancipation that included sizable compensation sums, including the British and French cases. Besides iterating this point, the conservative press also underlined (and accelerated) another ongoing phenomenon: the transition of the landed elite to the Republican Party. The indemnification campaign, despite its ineffectiveness in changing the terms of abolition, resulted in an important moment in the reconfiguration of the landed elite's political formations.

This shift of the landed elite to the Republican Party had grave consequences on Brazilian politics in the late 1880s, leading up to the military-republican coup that ousted the constitutional monarchy in November 1889. Founded in 1870, Brazil's Republican Party came of age more under the influence of positivist ideology than the historical liberalism traditionally associated with the French Revolution. The party, while it opposed slavery on the grounds of its antiquated features, did not list abolition among its objectives in 1870. Republicans' most common goal was federalism.

This was in large part due to the important presence of São Paulo's coffee planters among its leadership ranks. To these planters, the federal and oligarchical features of positivist republicanism coincided with their aspirations for greater political power. In the northeast, republicanism found strong adherents among a younger generation drawn to its scientific and modern banner. However, historical variants of republicanism still resonated in Recife, Bahia, Fortaleza, and the national capital, and these three strains – planters' republicanism, modernizers' republicanism, and historical republicanism – coexisted with and infused abolitionist mobilizations.

The processes of consolidating these different republicanisms extended into the 1890s and early 1900s. For our purposes, the landed elite's turn to the Republican Party after May 13 sheds light on more than just their resentment toward the monarchy; it also illuminates the convergence of their and the positivists' beliefs about restricted political participation, and reflects the continuing role of the abolition issue in shaping republicanism. Prior to 1888, the antislavery movement galvanized Republicans; after 1888, a negative perception of the abolition law unified their objectives. Almost a year after the indemnification campaign, Republicans sold cigars in Recife labeled "Indemnization or Republic."

The abolition narrative became integral to Afro-Brazilian political activities. Like the abolitionist mobilizations, the Black Guard was a national phenomenon comprised of locally focused groups. Prominent abolitionists figured among it, including the mulatto José do Patrocínio in Rio de Janeiro and the white José Mariano in Recife. It counted on men and women from different socio-economic backgrounds, though it was largely comprised of blacks and mulattos. It was both celebrated and reviled because of this "popular" and "black" character. It was ardently devoted to the monarchy, and, most importantly, to Princess Regent Isabel for her role in hastening abolition. In the national capital and other major cities across Brazil, like São Paulo, Salvador, and Recife, the Black Guard manifested itself in political debates. It represented the most militant response to the growing Republican movement. The Black Guard organized counter-demonstrations to protest against Republican political candidates, fostering spaces for citizens to perform citizenship. The Black Guard, in the Republicans' views, magnified everything that appeared dangerous about mass political participation.

Beyond the Black Guard, freedpeople's everyday struggles for autonomy and inclusion played a key role in heightening political tensions after abolition. They challenged municipal vagrancy laws; some moved to cities, while others moved back to rural areas to be near family and familiar surroundings. They switched employers according to their own criteria, lived with whom they wanted, and through the combination of these actions made visible their own perspectives about freedom. It is important to note that, due to historically high levels of manumission and the marked decrease of the slave population over the preceding decades, these various forms of contestations had been a feature of political life in advance of abolition. As significant as these initiatives were on a personal level, their cumulative repercussions drew from the sustained nature of these challenges since the last years of slavery, and from the surrounding political changes taking place in the post-abolition context that rendered these familiar challenges in a new light.

Historians working primarily with police and judicial records have painstakingly recovered dozens upon dozens of instances of bitter disputes between former slaves and their former owners. It is clear that freedpeople went to great legal lengths to establish property ownership, to affirm the boundaries around their labor obligations, and to contest public acts of racism. From rural areas in the Bahian and Pernambucan hinterlands to the coffee plantation zones in Rio de Janeiro and São Paulo, freedpeople's activities are stamped across the historical record. The testimonies, buried pages deep into these files, make apparent that race was a central prism through which these interactions unfolded.

To many freedpeople, it became a strategic imperative to publicly downplay their past slave identities, so as to undercut prevailing tendencies to apply the stigmas of enslavement onto a stigma of blackness. It was not that they tried to shed their "blackness," per se, as Hebe Mattos argues, or that they aspired for "whiteness," but that they were trying to reconstruct blackness around ideals of autonomy, dignity, and equality.

The explicitly "black" forms of activism tied to the Black Guard and freedpeople's resistance also influenced changes in the public use of racial languages. Free and freed blacks and mulattos had long been politically active, and the abolition of slavery transformed perceptions of black politics. Even though slave-owning was obviously no longer a basis for affirming one's status, an association with the slave past still stigmatized afro-descendants. Compared to preceding decades, public references to both "blacks" and "Africans" became more apparent. In pointed critiques of how black activism was the consequence of the "disorderly" nature of abolitionism, the landed elite focused on "black" political participation when denouncing the broader effects of wide political participation.

Equally as problematic was the use of the word "Africans" when referring to Afro-Brazilians, as this wording located them outside the parameters of national membership. It was becoming increasingly evident that race was a more central way to signify social conflicts. Yet, we should not forget the fact that the remaking of racial identities unfolded beyond a strictly former slave/owner binary. The sizable international and national migrations in the late nineteenth and early twentieth centuries influenced local understandings of race. That is, abolition did not just reconfigure "blackness"; it also changed constructions of "whiteness," "Brazilianness," "foreigner," "Bahiano," and "Paulista."

The post-May 13 conservative reactions across Brazil reflected the popular political repertoire that the abolitionist social movement had invented and consolidated. To point to the decline of abolitionist associational activism as indicative of abolitionism's limited scope is to miss the broad ways in which it expanded the political field. This oft-mentioned critique of the movement is accurate only in its most literal sense: the overwhelming majority of abolitionist societies proper did dissolve around or not long after May 13. The critique ignores the continuation of other abolitionist-related strains of activism like the Black Guard, and obscures the longer-term political effects that those associational experiences had on its younger participants. Manoel da Mata Monteiro Lopes, for example, who rose to national prominence in republican Brazil, and became in 1909 the first representative to congress to explicitly present himself as a "black" politician, launched his public activism as leader of an abolitionist society in late 1880s Recife. An afro-descendant and law student, Lopes' involvement with the movement shaped later political views; notably, in 1909, he delayed his election celebrations for several weeks to have the commemorations occur on the anniversary of May 13.

Important social interventions related to abolition that surfaced in the aftermath of May 13 had deep roots in the movement's structure, networks, and resources. The creation of special schools for former slaves is among the most notable. These schools – in Recife, Fortaleza, Salvador, Rio de Janeiro, and São Paulo – were developed as private/public initiatives. Public school teachers involved with abolitionism drew on private (and little public) financing and stayed open for years. In Salvador, for example, they lasted as part of a post-emancipation project until at least the early 1900s. These initiatives became an important means for resignifying blackness around ideas of educational achievement.

The scores of abolitionist associations that formed nationwide between the 1860s and 1880s only strengthened the overall culture of associations into the twentieth century. The ties between abolitionist organizing and the labor mobilizations of the turn of the century still need further exploration, not only in relation to the individuals who may have comprised both, but also in terms of the forms of making public politics that may have endured, such as the continued politicization of popular cultural spaces. Along these abolitionist-labor connections, however, we should not assume a story of linear political gains, given that labor struggles, especially in the southeast, highlighted the fact that freedpeople remained both outside and excluded from some attempts at unionizing. Broadly, with renewed scholarly interest in questions of citizenship and political formations, it is likely that we will soon learn more about the rich and complex trajectories of abolitionism beyond May 13, which will also expand our historical understandings of the breadth of interracial activism that so defined that phenomenon.

CONCLUSION

Brazilian reckonings with the slave past and with modern-day slavery are very much a part of the nation's recent history. Like the abolitionist mobilizations of the nineteenth century, the current waves of activism have sparked wider debates related to citizenship and transformed political practice. A black political movement re-emerged in the 1980s and publicly called into question everything from the relevance of May 13 celebrations to contemporary, structural racial disparities. Other interracial coalitions of journalists, educators, students, and labor leaders have played a pivotal role in formulating demands for fuller black political inclusion, expanded educational and land rights, and a general reappraisal of blackness. Notably, Brazilians represented themselves as a non-white nation for the first time ever in the 2010 census. Mixed-race people accounted for 43 percent and blacks nearly 8 percent, a phenomenon which was shaped in part by the country's economic success during the preceding ten years. Yet, this level of affirmation also illuminates the longer struggles for civil rights that crystallized around the events marking the 1988 centennial of slave emancipation.

The mass black and interracial protests of 1988 sparked the most profound public debates on racial inequalities in Brazilian history. In capital cities alone, scholars noted roughly 1,700 events. The abolition theme permeated every facet of daily life. It was the subject of film festivals, television series, public works projects, carnival, music, tourism, and theater. These wide and varying reflections on the history of abolition and its legacies coincided with, and inflamed, parallel debates about citizenship that also surfaced in 1988 (the year when Brazil replaced the constitution of the dictatorship era of 1964 to 1985). The constitution's recognition, for example, of descendants of fugitive slave communities to make claims on those lands arose from this context of increased black political agitation. The Black Movement also decried the significance of May 13 in terms of its importance to Afro-Brazilian history, given enduring racial inequalities, and argued instead for the appropriation of November 20, in memory of the seventeenth-century quilombo leader, Zumbí. In 2010, former president Luiz Inácio Lula da Silva declared November 20 a national holiday.

Brazilians born in the 1980s and 1990s have a much different perspective of the country's African heritage and black present than their parents and grandparents. Stemming from the wide social reckoning with the legacies of abolition, university and grade-school educators alike have thoroughly reassessed the dominant narratives surrounding slavery, current racial dynamics, and Brazil's relationship to Africa. A 2003 federal law mandated the inclusion of African and Afro-Brazilian history and culture in school curricula, which also stimulated more professional study of such areas in post-graduate programs.

Beyond diversifying the curriculum, university classrooms are more diversified as a result of affirmative action policies of the last decade or so. Such initiatives have yet to be consolidated at the federal level, but most, if not all, states have adopted specific measures to ensure greater racial, gender, and socio-economic representation in higher education. Not all focus on race, per se, but this movement for affirmative action is another example of the broad engagement for civil rights that emerged in the late 1980s in relation to the centennial of abolition.

In closing, it is crucial to underscore that Brazil's abolition of African slavery did not spell the end of forced, unfree labor practices. By twenty-first-century standards, as derived from the United Nations' 1948 Universal Declaration of Human Rights, there are more people enslaved today around the world than there were during the height of African slavery, though their estimate comprises a smaller share of the overall world population. For reference, Latin America and the Caribbean are the regions with the smallest proportion of people held in captivity, but national and international organizations estimate that some 20,000 to 25,000 people are enslaved in Brazil. This number includes those caught in debt bondage, forced marriage, and child labor exploitation, among other criteria. Such practices have occurred mostly in rural areas of Brazil, but with increased regional migration and international immigration, urban centers have also been sites for enslaving factory workers.

Since the early 2000s, however, the government, in conjunction with NGOs and a host of other associations, has prioritized this issue. Among other measures, it publishes a biannual "dirty list" with the names of individuals and organizations that are caught enslaving others. The approval of the constitutional amendment alluded to at the outset of this chapter strives for more stringent penalties against offenders. The government wants the power to confiscate the property of slavers, and to redistribute it among said workers. A law is needed, however, to put the amendment into practice, and this process is still unfolding.

Broadly, the public struggles for everyone's equality is a legacy of the abolitionist mobilizations. Just as the fight to end African slavery was deeply embedded in ongoing debates about the nation's political future, today's dealings with both the consequences of the slave past and with modern slavery are equally as consequential in shaping the terms of Brazil's vibrant democracy.

A GUIDE TO FURTHER READING

Albuquerque, Wlamyra R. de, *O jogo da dissimulação: Abolição e cidadania no Brasil* (São Paulo, 2009).

Alonso, Angela, *Flores, votos e balas: O movimento abolicionista brasileiro, 1868–1888* (São Paulo, 2015).

Butler, Kim, *Freedoms Won, Freedoms Given: Afro-Brazilians in Post-Abolition São Paulo and Salvador* (New Brunswick, NJ, 1998).

Castilho, Celso Thomas, *Slave Emancipation and Transformations in Brazilian Political Citizenship* (Pittsburgh, PA, 2016).

Castro, Hebe Mattos de, *As cores do silêncio: Os significados da liberdade no sudeste escravista* (Rio de Janeiro, 1995).

Chalhoub, Sidney, *Visões da liberdade: Uma história das últimas décadas da escravidão na corte* (São Paulo, 1990).

Cowling, Camillia, *Conceiving Freedom: Women of Color, Gender, and the Abolition of Slavery in Havana and Rio de Janeiro* (Chapel Hill, NC, 2013).

Drescher, Seymour, "Brazilian Abolition in Comparative Perspective," *Hispanic American Historical Review*, 68 (August 1988): 429–60.

Grinberg, Keila, *Liberata, a lei da ambigüidade: As ações de liberdade da corte de apelação do Rio de Janeiro no século XIX* (Rio de Janeiro, 1994).

Machado, Maria Helena Pereira Toledo, *O plano e o pânico: Os movimentos sociais na década da abolição* (São Paulo, 1994).

PART IV

AFTERMATH

CHAPTER 22

THE AMERICAN CIVIL WAR AND ITS AFTERMATH

PETER A. COCLANIS

Scholars today are less confident than they have been in a long while about many matters relating to the American Civil War and its aftermath. This is so for a variety of reasons. Some see the roots of such uncharacteristic scholarly humility in powerful intellectual currents, most notably, in the epistemological challenges raised during the recent, but now much-dimmed, postmodernist movement, particularly the movement's assault on the idea of grand narratives. Similarly, others point to today's rapidly intensifying methodological critiques of standard economics, which have led an increasing number of economic historians, especially younger scholars, to believe that we are asking the wrong questions, measuring the wrong things, and/or misreading or drastically simplifying the motivations animating human economic behaviors. Still others view the war and its aftermath differently because the simultaneous rise of both global and micro history as fields has changed the levels of refraction in which we view – and interpret – American developments, while still others have become interested in studying questions, issues, groups, and themes that don't fit comfortably, if at all, into the interpretive architecture that once so solidly framed our understanding of the war, emancipation, and all that. As a result, one thing we can say with some certitude, with a nod to Marx, is that much of what we once considered solid about the war and its aftermath has melted into air.

This situation, however, is not necessarily a cause for despair. Speaking broadly, the main political and economic contours of the postbellum South are still visible. Moreover, we now know a great deal more about the (growing number of) subjects at hand than we did a generation ago. Excellent work continues to be done that treats or overlaps with – or at least touches upon – standard themes. And advances in technology have allowed us at once to access and assess, manipulate, and incorporate amounts of data that previous generations would have found unfathomable. Thus, while we proceed with some caution, we do so with excitement, certainly not while whistling in the dark.

A generation ago, things were different. In retrospect, the publication in 1988 of Eric Foner's magisterial *Reconstruction: America's Unfinished*

Revolution, 1863–1877 – which at once encapsulates and extends earlier revisionist treatments of the era – marked the apogee of that interpretative tradition. Acknowledging and at times taking on so-called post-revisionist critiques in his massive study, Foner provides a skillful blend of political and social history that highlights the positive dimensions of Reconstruction, however short-lived, *to wit*: the federally backed efforts after the war to secure racial equality in the South, to incorporate newly emancipated African Americans as citizens into the body politic, and to create and defend a legal regime and a system of labor relations in the region that would allow African Americans far greater economic independence, opportunity, and autonomy than was the case under slavery. Overall, Foner succeeds in keeping freedmen (if not always freedwomen) front and center and labor relations and class formation at the fore. If in time many of the efforts promoted by the federal government failed or were scaled back for reasons ranging from inattention to the rise of competing concerns to tenacious, often violent opposition, the efforts themselves were laudable and in some cases unique in their radicalness, and put in place some statutes and constitutional mechanisms that endured for later redeployment in more propitious days. So rich was Foner's account of Reconstruction – and so consonant with the scholarly consensus in the late 1980s – that in the wake of *Reconstruction*, many historians believed that there was little more to say about the era, whose once "dark and bloody ground" had been pacified and perhaps even rendered hallowed by a supremely talented historian.

Similarly, by the late 1980s most economic historians believed that they had a good sense of the difficult postbellum transformation of agricultural labor systems and labor relations occasioned by emancipation. If scholars disagreed on the timing and causes of the transformation, most accepted the proposition that after a relatively short period of flux, new labor patterns came to characterize most parts of the rural South, with the vast majority of African American agriculturalists occupying positions on a metaphorical agricultural ladder, whose firmly-set rungs went in ascending order from wage labor to sharecropping to tenancy to land ownership. Careful scholars were quick to add that white agriculturalists increasingly found themselves positioned on the ladder as well, but virtually all economic historians c. 1990 believed that the metaphor accurately captured the system of labor relations that emerged in the South after the war.

To be sure, economists are naturally argumentative and debates continued over hows and whys. Most neo-classically oriented scholars, for example, believed that the ladder, particularly the positioning of farmers on the sharecropping rung, was "an understandable market response" to postbellum economic conditions. On the other hand, scholars coming from political-economy and institutional traditions – Roger Ransom and

Richard Sutch, most notably, in their much-acclaimed 1977 study, *One Kind of Freedom: The Economic Consequences of Emancipation* – attributed sharecropping in large part to market distortions occasioned by racism and "flawed institutions." But it seems fair to say, with a nod to Genesis 28: 12, that most members of the (economic) flock c. 1990 believed in the efficacy of the ladder metaphor in explaining and interpreting the agricultural transformation of the postbellum South.

Moreover, there were other broad areas of economic agreement a quarter of a century ago. No one questioned the fact that the southern economy was in disarray coming out of the war and remained very poor through the remainder of the nineteenth century. Some scholars, it is true, argued that the South rebounded a bit in the 1870s and 1880s and that some sectors (manufacturing, for example) grew fairly rapidly after that time, but no one tried to make the case that the region was – in a North American context – anything other than poor and technologically backward in 1900. And regarding the impact of the Civil War on the US economy as a whole: Few scholars twenty-five years ago gave much credence to the supposedly hoary Beard-Hacker line that the Civil War served as a revolutionary punctuation point in the country's economic history, at once marking and causing the nation's transformation into a major industrial power in the decades after the war.[1]

But over the course of the last twenty-five years, "something happened" –to employ the title of Joseph Heller's 1974 novel – or, more accurately, a number of things happened that brought to an end some of the areas of consensus discussed above. In part, of course, this was to be expected. Scholarly capital can be "crowded out" for only so long, even by great works on the Civil War and its aftermath such as those produced in the 1970s and 1980s. We thus see numerous extensions and qualifications to the interpretations that reigned c. 1990 – some major, some more minor – as well as somewhat scholastic exercises in gap-filling (including at times, alas, the filling of "much-needed gaps!"). Moreover, we also see at times, perhaps as a result of intentional misreading *à la* Harold Bloom's anxiety-of-influence line, rather strained attempts by some to differentiate themselves from Foner or Ransom and Sutch – or Michael Perman, Robert Higgs, or Gavin Wright, etc., for that matter – by challenging reduced and oversimplified versions of major works. All in

---

[1] Charles A. Beard and Mary R. Beard, *The Rise of American Civilization* (New York, 1927), Vol. 2, pp. 52–121; Louis M. Hacker, *The Triumph of American Capitalism: The Development of Forces in American History to the End of the Nineteenth Century* (New York, 1940), chs. 24, 25, 26, and App. A. For seminal critiques of the Beard-Hacker interpretive line, see Thomas C. Cochran, "Did the Civil War Retard Industrialization?" *Mississippi Valley Historical Review* 48 (1961): 197–210; Stanley L. Engerman, "The Economic Impact of the Civil War," *Explorations in Economic History*, 3 (1966): 176–99.

hopes of creating a little interpretive space for themselves, as it were. But, by and large, the new views sprung from the fertile ground tilled in the first paragraph of this chapter – new approaches, new questions, paradigms lost and found – and it is to such ground that we shall now turn.

It is perhaps appropriate, first of all, to reiterate that, while a good deal of what we thought we knew about the Civil War and its aftermath has been called into question in recent decades, scholarly views regarding the broad contours of the economy of the antebellum South and of the region's economy between 1860 and 1900 haven't shifted all that much over the last twenty or twenty-five years. Our views on such contours had been fundamentally recast in the 1960s, 1970s, and 1980s by a talented cadre associated with the "new economic history," and this recasting, often corroborated and fleshed out by newer studies, has generally remained set. Thus, most scholars continue to view the antebellum South as a diverse area, but one dominated economically by plantation slavery. Contrary to the assertions of today's "new historians of capitalism," most scholars writing on the South have long embedded slavery in a market frame, viewed the plantation sector as capitalist in nature, and emphasized the production therein of a small number of export staples by enslaved laborers. Almost everyone agrees that the region was a dynamic, rapidly growing area, while scholars continue to be divided – as they have been for a half-century now – regarding the question of whether or not the South, which was wealthy by the standards of the day, was poised to make the transition to self-sustained development.

Similarly, almost everyone still agrees that the southern economy was transformed by the Civil War, that relative decline accompanied said transformation, and that the South c. 1900 was impoverished, marred by isolated labor markets and flawed institutions, sorely lacking in what we would now call technology networks and innovation communities, saddled with a retrograde agricultural sector, short on financial capital and deficient in human capital. Scholars now disagree more on the relationship between pattern and variation, on matters of timing, and on the weighting of the specific variables involved in the southern economy's relative decline. They do not, however, disagree on the question of the region's relative economic decline itself.

With these contextual considerations in mind, let us turn to our main quarry: the Civil War and its aftermath. As suggested at the outset, over the past generation scholars have emphasized just how difficult it is to capture or even at times to catch sight of said quarry. What is the proper unit of analysis to employ? Shall we stick to the South? If so, what South? The Confederate States of America (CSA)? Or shall we include the border slave states as well? What about the war and its aftermath in the North, and, as scholars such as Heather Richardson in particular have asked, what about the West?

Complicating matters further is the fact that even if we stick to the South, the region comprised populations whose experience (and perceptions) of the war and its aftermath were, shall we say, very different. To the roughly 40 percent of the southern population that was enslaved in 1860, the proposition that the South "lost" the Civil War would have seemed ludicrous, but the conventional narrative has until recently been framed in that way. To former slave-holders and, likely, to most of the region's white population, however, the "South" did lose the war, and their experiences and perspectives should not and cannot be minimized even as we broaden our operating frame and empathies as we should. And so far we have just begun peeling the onion, so to speak, because, as beavering scholars keep reminding us, the war and its aftermath also meant different things to men and women, young and old, rich and poor, rural dwellers and urbanites – distinctions which were often overlooked or glossed over by previous generations of scholars.

We have learned as well that both the periodization of the "war" and the concomitants and effects traditionally associated therewith may need revising. History is always related, some would say dialectically, to the present. The recent experience of the United States in Iraq has led some scholars – my long-time collaborator, David L. Carlton, among them – to suggest that the years after 1865 may be more accurately described not as the "post-war" period, but as the "insurgent" phase of the conflict that began officially in April 1861. One could argue that this phase lasted from 1865 to 1867, but one could also argue that it ran all the way through Reconstruction, and maybe even later. An intriguing reconceptualization to say the least. Some might push further, in fact, and argue that there was also an insurgent phase *before* Fort Sumter – a phase which began in October 1859 at Harpers Ferry, Virginia, but you get the point.

Another provocative line of inquiry opens up when we recognize the fact that at approximately the same time that the United States was going through the secession crisis and "the Civil War and its aftermath," the nation was also going through an economic/business transformation that was related in some ways to the political-military crisis, but nonetheless basically independent of it. This transformation – first identified by and still most closely associated with Alfred D. Chandler, Jr. – essentially entailed the gradual emergence between roughly the 1830s and 1900 of a national market and the rise over time, as a result of a series of organizational and institutional responses to the new market thereby created, of what we now refer to as "big business" in America. To be sure, there have been numerous challenges to the Chandlerian narrative in recent decades, but no one gainsays the fact that accelerated market expansion and market integration powerfully influenced the course of American economic and business history beginning in the 1830s and 1840s. Many of the economic and business developments in the South in the postbellum period – developments that historians have traditionally attributed to "the war" or to "its aftermath" – are more accurately seen as the result of largely autonomous forces associated with long-term market expansion and integration. Who knew? At least some economic and business historians, for starters.[2]

None of the comments above is intended to suggest that conventional questions relating to the Civil War and its aftermath have passed their "sell-by" dates, merely that it's not as easy to feel confident in our approaches or answers to them. Viewed in this way, Churchill's famous 1939 observation about the difficulty of forecasting Soviet Russia's behavior – behavior that he saw as "a riddle, wrapped in a mystery, inside an enigma" – seems relevant to our interpretive task here.

One of the principal takeaways from the discussion above is that the Civil War, emancipation, and the economic and political reconstruction/reconstitution of the South/nation are inexplicable without grounding these developments in the history of American capitalism. Without the expansion, diffusion, deeper penetration, and ever-increasing elaboration of capitalism in North America and other parts of the Atlantic World, tensions between the ideologies of free labor and slave labor in the Atlantic World would not have arisen. As historians of antislavery have long pointed out, the movement against, first, the slave trade, then slavery itself was at least in part a concomitant of the capitalist project. One doesn't find much antislavery sentiment, nor little in the way of humanitarian sensibility (to use Thomas Haskell's term) reproachful of slavery until capitalism had raised material living conditions sufficiently to create a sizable bourgeoisie in certain areas, for a significant part of which moral concerns began to trump economic issues. To invoke Haskell again, for significant segments of the bourgeoisie, technological and material improvements associated with capitalism had so shrunk "the realm of necessity" that questions related to "morality" – "ought" questions, as it were – emerged among some populations as priorities, antislavery among them.[3]

Thus, the origins of – ok, to be completely fair – *one* of the main wellsprings for both the onset and the ultimate success of the global movement against chattel slavery and other forms of coerced labor during the period between the late eighteenth and late nineteenth centuries.

[2] Alfred D. Chandler, Jr., *The Visible Hand: The Managerial Revolution in American Business* (Cambridge, MA, 1977).
[3] Thomas L. Haskell, "Capitalism and the Origins of the Humanitarian Sensibility," *American Historical Review*, 90 (1985): 339–61 and 547–66.

Indeed, the expansion and further elaboration of capitalism – and the brand of morality commonly associated therewith – has fostered or at least enabled continued efforts against unfree labor right down to the present day in parts of the world where forms of the institution or analogs thereof are still said to exist. Though such efforts have generally been lower in profile than they were during the nineteenth century, they sometimes have risen significantly in prominence, as is the case today due in large part to high-profile scholar/activists such as Kevin Bales and organizations such as Free the Slaves and Anti-Slavery International.

Most scholars begin their stories of the modern antislavery movement *qua* movement in the 1770s and end their accounts with the tapering off of the movement in the 1890s or early 1900s. Over the course of time, it had achieved monumental success against chattel slavery and had contributed substantial moral weight to forces ending other systems of unfree labor – serfdom in Central/Eastern Europe and Russia, *corvée* labor in many areas, and the *cultuurstelsel* on Java come immediately to mind in this regard – all over the world. Antislavery ideologies were instrumental as well in reforming post-emancipation labor systems involving South Asian workers – both indenture schemes and labor contracted under the *kangani* and *maistry* systems in Malaya and Burma respectively.

The antislavery movement, like most movements, was diverse, as were its strategies, tactics, and results. Speaking broadly, chattel slavery, as Eric Foner among others has pointed out, came to an end in one of three ways during the "long" century of fervid antislavery activity: through revolution, legislation, or war. To be sure, such categories can blur at times, making it difficult to make precise distinctions among these three means of emancipation, most notably, when attempting to categorize how emancipation came about in parts of Latin America during the era of the wars for independence. Nonetheless, it is possible to draw clearer distinctions about the manner in which emancipation occurred in most other areas. Generally speaking, where the abolition movement succeeded, emancipation came about through legislation, often gradually with compensation for owners, but never for those being freed. Abolition and emancipation occurred under other circumstances in Saint Domingue, via revolution, and in the American South, via war.

As for abolition/emancipation in the American South, though most writers over the years have argued that ending slavery was not a primary goal of the US government at the commencement of hostilities in April 1861, James Oakes has recently argued otherwise. In *Freedom National: The Destruction of Slavery in the United States, 1861–1865*, Oakes makes a compelling case that Lincoln began his presidency in 1861 committed to a strategy designed to end slavery in the United States – a strategy which was supported by his party and accurately perceived by secessionist leaders in the South. The strategy was quite comprehensive, with short-term and longer-term dimensions, and could in many ways be likened to an aggressive containment strategy, intended to create a "cordon of freedom" in the United States, by at once eliminating the possibility of any further expansion of slavery, chipping away at the institution whenever and wherever possible (as in the border states after secession), and by continuing the moral onslaught against slavery and its defenders.[4] Viewed in this way, secessionist leaders were not so much hysterical, much less eaters of fire, but prescient defenders of a species of property at significant risk.

Whether one accepts Oakes' argument or prefers to see Lincoln's movement to end slavery as ad hoc, coming about more gradually, and largely due to wartime exigencies, the facts on the ground were such that slavery began to dissolve and "Reconstruction" began in parts of the South, shortly after the onset of the war, first and most famously in the fall of 1861 after Union forces secured the heavily slave-populated plantation district encompassing Beaufort and the Sea Islands of South Carolina with their victory in early November at the Battle of Port Royal. Even earlier, slaves fleeing from their masters in other parts of the South were being treated as "contraband of war" and not returned, and slavery's hold slipped further – not just in the CSA but also in the Union – in the spring of 1862 with the fall of New Orleans and much of eastern Louisiana to Union forces and with the passage of legislation providing for the emancipation of slaves (with compensation for their owners) in Washington, DC. Throw in the so-called Confiscation Acts of 1861 and 1862, which loosened still further the hold of slavery in the South, and one begins to see just how far slavery had already been compromised before the issuance of the Preliminary Emancipation Proclamation in September 1862, much less the final version on January 1, 1863. Thence, slavery increasingly gave way, so much so that many historians have traditionally begun their "Reconstruction" narratives in 1863 rather than 1865, though, as we have seen, one can, if one so chooses, begin shortly after "the war came."

Before moving on to issues relating to emancipation per se, a few words are in order about the economic cost of the war itself, an important and provocative question that hasn't drawn too much attention in recent years. Unlike the broader question of the economic impact of the Civil War, careful assessments of its monetary cost have proven rare. In some ways, this is not surprising, for it is both a difficult technical exercise to attempt to calculate the myriad costs related to the war, but it seems a bit unseemly to many to calculate the monetary value among other "costs" of hundreds of thousands of human lives cut short. Thus, for the most part, we still rely

---

[4] James Oakes, *Freedom National: The Destruction of Slavery in the United States, 1861–1865* (New York, 2013).

today on the estimates produced by Claudia Goldin and Frank Lewis in the 1970s – first in 1975, with a revision in 1978.[5] This is not the venue to probe deeply into their assumptions and methods, but to present their findings and briefly to contextualize the magnitude of the same.

What Goldin and Lewis hoped to do in their project – and in fact did do –was to get beyond true, but vague statements that the Civil War cost "a lot" by adding some monetary meat to such skeletal claims. In so doing, they broke down the costs of the war into two subcategories: direct costs and indirect costs. The former referred mainly to the monetary costs of war-caused destruction to "physical and human capital," i.e. the monetary value of the property destroyed and human lives lost due to the war. They also attempted to calculate what they called the "indirect" costs of the war: the monetary value of the impact of the war and "related events" on northern and southern consumption up until 1880. To calculate the indirect costs, they constructed a hypothetical US consumption stream, based on trend rates, from 1860 to 1880, then measured the consumption streams actually achieved in the North and South during that period. The difference between the hypothetical and actual streams, they suggested, can be considered the indirect cost of the Civil War to the United States.

In their revised 1978 estimates, Goldin and Lewis put the direct costs to the South – which they define as the CSA, plus an adjustment for West Virginia – at about $3.29 billion (1860 dollars in 1861) and the indirect costs up to 1909 at about $9.48 billion (ditto). Although these estimates were controversial, everyone involved in the debate was basically talking about similar levels of magnitude – billions rather than millions. Whatever the actual cost – and the scholarly community owes Goldin and Lewis much for their bold attempt at measurement – the upshot is that the total cost of the war was staggering. Employing the appropriate *measuringworth. com* conversion tool ("economic power") on Goldin and Lewis's upper-level figure (for indirect costs), we find that the total cost of the war for the South is equal to about $37.6 trillion in 2014 dollars or a figure a little over twice the size of US annual GDP in 2014! And this cost estimate may be low. If demographic historian J. David Hacker's 2011 estimate of the number of deaths due to the war is correct – and most specialists currently believe that it is – the total number of deaths rises from 618,222, long the

[5] Claudia D. Goldin and Frank D. Lewis, "The Economic Cost of the American Civil War: Estimates and Implications," *Journal of Economic History*, 35 (1975): 299–326; Claudia D. Goldin and Frank D. Lewis, "The Post-Bellum Recovery of the South and the Cost of the Civil War: Comment," *Journal of Economic History*, 38 (1978): 487–92. Note, however, that Peter Temin has argued that Goldin and Lewis's cost estimates for the South are overstated. See Peter Temin, "The Post-Bellum Recovery of the South and the Cost of the Civil War," *Journal of Economic History*, 36 (1976): 898–907; Peter Temin, "Reply to Goldin and Lewis," *Journal of Economic History*, 38 (1978): 493.

estimate employed, to about 750,000, an increase of over 20 percent.[6] This means that Goldin and Lewis's estimate for the direct costs of the war, which includes the value of human lives truncated prematurely by war-related deaths, would have to be raised considerably.

Given the profound monetary – not to mention spiritual and psychological – cost of the war, it is interesting to speculate about whether the adversaries still would have gone to war had they had any sense in advance of the final numbers involved. Maybe, maybe not, but one thing is clear: Few Americans (particularly African Americans) today would argue that abolition, emancipation, and freedom were not worth the cost.

In a brilliant set of lectures published over thirty years ago under the title *Nothing But Freedom: Emancipation and Its Legacy*, Eric Foner captured in a most memorable way one principal result of slavery's war-induced demise. Contrary to the hopes of many, freedmen and women came out of slavery, as former Confederate general Robert V. Richardson accurately put it, with "nothing but freedom." Although they were for a variety of reasons soon to gain much – at least for a time – emancipation and freedom at the onset were narrowly and aridly defined in pinched, some would even say craven, formalistic terms.

Not that freedom so scantily clad should have been completely surprising. None of the areas that had emancipated enslaved populations in the Western Hemisphere prior to the Civil War had done particularly well by those emancipated, and, in defense of the Civil-War-era emancipation in the United States, at least we didn't begin by freeing only slaves aged 60 or over – that is, superannuated slaves who had to be maintained until death – as was the case in Cuba and parts of Brazil in the 1870s and 1880s. That said, there was no compensation, let alone reparations paid to freedmen and women during the Civil-War-era emancipation in the United States, little lasting land redistribution except in a few areas, most notably in the Beaufort–Saint Helena–Port Royal area of South Carolina, with wartime and early post-war land-redistribution schemes in most other parts of the South soon reversed.

In the Civil-War-era emancipation, the word "emancipation" was taken quite literally: to free from restraint, to free from bondage. Full stop. In making freedmen more or less *sui juris*, but by no means enabling them readily to acquire the types of capabilities required for full citizenship, the lines demarcating the meaning of freedom were clearly drawn. Indeed, both the Latin roots of the word "emancipate" (essentially, to take or transfer out of the hands of) and one of the less widely used modern definitions of the word – to release from paternal care

---

[6] J. David Hacker, "A Census-Based Count of the Civil War Dead," *Civil War History*, 57 (2011): 307–48.

and responsibility and render *sui juris* – are instructive in this regard. Nothing but freedom indeed.

If emancipation in the postbellum South resulted, as elsewhere, in two key struggles – one over the constitution and character of the civil/political rights of those who had been freed, and the other over the arrangement of a new system of labor relations wherein freedmen and women would make their ways – these struggles were not the only things going on during the decades after the war, nor for that matter the only developments that affected said struggles. We must, in other words, guard against the *post hoc ergo propter hoc* ("after this, therefore because of this") fallacy – assuming that mere succession in time implies a causal relationship – as we proceed. For starters, during the "postbellum era," partially, even largely autonomous developments such as the growth of a national market and the global integration of markets for agricultural commodities (including cotton, sugar, and rice) were proceeding apace, indeed, accelerating in the second half of the nineteenth century. The latter development was at once rendered possible and marked by declining transportation, information, and transaction costs resulting from improvements in the organization and productivity of the maritime sector, the rise of steam (and later steel-hull) shipping, the opening of the Suez Canal, the laying of transoceanic submarine telegraph cables, and the *Pax Britannica*, etc., as many economic historians have well chronicled, and by European imperial projects around the world, which most have not.

Regarding this last point: although the argument – famously associated with C. Vann Woodward – that the South became an economic colony of the North in the decades after the Civil War is certainly debatable, Eric Hobsbawm's characteristically provocative (if a bit overdrawn) observation certainly merits a brief look while we are discussing the Civil War and its aftermath. According to Hobsbawm, one of the most important results of the American Civil War, considered in world historical terms, was "the transfer of the South from the informal empire of England (to whose cotton industry it was the economic pendant) into the new major industrial economy of the United States" – the economy of which was dominated, of course, by the victorious North.[7]

And before we return to southern soil, let me point out that a number of recent writers on the war and its impact have emphasized some of the international dimensions, inflections, or concomitants of the same, particularly the increasingly powerful American nation state's attempts to project (imperial) power whether in the American West, in Alaska, or in the Caribbean. That said, while the words "world historical terms" are still

---

[7] C. Vann Woodward, *Origins of the New South 1877–1913* (Baton Rouge, LA, 1951), pp. 291–320; Eric J. Hobsbawm, *The Age of Capital: 1848–1875* (New York, 1975), p. 82.

fresh in our minds, it would be nice if US historians, even those with an internationalist bent, spoke with a little more humility (and worldliness) when discussing the war. For example, for all the talk of the carnage of the American Civil War – and there was indeed plenty of carnage – it is worth noting that during another mid-nineteenth-century conflagration, the Taiping Rebellion in China (1850–1864), at least 20 million lives were lost, and perhaps as many as 30 million.[8] China had a population of roughly 400 million in the middle of the nineteenth century, and the United States, around 31 million in 1860. A little quick math demonstrates that in percentage terms the death figures in China, even using the lowest estimates, were over twice as great as the totals in the United States. And the Chinese death estimates do not include lives lost in several other Chinese rebellions shortly thereafter. In other words, at least for some purposes, a bit of perspective helps.

So that this does not turn into a gruesome exercise in comparative morbidity and mortality, let us return to the twin struggles that dominated the South after the war, starting with that over the constitution and character of the civil/political rights of the emancipated slaves. On the surface, important aspects of this story still sound much as they did a generation ago: distinct patterns associated with different periods; bold, unprecedented initiatives that for a time translated into full citizenship (including voting and office-holding rights) for freedmen, laying the foundations for a true bi-racial political democracy; the overturning of said initiatives and reversal of democratizing efforts by reactionary elements, often through violence, despite (or because of) impressive policy achievements, wherein freedmen and women often played central roles.

That said, the older story has changed in significant ways. The periodization has shifted a bit, as scholars have increasingly focused more attention on the story's margins or incorporated the conventional "Reconstruction" framework into larger, more expansive and elastic narratives. For example, initiatives undertaken during the war, however piecemeal and ad hoc, have risen in relative importance, and in temporal terms the span of the story has continued to stretch. "Reconstruction" per se, traditionally bracketed by the years 1865 and 1877, and later broadened so as to incorporate events from 1862 or 1863 until 1877, now often extends from 1861 to 1880 or even 1890. Moreover, scholars are increasingly

<hr />

[8] On the Taiping Rebellion, see, e.g., Stephen R. Platt, *Autumn in the Heavenly Kingdom: China, the West, and the Epic Story of the Taiping Civil War* (New York, 2012). Note that Pratt puts the death total at "at least twenty million." Some writers employ a much higher figure. John King Fairbank and Merle Goldman, for example, suggest that the total death count for the Taiping Rebellion and assorted smaller revolts in China during the 1860s and early 1870s may have been as high as 60 million. See John King Fairbank and Merle Goldman, *China: A New History*, enlarged edn. (Cambridge, MA, 1998), pp. 214–16.

THE AMERICAN CIVIL WAR AND ITS AFTERMATH 525

re-conceptualizing things so as to view the entire era from the Civil War until the 1920s or even into the 1930s as constituting one integrated, if sequenced, political/economic period in the South. Similarly, some influential scholars – Steven Hahn comes to mind – have insisted that important post-war questions (those relating to African American politics and political behavior in the South, for example) can best and perhaps only be understood by rooting the story in slavery times.[9]

If the periodization of the political story has changed, so have the relative roles of certain events and actors. To be sure, none of this is to suggest that anyone has proposed the jettisoning of major themes and punctuation points such as the Confiscation Acts, the Port Royal Experiment, the Emancipation Proclamation, the Presidential Reconstruction, the Radical Reconstruction, the Reconstruction amendments, and the so-called retreat from Reconstruction. Indeed, though downplayed in significance in recent decades, even the Compromise of 1877 has survived. What has often changed is the level on which such themes are studied, and the relevant subjects of study.

Over the past twenty years, we've seen much more work on the ways in which the themes mentioned above played out on the local and, in some cases, even the micro level, and women, formerly bit players in the political story, now play much more prominent roles. That women now do so is due in part, of course, to the general rise of gender as a unit of historical analysis, but also to the widespread adoption of much more capacious approaches to politics and the political than was the case in previous generations. Whereas the political realm once typically extended from treatise to tract and from the stump to the polling place – with some "daring" scholars extending the realm so as to include in some cases the street and the sword as well – women's historians and historians of gender have pushed ever further. Recent work in this vein has fruitfully expanded the political realm so as to incorporate as well activities in civic clubs and organizations, family power dynamics, questions relating to management of the household economy, and – with evocations, however faint, of *Lysistrata* – of authority wielded from the bedroom (albeit *sans* sex strikes apparently).

As with gender, so, too, with class and race. Such considerations, often dovetailing with gender concerns, have come increasingly to the fore in discussions of Reconstruction politics, and scholars have been much more careful about making broad claims about who did what to whom and why. Qualifiers are now much more common in political scholarship on the postbellum period: Middle-class white women often *believed* X, African

---

[9] Steven Hahn, *A Nation under Our Feet: Black Political Struggles in the Rural South from Slavery to the Great Migration* (Cambridge, MA, 2003).

American women in sharecropping families *tended to do* Y, and white yeoman farmers in non-plantation districts largely *voted* for Z. The particulars of the above examples bring us, more or less logically, to perhaps the biggest change of all in recent years in the political story of Reconstruction, to wit: the dramatic reframing of matters regarding historical agency.

Agency – the concept that launched a thousand careers – is simple to define, difficult to measure, and, alas, in recent decades nearly impossible to escape. In broad terms, agency, used in a historical sense, refers to the ability of an individual or group not only to act in his, her, or its own behalf, but also to affect, impact, shape – or, in the hands of its most zealous proponents, largely to determine – the developmental path of said individuals or groups. The use of the concept in historical work has been building for several generations, and has generally been employed by scholars with regard to groups – women, workers, African Americans, etc. – previously overlooked, glossed over, or rendered voiceless or powerless in standard treatments. I use the term "generally" advisedly because some scholars have gone so far as to bestow agency upon animals, plants, the sea, weather phenomena, etc., as well, but here we shall limit our comments to questions regarding the agency of *homo sapiens*. Up to a point, scholars employing the concept in this more limited way have performed an important service in so doing: clearly, every individual and every group is capable of acting to some extent in ways that express their preferences, and serve their interests and values. Point taken. But in many, if not most, cases, agency proponents considerably underestimate the obstacles and constraints impeding human volition. More problematic still is the fact that they feel it incumbent upon themselves to overcorrect and overcompensate, and, in so doing, to romanticize, sentimentalize, uncritically celebrate, and in extreme cases, to apotheosize seemingly pluperfect subalterns and members of subaltern groups.

African American history has been one area marked, some would say plagued, by hagiographic works. Such works overstate the power of enslaved African Americans vis-à-vis their supposedly hoodwinked or cowed masters under slavery, or tendentiously contend that during the Civil War the enslaved, *pace* Mr. Lincoln and the Union army, virtually freed themselves, or monochromatically depict freedmen and women during the radical phase of Reconstruction as "heroes of their own lives," responsible for much of the social progress that occurred in the benighted South during that phase, but largely absolved of responsibility for any of the defeats or disappointments.

There are obviously elements of truth in all of these claims and they are often cleverly cast, but on close inspection there is a certain illogic to them all. If African American slaves had so much bargaining power and if masters were so weak, why was there so little overt slave resistance, let alone violent resistance, in the antebellum South? If slaves virtually freed themselves during the war, why was the timing and geography of emancipation so closely correlated to governmental actions by the Union and troop movements of Union forces? If the newly emancipated had so much agency during the radical phase of Reconstruction, why did that phase end so quickly, to be followed by what many still consider the "nadir" of race relations in US history? What conditions, institutions, and actors facilitated African American agency and, as important, rubbed much of it out?

The most likely answers to such questions, taken together, suggest that maybe African Americans didn't have so much agency after all, or that in a relative sense they possessed fewer degrees of freedom than other individuals and groups. Not, I might add, because such individuals or groups were nobler or more heroic (quite the contrary in many cases), but because the way in which history had unfolded had led to power asymmetries that often overwhelmed – outgunned, might be the more appropriate verb here – whatever agency African Americans, slave or free, may have possessed. In the context of Reconstruction, writers such as Richard Zuczek, Nicholas Lemann, and Stephen Budiansky, and, most recently, J. Michael Rhyne, James Illingworth, and Douglas R. Egerton, have demonstrated the powerful role that violence played in shaping Reconstruction outcomes, with white conservatives by and large maintaining (or recovering), if not a monopoly on violence, then nothing less than oligopolistic control. Given this fact, it is not surprising that the role of African American volition in determining the southern political order was circumscribed and that, with regard to the resistance/accommodation dialectic, accommodation may have been the most that African Americans could hope for more often than not.

For the sake of argument, let us assume that I am wrong in this regard, and that African Americans did have more agency during Reconstruction than I have suggested. If so, it's certainly high time for historians to elaborate much more fully than they have done to date on the failings of African American politicians during the period, on the corruption in which they partook, and on the flawed political strategies and tactics among newly empowered freedmen and women that must then have contributed mightily to Radical Reconstruction's wane and ultimate defeat. Michael Fitzgerald made many of these points in an important essay published in 2006 and, unfortunately, we are still waiting for answers. This is not to suggest that I agree with Adam Fairclough, who in a provocative 2012 piece suggested that in retrospect the push for black civil/political rights, including voting rights, during Reconstruction may have been a tactical error – I have too much veneration for the Fourteenth and Fifteenth amendments to follow Fairclough there – but to suggest that history is too complicated and important to exclude the actions and behaviors of even those with whom we naturally empathize from the closest empirical scrutiny. All too often, however, agency has meant a free historical pass.[10]

Clearly, then, important questions regarding civil/political issues in the aftermath of the war remain open – or merit reopening. The same can be said regarding the transformation of labor relations. In this realm, economists and historians over the past twenty-five years or so have produced some very good work, which has succeeded admirably in complicating earlier stories. As of yet, however, no one has brought together all of the new studies into a compelling synthesis that has captured the imagination of the current generation as did works by Roger Ransom and Richard Sutch and by Gavin Wright in the 1970s and 1980s.

That no such synthesis has been written is due to several factors. Much of the new work that has appeared has been of the dismantling variety, taking down earlier interpretive structures piecemeal, brick by brick, rather than in a manner akin to demolition via wholesale implosion by the Cleveland Wrecking Company. Thus, however compromised, large parts of the older structures remain more or less intact. It is also true that, in a relative sense at least, fewer scholars seem to be working on questions relating to the economic history of the postbellum South, particularly on questions relating to class formation, agricultural social structure, income/ wealth, economic efficiency, and inequality. Why? First, because empirical work on such questions often requires a large amount of data, much of it quantitative in nature. Second, because in the field of history, at least, the "cultural turn" that lasted between about 1980 and the early years of the twenty-first century seemed to many to render quantitative research, if not studying the material world, at once *passé* and *déclassé*.

All of this said, what *have* we learned? One thing for sure – not to generalize so cavalierly (or in Yankee fashion for that matter!) – about any question relating to the economic aftermath of slavery in the South. Whatever we're speaking about, scholars have been quick to point out that answers vary according to variables relating to geography, demography, timing, gender, crop cultivated, local political structures, etc. Whereas we once talked of the emergence over time of relatively standard

[10] Michael W. Fitzgerald, "Reconstruction Politics and the Politics of Reconstruction," in Thomas J. Brown (ed.), *Reconstructions: New Perspectives on the Postbellum United States* (New York, 2006), pp. 91–116; Adam Fairclough, "Was the Grant of Black Suffrage a Political Error? Reconsidering the Views of John W. Burgess, William A. Dunning, and Eric Foner on Congressional Reconstruction," *Journal of the Historical Society*, 12 (2012): 155–88. See also *Journal of the Historical Society*, 12 (2012) for responses to Fairclough's controversial essay by J. Mills Thornton, Michael W. Fitzgerald, and Michael A. Ross and Leslie S. Rowland, as well as a rejoinder by Fairclough.

labor contracts, of an "agricultural ladder" more or less characteristic of the postbellum South, of the relative status in the rural social structure of wage workers/croppers/tenants and landowners, of *the* economic strategy of freedmen and, indeed, of the white yeomanry, we don't do *any* of these things any more. Historical sociologist Martin Ruef has recently emphasized the role that uncertainty played in the postbellum South; that same condition can be said to characterize the general state of scholarly work on the postbellum South today.

For example, many scholars now stress the fact that the South was characterized by a bewildering variety of labor contracts and formats, and that even as of 1880 – the date Gavin Wright gave for the ending of the post-war disequilibrium and the emergence of a new equilibrium – the region's labor system was, or, more accurately, labor systems were, still in flux. Many now argue, moreover, that the region *qua* region was characterized by no one agricultural ladder, and contend either that the ladder metaphor is inappropriate or that ladders differed by region/crop/time period.

Scholars have also recently pointed out that the rural social structure did not ipso facto run from poor wage worker on one end of the scale to relatively wealthier tenants and landowners on the other (though this was often the case), and that wage work was sometimes preferred and more remunerative than other types of labor arrangements. While on this subject it should also be noted that Harold Woodman and others have made the important point that earlier writers often misinterpreted and as a result misrepresented said social structure because they failed fully to distinguish the legal differences between sharecropping and tenancy.[11]

Other scholars, furthermore, have made the equally important point that we considerably reduce and simplify the economy of the postbellum South – just as the census takers did in the late nineteenth century – by considering people solely as agriculturalists when they often were employed intermittently, seasonally, or regularly, in various other non-agricultural activities, whence they made large proportions of their annual incomes.

With this in mind, it is not surprising that the manner in which we think about income-generation strategies has become more complex regarding both African American and white households. The operative word here is *complex*, for in some ways rural labor markets in the South in the late nineteenth century – always forming and reforming, constantly evolving, with twist after twist, novelty after novelty – seem to be captured better by *complexity economics* than by conventional approaches. Rather

[11] See Harold D. Woodman, *New South – New Law: The Legal Foundations of Credit and Labor Relations in the Postbellum Agricultural South* (Baton Rouge, LA, 1995).

than a new equilibrium emerging in 1870 or 1880 or even later, that is to say, what we may have is a state of perpetual disequilibrium.

Let us consider the range of possibilities regarding labor relations, for example. Broadly speaking, two basic points from the earlier literature remain in place, particularly when we are speaking about the immediate aftermath of the war, to wit: (1) planters typically supported and tried to impose tightly controlled labor schemes that resembled slavery as much as possible – so-called squad and gang systems, for example; and (2) African Americans, for their part, generally preferred and bargained hard for labor arrangements that offered as much independence, autonomy, and freedom from close supervision and monitoring as possible. Similarly, most recent writers continue to believe that the systems (not system) of labor relations that emerged resulted from various, local, on-the-ground negotiated compromises, whether formal or informal, between planters and workers, but often facilitated, even mandated, by various other parties (the Freedmen's Bureau, other governmental officials, organizations we would now refer to as NGOs such as the Union Leagues, creditors, etc.), which compromises reflected broader (and continually evolving) economic and social conditions in the region. One such condition in the immediate post-war years – and for considerably longer in most parts of the South – was, of course, the profound shortage of credit and capital more generally, which many still believe helps to explain various types of non-monetary contractual arrangements entered into by planters and workers, sharecropping and share-tenancy, most notably.

That is pretty much where the current consensus regarding labor relations ends. And even the above generalizations are tenuous. For example, while it is clear that there was a shortage of credit and capital in at least parts of the postbellum South at least some of the time, there were a large number – and perhaps sizable proportion – of African American agricultural laborers in the region working for cash wages in the decades after the war. A host of scholars has demonstrated that this was the case in parts of the South where the "cash" crop was rice or sugar, and Laura Edwards has also shown this to be true in some tobacco-growing areas. Perhaps even more surprising, wage work was also quite important in at least some cotton-growing areas, as Robert Tracy McKenzie has shown in his empirically rich (and grossly under-appreciated) 1994 study of agriculture in Civil-War-era Tennessee.[12]

Complicating matters further is the fact that our understanding of sharecropping and tenancy, once considered the pillars on which most interpretations of the agricultural economy of the postbellum South rested,

[12] Robert Tracy McKenzie, *One South or Many? Plantation Belt and Upcountry in Civil War-Era Tennessee* (Cambridge, 1994).

seems increasingly questionable. We now realize or at least acknowledge that in most cases we know little about power dynamics on the ground or discrete bargaining relationships, much less about the supply mix provided to tenants and croppers by landowners and/or merchants ("the furnish"). Moreover, as alluded to just above, Harold Woodman, after a careful analysis of Southern legislation and legal records regarding sharecropping, demonstrated twenty years ago now that croppers were generally treated by the law as *wage* workers, not tenants as many scholars had previously assumed, which meant that whatever portion of the crop went to the cropper (not always half, by the way, as is also sometimes assumed) was treated legally as a *wage* earned by an agricultural *employee.* Though many scholars have subsequently followed Woodman's lead, the importance of the distinction has not fully penetrated into general discussions of the postbellum economy, which is unfortunate, particularly in light of the fact that, in addition to croppers, so many other agriculturalists in the period seem to have been working for wages.

Other aspects of sharecropping – and the agricultural ladder more generally – have increasingly been questioned, as scholars have delved deeper into the black box that is the postbellum southern economy. The fact that the government made no formal distinction between croppers and share tenants until the 1920 census had often led to interpretive confusion, and as scholars in recent decades have at once recognized this problem and attempted to adjust for it, some of our earlier beliefs about the rural social structure of the South have been found wanting. No complete, much less completely satisfying, new interpretation has yet emerged, but, drawing from a number of studies, it now seems likely that there were more African American wage workers *and* landowners than we previously believed, fewer sharecroppers, and more variation in the types of tenancy arrangements possible.

New research has further destabilized our understanding of what we thought we knew about the inner workings of the southern economy after the war. A case in point: Scholars have increasingly come to realize that rural Southerners often made ends meet via a variety of economic activities, and that we reduce the complexity of both the rural southern economy and the income-generating strategies of rural households by attempting to treat all individuals who farmed simply as "farmers." Many so-called farmers, blacks and whites alike, are better seen as members of flexible, if often precarious, rural workforces, people who moved opportunistically in and out of a range of formal and informal economic activities.

In addition to farming, such workers, regardless of the particular "rung" on the ladder occupied, might spend part of the year in lumbering, in laying railroad tracks, in working in turpentine orchards, or mining phosphates on rivers or land. They likely spent time hunting and fishing, and if they had a mule and wagon, probably made a little money hauling goods. They might also have worked now and then at a local cotton gin or, a bit later, crushing cotton seed for oil. And, if the economic geography was right, either they themselves or other members of their households might have spent some time in town or at a rural crossroads hawking meat, fish, vegetables, and eggs. In pursuing such activities, they likely spent at least part of the year off-site, away from their farm houses/shacks, whether living rough, in cheap accommodations, or in barracks such as those set up for workers (wage workers, I might add) in the phosphate industry. Does the metaphor of an agricultural ladder do justice to income-generation strategies so complicated as this? I think not, and others join me in so thinking.

And things get considerably more complicated still when one disaggregates by gender, type of rural setting (plantation belt or non-plantation belt), crop cultures, and time period, and remembers that African Americans also flocked to Southern cities and towns after the war. One example here must suffice relating to freedwomen after emancipation. Though most scholars still accept Ransom and Sutch's very important point about the withdrawal of a considerable number of African American female laborers from field work after the war – which contributed significantly to the relative decline in overall African American labor inputs in field labor in the postbellum period and, alas, perhaps to increased indebtedness in African American farm households – a generation of scholars since 1990 has fleshed out the story of African American female labor after the war. In so doing, it has detailed the many formal and informal economic activities in which females participated, activities ranging from part-time field work to butter/egg production for local markets to domestic service to childrearing/household economic management, with most freedwomen incorporating some or even all of these remunerative and non-remunerative activities into their work routines.

The "remix" above captures at least in part the complexity of the rural labor system and rural labor relations in the South in the aftermath of the Civil War. Think about it for a moment: Wage work in staple crops by the task, day, week, or month. The so-called two-day or three-day system was used in coastal South Carolina and Georgia, whereby freedmen and women often worked two or three days a week in rice or (Sea-Island) cotton for a planter in exchange for a plot of land and housing. A variety of sharecropping arrangements (generally involving different terms and percentage shares for the cropper and landlord) and tenancy forms (share tenancy and cash tenancy, most notably) emerged. Landowning freedmen and women farmed their own land, while often also working some for white planters or business operators (in the phosphate and fertilizer industries, for example). Individuals in all of the above "boxes" also pursued a panoply of other economic activities.

Earlier in this chapter I alluded several times to matters of geography, and spatial concerns have risen in prominence over the past generation.

Given the thrust of the argument presented thus far, such concerns pose further challenges to earlier views. Scholars in recent decades have taken pains to distinguish between political and economic developments occurring in the South's plantation belt and in non-plantation parts of the region. In the latter, areas wherein there were many white small farmers and small farms, overall agricultural patterns were often very different than in heavily African American areas in the plantation belt.

In non-plantation-belt areas, it is clear that the worlds of white small farmers and African American small farmers *both* changed significantly over the course of the Civil War era. Many of the changes affecting the world of white small farmers – the expansion and elaboration of American capitalism, international demand patterns (particularly demand for cotton), new land-tenure patterns, credit and capital shortages, the imperatives driving greater specialization in cotton, etc. – also affected African American farmers, albeit to different degrees and sometimes in different ways. There is still considerable difference of opinion over the relative weight of race vis-à-vis economic variables in determining differential patterns and outcomes for white and black farmers in such areas. Clearly, much remains unclear – more local studies need to be done – but scholars today are increasingly aware of the issues at hand.

Scholars studying the plantation belt have also devoted more attention to spatial concerns. Such attention has already paid rich dividends and has the potential to pay even more. For example, we now have many more empirical studies on areas in the plantation belt that specialized in crops other than cotton, i.e. in rice, tobacco, and sugar, which have allowed us to offer more nuanced assessments of developments in the "plantation sector" in the aftermath of slavery. And, speaking spatially, there is more low-hanging fruit to be picked. Studies on the ways in which enslaved African Americans in the antebellum period conceptualized space, neighborhoods, and community have important implications for the postbellum period, especially as economic space was reconfigured as a result of the break-up of centralized plantations in many parts of the South and the creation of decentralized "neo-plantations," which led to more dispersed settlement schemes. Stay tuned.

While on matters spatial, it is also important to note that the factors famously referred to by George W. Pierson many years ago as the three Ms – mobility, migration, and movement – affected African Americans as well as other Americans after the war.[13] Until relatively recently, most scholars had emphasized the limited impact the three Ms had on freedmen and women, stressing instead the constraints imposed by institutions such as sharecropping, debt peonage, and convict leasing. Though no one denies that such constraints

[13] George W. Pierson, "The M-Factor in American History," *American Quarterly*, 14 (1962): 275–89.

were real, a number of writers in recent years have suggested that the mobility of many, if not most, freedmen and women in the postbellum period was greater than previously believed. Certainly, fewer writers today would argue that the complex and variegated socioeconomic arrangements in the South after the war were closely akin to "a new system of slavery," the description used by Hugh Tinker in referring to exploited Indian labor, mainly indentures, in various European plantation colonies after slave emancipation.[14]

Similarly, most scholars today believe that mobility was one factor that limited the likelihood that "territorial monopolies" – to employ Ransom and Sutch's famous concept – overseen by rural merchants wreaked economic havoc on either African Americans or, more broadly, the postbellum South. Anyone who has tried linking African Americans in census population schedules in the post-war period or, for that matter, anyone with the slightest familiarity with the world of Nate Shaw/Ned Cobb would testify that there was a whole lot of movement going on. That said, most such movement was local, and almost all of it was regional. As Gavin Wright suggested almost thirty years ago, there were some rational economic reasons for the limited movement of African Americans out of the South during the postbellum period (see below). Such reasons, ironically, help to explain the low wage levels in the region and perhaps even what Wright sees as the "dual labor market" that powerfully shaped the developmental trajectory of the South (and the United States) for decades after the war.

Stepping back a bit, what you seem to find in essence is a situation in the South wherein over time, after a period of jarring disequilibrium with emancipation, a somewhat more stable regime of labor relations emerged. Conditions in this regime may or may not have been such as to merit designation as a new equilibrium, but they were certainly more patterned than they had been. The new regime was marked by the numerical dominance of poor agricultural workers, both African American and white, working on a mix of small and large units (mostly the former) under a variety of contractual and tenure schemes. The units worked were undercapitalized, technologically backward, and inefficient. The regime was also marked by power asymmetries of various kinds. Most agricultural workers (even landowners) were subject to considerable economic and extra-economic pressure from creditors and merchants, which narrowed their degrees of freedom, compromised their independence, and often led them via perverse incentives into decisions regarding crop mix (or often the lack thereof), treatment of resources, and time horizons that were inimical to their interests.

In the case of workers, said power asymmetries were not absolute. Dissatisfied workers could try to bargain for better contractual terms, or

[14] Hugh Tinker, *A New System of Slavery: The Export of Indian Labour Overseas 1830–1920* (London, 1974).

at the margin change the job mix in the "portfolios" of economic activities in which they were normally engaged. They could also vote with their feet and try to create better situations for themselves by working for other landlords, or moving away. "Away" seldom meant very far, however, for powerful economic forces – most notably, one's reputation, which was often a worker's principal form of collateral when seeking credit – as well as non-economic factors (kith, kin, affective ties, etc.) acted to keep the vast majority of rural workers in the general vicinity and almost always in the South. What you get, then, is a labor-relations regime far better than slavery. Nothing but freedom is an apt phrase, but freedom wasn't nothing after all. That said, the new regime, however different, was still marked by tight controls on poor workers bereft of a sufficient stock of weapons (including so-called weapons of the weak) to change the game in the South. Indeed, that game wouldn't be changed until the 1930s, when the labor relations regime and the rest of the retrograde agricultural system established in the South after the Civil War finally collapsed in the wake of the Great Depression. But we are getting ahead of ourselves, for there were other late nineteenth-century power asymmetries that also bear note.

First of all, landlords and merchants in the postbellum South were hardly autonomous economic actors, but cogs in much larger wheels and circuits involving credit and commodity chains in both an emerging national market and an increasingly global market for agricultural commodities. However powerful they may have looked to agricultural wage workers and croppers, they themselves were often bit players on the larger stage. Not for nothing were levels of per capita income in the South but half the national average in 1900 and, after rising slightly in the early twentieth century, back at that same level in 1930.

Whether or not we would rather refer to the Southern economy as "colonial" in the decades after the Civil War, its developmental progress definitely was shaped – and in some important ways impeded – by its double-edged propinquity to the victorious North, which was urbanizing, industrializing, and modernizing rapidly, and, as important, had at once captured and for a long time succeeded in retaining control of the levers of political economic power in an increasingly powerful national state.[15] At the same time, the South was increasingly enmeshed in what had become truly global markets for the principal agricultural commodities it produced. Agricultural globalization affected southern agriculture profoundly – remember that in the late nineteenth century most of the southern labor

[15] Woodward, *Origins of the New South*, pp. 291–320; David L. Carlton, "The Revolution from Above: The National Market and the Beginnings of Industrialization in North Carolina," *Journal of American History*, 77 (1990): 445–75; David L. Carlton and Peter A. Coclanis, "The Uninventive South? A Quantitative Look at Region and American Inventiveness," *Technology and Culture*, 36 (1995): 220–44.

force was comprised of farmers of one type or another – albeit in cross-cutting ways, differing crop by crop. The region was the world's largest and most competitive exporter of cotton and was able to retain its supremacy in this crop – by far the leading export of the United States – even as the growth rate of demand for cotton fell and relative prices fell. Southern tobacco was competitive in several segments of the global tobacco market and, with the growth of the domestic market increasing rapidly in the late nineteenth century as a result of the rise of a new product category – cigarettes – tobacco farming in the South demonstrated some vitality.

The situation was decidedly different for sugar and rice, the region's two other principal market crops. The Southern sugar industry, centered at the time in southeast Louisiana near the climatic limits for cane-sugar production, was long a marginal participant in the international sugar market, and, after the Civil War, the industry survived via tariff protection and by gradually modernizing and becoming more capital-intensive. Things were even more dire for the region's rice industry. This industry, which was centered in the South Atlantic region, was already in relative decline well before the Civil War as low-cost Asian sources of supply were increasingly incorporated into and soon out-competing US rice in the principal Western markets in Northern Europe. Ever-increasing competitive pressure from Asia, coupled with problems invigorating production in the South Atlantic region in cost-effective ways after the war, resulted over time in the complete collapse of labor-intensive paddy-rice production in South Carolina and Georgia, and the gradual emergence after the mid-1880s of a new capital-intensive rice industry in the "Old Southwest" – first, in southwest Louisiana, and a little later in southeast Texas and east central Arkansas – the principals in which were largely white farmers who had migrated from the Midwest, and, to a lesser extent, from England and Germany.

Though the "rice revolution" in the Old Southwest – and later in the Sacramento Valley of California – "saved" the US rice industry and though US rice from these areas eventually became quite competitive on international markets, between 1860 and the First World War – the period, that is to say, wherein labor-intensive production of paddy rice by African American workers in the South Atlantic states died – the United States, despite high postbellum tariffs imposed on imported rice, became a major net importer of the commodity.[16] So, one can see, then, that despite the fact that planters and merchants in the South may have seemed to have

[16] Peter A. Coclanis, "Distant Thunder: The Creation of a World Market in Rice and the Transformations It Wrought," *American Historical Review*, 98 (1993): 1050–78; Peter A. Coclanis, "White Rice: The Midwestern Origins of the Modern Rice Industry in the United States," in Francesca Bray, Peter A. Coclanis, Edda L. Fields-Black, and Dagmar Schäfer (eds.), *Rice: Global Networks and New Histories* (Cambridge, 2015), pp. 291–317.

possessed commanding power and authority when viewed by a wage worker mired in mud or a cropper holding a hoe, the agricultural sector of the South in the late nineteenth century was largely dysfunctional and eventually had to – and did – go. The fact that it finally did go – in the 1930s – was due to many factors, perhaps the two most important of which – the withering away of the nation's dual-labor market and the onset of the Great Depression – didn't begin until well after our story's formal close.

I now add a few words as a kind of denouement on the post-war trajectory of the Southern economy and on the impact of the Civil War on the US economy, of which the South was (once again) part. Regarding trajectory: Scholars are somewhat divided on the course of the southern economy after the war, not on its relative decline from its performance in the late antebellum period, but on the timing and reasons for its lapse into stagnation. While some see the entire postbellum period as a downward spiral or even free fall for the economy of the South, others see a certain fluidity, even dynamism in the region in the 1870s and particularly in the 1880s, before such conditions were closed off in the 1890s.

The latter question – on the broader economic impact of the Civil War – has engendered a large, interesting literature with distinguished scholars taking very different, sometimes diametrically opposed, interpretative positions. This is not the time or place to plumb this literature's depths. Let it suffice to say that some scholars have argued that the war had very positive short-term and/or long-term impacts on the US economy, while others have argued precisely the opposite, i.e. that the war on balance had a negative impact on the performance of the US economy.[17]

The varied positions adopted rest largely upon the variables considered, the way in which such variables are measured, and the time frames adopted for said measurements. Compelling arguments have been made for both the positive and negative cases by historians and economists alike. If I had to choose sides, I would probably split the difference and say that, though in the short-to-intermediate runs, the economic effects of the war were likely negative, the long-term effects of the Union's victory were positive. The North's victory helped foster and facilitate a stronger, more activist centralized state led by capitalist groups favorable to manufacturing interests. Said victory hardly ended the political and economic power of southern conservatives, the outcome for which many Republicans for a time at least had worked assiduously. But, by limiting the influence of southern conservatives in national politics, the war clearly inhibited the

---

[17] See the works cited in n. 1, for example. For further insight into the debate, see Roger Ransom, "Economics of the Civil War," in Robert Whaples (ed.), *EH.Net Encyclopedia*, August 24, 2001, http://eh.net/encyclopedia/the-economics-of-the-civil-war/.

degree to which they could obstruct the agenda regarding capitalist modernization, without which America's economic will to power and, withal, its rise to great-power status would have been delayed or even waylaid.[18]

And most important of all, said victory put paid to the enormity that was slavery. In the aftermath of the Civil War, "[h]ow selfish soever man may be supposed" – Adam Smith's words in *The Theory of Moral Sentiments* – such selfishness in the United States would never again be expressed via the legal right to hold human beings as chattels. In the face of the questions raised in this chapter and the uncertainty evoked, let me leave readers with one enduring proposition, the truth of which marches on even in today's troubled times.

A GUIDE TO FURTHER READING

Agricultural History. Special Issue: "African Americans in Southern Agriculture, 1877–1945," 72 (1998).

Baker, Bruce E. and Brian Kelly (eds.), *After Slavery: Race, Labor, and Citizenship in the Reconstruction South* (Gainesville, FL, 2013).

Brown, Thomas J. (ed.), *Reconstructions: New Perspectives on the Postbellum United States* (New York, 2006).

Coclanis, Peter A., "Slavery, African-American Agency, and the World We Have Lost," *Georgia Historical Quarterly*, 79 (1995): 873–84.

Coclanis, Peter A., "In Retrospect: Ransom and Sutch's *One Kind of Freedom*," *Reviews in American History* 28 (2000): 478–89.

Davis, David Brion, *The Problem of Slavery in the Age of Emancipation* (New York, 2014).

Edwards, Laura F., *Gendered Strife and Confusion: The Political Culture of Reconstruction* (Urbana, IL, 1997).

Egerton, Douglas, *The Wars of Reconstruction: The Brief, Violent History of America's Most Progressive Era* (New York, 2014).

Explorations in Economic History. Special Issue: "*One Kind of Freedom* Revisited," 38 (2001).

Foner, Eric, *Nothing but Freedom: Emancipation and Its Legacy* (Baton Rouge, LA, 1983).

Foner, Eric, *Reconstruction: America's Unfinished Revolution, 1863–1877* (New York, 1988).

Glymph, Thavolia, *Out of the House of Bondage: The Transformation of the Plantation Household* (New York, 2008).

Hahn, Steven, *A Nation under Our Feet: Black Political Struggles in the Rural South from Slavery to the Great Migration* (Cambridge, 2003).

[18] See, e.g., Richard Bensel, *The Political Economy of American Industrialization, 1877–1900* (Cambridge, 2000).

Kyriakoudes, Louis, "Lower-Order Urbanization and Territorial Monopoly in the Southern Furnishing Trade: Alabama, 1871–1890," *Social Science History*, 26 (2002): 179–98.

McKenzie, Robert Tracy, *One South or Many? Plantation Belt and Upcountry in Civil War-Era Tennessee* (New York, 1994).

Ransom, Roger L. and Richard Sutch, *One Kind of Freedom: The Economic Consequences of Emancipation*, 2nd edn. (New York, 2001; 1st edn., 1977).

Rodrigue, John C., *Reconstruction in the Cane Fields: From Slavery to Free Labor in Louisiana's Sugar Parishes, 1862–1880* (Baton Rouge, LA, 2001).

Ruef, Martin, *Between Slavery and Capitalism: The Legacy of Emancipation in the American South* (Princeton, NJ, 2014).

Woodman, Harold D., *King Cotton and His Retainers: Financing and Marketing the Cotton Crop of the South, 1800–1925* (Lexington, KY, 1968).

Woodman, Harold D., *New South – New Law: The Legal Foundations of Credit and Labor Relations in the Postbellum Agricultural South* (Baton Rouge, LA, 1995).

Wright, Gavin, *Old South, New South: Revolutions in the Southern Economy Since the Civil War* (New York, 1986).

CHAPTER 23

DEPENDENCY AND COERCION IN EAST ASIAN LABOR, 1800–1949

PAMELA CROSSLEY

In the nineteenth century, two trends came together to erode the traditional patterns of slavery, servitude, and other forms of coerced labor in East Asia. First were economic and political changes that undermined demand for traditional unfree labor and dissolved its legal foundations. In Japan, the Meiji Restoration of 1868 ushered in a series of laws that by 1871 had destroyed the traditional caste system, abolished slavery and untouchable status, and created basic laws requiring wages for work. In Korea, a series of reforms beginning in 1894 and concluding in 1897 eradicated much of the traditional social hierarchy and all forms of legal slavery. China's Qing Empire attempted a similar series of radical reforms between 1907 and 1911, which included the abolition of slavery. In each of these events, the legal structures and much of the residual social systems that had defined inferiority and dependency in East Asia were destroyed. The result was an East Asian labor system more controlled by the forces of urbanization, industrialization, and imperialism, and also more open to manipulation by, in particular, the Governments of China and Japan. Second was the progressive intrusion of European, and later American, treaty requirements and business practices; as the earlier systems disintegrated, new forms were constructed, often on the same foundations. Contract and indentured labor together with reconstituted forms of subordination for women emerged, integrating the rapid political, social, and economic changes of East Asia with global networks supplying labor to developing regions.

THE END OF TRADITIONAL BONDAGE

The collapse of the traditional orders in East Asia ended some ancient forms of enslavement permanently, particularly military slavery, bond-servitude, and eunuchry that had marked Qing China and to a lesser degree Joseon Korea. These forms of bondage were based upon intimacy with the master and the master's household, dependency on the master, and social neutering that, as noted by Orlando Patterson, made the eunuch in particular the "ultimate slave."[1] In the post-imperial world of

[1] Orlando Patterson, *Slavery and Social Death: A Comparative Study* (Cambridge, MA, 1982), pp. 315–410.

the early twentieth century, surviving military slaves (the Eight Banners[2]), bondservants, and eunuchs had disparate fates, but all inspired foreign observers – and particularly the Japanese, who did not have a history of these particular forms of enslavement – to regard China and Korea as backward and obscurantist, seriously in need of the tutelage of progressive colonial powers.

From an early point the Eight Banners of the Qing Empire were transformed by circumstances from a conquest caste to an occupying constabulary. By the end of the seventeenth century, about half of the total population of the Eight Banners was concentrated at Beijing and some of the old installations in Manchuria. The remainder were distributed through the other provinces as peacekeepers and occasionally as defenders of the borders. By 1700, significant issues had arisen regarding the continuous supplies of cash and grain to the garrison populations across the empire. Despite attempted interventions by the court – among them occasional extraordinary payments intended to amend the arrears in payments, attempts to ease credit for Banner officers, tighter regulation of rice brokers and pawn shops who dealt with the Bannermen, and prescribed relocation of Bannermen to more promising farmland – the growing Banner population was steadily impoverished on its fixed income. With few exceptions, the populations of the Banner garrisons were marginalized not only economically, but also professionally and politically.

In the aftermath of the Taiping War that concluded in 1864, the virtually bankrupt state considered cutting off support to and emancipating the entire population of Bannermen. The prospect of hundreds of thousands of rootless Bannermen turned out into society prevented the court from adopting such a policy. When the war that led to the end of the empire broke out in 1911, Bannermen still living in the garrison compounds or wearing their uniforms became targets of violence from revolutionary soldiers and roving mobs. A law of the new Republic in 1912 referenced the Bannermen (as Manchus) in the same terms as other distinct cultural groups, protecting their safety and property without reference to their former status as legally encumbered military slaves of the Qing emperors. A small number of Bannermen continued to live in the Forbidden City as guards and officials, under their traditional terms: some were guards of the surviving Qing Emperor Puyi; some later accompanied Puyi on his sojourn at the Japanese embassy in Tianjin, and ultimately to his installation as

[2] The institution of hereditary, dedicated military slaves pre-dated creation of the Qing imperial state in 1636. Whole families were obligated in perpetuity, and after the middle of the seventeenth century were separated into divisions based on increasingly rigid criteria of genealogy. For general background, see "A Guide to Further Reading" at the end of this chapter.

president in 1932 (and later emperor) of the Manchkuo puppet state. A much larger number of Bannermen, particularly those regarded as skilled in marksmanship, trench fighting, and weapons manufacture, joined the armies of the military governors – the "warlords" – who dominated most provinces of China from the last Qing decades through the period of the Chinese Republic (1912–1949).

Qing bondservants (*booi aha*, 包衣), who served the emperors directly as farm laborers, footmen, secretaries, and managers of imperial monopoly enterprises such as silk, porcelain, and salt brokering, were a subset of the Bannermen. They had an unusually close connection to the emperors and the imperial family, and often were assigned to manage the households of imperial princes and their descendants. There is reason to believe that the size of the population of bondservants, unlike the Bannermen as a group, was stable at least until the mid eighteenth century and thereafter grew somewhat, due to the demands of managing the growing number of residences of the emperors and the imperial family as an extended group. At the end of the nineteenth century, the role of bondservants became more prominent, particularly in education. They are known to have managed a Beijing preparatory school that supplied students to the newly founded Metropolitan University in 1898, and were active in founding new schools for girls in Manchuria, as well as rehabilitation programs for opium addicts and those with minor criminal records among the larger Banner population. With the exception of those chosen to stay on in the Forbidden City until 1923, the legal status of bondservants ended with the abdication by Puyi in 1912.

Into the early twentieth century, eunuchs were living reminders of one aspect of imperial-era subordination, both in China and in Korea. The fall of the Qing Empire in China and of the Joseon dynastic order in Korea destroyed the legal basis of castration and also eradicated the incentives that had led to a significant number of boys or young men being privately castrated by their families, as well as those who sought castration themselves, as a possible avenue to employment at court. Eunuchs in China were given poetic or comical names obliterating their family origins. They had no legal recognition of their marriages or adopted children, and no legal right to choose their duties. They lived officially ostracized from civil society, in the same manner as other individuals who had been physically maimed or marked as slaves. Escape from the palace compound invited severe punishments for themselves, their families, and any who might harbor them. In some periods, depending in part on the attitudes of the dynasty in power, the proximity of eunuchs to the emperor's daily life could allow literate, talented individuals among them to rise to positions of great power, wealth, and influence.

Qing emperors and advisors railed against the role of eunuchs in the political life of the Qing predecessors, the Ming, and frequently uttered admonitions against permitting eunuchs to attain any status or influence. Moreover, the role of bondservants has sometimes been assumed to have prevented the dominance of eunuchs in palace and court life. But the first Qing emperor to sit in Beijing evinced a willingness to permit eunuchs in the imperial household. The complexity and managerial demands of the Qing residences at Beijing and Manchuria outstripped the abilities of the bondservants alone. As the need for eunuch services rose in the eighteenth century, so too did the ranks of newly recruited men and boys in response to salaries comparable to those received by Bannermen, who were expected to support whole households on their pay. As eunuch numbers grew, and as the Qianlong (1736–1795) emperor's court became pervaded by various kinds of corruption and incompetence, the influence and independence of the eunuchs increased. In 1813, eunuchs were blamed for opening the gates of the Forbidden City to Eight Trigrams rebels who intended to assassinate the Jiaqing (1796–1820) emperor. Perhaps as a response, in the Daoguang reign (1821–1850), eunuchs were put under strict surveillance and their privileges reduced. Castration and impressment as eunuchs remained an important punishment of the sons of rebels, famously imposed upon the sons and grandsons of the Kashgar secessionist Yakub Beg after his death in 1877. In the later nineteenth century, it appears that eunuchs again increased their role in the lives of the emperors, culminating in the career of Li Lianying (1848–1911), who until the death of the Empress Dowager Cixi in 1908 hugely enriched himself by bribes and blackmail.

In Korea, eunuchs had different roles. They had been introduced to the court of the Korean state of Goryeo from China in the tenth century, but the scale of Korean court and government did not afford the same opportunities as China for the rise of politically influential eunuchs. The total numbers of eunuchs in Joseon Korea was probably in the hundreds, as contrasted to tens of thousands in Qing China. If married before castration, Korean eunuchs could remain legally married, and if they married after castration and adopted sons these were also legally recognized. Korean eunuchs generally had some degree of literacy and were tested each month on their reading skills and knowledge of basic texts. Palace eunuchry was outlawed in the very late Joseon legal reforms of 1894. Unlike their counterparts in China, eunuchs who survived the Joseon dynasty lived with their families and generally integrated into society in the very early twentieth century.

After 1912, a residual population of eunuchs remained, primarily in Beijing, for most of the twentieth century; they were persistent objects of gossip, of foreign curiosity, and social criticism. The last known surviving eunuch was a minor celebrity when he died at Beijing in 1996, and his story recalled the experience of boys from poor families who had undergone speculative castration (in this case, performed by his father) in hopes

of gaining even the most humble employment opportunities in the Forbidden City. Like other eunuchs, he retained a small casque in which his
genitalia were preserved, to be buried with him. But in the Cultural
Revolution of the late 1960s his family feared political retribution because
of their association with him (a living relic of the "feudal age"), and
destroyed the remains before they could be discovered.

THE TRANSITION TO COMMERCIAL AND CONTRACT LABOR

In eighteenth- and nineteenth-century China, the mechanisms of an
increasingly fluid labor market prompted government attempts to regulate
and moderate slavery, particularly in the agricultural sector. Self-
enslavement contracts, sometimes privately affirmed and never registered
with the state, were common methods of escaping homelessness or acquit-
ting debt. Famously, the Yongzheng emperor in the early eighteenth
century had clarified the terms of indentured servitude and slavery, while
markedly reducing the numbers of workers regarded as slaves, in the
Yangtze Delta.[3] There, rising rents and taxes together with relatively
intense commercialization of agriculture had forced hundreds of thousands
of legally free farmers into compulsory labor as a result of debt. The
imperial court ordered that the criteria of enslavement generally and of
free or bound status of individuals be clarified, in order to prevent leading
landowners from enjoying profits from the labor of those illegally or
covertly enslaved. It remained a matter of comment in Qing law thereafter
that the specific distinctions of slavery should be scrupulously observed
and the poor should not be manipulated into enslavement. This reduced
the number of slaves in the Yangtze Delta, but to the end of the Qing
period, farmers, laborers, and small businessmen who incurred debt to pay
taxes or rent often voluntarily contracted themselves into slavery, always
with the slight hope of buying back or challenging the contract. Mining
labor was a mixture of wage labor and convict labor, and like agriculture,
presented a contrast to factory labor (generally for porcelain and textiles),
where wages had been gradually commercialized and conditions had
improved since the seventeenth century.

   Unlike China, Korea and Japan were still, to a significant degree, caste
societies into the early modern period. Korea's institutions of coercion and
dependency were similar to China's in institutional contours and in
terminology, but the social context was different. Slave status in Korea
was hereditary and overwhelmingly civil – while Joseon Korea had a
military organization superficially patterned on the Eight Banners system

---

[3] W. T. Rowe, "Social Stability and Social Change," in W. J. Peterson (ed.), *The Cambridge History
of China* (Cambridge, 2002), Vol. 9, pp. 473–562.

of the Qing. The military population was common-born and recruited, and at intervals was free to leave the military for other work. The majority of the Korean population was of commoner status (*sangmin* 常民), but 25 to 30 percent may have been low-born, or *cheonmin* 賤民, which corresponded to the proportionally much smaller (but numerically vastly larger) Chinese class of *jianmin*. As in China, the low-born caste were not exclusively slaves. They also included executioners, nightsoil carriers, shamans, Buddhist monks and nuns (who had abandoned conventional family life), prostitutes, and indentured female entertainers (*gisaeng* 妓生). A distinct caste of untouchables, called *baekjeong* 白丁, were butchers and leather workers believed to be descended from nomads and required to live in segregated districts. The majority of *cheonmin*, however, were slaves, most commonly called *nobi* (from Chinese *nupi* 奴婢). Privately owned slaves worked the fields and kept the houses of the aristocracy or wealthier commoners. Convict slaves were owned by the state and either worked the royal estates or served in the stations that maintained the roads and collected transit taxes.

Though the terminology of Korean slavery paralleled that of China, the basic practices were strikingly different. Contracts were less common than in China, except for *sangmin* who had personally sold themselves into slavery because of debt. Most *nobi* were born to the status, were marked visibly and indelibly, had no surnames, could not enter into legitimate marriage, and could be sold by aristocratic owners or traded to the state as tax or tribute. Registration at birth was required in both China and Korea, and on contact with the state – as when paying tax, reporting for *corvée*, or appearing before a magistrate – the status would always be reported as part of the identity, often before the name. In both China and Korea, low-born status – that is, eligibility to be enslaved – was strongly marked in one or more ways: tattooing, non-debilitating mutilation, or dress. In Korea, men between 15 and 70 years of age – the years of military service – were required to make their own tags with their identity information, and to have them endorsed by a magistrate. The identity tags made and worn by *cheonmin* were required to be larger than those of other castes and to be made of a common wood. This registration system was credited not only with magnifying the psychological dimensions of caste identity, but also with making the recapturing of fugitive slaves more efficient. *Cheonmin*, including *nobi*, could in unusual instances become wealthy on tips or booty, and could own slaves of their own. But, except by the subterfuge of forging a genealogy, they could not enter the ranks of commoners. Persons marked on their bodies faced lives on the margin in the civil societies that emerged from the collapse of traditional servitude with the 1896 to 1897 reforms in Korea and the revolution of 1911 to 1912 in China.

Though Japan shared Korea's basic social structure in the seventeenth and eighteenth centuries, and had a large caste of untouchables, historians estimate that not more than 5 percent of the population was enslaved (as *nuhi*, taken from the Chinese term) in this period. They were largely captives taken in the country's many internal wars. In 1590, the military government of Japan issued decrees establishing new rules for many aspects of social and economic activity, and banned civil slavery. The new laws applied primarily to persons who had been sentenced through the judicial system to forced labor in mines or newly opened agricultural land.

Civil slavery affected only a small number of commoners in Tokugawa Japan, but the much larger class of "untouchables" – the so-called *eta* 穢多 or "very polluted" – experienced social disenfranchisement. The historical origins of the *eta* are obscure, as in the case of the *baekjeong* of Korea, but most likely comprised war captives, refugees or other homeless people, orphans, and convicts. *Eta* were not permitted to own land or farms, and were compelled by circumstance to work in the unsanitary, bloody, or otherwise unsavory trades that were regarded as spiritually degraded. This in fact excluded the *eta* (like the *baekjeong*) from many forms of work performed by slaves in Japan, Korea, and China. The *eta* were regarded as physically intolerable, required to wear distinctive clothing, and forced to live in segregated districts (the inspiration for one of their designations in the twentieth century, the *burakumin* 部落民, or "people of the villages"). Their marriages were recognized, if poorly documented, but the value of their lives – if they should be murdered, killed by accident, or maimed to the point of losing livelihood – was traditionally "one-seventh" that of a commoner, and was specifically fixed at that rate in a law of 1859. Although inferior to all other classes of society, *eta* were not the personal subordinates or property of other Japanese – the likely reason being that their persons had no particular compensatory value. They remained in their despised occupations and could not enlist or engage in commerce.

Servitude and slavery were concentrated in the agricultural sectors of China, Korea, and Japan, which in the nineteenth century were profoundly disrupted. In China, exhaustion of farmland and deterioration of the water systems had already created stress in certain regions by the early 1800s. This became one of several factors driving a series of rural revolts which culminated in the Taiping War (1850–1864), which historians now believe had a death toll of between 20 and 40 million. Much of the country's most valuable cropland was destroyed and abandoned, some of which still lay uninhabited a generation later. Cities such as Shanghai and Hangzhou had their populations swollen by two or three times their previous size, as refugees waited for shelter, food, and medical care. In such circumstances, the poorer laborers of afflicted areas were eager to seek new opportunities for work, as well as take advantage of the chaos to escape servitude. Some could be absorbed by new urban enterprises – transportation, sanitation, prostitution, work on the docks, or in warehouses – especially in the "treaty ports" that had been created through a series of treaties forced upon the Qing Government by Britain, the United States, France, the Swedish Union, Austria-Hungary, Belgium, and, ultimately, Germany and Russia. Farmers who were free of debt, or so dislocated by war that their debt obligations could not be traced, could relocate to the cities if they applied for permission or bribed the appropriate officials. But even indebted farmers (or their children) could now be contracted to urban enterprises and thereby generate a new source of income for their landlords.

Enforcement of such long-distance exploitation was a problem, but not an insuperable one. In the Chinese countryside, and increasingly in the cities, landlords employed informal organizations to force farmers to pay inflated taxes (usually passed on from landowners), high rents, interest, and loans. On the other hand, farmers could hire informal organizations to protect themselves from the demands of landowners and officials. Often, these were one and the same. Foremost among them were the so-called "secret societies." They were lineage- and village-based, often hidden from the authorities, met infrequently and always in secret, and used terror tactics and blackmail to achieve their ends. Some, such as the Heaven and Earth Society, specialized in providing transportation, employment, and protection (all for frequent payments) for laborers working as barge-pullers and cargo carriers along the Grand Canal that ran between the Yangtze Delta and Beijing. Secret societies were factors in riots and rebellions in the later eighteenth and early nineteenth centuries. They were adept at melting into the countryside or into the city tenements as the authorities suppressed the insurgencies, and they sustained themselves by legitimate peddling and manual labor, as well as extortion and thievery.

THE TRAFFICKING OF LABOR OVERSEAS

From its beginnings and certainly after the rapid increase of trade in the 1840s, the traffic in indentured Chinese laborers was an integral part of the same network that transported opium, other drugs, and, increasingly, armaments. Transoceanic ports at which large numbers of laborers landed – Cape Town, San Francisco, Lima – also became centers of the international drug trade. Before the 1840s, the Qing Government had repeatedly banned emigration. But this law, like similar legislation banning the import of opium, was generally disregarded. Overseas indentures were originally modeled on domestic contracts that were both widely used and legal. After the first treaty between the Qing Empire and Britain in 1842, the gradual intrusion of foreign trade practices further complicated the legal status of overseas labor migration. The Qing Government passed its own explicit ban on contract labor export in 1873 and in subsequent years signed international treaties affirming the ban internationally. Brokers then disguised the practice as a self-financed free labor scheme, keeping double books, and using criminal gangs to enforce the terms.

Though commentators at the time (and some historians since) have assumed that China's large population made the export of labor necessary and advantageous, there is no obvious correlation between population density in China and the Chinese sources of exported laborers. Nor is there evidence that more efficient inland transportation enabled the flow of Chinese laborers to the coast. Rising population in China's eastern coastal provinces and development of commercial enterprises both in the cities and the countryside had resulted in improved infrastructure from the sixteenth century onward. But the impact of this had been on internal commerce, particularly on China's northwest and the western border area, which today is encompassed by Sichuan province. Early emigration was to Taiwan and then extended to Vietnam, the Malay Peninsula, the Philippines, and Indonesia, where by the end of the seventeenth century there were probably 50,000 Chinese in Java and perhaps 100,000 in Jakarta. Migrants were small farmers, merchants, or the servants of merchants, seeking land or trade opportunities. There were infrequent but very bloody massacres of the Chinese merchant and labor communities in Indonesia in particular; perhaps most spectacular was the murder in 1740 of over 10,000 Chinese in Batavia. The Qianlong Emperor (r. 1736–1795) of the Qing pronounced himself uninterested in their fate, since in his view they had absconded from China in search of profit.

From the early sixteenth century, when the Portuguese established their base at Macao island off the coast of Guangdong province, Portuguese ships and labor brokers were active in transporting migrants to Portuguese possessions in South Asia, Africa, and the Americas. Spanish and Dutch ships quickly joined in the traffic. For the early 1600s, there is evidence of Chinese technicians and gardeners being imported into Mexico and Peru, and a hundred years later Chinese miners were in the gold-producing regions of Brazil. By the late eighteenth century, when Britain established a colony at Penang in Malaysia, British ships had joined the trade, and by the mid-1800s, French, Italian, Belgian, and American ships were all prominent in the transport of Chinese labor across the Pacific. But the threshold of the sharp rise of Chinese migration was the conclusion of the Opium War of 1839 to 1842 and the subsequent establishment of the British colony at Hong Kong. Most of the laborers sent abroad in this period were natives of Guangdong province, specifically its "Four Counties" region on the coast near the city of Canton (Guangzhou) – lightly populated in comparison to the southeastern China coast. Labor brokers with links to the Portuguese colony at Macao and the British colony at Hong Kong targeted this region in the aftermath of the 1842 Treaty. From this point, British shipping and commerce overwhelmed the much older Portuguese trade, and Britain assumed Portugal's role in the export of Chinese labor. This new system supplied Chinese contract labor through to 1874 (when the 1873 Treaty went into full effect).

Chinese and British brokers seeking laborers for the warehouses, docks, rubber plantations, and tin mines of British Malaya and the Dutch East Indies oversaw the increased outflow of workers. They used a "credit ticket" system, meaning that a Chinese broker in Guangdong province would lend the laborer enough to pay for ship passage, and upon landing the broker would sell the loans to local employers at a profit, leaving the workers deeply in debt to strangers, and running up additional debt at rates of 50 to 100 percent per year. A minority of the sojourners had paid for their passage by borrowing from family, on the expectation of making enough both to pay off the loan and to return with enough for a land purchase and marriage; this minority was the originator of the remittance system in China, whereby Chinese laborers all over the world subsidized their families at home, a system that has continued through to the twenty-first century. By the 1920s, the credit ticket system had produced the so-called "coolie" trade, the mass transport of destitute Chinese laborers. Various etymologies have been proposed for the word "coolie," not least its Chinese version of *kuli* 苦力 ("bitter strength"), but it is most likely an Urdu word, derived from Turkish *kul* (slave, servant, property). In China, the system was referred to as a "piglet sale" (*mai zhuhai* 賣豬仔). Workers awaiting emigration in Macao and Hong Kong, as well as coastal cities in Fujian province, were crammed into huts the Chinese called "pig sties" (*zhuhai guan* 豬仔館), some of which can still be seen in Macao.

The basic forces behind expansion of the system are suggested by three global trends. First was European and US abolition of the slave trade bookended by Denmark in 1802 and Portugal in 1836, but with the slave trade continuing to 1867 in Cuba. This was followed by outright abolition of slavery, starting with Britain in 1833 and concluding with Brazil in 1888. Second is the roughly coterminous expansion of sugar plantations throughout the islands of the Indian Ocean, the Malay Peninsula, Indonesia, Australia, the Pacific Islands, South America, the Caribbean, and Southern Africa. Beginning in the early nineteenth century, plantation owners used convict labor to supplement slave labor. To meet rising demand, a system for recruitment of Indian labor for distribution to British colonies developed in the 1830s, based on five-year contracts and transport at the employer's expense. The third trend was improvements in transoceanic travel, which lowered transportation costs. Settlement of the west coasts of North and South America combined with development of more efficient steamships led to the development of new routes across the Pacific. Migrant labor could now be expected to arrive in weeks instead of months.

After 1842, Chinese labor began to fill some gaps in the rising global shortage of agricultural workers and miners. Global labor migration changed dramatically. North America was industrializing, and received more immigrants than any other part of the world, overwhelmingly of European origin. Southeast Asia and the Indian Ocean colonies, the second largest recipient region after the Americas, remained in need of agricultural and mining labor. This was primarily the zone fed by Indian and Chinese labor. Of all Chinese exported labor, 90 percent went to Southeast Asia in the period 1840 to 1940, with the Malay Peninsula receiving the greatest concentration. Historians have noted the tendency of labor brokers to direct Chinese and Indians toward agriculture and mining in the tropical regions (while Europeans headed for industrializing cities). According to Portuguese Government records, between 1864 and 1874, 182,000 Chinese laborers were shipped from Macao, of whom about 95,000 went to Cuba and about 83,000 to Peru. In those regions of tropical or near-tropical plantation and mining venues, Chinese labor had a transforming effect.

John Vincent Crawford, the British Consul in Havana for many years, drew up figures on the traffic. His records suggest one aspect of the hardship experienced by these laborers, but they relate only to the legal trade. The dimensions of the illegal trade are not precisely known, though Chinese officials commented frequently on the abduction or recruitment of Chinese by unlicenced brokers and the smuggling of people along with untaxed goods. At destinations, too, officials remarked upon the problem of excess and untaxed workers being smuggled ashore, while landowners complained about workers who were abducted or enticed to abscond before the employers who had paid their fares could have them transported to their intended place of work. A minority of the Chinese outflow was formally indentured, with the rest on their own contracts. Yet, the treatment of recruited laborers, usually secured by Chinese brokers, was not greatly different from the way in which slaves were traditionally treated. They were stripped for examination, penned in outdoor enclosures while awaiting transport, identified by numbers instead of names, and were stamped with a letter indicating their destination, always chosen for them by the broker.

For a very large portion of the men going into the system, the distinction between voluntary or forced participation may have been meaningless, since indebted tenants from rural China may have had no choice but to enter the system faced with the option of the sale of their families into slavery. Overall, it appears that conditions in Peru were the most brutal. Guano and sugar were the two great industries in Peru, both were starved of labor. In the 1840s, the fertilizing properties of guano in particular were recognized around the globe. American tobacco plantations, Jamaican sugar plantations, and European, Australian, and South African farms were demanding guano, and the labor needs of Peruvian guano entrepreneurs rose accordingly. In the absence of native laborers and African slaves, indentured Chinese constituted the majority of the worker inflow, and their working conditions seemed a continuation of the conditions for slaves before them. The element of virtual slavery was particularly pronounced for the very few women who moved through the coolie transport system. A Cuban census of 1861 counted 1.6 Chinese women for every thousand men, and Cuban newspapers sometimes announced that women and girls would be included in the next auction of incoming indentured. No woman could have left China legally as a contract laborer, and wives were forbidden to emigrate. Most of these female migrants would have been sold by parents or husbands, or abducted and forced to sign contracts that obligated them to virtual lifelong prostitution – a booming industry in China's treaty ports after the 1840s.

In 1856, when global suicide rates for men averaged about 90 per million, the rate among indentured Chinese in Cuba and in British Guiana was estimated to be 800 per million or higher (compared to 250 per million for Indians in the same environment). Perhaps 10 percent of vessels carrying Chinese laborers across the Pacific in the mid nineteenth century experienced revolts. Britain banned participation by its flag carriers in the traffic to Cuba and Peru in 1855; thereafter, the Portuguese handled the transportation of Chinese to the non-British Caribbean on their own. Conditions aboard ships generally improved, and voyage mortality dropped by half from the 1850s to the 1870s. Nevertheless, the problems of abduction or deceit by Chinese underground organizations or foreign recruiters persisted. A Peruvian ship transporting Chinese laborers called at Yokohama for supplies in 1872; Japanese inspectors determined that the Chinese aboard had been abducted or otherwise coerced and returned them all to China. Workers reported that the free laborers, once aboard the ships, were forced to sign contracts of indenture or be flogged. The treatment, and subsequent losses by workers who had expected to save up enough to change their lives, caused repeated unrest in China's coastal cities – primarily Xiamen, Guangzhou, Fuzhou, and Shanghai – where recruiting was most intense. Many families received reports that their husbands or sons, on encountering conditions at their destinations, had committed suicide.

When, in 1869, Chinese laborers from Peru petitioned the Qing Government in Beijing to intervene to improve their conditions, the court's response was identical to the Qianlong Emperor's response to the slaughter of Chinese workers in Batavia a century earlier: The laborers had all emigrated illegally for profit, and were of no interest to the empire. But by the 1870s, the Qing Government, led by Yixin (Prince Gong), took a dramatically different view. The government sent officials to the ports, and even to Cuba and Peru, to investigate the conditions of overseas workers. In 1874, these commissioners reported that four out of five Chinese laborers in Cuba claimed to have been abducted or recruited by deceit. After agreements between the Qing and the United States and Portugal in 1874, departures from Macao ceased and the last legal shipment of Chinese indentured laborers left for the Americas. In 1877, a treaty with Spain based on investigations by the Chinese Government confirmed that the coolie trade to Cuba would not be revived, and in addition established legal minimum standards of living for the Chinese laborers who were already there.

While the Qing court claimed humanitarian concerns were behind its reversal in attitude toward the conditions of exported workers, there had in fact been pressure for decades from foreign governments claiming that import of Chinese labor – and the retention of those laborers in conditions of destitution and dependency – was disturbing the development of domestic labor markets. Not only opium, but prostitution, gambling, and bubonic plague were believed to be in some way caused by the rising numbers of coolies working the docks, mines, roads, railroad tracks, and orchards. In Malaysia, in the 1870s, about half of all arriving Chinese laborers were on the "credit ticket" system, but direct competition with local workers was minimal. Throughout much of Southeast Asia, Chinese merchants were often privileged by colonial administrations and segregation between immigrant and native populations was often enforced (as in nineteenth-century Indonesia), allowing even the poor Chinese populations to enjoy safety. But in the Americas, economic and cultural crises associated with the transition from slavery to free labor combined with racism to crystallize hostility to Chinese labor. Cuba required Chinese who had fulfilled their contracts to either return to China or enter into new contracts of indenture; they were not permitted to participate freely in the economy or take rights of residence. Very few appear to have had the means to buy passage back to China, and so they were in a perpetual cycle of coercion. In Peru, where there were perhaps 100,000 Chinese laborers, riots spread in the 1850s, demanding an end to Chinese contract labor and the abuses that accompanied it. At the time, the Chinese Government ignored requests from both Peru and the United States to ban the trade. It was Portugal that responded, by investigating labor brokering and export via Macao, and subsequently banning the trade in December 1873. The Qing Government followed immediately with its ban.

The subject was particularly sensitive in the United States; like Cuba and Peru, the United States was making a transition from slavery to free labor, but unlike the European possessions in Southeast Asia and the Indian Ocean, the United States was not overseen by a colonial administration able to restrain public opinion. In the 1850s, American planters joined British colleagues in Hawaii in offering signing bonuses and relatively high wages to about 400 Chinese laborers. From that time to the American overthrow of the kingdom in 1898, East Asian laborers who had paid their debts were offered full rights of residency in the islands; the vast majority stayed. William Makepeace Thackeray foresaw the labor network extending to North America, where he anticipated that it would undermine slavery, as it was already doing in Peru. In 1853, he wrote to his mother from the US, ". . . scores of Celestial immigrants may be working in the cotton and tobacco fields here and in the West Indies Islands. Then the African Slave will get his manumission quickly enough."[4] Virtually as Thackeray's letter was being delivered, the population of workers of Chinese origin in the United States exploded from a few hundred to about 20,000, as contract laborers arrived to work the goldfields of California; that same year, California banned the "credit ticket" system and permitted arriving laborers to seek new employers if they wished. A local regulation of 1862 forced labor brokers to pay a high tax on each imported worker from China. By the early 1860s, Chinese workers who had paid off their debts entered railroad construction or set up their own businesses along the West Coast. But tensions rose when, in the 1870s, Chinese workers were willing to replace striking farm workers in California.

The abolition of slave labor in the American South spread concern after the Civil War that Chinese immigrants would work on plantations, a factor behind the US passage of the Chinese Exclusion Act of 1882 – which in fact did not exclude all Chinese, but only Chinese laborers. But the law did not quell mass violence against Chinese miners and railroad workers, which in the mid-1880s spread through California, Colorado, Wyoming, Oregon, and Washington State. The Act was renewed in 1892 and made permanent in 1902, by which time the number of Chinese resident in the United States had fallen from 105,000 to 90,000. The ban on Chinese labor immigration was extended to Hawaii when it became an American territory in 1898, and to the Philippines when it became an American colony the same year. It was not repealed until 1943, when the Republic of China – then fighting together with the United States against Japan in the Second World War – renegotiated all the provisions of the "unequal treaties" imposed upon China by the United States, beginning in 1844.

---

[4] William Makepeace Thackeray to his mother, Washington, DC, February 13, 1853, quoted in David Northrup, *Indentured Labor in the Age of Imperialism* (Cambridge, 1995), p. 16.

MODERN DISCIPLINE OF DOMESTIC AND EXPORTED LABOR

In the 1920s, agricultural and urban labor across East Asia was increasingly organized in attempts to improve conditions. In the countryside, these organizations were partly a legacy of the traditional village organizations that had resorted to rent strikes and sometimes violence to resist the predations of landowners and officials. But from the beginning of the twentieth century, activists inspired by agrarian socialism, anarchism, and later Marxism moved to the countryside to run schools and organize more effective rent strikes. These efforts became more urgent in the late 1920s, as a series of famines struck the Chinese countryside. In China, these activists were often specifically combating the remnants of traditional agricultural slavery, along with footbinding and general deference to landowners. For the military governors taking control of the Chinese countryside in the 1920s and 1930s, labor organizing could be regarded as intolerable, whether it was sponsored by the Communists or the Nationalists. The famous organizer Peng Pai, who had annoyed landlords in Guangdong province for years while leading strikes and providing rights to education for tenant farmers, was imprisoned and executed by the Nationalists. In Japan, independent farming was more common, tenancy was relatively low, and in the early twentieth century land reform had accelerated, along with commercialization and partial mechanization. Here, political organizing was focused on demanding government regulation of the prices of staple crops, and was most effective in the late 1920s, the last years of representative government in Japan before the militarization of the government in the 1930s. Rural organizing was particularly complex in Korea, where long-standing traditional resentment of landlord demands was combined in the 1920s with anger over landlords selling their holdings to Japanese land-holding conglomerates, thereby making the owners and managers of the land foreign imperialists. Korean farmers organized resistance that culminated in a series of strikes in 1929.

Frequently, the organizations of rural farmers seeking lower rents, more ownership, and fair prices were integrated with urban organizations that included rickshaw pullers, nightsoil carriers, and messengers, in addition to factory and dock workers. Throughout East Asia, most urban dwellers still had strong connections to their rural roots, and strikes over farmers' concerns would attract the support of urban workers and students. This was reinforced by the exposure of urban workers in the Chinese "treaty ports" to the presence of foreign entrepreneurs, security guards, soldiers, and missionaries. Both Nationalist and Communist organizers (the latter frequently guided from afar by the USSR Comintern after 1921) linked the economic privileges of foreign imperialists to the struggles of farmers dealing with falling grain prices in the 1920s. Urban workers – who included women working in the textile industries across East Asia at about half the wages of men – protested low wages, unfair competition, and unsafe working conditions. Following the military industrialization of both China and Japan in the late nineteenth century, the First World War was a spur to further heavy manufacturing across East Asia, since machine tools and chemicals were no longer easily available from European suppliers. This produced a few centers of dense industrialization – the combined cities of Wuhan on the Yangtze River in China, the port of Yokohama in Japan, and the Korean ports of Injeon and Busan, all of which attracted labor from the countryside. But by far the greatest number of workers in the early 1920s were involved in light industries, particularly textiles, and both the numbers and the expectations of urban workers rose.

The degree to which labor in industrial centers of East Asia in the period between the late 1890s and the end of the Second World War can be considered free or competitive is murky. Japan had by formal or informal means acquired major investments in – and often direct control over – land and industry in China and Korea. Taiwan became a Japanese colony in 1895, and Korea a Japanese protectorate in 1905 and a colony in 1910. In Japan itself, the *zaibatsu* – huge corporations integrating banking, raw material acquisition, and manufacturing – gained increasing control over the government and collaborated more and more closely with rising factions of militarists. In the case of China, Japan had used threats of force during the First World War to become a major creditor of the Chinese Government and a privileged investor in China's cotton and silk manufacturing. As a result of its own successful industrialization and its ability to manipulate the Chinese industrial sector, Japan was able to maintain its cotton textile output at about twice the amount of China's through the first three decades of the twentieth century. Chinese workers found they had little power to raise wages or expand employment. But cotton workers still had much greater stability than those in silk manufacture. In the first three decades of the twentieth century, Japan's manufacture of raw silk overtook that of China and Italy, and along with colonial Korea, led the world by 1930. The result was unemployment and immiseration for workers in many parts of China during the 1920s. But the global crash of the market for raw silk in the early 1930s brought a similar crisis to Japan; through all of East Asia, the industrial crises caused by disruption of the global market spurred intensified conflict between increasingly socialist labor organizations and increasingly authoritarian governments.

Dissatisfaction with labor conditions and employment prospects across East Asia contributed to a spike in emigration in the 1920s, reaching a peak of 700,000 Chinese in 1926.[5] The traditional patterns of trade and

[5] A. M. McKeown, "Chinese Emigration in Global Context," *Journal of Global History* 5 (2010): 95–124. McKeown's figures show a steady rise through the nineteenth century and a steep drop during the first decade of the Republican era (1911 to 1921, with a surge through the 1920s, ending with the global

transport drew a great majority toward Southeast Asia, as in earlier times, but there were significant differences. The Philippines were now under American control, and subject to the American restrictions on Chinese labor, but with no control over Filipino migration to the United States. The same restrictions also applied to Hawaii. In addition, an American law of 1924 (kept in effect until 1952) severely limited the import of Japanese and Korean labor. Hawaii attempted to lure Scandinavians and Poles to offset resident Chinese, Japanese, and Koreans. After creation of the Commonwealth of Australia in 1901, the Chinese who had come earlier to mine gold were expelled because immigration was restricted to white Europeans. The Union of South Africa, at its founding in 1910, ordered all Chinese immigrants to return to China. To meet their own labor demands, the United States, Canada, South Africa, and Australia offered subsidies to Europeans wishing to immigrate. In such circumstances, it was not only the traditional structure of labor migration from East Asia, but the positive restrictions imposed by the United States and new countries emerging from the British Empire that restricted most Asian emigration to tropical Asia, particularly Indonesia and the Malay Peninsula. Trans-Pacific labor migration for East Asians generally was focused on Peru, Bolivia, and Brazil.

The role of the new governments of East Asia in the control of labor – whether within colonially managed zones such as Korea and Taiwan, or regulating emigration – is striking, particularly in the development of Hawaii. Before 1853, Hawaiian agricultural labor had been overwhelmingly native, though the decline in the native population and the increasing profitability of Hawaiian agriculture raised the demand for labor. A new Board of Immigration was founded in 1864 to promote the importation of agricultural laborers, particularly from China, with the acquiescence of the Chinese Government; the population of workers in Hawaii of Chinese origin, overwhelmingly agricultural laborers, surpassed 18,000 by 1882.[6] In the 1880s, the stream of Chinese laborers was augmented by Japanese, of whom 30,000, all indentured, arrived between 1885 and 1899. The Japanese Government set up its own agency to manage the export of indentured labor to selected locations.

The Chinese Government permitted the completion of old indenture contracts and acquiesced in the recruitment of ostensibly voluntary labor for foreign locations, particularly Southeast Asia, where a faction within

depression of 1931). While the totals for North America and Africa fell steadily between 1882 and 1921, they also increased during the 1920s. The overwhelming majority of labor emigrants went to the European colonies of the Philippines (before 1898), Malaya, and the Dutch East Indies.

[6] Eleanor Nordyke and Richard C. K. Lee, "The Chinese in Hawai'i: A Historical and Demographic Perspective," *Hawaiian Journal of History*, 23 (1989): 196–216, esp. 202.

the late Qing Government were working to undermine French and British colonialism. By 1887, the number of still-indentured Chinese laborers in the Malay Peninsula was just over 25 percent of all Chinese laborers there, and in 1890 may have fallen as low as 2 percent. British corporations sought Chinese labor in China, Malaya, and Singapore; as many as 64,000 contracted Chinese are known to have been employed in the gold mines of Transvaal between 1904 and 1906 under the terms of a new labor convention between the Qing and British Empires. Germans were also recruiting Chinese under the new system to work on their plantations in Western Samoa.

In Japan, as the Meiji Government encouraged industrialization and a certain amount of urbanization, labor surpluses threatened to drag down wages and economic growth. The Japanese Government not only encouraged a labor exodus, but managed it, monitoring foreign labor recruiters, inspecting overseas venues, negotiating wages, and regulating loans. But when Japanese labor needs increased in the very early 1880s, the government stepped in to lower the number of workers going overseas. In this way, the Japanese Government was able to mitigate urban poverty and disorder, exercise some control over wage fluctuations, and avoid the humiliation experienced by the Qing Empire when it could not protect its people from being forced into virtual slavery overseas.

Competition by poor Japanese to get into the overseas network was sometimes intense. In 1885 – in the middle of grinding rural depression and sharply rising tenancy rates – a government recruitment initiative seeking a thousand workers for three years in Hawaii was flooded with 28,000 applicants. In 1894, the Japanese Government gave up its monopoly on recruitment, but continued to regulate private labor export companies. By 1907, the numbers of Japanese entering Hawaii had jumped to 125,000. In that year, a proposed American regulation would have severely limited Japanese labor migration to California, but the Japanese Government agreed to voluntarily restrict the numbers; thereafter, surplus Japanese workers were directed to Peru and Brazil (which by 1924 were receiving 21,000 and 26,000 Japanese laborers respectively per annum), though the inflow into Hawaii was not affected. Japanese domination of the Korean Peninsula from the 1880s also permitted more precise coordination of labor distribution. Distressed Japanese farmers could be relocated to undeveloped parts of Korea (and, after 1931, to Manchuria), while Koreans could be recruited or coerced to work new Japanese mining, smelting, and railroad construction enterprises in Korea. Labor managers could also sweep Korean laborers into scheduled emigration to trans-Pacific destinations, and in the early twentieth century Korean laborers began arriving at the sites most favored by Japanese labor brokers – Hawaii, Peru, and Brazil. Japanese men working in Hawaii, the Philippines, and in the

Continental United States could be joined by their wives; after Korea became a Japanese colony in 1910, this provision was also extended to Koreans.

Despite government oversight and management of some aspects of the international labor market, the scope of criminal involvement continued to widen. Japan's colonization of Korea extended the existing need for false passports and health certificates, extortion of money from laborers, money laundering, prostitution, and the restrictions of workers' movements and activities. The result was that the Japanese criminal gangs – the *yakuza*, who were 70 percent of *eta* origin – became ubiquitous in the overseas diaspora of Japanese labor. In China, the lack of an effective central government after 1912 left hundreds of thousands of workers open to forced recruitment and lack of protection at work sites. Warlords could profit from mass contracts and loans to the families of exported laborers, just as landlords had in the imperial period. Gangsters, private recruiters, and even missionaries all became involved, and at the local level warlords often manipulated the recruitment systems to keep the best workers for themselves and shift the starving, opium-addicted, or dangerous to other provinces or other countries. Though women remained a tiny portion of the migrants, their numbers spiked at the same as those of men in the 1920s. The proportion of women moving through the system to rural venues declined, but the numbers going to cities such as Jakarta, Cape Town, Bangkok, and Havana, and to locations in Europe increased. Prostitution in particular, based in significant part on abduction and fraud, pulled Chinese women into a separate network that, like other forms of overseas labor recruitment, existed in a milieu suspended between government registration and regulation on the one hand and organized crime on the other.

With the outbreak of the First World War, the Chinese Government was able to use the infrastructure of the contract labor system to supply 150,000 support workers to England and France, in hopes that after the war the victors would help the Republic of China regain sovereignty over lands dominated by Japan, as well as held by the Allies themselves. These hopes were dashed, leading to public outrage in both Korea and China in 1919. Thereafter, the Chinese Government was unable to use the contract labor system to its benefit. But through the Republican period, private remittances by overseas Chinese provided farming families with the small margins needed to survive famine or bribe local officials. In 1930, total remittances amounted to almost $95 million (of which nearly half may have come from the relatively small population of Chinese residents in North America). As in earlier eras, most came from wealthier students, professionals, or patriotically minded gangsters, but a third of the money received went to the Four Counties in Guangdong province that had historically provided the core of the indentured and contracted export labor. In turn, the remittance industry created new profit opportunities for both criminal networks and honest brokers, since cash transmitted via goods or promissory notes had to be redeemed inside China. The central government opened special bank branches in Singapore and New York in 1936 to handle remittances directly, and the next year – as Japanese invasion loomed and remittances from overseas Chinese increased – it opened new branches across Southeast Asia and Indonesia. Beyond that, the central government could do little to gain from overseas contract labor or to ameliorate the conditions under which Chinese people were still laboring overseas.

In Japan, the government had maintained a role in monitoring remittance income by Japanese workers and encouraging its investment in regional industries. Though the numbers of Japanese participating in international contract labor was very small in relation to the Chinese, Japan quickly learned to use export labor systems to help stabilize its domestic economy, as well as gather and organize remittances to fund industrialization and commercialization. Because Japan was a rising naval power in the late nineteenth and early twentieth centuries, it could negotiate with governments such as the United States to win certain accommodations for its exported workers, both Japanese and Korean. Nevertheless, Japan could not overcome the tendency of the system to function outside the scope of legal monitoring and correction. In Japan, as in China, criminal networks combined labor contracting with drug and weapons running as well as prostitution to create part of the infrastructure of twentieth- and twenty-first-century human trafficking.

CONCLUSION

After forms of bondage peculiar to the imperial period in East Asia died along with traditional legal systems, a global market began to create new dimensions of free and independent labor. The vast majority of laborers stayed on their traditional land or migrated to the cities. In China, for instance, the total leaving for overseas between 1840 and 1940 was probably lower than 50 million, a small figure in a population that was probably about 450 million in 1840 and twice that size in 1940. At home, laborers attempted at the dawn of the twentieth century and in the following decades to change their conditions through labor organizing. In the 1920s in particular, they began to make some progress in political visibility and influence, but the economic hardships and political radicalization of the 1930s inhibited the momentum and very many, if not most, agricultural workers across East Asia reached the mid-1930s indebted to landlords and crushed by collapsing national and international demand for anything but basic staples. For urban laborers, attempts to organize for better wages and conditions made them targets of government suspicion that Communists under the control of the Soviet Union were using the labor movements for subversive ends. In China, the Nationalist Government violently suppressed strikes in 1925, and in 1927 and 1928 conducted an extermination campaign against Communist organizers who had been active in both the countryside and the cities. In Japan, suspicion of the labor movements helped catalyze persecutions of academics, writers, and politicians in the early 1930s by right-wing militarists. In Korea, rural and urban organizing by local leaders continued well after the colonization by Japan in 1910, braving draconian suppression and reprisals by both the Japanese military and the security police.

The minority of East Asian laborers who participated in the early globalization of labor and migration had a significant effect on the societies to which they migrated. The coolie system remains the focus of a great deal of historical discussion, but the assumption that this system was the most exemplary form of nineteenth- and twentieth-century unfree labor may not be well founded. Most indentured Chinese laborers of the later nineteenth century remained in China, often with deepening debt sinking them into the grip of landlords, criminals, and warlords, or they migrated to the cities where they experienced poverty and abuse. But workers leaving China, whether coerced or under their own initiative, hastened the demise of African slavery in some places, and smoothed the transition away from slave labor in others. They aided the take-off in industries such as mining, shipping, and railways. And remittances from Chinese, Japanese, and Korean overseas workers financed much of the survival of family enterprises in China during the late nineteenth and early twentieth centuries and the industrialization of Japan. In virtually all host societies, these workers faced racism and increased social tensions. They played an unwilling, but critical, role as objects of public discourse reconfiguring legal and social concepts of race and status, freedom and inclusion, and control of borders as an expression of national sovereignty.

A GUIDE TO FURTHER READING

For studies of institutions of servitude in China, see:

Crossley, P. K., "Slavery in Early Modern China," in David Eltis and Stanley L. Engerman (eds.), *The Cambridge World History of Slavery* (Cambridge, 2011–2017), Vol. 3 (1420–1804), pp. 186–215.

Schottenhammer, Angela, "Slaves and Forms of Slavery in Late Imperial China (Seventeenth to Early Twentieth Centuries)," *Slavery and Abolition*, 24 (2003): 143–54.

A major source on Japan is Thomas Nelson, "Slavery in Medieval Japan," *Monumenta Nipponica*, 59 (2004): 463–92, and for Korea see Kim, Bok Rae, "Nobi: A Korean System of Slavery," in Gwyn Campbell (ed.), *Structure of Slavery in Indian Ocean Africa and Asia* (London, 2003).

For traditional servitude, see:

Anderson, Mary M., *Hidden Power: The Palace Eunuchs of Imperial China* (Buffalo, 1990).

Crossley, Pamela Kyle, *Orphan Warriors: Three Manchu Generations and the End of the Qing World* (Princeton, NJ, 1990).

Kutcher, Norma A., "Unspoken Collusions: The Empowerment of Yuanming Yuan Eunuchs in the Qianlong Period," *Harvard Journal of Asiatic Studies*, 70 (2010): 449–95.

Taisuke, Mitamura, *Chinese Eunuchs: The Structure of Intimate Politics*, trans. Charles A. Pomeroy (Tokyo, 1970).

For histories of women in various contexts of dependency, see:

Herhatter, Gail, *Women in China's Long Twentieth Century* (Berkeley, CA, 2007).

Sommer, Matthew H., *Sex, Law, and Society in Late Imperial China* (Stanford, CA, 2000).

Yeung, Sau-Chu Alison, "Fornication in the Late Qing Legal Reforms: Moral Teachings and Legal Principles," *Modern China*, 29 (2003): 297–328.

On the role of indenture, contract labor, and political violence in migration, see:

Irick, Robert L., *Ch'ing Policy toward the Coolie Trade: 1847–1878* (Taipei, 1982).

Patterson, Wayne, *The Korean Frontier in America: Immigration to Hawaii, 1896–1910* (Honolulu, 1988).

On the forced laborer's experiences, see:

Glick, Clarence, *Sojourners and Settlers: Chinese Migrants in Hawaii* (Honolulu, 1980).

Glosser, Susan L., *Chinese Visions of Family and State, 1915–1953* (Berkeley, CA, 2003).

Ling, Huping, *Chinese Chicago: Race, Transnational Migration, and Community Since 1870* (Stanford, CA, 2012).

Rojas, Carlos, *Homesickness: Culture, Contagion and National Transformation in Modern China* (Cambridge, MA, 2015).

Yun, Lisa, *The Coolie Speaks: Chinese Indentured Laborers and African Slaves in Cuba* (Philadelphia, PA, 2008).

CHAPTER 24

GENDER AND COERCED LABOR

PAMELA SCULLY AND KERRY WARD

INTRODUCTION

By highlighting gender, this chapter contributes further to our understanding of coerced labor from the beginning of the nineteenth century to the present. Gender and coerced labor provide a conceptual framework rather than being a synonym for adding women to existing topics. Following Joan Scott, we understand gender as an analytic category that helps historians make sense of how ideas and practices about masculinity and femininity shaped people's experiences and also helped construct broader patterns of labor, sociability, and politics. Laboring itself is a gendered experience and forms of forced labor have been also particularly gendered in ways that constrained the lives of men and women who experienced specific forms of coercion. This chapter therefore focuses on the way in which gender and the changing nature of masculinity and femininity shaped broad social patterns of coerced labor globally. We write with broad brushstrokes to outline both chronological trends and themes, as well as changes over time.

Struggles over the relationship between gendered individuals, their labor, and the claims of the state in particular were contemporary with the emergence of these forms of labor in the course of the nineteenth and early twentieth centuries. If we look at coercion as an analytical category, not only as the legal understanding of a form of labor, then it includes many different terms of labor including slavery, various forms of indenture, convict labor, waged labor, and forced sex work. This is why so many of the forms of coerced labor were open to accusations that they were a new form of slavery. An analysis of forced labor and gender in the nineteenth century thus has to take into account both formal slavery and emerging forms of indenture and other forced labor regimes that supplanted slavery.

Our initial impression of the existing literature on gender and coerced labor is that there is much room for more gendered historical research, as well as for synthesis. The last two decades have seen considerable research on gender as a category of analysis in slavery and emancipation, especially in the British Atlantic World, and the United States, on indentured servitude in the Caribbean, and on the gendering of waged industrial labor. There is also a rich scholarship on women's experience and the creation of gendered roles of femininity and masculinity in penal transportation and convict labor in colonial Australia. Paradoxically, women's and girls' experience of coerced sexual labor has come to focus on recent global campaigns against modern human trafficking. Analyses of other forms of coerced labor, particularly penal labor in colonial empires and modern states, have demonstrated acute awareness of race and ethnicity, but less so of gender. This chapter is therefore a preliminary attempt to pull together different themes through the analytical thread of gender, and to suggest areas and ideas which could be further explored.[1]

The ending of the transatlantic slave trade, and the ongoing practice of slavery in other parts of the world, involved contestations about the meanings of masculinity and femininity. We focus on changing legal statuses to define "forced labor" from the era of legal slavery, through the process of formal emancipation, and the emergence of illicit bondage and state-sanctioned forced labor. This includes the changing definitions of slavery from the mid nineteenth century to the present because the emergence of international laws prohibiting slavery became more inclusive of forms of forced labor other than chattel slavery. The only category of bonded labor to become universally illegal by the end of the twentieth century was slavery, but as Kevin Bales' chapter demonstrates, that did not end slavery as a practice.

SLAVE SYSTEMS AND COERCED LABOR IN THE LONG NINETEENTH CENTURY

As Gwyn Campbell and Alessandro Stanziani have detailed in their chapter for this volume, various forms of coerced labor in Africa, the Middle East, and India persisted during the nineteenth century, most especially the ubiquity of debt bondage. The Atlantic slave-trading economy took decades to end, and overlapped with moves toward formal emancipation across different parts of the world. For example, the Danes and the British abolished the trade first, but the Portuguese Atlantic slave trade continued to Brazil through to mid-century, with the source of slaves from Africa moving from West Africa to West-Central Africa and East Africa. Slave emancipation in the British Empire began in the 1830s, long before the

---

[1] For overviews, see Pamela Scully and Diana Paton (eds.), *Gender and Slave Emancipation in the Atlantic World* (Durham, NC, 2005); for Australia, Angela Woollacott, *Gender and Empire* (London, 2006), ch. 2; Anne Summers, *Damned Whores and God's Police: The Colonization of Women in Australia*, 3rd edn. (London, 2003); Monica Perrot, *"A Tolerable Good Success": Economic Opportunities for Women in New South Wales, 1788–1830* (Sydney, 1983); Annette Salt, *These Outcast Women: The Parramatta Female Factory, 1821–1848* (Sydney, 1984).

formal ending of slavery in Brazil in 1888, and, finally, in parts of West and Central Africa in the twentieth century. Slavery and coerced labor practices in Africa accompanied the expansion of European colonialism, together with the growth of plantation agriculture despite laws against colonial slavery. However, slave-trading patterns changed and were in some cases extended during the nineteenth century as commodity production for the world market stimulated the demand for coerced labor. The long-standing slave trade along the East African coast to the Middle East and South Asia was actively suppressed by the British Navy and its allies in the nineteenth century, along with the Atlantic slave trade. Indigenous systems of slavery in Africa, the Middle East, and Asia, however, continued well beyond the era of formal emancipation in India in 1843 and the criminalization of slave holding there in 1860.

The growth of Hong Kong and the Straits Settlements under British rule in the nineteenth century resulted in the expansion of an illicit slave trade in men for plantation labor and women largely for domestic service and prostitution. British colonial officials did little to intervene in this trade, particularly as Dutch colonial slavery was not abolished until 1860 in its Asian colonies and, as Eric Tagliacozzo has demonstrated, the borders between Asian states and European colonies were fluid and permeable, allowing for illicit slave trading. Indigenous forms of bondage were explicitly tolerated in European colonies well beyond formal emancipation, first because European colonial officials had difficulty determining whether or not forms of bondage and labor practices constituted slavery, and, second, because European rule was often partial, nominal, or non-existent in areas with active slave trading and slavery. Debt bondage and *corvée* labor was widespread in the region. In Southeast Asia, colonial slavery was generally abolished by the end of the nineteenth century, but European colonial powers were unable to suppress a widespread and active slave trade in the archipelagic regions. Slavery was not abolished in China until 1910. An extensive slave trade in men and women existed in Central Asia well into the twentieth century.

Simultaneously with the emergence of anti-slave trade laws in European empires, the long nineteenth century involved not only profound changes in the nature of labor itself – due to the gradual spread of industrialization and increased urbanization – but also the gendered nature of labor as state laws began to restrict or prohibit the use of child or female labor in specific industries. These processes coincided with changing gender roles whereby some work was feminized and other jobs were increasingly masculinized and reserved, sometimes by law, for men. Sanctions against child labor and the definition of childhood as a legal category that precluded some forms of paid labor gradually removed children from the regulated workforce. These labor laws coincided with the emergence of labor unions that themselves tended to be dominated by men and sought to exclude women from their ranks. Only during times of war with its conscription of men were women able to access factory and health-care employment, usually through voluntary recruitment via state agencies.

Men had long comprised two-thirds of those enslaved into the Atlantic slave trade, and this continued throughout the nineteenth century, with most slaves being shipped to plantation economies to meet the demand for agricultural labor. The perspectives of slave-holders, which associated outdoor labor with masculinity, helped shape this gender order. Given that many sub-Saharan African societies depended also on women's agricultural labor, historians have argued that the gendering of the Atlantic trade arose from both push and pull factors. Studies of plantation labor, however, show that many women were very much involved in such labor. In Jamaica, for example, by the 1820s, women often made up the majority of workers in labor gangs, with some men being involved in what was described as skilled labor. In tobacco regions in the US South, slave women worked alongside enslaved men, in addition to doing other work assigned by gender, such as cooking, weaving, and nursing.[2]

The slave trade to the Islamic world had long been different: with women and children in more demand, because of the prevalence of domestic slavery. However, in the nineteenth century, as maritime slave trading became illegal or more closely monitored, there was downward pressure on the age of slaves, with children comprising a greater proportion of slave cargoes than in previous centuries, particularly in the East African maritime slave trade.

James Warren has traced the expansion of the slave trade in the nineteenth century due to the growth of European and Chinese commerce. This occurred particularly in Borneo and the Southern Philippines regions where indigenous polities, especially in the Sulu Sultanate, continued raiding coastal and maritime local populations for slaves – men and boys for commercial maritime, agricultural, and other forms of labor, while women and girls bore the extra burden of domestic and sexual servitude, but with the potential for cultural and social integration through conversion to Islam. In the late nineteenth century, the practice of parents selling children in times of economic hardship was still widespread, though in East Asia girls were considered less valuable than boys and were therefore more likely to be sold away from the parental household and

---

[2] David Eltis and Stanley L. Engerman, "Fluctuations in Sex and Age Ratios in the Transatlantic Slave Trade, 1663–1864," *Economic History Review*, 46 (1993): 308–23; James A. Delle, "Women's Lives and Labour on Radnor, a Jamaican Coffee Plantation, 1822–1826," *Caribbean Quarterly*, 54 (2008): 7–23; Anthony Reid (ed.), *Slavery, Bondage and Dependency in Southeast Asia* (Saint Lucia, 1983).

re-incorporated into the domestic sphere as servants and/or concubines. Many were also placed into prostitution through this social practice. In Thailand, King Chulalongkorn (Rama V) instituted the gradual abolition of royal *corvée* and debt slavery, culminating in the Slave Abolition Act of 1905.

Women and children of both genders made up the majority of slaves traded in the Indian Ocean World. Though many were transferred across slave systems, the majority were held in forms of bondage in their own societies, where in many cases cultural prohibitions against selling them outside their own communities existed. These systems of unfree labor did not, for the most part, replicate the commodification of chattel slavery. Women slaves in Islamic societies who were the concubines of their masters theoretically had rights to receive support, manumission, and freedom for children born of sexual union. While European colonial slavery in the Indian Ocean region declined and was eventually abolished during the nineteenth century, the transfer of slaves from indigenous to colonial slavery had involved a change of their legal status into chattel slaves.[3]

The abolition of the British African slave trade in 1807 and then the legal abolition of slavery itself in 1834 inaugurated complex debates over the meanings of labor. The ending of the trade caused Britain to begin policing of other countries' slave ships and created a whole new category with the Orwellian name of liberated Africans. The fate of liberated Africans differed significantly according to where they were first liberated and where they were settled. While the majority who remained in Sierra Leone were not indentured, those taken elsewhere were more accurately called recaptives. Many liberated Africans were slave captives taken by the British Navy off the slave ships of those countries still engaging in the slave trade and deposited as bonded laborers on other parts of the African coast, as well as in the British Caribbean. This was an unusual intermediate category of labor specific to the Atlantic World and a small number of Indian Ocean colonies. With the exception of Sierra Leone, the British Navy did not return all captives to the areas where they had been forced on board ship. The Navy distributed between 150,000 and 200,000 liberated captives to colonies and settlements throughout the Atlantic World. The status of recaptives thus confuses the delineation of free and coerced labor and highlights the uneven histories of emancipation in the British Atlantic. In many respects, many recaptives endured a form of slavery, with no or

[3] Gwyn Campbell, Suzanne Miers, and Joseph C. Miller (eds.), *Children in Slavery through the Ages* (Athens, OH, 2009); James Warren, *The Sulu Zone, 1768–1898: The Dynamics of External Trade, Slavery, and Ethnicity in the Transformation of a Southeast Asian Maritime State*, 2nd edn. (Singapore, 2007).

little control over the destination to which they were sent, and very little autonomy once they arrived, at least in colonial settlements. The fate of the Saro (Afro-Brazilians) and the Congo who settled in Nigeria and Liberia, respectively, offers a more upwardly mobile trajectory. Captives were absorbed into local slave and emancipated societies in conditions of indentured servitude, as happened in the Cape Colony, Jamaica, Trinidad, and Guiana, absorbed into the ruling class, as in Liberia, and became important commercial leaders, as in Nigeria.

Examination of the African Origins database shows that about two-thirds of the recaptives were men. This makes sense given the general dominance of men enslaved into the trade. Of the 91,141 people identified in the database, some 29,635 were women. However, as Nwokeji and Eltis pointed out in their initial discussion of the records, some masculine names today seem to have been female names in the nineteenth century; and practices regarding daughters in some African communities meant that a younger daughter might have been given a male name. Thus, one has to proceed with caution.[4]

GENDER AND SLAVE EMANCIPATION: LIBERATING THE FAMILY?

Slave emancipation, as explained below, was an inherently gendered project, and thus a site of great contestation, involving ideas of labor, masculinity and femininity, class, and race. In the 1820s and 1830s, the British slowly moved toward ending slavery in the Cape Colony, Mauritius, and their Caribbean slave-holding colonies, through a series of amelioration proclamations, and finally the end of slavery with a four-year apprenticeship period from 1834 to 1838. As Pamela Scully has discussed in her book *Liberating the Family?*, tensions about working-class women's place in a wage labor economy shaped emancipation struggles. Abolitionists in England and the colonies had long imagined slave emancipation as a gendered project, which would liberate women into a patriarchal family, thus restoring the proper gender order and

---

[4] http://www.african-origins.org/. Daniel Domingues da Silva, David Eltis, Philip Misevich, and Olatunji Ojo, "The Diaspora of Africans Liberated from Slave Ships in the Nineteenth Century," *Journal of African History*, 55 (2014): 347–69; Lisa A. Lindsay, "'To Return to the Bosom of Their Fatherland': Brazilian Immigrants in Nineteenth-Century Lagos," *Slavery and Abolition*, 15 (1994): 22–50; William E. Allen, "Liberia and the Atlantic World in the Nineteenth Century: Convergence and Effects," *History in Africa*, 37 (2010): 7–49; G. Ugo Nwokeji and David Eltis, "The Roots of the African Diaspora: Methodological Considerations in the Analysis of Names in the Liberated African Registers of Sierra Leone and Havana," *History in Africa*, 29 (2002): 365–79, 375–6; Monica Schuler, "Liberated Central Africans in Nineteenth-Century Guyana," in Linda M. Heywood (ed.), *Central Africans and Cultural Transformations in the American Diaspora* (Cambridge, 2001), pp. 319–52; and the essays in Gwyn Campbell (ed.), *The Structure of Slavery in Indian Ocean Africa and Asia* (London, 2004).

sexual economy, both of which had been upended by slavery. One vision of forced labor after emancipation envisioned nuclear families, grounding the experiment with emotional bonds, which would take women out of the labor force. Formerly enslaved people also affirmed the importance of family to freedom, seeing emancipation as bringing freedom from forced labor, and particularly freedom for women to escape the bonds of harassment and sexual violence. Ideologies of gender, however, clashed with the pull of class: the emancipation of women's labor from the plantations was not what the former planter class desired: rather, they hoped that men would compel their wives to work for wages on plantations. As Thavolia Glymph has shown, gendered imaginings of former enslaved people and of missionaries conflicted with former planters' expectations of the exercise of formal as well as psychological power: the stage was thus set for struggle over the meaning of free labor and of gender.

The years of apprenticeship from 1834 to 1838 wrote ideas of femininity and masculinity into law: laws favored less harsh treatment of women, legislated against the sale of minor children from their mothers, and eventually recognized the family bond and slave marriages. Women in particular fled farm labor unless they and their family gained access to independent smallholdings. They sought autonomy from plantation labor by engaging in marketing or laundry and other work. During the period of apprenticeship, which was supposed to teach freed people to be good waged workers, it became clear that the formerly enslaved people wanted to move away from working on plantations, in whatever status, and move to independence.[5]

In the US South after the Civil War, similar gendered struggles over the meaning of freedom took place. Freedwomen and former slave-holding women battled to define the new relations of freedom and labor. Many freedwomen left the plantations. Those who stayed fought to organize labor in conditions of their choosing, including the time it took to do particular types of labor. With the ending of Reconstruction and the coming of Jim Crow in the late nineteenth century, however, life for the many African Americans living in the rural South became a struggle for survival caught, as Jacqueline Jones has stated, "in a cash-crop economy based upon a repressive labor system." In the South, cotton, produced now on smaller farms, some by sharecropping arrangements, still dominated the economy and in that setting both black and white tenants struggled to

[5] Pamela Scully, *Liberating the Family? Gender and British Slave Emancipation in the Rural Western Cape, South Africa, 1823–1853* (London, 1997); Bridget Brereton, "Family Strategies, Gender, and the Shift to Wage Labor in the British Caribbean," in Pamela Scully and Diana Paton (eds.), *Gender and Slave Emancipation in the Atlantic World* (Durham, NC, 2005), pp. 143–61.

maintain autonomy over the labor of family members. Working under conditions bordering on coercion, men, women, and children all worked, with women laboring in the fields as well as at home. The great migration of African Americans out of the rural South to the urban northeast, Midwest and west that fundamentally altered these gendered labor patterns did not begin until the early twentieth century.[6]

The end of slavery in Latin America took place in two phases, with first the suppression of maritime slave trading and slavery in several newly independent nations in the first half of the nineteenth century, and then with the long process of slave emancipation that accelerated in the second half. For example, during the 1830s and 1840s, over 760,000 African slaves were brought to Brazil in the illegal slave trade. Of these, around 11,000 had been found on board detained slave ships and though technically emancipated were forced to labor for either private employers or the state. Manumission and free womb laws often gave women opportunities to use their reproductive labor as a path to maximizing their own freedom or that of their children. The gendered division of labor on plantations, however, was not as distinct as within urban settings, where women dominated domestic work, marketing, and prostitution. Emancipation in many former Latin American colonies was tied into independence struggles, resulting in gendered citizenship rights that subordinated women's labor to male control within family structures.[7]

Across the world, slavery slowly gave way in the course of the nineteenth and early twentieth centuries to other forms of labor, often coerced and always gendered, with men making up the majority of coerced laborers in these settings. Imperial and colonial states helped shape these labor systems through the use of contract labor, including indentured servitude, penal transportation, convict labor, and forced recruitment of naval and military labor. These forms of forced labor existed simultaneously, but their particular forms and legal status differed over time and place. For people who experienced this form of labor, the boundaries between consensual contract and coercion were not always clear. Wage theft and breach of contract conditions amounting to forced labor were commonplace even if the indentures were limited in duration. The two major forms of forced labor that emerged comprised a reliance in the Americas on indentured labor regimes from India and China and the extension of convict transportation and penal slavery.

---

[6] Jacqueline Jones, *Labor of Love, Labor of Sorrow: Black Women, Work and the Family from Slavery to the Present* (New York, 1985), pp. 80–2; Thavolia Glymph, *Out of the House of Bondage: The Transformation of the Plantation Household* (Cambridge, 2003).

[7] Beatriz G. Mamigonian, "A Harsh and Gloomy Fate: Liberated Africans in the Service of the Brazilian State, 1830s–1860s," in Dawne Y. Curry, Eric D. Duke, and Marshanda A. Smith (eds.), *Extending the Diaspora: New Histories of Black People* (Champaign, IL, 2009); Pamela Scully and Diana Paton, "Introduction," in Scully and Paton (eds.), *Gender and Slave Emancipation*.

INDENTURED LABOR

As David Northrup has shown, the period from the early 1800s through the 1920s witnessed one of the largest forced movements of individuals the world has seen. Some 5.5 million individuals were sold from Africa to the Americas and Asia, while 2 million people became indentured laborers in places far afield from their natal homes. Both Europeans and peoples from Asia entered into indentured labor agreements, many of them by force. The initial term of these indentures was fixed in time. For many others from Africa and parts of Asia and the Pacific, indenture was often extended in time and turned into a form of lifelong bondage. Overall, it was a labor system that in practice maximized the vulnerability of laborers to coercion. Though there were more provisions made for Indian male indentured servants to be accompanied by their wives and children, indentured workers were overwhelmingly men who migrated without their families.

Well over 1 million Indian indentured laborers were transported across the globe before this form of migration was ended in 1917. French colonial officials began recruiting indentured Indian male laborers from Pondicherry for contracts on Réunion plantations in 1829 and for the French Caribbean colonies in the 1860s. After the legal emancipation of slaves in the British Empire in 1834, demands to extend the indenture system to former slave colonies increased, and by 1838, 25,000 indentured laborers had been sent to Mauritius. Clare Anderson reports that of the 15,000 laborers from India, only 1 to 2 percent were women. Only in mid-century, as a result of legislation, did women make up at least 40 percent of the indentured laborers. Abuses of the system and accusations of its similarity to slavery caused the British Government to briefly ban indenture between 1839 and 1842. But pressure from colonial employers resulted in the reopening of the trade in indentured servants to Mauritius and their extension to the Caribbean from the mid-1840s and to Natal from 1860. British Government reforms in the indentured contract system included stipulations designed to address the gender imbalance of indentured servants by demanding that one-quarter or more of indentures had to be assigned to women. In Hawaii, 93 percent of contract laborers were men, though Hawaiian planters encouraged them to bring their wives and children with them.[8]

Gender helped define the emerging unfree labor systems across the British Empire. Caribbean planters might have relied on women's agricultural work, but they still saw men as the primary labor force in agriculture. Thus, when the plans to bring indentured workers from India were first

---

[8] David Northrup, *Indentured Labor in the Age of Imperialism, 1834–1922* (Cambridge, 1995); Clare Anderson, "Unfree Labour and Its Discontents: Transportation from Mauritius to Australia, 1825–1845," *Australian Studies*, 13 (1999): 116–33, 120.

discussed, planters did little to recruit women. In fact, they were actively hostile. In addition, there was no initial intention of allowing Indian laborers to stay permanently, and the presence of Indian women was seen as dissuading men from returning to their home country. As Madhavi Kale has shown, however, the Indian Government insisted that women be allowed to go and made this a condition of allowing the indenture system. As a result, both men and women came as indentured laborers, though women constituted only between a fifth and a quarter of individuals recruited into the system.[9] A small proportion of women were recruited as domestic workers with indentured contracts.

The massive global transfer of labor from tropical Africa, South and East Asia, and the Pacific Islands to the Americas, Caribbean, Pacific Islands, South Africa, and Australia was deeply gendered, with men being the primary labor recruited for overseas work contracts. The building of the post-emancipation world was also gendered. As had been the case under slave systems, ideas about male and female roles and capacities informed the ways in which participants crafted emerging forced labor regimes. For example, when William Gladstone initially proposed the indenture scheme to make up for the flight of freed people anticipated (and realized) on emancipation, he advocated bringing both men and women as laborers from India. He did propose to pay women less, in accordance with the perspective that women's labor was not as valuable.

To discipline workers after the ending of slavery, the British invoked the metropolitan Master and Servant Laws. Premised on the notion of contract, these laws focused on the relations between employer and worker. As Douglas Hay and Paul Craven have pointed out, master and servant law can be seen as a form of imperial statute law, focused on judicial enforcement and punishment, including flogging. For workers caught up in the workings of master and servant legislation, the theory of free labor often turned into an experience of forced labor. In Guiana and Trinidad, indentured laborers from India were subjected to this legislation, and experienced "stunningly high rates of penal enforcement."[10] In the Caribbean and South Africa, the enactment of master and servant legislation targeted former enslaved people to minimize alternative opportunities for men and women in the workforce and to compel women to remain in domestic service. Chinese workers in Hawaii, brought under contract, were subject to the Master and Servant Act of 1850.

[9] Madhavi Kale, "Projecting Identities: Empire and Indentured Labor Migration from India to Trinidad and British Guiana, 1836–1885," in Peter van der Veer (ed.), *Nation and Migration: The Politics of Space in the South Asian Diaspora* (Philadelphia, PA, 1995), pp. 73–91.

[10] Douglas Hay and Paul Craven (eds.), *Masters, Servants, and Magistrates in Britain and the Empire, 1562–1955* (Chapel Hill, NC, 2004), p. 4.

An illicit slave trade in men developed in the late nineteenth century in the Pacific Ocean, mainly from the Melanesian archipelagos to Australia and from the Polynesian Islands to Peru. Because of the small populations of many of these island groups, some communities suffered devastating population losses. One pattern involved the kidnapping or coercion of male Pacific Islanders who were shipped to the Australian colony of Queensland to work on sugar plantations and farms in northern New South Wales. While many Pacific Islanders were induced to sign three-year indentured labor contracts to work in Australia, these contracts were often not honored and the Pacific Islanders were not paid their wages. The forced and fraudulent recruitment of Pacific Island laborers was commonly referred to as "blackbirding" and invoked contemporary accusations of slave trading, inducing the British government to introduce the Pacific Islanders Protection Act in 1872. This did not halt the practice. Immediately after Australian Federation in 1901, the government passed the Pacific Island Labourers Bill as part of the implementation of the White Australia Policy, resulting in the systematic forced deportation of Pacific Islanders from Australia during the first decade of the twentieth century.[11]

PENAL LABOR

Penal transportation and convict labor were other forms of coerced labor that expanded during the nineteenth century. British colonies in Australia founded on penal transportation and convict labor initially had profound gender imbalances, with men outnumbering women by over four to one in the nineteenth century. This gender imbalance created conditions for both sexual exploitation and social mobility for convict women, whose sexual and domestic labor was at a premium because of their scarcity. Penal labor often overlapped with other categories of coercion and punishment. In every case, penal labor was fundamentally gendered. Men were subject to this form of punishment far more often than women.

Clare Anderson has argued that in many colonies convict labor was tied into and overlapped with not only the end of slavery, but also with systems of indentured servitude. In the case of colonial Mauritius, French plantation owners sought new sources of cheap labor after the abolition of the slave trade. British colonial officials wanted to remove criminals and political prisoners from its areas of control in India, resulting in the penal transportation of male prisoners from India to Mauritius for labor on private plantation and public works. The beginning of the indentured

[11] See the essays in Brij V. Lal and Kate Fortune (eds.), *The Pacific Islands: An Encyclopedia* (Honolulu, HI, 2000); and Donald Denoon and Malama Meleisea (eds.), *The Cambridge History of the Pacific Islands* (Cambridge, 1997).

servitude system lessened the pressure on colonial labor markets in places like Mauritius and the Caribbean and therefore made convict labor less desirable for the British colonial government, given the added costs of transportation and surveillance. Penal transportation from India was extended to other British Indian Ocean colonies as male prisoners were sent to labor, particularly on public works, in the Andaman Islands and in the Straits Settlements. The phasing out of the use of penal transportation of men and women as a strategy to bolster European populations in overseas colonies of the Portuguese Empire from the mid eighteenth century did not entirely end the system. Though the use of internal exile and the evolution of modern prisons in Portugal increased during the nineteenth century, convicts were still sent to forced labor in Brazil until that country's independence in 1822, and for the years from 1822 to 1932 to Angola, and, in the French case, to French Guiana (Cayenne) until 1939. Timothy Coates demonstrates that internal mechanisms for penal transportation between colonies persisted, with convicts being sent to Angola or convicts from Angola being sent to Mozambique. The abolition of slavery in Latin American countries also generated an increase in forms of coercive labor practices aimed at economically marginal people, including the use of male penal labor, forced impressment for men, and forced domestic servitude for women and children.[12]

Coerced military labor and particularly palace servitude performed by men in China and to a lesser extent Korea was, until the late nineteenth century, sometimes accompanied by castration, which was also a punishment for criminals and rebels, who then became bonded laborers. Eunuchs were a small minority of the officials in some palace cultures, a practice that faded out during the nineteenth century in the Ottoman Empire, Kongbaung Burma, and Nguyen Vietnam. However, military impressment and penal servitude were not accompanied by castration in most other societies.[13]

Spurred on by urbanization and industrialization in the nineteenth century, vagrancy laws instituted by many European states provided legal mechanisms to incarcerate the poor and compel them to labor for the state,

---

[12] Clare Anderson, *Convicts in the Indian Ocean: Transportation from South Asia to Mauritius, 1815–1853* (London, 2000); Elizabeth Anne Kuznesof, "Domestic Service and Urbanization in Latin America from the Nineteenth Century to the Present," in Dirk Hoerder and Amarjit Kaur (eds.), *Proletarian and Gendered Mass Migration: A Global Perspective on Continuities and Discontinuities from the 19th to the 21st Centuries* (Leiden, 2013).

[13] See Crossley, "Dependency and Coercion in East Asian Labor, 1800–1949," in this volume. The castration of boys with exceptional singing voices, for performance in commercial opera or in the Vatican choirs of the Catholic Church, became increasingly rare in the nineteenth century. Though not widespread, this European cultural practice constituted a form of coerced labor, as young boy singers who were castrated to preserve their pre-adolescent voices did not choose their fate as feminized castrati. Naomi Adele Andre, *Voicing Gender: Castrati, Travesti, and the Second Woman in Early Nineteenth Century Italian Opera* (Bloomington, IN, 2006).

subjecting them to convict labor or penal transportation, and also provided the legal means to impress young men into military service. England, France, Spain, and Portugal had used vagrancy laws during the early modern period for penal transportation to the colonies, particularly in the Americas and the Caribbean and, in the Portuguese case, to their colonies on the west coast of India, Goa, Amazonia, and Africa. During the nineteenth and twentieth centuries, colonial vagrancy laws as well as other punitive laws aimed at indigenous populations in European colonies were explicitly designed to compel people into the wage labor market, but in many cases they were used as unpaid penal labor. Vagrancy and labor contract laws criminalized workers who sought to maximize their mobility, thereby forcing them to submit to employers and to the state. For example, the Vagrancy Act and Master and Servant statutes passed in South Africa during the second half of the nineteenth century criminalized both lack of employment and breach of contract by individual workers.

Vagrancy laws hinged on a particular conception of masculinity: that adult men had to have jobs: to be otherwise was not to fully embrace proper manhood. In Europe and the United States, many of these young men were demobilized soldiers and displaced workers who lost their jobs in the periodic economic downturns of the late nineteenth and early twentieth centuries. Women were a tiny minority of this large itinerant workforce, and tended to be incarcerated locally and channeled into charity organizations that compelled them to work as a means of their "redemption." After the American Civil War, vagrancy laws were used in a racialized pattern whereby young, single white male vagrants categorized as "tramps" were incarcerated during the "off season" for casual employment across the whole country. By far the most systematic use of vagrancy laws in the United States to create a bonded labor force during the nineteenth century took place in the aftermath of the Civil War, with the Black Codes. The withdrawal by African Americans of their labor from white Southern employers, often former slave-owners, resulted in the imposition of annual labor contracts to avoid vagrancy charges, a system which lasted until the 1940s. As a result of the Black Codes, the later emergence of convict-leasing in the Southern states was specifically aimed at generating African American male prisoners for hiring out as cheap manual laborers to private employers and generating a profit for state legislatures. The system lasted well into the twentieth century in some states and resulted in the massive increase in African American male incarceration rates.[14]

[14] Timothy Coates, *Convicts and Orphans: Forced and State-Sponsored Colonizers in the Portuguese Empire, 1550–1755* (Stanford, CA, 2001); A. L. Beier and Paul Ocobock (eds.), *Cast Out: Vagrancy and Homelessness in Global Historical Perspective* (Columbus, OH, 2009).

The global context of convict labor and penal transportation predominantly involved men; women were always in the minority. While impressment of men into British naval service had largely faded by the end of the Napoleonic Wars, it had been one of the causes of the War of 1812 and it was still legal for much of the century. It could be argued that many young, male, liberated Africans were pressed into military service, for example, in the Royal Africa Corps and the West India Regiment, as well as on British naval vessels. In Australia, as in other convict transportation networks, the prisoners who were moved were overwhelmingly male. The disproportionate sex ratio means that social mobility in Australia among the white community was gendered. The shortage of white women created opportunities for social mobility for women through marriage: marriage with aboriginal women was also socially sanctioned in colonial society. Because the Australian colonies were reserved for white (male) labor in contrast to so many other countries, men were able to move out of the penal or coerced state into citizenship.

In the twentieth century, state-sanctioned forms of gendered forced labor have been especially apparent in the use of convict labor and military conscription – both of which targeted men. One of the significant changes in the second half of the twentieth century was the neutralization of gender as a basis of military conscription in many states that have laws on gender equality and use of conscription as a form of civil service for youths. Men overwhelmingly dominate systems of conscription for active military duty, whether by the state or by non-state militias. Women have been coerced or kidnapped into sexual servitude by military forces in some cases of civil war, as well as by non-state militias in conflict zones.

GENDER AND FORCED LABOR UNDER COLONIALISM

The twentieth century brought new forms of coercion – political, economic, and social – and in some places the continuation of slavery, if sometimes under a different name. Suzanne Miers has documented the continuance of slavery, and debates its continuance in the twentieth century. As she notes, chattel slavery still existed across the world at the dawn of the twentieth century, but by the start of the First World War, had by and large been legally ended. The colonial solution was to allow enslaved people to free themselves. "Many slaves did leave, but probably the greater number stayed where they were, but over time renegotiated their terms of service."[15] In the twentieth century, we see echoes of the

---

[15] Suzanne Miers, *Slavery in the Twentieth Century: The Evolution of a Global Problem* (Lanham, MD, 2003), p. 445.

negotiations that people had undertaken during the period of apprentice-ship in the 1830s.

For much of Africa, the late nineteenth century saw the launch of colonialism. Various European powers consolidated their claims to terri-tories across the continent increasingly coveted as wellsprings of natural resources and potential markets for industrializing nations. Given what we know of the fate of free labor after the ending of slavery, it is not surprising that the colonial era, which lasted up until the 1960s, both entrenched earlier patterns of unfree labor and created new ones. And also, as before, ideas about gender, labor, and family influenced the ways in which individuals experienced coercion.

The historiography of French West Africa has pioneered in the study of gender and forced labor. The colonial era saw a rise in coerced labor with particular gendered dimensions. The French state forcibly recruited men to work for the colonial project through a whole host of different forms of coerced labor, or *corvée*. This included requisition, which forced men to work on particular projects; forced labor for the colonial state, often coordinated through chiefs; and the "deuxième portion du contingent" which was a form of military service in which men could be made to labor in areas of the economy outside military service and penal labor. Men were targeted as laborers in such labor schemes, which included working as porters and laborers on railway construction, as well as on colonial build-ings, repairs of infrastructure, and on rice and cotton plantations. The French also solved their difficulty in accessing labor for the colonial project by creating so-called free villages, similar to the earlier British policy of resettling recaptives in places that would benefit colonial regimes. For example, as Babacar Fall has shown in French Sudan, the authorities settled some 17,600 liberated captives in ninety-eight villages along the path of the railway to provide labor as needed.[16]

Women also were caught up in the coercive labor regimes of the state and in contests between different big men. Colonial officials sought to "free" women into the labor market. African elders sought to control women's labor for their own ends. For many women, the contestation occurred around marriage and its connection to forms of labor obligation. Thus, in West Africa, debates about marriage were often debates over labor and, particularly, access to female labor. Women either owed their labor to their natal family or to that of their husband. When women used newly established native courts to try to advocate for their independence, this

[16] Alice L. Conklin, "Colonialism and Human Rights, A Contradiction in Terms? The Case of France and West Africa, 1895–1914," *American Historical Review*, 103 (1998): 419–42; Babacar Fall, "Social History in French West Africa: Forced Labor, Labor Market, Women and Politics," South-South Exchange Programme for Research on the History of Development (SEPHIS, 2002), p. 7.

threatened claims to their labor. By 1914, women seeking divorce were increasingly being forced to return to their husbands and thus to particular labor relationships.[17]

In South Africa, the fundamentally coercive nature of state laws regarding African labor from the colonial era through segregation and apartheid makes for uneasy distinction between free and forced labor. From the late nineteenth century, well before the rise of apartheid with its legal forms of coercion, chiefs worked with employment bureaus to supply men's labor to the mines. In the course of the twentieth century, in many rural communities, migration to the mines for long periods of work became part of what it meant to be a man. Mining labor, which if not exactly coerced, can be understood as operating in a coercive environment. It came to inform male dress codes, dancing forms, and politics, as well as new sexual identities. From the 1950s, pass-laws reinforced existing gendered patterns of coercion: women were forced into ill-paying work as domestics in rural as well as urban areas, while men primarily were employed in industry. Apartheid's separate development policies in the 1960s created conditions of structural violence which make it difficult to see any labor as free. Men and, increasingly, women were forced into labor because of the threat of starvation in the increasingly impoverished homelands.[18]

FORCED SEX WORK AND SEXUAL SLAVERY

Various slave systems made rape and other forms of sexual violence integral to the maintenance of slave-holder authority, and were a means of making the slave population self-reproducing. As Donna Guy has pointed out, sex work has rarely been studied as part of labor history, much less as part of the history of coerced labor, outside formal slave systems.[19] Women continued to be coerced into forms of sex work. These forms of sex work included forced prostitution, the rise of sexual slavery linked to patterns of

---

[17] Martin Klein and Richard Roberts, "Gender and Emancipation in French West Africa," in Scully and Paton (eds.), *Gender and Slave Emancipation in the Atlantic World*, pp. 162–80; Emily S. Burrill, "'Wives of Circumstance': Gender and Slave Emancipation in Late Nineteenth-Century Senegal," *Slavery and Abolition*, 29 (2008): 49–64.

[18] Isak Niehaus, "Renegotiating Masculinity in the South African Lowveld: Narratives of Male-Male Sex in Labour Compounds and in Prisons," *African Studies*, 61 (2002): 77–97. On masculinity in South Africa, see Robert Morrell, "Of Boys and Men: Masculinity and Gender in Southern African Studies," *Journal of Southern African Studies*, 24 (1998): 605–30.

[19] Darlene Clark Hine, "Rape and the Inner Lives of Black Women in the Middle West," *Signs*, 14 (4) (1989): 912–20; Pamela Scully, "Rape, Race, and Colonial Culture: The Sexual Politics of Identity in the Nineteenth-Century Cape Colony, South Africa," *American Historical Review*, 100 (1995): 335–59.

migration, and, in the twentieth century, the emergence of sexual slavery as part of military regimes in Germany and the Japanese Empire.

Prostitution was integrally tied to the gendering of other patterns of forced labor and immigration in the nineteenth century. For example, in California, out of the 100,000 Chinese immigrants, only some 8,848 were women, though this was not peculiar to forced migration in general. This gender imbalance was common for frontier populations. By 1854, gangs, or tongs, had established control of the trade in women, bringing young women from China to work in brothels. The traditional *mui tsai* system of selling poor young Chinese girls for domestic service left these children vulnerable to sexual abuse and forced prostitution. Recruitment ran the gamut from outright sale into slavery to promises of employment contracts. Teresa Arnott and Julie A. Matthaei show that in 1870, most Chinese women in San Francisco worked as prostitutes in "slave or semi-slave conditions." Abolitionists in the late nineteenth century began to equate the *mui tsai* system with slavery, particularly in British colonies in Asia, as young girls were being exploited in the huge sex trade that flourished in the region alongside the growth of the entrepôts like Singapore and Hong Kong. British colonial officials claimed that this form of female domestic servitude fell under customary law and they did not intervene systematically, especially because prostitution was considered a necessary and natural aspect of gender relations. The British abolished the system in Hong Kong in 1929 – after the 1926 International Slavery Convention was instituted under the auspices of the League of Nations.[20]

In the twentieth century, war provided a basis for the expansion of coerced sex work. As emerging research is showing, the SS forced women in concentration camps into prostitution, a clear form of sexual slavery. Before and during the Second World War, the Japanese instituted a vast system of sexual slavery as part of a military regime throughout their empire. Sex slaves, known by the Japanese under the euphemism "comfort women," were moved throughout the Pacific region to cater to soldiers. About 80 percent of the women enslaved were from Korea, but females from occupied regions such as Burma, Indonesia, and the Pacific Islands were also forced into prostitution.

Some 200,000 women were sold into slavery in the Japanese Pacific theater of war under pretenses of finding work that would help their families; others were simply kidnapped. The low status of women appears to have set the context for young women originally trying to seek employment. But they did not sign up for slavery. Conditions were appalling for women, more akin to gang rape than anything that could be called sex

---

[20] Teresa Amott and Julie A. Matthaei, *Race, Gender, and Work: A Multicultural Economic History of Women in the United States* (Boston, MA, 1991).

work. In 1996, the United Nations' special rapporteur on sexual violence called the system "sexual slavery," while the author of the UN Report on Wartime Slavery called the comfort women system a series of "rape centers."[21]

HUMAN TRAFFICKING

The scrutiny of the *mui tsai* system in the late nineteenth century coincided with the emergence of a much larger global campaign around "white slavery." This campaign was framed as a moral panic about the vulnerability of young white women migrating for economic purposes and entering into the urban workforce, then being "lured" into prostitution. The white slavery issue intersected with feminist debates about female sexuality generally, women's choice in terms of sex work, and the state regulation of prostitution. The public campaigns painted lurid stories of white women being kidnapped and tricked into prostitution by pimps who shipped them across the globe.

The campaign was deeply gendered and racialized, with the only "victims" being white women, and the specter of black and Asian men buying sex from white prostitutes fueled the moral outrage. Legislation aimed at surveillance and the restriction of such forms of prostitution was passed in Britain in the late nineteenth century and in the United States under the Mann Act of 1910. International conferences on white slavery were organized in Europe from the 1880s onward, culminating in the 1904 International Agreement for the Suppression of "White Slave Traffic," the 1910 International Convention for the Suppression of the White Slave Traffic, and the 1921 International Convention for the Suppression of the Traffic in Women and Children, under the auspices of the League of Nations. The latter convention, while incorporating the rhetoric of white slavery as the forced prostitution of white women, also focused on the trafficking of children of both genders.[22]

International conventions for the suppression of slavery have been passed regularly during the twentieth century, first under the League of Nations and subsequently by the United Nations under the 1956 Supplementary Convention on the Abolition of Slavery and the 2000 Protocol to Prevent, Suppress and Punish Trafficking in Persons, Especially Women and Children (under the Palermo Protocols). However, "human

---

[21] Sonja Hedgepeth, *Sexual Violence against Jewish Women during the Holocaust* (Philadelphia, PA, 2010); Sarah Soh Chunghee, *The Comfort Women: Sexual Violence and Postcolonial Memory in Korea and Japan* (Chicago, IL, 2008).
[22] Stephanie Limoncelli, *The Politics of Trafficking: The First International Movement to Combat the Sexual Exploitation of Women* (Stanford, CA, 2011).

trafficking" as an international discourse only emerged around the 1990s and the growth of campaigns against human trafficking in many cases mirrors the discourses of the moral panic that attended the white slavery campaigns of the late nineteenth century. The focus on trafficking in young girls is particularly apparent in the United States, where legislation has conflated underage prostitution (of both genders) with sex trafficking. International and local awareness of other forms of gendered coercion have also come into focus under the contemporary rubric of "human trafficking" and "modern slavery" as legislation against some forms of formerly legal coerced labor that have been examined in this chapter have been reclassified as slavery.

CONCLUSION

As we have seen, gendered forms of bonded and forced labor were, and are, ubiquitous throughout the nineteenth and twentieth centuries. We have witnessed changes in the legal status of bondage from slavery as a legal labor regime to an illegal practice. However, slavery continued in various forms throughout the twentieth century. The Slavery Convention of 1926, and the Forced Labor Convention of 1930, sought to clarify policy on coerced labor. The complicity of multinationals, such as Firestone in Liberia, in using forced labor helped to create some of the context for international focus. And as Kevin Bales has shown, in the twenty-first century, tens of millions of people experience conditions of labor that are clearly coerced. The gendered implications of the debates on coercive practices are still unclear, though media attention focuses largely on the exploitation of children, especially girls in sexual bondage. In 2011, about 70 percent of human trafficking victims were women and girls.[23]

The shift in the scale of global migrations from enslaved to overwhelmingly free has changed the debate about gender and forced labor. Forced global migrations have been proportionally smaller, but have had significant impacts on the destination regions, as we have seen with regard to indenture in the Caribbean, and the nature of penal settlement in Australia and the United States. War and sexual slavery have been an important part of women's experience of forced labor in the twentieth century. There is also much to say about the voluntary global migration of working-class women from South and Southeast Asia to the Middle East and elsewhere, into conditions that for many are very much coerced. As Kamala Kempadoo remarked, "A 1996 ILO report describes the 'feminization' of

---

[23] Bales quoted in Miers, *Slavery in the Twentieth Century*, p. 445; UNODC, "Percentage of Trafficking Victims Worldwide in 2011, by Gender and Age," www.statista.com/statistics/300796/percentage-of-trafficking-victims-worldwide-by-gender-and-age/ (accessed December 2, 2015).

international labor migration as 'one of the most striking economic and social phenomena of recent times.'"[24]

Gender and coercion have come full circle from the beginning of the nineteenth century – with the first abolition movement, to the beginning of the twenty-first century – with a new abolition movement. The terms of how we identify coercion have changed: the discussions over the title of the United Nations Working Group on Slavery (formed in 1975) in the late twentieth century show some of the parameters of this discussion. In 1987, the name was changed to "The Working Group on Contemporary Forms of Slavery," which spoke to the breadth of coercion considered under its purview, including debt bondage and the sale of children. This group has now been replaced by a Special Rapporteur on Contemporary forms of slavery, concerned particularly with causes and consequences. The group defines its mandate as:

debt bondage, serfdom, forced labour, child slavery, sexual slavery, forced or early marriages and the sale of wives. As a legally permitted labour system, traditional slavery has been abolished everywhere, but it has not been completely stamped out. There are still reports of slave markets. Even when abolished, slavery leaves traces. It can persist as a state of mind – among victims and their descendants and among the inheritors of those who practiced it – long after it has formally ended.[25]

The degree to which the forms of coercion explicitly involve girls, and women's status in relation to men is striking. Gender has remained at the heart of our practices and understandings of coerced labor.

A GUIDE TO FURTHER READING

Anderson, Clare, *Convicts in the Indian Ocean: Transportation from South Asia to Mauritius, 1815–1853* (London, 2000).

Chunghee, Sarah Soh, "From Imperial Gifts to Sex Slaves: Theorizing Symbolic Representations of the 'Comfort Women,'" *Social Science Japan Journal*, 3 (2000): 59–76.

Coates, Timothy, *Convict Labor in the Portuguese Empire, 1740–1932: Redefining the Empire with Forced Labor and New Imperialism* (Leiden, 2014).

Miers, Suzanne, *Slavery in the Twentieth Century: The Evolution of a Global Problem* (London, 2003).

Northrup, David, *Indentured Labor in the Age of Imperialism, 1834–1922* (Cambridge, 1995).

---

[24] Kamala Kempadoo, "Globalizing Sex Workers' Rights," *Canadian Woman Studies*, 22 (2003): 143–50.

[25] www.ohchr.org/EN/Issues/Slavery/SRSlavery/Pages/SRSlaveryIndex.aspx (accessed December 2, 2015).

Scott, Joan W., "Gender: A Useful Category of Historical Analysis," *American Historical Review*, 91 (1986): 1053–75.

Scully, Pamela, *Liberating the Family? Gender and British Slave Emancipation in the Rural Western Cape, South Africa, 1823–1853* (London, 1997).

Scully, Pamela and Diana Paton (eds.), *Gender and Slave Emancipation in the Atlantic World* (Durham, NC, 2005).

Tagliacozzo, Eric, *Secret Trades, Porous Borders: Smuggling and States Along a Southeast Asian Frontier, 1865–1915* (New Haven, CT, 2006).

Woollacott, Angela, *Gender and Empire* (London, 2006).

CHAPTER 25

COERCED LABOR IN TWENTIETH-CENTURY AFRICA

RICHARD ROBERTS

Labor coercion has been a central feature of social and economic life in Africa in the twentieth century. Such coercion has taken many forms, with changes over time. Varieties of labor coercion reflected imperfections in the African labor market, the place of Africa in the evolving global market for commodities and raw materials, the varieties of colonial and post-colonial states, rebel movements in the late twentieth century, and the re-articulation of cultural norms regarding gender and generation in mobilizing domestic labor. The persistence of coerced labor in Africa reflects the complex ways in which colonialism and global capitalism interacted with ongoing changes in Africa, yielding a mosaic of different labor regimes. Coerced labor, paying meager wages, and applying non-market forms of compulsion offered employers short-term economic benefits, but contributed little to the growth of consumption in Africa, thus limiting the development of market forces. The end of slavery, which took place under pressure from deeply ambivalent colonial states, contributed to new forms of mobilizing labor, including trafficking in people that continued throughout the twentieth century and persists to this day. Increasingly from the interwar period, international institutions and non-government organizations put pressure on colonial and post-colonial states to reduce their complicity in coerced labor.

Colonial officials, European and African capitalists, African chiefs, rebel leaders, and household heads all drew on various forms of coerced labor to yield profits, expand production, build infrastructure, staff armies and support services, perform domestic chores, and enhance patriarchy. To capture the range of coerced activities, this chapter draws on two different historiographical traditions: (1) the robust literature on the "end" of slavery, as well as the varieties of post-emancipation adaptations, which includes studies on trafficking, pawning, apprenticeship, and forced marriages; and (2) the rich literature on state-sponsored forced labor, which is distinguished by the direct role of the state in mobilizing coerced labor. During the post-colonial period, coerced labor was a prominent feature of many state-sponsored development schemes and many rebel movements.

This chapter begins with a survey of the imperfections in labor markets and examines the range of state-sponsored coerced labor in colonial Africa. The colonial state used a range of compulsions to recruit labor for specific purposes or economic sectors, which had significant gendered characteristics. The chapter explores the role of forced marriages in mobilizing coerced labor for household economies. It then examines the rise of a new humanitarian sensibility in the interwar period and the role of new international organizations, such as the League of Nations and International Labour Organization, which put periodic pressure on colonial states regarding their role in mobilizing forced labor and complicity in what was officially called "practices analogous to slavery." Decolonization accelerated the end of colonial era coerced labor, but introduced newer forms including those linked to post-colonial development projects. During the last quarter of the twentieth century, rebel movements intensified their use of coerced labor, including sexual slavery.

COLONIALISM AND COERCED LABOR

When the active phase of the Scramble for Africa ended in the late nineteenth century, nearly all sub-Saharan Africans were engaged in agricultural, pastoral, fishing, and hunting pursuits. Most of these pursuits were seasonal and provided significant opportunities for diverse commercial, artisanal, mining, and small-scale manufacturing work that fed regional and long-distance trade in Africa and overseas. There were scattered pockets of dense urban, political, and religious agglomerations that supported full-time military, bureaucratic, religious, commercial, and mining specialists. With its much longer history of colonization, South Africa had already developed centers of mining and urban development. Elsewhere, nascent colonial states established burgeoning central places of bureaucracies, harbors, commerce, and communication. In general, these urban pockets swelled seasonally as rural workers streamed in to add labor to infrastructural projects only to dwindle again when the planting, herding, or fishing demands resumed.

Precisely because most Africans could secure at least a part of their livelihoods from rural activities, those seeking African labor had to provide incentives to induce Africans to leave their farms, herds, or artisanal activities. Even those Africans who migrated to the expanding urban areas to take jobs during the interwar years with the expanding colonial bureaucracies and those whose jobs in mining areas were "stabilized" by long-term employment and family housing very often invested resources in rural homelands in order to retain ties to kin and rural resources. Employers seeking African labor turned to many different strategies to induce Africans to sell their labor. These different strategies changed over time in response to world markets for African commodities, but also in terms of how different colonies were integrated into both world markets and imperial economies.

In the 1970s, Samir Amin proposed an influential typology of the modes of colonial Africa's integration into imperial economies.[1] Framed within the broad reductionism of underdevelopment theory, Amin provided a schematic historical view of three generalized modes of Africa's divergent forms of integration into the world and imperial economies: (1) Africa of the colonial economies, which were characterized by African peasants producing agricultural commodities that were funneled through European merchant houses; (2) Africa of the concession-owning companies in which the colonial state ceded vast tracts of land (and the Africans living on them) to private companies in exchange for rents; and (3) Africa of the labor reserves in which colonial policy "enclosed" on "reservations" entire ethnic groups, thus providing a reserve army of short-term male labor. Despite different imperial policies, all colonies falling within these broad modes shared common core economic and labor policies. We might want to consider these modes as zones because they also applied to different regions of Africa. The Africa of the colonial economies was the peasant regions of coastal and close hinterland West Africa and some regions in East and Central Africa that promoted African peasant production. Even the emergence of capital-intensive mining in Kimberley in South Africa in the 1870s, which would fit Amin's labor reserve mode, stimulated the rise of the South African peasantry, whose increased production fed the expanding urban markets for food only to be crushed by pressure from both mining capital and settler farming interests to secure cheap African labor.

In his discussion of the Africa of labor reserves, Amin established the framework for two further modes of integration that he did not identify as such: the Africa of the mining regions and the Africa of settler economies. The Africa of the mining regions, principally South Africa and the copper belt in Katanga and Northern Rhodesia, was directly linked to labor reserves precisely because of mining capital's interest in securing cheap, unskilled African labor on temporary contracts. The Africa of settler economies was also linked to African labor reserves because settler agriculture depended upon eliminating African peasant competition for export markets and in obtaining cheap agricultural labor. Settlers were prominent in South Africa, Kenya, Southern Rhodesia, Angola, and Southwest Africa. During different periods, pockets of settlers exerted significant influence in Tanganyika, Northern Rhodesia, Nyasaland, Mozambique, Belgian

[1] Samir Amin, "Underdevelopment and Dependence in Black Africa-Origins and Contemporary Forms," *Journal of Modern African Studies*, 10 (1972): 503–24.

Congo, Italian Somaliland, Madagascar, Mauritius, and Cameroon. Similarly, there were vast areas of the West African interior that served as labor reserves for African smallholders near the coasts who were expanding production for export. These "modes" were ideal types that were rarely identifiable as such in real historical cases. Moreover, multiple modes could coexist within zones, so that African peasant production coincided with labor reserves. Concession zones had vast areas where African peasants continued to produce for regional markets and they often sold their labor to mining enterprises on short-term contracts. Qualifying Amin, Frederick Cooper argued that nineteenth-century colonization should be seen as a period of deglobalization through which areas formerly integrated into world or regional economies were progressively integrated into narrower imperial economies.[2]

We can also identify four general patterns that shaped colonial labor policies. First, colonial states were under enormous pressure to yield benefits for the mother country and to reduce operating costs as much as possible by generating revenue through taxing imports and exports and by imposing personal income or head taxes on Africans. Second, employers of labor and buyers of African produce wanted to maximize profits given the high costs of fixed capital and of transport to imperial markets. Third, most Africans were reluctant to sell their labor for the wages being offered. And, finally, African peasants often had alternatives to colonial labor and export markets. In French West Africa, for example, despite enormous efforts by the colonial state to promote cotton production for export, most peasants sold their cotton for higher prices in local markets where it fed a thriving handicraft textile industry. These factors contributed to the deep imperfections in the labor and commodity markets in colonial Africa and forced colonial states to intervene through various degrees of compulsion. In the following section, we explore some of the mechanisms that colonial states used to generate revenue, labor, and exports.

WEAK COLONIAL STATES, TAXES, AND LABOR

Although European colonial powers managed to establish military hegemony over most Africans, colonial states' capacity to exercise their power was unevenly distributed over space. Many areas remained relatively isolated from direct colonial control. Precisely because European colonial power was thinly stretched throughout much of Africa, colonial officials often resorted to violence to achieve their ends. With a few celebrated exceptions, Europeans won all military contests with Africans with relative ease.

---

[2] Frederick Cooper, "What Is the Concept of Globalization Good For? An African Historian's Perspective," *African Affairs*, 100 (2001): 189–213.

Success on the battlefield and superior military might did not mean that colonial states easily accomplished their goals of governing and generating wealth. Some scholars have argued that far from being hegemonic, colonial states struggled with deep weaknesses and contradictions.

Bruce Berman described the colonial state as Janus-faced: On the one hand, there was the weak colonial state that was hobbled by inadequate resources, had little coercive force, and struggled "to maintain a precarious sovereignty over contending interests." On the other hand, the strong colonial state continually expanded its bureaucratic apparatus and intervened in ever-widening areas of colonial political economy in order to serve settler interests and to contain and suppress indigenous social forces. Crawford Young argues that if the colonial state's performance up until the Second World War is measured primarily by military challenges to its hegemony and its ability to secure local sources of revenue, then almost all colonial states in Africa were "strong." Mahmood Mamdani points to the decentralized, rural character of colonial hegemony in twentieth-century South Africa, where with the backing of white officials, rural chiefs reigned with few constraints. These chiefs became "decentralized despots" who contributed to the creation of an authoritarian colonial regime. The state's ability to intervene significantly in the lives of its subjects varied temporally and spatially. The colonial state "broadcasted" its power – its ability to intervene significantly in the lives of its subjects – most effectively in capital cities and colonial centers of power; the power of the colonial state extended weakly, if at all, to the vast, rural hinterlands. Far from being able to broadcast its power uniformly, some characterize colonialism as a process prone to contradictions, fragilities, and deep structural weaknesses, with a constant struggle to generate sufficient revenue locally to pay for colonialism without relying on metropolitan resources.[3]

Without substantial resources from the metropole, colonial administrators in Africa adapted local, African institutions to serve their purpose. Despite their different native policies, all colonial powers developed forms of indirect rule that responded to the need to construct a colonial administration "on the cheap." All became dependent upon African chiefs, intermediaries, and employees for administrative service and revenue generation. Some revenue came from excise taxes collected on imports and exports. The other stream of revenue came from direct taxes in the

[3] Bruce Berman and John Lonsdale, *Unhappy Valley: Conflict in Kenya and Africa*, 2 vols. (Athens, OH, 1992); Crawford Young, *The African Colonial State in Comparative Perspective* (New Haven, CT, 1994); Mahmood Mamdani, *Citizen and Subject: Contemporary Africa and the Legacy of Late Colonialism* (Princeton, NJ, 1996); Sara Berry, *No Condition Is Permanent: The Social Dynamics of Agrarian Change in Sub-Saharan Africa* (Madison, WI, 1993).

form of either head or hut taxes. Collecting taxes was, however, not easily accomplished. Colonial violence manifested itself in the episodic or systematic use of violence to force Africans to work for the new colonial economies and pay taxes. Africans often experienced colonialism first through taxes, which drew them more closely into the new colonial order and contributed to major uprisings in colonial Africa in the late nineteenth and early twentieth centuries.

All colonial powers shared a lack of European personnel to collect taxes directly, so that they used various African intermediaries to collect taxes on their behalf. The classic model of British indirect rule rested on the assumption that pre-colonial African political institutions were sufficiently robust to collect taxes. Indirect rule thus worked best where pre-colonial states were highly centralized and bureaucratized. This assumption, however, rarely meshed with the realities of African pre-colonial states. And it certainly did not map neatly onto societies that had deeply divided political factions, such as Buganda, or diffuse ones, where no single individual held power and authority. This model worked best in Northern Nigeria, where the administrative architecture of the Sokoto Caliphate managed the local population and collected taxes, which they had done before conquest. This model failed miserably in many parts of the Congo Free State, where small communities had only marginally developed political hierarchies. In the Congo Free State, the state delegated tax collection to its military wing – the Force Publique – or to its concession owners, who in exchange for a rent payable to the state became the lords of vast tracts of land and their inhabitants. Without finding pre-existing headmen to collect taxes and mobilize labor, the Force Publique and the concession owners turned to extreme violence to extract taxes whether in commodities or labor.

By the beginning of the twentieth century, the annual tax campaign had become a regular part of life under colonial rule. This was when African chiefs, sultans, kings, and headmen were pressured to collect taxes from their communities. Failure to pay taxes ushered in a painful and sharp visit from the colonial military, which seized livestock, grain stores, and sometimes people that often exceeded the value of the community's tax responsibility. Africans had five primary means of generating the cash needed to pay taxes: they could sell their crops, assuming that there was demand for them; they could plant new crops that had market demand within the colonial economies; they could extort commodities and cash from their neighbors or underlings; they could sell their labor to the emerging mining, urban, and capitalist agricultural sectors; or they could migrate to regions where the pressures to pay taxes were, at least temporarily, less acute. In zones of settler agriculture, the colonial state coerced Africans not to grow crops that would compete with settlers' output. Moreover, unequal access to transportation raised costs and reduced the value Africans received for their crops.

Colonial officials often faced unintended consequences in response to policies designed to encourage export crops as in the case of the extension of the railway to Kano in Northern Nigeria, which had long produced cotton and cotton goods for regional and long-distance trade. British promoters expected African peasants to expand cotton production for export to Britain. Northern Nigerian peasants did indeed expand production for export, but they did not produce cotton. Instead, they produced peanuts because these were easier to produce than cotton and returned more value on labor. Most commercial agriculture, however, was located closer to export facilities, since railroads were still few and freight rates high.[4]

The discovery of diamonds and gold in South Africa in 1867 and 1886, respectively, stimulated Africa's gold rush and inspired European imperialists to think of Africa as a vast treasure trove with fortunes waiting to be discovered. Gold and diamonds were discovered elsewhere in Africa, but not on the scale of the large, concentrated, and lucrative mines of South Africa. Nonetheless, gold mines were established in Southern Rhodesia, the Gold Coast, the French Sudan, and Tanganyika among other places. Copper, which was crucial to the global electrification and communication of the twentieth century, stimulated enclaves of development in the copper belt of the Congo and Northern Rhodesia. Deposits of gold, diamonds, uranium, as well as other rare minerals, were discovered later during the colonial era.

Mining required both capital and labor. Whether there was significant capital investment or little investment in heavy machinery, mining capitalists wanted cheap labor. The cheaper the labor, the higher the potential profits. Conditions of mine work were often so onerous and wages so low that few workers wanted to stay on beyond the terms of their contracts. Most Africans preferred to return to their wives and families in their rural homelands as soon as possible. In this manner, the colonial pattern of circular migration was born.

Colonial economists advanced the concept that African workers were essentially motivated by certain "targets," and once they achieved their goals, they quit working and returned home. This concept of the target worker became an excuse for employers to keep wages low; if they paid higher wages, workers would achieve their goals sooner, quit, and thus

---

[4] Jan Hogendorn, "The Cotton Campaign in Northern Nigeria, 1902–1914: An Example of Public/Private Planning Failure in Agriculture," in Allen Isaacman and Richard Roberts (eds.), *Cotton, Colonialism and Social History in Sub-Saharan Africa* (Portsmouth, NH, 1995); Richard Roberts, "Africa and Empire: The Unintended Consequences," in Toyin Falola and Emily Brownell (eds.), *Africa, Empire, and Globalization: Essays in Honor of A.G. Hopkins* (Durham, NC, 2011).

leave employers scrambling for new workers. Some workers did indeed have targets in mind, but the conditions of work and the poor pay meant that few had long-term interests in remaining in those jobs.

Circular migration of Africans was a rational response to a bad situation. Even though agricultural work was hard and the profits usually slim, African peasants worked for themselves or their families. By working for their families, these Africans also invested in their futures, because they expected that their sons would also work for them. The French anthropologist Claude Meillassoux argued that elders whose sons migrated in search of work also had to work hard to develop incentives to encourage them to return to their rural homelands. Inherent tensions between generations and ideologies of kinship were strengthened during the colonial period. Recent research has shown how rural homelands continue to exert a significant force in shaping migrants' behavior, especially ritual ties to their homelands and the continued flow of remittances.[5]

Migrant labor and colonial economic and political policies transformed rural areas. Two processes were at work here: the first was the growing power of African chiefs; and the second was the corrosive process of rural poverty. The need to find African intermediaries to collect taxes and organize labor for rural projects such as road building, dams, and other infrastructure led to the emergence of "rural despots." Rural despots were chiefs and headmen who served as intermediaries of the colonial state and helped to codify "customs" that served their interests and those of other senior men. Colonial rule thus contributed to chiefs becoming rural despots. However, in many areas of Africa, a chief who became too despotic might find that his subjects fled to neighboring communities, to different colonies, or remained in the burgeoning colonial urban centers.

The second conjoined process was the progressive impoverishment of rural areas, especially those areas far from zones of commercialized agriculture. In these areas, the periodic absence of labor migrants led to declines in labor available to peasant families and thus to declining agricultural output. Care for the weak, the infirm, the very young, and the very old became precarious. Moreover, since the cash these returning migrants brought back was most often turned over to elderly male household heads, and circulated within tight bounds of matrimonial exchanges, few resources remained to invest in agricultural modernization such as new technologies of production and new crops. In some parts of Africa, the arrival of European settlers blocked access to new and more fertile lands. Since relatively few women participated in labor markets, many women experienced increasing poverty. This is what Ester Boserup called the

---

[5] Claude Meillassoux, *Meal, Maidens, and Money: Capitalism and the Domestic Economy* (Cambridge, 1981); Charles Piot, *Remotely Global: Village Modernity in West Africa* (Chicago, IL, 1999).

feminization of poverty and it increased dramatically during the course of the twentieth century. Progressive impoverishment of rural areas pushed more men and eventually women into the labor force and into the expanding urban areas of mid-century colonial Africa.[6]

While men dominated migration and shaped the circular patterns, during the interwar years more women began migrating. Some traveled together with their husbands, thus providing greater stability to male migration and leading to longer-term residence in migrants' destinations. Single women also sought to escape pressures of rural patriarchy and poverty. Most unattached women moved to urban areas, where they entered the informal economic sector as hawkers of foodstuffs, brewers of beer, and prostitutes. In a world dominated by single migrating males, the provision of sex and domestic services provided women with the means to survive. Many of the prostitutes accumulated savings that enabled them to buy urban property and expand their entrepreneurial skills. Other single women migrated to mines, where they set up small establishments that served beer and provided sociability. Beer provided mine workers not only with calories, but also alcohol to numb the misery they experienced on the job.

By the end of the Second World War, the pace of industrialization and urbanization expanded dramatically. The growth of urban Africa coincided with the massive expansion of the informal economy. Given the weak nature of the colonial state, most economic activities existed below the state's capacity to see, monitor, and tax them. The informal economy was by far the largest sector of economic enterprise and activities. The informal sector consisted of small-scale artisans; vendors of commodities needed by urban dwellers; tailors who worked out of their homes; garbage recyclers; workers in the transport sector involving the movement of people and goods in privately-owned trucks, carts, and cars; and people providing all kinds of services that kept cities buzzing. Coerced labor of many kinds – apprentices, pawns, servants, students – were widespread in the informal urban sector.

VARIETIES OF COERCED LABOR IN COLONIAL AFRICA: THE "DOMESTIC" ECONOMY

Coerced labor was a feature in all of Africa's "domestic" economies. By domestic economies, I include households as well as rural and urban communities that largely serviced regional economic demands. The distinction between domestic and export-oriented is artificial because of the

---

[6] Ester Boserup, *Women's Role in Economic Development* (London, 1970).

significant labor and commodity flows between these sectors and because the persistence of the "domestic" sector subsidized the economic activities in the export sector. The sources of coercion could be domestic – stemming from household heads, elderly men, elderly women, husbands, or clerics: it could also come from the state or the state's proxies. Within the domestic economy, the end of slavery was a major transition, though trafficking in women and children continued to provide streams of coercible labor.

Students of slavery in Africa do not know with any precision the numbers of slaves in Africa at the beginning of the twentieth century. The proportion of slaves in various African communities ranged from a tiny share to upwards of half. Slavery in Africa had deep roots, but expanded during the nineteenth century with the gradual decline in demand for slaves in the Atlantic, Mediterranean, and Indian Ocean worlds. Fresh from the Berlin Conference of 1884 to 1885 and the Brussels Act of 1890, where European powers committed themselves to prohibiting the slave trade, colonialism was linked with the humanitarian impulses of antislavery. But most colonial powers did little to enforce their commitments. Slavery and the slave trade persisted throughout the twentieth century, though the scale of enslavement and the slave trade within Africa diminished from its heights during the trans-Atlantic and trans-Saharan trades.[7]

From the British abolition of slavery in its crown colony of South Africa in 1833, where a relatively short transition through apprenticeship operated, to the most recent abolition of slavery in Mauretania in 2008, the end of slavery occurred over a sustained period. In most colonies in Africa, the colonial state prohibited new enslavement and removed the legal foundations of masters' claims on their existing slaves in the colonial court system. Even if they wanted the end of slavery to yield an industrious working class or peasantry, colonial states could not orchestrate the transitions. In general, former slaves chose either to leave their former masters or remain with them. Within these two poles, former slaves and former masters had a wide range of choice shaped by many factors: gender, available land, security, etc. Former male slaves had relatively more social mobility than former female slaves, who still needed male guardians. Many female slaves remained with their former masters as concubines.

In the course of the twentieth century, women and children, who could be more easily disguised as household members, increasingly composed the largest share of trafficked people. Trafficking fed the demand from male household heads eager to invest in coercible dependents and because of the

---

[7] Paul E. Lovejoy, *Transformation in Slavery: A History of Slavery in Africa*, 3rd edn. (Cambridge, 2012); Suzanne Miers, *Slavery in the Twentieth Century: The Evolution of a Global Problem* (Walnut Creek, CA, 2003).

range of domestic, agricultural, and small-scale manufacturing roles that women and children provided. Various incarnations of patriarchy also fed demand for unfree women. Women are valued for their sexual services, their reproductive capacity, and for their labor power. They often found themselves in slave-like conditions, whether they were purchased or not. Children were also more easily socialized into dependent and subordinate roles. Demand persisted also because of the range of services provided by trafficked children. Late twentieth-century child labor scandals in the Ivory Coast cocoa plantations revealed the widespread use of coerced labor of children trafficked across borders.

The end of slavery rejuvenated older African institutions of coerced labor. This included pawning and various forms of apprenticeship. Pawning was a form of bonded labor that has a deep pre-colonial tradition. In an environment where real property was relatively scarce, the principle collateral for loans was people. Pawning differed from slavery in the sense that the individual remained a member of his or her lineage and was redeemed once the loan was repaid. The pawn's labor was obligatory and was considered to be the interest on the loan until repayment. In the colonial period, women and children were pawned to raise money for taxes. As was often the case with girls, they were married to their creditor and the bridewealth paid off the debt. Pawnship was tied closely to marriage, especially forced marriage, and pawns were subject to significant domestic and sexual violence.[8] Perpetual servitude could often stem from ritual punishment for crimes, most notably in the case of *trokoisi* among the Ewe of Togo, Ghana, and Benin. Children were recruited as apprentices in exchange for learning skills and subsistence.

Some aspects of the wide range of marriage practices in Africa resemble slave-like practices. This was especially true regarding consent in marriage, child marriages, bridewealth, and labor obligations of marriage. Missionaries, colonial administrators, anthropologists, social reformers, and anti-slavery activists during the twentieth century all raised concerns about forced marriages. These concerns were articulated in the context of colonial civilizing missions. With the establishment of the League of Nations, forced marriage was seen as a practice similar to slavery.

Marriage is a central institution in African societies, but its forms and meanings have changed over time. Bridewealth and early female marriage were core components of marriage. Bridewealth was a strategic investment that built and maintained webs of kinship and organized and controlled labor. Bridewealth often involved the transfer over a number of years of

---

[8] See the essays in Paul E. Lovejoy and Toyin Falola (eds.), *Pawnship, Slavery, and Colonialism in Africa* (Trenton, NJ, 2003); Benjamin N. Lawrance and Richard Roberts (eds.), *Trafficking in Slavery's Wake: The Experience of Women and Children* (Athens, OH, 2012).

goods (grain, livestock, and cash) and services (weaving, herding, and occasional farm work) from the husband's kin to those of his bride. In return, the husband and his kin group received the rights to the bride's labor power, her reproductive capacity, and her domestic services. The value of bridewealth changed over time as African regional economies were drawn ever more fully into colonial and global ones. Many regions of colonial Africa experienced a "marriage crisis" as the value of bridewealth increased significantly. Husbands often understood the higher value of bridewealth to confer on them fuller control over their wives' labor and sexuality and enhanced patriarchal authority. At the same time, economic pressures often limited the ability of husbands to pay bridewealth and contributed, particularly in the post-colonial period, to a rise in long-term domestic relationships that did not attain the status of marriage. Because bridewealth flowed from the groom's kin to the bride's kin, women's consent was rarely sought. Social expectations of marriage and the early age of marriage made women vulnerable to coercion. Colonial administrators faced considerable pressure from missionary societies, activist groups in the metropole, and the liberal press to prohibit child marriages. Age, consent, and coercion were thus deeply entwined in debates about African marriages.[9]

COERCED LABOR IN COLONIAL AFRICA: STATE-SPONSORED COERCION

Reliance on forced labor was one of the outcomes of what the colonial state saw as Africans' failure to utilize the labor market. Whenever possible, Africans sought to avoid employment in the mines, plantations, and settlers' farms. Precisely because they had alternatives to selling their labor at the low rates offered by employers, the settlers, capitalists, and colonial administrators put pressure on the state to organize a supply of coerced labor. Compulsion became a central feature in the colonial economy. Compulsion manifested itself differently in response to demands for labor in different parts of the continent and for different economic sectors. The International Labour Organization argued that head or hut taxes, so necessary to the funding of colonial states, constituted an "indirect form of forced labour, since only through paid employment could many Africans hope to find the necessary money."[10] Taxes were only one form of compulsion among many used by colonial states.

Colonial states were under pressure from metropolitan governments to generate revenue and commodities that would benefit the mother country

    [9] Anne Bunting, Benjamin N. Lawrance, and Richard Roberts (eds.), *Marriage by Force?: Contestation over Consent and Coercion in Africa* (Athens, OH, 2016).
    [10] International Labour Office, *African Labour Survey* (Geneva, 1958), p. 295.

and promote ideological justifications for colonialism. Paradoxically, many colonial states justified the Scramble for Africa in the later nineteenth century as part of their efforts to end the slave trade and slavery and to promote African commerce, only to resort to forced labor to build the infrastructure that would enable the colonial project. Forced labor was therefore a prominent feature in all of colonial Africa. Though compulsion took place in rural areas through pressure from village chiefs, through the barrel of a gun from colonial officials, or through pressure from colonial officials who were assisting private labor recruiters, the conditions African workers found themselves in differed depending upon whether the employment was in public works, mining, settler agriculture, or concession companies that controlled vast tracts of land. The means of recruitment, therefore, also differed.

Five types of forced labor have been identified in French West Africa: requisitioned labor, which was generated by direct pressure on African chiefs to provide male labor; prestation, which was a form of direct labor tax for a fixed number of days per year; the so-called "second portion" of the annual military draft, selecting not-quite able-bodied males for public works labor, though some labor was funneled toward private enterprises; penal labor, which was a widely used form of coerced labor often for public works, but sometimes hired out for private enterprise; and forced cultivation of certain crops, especially those deemed essential for "national security" and colonial development.[11] We should also include two additional categories: indentured labor and military conscription. Though Africa was often a source of the outflow of indentured labor, indentured-laborers were also imported into South and Eastern Africa in the mid nineteenth and early twentieth centuries. Military conscription was a mechanism of coerced recruitment into the military and widely used throughout the world. Both voluntary enlistment and coerced conscription took place in Africa during conquest and the two world wars. Forced labor always involved extra-economic pressure, but the nature of the forced labor differed according to the context in which it was performed and the length of time it required. Moreover, the forms of forced labor changed over time, especially with the establishment of the League of Nations and the International Labour Organization.

REQUISITIONED LABOR

The Scramble for Africa was relatively short-lived. Once primary African resistance to conquest was crushed, colonial officials found themselves in

[11] Babacar Fall, "Le travail forcé en Afrique Occidentale Française (1900–1946)," *Civilisations*, 41 (1993): 329–36.

charge of vast territories with few natural waterways and harbors. The colonial state immediately confronted the need to build infrastructure: ports, railways, roads, dams, bridges, telegraphs, barracks, etc. They also confronted the need to transport materials over long distances, thus requiring porters. Porterage and infrastructure construction required labor. Some labor could be drawn from colonial troops, but the bulk fell to Africans forced into this labor service. Most of the infrastructure was built using simple hand tools, meaning that the labor was hard and dangerous. All colonial states used some form of requisitioned labor for this purpose. The most common method was for colonial officials to instruct village chiefs to produce a certain number of workers. In French West Africa, Africans requisitioned for labor received a daily ration of food if their work took them more than five kilometers from their homes. Sometimes requisitioned laborers received token cash payments. In British colonial Africa, women and children formed part of the requisitioned labor on infrastructure, especially road work. Few formal rules governed requisitioned labor during the first two decades of colonial rule. By 1912, however, colonial governors began to enact legislation limiting the numbers of days per year individuals could be required to work for the colonial state and prohibiting women's and children's labor on state projects. Britain abolished the provision of requisitioned labor to private enterprises in 1908, but retained it for building and maintenance of roads, bridges, sanitation, and irrigation.

Most requisitioned labor flowed through chiefs, who often had wide latitude in choosing recruits and could favor friends and kinsmen and harm rivals. In Kenya, chiefs thus became "big men" and essential allies of the colonial state. In 1919, the governor issued a circular instructing government officials in charge of native areas to use all lawful means to "induce" able-bodied males into the labor market, especially the labor-scarce settler agricultural sector. The Colonial Office ultimately repudiated this circular, though other labor coercive mechanisms, including the *kipande* (identity card) and restrictions on breaching labor contracts, effectively limited free labor. In French colonies, chiefs requisitioned labor for infrastructure, but also in French Equatorial Africa for use on private plantations and concession companies. In FEA, chiefs requisitioned over 127,000 workers to build the Congo-Océan railway. Chiefs in Upper Volta requisitioned 22,000 workers to build the Thiès-Kayes railway in the early decades of the twentieth century and then thousands more to build the massive irrigation works of the Office du Niger in the 1930s. Chiefs in Gabon requisitioned labor for the private lumber concessions.

Though we cannot draw a direct causal connection between the rubber scandal in the Congo Free State and the enactment of rules limiting requisitioned labor, the timing suggests that the scandal had significant implications for labor regimes in the rest of Africa. In 1891, King Leopold decreed the *régime dominal* in which the state acquired all vacant land and all the products on that land. Central Africans did not practice freehold in the terms Europeans understood and thus Africans were considered trespassers on state land, subject to fines and imprisonment. By 1892, the Congo Free State ceded vast tracts of state land to European companies in exchange for rents. Demand for rubber and ivory in Europe was booming due to the transportation revolution (bicycles, cars, trucks) and middle-class consumption of leisure (pianos and billiards) and for use as false teeth. Not surprisingly, the concession owners turned to requisitioned African labor, eventually requiring that Africans work for the state or the concession companies for up to 280 days per year. Such labor requirements threatened Africans' agrarian economies, which had been eroded by the vacant land alienation decree (*régime dominal*). Few Africans came forward willingly. The state turned to the Force Publique, the African army of the Congo Free State, to secure African labor, resulting in the horrendous crimes and massive death toll that Roger Casement, E. D. Morel, and William Henry Sheppard made public in Europe. The Belgian Parliament held an independent inquiry into the abuses in the Congo in 1905, and in 1908 Parliament voided Leopold's claim to the Congo and annexed the territory. Concerned about continued loss of African population, the Belgian Congo introduced laws limiting requisitioned labor and prohibiting labor recruitment from regions suffering extreme depopulation. Existing Congo Free State concessions were canceled, but new ones were auctioned off. Concession companies remained a significant feature of the Belgian Congo's economy and they continued to rely on requisitioned labor.

It is important to distinguish between requisitioned labor for public works projects and for private enterprises. The work was harsh and brutal in both sectors. Demand for requisitioned labor put direct state pressure on village chiefs, who mediated between colonial states and broader African communities and who had to balance state pressures for workers and the well-being of the village. Chiefs were actively complicit in this process and they benefited from their enhanced authority. In many areas of colonial Africa, village and canton chiefs used unpaid requisitioned labor on their own fields. The freed slave villages in French West Africa during the era of conquest, where slaves of France's enemies were sent, often formed a reserve army of porters and workers on infrastructure.

PRESTATION OR LABOR TAX

Prestation was a form of annual labor tax in which all able-bodied men were required to perform labor on public works for a set number of days.

Both the French and British established fixed terms for *corvée* labor before the First World War. In French West Africa, legislation set the maximum number of days of obligatory labor, but gave the various colonies latitude in setting the exact duration. In Senegal, Africans were obliged to work eight days per year, while in the French Sudan, it was fixed at twelve days. Prestation labor in Senegal was reduced to four days in 1922. In FEA, a labor tax was introduced in 1918 and set at seven days per year, but due to continued labor shortage, in 1925 it was raised to fifteen days in response to railway construction. Food was supplied only to those working more than 30 kilometers from their homes. Legislation also prohibited the exaction of *corvée* labor between planting and harvesting, thus making the annual *corvée* a dry season requirement. Under Belgian colonial rule, a more systematic and greatly reduced *corvée* was imposed in the Congo. Just as France, Britain, and Belgium were limiting *corvée* labor, however, Angola increased its labor tax and became the subject of an international scandal. In 1906, Henry Nivenson published a scathing critique of the abuses of forced labor in Angola in the aftermath of the Congo scandal. Prestation persisted in French Africa until the Brazzaville Conference in 1944, when Charles de Gaulle rewarded Africans for their support of the Free French with the promise to repeal the hated labor tax and the *indigénat* (the system of administrative punishments), which took effect in 1946.

MILITARY CONSCRIPTION

Demand for men to fight, to carry war materiel, and to grow crops that were essential to the war effort during the First World War led to significant and sustained intervention in African economies. Britain, France, and Belgium increased the recruitment of African soldiers. France turned to the draft to recruit Africans for the front in Europe; Britain increased its voluntary recruitment of soldiers primarily for the military campaigns in Cameroon and East Africa. In the absence of railways, war materiel, food, and shelter had to be carried overland. David Killingray argues that far more Africans were forcibly recruited as laborers for the war effort than all of the workers forcibly recruited for the mines, concessions, plantations, and settler farms in Africa. He argues that forced recruitment "stripped bare" the African populations in large areas of Eastern Belgian Congo, Rwanda, Uganda, Kenya, German East Africa, Northern Rhodesia, Nyasaland, and the northern regions of Portuguese East Africa. He estimates that half of the total male population of the African reserves in Kenya had been forcibly recruited; overall, Britain had conscripted over half a million men in its

African colonies by 1918.[12] Belgium increased recruitment of Africans for the Force Publique and the carrier corps, which played crucial roles in the defeat of Germany in Rwanda and Burundi. By 1918, however, pressure for recruitment decreased, except in French Africa.

France, which had suffered massive losses of young men during the First World War, decided to continue with annual military recruitment in colonial Africa. Throughout the 1920s and into the 1930s, French colonial states discovered that they could use the annual military draft to identify two categories of young men: those able-bodied recruits for the military and those deemed too unhealthy to serve. Those considered healthy were subject to a lottery system out of which would flow military recruits for a three-year stint in the Tirailleurs Sénégalais. Those not selected were placed in a vague "reserve army" category. During the interwar period, France sought to promote colonial economic development through massive public works projects, but faced the challenge of finding adequate labor for these projects. In 1928, French officials turned the "reserve army" of healthy recruits into the "second portion" of military recruitment, but directed them to public works, including the massive irrigation scheme of the Office du Niger and for building the Thiès-Niger railway. Men in the second portion, which was the largest share of this population, were drafted into two-year "contracts" for public service. The French West African model of the "second portion" military recruitment for public works was modeled on one started in Madagascar two years earlier. On average, nearly 3,000 men annually were conscripted into second portion labor between 1928 and 1946, when it was finally abolished. Military conscription resumed in many colonies with the outbreak of the Second World War.

FORCED CULTIVATION

Given that most Africans farmed at least part of the year, colonial states turned to force to coerce Africans to grow certain crops. But there was a deep paradox here: most African farmers responded positively to price incentives and innovations in transportation by increasing their output and bringing their crops to market. This was certainly the case with palm oil, peanuts, and cocoa in West Africa, and sesame and coffee in East Africa.

[12] David Killingray, "Labour Exploitation for Military Campaigns in British Colonial Africa 1870–1945," *Journal of Contemporary History*, 24 (1989): 483–501. See also Myron Echenberg, *Colonial Conscripts: The Tirailleurs Sénégalais in French West Africa, 1857–1960* (Portsmouth, NH, 1991); and Timothy Parsons, *The African Rank-and-File: Social Implications of Colonial Military Service in the King's African Rifles, 1902–1964* (Portsmouth, NH, 1999).

Most of the crops or commodities colonial authorities demanded as part of this regime of coercion were those in high demand in Europe. Rubber was one of these commodities in the late nineteenth and early twentieth centuries, which fed a growing demand for bicycle tires, among other products. This demand put pressure on the regions of Africa where wild rubber flourished, especially the Congo. Among the worst abuses was the forced collection of wild rubber in the Congo Free State discussed above. Individually or as a community, Africans were assigned quotas of wild rubber and failure to meet those quotas led to severe punishment. Vegetable oils derived from palm kernels and peanuts did not seem to warrant coercion, since peasant producers responded to price incentives. Cotton, a commodity in demand in metropolitan economies, was the crop most susceptible to coerced cultivation.

Demand for cotton in Europe expanded rapidly with mechanization of the textile industry during the second half of the nineteenth century. Since cotton does not grow in temperate European climates, industrialists had to draw on supplies thousands of miles away. Early in the nineteenth century, cotton from the American South fed the growing demand for raw materials in Europe. However, the American Civil War led to a major raw materials crisis for industrializing Europe and contributed to economic and political instability there as factories closed and workers were laid off. The Scramble for Africa coincided with European economic recovery and provided new opportunities for Europeans to have colonies supply their metropoles with crucial raw materials.

Coerced cotton production took many forms. Because African peasants had a keen sense of the labor requirements of various crops, they planted based on expected yields and prices. Cotton was usually not their choice. Cotton was labor-intensive, often interfered with the production of food crops, and, at times, fetched higher prices locally than in the export market. Colonial officials were mostly disappointed by the quality and quantity of cotton delivered for export and they increasingly turned to more coercive means: forcing peasants to cultivate new varieties of cotton, bring their harvest to market, and often to sell their harvest at fixed prices.

Perhaps the most coercive cotton regime emerged in Portuguese Angola and Mozambique. Despite the relatively small metropolitan cotton textile industry, colonial officials were under significant pressure to meet its requirements. In 1928, Angola and Mozambique provided only 2 percent of the Portuguese supply of cotton. By 1946, these colonies produced 95 percent of Portugal's demand for raw cotton. But the cost to African peasants was extremely high. The colonial state put enormous pressure on African chiefs and headmen to force African peasants to cultivate cotton despite its low yield and its substitution for subsistence crops. By 1944, vast tracts of Mozambique were formally directed as cotton concessions and well over 800,000 Mozambicans were forced to cultivate cotton and bring their harvests to official markets, even as prices fell. Mozambique achieved such results only through a brutal regime of labor control and punishments imposed by African headmen and police.[13]

Africans faced forced cultivation on smaller scales everywhere. Most prominent were the "chief's fields," sometimes called the "champs de commandant" (fields of the colonial district officer). Some of these fields were designated as experimental, where new crops were grown to assess their economic and agronomic viability. But chiefs throughout colonial Africa benefited from their control over requisitioned labor and directed village labor to their own fields. This was a central part of the "bargains of collaboration" that provided incentives for elite Africans to serve their colonial overlords.

Prison Labor

Created to discipline and punish, prisons in colonial Africa provided a stream of coerced labor for public works and private enterprise. Prisoners everywhere were under compulsion to work for the maintenance of the prison. Female as well as male prisoners worked in gendered roles within the prisons. Minors were increasingly separated from adults and sometimes sent to agricultural colonies, where they worked as part of their rehabilitation. In most colonies, prisoners were compelled to labor as part of their sentences. In French Guinea, prisoners were obliged to work five days a week. In French Equatorial Africa, prisoners were transferred to work for expatriate logging companies and other concession owners. In British colonial Africa, a parallel system of prisons – one for the native administrations and the other the central government prisons – funneled prisoners into different labor pools: one for native authorities' public and often private needs; and the other for public works primarily. In some cases, as in South Africa, where the prison labor system was highly developed, prisoners working for private enterprise were paid a nominal wage, but this wage was actually paid to the prison administration as a way of financing the prison system.

South Africa developed the most comprehensive prison labor system. From the founding of the Cape Colony, prisoners worked on public works. South African prisons developed two methods for using prison labor other than for public works. The first was the contract system, where

---

[13] Allen Isaacman, *Cotton Is the Mother of Poverty: Peasants, Work, and Rural Struggle in Colonial Mozambique, 1938–1961* (Portsmouth, NH, 1996); Richard Roberts, *Two Worlds of Cotton: Colonialism and the Regional Economy in the French Soudan, 1800–1946* (Stanford, CA, 1996).

light manufacturing was conducted within the prisons. On Robben Island, for example, prisoners produced dried seaweed that was sold internationally. The second was the lease system, whereby prisoners were hired out to private enterprises. At the beginning of the twentieth century, De Beers diamond mining at Kimberley was the largest employer of leased prison labor in South Africa. After the South African War, the gold mines of Witwatersrand increasingly used prison labor. The 1913 Natives Land Act meant that white farmers found recruiting cheap African labor more difficult. With the massive increase in incarceration due to pass-law violations, especially after the development of apartheid, the South African prisons faced severe overcrowding and escalating expenses. To reduce both, the prisons increasingly used the lease system to funnel prison labor to white farmers. In the 1950s, more than 200,000 prisoners annually were released on parole to white farmers for whom they were forced to work. These were termed "farm-jails."

INDENTURED LABOR

Indentured labor was a public-private system that funneled millions of workers around the world from the 1840s through the 1920s to meet demands for labor largely in tropical agriculture in the aftermath of the abolition of slavery. Hugh Tinker has labeled indentured labor a "new system of slavery," wherein laborers worked for little more than maintenance in brutal conditions not of their own choosing. Revisionist approaches have suggested that indentured labor involved contractual bondage of limited duration and offered some choice at the moment of recruitment. Others have argued that few laborers were made aware of the labor conditions they were to enter or the exact terms of their contracts. Even if laborers were not forced to sign contracts, many faced severe poverty and had few alternatives.

Indentured labor was not a significant part of the African coerced labor scene; its most significant presence was in the sugar sector of Natal, South Africa, where South Asian indentured workers were recruited to build this new sector in the absence of a steady stream of African wage labor. Between 1875 and 1911, more than 145,000 Indian indentured workers were imported into Natal to augment the 6,450 Indian indentured workers who had been imported at the beginning of the sugar boom. In the late nineteenth century and the early decades of the twentieth century, nearly 40,000 Indian indentured workers were imported into East Africa for railway construction. Between 1904 and 1907, 63,695 indentured Chinese laborers were recruited to work the gold mines of the Witwatersrand in part to undercut the growing tendency of African workers to resist mine owners' demands for disciplined low wage workers. During this period,

Chinese indentured laborers constituted 35 percent of the total labor force on the Rand, but as the Chinese demanded stronger labor protections, the experiment was abandoned.

By far the largest numbers of indentured workers were imported into the Indian Ocean islands of Mauritius and Réunion, which emerged as major sugar producers in the aftermath of decline of sugar production in the Caribbean. Together, these Mascarene Islands imported 527,402 indentured Indians of whom 86 percent went to Mauritius; 34,219 indentured Africans almost all of whom went to Réunion; and slightly over 2,000 indentured Chinese. Some indentured workers renewed their contracts; others returned home; and a significant number sought out other forms of livelihood on the islands once their contracts ended. In all cases, during the period of indenture, these workers were unable to change employers on their own, but could be sold by planters, and many were subject to harsh conditions and brutal punishments. By 1922, due mainly to pressure from India, indentured labor was largely ended.

COERCED LABOR, INTERNATIONAL SCRUTINY, AND NEW HUMANITARIAN SENSIBILITIES

Following the First World War, the Paris Peace Accords led to the establishment of the League of Nations, with the Mandate system governing the seized colonies and territories of the defeated powers, along with the International Labour Organization. There emerged a vague commitment to "secure fair and humane conditions of labor" at home and in the mandated territories, which also meant dealing with the persistence of slavery. In Mandated Territories, members of the League committed themselves to "prohibit all forms of forced or compulsory labor, except for essential public works and services, and then only in return for adequate remuneration," as well as to "secure and maintain fair and humane conditions of labor for men, women, and children." Religious and secular humanitarian groups as well as international diplomatic posturing regarding whether to admit Ethiopia into the League pressured the League to establish the Temporary Slavery Commission, which was to inquire into the "resurgence" of slavery, especially in Africa. In 1922, the Commission requested information from all member states to provide information on slavery. Building on the 1919 Saint Germaine-en-Laye convention, which committed Britain, France, and Belgium to "secure the complete suppression of slavery in all its forms, and of the slave trade by land and sea," the Slavery Commission used the information it received to issue a Slavery Convention in 1926. The Convention pledged its signatories "to prevent and suppress the slave trade and to progressively bring about the complete elimination of slavery in all its forms." It defined slavery as "the status or condition of a person over whom any or all of the powers attaching to the right of ownership are exercised." The Convention also identified child marriage as a form of slavery. The Convention delegated to the ILO the task of investigating forced and compulsory labor and proposing means to prevent such labor from becoming similar to slavery. The League's Assembly also declared that forced labor should be resorted to only when free labor "could not be obtained" and be exceptional, not regularized.

In response, the ILO established a Committee of Experts on Native Labour. These experts included colonial administrators, some of whom had served on the Temporary Slavery Commission. It also included representatives from labor and business. By 1930, the Committee of Experts produced a Convention that defined forced or compulsory labor as "all work or service which is exacted from any person under the menace of any penalty and for which the said person has not offered himself voluntarily." The Convention excepted military conscription, service in case of emergency, penal labor, and "the normal obligations of members of the village community," such as keeping paths open. Forced labor for private enterprise and for underground work in mines was expressly forbidden. France, Belgium, and Portugal signed on with "reservations," thus providing legal coverage for the persistence of such practices. Some leading colonial officials argued that temporary forms of forced labor "educated" Africans about the value of work. Portugal under Salazar increased the incidence of compulsory labor in its effort to promote the economic development of its African colonies.

By 1930, the League began to investigate complaints of compulsory labor recruitment and transport under government oversight from Liberia to Fernando Po. This commerce in coerced labor was at least three decades old and fed the growing demand for labor on cocoa plantations in Fernando Po. Liberians were forcibly recruited and sold to Fernando Po planters. The League's investigation revealed widespread official government complicity in this trade in coerced labor and this resulted in a scandal that rocked the Liberian Government. The League's investigation did not, however, look into the emerging compulsory labor recruitment for the Firestone Rubber plantations in Liberia. In 1926, 76 percent of the 10,500 workers on the rubber plantations had not signed on voluntarily.

The 1920s also witnessed the emergence of a new humanitarian sentiment that was linked to the growing international women's movements and to the maturation of new forms of documentary reporting, which further opened colonial practices to scrutiny and debate. Travelers' accounts, such as those by André Gide on the labor abuses in Chad in the late 1920s, and journalistic reporting from the colonies, sometimes embarrassed colonial officials and often inflamed public outrage. The election of reformist governments in several European metropoles contributed to increased attention to colonial reforms. The deepening of the Depression in the 1930s and the rumblings of war blunted the potential reforms in Africa regarding forced labor and slavery. In some areas, the Depression, which had sharply reduced peasant and worker incomes, led to the resurgence of forced labor practices such as pawning in order to secure cash for taxes.

The outbreak of the Second World War witnessed the return of military conscription and forced cultivation in many African colonies. With the fall of France in 1940, most of colonial Africa remained with the Vichy regime (French Equatorial Africa sided with the Free French) and Vichy's corporatist ideology provided justification for forced labor in the "public interest." Under Vichy, forced labor in French West Africa reached unprecedented levels. Fascist Italy intensified compulsory labor as well. In British Southern Rhodesia, all males aged between 18 and 45 who were unemployed (i.e. not working for someone else) for three months or longer were conscripted by the state and funneled into settler farms. In both Rhodesias, Africans were conscripted both in the military and into the "Labour Corps" to be used as colonial officials deemed necessary for building of new air bases, which trained pilots and crew for the Royal Air Force, food production, commodity production, and for public works more generally. Scholars estimate that 50,000 to 100,000 Africans were conscripted into the various Labour Corps each year from 1942 to 1945. Britain's loss of its Far Eastern colonies to the Japanese led to an intensified focus on African colonies as a source of food and commodities through the mobilization of "non-combatant labor." The conditions of such labor were purposely left vague. This was especially true in East and Central Africa, where this region's production of rubber, sisal, and pyrethrum led to labor conscription with harsh penalties for desertion and resistance to recruitment. In Nigeria, conscripted labor was used in the Jos tin mines. Compulsory labor coincided with sustained droughts and crop shortfalls in East and Central Africa, which contributed to recruitment resistance and anti-colonial agitation.

The end of the war led to a series of major colonial reforms and to investment in development programs. Both France and Britain set aside considerable funds for investment in colonial development. All remaining colonial powers invested in higher education for the first time. Peace also saw the creation of new international organizations, such as the United Nations, which following the revelations of Nazi war crimes and widespread use of forced labor, contributed to the new international conventions on human rights. The United Nations' Universal Declaration (1948) called yet again for the abolition of all forms of slavery, servitude, and the trade in slaves. Recognition of the continued presence of forms of unfreedom among UN member states led to the Supplementary Convention on the Abolition of Slavery, the Slave Trade, and Institutions and Practices Similar to Slavery in 1956, which included debt bondage, serfdom, unfree marriages, and exploitation of child labor under prohibited practices. Defining the relationship between ordinary and exploitative child labor led to the 1989 Convention on the Rights of the Child and to the International Labour Organization Convention Concerning the Prohibition and Immediate Action for the Elimination of the Worst Forms of Child Labour (1999). In 2000, the United Nations passed the Protocol to Prevent, Suppress and Punish Trafficking in Persons, Especially Women and Children. The 1990s and the first decade of the twenty-first century witnessed the proliferation of international conventions against trafficking, the development of international case law regarding trafficking, and individual countries' efforts to legislate and enforce anti-trafficking laws. Following the collapse of the former Soviet Union, a new wave of humanitarian sentiment has focused on sex trafficking. Sex trafficking, however, is only a relatively small part of a much wider trafficking in unfree women, men, and children in Africa and throughout the world.

COERCED LABOR IN POST-COLONIAL AFRICA

Many African nationalists heralded the end of colonial rule as the liberation of Africans from the chains of colonialism and forced labor and promised that independence and economic development would benefit all. Within a decade of the first wave of independence of the late 1950s and early 1960s, civil wars, military coups, economic mismanagement, and corruption undermined these promises and bred deep resentments. Liberation movements struggled against the remaining colonial and settler colonies of Guinea-Bissau, Angola, Mozambique, South Africa, South West Africa, Rhodesia, and Ethiopia, which had annexed Eritrea. Secessionist movements broke out in Nigeria, the Congo, and Ethiopia, among other states. In this context, nation states, secessionist movements, and rebel movements turned to varieties of coerced labor. Virtually all independent states retained various forms of coercion in rural areas to sustain production of export crops and the supply of cheap food to the expanding urban centers in their effort to buy political peace from politically volatile urban dwellers.

In 1967, independent Tanzania launched an ambitious economic development program that President Nyerere called *ujamaa*, a Swahili term referring to community or extended family. It became a shorthand for a linked set of political and economic reforms that was intended to yield prosperous and self-reliant rural villages centered around the provision of clean water and sanitation, access to community-owned farming machinery, and public education. Tanzanian peasants, however, were less convinced about the value of moving from their farms where they under-stood the micro-endowments of various terrains to the new ujamaa villages often far from their homes. Frustrated with peasants' tepid response, the state turned to violence to compel peasants to move. By 1973, under Operation Ujiji, the military was used to uproot peasants and force them to relocate to ujamaa villages. Faced with continued deterioration of rural and urban standard of living and with pressure from World Bank and International Monetary Fund structural adjustment programs, in 1985, Tanzania finally abandoned many aspects of ujamaa.[14]

In 1961, the Eritrean Liberation Front began a thirty-year war of liberation against Ethiopia's annexation of Eritrea. The ELF created a highly disciplined army and support system that ultimately prevailed against a much stronger Ethiopian military. In 1991, Eritrea had become an independent country with an ambitious economic development agenda. To further build a sense of national identity, Eritrea instituted compulsory military service for all Eritrean men and women between the ages of 18 and 40. Such service consisted of six months of military training and twelve months of active service. Eritrea was making consid-erable strides toward its goals when war with Ethiopia broke out again in 1998. In 2000, peace accords were signed to end hostilities, but the Eritrean Government did not demobilize its vast military. Instead, it extended compulsory military service indefinitely under the label of the Warasi-Yikaalo Development Campaign. Designed to be a "school of the nation," WYDC was supposed to provide labor for development projects in the national interest, but it morphed into a "modern form of slavery." Men and women in WYDC worked "under menace of penalty" (the classic ILO formulation of forced labor) and were subject to periodic police round-ups.[15]

Smaller-scale coercion continues in many rural areas of independent Africa where chiefs continue to exert "traditional authority" over presta-tion. Some of the most egregious cases can be found in post-apartheid South Africa, where basic human rights are enshrined in the constitution. However, the constitution also recognizes the traditional authority of rural chiefs, who use unpaid "tribal levies" to work on village projects, including the chiefs' own fields. Tribal levies are essentially forced labor.

A central feature of the late-twentieth-century roving rebel movements in Africa has been the "civilianization" of armed conflict. Rebel move-ments in Sierra Leone, Liberia, Mozambique, Northern Uganda, Somalia, and the Democratic Republic of the Congo have preyed particularly on

---

[14] James C. Scott, *Seeing Like a State: How Certain Schemes to Improve the Human Condition Have Failed* (New Haven, CT, 1998).

[15] Gaim Kibread, "Forced Labour in Eritrea," *Journal of Modern African Studies*, 41 (2009): 41–72.

boys and often girls as child soldiers and girls as "bush" wives. As many as 120,000 children may have been forcibly recruited into these rebel movements. In the Ugandan Lord's Resistance Army, which abducted 25,000 children, child recruits constituted 70 to 80 percent of the force, with girls composing about a third. Two to three thousand girls were forcibly recruited into the Revolutionary United Front in Sierra Leone. While some girls fought, most were forced into marriages to provide sexual, domestic, and reproductive services. Fifty percent of the bush wives in the RUF were under 15 years old. In Somalia and Northern Nigeria, the al-Shabaab and Boko Haram rebel movements have abducted schoolgirls and forced them into marriages to rebel fighters as a means of undermining Western education and of providing sexual and domestic labor. In the eastern regions of the DRC, girls and young women abducted by combatants have been taken to bases in the forest where they are forced to provide sexual services and domestic labor.

CONCLUSION

Coerced labor was a prominent feature of sub-Saharan African social, economic, and political life in the twentieth century. Because Africans usually retained ties to rural areas during most of the colonial period and therefore had access to agricultural land, few willingly entered the labor markets where wages were low and working conditions dangerous. The end of slavery was a long process that led to new or rejuvenated forms of coerced labor to meet the needs of household heads in rural areas. Colonial states turned to compulsion to force Africans to enter the labor markets, pay taxes, and provide forced labor for public works. Indirect rule enhanced the powers of chiefs as they provided taxes and labor to colonial states and private enterprises. In some areas, colonial states further constrained workers' mobility through pass-laws and severe punishments for breaking contracts. Colonial states also turned to wartime recruitment of soldiers and porters and forced those remaining in rural areas to produce crops for the war effort. The emergence of the League of Nations and the International Labour Organization led to new measures to combat coerced labor and practices analogous to slavery. But demand for coerced labor persisted and new mechanisms emerged to meet this demand.

Coerced labor did not disappear with decolonization. Indeed, many independent nations retained colonial era programs of forced cultivation and *corvée* labor for development projects. Political and economic instability in post-colonial Africa led to the rise of rebel movements, which relied on many forms of coerced labor to survive. As long as demand for cheap commodities and for submissive dependents persists, so will the availability of coerced labor in its many guises.

A GUIDE TO FURTHER READING

Berman, Bruce and John Lonsdale, *Unhappy Valley: Conflict in Kenya and Africa*, 2 vols. (Athens, OH, 1992).

Boserup, Ester, *Women's Role in Economic Development* (London, 1970).

Bundy, Colin, *The Rise and Fall of the South African Peasantry* (Berkeley, CA, 1979).

Bunting, Anne, Benjamin Lawrance, and Richard Roberts (eds.), *Marriage by Force? Contestation over Consent and Coercion in Africa* (Athens, OH, 2016).

Campbell, Gwen, Suzanne Miers, and Joseph C. Miller (eds.), *Children in Slavery* (Athens, OH, 2009).

Cook, Allen, *Akin to Slavery: Prison Labour in South Africa* (London, 1982).

Fall, Babacar, "Le travail forcé en Afrique Occidentale Française (1900–1946)," *Civilisations*, 41 (1993): 329–36.

Ferguson, James, *Expectations of Modernity: Myths and Meanings of Urban Life on the Zambian Copperbelt* (Berkeley, CA, 1999).

Isaacman, Allen, *Cotton Is the Mother of Poverty: Peasants, Work, and Rural Struggle in Colonial Mozambique, 1938–1961* (Portsmouth, NH, 1996).

Lawrance, Benjamin and Richard Roberts (eds.), *Trafficking in Slavery's Wake: The Experience of Women and Children* (Athens, OH, 2012).

Lovejoy, Paul and Toyin Falola (eds.), *Pawnship, Slavery, and Colonialism in Africa* (Trenton, NJ, 2003).

Meillassoux, Claude, *Meal, Maidens, and Money: Capitalism and the Domestic Economy* (Cambridge, 1981).

Miers, Suzanne and Richard Roberts (eds.), *The End of Slavery in Africa* (Madison, WI, 1988).

Mkandawire, Thandika, "The Terrible Toll of Post-Colonial 'Rebel Movements' in Africa: Towards an Explanation of the Violence against the Peasantry," *Journal of Modern African Studies*, 40 (2002): 181–215.

Roberts, Richard, *Two Worlds of Cotton: Colonialism and the Regional Economy in the French Soudan, 1800–1946* (Stanford, CA, 1996).

White, Luise, *Comforts of Home: Prostitution in Colonial Nairobi* (Chicago, IL, 1990).

Young, Crawford, *The African Colonial State in Comparative Perspective* (New Haven, CT, 1994).

CHAPTER 26

INDENTURE IN THE LONG NINETEENTH CENTURY

ROSEMARIJN HOEFTE

INTRODUCTION

Indentured labor is frequently associated with the abolition of slavery, but it was not a new phenomenon in pre-colonial Asia and in the Atlantic.[1] However, it is true that in the nineteenth century the expanding global sugar market and a shortage of cheap, servile labor revived the system. The abolition of the slave trade and slavery and the subsequent actions by the imperial powers, particularly Great Britain, had enormous worldwide consequences. The "new" indenture system relocated millions of Asians to work under contract on sugar plantations in the Caribbean, Peru, Hawaii, Réunion, Fiji, and Mauritius. In addition, temporarily, Asian indentured laborers were often used in the exploitation of natural resources or in other jobs demanding hard physical labor in new economic activities. Examples of such activities were the exploitation of guano in Peru and rubber production in Southeast Asia and Brazil. This underlines the point that Asian indentured labor was also used in Asia itself. In fact, the overwhelming majority of Asian indentured migrants did not travel outside South and Southeast Asia. Increasing colonial intervention and expansion transformed regional economies, pushing people out, but also creating new Western enclaves of labor-intensive production.

The majority of the indentured laborers signed a contract binding them to an employer for a specified time period. The system of indenture curtailed the freedom and mobility of the workers, who could not easily disengage from the contract when criminal laws reinforced it. Refusal or inability to work, misbehavior, or other transgressions of disciplinary codes were punishable breaches of contract. In those cases, the indentured workers were subject to fines, hard labor, incarceration, or an extension of the period of service.

Indenture is one of many forms of bound labor, including debt bondage, convict labor, and *corvée* labor. These forms of labor mobilization

---

[1] Indentured labor existed in the seventeenth-century British and French Caribbean where debt servants, political and religious dissenters, criminals, etc. were put to work. With the expansion of the sugar plantations, enslaved Africans became the preferred labor force.

merit separate coverage. Here, I will only use the term "indentured labor" and not "contract labor," as this term may be confused with other forms of labor contracts. The indentured laborers were often called "coolies." The origin of the word "coolie" is unclear; it might be from the Hindi and Telugu *kūlī* meaning "day laborer," and is probably associated with the Urdu word *ḳulī* or "slave." In the nineteenth century, it became a common European term to characterize an unskilled physical laborer of Asian origin. In some areas, such as South Africa, it even could mean anyone of Asian descent. In this chapter, the word will not be used, except when in quotations or official terminology, because of its association with negative and racist stereotypes.

The British were the pioneers in organizing the nineteenth-century intercontinental system of indenture. Even before pressuring other European nations to follow their lead in banning the slave trade, in 1806 the British were the first to ship 200 indentured Chinese to Trinidad for a five-year period of "industrial residence," a euphemism in the same league as the term "apprenticeship." The system really took off in the 1830s, when slavery and apprenticeship came to an end in the British Empire, and the British shipped thousands of Indian indentured workers to their colonies in Asia and the Caribbean. Planters argued that only massive, regular imports of malleable labor could save their enterprises. Indian indentured migration thus was closely tied to the expansion of the tropical regions and the abolition of slavery in the Empire.

However, it is misleading to regard indentured servitude as an intermediate stage in a linear process from slavery to free labor. Though indenture often came on the heels of abolition and apprenticeship, and thus developed at times throughout the world, it did not always follow slavery. Cuba is an example of a different mixed labor system where Chinese indentured laborers were imported before the abolition of slavery, while Hawaii and Fiji used contracted indentured laborers without ever resorting to slave labor. Nor did indentured labor preclude the hiring of free labor. Thus, free, indentured, and slave labor could exist side by side in the same economic setting.

As was the case with slavery, abolition of indenture took place at different times. The Chinese indentured out-migration of labor was banned as early as 1874. In India, indenture was abolished in 1917, while in Indonesia (the Netherlands East Indies) the penal sanction was repealed in 1931. This also affected labor relations with Javanese indentured migrants in the Dutch Caribbean colony of Suriname. That last mentioned indentured labor influx from Indonesia is frequently forgotten, encouraging the mistaken assumption that Indian abolition entailed the end of all Asian indentured migration to the Americas.

SYSTEMS OF INDENTURED LABOR

It is important to note variations in the indenture systems at different times and locations. The dynamics of the political economy of the various regions using indentured labor largely determined the arrangements with the workers. Several kinds of arrangements could operate simultaneously, thereby further undermining the idea that indenture was a monolithic system. This complexity means that it is not always easy to distinguish indentured labor from other forms of unfree labor. The one factor that all forms of indenture had in common, however, was coercion.

The nature of coercion in the various forms of indenture was, and still is, a matter of debate. The question of whether indenture more closely approximated slavery or free migrant labor has been disputed for over two centuries. Looking at recruitment procedures, transportation, contract obligations, and enforcement, many contemporary observers, as well as antislavery activists, and more recently scholars, have likened indenture to slavery. They underlined the fraud and abuse used to recruit laborers and the arduous working conditions. In his influential study, *A New System of Slavery*, on Indian indentured labor Hugh Tinker concluded that indenture "replicate[d] the actual condition of slavery."[2] Others, however, have stressed the voluntary nature of accepting employment in the indenture system and have also pointed to the greater economic opportunities available to migrants at their destination. They viewed the abuses and malpractices as incidents in the earliest, unregulated phases of indentured migration. They argued that high mortality rates were not the result of working conditions and abuse, but of epidemiological factors. Rather than comparing Asian indenture to slavery, these "defenders" likened it to European nineteenth-century overseas migration to the Americas and Australia.[3] More recently, scholars have positioned the system within the wider framework of the prevalent master–servant relations in Britain, which existed well into the nineteenth century.[4]

Despite the fact that both slavery and indentured labor are forms of unfree labor and are often associated with back-breaking work on plantations, it is questionable whether the equation between the two is correct. The main differences are that indentured laborers did not become the legal property of their employers (who were often their owner in the case of

[2] Hugh Tinker, *A New System of Slavery: The Export of Indian Labour Overseas 1830–1920* (London, 1974), p. xiv.
[3] See, e.g., several publications by Ralph Shlomowitz on epidemiology, mortality, and indenture and Pieter C. Emmer on Indian indentured labor in Suriname.
[4] See, e.g., Steinfeld, who states that "strict labor contract enforcement through nonpecuniary pressure ... was an integral feature of English wage labor in the nineteenth century," Robert J. Steinfeld, *Coercion, Contract, and Free Labor in the Nineteenth Century* (Cambridge, 2001), p. 9.

slavery) and that there was a time limit to the contracts, which also prescribed the rights and duties of laborers and employers, albeit in Western terms. Indenture was a compulsory labor system, which was enforced by so-called penal sanctions, which made neglect of duty or refusal to work a criminal offense. Importantly, the enforcement of contracts, their supervision by authorities, the quality of indentured life in general, and labor conditions in particular, varied across time and space.

In recent decades, numerous publications have appeared with case studies of indentured labor relating to specific places of origin or destination, to specific economic activities, or to specific ethnic groups, often in a single place. These studies provide details about the experiences of indentured migrant laborers in particular settings, but often lack a comparative perspective showing the variations across time, geographical space, industry, and ethnic group. The number of more comprehensive comparative studies is limited, particularly those that examine diasporas from India, China, and Java.

ORIGINS, DESTINATIONS, AND RECRUITMENT

The nineteenth century saw a global movement of commodities and people, and of the capital required to accomplish this. The Industrial Revolution transformed "not only economic structures and social relations within the countries where the process was taking place, but also the momentum of global migration and the course of empire throughout the century."[5] Steamships made it possible to move great numbers of people across the oceans and beyond traditional areas of migration. The Caribbean Nobel Prize winner in economic sciences, Sir Arthur Lewis, distinguished two enormous streams of international migration: 50 million people leaving Europe for temperate climate zones to work in agriculture, industry, and construction, and another 50 million leaving East and South Asia to toil in the tropics producing agricultural goods and extracting minerals. This international and racial division of labor which took place within the framework of late colonialism or neo-colonialism includes the young republics in Latin America.

The growing demand for labor in mineral, industrial, infrastructural, and urban projects and on plantations could only be met because an increasing number of individuals were pushed to migrate because of

---

[5] Walton Look Lai, "Asian Diaspora and Tropical Migration in the Age of Empire: A Comparative Overview," in Walton Look Lai and Tan Chee-Beng (eds.), *The Chinese in Latin America and the Caribbean* (Leiden, 2010), p. 35; and Walton Look Lai, "Asian Contract and Free Migrations to the Americas," in David Eltis (ed.), *Coerced and Free Migration: Global Perspectives* (Stanford, CA, 2002), pp. 229–30.

hardship in their homelands and were pulled by the lure of opportunities in places of which they had previously probably never heard. The new indentured labor migration was a product of changing socioeconomic and political realities in the countries of origin, the extant patterns of (bound) labor migration, and the imperial nexus providing the legal and logistical basis (including recruitment and transport) for this type of migration. In short, old and new factors fused in this process, and the mix varied in the different areas of the migrants' origin. The most important supplying countries – India, China, and Java – had a long history of regional labor migration, while in other sending areas such as Japan and the Pacific the end of international isolation and overseas migration were intertwined. Another determining factor was demographic pressure in those areas where there simply was not enough land or work to support the growing population. Whatever the differences, the common factor was that all areas of supply were changed by the increasing economic and political power of Western empires.

The state intervened in the mobilization of labor for private enterprises. The state extended its authority by controlling the recruitment and migration process in the sending countries and the labor conditions in the destination centers. The efficiency or ability of the state to extract labor varied from country to country and over time. Important factors included the size and competence of bureaucracies, the moral attitude toward indentured servants among civil servants, and the geographic location of the sites of indentured recruitment or labor relative to centers of control.

Africa was the source of the first indentured migrants, but it turned out not to be a major supplier. Few people were inclined to move on account of extant socioeconomic conditions at home. Some British colonies recruited Africans freed from intercepted slave ships or liberated Africans in Sierra Leone, a British West African colony. According to David Northrup, approximately 60,000 indentured Africans left for the British, French, and Dutch Caribbean, 50,000 for Indian Ocean Islands, and 97,000 for other parts of Africa.[6]

The largest supplier was India, where Great Britain oversaw the recruitment, transport, and overseas labor conditions of more than 1.3 million indentured migrants, 900,000 of whom were transported to British colonies in Asia and the Caribbean. Imperial regulation and control checked the number of abuses, without being able totally to eliminate foul play.

---

[6] In addition to his chapter in this volume, see David Northrup, *Indentured Labor in the Age of Imperialism, 1834–1922* (Cambridge, 1995), p. 49; see also Northrup, "Freedom and Indentured Labor in the French Caribbean, 1848–1900" in Eltis (ed.), *Coerced and Free Migration*, pp. 208–14 for detailed information on labor recruitment in Africa. In addition to this African migration, a group of 30,000 Portuguese from Madeira were indentured in British Guiana and another 10,000 in Hawaii.

Indian indentured migration was directly tied to expansion of capitalist enclaves in the British orbit in the nineteenth century. The reach of London showed also beyond the Empire, as in Suriname, when in 1875 the government suspended recruitment for the Dutch colony following complaints by the British consul in Suriname concerning the health of the migrants and the inadequate system of justice. In the French colonies, the trade was banned in stages, beginning with French Guiana in the late 1870s, on account of maltreatment.

Indian indentured migration was not a new phenomenon in the nineteenth century, as traders and laborers had previously traveled to other parts of Asia or East Africa. Their number included enslaved who toiled on French plantations in Réunion and Mauritius and convict laborers in British colonies in Southeast Asia. What was different in the nineteenth century, however, was the origin of the new migrants, as they no longer came from coastal areas, but from inland communities.

After the first recruiting efforts by the French, looking for laborers for Réunion in the late 1820s, indentured migration expanded when planters from the island of Mauritius (which was British from 1810) turned to Indian labor after the abolition of slavery in 1834. Within five years, more than 25,000 Indians had been transported to Mauritius. This island offers an interesting case study of planters' reactions to the abolition of the slave trade and slavery. In contrast to the British Caribbean, illegally imported African enslaved continued to reach Mauritius until the late 1820s. They were followed by imports of Indian indentured workers. Local planters were confident that their business would boom with these migrant laborers who were considered cheaper, more productive, and easier to control than the formerly enslaved. But compulsion of labor trumped all the other factors in the choice of workers.

The optimism of the Mascarene planters had two linked effects: it inspired Caribbean planters to recruit Indian labor, but it also raised red flags among reformist British officials who were concerned about a new forced labor trade. The latter expressed humanitarian concern about abuses in Mauritius (where migration was suspended from 1839 to 1842), but they were particularly worried about allowing migration to the Caribbean as comparisons to the Middle Passage and a new system of slavery were to be expected from the vigilant antislavery societies. However, the Caribbean request for Indian labor could not be denied after Mauritius was allowed to import Indian workers again. In late 1844, a law allowing Indian emigration to British Caribbean colonies was passed; a few months later, the first ship with Indian laborers sailed for the Caribbean.

The terms of indenture changed over time. This first group leaving for the Caribbean was not made to sign a contract before departure, or even on arrival, but soon contracts signed in advance were legalized in all colonies. The terms of indenture also changed: in 1849, Mauritius made the minimum length of the labor contract three years; the Caribbean followed this policy. When some colonies provided a free return passage after completing a minimum of five years under contract, the five-year contract became standard in the Caribbean in 1862. When the system was firmly in place, the number of destinations, including non-British colonies, expanded. Indentured Indian immigration was legalized for Natal and Réunion (1860), the French Caribbean (1865), Suriname (1873), Fiji (1879), and East Africa (1895). It took the French more than a decade to convince the British of their good faith in protecting the rights of Indian indentured immigrants. The British finally consented on the condition that the Indians would be entitled to free return passage after only five years rather than the ten years then required in British possessions. Later, this same rule would apply to Dutch recruitment in India.

The number of intercontinental indentured migrants was less than 10 percent of the total number of indentured and non-indentured departures from India. Major Asian destinations such as Ceylon, Burma, and Malaysia attracted millions; annual departures climbed to over 425,000 in the last decades of the century. The seemingly endless supply of Indian migrants was the result of demography and overpopulation, political unrest, economic changes, and famine and other natural disasters which set millions on the move looking for work and shelter in the cities, where many would be lost and thus a potential prey for recruiters. Infrastructural changes, including the building of railroads, made easier the movement of people to the cities and also to the depots in the ports. Though it is difficult to pinpoint the exact reasons for migration, emigration data suggest that the Indian Rebellion of 1857 led to a peak in overseas departures.

In the places to which migrants were destined, a commonly held view was that the indentured immigrants came from the lowest stratum of Indian society. For example, Dutch officials contended that Suriname recruited the "scum of the earth." However, during the entire period of indentured migration, experienced officials in India (but also in Suriname) stated that the migrants represented an average sample of the rural population. Not all migrants were country folk; some had urban roots. Experienced officials reported difficulty in recruiting women. The most numerous groups of females willing to sign consisted of widows.

As stated previously, it is hard to gauge individual motives for signing a contract of indenture, but the army of recruiters played a crucial role in this decision. The actual recruiting was done by the so-called *arkatia* or unlicensed recruiter, who looked for candidates in busy places like markets, railway stations, and temples. According to Hugh Tinker, the *arkatia* worked within a local radius; he relied upon his local knowledge and local contact. He knew who was in trouble, who had fallen out with his family, who was in disgrace, who was wild or wanton. If a big man wanted to get rid of a trouble-maker, the arkatia was in contact. If the police were making things hot for anyone, he was in the know. Seldom – hardly ever – did the arkatia venture into the village to seek out his prey: this was too dangerous. The village folk would certainly beat him up if he showed his face within their walls.[7]

The *arkatia*, who received a fee for every recruit, often painted a deceptive picture, promising riches and concealing the long voyage across the *kala pani* (the black water, the crossing of which is a taboo in Indian culture) or the penal system. When successful, he handed the candidate over to the licensed recruiter, also an Indian, who took care of the administrative process and forwarded the recruit to the ports of Madras or Calcutta. South Indians, including many Tamils, predominantly migrated to South and Southeast Asia, Natal, and the French colonies. Tamils were characterized as submissive and in Malaya they were considered a counterweight against the laborers from elsewhere.[8]

All officials in the chain of command were more or less dependent on the premiums paid for each migrant. The recruiters were the weakest link. The *arkatia* and the licensed recruiters were closely connected: an *arkatia* who obtained a license became a recognized recruiter, while a recruiter who lost his license became an *arkatia*. This practice and the prospect of high wages, a promise too readily believed by the migrants who were looking for an escape hatch, were the main permanent problems of indentured migration in India. Once entered into the system, it became hard to run away.

Like India, China had a long tradition of labor migration, which took on new dimensions in the nineteenth century. And as in India, demographic, socioeconomic, political, and ecological pressures explain the growing willingness to leave. Finally, in both India and China, a majority of the migrants originated from specific sending areas. Historically, the southern coastal provinces of Guangdong and Fujian were the main areas of recruitment. In the nineteenth century, migrants to Southeast Asia came from Fujian, while Guangdonese dominated the labor trade to the western hemisphere.

---

[7] Quoted in Tinker, *A New System of Slavery*, p. 122; see also other examples on pp. 123–4.

[8] Principal destinations of Indian labor in the period 1838 to 1924 were (in rounded figures): Ceylon – 2,321,000; Malaya – 1,754,000; Burma – 1,164,000; Mauritius – 455,000; British Guiana – 239,000; Natal – 153,000; Trinidad – 150,000 (144,000 indentured); French Caribbean – 79,000; Réunion – 75,000; Fiji – 61,000; East Africa – 39,500 (32,000 indentured); Jamaica – 38,600 (36,500 indentured); Suriname – 34,400; and other British Caribbean – 11,200. Figures are from Northrup, *Indentured Labor*, Map 6, p. 53. Note that most of the data are for labor migration, not just indentured migration. The figures for regional migration to Ceylon, Burma, and Malaya are likely to be inflated by the inclusion of re-migrants (Northrup, *Indentured Labor*, p. 64).

Not all migrants were transported directly to their destination; rather, they traveled via other regional or imperial connections. For example, the Chinese for Suriname sailed from Java. In the nineteenth century, various forms of coerced migration existed simultaneously with debt to a third party being a common denominator. To further complicate matters, there were also two kinds of indenture arrangements, one run by the British Government and the other privately organized for Cuba and Peru, operating out of Macao. The main formal differences between the "credit ticket" (which advanced money for transportation and other expenses) and indenture systems were the nationality of recruiters (native or Western) and the nature of obligations. For indentured migrants, the passage was free, but was to be reimbursed in kind in the form of labor for a fixed period of time. The so-called *kangani* system in Southeast Asia was more informal and based on kangani or labor headmen who went back to their home communities to recruit people. These new recruits were not under indenture, but had made personal commitments with the kangani.

Immediately after the banning of the slave trade in 1807, the British showed interest in Chinese workers with their reputation for stamina and endurance. Yet, after the failed experiment in Trinidad in the early nineteenth century, the next transport of indentured Chinese to overseas European colonies took place only in 1843, when the planters' demand for labor overcame the racial antipathy of planters and the fact that recruitment was technically illegal under Chinese law. The first shipment brought 582 indentured Chinese from Singapore to Mauritius; the trade soon expanded in volume and destinations.[9] In 1850, the British Government granted permission to its Caribbean colonies to obtain Chinese indentured labor, but the recruitment costs were appreciably higher than in India, thus making this an expensive form of labor. In total, some 2 million Chinese traveled beyond Asian shores, but even this estimate represents only a modest part of total Chinese migration. In contrast to the Indian labor trade, which was largely directed to other parts of the British Empire, Chinese migrants left for a larger number of countries and colonies with different historical, political, legal, and socioeconomic histories, and as far apart as the Caribbean and Australia.

Recruitment in China was one of the main reasons for the ill repute of indentured migration. In particular, the system for Cuba and Peru, known

---

[9] The main destinations of Chinese indentured labor were: France (1917–19) – 140,000; Cuba (1847–73 and 1901–24) – 138,000; Peru (1849–75) – 117,000; Transvaal (1904–07) – 64,000; Hawaii (1852–99) – 34,500; and Australia (1848–80) – 6,000. Australia received 100,000 legally free Chinese laborers, Cuba another 17,000, and Hawaii another 18,500. The United States, mainly California, imported 348,000 "legally free Chinese." The main regional destinations of all types of labor were: Malaya (1881–1915) – 5,750,000; Philippines (1876–1901) – 325,000; Siam (1876–1901) – 310,000; and the Netherlands East Indies (1876–1901) – 86,000. Source: Northrup, *Indentured Labor*, Map 7, p. 61.

as *la trata amarilla* or the yellow trade, "virtually ignored the provisions of the law and kept condoning its numerous violations by recruiters (Chinese), shippers (of all nationalities), and planters and their agents."[10] In 1847, the first Chinese indentured laborers arrived in Havana, and soon after Peruvian entrepreneurs followed the Cuban example. The Spanish and Peruvian governments granted exclusive licenses to merchants to import Chinese indentured laborers on assignment. These merchants auctioned off the immigrants upon arrival. Contracts, printed in Chinese and Spanish, for the Cuban sugar plantations and guano islands in Peru lasted eight years. After 1855, the British, officially for humanitarian reasons, banned other nations from using their treaty ports, but competition for labor played a role. The British themselves continued to send indentured Chinese to British possessions in Australia and the Caribbean. The Spanish and Peruvians subsequently moved their trade to Portuguese Macao; Guangdong and Fujian remained the most important areas of recruitment.

Local agents hired Chinese sub-agents, so-called crimps, and even sub-sub-agents to do the actual recruiting. They tried to round up enough eligible men to meet their quota. As elsewhere, coercion, abuse, fraud, and deception about the final destination and the contract were oftentimes used to lure men to sign up. Spanish and local officials contended that in the late 1850s, 90 percent of the indentured migrants boarded ship against their will. Scandals about corruption, kidnapping, and other abuses prompted investigations uncovering even more irregularities. The sub-agents, locally despised as "pig brokers," were seen as the major culprits. Chinese contract migration was depicted as a new slave trade.

The principal problem was the lack of a well-structured mechanism of control. In the 1860s, a series of treaties between Chinese and Western authorities were concluded to regulate the trade. In 1874, the profitable "yellow trade" was banned, but this was not the end of bound overseas migration, as yearly hundreds of Chinese indentured laborers were shipped to Australia throughout the 1880s. In the early twentieth century, the labor trade revived under more strict bilateral agreements; the main recipients were the plantations in Cuba, the gold mines in Transvaal, and especially France in the final years of the First World War.

Indentured migration from Java started later than in India or China and continued for a longer period of time. As was the case in the rest of Asia, there already existed a tradition of migration and laws to control labor. The growth of indentured labor was a product of the rise of a pioneering export economy throughout the Dutch East Indian or Indonesian archipelago,

---

[10] Look Lai, "Asian Diaspora," p. 52.

particularly in Sumatra and Kalimantan in the western so-called Outer Islands from the 1870s. Whereas Javanese sugar and coffee had traditionally been the main pillar of the colonial export economy, in the early twentieth century the momentum shifted to the tobacco and rubber plantations in East Sumatra (Deli), the oil industry in Palembang (South Sumatra), coal mines in West Sumatra, and the oil and rubber industry in Southeast Kalimantan. In addition, tin from Belitung and Bangka, and copra, rubber, pepper, and coffee from North and West Sumatra and Riau were exported globally. All of these locations became destinations for indentured labor, but it was Deli with its frontier capitalism and boom-bust cycles that gave the system a bad name in contemporary official reports, in the colonial and nationalist press, and even in novels. Mortality on the Deli plantations was infamously high, with annual death rates at sixty to seventy per thousand in the 1890s. Later, improvements were reported, but the figures fluctuated, with some years recording an alarming number of deaths. In the 1920s, mortality rates fell below ten per thousand.

Given that the small local population was loath to work on European-managed enterprises, labor had to be recruited elsewhere. Densely populated Java was the obvious source, but planters were reluctant to ship off workers to other islands. Therefore, the first large influx of indentured laborers consisted of Chinese who were recruited in Malaya. Later groups came straight from China as the Malayan supply turned out to be too small. The reputation of the Chinese workers was not all positive: they were lauded as hard workers, but also branded as demanding and rebellious. Consequently, the call for Javanese indentured laborers, who were stereotyped as slower but submissive, gained strength now that the plantations were expanding at a rapid rate. By the second decade of the twentieth century Javanese indentured laborers outnumbered Chinese migrants in the Outer Islands.

There existed several overlapping systems of recruitment in Java: informal indigenous networks, commercial agencies, and employers. As in India and China, overpopulation served as a push factor in Java. And as in the other sending territories Java had a long tradition of labor migration through informal networks. Brokers, who organized pilgrimages to Mecca, also employed professional recruiters to arrange for Javanese temporary labor migration to plantations in Malaya and British North Borneo, and later New Caledonia and French Cochin China. However, the expanding economy in the Outer Islands meant that the informal local networks were inadequate to meet the growing demand for labor. After 1900, two commercial firms were additional players in the recruitment market. Recruitment for Suriname, too, was in these commercial hands. After much cajoling by Surinamese planters and authorities, the colonial government in Batavia (present-day Jakarta) in 1890 finally consented to indentured immigration to the Dutch Caribbean colony of Suriname. In total, almost 32,000 Javanese indentured migrants left for the West in the period 1890 to 1932. In 1939, another 990 free Javanese disembarked in Suriname, but that was the last group to arrive in the West. For Suriname, the length of contract was five years, while for the Outer Islands it was often three years or less. The commercial organization was similar to the Indian system with European recruiters, local agents, and henchmen (*handlangers*). The latter two groups were the actual recruiters who approached potential indentured laborers in villages and towns, targeting in particular crowded markets. The agent and his henchmen were each paid a premium for every recruit.

Critics of indentured migration disapproved of recruitment procedures in Java from the very beginning. Recruiters were accused of irregularities, including luring people with false promises, and illegal procedures. The reputation of the recruiters was so bad that Javanese aspiring to become members of the twentieth-century nationalist Islamic organization Sarekat Islam had to swear that they "would not steal, would not recruit, and would not lie."[11] In 1907, the Dutch labor inspector D. G. Stibbe reported as follows:

Recruitment in the interior is nowadays in the hands of a gang of unscrupulous extortioners (excluding, of course, the recruitment agencies), who, wholly under false pretexts and promises persuade the naive village man to emigrate; by duplicity lure women away from their husbands; and children from their parents. When the illicit recruitment, which through lack of Government regulations has attained very high levels, is added to this it is essential that the present situation should be brought to an end as soon as possible, both in the interests of the population, and of the migration itself, and in the interests of our reputation as a civilized nation.[12]

Other civil servants likewise reported regularly through official reports and articles about malpractices which were intended to undermine the bureaucratic control mechanisms. Other official requirements, such as the official registration of the identity and place of origin of each migrant, were often ignored. Recruits were transported to depots where they had to sign their contracts.

The seaports of Batavia, Semarang, and Surabaya were the foremost areas for recruitment, and it was here that the supervising recruitment commissioners were stationed to check procedures. The majority of the

---

[11] J. W. Meyer Ranneft, "De misstanden bij de werving op Java," *Tijdschrift voor het Binnenlands Bestuur*, 47 (1914): 62.
[12] Quoted in Vincent J. H. Houben, "Before Departure: Coolie Labour Recruitment in Java, 1900–1942," in Vincent J. H. Houben and J. Thomas Lindblad (eds.), *Coolie Labour in Colonial Indonesia: A Study of Labour Relations in the Outer Islands, c. 1900–1940* (Wiesbaden, 1999), p. 30.

recruits, however, originated from the densely populated rural parts of inland Java, indicating the migratory background of the recruits. In Java, the recruits were labeled as socially marginal, but in reality the social and professional background of the migrants for the Outer Islands as well as Suriname was more mixed. The flow of migrants to Suriname was exceedingly small compared to that to East Sumatra: Deli in its economically most prosperous years imported annually as many Javanese indentured immigrants as Suriname did in a forty-year period.

Around 1910, a third system in the recruitment of Javanese laborers came into operation. The constantly growing demand for labor encouraged employers to organize their own recruitment system in Java. This so-called *laukeh* (old hand) system, legalized in 1915, focused its activities on the social network of experienced labor migrants with a good track record. Not the *laukeh*, but their plantation managers, were licensed to recruit. The Department of Labor Inspection, in the person of the previously mentioned D. G. Stibbe, was the *auctor intellectualis* of the program that was similar to the kangani system in Malaya. The idea was that the reputation of recruitment and "coolie labor" would improve if a relative or acquaintance could be held accountable for the process. In turn, this was expected to lead to higher recruitment numbers. A weakness in this personal recruitment system was the lack of qualified *laukeh* recruiters. Needless to say, this system was not a realistic option for Surinamese planters. In effect, the old commercial recruitment continued, resulting in two different but identical systems operating next to each other, and often using the same recruiters.

The colonial state had a heavy hand in the system of indenture in both the administrative infrastructure and the legal framework. From the 1880s onward, a number of so-called Coolie Ordinances regulated the terms and obligations for indentured work in the Outer Islands. It should be noted that indentured labor did not exist in Java itself. The first Ordinance only applied to East Sumatra, but was later extended to other Outer Islands as well. The Ordinances regulated the organization of recruitment, transportation, conditions in depots, medical care, and supervision of the signing of the contracts. The Department of Labor Inspection was in charge of implementation of the Ordinances, but the number of inspectors and commissioners was never large enough to be an effective force in an ever-growing jungle of bureaucratic procedures. Moreover, the ambiguity of the extant rules ensured there was often a serious gap between theory and practice.

In Indonesia, the common term for an Asian worker was "coolie," and the labor system recognized three categories: "contract coolies" (who had signed a contract with a penal clause, subject to criminal jurisdiction if warranted), "free coolies" (who had signed a contract without the penal sanction, but who were certainly not free laborers), and casual workers (who did not fall under the Coolie Ordinances). It became increasingly common to not sign work contracts in Java, thus circumventing official checks. This type of migration was categorized as "free recruitment" because this labor contract did not include the penal clause. This type of "free" labor, often attracting time-expired indentured laborers, gained ground in the 1920s. By then, about one-tenth of the immigrant labor population in East Sumatra was "free."

Total "coolie" employment in East Sumatra rose from 110,000 in 1910 to 190,000 in 1913 and 300,000 in the late 1920s. Of these, 85 percent prior to 1917, 80 percent in 1920, and 57 percent in 1929 were "contract coolies." Around 1920, the companies made the definitive shift from Chinese to Javanese labor. At the turn of the century, two-thirds of the laborers had been Chinese and one-third were Javanese. In the boom years of the 1920s, when the rubber estates expanded rapidly, Chinese laborers were recruited for specialized and better-paid tasks. The shift to Javanese labor also meant that more women were recruited. The female labor force clearly was supplementary, as women were the first to be fired when the economy turned for the worse. The sex ratio was unbalanced at the plantations, but this imbalance was even greater in the oil industry and in the coal mines. During the bust caused by the Great Depression, the labor force consisting of "free" and "contract coolies" was reduced by almost 45 percent.

Labor conditions in other Outer Islands varied and did not allow for much comparison. For example, the oil industry offered the "best" contract with higher wages and better social provisions, while the climate in Lampung was unhealthy, with higher than average mortality rates. What indentured laborers outside East Sumatra had in common was that they usually worked in economic enclaves, located far from population centers and not in mainstream economic activities. Consequently, they were not only socially but also geographically marginalized. The setting up of new enterprises in remote and virgin areas added an extra dimension to already difficult labor conditions.

Japan and the Pacific Islands were places of origin of smaller numbers of indentured migrants. In Japan, the Meiji Government's opening of the country from 1868 led to an unprecedented international migration of indentured laborers and free migrants. The main destination was Hawaii, which saw the arrival between 1868 and 1900 of approximately 65,000 indentured Japanese. Though the United States had banned indentured contracts in 1885, Japanese immigrants were still in bondage as they were in debt, often for brokerage and transport services, to the contracting agencies. When in 1908 the United States restricted Japanese immigration, the flow turned to Peru, which received a total of 18,000 Japanese indentured migrants.

Recruitment in the Pacific Islands was known as "blackbirding" – the use of force and fraud by private agents. From the 1880s, the migration process was monitored by the British administration, which reduced major abuses. The majority of the indentured islanders came from Melanesia. More than 80 percent of the migrants were transported to plantations in Queensland (which alone received more than 60,000), to Fiji, and to the nickel mines in New Caledonia. In Fiji, more than 60,000 Indian indentured migrants, *Girmitiyas*, were imported when competition for Melanesians created a labor shortage and drove up recruitment costs. In the end, indentured Indian laborers vastly outnumbered the imported Pacific Islanders in Fiji.

The emergence of plantations in the western Pacific was fueled by the decline in cotton production in the US South during the Civil War and thus the abolition of slavery there. Cotton turned out to be a transitional crop, and soon was overtaken by sugar and copra. The indentured labor trade was closely linked to existing trading networks and maritime labor practices. In contrast to other processes of indenture, the Melanesians did not sign a written contract; their recruitment was based on oral agreement. Another difference was that the labor trade in the western Pacific lacked the infrastructure of other source areas and depended on beach-based exchanges between recruiters and potential candidates.

Despite the large number of migrants to destinations far outside their region of origin, the overwhelming majority of the skilled and unskilled Chinese, Indian, and Javanese migrants remained in South and Southeast Asia.[13] Their migration was over a relatively short distance, often preceded by internal migration to urban areas, caused by the transformation of local and regional economies. Transportation improvements facilitated both types of migration flows.

THE CONTRACT

The contract of indenture, which minimally listed the name of the laborer, regulated the legal relationship between worker and employer, stipulating a number of obligations for both parties. Its content varied over time, area, and economic branch, but the main clauses concerned the length of the contract and the number of working hours and days, as well as wages. The length of contract varied over time and in different areas and responded to the costs of recruitment and transportation. Employers recouped their initial costs by the work of the indentured. The higher the costs, the

---

[13] Look Lai, "Asian Diaspora," pp. 38–9, states that 6.5 million of the 7.5 million Chinese and 5 million of the 6.3 million Indian migrants remained in the region. Only a minority was actually indentured.

longer the contract would run. Chinese labor for Cuba and Peru was the most expensive and eight-year contracts were the standard. Intra-Asian recruitment and transportation costs were the lowest, resulting in contracts of three years or less.

Additional stipulations prescribed that the employer had to provide housing and medical care at his own expense. The worker could not leave the premises of the enterprise without consent. The core of the indenture contract was the penal clause, which subjected the worker to criminal jurisdiction in case of a breach of contract by refusing work or other infractions threatening labor discipline.

Actual surveillance of contracts was in the hands of civil servants who were the backbone of the (colonial) state in both the source and receiving areas. They could play an important role in supervising and checking the system, but they were not always united in their philosophy and operations. Required to keep the economic forces behind the systems in mind, some officials had greater cultural affinity with the Western employers, while others also tried to maintain a certain degree of autonomy in relation to the enterprises. Thus, besides official rules and regulations, the size and quality of the controlling bureaucracy and the personal efficiency of civil servants determined the level of inspection and the enforcement of the rules. The policy of these monitoring agencies could also shift over time. As the case of Deli shows, when in 1904 the government installed the Department of Labor Inspection to supervise working conditions, the goals of the agency shifted from eradicating the most excessive and obvious abuses to improving material conditions such as wages and health care.

Indian immigrants in non-British territories had the right to claim the assistance of the British consul. Communication with this official was free and without restrictions. Indentured laborers could request his help to appeal against the decisions of the highest local authorities. The consul could also report on shortcomings in the living and working conditions of Indians under indenture. In Suriname, planters and colonial officials identified the role of the British consul and the right of appeal as one of the major reasons for the perceived lack of submissiveness of the Indian labor force and a reason for promoting immigration from Java. Indonesian scholars later claimed that some Indians felt superior to the Javanese because of the protection they enjoyed from the British consulate.

Though the contract stipulated a fixed wage, the wages actually paid out could lead to conflict as "official" and actual wages often differed. According to many arrangements, the indentured laborers could be paid on the basis of days or hours worked or the number of tasks completed. Generally, employers preferred to pay for each finished task in order to increase labor productivity. Employers thus defined a task as the work an average laborer could perform in one day. The management argued that they were acting according to the contract. Indentured workers, however, frequently complained that the tasks assigned were too heavy to finish in one day, particularly when weather conditions such as heavy rain made their work even harder. Thus, employers and indentured laborers, sometimes supported by colonial officials, differed on what a worker could do in one day. The arbitrary definitions of an "average worker" and "average performance" were the main elements in wage conflicts. In practice, wages and thus the capacity of indentured workers to accumulate savings varied enormously, depending on their health and stamina, their experience, the type of work they undertook (with overseers, for example, earning more), or opportunities to gain extra income from other activities. Moreover, to obtain a clear measure of any earnings, income needed to be compared to the local cost of living. In many instances, the price of rice was an important determinant of the actual standard of living of the laborers.

After expiration of their contracts, laborers had several options: to sign a new contract, to return home, or to find employment elsewhere. The last option could be restricted as former indentured migrants were explicitly prohibited from working in certain industries to protect the non-immigrant population. Gold mining in Suriname is but one example. Many contracts included free return passage to convince those signing up of the, at least in theory, finality of the agreement. Many factors influenced decisions about whether to return or to stay. They included the formation of family and other relations in the host country, the power of the caste system in the case of Indian migrants, a failure of meeting savings goals, or the irregular sailing of return ships which caused time-expired migrants to incur debts. Distance from the homeland could also play a role in the decision to return. In Cuba and Peru, free return was not part of the contract and the high cost of the voyage made it difficult to return. In contrast, the overwhelming majority of Indian migrants in the Mascarene Islands repatriated. In the late nineteenth century, many Caribbean governments offered former indentured workers plots of land to populate the colony and to further develop smallholding agriculture. Repatriation rates varied through time among ethnic groups and destinations, and according to economic opportunities in places of destination and of origin.

RECEPTION IN HOST SOCIETIES

Governments and employers determined the conditions of the labor contracts, but the migrants themselves also shaped conditions in their new, possibly temporary, homes. Their places of work were often spatial and social enclaves. Upon arrival, most newcomers were allocated to their employers, but in some cases, including Cuba and Peru, slavery-style auctions were common. The arrivals had to adjust to a new environment, including different diseases, diet, work rhythm, culture, and social stratification.

Needless to say, circumstances varied by territory, time period, and product. In Peru, for example, the mortality rate among Chinese migrants was exceedingly high, but it is unclear whether this was caused by ill treatment and malnutrition or the encounter with a different disease environment. The organization of production and the profitability of the enterprise had a great impact on labor conditions and levels of well-being. A common denominator was a clearly defined hierarchical organization demanding unconditional discipline and obedience. Moreover, language differences increased the sense of alienation of contract workers from their employers. Yet, management cultures could vary by economic sectors or even among employers. Another important factor was the macro-economic climate. Rapid economic expansion might lead to increased workloads and mounting tensions, lower health standards, and more crowded housing. It is a matter of debate whether material conditions such as housing, medical care, drinking water, and food provisions improved over time. Finally, factors such as age, experience, social relations, and the physical state of migrants influenced how well and how quickly they might adjust.

Specific case studies, whether for particular places, ethnic groups, or economic sectors, reveal little about individual experiences, though there are some indirect indicators. Frustration about the circumstances in which they found themselves may have prompted a variety of reactions, ranging from gambling and drug taking to suicide or even rebellion. Heavy workloads and poor wages were often the main reasons for discontent. Desertion, that is leaving the enterprise without consent, was a clear act of dissatisfaction with prevailing conditions relative to opportunities elsewhere. One notorious case was the maltreatment of workers at a Japanese enterprise in Deli where the desertion rate reached 18.5 percent in 1925. Deserters could stay relatively close to their official place of employment, but could also cross state lines, as was the case with a growing number of Indians escaping Trinidad for Venezuela in the 1870s or with the Japanese in Mexico, some of whom escaped to the United States in the first years of the twentieth century.

Other obvious forms of protest, certainly to the outside world, were personal attacks on supervising staff or mass strikes and rioting. In case of open defiance, the army or police might be used to suppress unrest. Particularly in the late colonial period, employers used allegations of anti-colonial agitation as an argument to call in the support of the state to curb unrest on their enterprises, sometimes with perverse consequences for their workers. In Indonesia, in the 1920s, the fear of agitation by alleged "outsiders," such as nationalists and Communists, led to ever-more regressive policies, which did not lead to better treatment of the workers. Where resistance was more covert, involving, for example, feigning sickness or not following orders, the penal sanction gave the employers the right to take recalcitrants to court, as such breaches of contract were deemed criminal offences. Open confrontations may have been more eye-catching, but the rates of convictions may have been a clearer indication of resentment. Finally, contemporaries had little awareness of cultural strategies of survival, such as forms of escapism, to accommodate to the new life in an unfamiliar setting.

Though often from different cultural backgrounds, indentured workers moving overseas tried to form communities within the new and often alien world in which they found themselves. Adaptation and sociocultural identity formation often went hand in hand, but uneven sex ratios, and in particular a low ratio of females, sometimes made it more difficult to (re)build communities and to generate a sense of well-being and stability. This was especially so among Chinese and Pacific Islanders, making it even harder for them to settle in the host society. The British Government ordered that specified quotas of women needed to be recruited, while Caribbean planters stated that they wanted women not for their labor power, but to tie the men to the plantations. The status of women within the indenture systems remains, however, debatable. Some have argued that women were at the bottom of a race-class-gender hierarchy, subject to exploitation by both employers and by men from their own group, while others have pointed to the opportunities for women in a society with a shortage of females.[14]

The arrival and settlement of different ethnic groups sometimes caused outbreaks of open racism. The migrants were often seen as intruders taking jobs, weakening the bargaining position of local workers, mainly, in the Caribbean, and thus lowering wages. In particular, Chinese laborers were frequently targeted, both during and after the indenture period, not only because of their ethnic distinctiveness, culture, and language, but also because of their perceived economic success. Not surprisingly, in times of economic crisis, migrants were often scapegoats accused of taking jobs at cut-throat wages and undercutting local entrepreneurs. Ethnic tensions may even have harmed development in post-colonial countries such as Trinidad, Guyana, and Fiji, where rivalry between descendants of indentured laborers and other population groups continues to provoke discussion about social exclusion, with important socioeconomic, cultural, and

---

[14] See the debate between Emmer and Hoefte on the position of Indian indentured women in Suriname in *Boletin de Estudios Latinoamericanos y del Caribe*, 42 and 43 (1987). A contemporary source on the topic is the report by James McNeill and Chimmam Lal, *Report on the Condition of Indian Immigrants in the Four British Colonies Trinidad, British Guiana or Demerara, Jamaica, and Fiji, and in the Dutch colony of Suriname or Dutch Guiana* (London, 1915).

political consequences. Outcomes vary, however, for whereas twenty-first-century Mauritius and Suriname provide examples of non-Asian countries where people of Asian descent form today the majority of the population, in other countries, such as Jamaica or the French Caribbean islands, the presence of indentured migrants has basically "vanished."

THE END OF INDENTURE

Like the abolition of slavery, the end of indenture did not occur simultaneously in each of the receiving countries. Moreover, as with slavery, the debate surrounding the end of indenture focused on freedom in general and the concept of free labor in particular. Temporal and geographical factors influenced debates over the meaning of free labor. What was lauded as free labor in one place at a particular time was often labeled as slavery by another name at other places at the same or different times. The system's abuses fueled the debate. This controversy is still visible in current publications. Proponents stressed and continue to stress that indentured migrants signed a contract out of their own free will, while opponents pointed to deceptive recruitment methods, the penal sanction, and the labor and living conditions in new host societies. Sometimes, governments acted on critical reports regarding labor conditions and the legal rights of the indentured workers, but calls for reform were often ignored on account of either the socially marginal position or the ethnic background of the indentured migrants. Ultimately, politics with a capital P and new socioeconomic realities made the difference. Hawaii was the first major receiving country where indentured labor was banned when the US Anti-Peonage Act (1867) prohibiting the "voluntary or involuntary servitude" was extended to the newly annexed islands (1898). However, it was in the sending countries where the rising nationalist tides signaled the end of the system. China was the first to act when in the 1870s the country adopted a more assertive policy and first regulated and then suspended the system, even though debt and other forms of involuntary migration to Hawaii, Natal, and Europe continued to exist.

Despite an official report from 1910 endorsing indenture as a free-labor system benefiting Indian workers, even while acknowledging large-scale use of penal clauses to enforce labor discipline, six years later the Indian Viceroy, Lord Hardinge, abolished the indentured trade. Indenture was seen, in Hardinge's words, as "a system of forced labour entailing much misery and degradation and differing but little from a form of slavery." Consequently, he urged "the total abolition of the system of indentured labour" in Fiji, Jamaica, British Guiana, Trinidad, and Suriname.[15] This

---

[15] Quoted in Northrup, *Indentured Labor*, pp. 144–5; Tinker, *A New System of Slavery*, p. 339, respectively.

volte face by the British authorities was prompted by increasing nationalist pressure in India. Following Mohandas Gandhi's protests in Southern Africa over the precarious legal position of Indians there, indentured labor became a vehicle for highlighting wider forms of discrimination against Indians by the British. During the Great War, indentured migration was thus abolished by London in order to save the British Raj.

Other developments leading to the international abolition of indentured labor were socioeconomic in nature. As stated in this chapter's introduction, the nineteenth century had witnessed two major, distinct streams of migration: from Europe to temperate settlements and from Asia to (sub) tropical lands. At certain places these streams converged, as for example in Australia and Southern Africa. Where at first the European settlers regarded indentured labor as an asset, soon they considered the growing number of non-Europeans as a threat to European rule and jobs. Consequently, by the turn of the twentieth century, governments in these settler areas restricted entry of non-Europeans by adopting discriminatory legislation and thereby promoting the interests of people of European descent at the expense of the Asian populations.

In the plantation zones, changing economic circumstances sometimes made bound labor unattractive, either because economic downturns and unemployment militated against continuing recruitment or because in some cases offered wages were high enough to attract non-indentured workers. In Java, both political and economic factors prompted abolition of the penal sanction and thus of the "contract coolie" system in Indonesia and Suriname in 1931. In 1925, the Dutch East Indian government decided to gradually phase out the penal sanction. This decision, however, triggered opposition against the penal sanction by Dutch labor unions, the International Labour Organization, and the US Congress and forced the government to revise its plans. Before the repeal of the penal sanction, 80 percent of the workers in East Sumatra were still "contract coolies," thus underlining how long employers held on to the system of indenture. Low wages and mass unemployment caused by the Great Depression, however, made the indentured labor system redundant in the Dutch colonies both in the East and in the West.

CONCLUSION

The indentured labor system exhibited temporal, regional, and industrial variations depending, among other things, on the prevailing colonial authority that managed it, production regimes in new host societies, the local labor history, laws and customs in both source and host areas, the strength of the entrepreneurial class, the state of demand for workers in host areas, and supervisory structures. Many kinds of arrangements were simultaneously at work in both sending and receiving areas. Studies of the different systems in operation reveal a complex picture with different shades of coercion and freedom and that borders between forms of labor were fluid.

In whatever regime one considers, it was evident that the level of coercion involved was determined from the outset by whether an individual was forced to leave or made his or her own decision to leave. In either case, the role of recruiters was crucial. Those recruiters "fished in two pools." First, they pursued mobile laborers in search of work and who were willing to consider the opportunities of new life elsewhere. Second, recruiters targeted more sedentary people living in villages. Chicanery could be a part of the process encouraging people to leave, and might include providing misleading information about work and contract conditions, as well as final destinations, especially if they involved traveling long distances overseas. The costs of recruitment and transport were ultimately reflected in the length of initial contract signed by migrants.

Indentured migrants faced onerous conditions on sugar plantations, a major destination for such migrants and one where employers had often previously been slave-owners and working conditions had historically taken a heavy toll on the enslaved. But decades after slavery had ended, working conditions for indentured laborers in new and expanding economic enclaves such as Deli were also arduous. The case of Deli shows that it is questionable to claim that economic buoyancy and prosperity for employers of labor naturally entailed better working conditions for bonded labor. After an initial period of trial and error in the first half of the nineteenth century, the indentured labor system reached both its historic peak numerically and its greatest diversity in the third quarter of the nineteenth century. Thereafter, the number of indentured migrants slowly declined, notably in the wake of the formal abolition of the system in China and India, but it still survived well into the twentieth century. Its final collapse came in the 1930s, with repeal of the penal clause in the Dutch East Indies in 1931, and its subsequent ending in Suriname, the last refuge of indentured labor in the Americas. Local histories of indentured migration and labor, detailing changes and differences across time and space, are important to understanding the complexities and nuances, as well as the aftermath.

The categorization of the revived system of indenture has been debated since its early-nineteenth-century beginnings. The system was hailed as free labor based on voluntarily signed contracts, but the fact that in many places it was a direct successor to slavery, with the mental legacy of that system as well as the material remnants such as slave barracks, made it suspect then and now. As with slavery, racism was a cornerstone of the indentured migration system, even though its depth varied across colonial settings and depended on global and local economic conditions influencing how employers, civil servants, and other population groups treated "foreign" laborers.

Despite these continuums, indentured labor was not an intermediate phase in a teleological development from slavery to free labor. Indentured labor existed in places without a history of slavery and in other settings where enslaved, free, and indentured laborers worked side by side. Indenture was a bound labor system based on a time-specific contract to a single employer, defining the rights and obligations of both employer and laborer. The indentured contract hinged on the penal sanction, enforcing the terms under criminal law, and ensuring the docility and malleability of the indentured laborer. The way in which the system was implemented showed clear variations in time and locality, calling for a nuanced approach to indentured migration and to labor.

A GUIDE TO FURTHER READING

Christopher, Emma, Cassandra Pybus, and Marcus Rediker (eds.), *Many Middle Passages: Forced Migration and the Making of the Modern World* (Berkeley, CA, 2007).

Clarke, Colin, Ceri Peach, and Steven Vertovec (eds.), *South Asians Overseas: Migration and Ethnicity* (Cambridge, 2009).

Drescher, Seymour, *The Mighty Experiment: Free Labor versus Slavery in British Emancipation* (Oxford, 2002).

Eltis, David (ed.), *Coerced and Free Migration: Global Perspectives* (Stanford, CA, 2002).

Houben, Vincent J. and J. Thomas Lindblad, *Coolie Labour in Colonial Indonesia: A Study of Labour Relations in the Outer Islands, c. 1900–1940* (Wiesbaden, 1999).

Kale, Madhavi, *Fragments of Empire: Capital, Slavery, & Indian Indentured Labor in the British Caribbean* (Philadelphia, PA, 1998).

Linden, Marcel Van der (ed.), *Humanitarian Intervention and Changing Labor Relations: The Long-Term Consequences of the Abolition of the Slave Trade* (Leiden, 2011).

Look Lai, Walton and Tan Chee-Beng (eds.), *The Chinese in Latin America and the Caribbean* (Leiden, 2010).

Northrup, David, *Indentured Labor in the Age of Imperialism, 1834–1922* (Cambridge, 1995).

Steinfeld, Robert J., *Coercion, Contract, and Free Labor in the Nineteenth Century* (Cambridge, 2001).

Tinker, Hugh, *A New System of Slavery: The Export of Indian Labour Overseas 1830–1920* (London, 1974).

CHAPTER 27

FORCED LABOR IN NAZI GERMANY AND THE STALINIST SOVIET UNION

ALAN BARENBERG

INTRODUCTION

Nazi Germany and the Stalinist Soviet Union created and operated forced labor systems that were among the largest in the twentieth century. In each case, coerced labor was part of a vast system of terror and economic exploitation that affected millions both within and outside state borders. In the popular imagination, Nazi and Stalinist forced labor often serve as the quintessential expression of each regime's fundamental nature, bent on the cruel exploitation, and often the physical annihilation, of its victims. Indeed, apparent similarities between the Nazi and Soviet systems of terror and exploitation are often invoked to demonstrate characteristics shared by both regimes, frequently stated in terms of their "totalitarian" nature. Yet, systematic investigations of forced labor in Nazi Germany and the Stalinist Soviet Union suggest that there were significant differences in how they operated, both in theory and in practice. This chapter will examine forced labor, both within each national context and in comparison to the other, from four perspectives. First, it provides a broad overview of each forced labor system, in terms of chronology, scale, and institutions. Second, it examines the place of each forced labor system within its respective society, focusing particularly on attempts to create and maintain social and spatial distance between forced laborers and ordinary citizens. Third, it analyzes mortality rates among forced laborers. Finally, this chapter discusses the end of each system and attempts to punish perpetrators and compensate victims.

This chapter takes a broad approach to the question of what populations should be considered forced laborers. It examines a wide range of populations that were exploited as forced laborers in Nazi Germany and the Soviet Union, including concentration camp prisoners, prisoners of war, ethnic and class deportees, conscripted foreign workers, and Jews subjected to forced labor. Toward this end, it explores the operation of a wide range of forced labor institutions, including not only concentration camps, but also exile villages, mobile labor "columns," and private factories. As such, this chapter attempts to understand the operation of forced labor more broadly in the Nazi and Soviet contexts and, in particular, how it fit into their respective social and economic orders. Acknowledging that there was great diversity both in the status of forced laborers and the institutions through which they were exploited, I argue that a broad examination of each system side by side reveals a great deal about the nature of Nazi and Stalinist forced labor and its place in each respective society.

STALINIST FORCED LABOR

The Soviet system of forced labor, what would later become known as the Gulag, existed from the early 1930s until the late 1950s. Institutionally, it consisted primarily of labor camps and exile settlements. The former, which included both "corrective labor camps" (ITLs) and "corrective labor colonies" (ITKs), held prisoners convicted of various crimes and given specific sentences, whereas the latter held members of population categories that were collectively subjected to terms of exile that were usually open-ended. In addition, during and after the Second World War, millions of foreign prisoners of war were subjected to forced labor within the Soviet Union in a parallel, but separate system. Over the course of its existence, the Gulag changed significantly in a variety of ways, including the size of its population, the targets of repression, and conditions within the various forced labor institutions. However, it remained an important source of economic capital for the Soviet state throughout the Stalin era, particularly when it came to colonizing remote parts of the Soviet Empire and exploiting natural resources.

The Gulag's creation was closely related to the launch of "the Great Break," Joseph Stalin's radical attempt to remake the Soviet Union. The First Five-Year Plan (1928–1932), which promised to rapidly transform Soviet agriculture and industry, saw a small system of prisons and camps grow into a massive penal empire. In particular, the decision to use any means necessary to induce peasants to join collective farms was fundamental in the spread of forced labor. During the ongoing collectivization operation, hundreds of thousands of alleged kulaks (wealthy peasants) were deprived of their property and deported to sparsely settled regions of the Soviet Union, particularly in Siberia and the Far North. By 1930, the Soviet police organs (the OGPU until 1934, from 1934 to 1946 the NVKD, and from 1947 to 1953 the MVD) had hundreds of thousands of politically suspect potential forced laborers at its disposal. A hastily established system of "special settlements" spread across the Soviet Union, with a population soon numbering well over a million. Such "special settlements" would serve as the prototypes for exile settlements for the three decades that followed.

Operations against peasant kulaks, intensified terror against "bourgeois specialists," and increased pressure to rapidly industrialize led to a rash of arrests during the First Five-Year Plan that rapidly expanded the size of the Soviet Union's prisoner population as well. Existing camps and prisons proved to be inadequate to house the new prisoners, and what was more, police officials saw the opportunity to transform the existing penal system into a large network of labor camps. Soon, hundreds of thousands of prisoners were engaged in a wide range of economic activities across the Soviet Union. By the middle of the 1930s, these camps formed a massive network, engaged in mining, construction, lumber, and, to a lesser degree, agriculture. These camps, in addition to prisons and "special settlements," were run under the Main Administration of Camps, a bureaucracy created in the winter of 1930 to 1931. Though its official nomenclature was frequently changed throughout Stalin's rule, its original acronym, Gulag, would later become a shorthand term for referring to the Soviet forced labor system as a whole.

From its inception, the forced labor of prisoners and exiles in the Gulag was seen as an essential resource to aid in the transformation of the Soviet Union from an economic backwater into a powerhouse. "Special settlements" and camps were considered to be tools of internal colonization, one of the methods that Soviet leaders had at their disposal to transfer populations and exploit remote natural resources. The connection between the Gulag and colonization was particularly explicit in early discussions regarding the system, but it remained an important part of the Gulag's mission throughout Stalin's lifetime. Given its size, the Gulag came to play an essential part in the Soviet economy. The Gulag population was never a significant proportion of the total labor force of the Soviet Union – in 1940, for example, the total population of camps, colonies, and "special settlements" was approximately 3 percent of the total labor force in the Soviet Union (this, as we shall see, was in clear contrast to the importance of forced labor in wartime Nazi Germany).[1] However, the Gulag played a key role in certain sectors of the Soviet economy, in particular in construction and the production of minerals.

That said, the Gulag cannot be seen solely as an economic institution. Though scholars have long debated whether the Gulag was primarily an economic, political, penal, or ideological institution, the system incorporated all of these elements. On one level, it was a penal system that housed a growing number of criminals of various kinds, from petty thieves to those convicted of the most serious treason against the Stalinist order. Indeed, it is important to point out that prisoners convicted of non-political crimes

[1] Figures derived from J. Arch Getty, Gábor T. Rittersporn, and Viktor N. Zemskov, "Victims of the Soviet Penal System in the Pre-War Years: A First Approach on the Basis of Archival Evidence," *American Historical Review*, 98 (1993): 1021; John Barber and Mark Harrison, *The Soviet Home Front, 1941–1945: A Social and Economic History of the USSR in World War II* (London, 1991), p. 215.

always outnumbered those convicted of political crimes. As a penal system, it was concerned with the rehabilitation of prisoners and exiles, in Soviet parlance "re-forging" (*perekovka*), with anywhere between 20 and 40 percent of Gulag prisoners released every year during Stalin's reign. Such a goal is reflected in the public face of the camps in the early 1930s, particularly the White Sea Canal construction project that was commemorated in a volume featuring many prominent Soviet writers. It is also apparent in the internal documentation that camp officials used to categorize prisoners. Thus, as historian Steven Barnes recently concluded, the Gulag was an "especially Soviet institution," in which ideology played an essential role in shaping attempts to reclaim the margins of Soviet society.

By the late 1930s, however, the priority of "reforging" prisoners and exiles was receding in the favor of isolation and economic exploitation, a process that intensified during and after the Second World War. Isolation was clearly the priority for hundreds of thousands of prisoners from the western borderlands, particularly from the Baltics and Western Ukraine, who were swept into the camps as the Soviet Union attempted to re-establish its authority after the war. It was also the clear priority during the second "wave" of deportations to Soviet "special settlements." Unlike the first, which had targeted kulaks on the basis of class, these were carried out against specific Soviet nationalities that were the subject of intense suspicion and scrutiny. The focus of these deportations was on diaspora nationalities with potential loyalties to fellow nationals outside Soviet borders, and also nationalities accused of actively collaborating with the Nazis. The first Soviet national group to be deported en masse was the Korean minority in the Soviet Far East, a group numbering 170,000 people, who were deported to Central Asia in 1937. This was followed by various wartime deportations, including Soviet Germans and Poles. Next came the so-called "punished peoples," six national groups from the Caucasus and Southwestern Russia accused of collaborating with the Germans. The group, which totaled 900,000 people, included virtually the entire Karachai, Kalmyk, Chechen, Ingush, Balkar, and Crimean Tatar populations in the Soviet Union. After deportation, the semi-autonomous "ethnic homelands" in which these groups had lived were eliminated. In 1948, the Supreme Soviet decreed that the wartime deportees would retain their status as "special settlers" permanently. Further, many categories of camp prisoners would be permanently exiled upon release. Thus, there was little "reforging" to be done with the waves of new prisoners and exiles in the post-war era.

Overall, it is estimated that 18 million people were imprisoned in Soviet camps and colonies, whereas 6 to 7 million were exiled. However, the population of the Gulag varied significantly from year to year over that time because of various campaigns that resulted in arrests/deportations, but also because of mortality, escape, and periodic releases of prisoners and exiles. The "special settlements" grew significantly over the first half of the 1930s during collectivization, reaching a population of 1.3 million at the beginning of 1932. The population then declined steadily until 1935, when there were approximately 973,000, and afterwards remained relatively steady until the beginning of the Second World War. During the first two years of the war, the exile populations fell as kulaks were released for frontline service. However, wartime national deportations swelled the population of the "special settlements" from 1943 onward. By October 1945, there were already 2.2 million "special settlers," and by the beginning of 1953, there were 2.7 million exiles in the villages.[2]

By contrast, the population of camps follows a somewhat more regular trajectory, growing in the 1930s (particularly after 1935), falling during the Second World War, and then growing once more until Stalin's death in 1953. In 1934, there were just over half a million prisoners in the Gulag. By 1935, this number had doubled. After the Great Terror of 1937 to 1938, it increased again to nearly 2 million. The Gulag prisoner population declined throughout the war due to high release rates and high mortality, falling to 1.2 million in January 1944. The population rapidly increased thereafter, reaching its zenith in January 1950, when there were over 2.5 million prisoners in the Gulag.[3]

The overwhelming majority of prisoners and exiles in the Gulag system were Soviet citizens. This was not the case, however, with a final group of forced laborers: foreign POWs captured during the Second World War. After the victory in the Battle of Stalingrad in early 1942, the Red Army began to capture tens of thousands of POWs each month, and Stalin was eager to utilize their forced labor to aid the war effort and rebuilding. A small minority of POWs was formally charged with crimes and sent to Gulag camps. A somewhat larger group was sent to "separate labor battalions" (ORB) controlled directly by the Ministry of Armed Forces. However, the vast majority were processed and then transported to camps within the Soviet Union to be exploited as forced labor by the GUPVI (Main Administration for the Affairs of POWs and Internees), another NKVD (later MVD) department. In the GUPVI camps, prisoners were employed in a wide range of economic activities, particularly construction, heavy industry, and defense production. This included not only high-profile building projects such as metro lines and hydroelectric stations, but also urban housing. POWs played a significant part of post-war reconstruction – estimates from the Soviet military archive suggest that POWs

---

[2] J. Otto Pohl, *The Stalinist Penal System: A Statistical History of Soviet Repression and Terror, 1930–1953* (Jefferson, NC, 1997), pp. 57, 59, 133.

[3] Getty *et al.*, "Victims of the Soviet Penal System," p. 1048.

contributed more than 1 billion "labor days" to the Soviet economy from 1943 to 1950, and in 1945 comprised nearly 4 percent of the total Soviet labor force.[4] Of all the components of Soviet forced labor under Stalin, the use of POWs most resembled Nazi labor practices, in that these were foreign citizens exploited to serve the domestic economy. At its height in early 1946, there were nearly 2 million POWs working to rebuild the Soviet Union, including 500,000 Japanese and 1.2 million Germans.[5] Overall, nearly 3.5 million POWs were subjected to forced labor in the Soviet Union from 1943 to 1950.

NAZI FORCED LABOR

Whereas the use of forced labor was systemic in the Soviet Union for three decades, Nazi use of forced labor was largely confined to the Second World War. The Nazi regime did establish concentration camps for its perceived enemies as it seized power in 1933 to 1934, but these camps were hardly analogous to the Soviet Gulag of the 1930s. First of all, the Nazi concentration camp system population was far smaller, and did not exceed one hundred thousand until 1942. Second, throughout the 1930s, prisoner labor in Germany was focused primarily on punishment, and therefore usually involved in activities of marginal economic utility. Instead, it was foreign civilians and POWs that became the basis of a vast system of forced labor that was a key part of the Nazi wartime economy.

There were ample precedents for the use of both civilian and POW foreign forced laborers in Nazi Germany. Germany had used Polish seasonal labor since the 1860s, and during the First World War approximately 500,000 Polish migrant workers were compelled to work in the German economy. Germany had also deployed POWs as forced laborers during the First World War. Such precedents were clearly important when the Nazi regime began to discuss the use of foreign civilian and POW forced labor during the late 1930s and early 1940s. These discussions were precipitated by rapidly changing economic conditions as Germany mobilized for total war. After sustained economic recovery in the second half of the 1930s, unemployment was no longer a problem in the German economy. Instead, there were now labor shortages, and planners feared that food shortages would soon follow. In the summer of 1938, the Nazi leadership was concerned with an impending agricultural crisis, driven to

---

[4] Stefan Karner, *Arkhipelag GUPVI: plen i internirovanie v Sovetskom Soiuze 1941–1956* (Moskva, 2002), p. 164; Barber and Harrison, *The Soviet Home Front, 1941–1945*, p. 215.

[5] Christian Gerlach and Nicolas Werth, "State Violence – Violent Societies," in Michael Geyer and Sheila Fitzpatrick (eds.), *Beyond Totalitarianism: Stalinism and Nazism Compared* (Cambridge, 2009), pp. 167–8.

a large degree by the urban economic boom that was luring workers to the cities from the countryside. As mobilization for war ramped up, labor shortages also spread to industrial production. By May 1940, for example, the armaments industry reported a shortfall of 1 million workers, and with increasing numbers of German men conscripted for the front, the prospect of finding such workers domestically was non-existent. At the same time, Nazi conquests opened the possibility of using foreign workers to make up for such shortfalls. Beginning with the annexation of Austria and Czecho-slovakia, and continuing through the Soviet invasion in 1941 to 1942, millions of foreign workers were made available as "booty" for the German economy. Thus, war was responsible both for generating shortages in the Nazi economy and providing the Nazis with an ever-expanding pool of potential coerced laborers, factors that profoundly shaped the course of Nazi forced labor policy and practices.

Polish civilians and POWs constituted the first significant group of foreign laborers deployed by the Nazis. By the end of 1939, 300,000 Polish POWs had been put to work in German agriculture. They were joined by civilians conscripted from the General Government (Nazi-occupied West-ern Poland), of whom a roughly equal number were subjected to forced labor in 1940. The number of Polish forced laborers would continue to increase thereafter. POWs and civilians from Continental Western Europe were conscripted following further Nazi conquests in the spring and summer of 1940. By October 1940, there were 1.2 million French and British POWs subjected to forced labor. Nazi allies also provided forced laborers: for example, by September 1941, there were 270,000 Italian workers in Germany. Finally, after the invasion of the Soviet Union in June 1941, millions of POWs and civilians were conscripted for forced labor. Despite frighteningly high mortality rates among foreign workers, particularly among Soviet POWs, by the summer of 1944 there were 7.6 million POWs and civilian workers performing forced labor in Germany, a figure that dwarfs not only the population of Nazi concentration camps, but also the Soviet Gulag and GUPVI. Though the majority of the forced laborers were men, there were 1.9 million women among them (one-third of the civilian conscripts), the vast majority of whom had been taken from the Soviet Union.[6]

Much of the Nazi leadership had significant reservations about employing foreigners in the Reich, particularly Poles and Easterners who were low on the Nazi racial hierarchy. Indeed, those in the leadership who argued for the increased use of coerced foreign labor had to overcome the forceful pursuit of Nazi racial policy by Himmler and others.

---

[6] Ulrich Herbert, *Hitler's Foreign Workers: Enforced Foreign Labor in Germany under the Third Reich* (Cambridge, 1997), pp. 62, 85, 95, 98, 296–7.

However, by 1940, labor shortages had become acute enough that compromises were reached regarding the conscription of Poles to the Reich. In order to make it ideologically palatable, the use of Poles as forced laborers was explicitly conceived as a short-term measure. Further, they would be limited to working in agriculture, and would be subject to an extraordinarily strict regime (see below). But the greatest turnabout in Nazi forced labor policy concerned Soviet POWs and civilians. The infamous *Generalplan Ost*, a plan for the Nazi colonization of Eastern Europe formulated from 1939 to 1941, had called for the removal of the vast majority of the Slavic population of Poland and the Western Soviet Union. Related plans for Nazi occupation of the Soviet Union explicitly called for the forced starvation of 20 to 30 million Soviet civilians so that food from the Soviet Union could be used for the needs of Germany instead. Such plans suggest that the Nazis did not see the Soviet population as a pool of potential labor. However, just as the exigencies of war brought a compromise on the use of Polish civilians and POWs, economic realities following the invasion brought a significant shift change in Nazi policy toward Soviet civilians. By September 1941, there was already a shortage of 2.6 million workers across the German economy. In October, Hitler ordered the widespread deployment of Soviet civilians and POWs for labor in the Reich. While genocidal policies against Soviet Jews and POWs continued, in 1942 authority for the deployment of foreign forced labor was shifted to Albert Speer's new Ministry of Armaments and War Production, with Fritz Sauckel appointed to a new position created solely for the purpose of coordinating foreign forced labor, General Plenipotentiary for Labor (GBA). The creation of the GBA indicated just how significant a priority the deployment of foreign labor had become. Sauckel and the GBA would preside over the conscription of millions of civilians from Soviet territories.

Foreign forced labor was an integral part of the German economy only from 1940 to 1945. But this relatively brief time span belies the fact that it played a much larger role in the overall German economy than forced labor ever did in the Soviet Union. By the summer of 1944, foreign laborers constituted over a quarter of the overall workforce in Germany. Further, foreign labor tended to be concentrated in certain sectors of the German economy that came to rely on it. For example, foreign workers (mostly Polish civilians and French POWs) constituted nearly half of the agricultural workers in Germany. In mining, metals, chemicals, and construction, foreign workers constituted nearly a third of the workforce. They made up over a quarter of the labor force in transportation. If we add to this the forced labor of concentration camp prisoners in construction and armaments, as well as the forced labor of Jews outside the concentration camp system (both discussed below), it is clear that forced labor played a central role in the Nazi wartime economy, far greater than the role of forced labor in the Soviet economy even at its height.

At the same time that the conscription of civilians and POWs from the Soviet Union intensified in 1942, the Nazi concentration camp system began a significant transformation that made it an important site of forced labor for the first time in its history. The system expanded rapidly, and the prisoner population exceeded 100,000 for the first time in 1942. By early 1945, the concentration camp population passed 700,000. This expansion was related to the two imperatives that now governed the system's operation. First, a policy to systematically exterminate Europe's Jewish population had emerged between the summers of 1941 and 1942, and concentration camps were key sites of extermination. Second, continued concerns about labor shortages and the inability of the Nazi economy to cope with the demands of total war led to the reorientation of the camps to maximize the economic exploitation of prisoners. For the first time, the concentration camp system was thoroughly integrated into the German war economy. Both extermination and economic exploitation were overseen by the new Business and Administration Main Office (WVHA) of the SS, run by Oswald Pohl. The move signified that the concentration camps were to be a part of an expanding SS economic empire.

The question of how to exploit prisoner forced labor resulted in significant conflict between the SS and industry leaders. Himmler and the SS foresaw prisoners working in factories and enterprises that would be directly subordinated to the WVHA. However, industrial leaders were loath to cede control to the SS. By 1943, a system emerged whereby concentration camp prisoners were "loaned" out to factories. In many cases, prisoners were transferred from main camps to satellite camps that were set up at construction sites and existing armaments factories. These industries then paid the concentration camps a daily fee per prisoner and were responsible for their upkeep, such as it was. These satellite camps spread rapidly and expanded from a few hundred at the end of 1943 to over 730 by January 1945. By the end of 1944, the majority of concentration camp prisoners were working in such satellite camps.[7] By 1944, Albert Speer, Minister of Armaments and War Production, had taken over responsibility for camp labor, a move that demonstrated both the importance of forced labor by concentration camp prisoners and the "triumph" of the satellite camps as a model.

---

[7] Jens-Christian Wagner, "Work and Extermination in the Concentration Camps," in Jane Caplan and Nikolaus Wachsmann (eds.), *Concentration Camps in Nazi Germany: The New Histories* (London, 2010), p. 135.

Jews were exploited as forced laborers not just in the SS concentration camp system, but also outside it. In fact, Jews were the largest inmate group in the SS camps only for a relatively short frame of time, in 1938 and again from late 1944 until 1945. Organized into "columns of Jews" (*Judenkolonnen*) by local labor offices, hundreds of thousands of Jews in Germany and occupied territories were forced to work on a variety of economic projects throughout the war. The spread of Jewish forced labor began in 1938 with a decisive shift in Nazi policies. Up until that point, the overall thrust of Nazi anti-Semitism had been to eliminate Germany's Jewish population through emigration. Yet, sustained anti-Jewish violence in late 1938 failed to bring about the desired emigration, and further, the absorption of new territories actually increased Germany's Jewish population. Thereafter, local labor administrations organized labor columns and camps for Jews in Germany and throughout occupied territories in the East. They tended to be much smaller scale than those that were formally part of the concentration camp system, and often operated only on a temporary basis in order to complete a particular economic task. The largest number of Jewish forced laborers were in occupied Poland, where there were more than 700,000 forced laborers at the end of 1940, though there were also large populations of Jewish forced laborers in Germany, Austria, and the former Czech lands. At its height, over 1 million Jews were subject to forced labor in this manner.

FORCED LABOR AND ITS PLACE IN STALINIST AND NAZI SOCIETIES

Both Nazi and Stalinist forced labor systems were seen as potentially dangerous sites for their respective societies. Each targeted populations that were considered to have the potential to corrupt ordinary citizens. In the Soviet case, this was largely a fear of criminal or political corruption that prisoners and exiles could inflict on law-abiding Soviet citizens, though later the fear of nationalist contamination became paramount. In the Nazi case, concentration camp prisoners and foreign laborers not only presented a political danger to German society, but also the danger of racial corruption. Thus, the Soviets and the Nazis attempted to create and maintain distance, both spatial and social, between forced laborers and ordinary citizens. Each used a wide variety of measures that depended both on the forced labor institution and the identity of the forced laborer.

The most obvious way in which the Stalinist and Nazi regimes attempted to create and maintain social distance between forced laborers and the general population was through confinement of the forced laborers to enclosed camps. One defining feature of the concentration camp is its spatial isolation. Gulag camp "zones" were surrounded by physical barriers, usually a single or double row of barbed wire fencing, with periodic guard towers from which prisoners could be shot if they attempted to escape. Nazi SS camps were also surrounded by barriers, which ranged from simple fences to sophisticated multilayered systems involving concrete walls, electrified fences, and moats. The purpose of such barriers was to dissuade escape attempts through intimidation and to physically prevent them. But such barriers did more than simply deter escapes – they also marked boundaries between the outside world and the internal world of the camps, which operated according to different rules. Further, such barriers were intended to conceal, as much as was possible, the world of the camp from that of the outside (and vice versa). Thus, scholars of the Gulag and Nazi concentration camps have focused on each system's isolation. Aleksandr Solzhenitsyn described the Gulag as an "archipelago," whereas Wolfgang Sofsky described Nazi camps as a "closed universe."

A majority of forced laborers in both the Stalinist Soviet Union and Nazi Germany were confined to camps of various kinds. Gulag prisoners in both ITLs and ITKs, as well as POWs in the GUPVI system, were held in enclosed spaces that followed the basic model of the Gulag "corrective labor camp" established in the early 1930s, though there was often considerable variation among them. In Nazi Germany, it was not only prisoners in SS concentration camps who were confined, but also Jews outside the SS camps, as well as many of the foreign civilians and POWs conscripted during the Second World War, particularly those in urban industrial areas. There was considerable variation in the size and layout of the camps themselves, as well as their evolution over time, making it difficult to generalize how forced laborers were confined in Nazi Germany. Indeed, even when speaking only of the SS concentration camps, historian Nikolaus Wachsmann concluded that they were "extremely diverse." Regardless of the variation, confinement and isolation were a major operating principle of all types of camps run by both regimes.

However, a significant proportion of the forced laborers in both the Stalinist Soviet Union and Nazi Germany were not confined to camps. In the Soviet case, millions of "special settlers" were exiled to villages in remote areas. They were not allowed to leave the area without special permission, and were required to check in regularly with the local authorities. However, their physical movements within such settlements were generally not regulated and they were free to interact with non-exile populations. While their places of exile were sometimes extremely remote, they were frequently sent to areas that already had significant local populations. Many of the foreign forced laborers in Nazi Germany were not confined to camps either. Civilians and POWs conscripted from Nazi-occupied "Western" countries were far less likely to be held in isolated camps, particularly those brought to Germany early in the war. Until 1941, the majority of foreign laborers worked in agriculture, and such workers lived on farms in relatively small groups, making it impractical to keep them in camps.

Because of their perceived potential to corrupt other populations, these unconfined forced laborers presented particular challenges for the Soviets and the Nazis. The Stalinist solution to this issue was largely geographical in nature: in order to keep exiles from interacting with other populations, they were usually sent to remote areas. In the 1930s, this often meant being sent to villages in Siberia or the Far North that were little more than "pencil points on a map," where prospects for survival were grim. The national deportees, on the other hand, were generally sent to Kazakhstan or Kyrgyzstan. Aside from their relative spatial isolation, regulations also assigned to "special settlers" subordinate legal, political, and social status. They were not only deprived of their civil rights, but they were also required by law to be engaged in "socially useful work." Thus, the Stalinist order used geography and variations in social and legal status to limit the potentially dangerous influence of unconfined forced laborer populations.

The Nazis, for their part, created a strict system of decrees to regulate the behavior of foreign laborers. This began with the conscription of Polish forced laborers in 1939 to 1940. Though there was acknowledgment among the Nazi leadership that forced labor by Polish civilians and POWs was necessary for the benefit of the German economy, there were also significant anxieties about employing racially "inferior" foreigners within the country. In order to address such concerns, the SS formulated the "decrees on Poles" (*Polenerlasse*). These rules subjected Polish forced laborers to strict regimentation in their daily lives, setting wages, limiting mobility, and creating a system of punishments for transgressions. Particular attention was paid to prevent social mixing between Poles and Germans. Potential sexual contact between Polish men and German women was an area of particular anxiety and was to be prevented by maintaining a gender balance among conscripts and by establishing brothels if this was not possible. The "decrees" required that Polish workers wear a Polish badge, which would later be the model for the "Jewish star."

As the conscription of foreign workers expanded, the "decrees on Poles" became a model for maintaining social distance between Germans and foreign workers. Strict regimentation was extended to other groups of foreigners, including both Westerners (for example, French, Italians) and Easterners (especially Soviets). Great care was taken to differentiate between the different kinds of foreign workers, creating a hierarchy that reflected Nazi notions of race, with Westerners on top and Easterners on the bottom. The strictest regulations of all were the "Decrees on Eastern Workers" (*Ostarbeitererlasse*), which applied to all Soviet citizens excluding those from the Baltics. Following the Polish precedent, Soviet workers had to wear a badge delineating their status. Racial hierarchies were also reflected in wages – foreigners from Western countries were supposed to receive equivalent salary and rations to Germans, whereas Poles were to receive 20 percent of German wages. Occupying the lowest rung in the hierarchy, Soviet citizens received the lowest wages, and sometimes were not paid at all.

Despite the creation and enforcement of elaborate systems of confinement and regulation of the behavior of forced laborers, recent research on both the Stalinist Soviet Union and Nazi Germany suggests that forced labor was neither isolated nor hidden in each society. This is easiest to see, of course, among forced labor populations that were not confined in camps. Soviet exiles lived intermingled with non-exile populations, attending the same schools and working at the same enterprises. While prejudices and social stigma were omnipresent, they were not enough to prevent interactions among those who lived and worked in close proximity. While it is clear that the practice of racism became "daily habit" in Germany, and discrimination against foreign laborers was met with passive acceptance by the majority of Germans, this does not mean that ordinary Germans were unaware of or uninvolved with foreign laborers. Considering the huge size of the foreign laborer population and its widespread distribution throughout Germany, it is indeed hard to imagine the strict social isolation of forced laborers. According to Ulrich Herbert, the city of Essen was an example of "how thoroughly the foreigners had been assimilated into city life." In March 1943, approximately one-quarter of the foreign workers in the city rented private rooms, whereas the rest were housed in a network of camps across the city.

In fact, camps and confined prisoners were integrated into the Stalinist and Nazi societies to a surprising degree. Gulag camps and colonies were frequently located in or near urban areas across the Soviet Union. Though prisoners were usually kept within enclosed camp "zones" surrounded by barbed wire and guard towers, most prisoners worked outside the camps, often alongside non-prisoners. As historians of the Gulag have begun to demonstrate, there was a constant flow of people, goods, and information between camps, colonies, and the "outside." Furthermore, there were often intimate social connections that crossed the barbed wire, whether in terms of romantic relationships, families, or friendships. Finally, the consistently high rates of release from Gulag camps and colonies (20 to 40 percent per year) suggests that the Gulag truly was a part of Soviet society, with a frequent circulation of people in and out of institutions of forced labor.

Nor were Nazi concentration camps truly the closed universe that is often described in memoirs and scholarly studies. Early camps such as Dachau and Buchenwald were established in cooperation with municipal authorities, with an understanding that cities and their citizens could benefit from the camp as a "municipal enterprise." With the proliferation of satellite camps after 1942 to serve the war effort, concentration camp prisoners became even more "visible" in German society, and social interactions, especially during working hours, became commonplace. Even Auschwitz, the camp that has come to symbolize both the closed world of the concentration camp and the Nazi enterprise of genocide, was closely linked with its surrounding community. Indeed, as Sybille Steinbacher has pointed out, Auschwitz represented more than a site of mechanized destruction to the Nazi regime: it was also a model community for German policies of colonizing the East. The town and the concentration camp were connected in a variety of ways.

In the final analysis, one can see the various means of creating and maintaining physical social distance between forced laborers and the general population in both Nazi Germany and the Stalinist Soviet Union as reflecting the anxieties of their respective regimes. Each was deeply concerned about the potential for forced laborers to corrupt the general population, whether politically, sexually, or racially. But there was also an important distinction in the relationships between the forced labor populations and the general populations of each state. Soviet forced laborers (except POWs) largely came from the population of the Soviet Union. Forced laborers in Nazi Germany, however, came almost entirely from the countries that were part of its external empire. This undoubtedly made it easier for the Nazis to create and maintain social distance between its citizens and forced laborers. Regardless, it is clear that both Stalinist and Nazi systems of forced labor were highly visible and an integral part of their respective societies.

FORCED LABOR AND MORTALITY

The Stalinist and Nazi systems of forced labor were not only among the largest in the twentieth century, they were also among the deadliest. Each system had millions of victims that did not survive. The following section will examine mortality rates in the Stalinist and Nazi forced labor systems side by side. However, comparisons between mortality in each forced labor system must be approached very cautiously. Stalinist forced labor was a significant phenomenon for twenty-five years, whereas Nazi forced labor was widespread only for five. Further, the goals of Stalinist and Nazi terror, to which these forced labor systems were intimately related, were starkly different. For the Nazis, the forced labor system was a necessary part of a broader plan to transform Germany and Europe through violence and mass extermination. For the Soviets, the physical annihilation of its enemies was rarely pursued explicitly. It emerged as a central goal only during moments of particular stress, such as during the "mass operations" of the Great Terror of 1937 to 1938, and even then it was targeted against certain population categories rather than against entire racial groups. The significant qualitative differences between the Nazi and Stalinist forced labor systems makes direct quantitative comparisons highly problematic. Nevertheless, trends in mortality are a key aspect in considering each forced labor system.

According to official statistics, somewhere between 1.6 and 1.7 million prisoners died in Gulag corrective labor camps from 1930 to 1956. In the 1930s, annual mortality rates were typically below 5 percent. However, they reached a high of 15.3 percent in 1933, a year of rapid expansion of the early camp system. In the 1940s, a clear trend emerged: death rates peaked during the Second World War and subsequently declined throughout the remainder of the decade. 1942 and 1943 represent the high watermarks for prisoner mortality in the Gulag, with annual death rates of 24.9 and 22.4 percent respectively, owing mostly to a catastrophic shortage of food in most camps. Mortality was much lower in the last two years of the war, 9.25 percent in 1944 and 5.95 percent in 1945. By the 1950s, the annual death rate had fallen below 1 percent, often lower than the general mortality rate for the Soviet population as a whole.[8] Though official mortality statistics almost certainly underestimate the total number of deaths, there is general consensus that these figures convey the scale of mortality. In all, approximately 10 percent of the prisoners held in Gulag camps died between 1930 and 1956.

Mortality data on Soviet "special settlers" are difficult to examine systematically, owing to poor record-keeping and high turnover. Mortality rates were extraordinarily high in the early 1930s when hundreds of thousands of kulak "special settlers" were being sent to build villages in remote locations with only the most minimal of preparation. Deaths throughout the "special settlements" reached a high water mark in 1933, when over 150,000 (over 13 percent) exiles died. Members of the ethnic minorities targeted for deportation in the 1930s and 1940s also suffered high rates of mortality, both during transportation and after arrival at their places of exile. Nearly 290,000 exiles died in special settlements from 1945 to 1950, the vast majority of them from 1945 to 1948. In 1945, for example, eleven times as many "special settlers" died as were born. Death rates among the deported nationalities were not equal, and those deported from the North Caucasus during the Second World War fared worst of all. Of the 575,000 Chechens, Ingush, Karachai, and Balkars deported in 1943 to 1944, 144,000 died in 1944 to 1948, an overall mortality rate of over 25 percent.[9] For both kulak and national "special settlers," death rates

[8] Iu. N. Afanasev and V. P. Kozlov (eds.), *Istoriia stalinskogo Gulaga: konets 1920-kh - pervaia polovina 1950-kh: sobranie dokumentov v semi tomakh* (Moscow, 2004), Vol. 4, p. 55.
[9] Pohl, *The Stalinist Penal System*, pp. 61, 106, 133.

peaked during and just after deportation, but fell considerably a few years after resettlement.

Mortality among POWs in the Soviet Union was considerably higher than among Gulag prisoners and exiles. According to official Soviet statistics, over 500,000 (nearly 15 percent) of all POWs in the GUPVI system died in Soviet captivity.[10] However, these records only include those POWs who survived long enough to be registered. Estimates suggest that 20 to 25 percent of POWs died during transfer, and a further 30 to 50 percent died within two months of capture.[11] Such high death rates were partially due to deliberate mistreatment, but were also caused by a total lack of organization and infrastructure in the nascent GUPVI system. Even among those POWs who survived long enough to be registered, some 119,000 died in 1943 alone, over half of the total. Nearly as many died in 1945, but by this time the number of POWs had increased to 2.9 million, making the death rate below 5 percent. Thus, POWs in the Soviet Union died at much higher rates than other forced labor populations, particularly in 1943 to 1944.

Many factors complicate calculating mortality rates for forced laborers in Nazi Germany. First, the scale of forced labor in Nazi Germany was much greater than that of the Soviet Union, and was also spread more broadly among camps, cities, towns, villages, and private companies all over the Reich and other Nazi-controlled territory. Second, though widespread forced labor was much shorter-lived than in the Soviet Union, there were rapid fluctuations in population size. Third, in the Nazi case, forced labor coexisted with the deliberate mass murder of a variety of populations, including Jews, Roma, and Soviet POWs. Can or should death through deliberate exterminatory policies be separated from death in captivity due to overwork, cruelty, or starvation? While it is possible in some cases to distinguish between those victims who were exterminated without any attempt to economically exploit them and those who died during their exploitation as forced laborers, in many cases such distinctions are impossible to draw. Hundreds of thousands of forced laborers were deliberately killed in mass executions after some period of economic exploitation. Further, many of the forced laborers belonged to the category of what historians Mark Spoerer and Jochen Fleischhacker have called "less-than-slaves," workers who were so legally and socially debased that they had few prospects of survival.

Due to the large number of foreign forced laborers and their use in a wide range of locations and industries, it is likely impossible to compile accurate mortality figures. But some observations are helpful in

---

[10] Karner, *Arkhipelag GUPVI*, p. 96.
[11] Gerlach and Werth, "State Violence – Violent Societies," p. 167.

determining mortality. First, Nazi racial prejudices and hierarchies had a significant effect on their chances of survival. Soviet POWs had the lowest chances of survival of any population of forced laborers, excluding Jews and other racial groups that were targeted for elimination. During 1941 and 1942, Soviet POWs were subject to a policy of physical destruction, and some 2 million Soviet POWs died in German captivity over this period.[12] Overall, 3.5 of 5.7 million Soviet POWs in German custody died over the course of the war, more than six out of every ten prisoners.[13] Soviet civilian conscripts fared significantly better than POWs, but still faced high mortality. Of 2.775 million Soviet civilians conscripted from 1941 to 1945, it is estimated that at least 170,000 died. Of 2 million Poles who became forced laborers, at least 130,000 died.[14] Overall, historian Adam Tooze has estimated that 2.4 million non-Jewish foreign workers died after January 1942.

Mortality was extraordinarily high within the SS concentration camp system. Of the 1.65 million people sent to concentration camps between 1933 and 1945, almost a million did not survive. This figure does not include an additional 1.1 million people who were murdered in the gas chambers at Auschwitz and Majdanek without being subjected to forced labor in the camps. As has been widely noted, the vast majority of the deaths took place from 1942 onward, when the camp system expanded rapidly and the economic exploitation of prisoners intensified. By 1944, over a quarter of a million prisoners were working to build a series of production facilities underground in caves and bunkers, in particularly murderous conditions. Survival chances were not much higher among the roughly equal number of prisoners who were "rented" out to private factories. Because the factories paid the camps a flat rate per prisoner per day, this encouraged overwork, neglect, and frequent "selections" to weed out weak prisoners. Death rates were higher still in 1945 as many camps were evacuated into Germany as the Allies marched toward Berlin. In Mathausen, for example, 12.5 percent of prisoners died *each month* between January and April 1945. Of the nearly three-quarters of a million concentration camp prisoners alive at the beginning of 1945, between one-third and one-half died by the end of the war.[15] The decision to economically exploit concentration camp prisoners in late 1942 did not lower mortality rates; in fact, it rendered Nazi concentration camps even more deadly.

---

[12] J. Adam Tooze, *The Wages of Destruction: The Making and Breaking of the Nazi Economy* (New York, 2007), p. 523.

[13] Ulrich Herbert, "Forced Laborers in the Third Reich: An Overview," *International Labor and Working-Class History*, 58 (2000): 195.

[14] Tooze, *The Wages of Destruction*, p. 523.

[15] Nikolaus Wachsmann, "The Dynamics of Destruction: The Development of Concentration Camps, 1933–1945," in Caplan and Wachsman, *Concentration Camps in Nazi Germany*, p. 35.

THE END OF NAZI AND STALINIST FORCED LABOR

The vast Nazi network of forced labor institutions ended with the German defeat in May 1945, though it had been in a state of growing crisis since the summer of 1944 due to Allied advances and aerial bombing. With many camps and factories destroyed, thousands of foreign workers were left without shelter. Hundreds of thousands of prisoners were sent on "death marches" from concentration camps in the Nazi eastern empire to Germany, and later, within Germany, in order to prevent them from falling into the hands of the advancing armies. In the last four months of the war, at least 250,000 prisoners died on such marches, and many of the remaining prisoners were in such poor physical shape that they died soon after liberation.[16] The arrival of Allied armies meant an end to forced labor, but did not immediately relieve the suffering of the civilians and former POWs. It would take months for the occupying powers to set up even the most basic facilities to house, feed, and care for the more than 11 million "displaced persons" (DPs) on German soil.

The issue of Nazi forced labor and its victims did not end with the repatriation of its victims. Almost immediately, questions of punishing perpetrators and compensating victims arose. The former issue was resolved, albeit in a limited fashion, by a series of legal proceedings against Nazi perpetrators and collaborators. The most important of the attempts at post-war justice were those organized by the International Military Tribunal at Nuremberg, a joint Allied effort. These were followed by a series of twelve trials organized by the US occupation authorities that lasted until 1949 and also by scores of national trials against accused perpetrators. During these proceedings, many Nazi and SS officials, as well as managers at major firms that had benefited from forced labor, were convicted of a series of charges, many of which were directly connected with a "program of slave labor." However vague the charges were and how narrowly the perpetrators were construed, there was some unequivocal acknowledgment of wrongdoing on the part of those convicted, something that is notably absent in the Soviet case.

The question of compensation of the forced laborers took considerably longer to resolve. Post-war negotiations on debts and reparations included some provisions for compensating victims, as did subsequent West German legislation. However, these applied only to victims who could prove that they had been on German soil during the war, and who subsequently became residents of countries willing to negotiate on their behalf with West Germany. But POWs were entirely excluded from

---

[16] Daniel Blatman, "The Death Marches and the Final Phase of Nazi Genocide," in Caplan and Wachsmann, *Concentration Camps in Nazi Germany*, pp. 167, 173.

compensation, as were virtually all forced laborers from the Soviet Union and Eastern Europe. Some Jewish survivors received compensation, but Soviet Jews and those who settled in the Eastern Bloc after the war did not. Except in limited cases, German private companies took no part in compensating those forced laborers that they had exploited. This situation changed significantly in the twenty-first century, however. After a series of lawsuits from victim groups, the *Erinnerung Verantwortung Zukunft* foundation ("Remembrance, Responsibility, and Future") was established in 2000, paying out 4.4 billion euros to 1.66 million former forced laborers in nearly 100 countries from 2001 to 2007.[17] Overall, it is important to note that while there has been both prosecution of perpetrators and compensation of victims, neither question was resolved quickly or definitively. This is particularly striking in the case of compensation, as the largest groups of forced laborers in Nazi Germany, Soviet POWs and civilians, did not receive compensation for over fifty years.

In sharp contrast to the Nazi case, the scale of Soviet forced labor actually increased at the end of the war, and though some forced laborers were released during Stalin's lifetime, most had to wait until the period following his death in March 1953 for freedom. Foreign POWs were held in the Soviet Union until 1948 to 1950, when most were repatriated to their home countries, with the exception of those convicted of war crimes, who were amnestied in 1955 to 1956. Most "special settlers" who had been exiled during the first wave of deportations against kulaks in the 1930s were freed from their terms of exile during and after the Second World War. However, it would not be until August 1954 that the exile status was officially lifted from the final group of former kulaks. Those "special settlers" who had been deported in ethnic cleansing operations from the late 1930s and 1940s were released en masse in the middle of the 1950s, with over 2.5 million people released from their terms of exile from 1954 to 1957. However, a number of the deported groups, including the Crimean Tatars, did not have their homelands restored and were forbidden from returning to their places of deportation. Many deportees from Western Ukraine and the Baltics had to wait until the end of the 1950s to be released from exile and, in fact, several thousand of them remained in exile into the 1960s.

The Gulag camp population declined sharply after 1953 as Stalin's successors attempted to reform the camp system and end the mass incarceration of "counterrevolutionary" prisoners. On March 27, 1953, an amnesty was announced that led to the release of approximately half of the Gulag's 2.4 million prisoners in a matter of months. This amnesty was

---

[17] "Origins of the Foundation EVZ", n.d., accessed February 2, 2015, www.stiftung-evz.de/eng/the-foundation/history.html.

followed by a series of measures in the mid-1950s that were intended to decrease the size of the camp population. In 1951, the Gulag had held just over 2.5 million prisoners, of whom about 580,000 were "counterrevolutionaries." By 1960, there were only about 580,000 prisoners in total, of whom less than 10,000 were "counterrevolutionaries."[18] But it is debatable whether or not forced labor by Soviet prisoners ever ceased to be a widespread practice. Labor remained a key part of Soviet penal theory and practice. By the late 1960s and early 1970s, over a quarter of Soviet prisoners participated in what historian Marc Elie has called "semi-forced labor." Further, forced labor continued to be a structural part of the economy of many regions throughout the Soviet period.

The Soviet case also contrasts with the Nazi case regarding the punishment of perpetrators and the compensation of victims. No one associated with the Soviet system of forced labor has been prosecuted for participation in the system as such. It was not until the advent of Perestroika in the second half of the 1980s that widespread public discussions of forced labor and Stalinist repression became possible, and despite initial enthusiasm for exposing the "crimes" of the Soviet regime, efforts for public reckoning have been ambivalent at best. The issue of compensation of victims has also been complex and contradictory. Former prisoners and exiles were entitled to economic compensation and to a full restoration of social and political rights only if they received a "rehabilitation" from the state confirming that they had been wrongly convicted. Whether or not a former prisoner or exile received "rehabilitation" depended not only on the circumstances of her or his particular case, but also on the broader political winds in Soviet society. Broadly speaking, there was considerable enthusiasm for reconsidering cases under Nikita Khrushchev (1955–64), but few rehabilitations for the next two decades until Gorbachev (1985–91). Financial compensation was extremely limited: a secret decree dating from 1955 made those "rehabilitated" entitled to two months' wages, and credit for time served toward pensions and regional bonuses. Overall, in the Soviet case the punishment of perpetrators has been notably absent, and the compensation of victims strikingly meager.

CONCLUSION

The forced labor of millions of civilians and POWs was a structural part of both the Stalinist Soviet Union and Nazi Germany. In each country, a wide range of populations was subjected to forced labor in a variety of

---

[18] Marc Elie, "Khrushchev's Gulag: The Soviet Penitentiary System after Stalin's death, 1953–1964," in Eleonory Gilburd and Denis Kozlov (eds.), *The Thaw: Soviet Society and Culture during the 1950s and 1960s* (Toronto, 2013), p. 119.

institutions. Unfree labor played a significant role in each country's economy, with prisoners and other populations ruthlessly exploited to drive the needs of production. However, forced labor was more than simply an economic expedient in both Nazi Germany and the Stalinist Soviet Union – it was also a key element in a program of transforming their respective societies into the utopian communities imagined by their leaders. Forced labor was often, but not always, performed in the setting of each state's extensive system of concentration camps. However, in both the Soviet Union and Nazi Germany there were millions of unconfined forced laborers and each state developed a system of regulations and hierarchies to isolate such populations and prevent the "contamination" of ordinary citizens. Both systems exploited millions of foreign POWs during the Second World War, a phenomenon that suggests that it was during the war that there was the greatest amount of convergence in Nazi and Soviet forced labor practices. Further, it is clear that in Nazi Germany and the Stalinist Soviet Union forced labor was both visible and deeply embedded in the existing social order.

Ultimately, however, when looking at Nazi and Stalinist forced labor side by side, the differences between them are just as striking as the similarities. Soviet forced labor was a phenomenon that lasted at least as long as the Stalin regime itself, with millions of prisoners and exiles from 1930 until the middle of the 1950s, whereas Nazi forced labor was primarily confined to the war years. Yet, the scale of Nazi forced labor, both in absolute and relative terms, was considerably greater than in the Stalinist Soviet Union. According to best estimates, by the middle of 1944 there were more than 11 million forced laborers in Nazi Germany, representing more than a quarter of its workforce.[19] By contrast, the total population of forced laborers in the Soviet Union reached a high point of just over 6 million prisoners, "special settlers," and POWs in 1946, representing approximately 8 percent of the working population. The populations subjected to forced labor by each regime also were separated by a key characteristic: the vast majority of Nazi forced laborers were not German citizens, whereas most Stalinist forced laborers were Soviet citizens (with the notable exception of POWs). The aftermath and legacies of both systems were also quite different: there have been significant, albeit incomplete, efforts to punish perpetrators and compensate victims in the Nazi case; in the Soviet Union, perpetrators have never faced a formal judicial process, and the compensation of "rehabilitated" victims has been much more limited. Finally, and most importantly, the two systems are distinguished by the ultimate ends of their policies of terror. The utopia that the

---

[19] Mark Spoerer and Jochen Fleischhacker, "Forced Laborers in Nazi Germany: Categories, Numbers, and Survivors," *Journal of Interdisciplinary History*, 33 (2002): 198.

Nazi regime was intent on creating necessitated the mass murder of millions of "racially inferior" populations, and forced labor was inextricably entangled with this goal. The Stalinist utopia, on the other hand, was a multinational empire, and was not pursued through a deliberate policy of mass murder. While Stalinist forced labor counted its victims in the millions, mass extermination of population categories was not among the regime's policies.

A GUIDE TO FURTHER READING

Barenberg, Alan, *Gulag Town, Company Town. Forced Labor and Its Legacy in Vorkuta* (New Haven, CT, 2014).

Barnes, Steven Anthony, *Death and Redemption: The Gulag and the Shaping of Soviet Society* (Princeton, NJ, 2011).

Bloxham, Donald, *Genocide on Trial: The War Crimes Trials and the Formation of Holocaust History and Memory* (Oxford, 2001).

Caplan, Jane and Nikolaus Wachsmann (eds.), *Concentration Camps in Nazi Germany: The New Histories* (London, 2010).

Elie, Marc, "Ce que réhabiliter veut dire," *Vingtième Siècle. Revue d'histoire*, 107 (2010): 101–13.

Getty, J. Arch, Gábor T. Rittersporn, and Viktor N. Zemskov, "Victims of the Soviet Penal System in the Pre-War Years: A First Approach on the Basis of Archival Evidence," *American Historical Review*, 98 (1993): 1017–49.

Geyer, Michael and Sheila Fitzpatrick (eds.), *Beyond Totalitarianism: Stalinism and Nazism Compared* (Cambridge, 2009).

Gruner, Wolf, *Jewish Forced Labor under the Nazis: Economic Needs and Racial Aims, 1938–1944* (Cambridge, 2006).

Herbert, Ulrich, *A History of Foreign Labor in Germany, 1880–1980: Seasonal Workers, Forced Laborers, Guest Workers* (Ann Arbor, MI, 1990).

Karner, Stefan, *Im Archipel GUPVI: Kriegsgefangenschaft und Internierung in der Sowjetunion 1941–1956* (Vienna, 1995).

Khlevniuk, O. V., *The History of the Gulag: From Collectivization to the Great Terror*, trans. Vadim Staklo (New Haven, CT, 2004).

Sofsky, Wolfgang, *The Order of Terror: The Concentration Camp*, trans. William Templer (Princeton, NJ, 1997).

Spoerer, Mark and Jochen Fleischhacker, "Forced Laborers in Nazi Germany: Categories, Numbers, and Survivors," *Journal of Interdisciplinary History*, 33 (2002): 169–204.

Tooze, J. Adam, *The Wages of Destruction: The Making and Breaking of the Nazi Economy* (New York, 2007).

Viola, Lynne, *The Unknown Gulag: The Lost World of Stalin's Special Settlements* (Oxford and New York, 2007).

CHAPTER 28

CONTEMPORARY COERCIVE LABOR
PRACTICES – SLAVERY TODAY

KEVIN BALES

Slavery is alive and well in the twenty-first century. The study of contemporary slavery, however, is beset with confusion, and when compared to the mature discipline of the history of slavery it can be seen, at best, as an emerging proto-discipline. Yet, the need for such an area of study is pressing, the extent of the crime of slavery is global, it exacts a terrible human cost, and in the globalized economy its products penetrate into the lives of a significant proportion of the world's consumers. At the same time, the extent of slavery and its economic impact have paradoxical features that engender both serious concern and optimism.

DEFINING SLAVERY

One area of confusion in the study of contemporary slavery is how it should be defined. In the past, the meaning of the word "slavery" was rarely debated. Most legal instruments and writing on the subject before the twentieth century did not set out to define slavery. The fundamental nature of slavery, the complete and exploitative control of one person (the slave) by another (the slave-holder) in which the slave was treated as property, was broadly understood and accepted. This acceptance was underpinned by many different legal, religious, social, or cultural justifications and rationalizations. Slavery was a long-lasting and ubiquitous part of many societies; its reality fixed and often enshrined in law. But with the end of legal slavery in most countries, there was a popular assumption that slavery itself had come to an end. It had not, but as a criminalized activity slavery moved into the shadows, and was often concealed by other names.[1]

In the 1990s and into the first decade of the twenty-first century, it can be said that slavery was "rediscovered." A key stimulus to this rediscovery was the end of the Cold War and the opening of national borders to greater international movement. Criminals were quick to exploit the

---

[1] See Douglas A. Blackmon, *Slavery by Another Name: The Re-Enslavement of Black Americans from the Civil War to World War II* (New York, 2008).

economic gradients that existed between the countries of the former Soviet Union and those of Western Europe and North America, as well as between the poorer countries of the Global South and the richer countries of the North. A rapid increase in trans-national organized crime after 1989 included the trafficking of human beings, as well as drug and arms trafficking. It was the relatively sudden escalation of Eastern European women in situations of forced commercial sexual exploitation in Western Europe and North America that fostered a sense that "human trafficking" or "sex trafficking" was a new and serious global issue.

In response to this emerging issue, new laws and international instruments were forged in addition to international conventions that had been in effect for decades. Many of these laws and instruments struggled to define their object, in large part because of the popular misconception that since "slavery" had been abolished, then the crime under consideration must be something else. For that reason, many of the new laws addressed not slavery, but "human trafficking." The UN Convention on Transnational Organized Crime, ratified in 2000, is a good example. It defines human trafficking as the overarching crime to be prohibited, and lists slavery as one of a subset of activities that make up the crime of "human trafficking." This conceptual and definitional confusion, repeated in other laws, arises because slavery itself is not defined in the Convention, but the definition of "trafficking" states that it is the movement of a person into a situation of control and exploitation. In other words, human trafficking is described as a conduit by which a person is taken into a situation of enslavement, yet the Convention defines trafficking as the crime, and slavery as but a possible part of that crime.

Similar definitions were enacted in a number of national laws. The result is that scholars who have looked to legal definitions to guide their exploration and analysis of contemporary slavery have become entangled in debates over what constitutes "slavery" in the twenty-first century, often to the exclusion of useful exploration of the reality of slavery within contemporary societies. A parallel, and equally unresolved, debate asks whether all prostitution is slavery, and whether "human trafficking" is simply another name for "sex trafficking" and excludes other forms of unfree labor.

An important antidote to this definitional confusion has been offered by a committee of experts that met to discuss and seek resolution of this issue in 2009 to 2011.[2] This group, consisting of international legal scholars, historians of slavery, and social scientists, reviewed existing definitions within international law to determine what might provide the greatest clarity and determine how to resolve the widespread confusion. The

---

[2] Conference held by the International Research Network on *Slavery as the Powers Attaching to the Right of Ownership*, Bellagio, Italy, 2010, papers for which were subsequently published as Jean Allain (ed.), *The Legal Understanding of Slavery: From the Historical to the Contemporary* (Oxford, 2012).

resulting consensus was that the definition of slavery given in the 1926 Slavery Convention of the League of Nations (later adopted by the United Nations) had both a sound conceptual and legal basis: "Slavery is the status or condition of a person over whom any or all of the powers attaining to the right of ownership are exercised."[3]

Building upon this definition, the committee then sought to elucidate the phrase, "powers attaching to the right of ownership" so that the attributes of any instance of suspected enslavement might be compared to the criteria inherent (but not explicit) within the 1926 Convention. To achieve this goal, the committee sought to accomplish two aims: (1) to situate the legal definition within the experiential reality of enslavement; and (2) to specify more clearly the attributes of ownership that apply to enslavement within the context of property rights.

To accomplish the first aim, the committee specified that:

The exercise of "the powers attaching to the right of ownership" should be understood as constituting control over a person in such a way as to significantly deprive that person of his or her individual liberty. Normally this exercise is supported by and obtained through means such as violent force, deception and/or coercion, with the intent of exploitation through the use, management, profit, transfer or disposal of that person.[4]

This additional specification to the 1926 Convention addresses the fundamental socioeconomic and legal dynamics between two actors (the slave and the slave-holder(s)) that constitute a situation of slavery. It forms a bridge between the lived reality of enslavement and the legal definition needed to specify and address this crime.

To accomplish the second aim, the committee drew upon the work of legal scholars, including Honoré and Hickey, who specify that instances of ownership within a context of legal property rights include, but are not limited to:

The right to possess, which, according to Honoré, is "the foundation on which the whole superstructure of ownership rests."[5]
The right to use, which is the right to enjoy the benefit of the possession.
The right to manage, which is the right to make decisions about how the possession is used.
The right to income, which is the right to profits generated by the possession.
The right to capital, which is the right to dispose of the possession, by transfer or destruction.

---

[3] 1926 Slavery Convention of the League of Nations, www1.umn.edu/humanrts/instree/fisc.htm.
[4] Bellagio-Harvard Guidelines on the Legal Parameters of Slavery, www.qub.ac.uk/schools/School ofLaw/FileStore/Filetoupload,651854,en.pdf.
[5] A. M. Honoré, "Ownership," in A. G. Guest (ed.), *Oxford Essays in Jurisprudence* (Oxford, 1961).

These legal attributes, or "instances" – control, use, management, and profit – are the central rights of ownership inherent (but not explicit) to the 1926 Convention as they are specified in the wider tradition of property law. At the same time, these attributes can be, in somewhat different language, used to define slavery by social scientists whose aim is not to locate a particular human activity within the rule of law per se, but rather to describe it as social phenomena.

FORMS OF CONTEMPORARY SLAVERY

A unifying definition is very much needed within the study of contemporary slavery because slavery takes many forms. These many forms are concealed behind criminal secrecy, customary practices, racist or tribal discrimination, economic rationalizations, religious justifications – any concept that can be adopted into a moral economy that rationalizes the complete domination of one person by another. This moral economy will not normally be the dominant cultural or legal context of a society (as it might have been the case historically), but a sub-culture that in some way defines enslaved people in a way that allows and explains their exploitation. The behavior of human traffickers and slave-holders, the "consumers" of slavery, will be more or less hidden depending on the extent to which the surrounding public also holds these views, or is simply apathetic to or ignorant of the presence of slaves.

While the "rediscovery" of slavery at the beginning of the twenty-first century was largely driven by media reports and law enforcement concerns about human trafficking in the rich countries of Europe and North America, the reality was that diverse forms of slavery had continued in many parts of the world relatively uninterrupted by legal prohibition. Hereditary forms of chattel slavery have never ended in such countries as Mauritania and Niger, only becoming less visible. Likewise, hereditary forms of slavery based upon collateral debt bondage continue for millions of persons in South Asia. In these cases, the concept of "debt" is used by the slave-holder to justify the enslavement, in spite of the fact that debt bondage slavery has been specifically illegal in all affected countries for many years. The capture and enslavement of children for use as "child soldiers" has continued in Afghanistan, Chad, Sierra Leone, the Democratic Republic of Congo, Sri Lanka, Liberia, Somalia, Myanmar, Northern Uganda, Southern Sudan, and in other conflict zones. Six distinct types of slavery, including forced marriage, were found in Eastern Congo in 2011,[6] some linked to the extraction and trade in "conflict minerals" which then flow into the global market for consumer electronics.

---

[6] The Congo Report: Slavery in Conflict Minerals, Free the Slaves and the Open Square Foundation, June 2011, www.freetheslaves.net/wp-content/uploads/2015/03/The-Congo-Report-English.pdf.

In addition, and as happened throughout the history of slavery, the form, methods, and uses of contemporary slavery regularly adapt to new economic circumstances and opportunities, often blended with traditional practices. There are forms of slavery linked to religious practices, such as *Trokosi* slavery in Ghana or *Devadasi* slavery in India. The widespread enslavement of children as household workers in Haiti, known as the *restavèk* system, is mirrored by the corruption of the traditional child placement or apprenticeship systems into forms of slavery in West Africa. And while it is often confused with arranged marriage, the violent capture and exploitation of women in forced marriages occurs worldwide and is protected by parallel tribal, customary, or religious legal systems.

The enslavement of citizens of a country by their own government also continues, usually referred to as "forced labor" or "state slavery." For example, the country of Uzbekistan in Central Asia sends most of its school and college students into the cotton fields for up to three months each year. These young people have no choice and are paid little or nothing for their labor and face severe punishment for resistance. Similar state-directed forced labor occurs in China, Sudan, and, until recently, Myanmar.

Patterns of enslavement also reflect contemporary business and labor practices. While enslavement can still be lifelong, many people are enslaved for much shorter periods to do specific tasks. There are two key reasons for the emergence of "just in time" slavery in a number of countries. The first reason is that the cost of acquiring a slave can be very low. Desperate for work, a potential slave needs only to be offered a job, chivied along with some food, and transported to the, normally isolated, work site. For the slave-holder, there's no actual purchase price, just the small upfront expenses of finding them, feeding them, moving them, and providing the tools and materials needed for the work. The cost of acquiring a slave is so low that the length of time to make a profit on their labor has shortened, in some cases, to as little as a month. For the criminals tearing out the forest, short-term slavery is a great way to maximize profits while minimizing risks. And the minimization of risk is the second reason for the emergence of short-term enslavement. In countries where the laws against slavery are more likely to be enforced, short-term slavery reduces the possibility of exposure and detection. There is another consequence of short-term slavery that helps the criminal slave-holder avoid arrest. It is the uncertainty felt by many who have been enslaved as to what, exactly, has happened to them. The slave-holder, over a shorter period, can play on the worker's sense of hope and obligation to maximize productivity. Once free, the exploited workers assume they've had the bad luck to have been held in such poor conditions and never received their wages.

For example, in countries where law enforcement is more effective, short-term enslavement is used by criminals to avoid detection and prosecution. In Brazil, poor landless rural men will be offered work in land clearance or agriculture. Removed from their home villages, they will be isolated and come under complete and violent control. They will be forced to work and not paid, and attempts to escape will be met with brutality or even murder. Poorly fed, worked to exhaustion, and exposed to disease, after a month or more of intensive labor they will be exhausted and often incapacitated. At this point, these temporarily enslaved workers will be taken away and dumped, or killed and buried in the forest they have been clearing.

A similar form of fraud leading to enslavement hides behind modern labor relations: contracts are offered that guarantee employment often in a foreign country, but when the workers arrive, they are enslaved. This type of enslavement leads to workshops and factories, construction, service work in restaurants, and agriculture – anywhere that the victim can be sufficiently isolated and controlled. This can be a highly profitable form of trafficking into slavery in that the victim is required to pay their own transport costs as well as a "recruitment fee" to a labor broker. This form of "contract" slavery is most often found in Southeast Asia, Brazil, some Arab states, and some parts of the Indian subcontinent. While these relatively short-term forms of enslavement are one way in which criminal slaveholders avoid detection, it is also a function of a key change in the economic equation of slavery.

THE COLLAPSE IN THE COST OF ACQUIRING SLAVES

Since the middle of the twentieth century, the cost of acquiring a slave seems to have fallen dramatically. In a clear reflection of the workings of supply and demand, the acquisition cost of slave labor has declined inversely with the rise in the global population. This process is little documented. The acquisition cost of human beings appears to have dropped from an historical average of around $40,000 (in 2016 dollars) to about $90 today. For example, the "prime field hand," the most common type of slave traded in the American Deep South during the antebellum period, cost, on average, $1,200 in 1850 dollars, which is equivalent to about $45,000 in 2016 currency. Today, most slaves can be acquired for $100 to $500, with the cost of acquiring a slave falling as low as $10. Given the large number of economic migrants anxious to take on any paying work, the cost of acquisition can often be reduced to the price of the food and travel needed to lure a worker to a place where they can be easily controlled and enslaved. After arrival, the enslaved person may be sold on to another slave-holder, but these sale prices also tend to be much lower than historical examples. This price collapse is supply driven.

Of the 7.1 billion people on the planet in 2012, about 900 million were living below the World Bank extreme poverty benchmark of $1.90 a day. Of this 900 million people, a significant proportion are also living in countries where the rule of law is either not effective or absent. Economically desperate, and without resources or the protection of law, the physically viable (thus, the most useful as slaves) are easily harvested from this pool of vulnerable potential slaves by those with access to the tools of violence and trickery and the willingness to use them. As population growth and increased vulnerability have flooded the market with potentially enslavable people, one result has been the collapse in the price of acquiring enslaved workers.

The demand for various types of enslaved workers is not well understood, but it is worth noting that the pool of potential slaves, some hundreds of millions of persons, continues to be much larger than the estimated 35.8 million people in slavery. This might reflect the impact of making slavery illegal, or the fact that slaves cannot normally be used in most types of regulated and inspected legal economic activity, or may be linked to the low efficiency of much slave-based economic activity. The gap between the supply of potential slaves and the demand for actual slaves requires further investigation.

MEASURING THE PREVALENCE AND EXTENT OF CONTEMPORARY SLAVERY

Until 2013, estimates of the number of people enslaved were based almost exclusively on secondary sources, often the records of governments or international organizations. This reliance on secondary reports of criminal activity made reliable estimation of slavery extremely difficult, if not impossible. As an illegal acitivity in all countries, slavery has become, to a greater or lesser extent, a hidden crime. Yet, it is not possible to estimate the extent of slavery within a population in the way that most crimes are measured.

For most crimes, the reported prevalence of a crime is compared with an estimate derived from a random sample survey to calculate that crime's "dark figure." The estimation of the "dark figure" for any crime (the number of actual instances of a specific crime as found by the crime survey minus the reported cases of that crime within a population) rests on the ability to conduct random sample crime surveys. The use of such crime surveys rests on the assumption that crime victims are victimized during a discrete, and presumably short-term, "crime event," and that they are able to report the occurrence of their victimization at a specific time and place in the past to a surveyor, even if the crime was not reported to the authorities. Because victim surveys do not address the question of the duration of the crime event, the crime of enslavement presents a special challenge to estimation because of its indeterminate duration.

The indeterminate temporal nature of the crime of slavery is one of its defining characteristics. Note that the *Bellagio-Harvard Guidelines on the Legal Parameters of Slavery* state that possession of one person by another can be demonstrated by the control exercised over the enslaved person, and that: "Fundamentally, when such control operates, it will significantly deprive that person of his or her individual liberty *for a period of time which is, for that person, indeterminate.*"[7] It is a fundamental part of the conceptualization of slavery that, once enslaved, a person cannot affect the period of their bondage except through the risk of attempting escape. And though it might be a *defining* characteristic that the exercise of control over an enslaved person has no expected time limit, this temporal facet of slavery is not mentioned in most official definitions. This fact points to a small paradox – that while the indeterminate length of enslavement over time "goes without saying," this fact also goes unacknowledged as to its effect on the estimation of slavery within criminal statistics.

Estimating the prevalence of slavery and the dark figure of the crime of slavery is especially problematic for, at least, three reasons. First, sexual assault is common within the crime of enslavement and the stigmatization of victims of sexual assault is known to foster an unwillingness to report being a victim of such crime. Second, there is the stigma or shame felt by victims of slavery that reduces their propensity to report the crime of enslavement, a factor that applies to men who are enslaved as well as women. Third, as explained above, at the initiation of the crime of enslavement it is difficult to predict how long the victimization will last. Throughout the indeterminate period of victimization, and unlike the victims of most crimes, the slavery victim is unavailable to be contacted and their experience recorded and counted and compared to official reports of crime. This challenging temporal dimension of slavery as a crime also tends to be ignored in the normal collection of criminological statistics. For these reasons, both the actual prevalence of, and the dark figure of, the crime of enslavement have hitherto lacked sufficient measurement or estimation.

In 2012 and 2013, an attempt was made to break through this measurement challenge by bringing a mixture of methods to the task of estimating global slavery. For the first time, random sample data on slavery and trafficking for some countries were available. These surveys asked

---

[7] Bellagio-Harvard Guidelines on the Legal Parameters of Slavery, qub.ac.uk/schools/SchoolofLaw/Research/HumanRightsCentre/Resources/Bellagio-HarvardGuidelinesontheLegalParametersofSlavery/ (emphasis added).

respondents if they or other family members had been victimized in human trafficking or slavery. These survey data were combined with secondary source estimates and then used as a basis to build statistical extrapolations of the prevalence of slavery in 162 countries, representing the majority of the world's population. These estimates were published in the 2013 *Global Slavery Index* and offered a total global estimate of 29.8 million people enslaved worldwide.[8] By 2016, the number of countries with representative random sample survey data on slavery prevalence had risen to twenty-seven, representing over half of the world's population.

The estimates developed for the Global Slavery Index included extent (the actual number in slavery in a country), prevalence (the proportion of a country's population in slavery), and estimates of the risk of enslavement as measured by thirty-three variables grouped along five dimensions. In terms of the extent of slavery, ten countries (India, China, Pakistan, Nigeria, Ethiopia, Russia, Thailand, the Democratic Republic of Congo, Myanmar, and Bangladesh) with the largest numbers of slaves accounted for 76 percent of the global total when taken together. India was estimated to have just under 14 million slaves within its borders. In terms of prevalence, Mauritania was estimated to have the highest proportion of its population in slavery, followed by Haiti, Pakistan, India, Nepal, Moldova, Benin, Ivory Coast, Gambia, and Gabon. The prevalence measure, combined with indicators of levels of human trafficking and child marriage, was used to calculate a ranking across all countries.

The risk of enslavement was measured using variables that reflected conditions or contexts that created vulnerability to enslavement. Conflict, for example, is a strong predictor of slavery in that it brings about a disruption in the rule of law and opens the door to violent exploitation, including the enslavement, of citizens. Corruption also breaks down the rule of law, and those without access to resources or influence are more likely to risk enslavement in more corrupt countries. At the same time, what could be termed very low levels of social capital, marked by illiteracy, food insecurity, lack of access to health care, and other indicators of extreme poverty, also create a vulnerabilty to enslavement. The five predictive dimensions through which the vulnerability or risk was measured were the stability of a nation-state, the level of protections given to human rights in each country, the level of economic and social development

---

[8] The *Global Slavery Index* is an annual publication of the Walk Free Foundation and can be found at www.GlobalSlaveryIndex.org. For more details of the methodology used in developing the global estimates, see: Monti Narayan Datta and Kevin Bales, "Slavery in Europe: Part 2, Testing a Predictive Model," *Human Rights Quarterly*, 36 (2014): 277–95; Monti Narayan Datta and Kevin Bales, "Slavery in Europe: Part 1, Estimating the Dark Figure," *Human Rights Quarterly*, 35 (2013): 817–29; and Kevin Bales, "International Labor Standards: Quality of Information and Measures of Progress in Combating Forced Labor," *Comparative Labor Law and Policy*, 24 (2003): 321–64.

Figure 28.1 Slavery Prevalence and Corruption

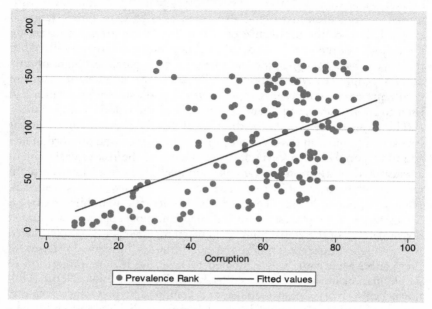

The dependent variable (y-axis) is Prevalence Rank, based on the 2014 Global Slavery Index. The independent variable (x-axis) is Corruption, based on the 2014 Corruption Perceptions Index from Transparency International. Corruption scores are coded so that a score of 0 represents the least amount of corruption and a score of 100 represents the greatest amount of corruption. Prevalence Rank is coded so that a rank of 1 represents the least prevalence of modern slavery, and a rank of 167 represents the greatest prevalence of modern slavery. $R^2 = 0.30$.

(including those measures of poverty and human development), the presence of antislavery policies, and the level of women's rights and discrimination. This first in-depth analysis of the risk of enslavement across most countries was important in that it helped to resolve outstanding questions concerning what might be the most appropriate interventions to eradicate slavery in two ways.

The first way in which risk estimation addressed outstanding questions was at the global level, to illuminate which factors are most strongly predictive of the prevalence of slavery. The charts in Figures 28.1 and 28.2 show variables that are significant predictors of the prevalence of slavery across 167 countries. The first chart shows the relationship between the prevalence of slavery and the level of corruption within a country. This is a strong, positive, and statistically significant relation that illustrates how corruption might act to diminish the effectiveness of the rule of law in ways that exacerbate vulnerability to enslavement by fostering a context of impunity for criminal slave-holders.

Figure 28.2 Slavery Prevalence and Human Development

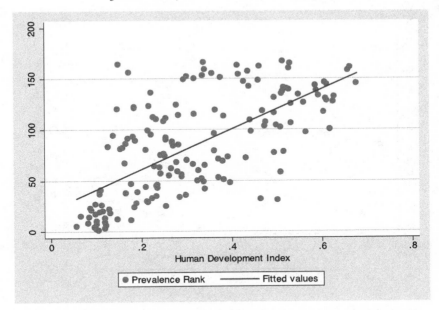

Note: The dependent variable (y-axis) is Prevalence Rank, based on the 2014 Global Slavery Index. The independent variable (x-axis) is the Human Development Index (HDI), based on the 2013 UN Human Development Report. HDI Scores are coded so that a score of 0 represents the best HDI, and a score of 1 represents the worst HDI. Prevalence Rank is coded so that a rank of 1 represents the least prevalence of modern slavery, and a rank of 167 represents the greatest prevalence of modern slavery. R^2 = 0.43.

Poverty and social deprivation are also often suggested to be predictors of modern slavery. Figure 28.2 illustrates and demonstrates this relationship between human development (as measured by the UN Development Program Human Development Index) and slavery prevalence. The level of a country's human development reflects its economic well-being, which in turn affects the chance of poverty and deprivation a citizen might face. On the other hand, higher levels of educational attainment, elevated health care, and the chance of effective citizenship (key measures of the Human Development Index) all tend to protect against vulnerability to enslavement.

A common pathway into slavery is through debt. When access to legal sources of credit is not possible, the poor and vulnerable will sometimes turn to other types of lending, even to the mortgaging of their own lives – debts that are often fraudulent and a conduit into slavery. Access to financial services can be crucial for upward social mobility. Without access to credit, there is often little the average family can do to improve its lot in life. Figure 28.3 examines the relationship between slavery prevalence (as measured by the

Figure 28.3 Slavery Prevalence and Access to Financial Services

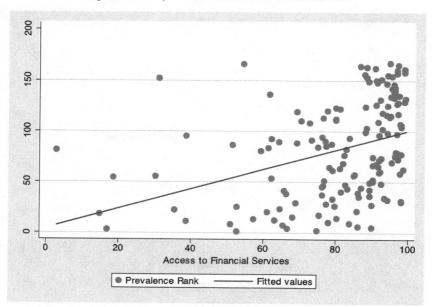

Note: The dependent variable (y-axis) is Prevalence Rank, based on the 2014 Global Slavery Index. The independent variable (x-axis) is Access to Financial Services based on 2013 data from the World Bank. Access to Financial Services scores are coded so that a score of 0 represents the best score, and a score of 100 represents the worst. Prevalence Rank is coded so that a rank of 1 represents the least prevalence of modern slavery, and a rank of 167 represents the greatest prevalence of modern slavery. R^2 = 0.63.

Global Slavery Index) and access to financial services that the average citizen can obtain in a given country (as measured by Patrick Honohan in 2007 for the World Bank).[9] The figure shows a negative relationship between access to financial services and the prevalence of slavery in a country. This finding is statistically significant (R^2 = .63) and suggests a strong relationship.

The second way in which this first in-depth analysis of the risk of enslavement addressed outstanding questions concerning the appropriate interventions to eradicate slavery is at the level of individual countries. By dividing the measurement of the risk of enslavement into five dimensions, a portrait emerges of the context in which slavery occurs. Clearly, those countries that score highly on all five dimensions of risk offer fertile ground for the emergence of slavery. A key marker of these countries is their high levels of conflict. The countries with the highest mean score for all

[9] See Patrick Honohan, "Cross-Country Variation in Household Access to Financial Services," *Journal of Banking and Finance*, 32(11) (2008): 2493–500.

CONTEMPORARY COERCIVE LABOR PRACTICES

dimensions of risk are all countries involved in current or recent internal conflicts: Somalia, Afghanistan, Democratic Republic of Congo, Eritrea, Zimbabwe, Central African Republic, Chad, and Sudan. At the time of writing, most countries in this grouping are in Africa, but this is a changeable list reflecting the flaring and diminishing of conflict. In the recent past, Bosnia would have been included in this unfortunate top catalog, and in 2016 Uzbekistan, Yemen, and Iraq were replacing some of the African states in which conflict had diminshed. The fundamental mechanism is that conflict shatters the rule of law, and whatever protection the law might bring to a population, at the same moment that parts of the population are being driven into extreme vulnerability through displacement or the collapse of infrastructure. The blatant adoption of enslavement as a tactical component of the war waged by the so-called Islamic State in Iraq in 2015 and 2016 is a brutal example of this mechanism.

Looking more closely at the individual dimensions of risk, for countries less troubled by conflict, other factors are also indicative of a context conducive to enslavement. For example, when the seven variables measuring the protections of human rights are combined and examined, they mark countries that are relatively stable and free from armed conflict, but at the same time create the risk of enslavement by failing to protect human rights. Good examples of such states are Turkmenistan, Uzbekistan, Yemen, Laos, Belarus, Tajikistan, and Saudi Arabia. The link between poverty and enslavement can also be noted by examining those countries where very low development (as measured by nine variables) creates a vulnerability to enslavement: Somalia, Sierra Leone, Burkina Faso, Niger, Ethiopia, Mali, Malawi, and Chad.

The presence or absence of specific antislavery and anti-trafficking policies also adds nuance to the understanding of the risk of enslavement. Clearly, for those regimes that provide very few legal and policy protections overall (such as Iran, Algeria, and Equatorial Guinea), citizens are vulnerable to a wide range of threats, including enslavement. But richer and more stable countries that tend to offer greater protections to their citizens, those which have failed to focus on antislavery laws and policies, are also shown to have a higher prevalence of slavery, such as Qatar, Russia, Moldova, Mexico, and Japan.

It can be seen that the statistical analysis of contemporary slavery is still in its infancy. Measures of correlation, or the ranking of states by individual variables, are simpler and less powerful ordinal and relational procedures. The use of more powerful inferential statistics has been limited by the lack of uniform and extensive data. The use of random sample surveys and better data collection in Europe, however, has provided data upon which one test of predictive modeling[10] was made.

---

[10] This analysis was first presented in Datta and Bales, "Slavery in Europe: Part 2."

Table 28.1 *Regression Analysis: Presence of Slavery and Human Trafficking in Europe*

	Coefficient
State Stability Risk	.031*
	(.015)
Women's Economic Rights	−.011
	(.181)
Freedom of Speech	−.207**
	(.009)
Access to Financial Services	.029**
	(.009)
Former Soviet Union	.022**
	(.006)
Population Over 60	.036**
	(.014)
Constant	.302
	(1.64)
R^2	.77
N	37

Notes: Robust Standard Errors in Parenthesis.
* $p < .05$
** $p < .01$

That test examined predictors of slavery in thirty-seven European countries. The measured variables that met selection criteria, demonstrated statistical significance, and tended not to violate too egregiously concerns over multicollinearity included *State Stability Risk*, *Women's Economic Rights*, *Freedom of Speech* (as a proxy for human rights protections), *Access to Financial Services*, whether a country was one of the states of the *Former Soviet Union*, and the proportion of country's population *Over the Age of 60* (an indicator or proxy for those countries with higher standards of living). The more well-off and "older" countries are also those which will have a greater demand for, and economic ability to procure, immigrant labor, as well as trafficked persons forced into commercial sexual exploitation. It should be noted that other variables were tested, but failed to demonstrate statistical significance in preliminary tests of correlation.

A regression analysis tested the hypothesis that the independent variables listed above would be likely predictors of the presence of slavery and human trafficking in Europe. See the analysis in Table 28.1.

While there is a general strong overall relationship between the proposed variables and the presence of slavery and human trafficking, the relationship between *Women's Economic Rights* for these European

Figure 28.4 Diagram of Causal Variables

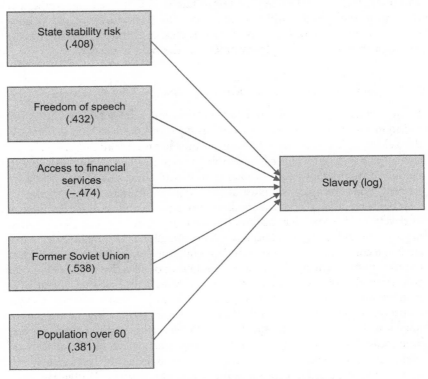

Note: (Standardized beta coefficients in parentheses.)

countries and the presence of slavery was not statistically significant, and this variable was then dropped from further analysis.

When the analysis was repeated without the measurement of women's economic rights, the predictive power, as measured in the beta coefficients, increased. The following path diagram shows the independent and statistically significant predictive power of each of five independent variables on the prevalence of slavery in thirty-seven European countries.

The importance of such tests is that they help to apportion the relative importance of causal factors, and thus point toward areas of potential intervention aimed at reducing the risk of enslavement. For example, a key division between the countries of the former Soviet Union and those of Western Europe concerns access to financial services and credit. Credit availability helps to prevent worker migration (legal, illegal, and through fraudulent trafficking) – and the lack of financial services proves to be a strong predictor of whether citizens of countries of the former Soviet

Union are caught up in human trafficking. At the same time, this simple and preliminary initial inferential test of factors that predict enslavement at the nation-state level simply demonstrates the immaturity of the field of studies of contemporary slavery. And this lack of empirical research is just one area in which further development of the field is needed.

EMERGING AREAS OF INQUIRY IN CONTEMPORARY SLAVERY

Because of its recent arrival as both a social issue and a field of study, the nature of inquiry into contemporary slavery has been rudimentary and general. As the field has grown, the specific relationships between contemporary slavery and other broad factors have been coming under greater scrutiny. If the broad field of contemporary slavery studies is immature, these sub-areas of study are nascent. Four examples will illustrate the opportunities for further study.

It has been noted above that conflict seems strongly linked to the appearance of slavery in locations that descend into civil or ethnic war. For all of human history, war and slavery have been regular companions. This includes the most ancient records of war right up to the "low-intensity" wars that mark conflict in the twenty-first century. If war is a conscious and collective pursuit of group aims through violence, in many wars one of those aims has been the enslavement of others. In other wars, slavery seems to be a by-product, a tactical choice, even a consequence unintended in the original and precipitating motivations to wage war. However, not all wars have included slavery and not all slavery has been located in the context of war. Questions then arise as to why some wars engender slavery and others do not, as well as questions concerning the changing nature of slavery in war as the nature of armed conflict has changed.

The dehumanization of the enemy or "the other" is well documented in both war and slavery. Dehumanization is termed one of the essential steps in the process that will lead to genocide. It is understood to be part of both individual and collective rationalization and justification that makes possible otherwise socially restricted, even forbidden, behaviors which culminate in the extreme violence expected in both the waging of war and the practice of slavery. The parallel practices of dehumanization in both contemporary conflicts, including those leading to genocide, and contemporary slavery generates questions about whether the extent or quality of dehumanization can be measured in such a way as to explore how it might predict the appearance of slavery in the context of war.

A second example of a sub-area of study within contemporary slavery concerns the enslavement of women.[11] It is the sexual use of slaves, in

---

[11] See Jody Sarich and Kevin Bales, "The Paradox of Women, Children, and Slavery," in Benjamin N. Lawrance and Richard L. Roberts (eds.), *Trafficking in Slavery's Wake: Law and the Experience of Women and Children in Africa* (Athens, OH, 2012), pp. 241–53.

particular, that marks and typifies the enslavement of women. Slaves tend to be reduced to the status of "other," slaves are worked to create economic wealth for their slave-holders, slaves are denied free will and expect and experience violence, but slaves that are women have added dimensions to their enslavement. While some male slaves are sexually abused, sexual assault is common for enslaved women. The bodies of men are also controlled in slavery, but it is primarily their ability to work that interests the slave-holder. Women do virtually all the types of work that male slaves do, but they also tend to be viewed as available for sexual use. In this way, women in slavery suffer an appropriation and control of the interior as well as the exterior of their physical beings. This assault also leads to the second key way in which the experience of slavery for women differs from that of men.

Not only does the slave-holder use an enslaved woman for pleasure, but he can also create in her body an extension of himself that will exploit her being from within. Upon birth, that child can be claimed as progeny, sold, or retained as a slave. For the enslaved woman, this is a kind of thievery of life itself transcending the loss of her own productive capacity. This appropriation of reproductive capacity also has a profound psychological impact, again one that has been little studied except as it has been explored through art and literature. Though the reproductive capacity of any slave can be used to a slave-holder's economic advantage, the reproductive exploitation of women slaves has no exact parallel in male enslavement.

Given the collapse in the acquisition cost of slaves, the rape of women slaves today may result in a child whom she will be forced to watch be malnourished, abandoned, or destroyed before her eyes. The relative worthlessness of slave infants opens a third determining factor of women's experience in slavery. With the exception of male slaves once used as eunuchs, male slaves tend to retain control of all of their biological functions in slavery, though their access to sexual interaction may be restricted. For female slaves, contemporary slave-holders regularly manipulate their reproductive biology. Abortion, sterilization, chemical controls, hysterectomy, female genital cutting, and the sewing up or other surgical alteration of the vagina are all potentially part of enslavement. Such manipulation and alteration extends to other parts of the anatomy as well. If male slaves are primarily seen as beings of labor potential, female slaves are seen in this way *and* as bodies that can be used in other ways: as sexual outlets, for their reproductive potential, and as items of conspicuous consumption. This leads to a paradox that deserves further investigation: while enslavement is the total control of one person by another, the enslavement of women achieves a totality exceeding that of men. This paradox also points toward one further understudied area in the enslavement of women, that of forced marriage. It could be argued that the most common and least understood form of enslavement of women in the past and today is forced marriage. This is a form of slavery almost entirely feminized and yet, unlike other forms of slavery, it has not been the target of the same legal and cultural responses and prohibitions afforded the forms of enslavement where men are included. Equally, it is an area of slavery that is global in its reach and yet is little understood and less studied. At this time, "forced marriage" lacks a clear definition, and no reliable prevalence figures exist.

A third example of a sub-area of study within contemporary slavery that is just emerging is an understanding of the relationship between environmental issues and slavery. Slaves have long been used in derivative industries such as mining and agriculture. As environmental concerns and regulations have placed more restrictions on destructive and polluting economic activities, criminal slave-holders have stepped into the resulting economic vacuum and often use slave labor. Around the world, and particularly in the tropics, slaves are being used extensively in illegal mining, deforestation, and highly polluting industries such as brick making. Global markets drive much of this slave-based and environmentally destructive enterprise. Shrimp, fish, gold, diamonds, steel, beef, sugar, cotton, timber, and minerals flow from enslaved workers into North America, Europe, Japan, and increasingly China. Slave-based deforestation, in particular, increases global CO_2 emissions. At the same time, environmental forces push indigenous peoples into greater vulnerability to enslavement. Desertification, habitat loss, flooding, and erosion can all push poor rural families toward migration and an increased likelihood of enslavement. Exactly how far environmental destruction drives slavery, and how far slave labor is being used in environmentally destructive ways has yet to be determined, yet one calculation of the environmental impact of slave-based enterprises suggests that slavery is a major contributor to climate change. By this measure, primarily through illegal deforestation, but including other highly polluting industries, slavery is emitting approximately 2.54 billion tonnes of CO_2 into the atmosphere, more than any country in the world except China and the United States.[12]

A final example of a relatively unexplored sub-area of contemporary slavery concerns the psychological impact of slavery on those enslaved. Many, if not most, victims of contemporary slavery suffer from post-traumatic stress disorder (PTSD). Moreover, while most PTSD in the general population results from short-lived trauma such as car accidents,

---

[12] Kevin Bales, *Blood and Earth: Slavery, Ecocide, and the Secret to Saving the World* (New York, 2016).

natural disasters, or being the victim of a single crime event, this is not the case with situations of enslavement and long-term abuse.

Such conditions can cause enslaved persons to lose their sense of personal efficacy and control and to become increasingly dependent on those who hold them captive, if merely to survive. Captivity brings the victim into prolonged contact with the perpetrator and creates a special type of relationship, one of coercive control. "In situations of captivity," writes psychiatrist Judith Herman, "the perpetrator becomes the most powerful person in the life of the victim, and the psychology of the victim is shaped by the actions and beliefs of the perpetrator." The methods of establishing control, she adds, are based upon "the organized techniques of disempowerment and disconnection . . . [so as] to instill terror and helplessness and to destroy the victim's sense of self in relationship to others." As victims become more isolated, they grow "increasingly dependent on the perpetrator, not only for survival and basic bodily needs but also for information and even for emotional sustenance."[13]

For such persons, a diagnosis of "Complex PTSD"[14] may be appropriate, applying to situations of long-term trauma where the victim is in a state of captivity, under the control of the perpetrator, and unable to flee. A diagnosis of Complex PTSD assumes that there has been a prolonged period of total control by another person of the victim. This diagnosis is important in that it recognizes a series of symptoms that reflect conditions found among survivors of enslavement and prolonged sexual abuse and that also have critical implications for their rehabilitation, reintegration, and their participation in the legal process.

While the symptoms of Complex PTSD have been described in both the narratives of past and present survivors of slavery, and in fiction that explores the lived experience of slavery, the psychological impact of enslavement remains little understood. No study of the specific nature of the trauma of slavery has been done, nor have trials explored what might be the best therapeutic responses.

RESPONSES TO CONTEMPORARY SLAVERY

While slavery has been a fundamental part of human history, it would seem that it is only now, at the beginning of the twenty-first century, that there exists the possibility of the eradication or the extensive reduction of

[13] Judith Herman, *Trauma and Recovery* (New York, 1997), pp. 74–5.
[14] The diagnosis was introduced in Herman, *Trauma and Recovery*. For a full definition of this, see Julia M. Whealin, "Complex PTSD – A National Center for PTSD Factsheet," www.svfreenyc.org/survivors_factsheet_97.html.

slavery as a human activity. The reasoning behind this assertion is based on a number of points, including the relative size and role of slavery in the global population and economy, and a reduction in the obstacles to abolition that existed in the past.

While measurements of the extent of slavery are difficult, as noted above, the consensus is that there are an estimated 35.8 million slaves in the world. This is a significant number, but it is also a very small proportion of the overall global population – specifically 0.0048 of a global population of a little over 7 billion. Likewise, assuming the estimate of global profits from forced labor made by the ILO,[15] noted above, of $150 billion and a global economy of about $87 trillion, then slavery as an economic activity represents 0.0017 of global economic activity. Put another way, in a comparison to public health risks, there are fewer people in slavery than people infected with HIV, and ten times fewer people in slavery than people who contract malaria per year. The point of these comparisons is simply to demonstrate that while slavery is non-trivial, it is proportionately a very small part of the global population and global economy.

The further comparison is that, while it cannot be precise, it can be assumed that slavery represented a larger proportion of both the population and the economy in the past, and that the trend is one of an ongoing diminution of slavery as a proportion of each. One example of that shift can be seen over time in the United States. In 1860, the estimated value of the nation's 3.95 million slaves, representing 12.5 percent of the US national population, was between $2.7 and $3 billion – far beyond the current proportions that slaves represent in the global population or economy. It is notable that the American Civil War caused the wealth of the South to fall by two-thirds, with slave emancipation accounting for half. In short, slavery is today a relatively small part of the global population and the global economy, its primary effects include severe human suffering, operating as a drag on economic and social development, and the enrichment of criminals.

The historical obstacles to the abolition of slavery have also been greatly reduced. Slavery is now illegal in every country and is condemned in widely ratified and enacted international laws. Within international law, the proscription of slavery is *jus cogens*, a peremptory norm from which no derogation is ever permitted. And if the laws of the past that supported slavery could be said to be based upon religious and social norms that regarded slavery as acceptable, support for slavery as both a matter of religious doctrine (with the exception of the so-

---

[15] International Labour Office, *Profits and Poverty: The Economics of Forced Labour* (Geneva, 2014), www.ilo.org/global/publications/ilo-bookstore/order-online/books/WCMS_243391/lang--en/index.htm.

called Islamic State or ISIS) and as a socially accepted norm has now collapsed.

If slavery is to be increasingly marginalized within our global economy and society, suggesting the possibility of eradication, it has to be noted that the necessary political will and resources to attempt full abolition are still lacking. In spite of the illegality of slavery in all countries, the resources devoted to its eradication are very small when compared to the costs of global campaigns for the suppression of illicit drugs or terrorism. One estimate of the cost of a significant reduction in the amount of slavery is $10.8 billion[16] over a period of twenty-five to thirty years. This estimate is based upon existing programs of liberation, rehabilitation, and social reintegration of slaves in different parts of the world. By comparison, for only the fiscal year 2014, the National Drug Control Strategy for the United States was budgeted at $25.4 billion.

The cost of helping slaves to freedom and a full life varies greatly. In South Asia, the cost of liberation and then helping an individual or previously enslaved family to achieve economic autonomy, basic education, active citizenship, and a sense of dignity can be as low as $200 over a period of one to three years. At the other end of the spectrum, in North America and Western Europe, those freed from slavery and supported in their rehabilitation and reintegration routinely require upward of $30,000 to support the process, more if extensive legal, medical, or psychiatric help is needed. The majority of slaves, however, are not in the most developed countries; the largest numbers are in South Asia and the poorer parts of Southeast Asia and Africa where the costs of liberation and reintegration are lowest.

The importance of this rehabilitation and reintegration process cannot be overemphasized. Perhaps no other country in the world so dramatically demonstrates the consequences of failing to follow liberation with reintegration as the United States. Without continuing access to adequate education and basic resources, it was very difficult for African American families to build the economic foundation needed for full participation and well-being in American society, as Engerman noted earlier in this volume. Generations of African Americans were sentenced to second-class status, exploited, denied, and abused. America has suffered, and continues to suffer, from the neglect and injustice perpetrated on ex-slaves. The long economic stagnation and lack of development of the Deep South after the American Civil War was due, in part, to the continued exclusion of ex-slaves from meaningful

---

[16] Kevin Bales, *Ending Slavery: How We Free Today's Slaves* (Berkeley, CA, 2007).

economic participation through systems that retained the effect, if not the legal characteristics, of slavery.

If the United States still suffers from the effects of a botched emancipation following 1865, it is becoming clear within the contemporary antislavery movement that effective rehabilitation and reintegration is crucial to bringing slavery fully to an end within communities where it occurs, disrupting the possibility of re-enslavement. Likewise, the second decade of the twenty-first century has the hallmarks of a watershed within global antislavery. Since 2012, significant new antislavery funders have emerged in the philanthropic arena. The Freedom Fund, for example, was launched in 2014 as a joint endeavor of three large charitable foundations to make grants specifically aimed at the liberation and reintegration of slaves. Seed funds of $30 million were committed, with an assumption of further funding up to, at least, $100 million. By the end of 2015, the Fund and their partners had liberated 6,642 people from slavery, and had a direct impact on 151,653 lives.[17] A relatively new campaigning organization, Walk Free, also founded in 2012, benefiting from much larger financial support than all previous antislavery groups, had achieved a global supporter base of over 8.5 million people by 2016. Linked to Walk Free, and supported by the same benefactors, an annual Global Slavery Index was launched in 2013 in order to provide the needed metrics to measure progress in contemporary abolition. All of these new initiatives help a global antislavery movement to grow and to press national governments to better resource and enforce their existing antislavery laws.

THE DYNAMIC FACT OF CONTEMPORARY SLAVERY

Slavery today, just like slavery of the past, is a dynamic economic activity that responds to changes in the market and its legal and social context. At the present time (2016), there are several areas of marked contrast in how slavery is understood and addressed. Recent social attitude surveys in the world's largest countries suggest that about two-thirds of respondents state that they are concerned or very concerned about slavery, human trafficking, and forced labor, though very few regard themselves as having sufficient knowledge about the issue. Most of those surveyed believe (rightly) that slavery exists in their country, and the majority state that they would not buy products known to come from slave workers. This indicates a broad public understanding that slavery exists and that it presents a challenge to fundamental notions of human rights.

---

[17] See Freedom Fund, 2015 Annual Report, http://freedomfund.org/blog/our-impact-in-2015/.

Yet, as is often the case with emerging social movements, public understanding is running ahead of governmental or business responses. The US State Department's 2014 Trafficking in Persons Report noted in a global count that there had been 9,460 prosecutions for slavery crimes, 5,776 convictions, and 44,758 victims identified in 2013. This suggests that only 0.0015 percent of all of those suffering in slavery were officially identified in 2013. A study by the Walk Free Foundation[18] found that for the twelve largest economies in the Organisation for Economic Cooperation and Development (OECD), spending on antislavery programs within their overseas development assistance budgets totaled about $US 124 million per year. The country making the largest annual contribution is the United States, spending an average of $US 68.7 million per annum, followed by Norway ($12.7 million), Japan ($11.2 million), Australia ($7.7 million), the Netherlands ($6.5 million), the United Kingdom ($5 million), Sweden ($4.3 million), Canada ($3.4 million), France ($1.8 million), Germany ($1.2 million), Austria ($1.1 million), and Finland ($200,000). Altogether, these countries devote about $78 billion to foreign aid, which means that less than 1 percent of their overseas aid budget goes to antislavery work.[19] Just three countries, the United States, Japan, and Norway, account for nearly three-quarters of the antislavery funding from the OECD countries.

The criminals who operate slave-based illicit enterprises adapt quickly to changes in law enforcement and international economics. E-commerce is a well-trodden path for slave-holders, as are the types of "just-in-time" or temporary enslavement noted above in Brazil. If there is a final paradox in contemporary slavery, it is that all but total, and often fervent, political and public agreement that it should be eradicated is accompanied by a scarcity of resources, political will, and official apathy. Clearly, there is still a long way to go and a fertile future for abolition.

In his survey of slavery and abolition in the Americas, David Brion Davis described the collective political will necessary to end legal slavery, a theme echoed in Seymour Drescher's book, *The Mighty Experiment*. If the will existed in some places in the past, then the question we face in the future is how abolition might be mobilized when cross-border intervention of the sort that Britain employed in the nineteenth century is no longer seen to be possible or acceptable.

[18] Martina Ucnikova, "OECD and Modern Slavery: How Much Aid Money Is Spent to Tackle the Issue?" www.antitraffickingreview.org/index.php/atrjournal/article/view/68/66.

[19] Based on 2012 ODA figures. See OECD, Aid Statistics, retrieved June 3, 2013, www.oecd.org/dac/stats/.

A GUIDE TO FURTHER READING

Bales, Kevin, *Blood and Earth: Modern Slavery, Ecocide, and the Secret to Saving the World* (New York, 2016).

Bales, Kevin, *Ending Slavery: How We Free Today's Slaves* (Berkeley, CA, 2007).

Bales, Kevin, Olivia Hesketh, and Bernard Silverman, "Modern Slavery in the UK: How Many Victims?" *Significance*, 12 (2015): 16–21.

Datta, Monti Narayan and Kevin Bales, "Slavery in Europe: Part 1, Estimating the Dark Figure," *Human Rights Quarterly*, 35 (2013): 817–29.

Datta, Monti Narayan and Kevin Bales, "Slavery in Europe: Part 2, Testing a Predictive Model," *Human Rights Quarterly*, 36 (2014): 277–95.

Murphy, Laura T., *Survivors of Slavery: Modern-Day Slave Narratives* (New York, 2014).

Murphy, Laura T., "Blackface Abolition and the New Slave Narrative," *Cambridge Journal of Postcolonial Literary Inquiry*, 2 (2015): 93–113.

Murphy, Laura T., "The New Slave Narrative and the Illegibility of Modern Slavery," *Slavery and Abolition*, 36 (2015): 382–405.

Shahinian, Gulnara, "Report of the Special Rapporteur on Contemporary Forms of Slavery, Including Its Causes and Consequences: Thematic Report on Servile Marriage," United Nations General Assembly, A/HRC/21/41 (July 2012).

INDEX